Employment and Work Relations in Context Series

Series Editors

Tony Elger and Peter Fairbrother

Centre for Comparative Labour Studies,
Department of Sociology,
University of Warwick

The aim of the Employment and Work Relations in Context series is to address questions relating to the evolving patterns of work, employment and industrial relations in specific workplaces, localities and regions. This focus arises primarily from a concern to trace out the ways in which wider policy making, especially by national governments and transnational corporations, impinges upon specific workplaces, labour markets and localities in distinctive ways. A particular feature of the series is the consideration of forms of worker and citizen organization and mobilization in these circumstances. Thus the studies will address major analytical and policy issues through case-study and comparative research.

PAYING FOR THE PIPER

Capital and Labour in Britain's Offshore Oil Industry

Charles Woolfson, John Foster and Matthias Beck

MANSELL

First published 1996 by
Mansell Publishing Limited, *A Cassell Imprint*
Wellington House, 125 Strand, London WC2R 0BB
PO Box 605, Herndon, VA 20172

© Charles Woolfson, John Foster and Matthias Beck 1997

British Library Cataloguing-in-Publication Data
Woolfson, Charles, 1946–
   Paying for the Piper: capital and labour in Britain's
offshore oil industry.—(Employment and work relations in
context)
1.Offshore oil industry—Employees 2. Collective bargaining
—Offshore oil industry 3. Labour disputes—Great Britain
I. Title   II. Foster, John, 1947–   III. Beck, Matthias
331.8′9′0422′33819′0941

ISBN 0 720 123488 (HB)
ISBN 0 720 12350X (PB)

Library of Congress Cataloging-in-Publication Data
Woolfson, Charles, 1946–
   Paying for the Piper: capital and labour in Britain's offshore
oil industry/Charles Woolfson, John Foster, and Matthias Beck.
      p.   cm.—(Employment and work relations in context)
   Includes bibliographical references and index.
   ISBN 0–7201–2348–8 (HB).—ISBN 0–7201–2350–X (PB)
      1. Offshore oil industry—Great Britain—Management. 2. Trade-
unions—Petroleum workers—Great Britain.   3. Offshore oil
industry—Accidents—Great Britain. 4. Offshore oil industry—Great
Britain—Occupational safety. 5. Continental shelf—Great Britain.
I. Foster, John, 1940–   . II. Beck, Matthias, 1964–   .
III. Title.   IV. Series.
HD9571.5.W664   1996
338.2′7282′0941—dc20   96–36069
                                                                 CIP

Typeset by BookEns Ltd, Royston, Herts
Printed and bound in Great Britain by Biddles Ltd, Guildford and King's Lynn

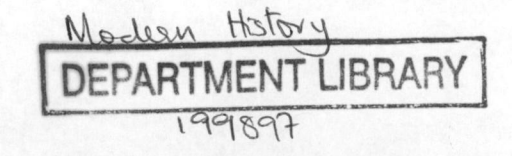

CONTENTS

TABLES

FIGURES

ILLUSTRATIONS

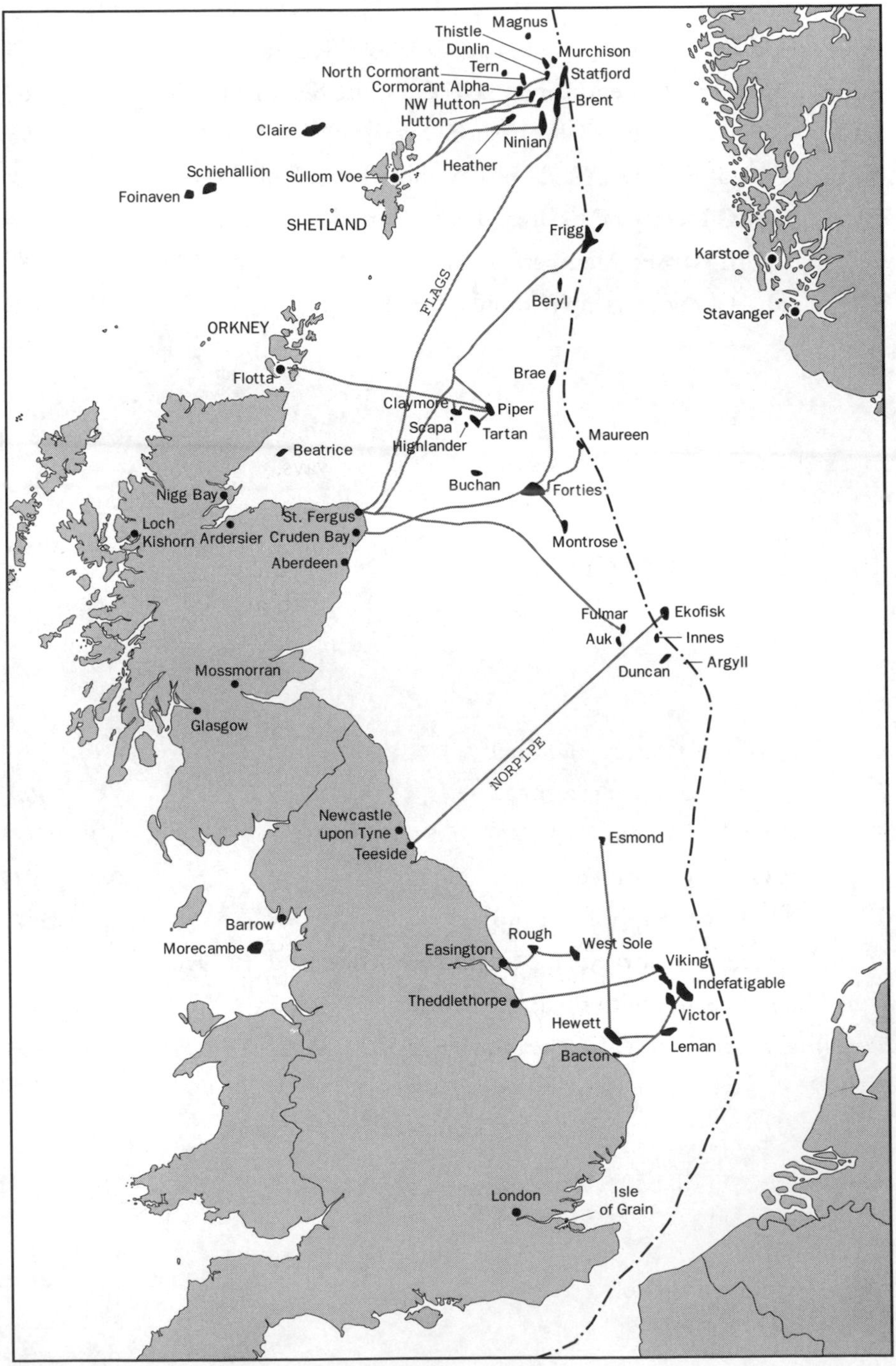

Illustration 1 *Map of UK Continental Shelf*

FOREWORD

Bob Ballantyne

I will not dwell upon my own experiences up to and during the Piper Alpha disaster; suffice it to say that Piper was, in many ways, no different from most of the other platforms that I worked on. This is especially so with regard to how it was managed. Occidental, not untypically, used 28 firms to supply labour on board Piper. Hired, not in the main for their technical expertise or for the depth of their understanding of health and safety issues, but because they were cheaper than the competition. Since the disaster the oil companies claim to have spent some five billion pounds on safety improvements. This raises the question – just what sort of condition were these platforms in that this kind of money had to be spent? Furthermore, with the squeeze once again being put on these contracting companies, to what sort of condition will the platforms be allowed to deteriorate in the future?

Like the coal industry, the oil industry is littered with the lives and blood of its workers. Tragedies such as Chinook, Cormorant Alpha and, of course, Piper Alpha weigh heavily on my mind along with many, many more. Sometimes as I speak these names I imagine the North Sea as a graveyard where people's dreams have been buried for the sake of wealth and power. This quest for 'black gold' has underpinned the nation's economy and enriched the multinational oil companies. In the space of less than ten years since the disaster, the oil companies have extracted £62 billion in gross trading profits from the North Sea. The total income derived from oil and gas sales since 1988 amounts to £104 billion. It is against these colossal sums that the safety spend should be assessed. Safety expenditure, even after Piper, comes to less than 5 per cent of income.

I remember, in the weeks after the Piper Alpha disaster, how my wife and I visited Tommy Lafferty, the local engineering union official at the AEU offices here in Aberdeen. Tommy was sitting in his chair absolutely shattered – he had just returned from one of the many funerals he had attended. His grief was palpable but almost eclipsed by a deep burning anger at the powerlessness that prevented challenge to a system which, as many had been saying all along, had made the disaster inevitable. 'Surely,' he pleaded, 'the world must listen now?'

This book charts how that challenge has been made. It does so by placing industrial relations in their proper context within the political economy and strategic imperatives which drive government and their co-venturers in the City of London and the boardrooms of the multinationals. Presented here for the first time is the definitive analysis of the labour and trade union movement's response to this unique industry. It is the most compelling case so far made that the movement's internal divisions can, and must, be bridged – not just in times of crisis arising from disaster, but permanently. As such it is an analysis which speaks to wider concerns facing the trade unions today both offshore and onshore.

Piper Alpha became a focal point for unity and the creation of the offshore workers' committee, the OILC, however fragile that unity may now appear in hindsight. The post-Piper campaigns of strike actions, vividly described here, show the workforce collectively challenging those who make the decisions – decisions which affect the working conditions and health and safety on which their lives often depend. The companies viewed these industrial disputes as irrational outbursts. Most commentators suggested that the strikes and sit-ins created 'losers' rather than 'winners'. This misses a vital point: to workers an industrial dispute is always a last resort which may cost them their jobs. But it also provides an opportunity to defend what they know to be important, no matter what the outcome is. Industrial action cannot ultimately be measured simply in terms of economic gain.

This dramatic story of Britain's offshore oil and gas industry is an authentic account of *our history* as offshore workers. But as a Piper survivor I am troubled by the unresolved question: who will ultimately control the still massive wealth which surrounds our shores and determines the lives of the people who continue to work there? This book suggests where we should be looking for that answer. At least then the price we have paid need not have been in vain.

Aberdeen
August 1996

ACKNOWLEDGEMENTS

The authors wish to thank the following people: Denys Blakeway, Eric Crockart, John Gillen, Martin Gostwick, Joe Hughes, John Kelly, Ronnie McDonald, Colin MacFarlane, Kenny Miller, Robert Moore, Daniel Vulliamy, David Walters, David Whyte. John Eldridge was kind enough to secure financial assistance on our behalf from the Fleck Foundation at a crucial stage of the research. We are also greatly indebted to Tony Benn for making available his invaluable archive, which made possible the reconstruction of some of the key points in the early offshore story.

Our deep gratitude goes to Eithne Johnstone for her invaluable contribution towards this book, which went well beyond the preparation of the typescript.

ABBREVIATIONS

AAIB   Air Accident Investigation Branch
ACAS   Advisory, Conciliation and Arbitration Service
ACOP   Approved Code of Practice
AEEU   Amalgamated Engineering and Electrical Union
AEU   Amalgamated Engineering Union (see CEU)
ALARP   As Low as Reasonably Practicable
ASB   Amalgamated Society of Boilermakers
ASTMS   Association of Scientific, Technical and Managerial Staffs
           (see MSF)
AUEW   Amalgamated Union of Engineering Workers (see AEU)
BALPA   British Airline Pilots Association
BIH   British International Helicopters
BNOC   British National Oil Corporation
BROA   British Rig Owners Association
BSJC   British Seafarers Joint Council (see NUS, AUEW, MNAOA,
           REOU)
CAA   Civil Aviation Authority
CBI   Confederation of British Industry
CEU   Constructional Engineering Union (see AEU)
CIMAH   Control of Industrial Major Accident Hazards
COSHH   Control of Substances Hazardous to Health Regulations 1988
COTA   Catering Offshore Traders Association
CRINE   Cost Reduction Initiative for the New Era
CROTUM   Commissioner for the Rights of Trade Union Members
CSEU   Confederation of Shipbuilding and Engineering Unions
DEn   Department of Energy
DTI   Department of Trade and Industry
EC   European Community
EETPU   Electrical, Electronic, Telecommunication and Plumbing
           Union
EPIU   Electrical and Plumbing Industries Union

EU	European Union
FAI	Fatal Accident Inquiry
FBU	Fire Brigades Union
FLAGS	Far-North Liquids and Gas System
FPIC	Fuel and Power Industries Committee (see TUC)
FSA	Formal Safety Assessment
GMB	General, Municipal and Boilermakers Union (see ASB)
HAZOP	Hazard and Operability Studies
HLO	Helicopter Landing Officer
HSC	Health and Safety Commission
HSE	Health and Safety Executive
HSWA	Health and Safety at Work Act 1974
HUMS	Health and Usage Monitoring System
IADC	International Association of Drilling Contractors
IRPA	Individual Risk Per Annum
IUOOC	Inter Union Offshore Oil Committee
LTA	Lost Time Accident
MNAOA	Merchant Navy and Airline Officers Association
MSF	Manufacturing, Science and Finance union (previously ASTMS)
MWA	Mineral Workings (Offshore Installations) Act 1971
NAECI	National Agreement for the Engineering Construction Industry
NECC	National Engineering Construction Committee (see AUEW, EETPU, ASB)
NEDO	National Economic Development Office
NOPEF	Norwegian Oil and Petrochemical Workers Union
NPD	Norwegian Petroleum Directorate
NRB	Not Required Back
NUJ	National Union of Journalists
NUM	National Union of Mineworkers
NUMAST	National Union of Marine, Aviation and Shipping Transport Officers
NUS	National Union of Seamen (see RMT)
OCA	Offshore Construction Agreement (Hook-up agreement)
OCC	Offshore Contractors Council
OCPCA	Oil and Chemical Plant Constructors Association (see OCC)
OFS	Federation of Oil Workers Trade Unions (Norwegian)
OIAC	Oil Industry Advisory Committee
OILC	Offshore Industry Liaison Committee

OIM	Offshore Installation Manager
OIUCC	Offshore Industry Unions Co-ordinating Committee (see OUCC)
OPEC	Organisation of Petroleum Exporting Countries
OPITB/O	Offshore Petroleum Industry Training Board/Organisation
OPRIS	Offshore Personnel Records and Information System (Shell)
OSD	Offshore Safety Division (HSE)
OSO	Offshore Supplies Office
OUCC	Offshore Unions Coordinating Committee (see OIUCC)
PED	Petroleum Engineering Division (DEn)
PFEER	Prevention of Fire, Explosion and Emergency Response Regulations 1995
POB	Persons on Board
PRT	Petroleum Revenue Tax
QRA	Quantitative Risk Assessment
REOU	Radio and Electronic Officers Union
RIDDOR	Reporting of Injuries, Diseases and Dangerous Occurrences Regulations
RMT	Rail, Maritime and Transport union (see NUS)
SAR	Search and Rescue
SJIB	Scottish Joint Industries Board
SRSCR	Safety Representatives and Safety Committees Regulations 1977
STUC	Scottish Trades Union Congress
TGWU	Transport and General Workers Union
TSR	Temporary Safe Refuge
TUC	Trades Union Congress
UCATT	Union of Construction, Allied Trades and Technicians
UDM	Union of Democratic Mineworkers
UKCS	United Kingdom Continental Shelf
UKOOA	United Kingdom Offshore Operators Association

INTRODUCTION

In the 1990s the British offshore oil industry underwent a profound change of direction. This shift irrevocably altered the character of the production regime on the United Kingdom Continental Shelf (UKCS), and with that, transformed the investment strategies of two of Britain's biggest multi-national companies, Shell and BP. In terms of corporate policy, the change of direction marked a new drive for market dominance by the UK oil majors within the European Union and a switch of investment priorities back towards the traditional overseas oil production bases that had been their staple prior to the 1970s. These changes were not limited in their impact to the oil industry itself. Because of the size of the industry and its linkages to the rest of the economy – over the past two decades the UKCS had absorbed between 10 and 20 per cent of all UK industrial investment – this transformation was of significance for the orientation of economic policy at governmental level.

This book investigates the crisis of industrial relations within the UKCS which precipitated these changes. This industrial relations crisis erupted after the world's worst offshore disaster, Piper Alpha in 1988, in which 167 oil workers died. The strikes which followed in 1989 and, more comprehensively, in 1990, were of a very special type. They did not immediately seek direct material gain. Rather, they questioned the totality of assumptions upon which the system of offshore production had been based: most fundamentally managerial authority and legitimacy in the area of health and safety.

By 1990 the overall death toll of the offshore industry since its inception had reached over 400. This made it the most dangerous industry in the UK. Piper Alpha exemplified one of the most unpalatable aspects of industrial production: the real human price to be paid for oil extraction. In the aftermath of Piper Alpha, many of the workforce mounted a challenge which rejected this price as having become unacceptably high.

The importance of this challenge was twofold. First, it demonstrated the circumstances in which a hitherto largely unorganized workforce in a non-union industry could become powerfully mobilized. Secondly, it revealed that even in such adverse circumstances labour has the potential to determine the course of events.

Organizing the offshore workforce had to overcome many obstacles. From the beginnings of the industry on the UKCS, offshore oil companies adopted an aggressively anti-union stance. An internal 1976 union analysis noted that oil companies, virtually without exception, employed a host of strategies to obstruct union organization. These included:

> The insistence on full ballots, not only for collective bargaining rights but also for simple representational rights; company initiated anti-union propaganda being spread in the run up to the ballot; prolonged delays in holding ballots, and delays in affording rights where the ballot has been successful; the setting up of staff consultative machinery to undermine the activities of *bona fide* trade unions … more favourable conditions of service to non-unionised areas and asking prospective employees their attitudes to trade unions. (ASTMS, 1976)

These observations applied to US and UK companies alike. In fact the document stressed the particular difficulties experienced not only with Esso (Exxon), but also with BP and Shell. The offshore industrial relations system was both a precursor and template for the non-union industrial relations system of the late twentieth century. From the 1970s to the early 1990s, Britain's offshore oil workers experienced a continuous line of disempowerment, blacklisting and victimization whenever they posed a challenge to the non-union structure of industrial relations.

Yet in 1989–90 this apparently all-powerful system of control broke down. We will argue that a critical element in this breakdown was the perception of how safety was managed. The legitimacy of the existing structure of safety control, both legislative and managerial, disintegrated in the eyes of both workers and, to an extent, management itself. In this process 'the class dimension' of safety was exposed (Carson, 1985).

A key characteristic of the legislative framing of safety issues has been the assumption that the protection of employees can be attributed to concrete physical objects and/or concrete measures and procedures. In this view, the industrial relations context and the rights and collective empowerment of workers do not figure in the safety equation. Workplaces are safe because certain provisions have been met – not because workers have rights in relation to management. According to Carson, this view is the product of a historical process of exclusion rather than a result of necessity or efficiency. In his article, 'Hostages to history: some aspects of the occupational health and safety debate in historical perspective', he has argued that the divorce of safety issues and corporate negligence from industrial relations was a deliberate strategy of nineteenth-century legislatures. Carson suggests that, when the Factory

Acts were established in the early to mid-nineteenth-century Britain, they served to deliberately obscure the 'class dimension of issues such as occupational health and safety'. Says Carson:

> Just as the introduction of 'classless', bureaucratic forms of policing absolved the new industrial bourgeoisie from the potentially explosive task of openly exposing its class position ... so factory legislation went some way towards performance of the same function with regard to conditions at the workplace. (1985: 64)

Carson proposes that:

> Factory legislation helped to 'defuse' or 'declass' the employer/ employee relationship at one of its most critical and socially obtrusive points, the price being extracted from industrial wage labour in terms of occupational injury and disease. More broadly, it served to 'mask' one of the potentially most unpalatable aspects of class relations in an industrialising society. It did so by purporting to pluck issues such as questions of occupational health and safety out of the fraught ... arena of industrial conflict, and making them a matter of 'classless' state regulation. As a result of the above processes ... an ideological separation between occupational health and safety as one category and industrial relations as another, took place. (1985: 65)

This separation has continued – despite subsequent changes in technological conditions and the technical framing of health and safety regulation. The fatal consequences of such a separation were highlighted by Piper Alpha and earlier accidents offshore. These accidents were palpably the consequence of authoritarian top-down management relying on formal physical procedures of safety compliance.

Piper Alpha marked the moment when, in the mass consciousness of the workforce, this artificial and ideologically-sustained separation evaporated. Workers recognized, and publicly said, that their colleagues' lives had been lost because of an autocratic workplace in which power had shifted wholly to the side of management. It was this issue of workplace power, and the right to trade union organization, that the subsequent strike action was about. Management maintained an exclusive prerogative over issues of safety, which was matched only by their determination to retain exclusive control over the work process by excluding unions. The unofficial movement which was formed, partly in response to the tragedy, returned to elemental industrial demands which questioned the totality of the established workplace regime rather than seeking incremental gains. The implications for the dynamics of unofficial action, changing forms of mass consciousness, and the permeability of sectionalist union identities are striking.

This breakdown in an industrial relations regime of a type that is now commonplace across much of British industry represents one side of our story. The other is its consequence for the wider political economy of the country's single most important industry. Workers striking in the UKCS did not achieve their principal goal of union recognition. Nor was health and safety made susceptible to the collective voice of workers. Management retained its overall prerogatives. But it had to do so in quite new ways. The tactical resolution of the strikes involved the employers in conceding quite disproportionate pay increases. For the contract workers who made up more than three-quarters of the workforce, the aggregate pay increase exceeded 40 per cent between 1989 and 1991. As much as anything, it was this increase in pay, together with the price increases imposed by the contractors, that brought to a head the wider politico-economic crisis of the UKCS of the early 1990s.

In 1992, the Department of Trade and Industry, together with the UKCS employers, embarked on a joint programme of industrial reorganization in the UKCS that in its scale is unique in modern British history. It is known by its acronym CRINE (Cost Reduction for the New Era). The rationale for this programme was a 50 per cent increase in operating costs which had occurred within the UKCS over the previous three years – an increase quite out of line with other oil provinces around the world. We will argue that the way in which this crisis was resolved directly reflected the perceived strength of the previous mobilization. Free market principles were abandoned. The government and the offshore employers worked in detail to transform technology, to minimize the reliance on labour offshore and to create a new management climate based on open communication. Safety culture became a key medium for restoring relations between the workforce and management. The emphasis was now on permanent core workforces and detailed involvement in the technical observance of safety compliance. This unparalleled attempt to restabilize the offshore industrial relations regime went hand in hand with fiscal policies that marked a decisive shift away from the previously very close involvement with the United States oil industry.

These changes themselves stand witness to the continuing power of labour. A highly individualized and authoritarian system of labour management disintegrated with remarkable speed and effect. A new system is now in place. Yet no more than its predecessor is it likely to ensure the final victory of individualism. The evidence from Britain's offshore oil industry suggests rather that those who seek to establish a system of wholesale labour incorporation will ultimately face the regeneration of new collective resistance.

PART I CAPITAL AND LABOUR

Chapter 1 examines the political and economic forces which have led to the making of the UK offshore oil industry in the 1960s and 1970s. We describe how its production system was developed on quite specific lines: no depletion controls, little phasing of investment over time and, largely in consequence, no creation of a locally owned infrastructure. We argue that the focus of offshore development was on rapid extraction of the oil resources on the UK Continental Shelf. This necessitated, in part, the predominant participation of US multinationals which brought with it the implantation of a US-type industrial relations system, sharply out of line with UK developments at that time.

Chapter 2 examines the conflicts which arose from this implantation of a US-type industrial relations system. These conflicts were multilayered. One layer of conflict was between the oil multinationals and offshore workers and their unions. UK unions, and to some degree the Labour government, expected the full and comprehensive extension of collective bargaining to this new industry. The oil multinationals, based on their experiences in other oil provinces, adopted a comprehensive union-avoidance strategy. Another layer of conflict arose between the client oil operators and their dependent contractors. What evolved was a small set of highly restricted bargaining agreements. While the unions initially approached the offshore sector with a cooperative anti-sectionalist agenda, the employers' concerted denial of bargaining rights, and later on, their strategic support for isolated bargaining agreements, brought to the fore inter-union sectionalist strife. Combined with the aggressive anti-union stance of the offshore multinationals, what resulted was an anachronistic industrial relations system, based on the arbitrary and uncontrolled exercise of managerial power in which both workers' rights and matters of safety were systematically neglected. Piper Alpha, as the inevitable outcome of these developments, fundamentally threw into question the legitimacy of the existing offshore production system. This was the essential ingredient for the period of massive labour unrest in the late 1980s and early 1990s, which we will discuss in the next part of our book.

OIL, IMPERIALISM AND THE BRITISH STATE: THE ORIGINS OF THE CRISIS

This chapter is concerned with origins. It will seek to identify the long-term economic and political factors which shaped the industrial relations crisis of the late 1980s. The immediate causes of this crisis were new and largely unexpected. They included the Piper Alpha explosion in 1988, the jump in oil prices in 1989 and the tightening of the labour market in 1989 and 1990. But to understand how these factors combined to create a major industrial crisis, and why it resulted in such profound changes, it is necessary to go back to the beginnings of the industry in the North Sea and beyond.

The UK sector had a number of unique features which are not quickly or easily explained. It possessed a health and safety regime which was quite different from that prevailing elsewhere in the UK. Its industrial relations practices were effectively implanted from the US. Its production system was developed on quite specific lines very different from those in the Norwegian sector: no depletion controls, little phasing of investment over time and, largely in consequence, no creation of a locally owned supply base. It was, in combination, these characteristics which produced the crisis of the early 1990s and which also meant that this crisis could not be resolved without structural change.

This chapter will begin by examining the historic relationship between the oil industry and the British State – a relationship which went back two generations before the discovery of North Sea oil. It will then assess the very special moment in the development of international oil politics at which it became feasible to exploit the UK sector, and finally look at what followed: the impact of oil on British politics in the 1970s and 1980s and the emerging contradictions which became manifest in the production system of the United Kingdom Continental Shelf (UKCS) by the end of the 1980s.

Oil and British Imperialism

Oil has always held a special and, at times, almost determining position within the development of modern British imperialism. Before the First World War oil's importance was strategic and military rather than economic. Technically, because oil had been adopted as fuel for the British navy, and enabled its ships to go faster and further than those of any competing navy, the security of oil supply came to be seen as essential for the security of Britain's empire and trade routes. *Pax Britannica* depended on it.

It was for this reason that Anglo-Persian Oil, later BP, became in 1913 the first major British firm in which the state took a controlling interest. Churchill, as First Lord of the Admiralty, insisted that the government gain a direct guarantee of supply by taking a 51 per cent shareholding in Anglo-Persian. In doing so, Churchill sought to insure the company against overseas take-over and also provided it with the capital needed to develop its supply network beyond its original acquisitions in Iran (Jack, 1968; Penrose, 1968).[1]

Only a few years before, in 1907, the biggest of Britain's oil companies, Marcus Samuel's Shell, had been taken over by Royal Dutch Oil to form an Anglo-Dutch conglomerate in which 60 per cent of the shares were held by the Dutch side. With ultimate control in the hands of a non-British national, Henri Deterding, this provided a worrying precedent for the British government. The navy needed absolute certainty of supply. Royal Dutch Shell was not seen to be totally reliable. Britain's only other oil company, Burmah Oil, although possessing a major shareholding in Anglo-Persian, was itself too small to supply the quantity of oil that would be needed in wartime. Hence the importance of Anglo-Persian Oil and the quite unprecedented step of taking it into state ownership (Goss, 1977; Jack, 1968; Jones, 1981).

The British government was only too well aware that oil, as an internationally traded commodity, had shown a strong tendency to monopolization. In the later nineteenth century one major player had emerged on the world scene, Rockefeller's Standard Oil. Standard Oil had already secured a monopoly over the American domestic market. Here it had used control over transport to achieve dominance. Physical access to oil in the USA was relatively easy. Many firms had sought to enter the field. The Rockefeller company had one major advantage. This was its ability to use its early technological lead in refining crude oil to buy up 90 per cent of America's refinery capacity by 1870. It was able to exploit this to strike deals with railway companies across America to secure preferential terms, and enable it to undercut and eliminate other firms. It was the resulting superprofits which then launched the company abroad (Odell, 1981; Roncaglia, 1985, Ch. 3).

Outside America, oil was in short supply and being produced in locations remote from the major industrial consumers. Oil was then available in commercial quantities only in the Dutch East Indies, the Russian Caucasus, Rumania, Persia and Turkish Mesopotamia (Iraq). Thus the struggle to monopolize control. Between 1907 and 1911 Standard Oil bought up or entered into cartel agreements with almost all other major owners: Nobel (Sweden) and Rothschild (France) who controlled the Caucasus, Royal-Dutch Shell (who controlled the East Indies and were seeking entry to Mesopotamia) and the Deutsche Bank interests that dominated Rumania (Lenin, 1971; Jones, 1981). This placed Anglo-Persian's concession on the Persian-Mesopotamian border in direct danger. There is some doubt among historians as to whether the state shareholding was strictly necessary to ensure security of supply or even whether oil was technically the most appropriate fuel for the navy. But of one thing there is no question. Without the British government shareholding, Anglo-Persian Oil would not have survived as an independent company.

For the British economy as a whole the importance of oil at this stage was, in purely economic terms, small. In 1913 it made up only 1.4 per cent of the value of UK imports and only 1.6 per cent of re-exports (Mitchell, 1962: 301, 308). The energy needs of the British economy were supplied overwhelmingly by the coal industry which then employed one in seven of all adult males in the country. Oil was of military importance. It enabled the navy to protect Britain's trade routes and above all the Suez canal through which passed over 30 per cent of all British exports, by value, in 1913 (Mitchell, 1962: 320). The pound sterling and the City of London depended on oil-propelled ships – not on oil as a commodity.

This was to change relatively quickly within the next few years. By 1920 petroleum made up 5 per cent of the value British imports and 2 per cent of re-exports – with much more being traded directly from the Middle East. Energy for industry, for electricity generation and for the rail network still came from coal. But motor transport was naturally dependent on imported oil. And the international trading profits of Anglo-Persian Oil, Royal Dutch Shell and Burmah made up almost 4 per cent of the profit income of the UK manufacturing firms by 1938 (Bamberg, 1994: 515; Feinstein, 1972: Tables 70–71).[2]

The ability of these oil firms to sustain their long-term position in the international oil market was throughout this period strongly dependent on direct state power. First, there was Britain's military grip on major oil-bearing territories – Iraq, Persia, and the feudal sheikhdoms of the Persian Gulf (and in a more neo-colonial form, in the Caribbean area where Britain held the major concessions in Mexico and Venezuela). Second, there was Britain's control of major oil-using markets: its own domestic economy and the dependent territories of its empire. These powers enabled the companies to strike cartel agreements within what was still a highly monopolized industry. Anglo-Persian entered into a pool agreement with Shell and Standard Oil (Esso) for the supply of the world market in 1928. Shell entered an agreement with Esso in 1933 for joint trading and exploration activity in the North West European market area (Corti and Frazer, 1983). These arrangements, which set production quotas and pegged prices at the US level plus transport costs, were never fully successful. Smaller American companies periodically broke ranks. But for years at a time, they did serve to regulate the market, and for the mid to later 1920s and again for the mid to later 1930s helped provide both Shell and Anglo-Persian with dividends of between 20 and 25 per cent annually (*Stock Exchange Year Book*, 1939).[3]

This trend to cartelization has remained remarkably consistent throughout the century. So indeed has the actual pattern of ownership. The same small group of companies that controlled the oil trade in 1914 still did so 50 years later. Three of these 'seven sisters' were direct descendants of Rockefeller's original company, Standard Oil. This had been broken up under anti-trust legislation by the US Supreme Court in 1911 in order to create smaller competing companies in each US state. The aim was cheaper, non-cartelized energy supplies for US industry. In practice only very limited change occurred. The stem company became Standard Oil of New Jersey, Esso and later Exxon, still the biggest world oil company. Standard Oil of New York later became Mobil. Standard Oil of California later became Chevron. In addition, two other US companies emerged using newly discovered Texas oil: Texaco and Gulf Oil – both originally financed and controlled by the Mellons, the Pittsburgh banking dynasty.

These five companies, Exxon, Mobil, Chevron, Texaco and Gulf, together with Royal Dutch Shell and Anglo-Persian (BP), made up the seven. At no point in the twentieth century have they controlled less than 60 per cent of the world's commercially marketed refined oil products. Usually it has been significantly more.

In order to understand the nature of the oil industry, it is important to explain how this dominance has been sustained over such a long period. The dominance of oil majors is not based in any simple way on the ownership of the reserves themselves. If it had been, the companies would have been displaced a long time ago. Long-term dominance has required a strategic control within the whole process of oil production and marketing. The oil industry involves a series of quite distinct stages, and it is the combined requirements of these different stages which has sustained dominance by very large firms. There is the control of access to reserves and command of the technology of exploration. There is the technological ability to extract. There is the capacity to transport oil – often over very long distances. There is the capital intensive process of refining. There is access to markets and the control of retail distribution. Typically this production chain will stretch across several countries, and, to be cost effective, demand the ability to handle large quantities of oil from different sources on a global basis and to operate simultaneously in markets for a wide range of oil products (Roncaglia, 1985).

There is also a final requirement. This is the ability to survive long periods of low profits. This is because of the special nature of the energy market. Oil is only one of a number of sources of energy: coal, hydro-power, nuclear energy. All compete. The demand for energy itself also fluctuates sharply. It depends on whether there is growth in the world economy, and whether a period of high energy costs has produced investment in energy saving (as occurred in the 1970s and 1980s). If the demand fluctuates strongly, so also does the supply. Periods of high energy cost will encourage new phases of exploration – bringing new producers into the market and again forcing down prices.

The giant oil companies are able to survive because they are big and because they operate strategically. They can use the periods of low price to weed out smaller rivals. They have the depth and range of investments to survive themselves, and harvest the very high profits available in periods of short supply. Most important of all, they are able to command the full length of the supply chain and, at particular periods, collectively assert control over one or other of its links. It is this that gives the big firms their periodic ability to influence price and consequently transform the oil trade into a source of superprofit.

Originally, in the United States, Rockefeller commanded refining and transport. It was the superprofits generated here over the quarter-century after 1870 that launched Standard Oil as a world company and financed Rockefeller's Chase Manhattan Bank. Globally, before 1914 it was control over supply. Between the wars, especially after the onset of the world slump, it was control over distribution networks. In the post-war world it was successively control over sources of supply, refining and distribution and over the technology of exploration and extraction, sometimes in combination and sometimes singly. Strategically, companies have to be ready to move quickly – and to plan for the next move but one.

In sustaining this dominance, the ability to call on state power has been essential. It is no accident that the dominant firms are based in the two states which were the victors in two world wars. The diplomatic claim to a 'national interest' in a particular territory has often meant no more nor less than access to its oil. The struggle over the control of the Persian Gulf in 1989–90 is the most recent example. This is not, of course, because governments are in any simple way tools of the oil companies. It is because modern states depend on oil economically and militarily. Since the First World War, ships, motorized transport, tanks and aircraft have all needed oil. Oil and gas have also tended to become progressively more important for economic competitiveness. This gives oil companies a very powerful leverage over governments.

From British Hegemony to Anglo-American Rivalry

In Britain's case, its victory over Germany in the First World War enabled it to consolidate its power over Germany's satellite, Turkey, and appropriate its colonial possessions. Mesopotamia (Iraq) became a British protectorate. Saudi Arabia became a client state alongside Britain's existing clients in the Persian Gulf. These moves gave Britain political control over the bulk of known oil reserves in the eastern hemisphere (outside the USSR). The outcome of the war also consolidated British control over markets in Africa and Asia. Anglo-Persian (BP) and Shell were the main beneficiaries. Preexisting access agreements struck before the First World War enabled the French company, CFP, and the American Standard Oil successors, Esso and Mobil, to consolidate concessions of their own in Iraq. The American majors Texaco and Socal (Standard Oil of California) were also able to buy up concessions in Saudi Arabia which at that point had no known reserves. But Britain and British-based firms were still dominant. For the British economy the importance of this oil was not just its scale. It was its cheapness, in terms of production costs, and its relative closeness to European markets. Between the wars the world price of oil was fixed to enable the US companies' home production base, where costs were up to ten times those of the Middle East, to produce at a profit (Barratt Brown, 1970: 236). Hence the particular profitability of the Middle East holdings for Anglo-Persian and Shell.

This gave these companies a very important position within British capital. They were among the country's biggest firms. At a time when many of Britain's overseas assets had been sold, when exports (particularly textiles and heavy engineering) had collapsed and when the fall in most commodity prices had reduced the profitability of other empire producers, the earning potential of these firms had increased sharply. They were closely interlocked at director level with the leading merchant banks, and, through this, with the Court of the Bank of England. Directors in the 1930s included Viscount Bearsted (of

Samuels), Viscount Weir, Sir Andrew Agnew, Sir Charles Wright, Frederick Godber, F. C. Tiarks, Sir John Lloyd, Sir George Barstow and Sir R. Waley Cohen (Aaronovitch, 1961: 84–9).[4] All were also directors of banking companies. In 1934, in recognition of the importance of these companies for the balance of payments and the pound sterling, a minute of agreement (the Treasury Minute) was reached between the Treasury and Anglo-Persian, Shell and Burmah that imposed an obligation to consult on all matters of mutual interest. Moreover, there was also a shift in the national base of Shell. Concerted steps were taken at governmental and City of London level to ensure that the control of Shell at director and shareholder level was brought much more closely under British aegis (Yergin, 1991; Bamberg, 1994). From the late 1930s it is probably more accurate to speak of Shell as a British company – though with significant American, Dutch and Swiss shareholdings (Penrose, 1968).

This was the scale of the change from 1914. Then the importance of oil was strategic: to defend the ships that carried British exports. In 1934 the stability of the pound still depended on ships coming through the Suez canal (and across the Atlantic) – but now they were the oil tankers themselves. For British capital, its two great oil companies represented the future. They were large, integrated and internationally organized. They brought together the control of natural resources, high technology and sophisticated product markets. Most important of all, they could match on a global scale the biggest of American companies.

This position of British dominance was eroded but not destroyed by the Second World War. For the two major aggressor powers, Germany and Japan, the acquisition of oil reserves was seen as a very important war aim. Neither had access to oil within their immediate territories. In both cases, their rulers saw their economic and military potential endangered by reliance on external suppliers. The US government also had a number of quite specific war aims. These included the elimination of protectionist tariff blocks (of which the biggest was the sterling area) and the ending of any restriction on access to the development of resources, of which the most valuable were the oil reserves within the British empire and its protectorates. The period from 1941 to 1945 saw intensive bargaining between America and Britain over the terms of the post-war economic settlement. Britain's dependence on American economic support meant that the war ended with Britain conceding on virtually all fronts. In terms of oil, America replaced Britain as the dominant power in the Middle East. Formally speaking, this was not so much the result of displacing Britain from its existing holdings (Iran, Iraq and Kuwait) as establishing Saudi Arabia as the major Middle East producer. By the early years of the war, the Americans had established that the scale of its reserves transcended all others. The role of the US government was to broker agreements whereby Saudi oil could be accessed and linked to European supply quotas. In particular, this involved revoking previous agreements with French and British companies in order to free Esso, Mobil and Chevron to join Socal and Texaco and form the Aramco consortium in Saudi Arabia (Funkhouser, 1951: 161–5; Yergin, 1991: 423–44).[5]

Strategic Role of Oil in the Post-war Era

Closely associated with this shift in the balance of power between Britain and the US, the ending of the Second World War also saw a new dimension entering the political economy of oil. This was the direct use of oil as a weapon in international diplomacy. Oil remained very important in a military sense. Its economic importance was greater than ever as industrial economies moved to fully motorized transport systems and began to use oil for industrial energy. What marked out the decades immediately following the Second World War was the degree to which these two facets were combined. Oil was now used to achieve the diplomatic objectives of the Cold War, and in doing so brought a still greater interlocking between the oil companies and government.

There were two main arenas for this diplomacy. One was in the Middle East itself. The other was the economic frontier of the Cold War – which stretched from Europe to Japan.

From 1947 the US embarked on a massive programme of economic aid to both Europe and Japan. In Europe, it was under the title of the European Recovery Programme (Marshall Plan). It involved the establishment of an elaborate administrative structure to oversee economic reorganization and to permit the immediate resumption of military production. An integral (though at that time covert) part of this programme was the supply of cheap energy. This oil came from Saudi Arabia whose immense reserves were exclusively under the control of Aramco. To supplement tankers, an oil pipeline was built at breakneck speed overland across Saudia Arabia and Syria to reach the Mediterranean. The US government made special allocations of steel to enabled this vast engineering feat to be finished by 1950 – a critical date for US military planners, who were at that time seeking to prepare a pre-emptive strike against the USSR before it achieved full nuclear capability (Cave-Brown, 1978).[6]

This oil, which was needed to fuel fast economic recovery in Europe and

Japan, was provided at a significantly lower price than that in the 1930s and hence was, to that extent, at the expense of the US oil majors. In return, therefore, the US majors were guaranteed a protected market inside the US that sustained US prices at roughly the same level as before the war. This policy of covert aid to Europe and Japan had a second aspect which also benefited the US oil majors in the longer run. It weaned these economies away from their previous reliance on coal and made them dependent on oil supplied from largely US-controlled reserves.

The other side of this policy was the diplomatic use of the oil companies in the Middle East itself. Here the old autocratic puppet regimes installed by the British were under threat from left-wing and nationalist forces. Persia, Iraq and Egypt were all teetering on the brink by the early 1950s. For the Americans the key country was Saudi Arabia – and the key problem was the reduction in the price of oil being supplied to the European market. By 1949 this was causing acute difficulties in relationships with the Saudi regime. A memorandum written in 1950 by Richard Funkhouser, then head of the US State Department Middle East Oil Desk (and by the 1970s US Consul in Edinburgh) summed up the situation thus:

> Rupture of the flow of Middle East Oil to normal markets ... would seriously affect US and allied economic, political and strategic interests. The problem is to develop lines of action to protect and maintain allied oil interests in the area and lines of action by which allied oil interests can help protect and preserve overall US interests in the area, e.g. removal of the sources of communism and attainment of overall US policy objectives such as economic and political stability, increased standards of living and the development of Western orientation. (US Senate, 1974: 142)

Already in the early 1940s the US government and oil companies had had to confront the political problems posed by movements for national self-determination. Following the Mexican nationalizations of 1938 (which were mainly at the expense of Shell), Venezuela threatened to follow suit in 1943. The Roosevelt government and Esso, faced with the loss of their major external source of oil, brokered a deal whereby income was split 50/50. Saudi Arabia was even more crucial after the war. The Assistant Secretary of State for Middle Eastern Affairs, George McGhee, negotiated a similar 50/50 deal in 1950 but one where the payment of Aramco was denoted as 'tax'. This enabled the companies to claim it back in total under US tax law – which left the companies no worse off. Similar deals were negotiated with Kuwait in 1951 and Iraq in 1952. The UK government was obliged to make similar concessions to its own oil companies (Yergin, 1991: 423–4).

Hence, as a complement to the supply of cheap oil to Europe, the oil companies acted as a channel to sustain the revenues of otherwise highly instable regimes. Ultimately, it was the US State which paid for this. In return, the oil companies got two things which only the US State could provide: military protection for the reserves and diplomatic clout for opening otherwise restricted markets in both Japan and Europe.

By the 1960s, therefore, oil had become integral to the world balance of forces and to the way in which the US government sustained its power. In some cases the oil companies acted as proxies for their government. Personnel tended to move freely between the oil companies and overseas US government agencies. And in terms of the overall dominance of the global economy, the dollar's status as world currency drew strength from the need of all countries to have dollars to buy oil (Bromley, 1991: 151–4).

For Britain oil remained no less critical. It had lost primacy in the international market to the Americans, but its straitened circumstances made oil more important than ever to its economic survival. Although the price of oil was lower, the UK companies compensated by expanding the volume of sales. The British client, Kuwait, was added to Iran and Iraq as a major oil source in the Middle East. Fields were developed in empire territories elsewhere, notably Nigeria, Brunei and Borneo. Shell continued to expand its control of refining and distribution in the empire and commonwealth. British Petroleum (as Anglo-Persian was called after 1954) concentrated on the European market.

Oil was the key provider of foreign currency during a period when the City of London was trying to re-establish itself as a world banking centre. Indeed, for the decade immediately after the war, oil assumed an importance for the British economy that matched the levels of the early 1980s. In 1953 the profit income of the oil companies constituted 14 per cent of the profit income of all UK industrial companies – with the rate of profit on capital at 24 per cent, double that of home industrials. For Anglo-Persian Oil alone the volume of profits, at constant prices, was almost four times as large in 1950 as in 1938 (Bamberg, 1994: 515; Barratt Brown, 1970: 248).

The relationship with the United States was inevitably a contradictory one. The Americans were direct rivals for the control of oil reserves, especially in the Middle East. America's diplomatic objectives – as in the 1956 conflict over Suez – were often in conflict with those of Britain. But ultimately Britain depended on US military might. The US provided the final safeguard in the Far East and the Persian Gulf. In 1953, the US directly contributed to the restoration of Anglo-Persian's oil assets in Iran by facilitating the overthrow of the progressive Mossadeq government (Yergin, 1991).

This ambivalence was repeated at the level of general political and economic relations. As such, the special character of Anglo-American economic relations directly affected Britain's post-war energy policy, and provides the immediate background for our story.

As part of the post-war economic settlement, the 1944 Bretton Woods agreement gave the pound the status of a reserve currency along with the dollar. It was a primary objective of the British government to use this status to re-develop the banking role of the City of London. To do this meant, initially, heavy reliance on US loans. Any longer-term independence could only come from a dramatic enhancement of Britain's export performance which in turn would involve competition with America's technologically far more advanced and productive multinational companies (Gardner, 1956). Any state subsidies were expressly denied by the terms of American aid. This was the dilemma facing Britain's policy-makers at the end of the war. In these circumstances Britain chose an indirect but very effective alternative route: the complete nationalization of its industrial infrastructure. Although there were powerful political reasons for the post-war nationalization, the particular way in which it was handled makes clear that these economic objectives were central. Transport and all forms of domestic energy production including coal, gas and electricity were taken into public ownership and comprehensively re-equipped. Pricing was placed strictly under government control and sct at levels that were highly advantageous to industrial producers. At least in the short run, the results were impressive. By 1950 British exports were 50 per cent higher, at constant prices, than in 1938 (Saville, 1993; Foster, 1993).

In this context, coal was particularly important. It was the only indigenous source of energy at a time when externally-sourced oil was earmarked for overseas currency earning. The redevelopment of coal was therefore given a strategic priority. Before the war, coal had been protected from competition by the imposition in 1934 of an import levy on oil. While the levy was lifted in 1947, during a period of acute coal shortage, coal continued to be seen as the basis of British energy policy and a protective import tariff was again imposed on oil in 1961 which effectively increased its domestic price by 25 per cent. In addition, the government embarked on an ambitious and very costly programme for the development of nuclear energy. Somewhat strangely, therefore, given the country's position in the world oil market, Britain remained considerably more dependent on coal as a source of energy than most of its major industrial rivals into the 1970s (Cazenove & Co, 1972: 80). For Britain's banking establishment and the

Treasury, oil's role was quite different. It was as a key provider of external currency and profit income.

So, to sum up. Externally-derived oil had been critical for Britain's economic and strategic policy-making for 50 years before the discovery of oil in the North Sea. As a commodity, its effective exploitation demanded transnational organization, very large scale capital concentration and the use of political and military power to sustain relations of dominance with client regimes. To this extent, the requirements of the oil industry matched quite exactly Britain's residual imperial strengths as well as its industrial weaknesses. The centrality of the industry was reflected in the degree to which the boards of the two big oil companies comprehensively interlocked with those of the leading merchant banks. After the war there was a further twist: the process of oil trading became locked into much wider structures for geopolitical dominance. While it was primarily the American oil majors that brokered the price and their tax transfers which set the ground rules for the new global relationships, the results were inevitably also critical for the British majors and their ability to sustain themselves as central vehicles for overseas earnings. Internationally, in terms of banking and commodities, Britain and the United States were joint beneficiaries of the resulting balance of world power – even though Britain suffered disproportionately from the accompanying return of Western Germany and Japan to industrial competitiveness.

Oil in the Sea: The Origins of a New Type of Alliance

By the 1960s, two interconnected problems threatened this post-war hegemony. The first concerned the structure of the industry. The protection of the US market and the tax clawback on overseas operations was designed to sustain the profit income of the oil majors. It also created a protected environment for the development of new oil companies in the United States – the so-called independents – and simultaneously propelled them overseas to reap the tax benefits (Yergin, 1991).[7] In consequence, the relatively regulated global oil-price structure of the early 1950s broke down. Although the global consumption of oil more than doubled between 1950 and 1960, the highly competitive market meant that prices fell by up to a third in the late 1950s, and continued to fall through the 1960s. This triggered the second contradiction: a political one. The purpose of the tax arrangements had been to compensate the oil companies for sharing profits with client governments. The fall in oil price, and of resulting income to friendly regimes, now brought new political problems. In Latin America, in North Africa and above all in the Middle East, American dominance no longer looked so certain. The Soviet Union was supplying oil technology. Nationalization began. In 1960 the Organisation of Petroleum Exporting Countries (OPEC) was formed – though its initial attempts to establish a producers' cartel had minimal effect.

These developments were matters of very considerable concern to the strategists of both the American government and the US oil majors. America was deemed to have enough oil for its own long-term needs. But it could not export. Its control of the world energy market depended on external sources. Eighty per cent of these were now within regions classified as politically instable of which the most worrying remained the Middle East. Here the deepening of the Arab–Israeli conflict had placed major question marks over the continuity of supply. To these concerns was added another: developments in the countries which had benefited from cheap oil supplies. In the 1940s and early 1950s, Japan, Germany, Italy and France were front-line states in the Cold War. Now they were emerging as industrial rivals. They wanted to be free of US-controlled energy and were seeking to secure their own supplies either through direct negotiations with Middle Eastern producers or, as in the case of Germany, through the imports from the Soviet Union.

Together these developments triggered a radical shift of policy. Henceforth, oil exploration was to be focused on politically stable areas, so that in the longer-term future the oil majors could draw a significant part of their supply from outside OPEC. In 1964 the Chief Executive of Exxon, Munroe Rathbone, ordered a $700 million programme of exploration in Canada, Alaska, Australia and the North Sea. At roughly the same time, John J. McCloy, then spokesperson for the US oil industry (and previously in the 1940s head of the European Recovery Programme in Europe), indicated this as the priority for all US oil companies (Sampson, 1976; Bromley, 1987). British Petroleum, hitherto highly dependent on Iran, had already initiated exploration in Alaska in 1959, largely in order to get access to the lucrative US market. Other oil majors developed similar programmes from the mid-1960s. The companies knew that oil in these locations was likely to be much more expensive. Its value was as a bargaining counter. It would give the oil companies a long-term leverage over the cheap oil and what was done with it. Long-term exploration outside OPEC areas was meant to give the US government and the US oil majors effective dominance over what still remained by far the biggest and cheapest source of oil: the Middle East.

The discovery of North Sea oil in 1969 was not, therefore, accidental. It was a product of the strategic planning required by the geopolitical character of the oil industry. And the conditions for its extraction were equally determined by such factors.

The existence of hydrocarbon deposits in the North Sea had been considered likely ever since the late 1950s when very major gas finds had been made in Holland. Initially the objective was natural gas – which could be extracted relatively cheaply from the shallow waters of the southern North Sea. From 1962 British and Norwegian governments were negotiating the territorial division of the North Sea, and in 1963/64 the Conservative government established a licensing system which gave it very considerable discretion to favour British companies. Territorial agreement on the UK Continental Shelf (UKCS) was reached in 1965, and at the same time the Wilson government negotiated gas supply agreements with BP, by which the Gas Board was to be the sole purchaser. Similar agreements were reached with some American companies in 1966. In licence allocation, preference was given to those companies which entered exploration and production partnerships with state companies such as the Gas Board and the Coal Board (Cameron, 1983: 192).

In this first, pre-oil, phase of the North Sea, there was considerable continuity with pre-existing domestic energy policy. The objective was national self-sufficiency. The concern was with energy costs for industry and to save foreign currency. Conservative and Labour governments both sought to maintain a very considerable degree of state control to ensure that the price and conditions of supply were fully regulated and to secure the involvement of British companies.

This is a measure of the contrast with the period after 1969. The extraction of oil from the North Sea occurred against a quite different background. It was not a matter of domestic energy policy. The way it was accomplished, both very fast and with the implantation of an external production regime, can only be understood on the wider canvas.

The first discoveries of commercial amounts of oil in non-OPEC locations occurred at roughly the same time. BP secured commercial discoveries in Alaska in 1968. Amoco struck oil in the UKCS in 1969. Phillips did so slightly later the same year in the Norwegian sector. In all these locations, the environmental conditions for extraction and delivery were extremely harsh. For the North Sea, the technology of deep-sea drilling was still at an early stage. For both Alaska and the North Sea, the capital costs were enormous, and the production cost per barrel would be such as to make oil from any of these locations totally uneconomic at the market rate of 1969 – then at its lowest since the war.

It is generally agreed that the initial success of OPEC in negotiating production quotas and increasing oil prices between 1970 and 1971 was not achieved without some co-operation from the oil majors (Sampson, 1976;

Odell, 1981: 113 and 230; Bromley, 1991: 151–4). These years represented the high point of trade rivalry and currency warfare between the United States, France and other European powers. In 1971 Nixon had broken the post-war gold–dollar link and set off a drastic devaluation of the US currency in which oil sales were denominated (Stadnachenko, 1975: 235). This made an increase in the dollar price of oil especially urgent for OPEC governments – and probably quite acceptable to the US government which saw higher energy costs as a further pressure on its industrial rivals.

This initial encouragement of OPEC was of course only tactical, and did not extend into 1972, when OPEC exploited existing production agreements to secure further price increases. It certainly did not apply to 1973, when the renewal of the Arab–Israeli conflict caused a leap in oil prices of unprecedented dimensions. The initial increase was, however, essential if the extraction of non-OPEC oil was to begin. By mid-1971 the rise in price was sufficient for the oil majors operating in the UKCS to action the development of the two big fields then discovered: Forties and Brent. Even then the risks and costs were very high. If oil was to be extracted on a scale that would impact on world markets with any speed, a massive and tightly bunched investment programme would be needed. In 1972 this was conservatively estimated as requiring the equivalent of 20 per cent of the UK's industrial investment for a decade. Such additional funds were quite beyond the resources of either the British government or the City of London, and were only conceivable as a result of a long-term strategic alliance between British and American capital.

The Rapid Extraction of Offshore Oil

It was this new type of relationship with US capital, and its strategic relationship to US government policy, which explains the special characteristics of the UKCS and why its development was so different from that of the Norwegian sector. The implantation of an external production regime, the exclusion of trade unions, the lack of an effective health and safety system, the disaggregated structure of management and the weakness of the indigenous supply base – all the key causes of crisis of the late 1980s and early 1990s – can be traced back to the very specific understandings achieved in the early 1970s. None was inevitable.

In Norway, we find almost exactly the reverse – even though oil was discovered at the same time, in the same conditions and in the same quantities. In the early 1980s Norwegian production was only 10 per cent that of Britain.

By the mid-1990s Norway was ahead. And it was Norway's path of development that was the obvious one if the sole objective was internal economic development. Norway's internationally competitive oil-technology industry currently stands witness to this. Norway insisted on depletion controls, strictly regulated and phased development and a direct state interest in each licence. Slow and regulated development was first and foremost vital for the viability of wider industrial economy. Without this, it was almost inevitable that the currency would rise in value to the detriment of industrial exports (proportionately a much bigger danger in Norway – but one ultimately experienced in the UK). Slow development was no less important if local industry was to gain the lead-in time to lodge itself in the high value, high technology sectors of oil supply. This was equally true for other aspects of Norwegian policy: the development of state-owned oil companies (awarding contracts to local suppliers), the insistence on Norwegianization (every external expert to be accompanied by a Norwegian), and the integration of the offshore industry into onshore industrial relations and health and safety practice. In Norway the offshore oil industry was not permitted to develop, as it had previously in all Third World locations, as an external implantation with a culturally distinct production regime. Such development would itself constitute a major barrier to local industrial penetration (Noreng, 1980; Andersen, 1993).

Yet this is precisely what did happen in the UK. The failure of the UK to take Norway's path of development, which might seem to have been the normal one for an already industrialized country, can only be understood in terms of what had gone before: the degree to which the world role of sterling and the City of London depended on the two great British oil companies, and the degree to which both these oil companies and the British government were locked into an existing special relationship with America. From 1971/72 this relationship became, for two decades at least, much closer.

The shift in terms of economic policy was both massive and, at the point of change, largely unnoticed and uncontested. The smoothness with which the British State swung round to this new alignment – and the almost complete lack of questioning by key establishment figures in the early 1970s – can only be understood when we recollect the institutional centrality of the oil companies within the British State and the key institutions of British capital.

For the inter-war period we noted the contribution of oil to Britain's balance of payments and a proportionately even greater contribution to the profit income of British capital. For long periods between the wars, the ratio of profits to share value exceeded 20 per cent. By the early 1950s this figure was even higher and, as we have seen, the volume of UK corporate profit income from this source had reached 14 per cent of the total. Aaronovitch has shown the degree of interlock of directors with the merchant banking sector for the 1950s. Key figures from the two UK oil majors sat on the boards of the three most active merchant-bank groupings – Hill Samuel, Morgan Grenfell and Lazards – or perhaps vice versa (Aaronovitch, 1961: 89). By 1972 this level of interlinkage was even more marked. The two major oil companies included among their directors key figures from fourteen major joint-stock and merchant banks – the Cobbolds, Keswicks, Inchcapes, Samuels, Geddes, Stevens (*Stock Exchange Official Year Book*, 1973/74). These directors included three present or future directors of the Bank of England.

The two UK oil majors therefore represented the country's biggest industrial concerns, which at the same time were at the centre of investment and banking and had direct access to strategic policy formation at the level of the Bank of England and the Treasury. The apparent ease with which a very specific path of development was adopted for UKCS oil can only be understood in this context.

Britain's oil was to be extracted at the fastest rate possible, with limited state control and in conditions of close commercial partnership between American oil companies and banks and those of Britain. This alliance was not just financial. It was practically embedded, as a matter of policy, in the system of production itself. Britain wanted United States capital locked in and sharing risk in the long run. The system of discretionary licensing, by which the government chose the licensees on non-market criteria, together with the very small size of blocks allocated, was used to ensure the creation of joint consortiums for the development of any field. And these partnerships, at the level of production, were underpinned by the supply of finance from the American banks and to a significant extent also by the American government. Britain's biggest company, Shell, formed a joint company with America's biggest, Exxon. The resulting company, Shell Expro, controlled around 35 per cent of all investment and output in the UKCS and was the dominant player in the UKCS for two decades until the early 1990s.

There was a threefold rationale for the formation of this alliance. First, there were the needs of the British oil majors themselves. As essentially colonial producers, they had been affected particularly badly by the tide of nationalization which had swept through the OPEC countries over the previous four years. It was now urgent that they re-establish their own independent sources of crude oil. Second, there were the needs of the City of London for foreign currency. By 1971 the balance of payments deficit was becoming a chronic threat to the stability of the pound and the City's banking role. The opening of the North Sea promised to reverse it. At this level the needs of the oil majors, the City and the Treasury coincided. The third element was one which American and British interests shared: the strategic need to secure sources of oil outside OPEC control. Access to such oil was of great importance both to the US and UK oil majors and to the American government. It became even more vital in 1972 and 1973, as France, Germany and Japan threatened to do direct deals with non-US suppliers of oil and to operate outside the terms of the US-led anti-OPEC body, the International Energy Agency (IEA). The sooner significant volumes of non-OPEC oil could be brought on to the market the sooner US dominance could be restored. The North Sea and Alaska, where BP held the dominant stake, were the main hopes.

There were two further implications which followed. If the object of getting oil out of the North Sea was to undercut OPEC, then speedy extraction was important for another reason also. Success would eventually result in a fall in price. Informed estimates of the early 1970s calculated that this would take between ten and fifteen years. Hence, enough oil needed to be extracted before prices fell to cover the capital costs of the original investment (Cazenove & Co, 1972: 94).[8] Within this strategic perspective, it made no sense at all to hold back production in order to retain reserves for the distant future. The other implication concerned the commercial partnership between Britain and America. Fast extraction demanded a prodigious level of capital investment very early. Estimates of how much were hazy at this stage. But everyone knew it would be immense, and in the event it amounted to nearly a quarter of the UK's industrial investment for the best part of a decade.[9] In 1971 such sums were quite beyond both the UK oil majors and the City of London. Accordingly, if the objective was to get the oil out quickly, most of the money would have to come from the US. Slow development might have been within the financial capabilities of the City of London. Fast development was not.

The New Alliance and US Involvement

These calculations – very specific to a particular moment in the development of international oil politics between 1970 and 1972 – underlay the policy decisions of these years. They marked a definite reversal of the North Sea policies of the previous Conservative government in 1963–64, which had sought to give very strong preference to British-owned companies (Robinson and Morgan, 1978; Jessop, 1983; Bromley, 1987).[10] They were also to a considerable extent irreversible themselves. There were two licensing rounds between 1969 and 1972. In these, a total of 388 blocks were awarded for the oil-bearing basins of the northern sector of the UKCS – comparable to the 475 in the two rounds of 1964 and 1965 covering the gas-bearing southern basin. Only 86 licences were awarded in the two further licence rounds of 1976–77 and 1978–79. The 388 blocks sold in 1969–70 and 1971–72 contained the great bulk of the oil-bearing territories east of the Shetlands (Atkinson and Hall, 1983; Cameron, 1983: Appendix 2). They were sold cheap. Total revenue was less than £40 million. They were sold under the terms of the 1964 Continental Shelf Act which gave the government only very limited controls over the way in which the blocks were used, and vested ownership of the recovered oil in the oil companies and ultimately in the bankers who put up the money. Liabilities were solely a 12.5 per cent royalty tax and Corporation Tax on profits. There was, in addition, a highly lucrative tax loophole. Both British and foreign companies could set overseas losses against earnings in the North Sea.

So these years were the critical ones for the future. It was at this point that a new type of alliance was forged between the United States and Britain that was no longer based simply on a general convergence of diplomatic and financial interests. The linkage with American capital now reached into the heart of the City of London. The two countries were jointly committed to a highly risky venture that involved both governments as well as the banking systems. In Britain's case the relative commitment was of course far greater; but strategically the venture was vital for both countries.

The licences sold between 1969 and 1972 gave US firms the majority: 54 per cent of the territory as against 32 per cent for the UK firms. In addition, most of the territory held by UK firms was either in direct partnership with US firms (as with Shell) or dependent on US banking finance. BP required £330 million to develop the Forties field – and of this 60 per cent came from the US banking system under a consortium headed by Morgan Guarantee. Twenty per cent was supplied direct by the US government.[11] In all £18 billion, over 60 per cent of the total capital cost of opening the UKCS, was borrowed from the US between 1972 and 1978 – making up almost half of the total overseas capital invested in Britain in these years. Getting a return on these loans added to the strategic pressure, in terms of balance of payments and control over oil markets, for quick results.

At industry level, the new alliance found expression in the United Kingdom Offshore Operators Association (UKOOA). This had existed as an informal association of UKCS oil companies since 1965. In 1973 it became a formal association recognized by the government as the prime negotiator on all matters concerning the industry. It included all major companies, the majority American, and maintained a monolithic unity until the crisis period of the early 1990s (UKOOA, 1987; Cameron, 1983: 104–7).

For the early 1970s, the industry's needs became the country's needs. Government responded. The first director of the Offshore Supplies Office, Norman Smith, describes the oil-related sector of the economy as being on a 'war footing'. During Heath's final days in Downing Street, when industrial electricity supply had been reduced to three days a week, it was the task of the Offshore Supplies Office to supply lists of firms engaged in oil-related work. For these factories alone, electricity was provided on a seven-day basis.[12]

The Implantation of a 'United States style' Production Regime

By the end of the decade around 30,000 people were employed directly in the North Sea, and as many again in support services onshore. Another 100,000 were in industries that significantly depended on the North Sea market.

What made the industry unique was the degree to which its production regime was transplanted virtually intact from its American base. This was so for its technology and its management structures, its systems of contract and supply, and even for those areas usually most susceptible to local modification: health and safety practices and industrial relations.

In some ways this implantation was, initially at least, almost unavoidable. Britain's international oil industry had until very recently been based in locales like the Middle East where oil was easily accessible and demanded little in the way of technology apart from ships to take it away. The high technology side of the industry was dominated by the United States. This stemmed from two historical peculiarities. First, there was the character of the US internal market: protection gave a profit premium to any reduction in the production cost of domestic oil. Second there was the strategic importance attached by the US government to external oil after the war. Matched with the sheer scale of the activities of US oil companies overseas, this produced an oil equipment and servicing industry which itself operated on an international scale. Initially, at the end of the war, it gained considerable government subsidy. In the 1960s, at which point the US industry controlled 80 per cent of the world market, the Department of Commerce still policed the industry against the transfer of technology to trade rivals (Feagin, 1990: 607; Hallwood, 1990: 63).

The organizational principle on which this supply industry operated, and had been operating since the 1940s, foreshadowed developments which were to take place in other industries in the 1980s and 1990s. It involved a radical contracting-out of the production process. Normally, over three-quarters of those employed would be the employees of specialist contractors and not of the oil company itself. This matched the needs of the operators, as the oil companies were technically called, in a number of ways. First and foremost, there was the phased character of the extraction process. Quite different sets of skills would be required at each stage in the cycle of exploration, development and production. Particularly in overseas locales, it was much cheaper to buy them in from a specialist than seek to supply them in-house. And it was certainly seen as safer that this specialist be an American-based transnational rather than risk giving local industries a grip on supply and technology – even if the country itself happened to be at that stage of development.

For political as well as economic reasons, therefore, there developed a strategic interdependence between the US oil majors and the giant oil contracting firms such as Brown and Root, Odeco and Marathon who originated the technology and owned the patents for advanced oil production. The contractors' ability to operate world-wide with an American-dominated global industry gave them the volume of work and cash flow needed for investment in technological advance. In theory at least the system of competitive tendering ensured that the services of the contractors could be purchased by the operators on the cheapest basis.

Accordingly, when the decision was taken to invest in the UKCS, the American oil majors brought with them their own contracting firms; and, because of the joint consortium arrangements, this involved the UK investors as well. Even in the solitary case of BP, which operated on its own in a number of fields, the company only employed core staff and relied on US-based contractors for the great bulk of the specialist services. Indeed, in the case of their first big investment, the Forties field, BP had no choice. The US government tied their share of the £330 million loan to the use of US suppliers. Hence, the fast development of the UKCS did not just mean reliance on American capital. It also meant, as the 1978 Report on the Financing of North Sea Oil stressed, dominance by American technology and management structures:

> North Sea oil has undoubtedly presented a number of difficult problems. The first is the strength of the international companies in the oil industry. Oil exploration and development are technologically very advanced operations. The expertise generally resides in established companies, or, if advances in technology are needed, can most easily be acquired by them. It is difficult therefore for new entrants to break into the industry. If development of the North Sea was to take place quickly, it was inevitable that it would be dominated at least initially by the established companies. (Wilson, 1978: 2)

Where previous American multinational investors in the UK had brought with them a factory, the oil majors brought with them a virtually complete industry. As in Third World locations, the personnel, usually down to foreman and supervisor level, would be American. The command structures, the relations between contractors, the pace of work, the conventions on health and safety were all American. Moreover, initially at least, local labour had only a weak purchase over the work process. With the exception of the steel fabrication and construction work, local workers were mainly used for tasks that required little prior skill.

This special 'external' character was something which the US operators were keen to retain for another reason also – one shared with their UK partners. This was to eliminate trade union interference with the production process. The period from 1969 to 1975 marked a high point of trade union militancy in Britain. The attempt by the Heath government to impose legal constraints in 1970/71 had gone a long way to repoliticize the trade union movement. In 1972 and again in 1974, at the very moments when the main investment decisions were being taken, the miners had used their power within another sector of the energy industry to enforce demands on wages and conditions. For the oil majors investing in the UKCS, continuity of supply was essential. The long-term value of oil from the North Sea was precisely to bring pressure to bear on OPEC. A unionized industry, where the flow of oil might be halted at any time, could not serve this purpose. The story of how attempts at unionization were thwarted is told in detail in the next chapter, but it is important to stress the centrality of this concern for oil investment in the UK sector. The American oil production and equipment industry had been among the corporate leaders of the process of de-unionization in the United States twenty years before (Kochan *et al.*, 1986: 58, 69). They certainly did not want to see unionization reappearing among their workers in Britain. The new US consul in Edinburgh, Richard Funkhouser, previously on the State Department's oil strategy desk at the height of the Cold War, briefed the State Department in detail on developments. Particularly after the return of a Labour government in 1974, the oil companies were acutely concerned about the growth of trade union influence (Yergin, 1991; Harvie, 1994).

Voices of Dissent

The point of interest is not so much the appearance of a US-style production regime in the UK. This was almost unavoidable. It was also present in the first phase of the Norwegian sector. It is the fact that this regime survived intact for two decades. In Norway, a deliberate policy of assimilation was initiated from the early 1970s and had become effective in most areas by the late 1970s (Noreng, 1980: 211). Norwegian health and safety and industrial relations procedures applied. Every external technical expert had to be accompanied by a Norwegian counterpart. The Norwegian state production companies sponsored the development of Norwegian supply firms. In the UK also there were steps in this direction, but they were defeated.

In Norway's case, these pressures came as much from Norwegian capital as from the labour movement. As both Noreng and Andersen make clear, Norwegian industry had its own very clear agenda for entry to the oil production market. Policies for state control and the Norwegianization of staffing and management were pursued as vigorously by Conservative governments as they were by the Social Democrats. In Britain quite similar interests did exist – and in the 1970s they had the potential for tactical alliance with Labour governments which had, on paper at least, even more radical commitments for public ownership than those in Norway. These interests were, however, outmanoeuvred. The comprehensiveness of their defeat between 1975 and 1981 is probably the most telling evidence for the centrality of the new alliance with US capital.

The disquiet about the existing course of development first surfaced in the all-party Commons Public Accounts Committee in 1972–73. The Committee first met on 15 May 1972 and continued meeting till January 1973 – a period during which the price of oil continued to rise dramatically, and when the terms of the third and fourth licensing rounds of 1970 and 1971 appeared totally derisory. The concerns of the committee, led by two Labour Party right-wingers, Edmund Dell and Howard Lever, were threefold. First, the licences had been sold on terms that bore no relation to the value of oil discoveries, with tax dispensations which meant that far into the 1980s very little income would accrue to the state. Second, British-owned industry appeared to be receiving little benefit from the massive investments being made. The best estimate, that made by the International Management and Engineering Group consultants (IMEG), was that between 25 per cent and 30 per cent went to UK-owned firms. Third, the Department of Trade and Industry section concerned with oil and gas appeared to have little independent information on costs or income and took what the oil companies told them at face value. The Public Accounts Committee report also made repeated reference to the much more active steps being taken by Norway to place the industry within some form of state control. Finally, the issue of depletion was raised – not decisively but as a warning note that the speed of development also involved important issues regarding the impact of an oil-related currency on the well-being of other sectors of the economy (Committee of Public Accounts, 1973: xxiv, xxvi, xxxi). All these fears were given even more pointed expression by Lord Balogh in his article in *The Banker* for March 1974. He effectively accused the government, or at least the relevant ministries, of collusion with the oil companies against the wider national interest, and argued for the creation of a National Hydrocarbon Corporation that would manage a state participation share in each field on Norwegian lines (Balogh, 1974: 281–8).

These pressures did indeed have some legislative impact. The effect of the Public Accounts Committee hearings was to compel the government to establish the Offshore Supplies Office in January 1973. During the last months of the Heath government considerable annoyance was felt in the Treasury, and by Heath himself, at the refusal of the British oil majors to assist the government during the fuel crisis. Even before the new Labour government came into power in March 1974, plans were being made to impose a somewhat tougher licensing and tax regime and possibly to initiate some form of state participation. The Labour Party, responding to a highly politicized trade union movement and wishing to impose some form of Social Contract incomes policy, spoke in terms of the 'public control' of oil and gas – an ambition translated into the British National Oil Corporation (BNOC) by Tony Benn as Secretary of State for Energy from 1975.

BNOC emerged very much as the corporatist vehicle that might – in other circumstances – have become the champion for the British industrial lobby. It was led by a previous managing director of Courtaulds, Lord Kearton. Its financial director, Alistair Morton, who had strongly corporatist views on the need for state industrial intervention, came from a background in industrial management and went on to head Eurotunnel. Its initial actions were to develop participation agreements that effectively saw the British government raising bank loans for smaller British oil companies and going out of its way to give special concessions to the biggest UK industrial conglomerate, ICI (Corti and Frazer, 1983: 176).

Yet, despite all this, not much changed. The first product of the parliamentary criticism, the Offshore Supplies Office, achieved remarkably little. It even failed to change the conventions for collecting statistics. The Public Accounts Committee had criticized the Department of Energy for collecting its statistics on supplies for the UKCS in terms of British-based and not British-owned companies. The Offshore Supplies Office, which inherited most of its staff from the Department of Energy, continued to produce statistics on exactly the same basis, and was consequently able to report very quickly that

its objective of 70 per cent British content had been achieved. Research conducted ten years later revealed that the percentage of input from British-
owned companies, as against US subsidiaries, remained exactly as it had at
the time of the IMEG report in 1973: less than 30 per cent. Moreover, with
one or two exceptions, the UK-owned imput was almost exclusively in the
low-technology, low value areas of catering and routine maintenance (Harris,
Lloyd and Newlands, 1988; Hallwood, 1990: Ch. 5).[13]

The Offshore Energy Technology Board, set up in 1975 by Benn to develop
technology in strategic areas of oil and gas extraction, was scarcely more successful. It had only limited funding as a result of the financial crisis of 1976,
and, probably more to the point, could identify very few UK-owned firms
that were willing to act as active partners and champions for technological
innovation (DEn, 1976a: 11–13). The US industry had got there first. The calculation of UK firms was, quite reasonably, that the very fast timetable set for
UKCS development meant that, by the time they had developed a technological competence, the most lucrative phase would be over.[14]

Some limited changes were also made to the legal and tax basis of licensing
in the 1975 Petroleum and Submarine Pipelines Act and in the 1975 Oil Taxation Act. The changes were, however, limited. The new Petroleum Revenue
Tax took a percentage of the market value of the oil produced, initially 45 per
cent, and could be periodically changed to reflect the price. The old tax loophole for the claiming of overseas losses was closed. Instead, companies were
allowed the right to claim the exploration and development costs involved in
producing that particular stream of oil. All these were to be recovered before
tax was paid. The Petroleum and Submarine Pipelines Act was intended to
give the government greater control over the process and speed of development, bringing the legal basis more closely in line with that in the Norwegian
sector. As the law stood previously, the government had no powers whatever
to enforce any form of depletion control over oil in licence blocks. The
Labour government, through its first Minister for Energy, Eric Varley, spent
most of its time reassuring the oil companies that the powers would not be
used. Specific guarantees were given that any discretionary powers, if ever
implemented, would only affect 20 per cent of the potential of any field,
would not apply to pre-1976 discoveries until 1982, and for subsequent discoveries would not come into force until 150 per cent of the costs had been
recovered. The logic of the legislation was ultimately reversed and presented
as an incentive for the fastest possible extraction over the years to 1982
(Cameron, 1983: 119).

The British National Oil Corporation, established in 1976, did make some
more significant inroads. It used its powers to gain commercial information

and, in a limited way, to engage in exploration and production. The small number of licences awarded in the two licence rounds of 1976–77 and 1978–79 gave to UK public sector companies up to 50 per cent of the very small amount of territory allocated. In pushing this through Benn certainly did annoy the American oil majors and their British partners. But BNOC singularly failed to break their grip. The aspiration of Tony Benn, and probably of Kearton as well, was to create a British state corporation which could ultimately play as dominant a role in the UKCS as Statoil did in the Norwegian sector. The Labour Party's election manifesto and its 1974 White Paper both called for some form of public control and direct participation. The outcome, however, was somewhat different. What BNOC eventually achieved was not control of the oil, let alone company assets, but of oil supply. It gained the right to buy 51 per cent of all oil produced, at a price which would not be to the disadvantage of the oil companies, in return for either writing off tax debts or providing a proportion of the capital needed for development. In this form, the government acted as broker and risk-taker for a proportion of the oil produced, in a way that was ultimately acceptable to the oil companies.[15]

These arrangements were hammered out between 1975 and 1977. They enabled the Labour government to say it had honoured its election pledge on public control. But the proportion of oil reserves controlled by the oil majors remained virtually unchanged. Despite the entrance of a few more smaller UK-owned companies including BNOC, the top five oil majors, Shell, Esso, Mobil, BP and Texaco, still produced over 60 per cent of the output. Through consortium arrangements these companies in fact participated in virtually all fields – and the major suppliers, employing up to 80 per cent of the workforce, also remained American. The structure of the industry and the character of its production regime stayed almost entirely intact. All this was in the face of a determined Secretary of State for Energy, and a Labour government representing a radicalized trade union movement.

This was no inconsiderable achievement for the oil companies. It can really only be understood in terms of the historical factors discussed earlier. If it had just been a matter of the US oil companies alone, they would have been very unlikely to have fared any better than in Norway. What was different was the centrality of the US alliance to the objectives of British finance capital: the degree to which the UK oil companies had long formed an integral part of the City of London, had direct links with the Treasury on account of their foreign exchange functions, had from the mid-1960s effectively colonized the government department overseeing the UKCS, and, finally, had reason, together with the City of London, to form a long-term strategic partnership with the US energy sector. It was this pre-existing and continuing influence of the UK oil majors that was crucial. The UK government had to face the united opposition of the UK oil majors and their merchant-banking allies as well as the US government.

There were groups within British capital at regional level who wanted to see a quite different path of development. They were joined by some in the leadership of the chemicals and synthetics industry who had always resented the oil industry's control of their feedstock. However, these groups had no clear path of influence. In the Conservative Party and the CBI much more powerful influences stood against them. In the Labour Party the position was scarcely better. In the 1960s Labour had championed industrial regenera-tion. In the 1970s it might have appeared as the natural vehicle for a 'national' oil policy. But between 1974 and 1979 it failed to deliver. Whenever Benn or BNOC appeared to be treading too closely on oil companies' toes, the oil men went straight to Wilson and Healey.[16] In 1975 the US Department of Commerce threatened to withdraw US-owned drilling rigs (Cameron, 1983: 99). The 1976 sterling crisis, in particular, gave ample opportunity for both the oil majors and British and US bankers to bring pressure to bear. Perhaps the most remarkable part of this story is that told in the next chapter. This is the degree to which it was possible for the oil employers to sidestep the Labour government's commitments on union recognition and, as part of this, to exempt the offshore industry from the new trade-union-based onshore health and safety regulations. For the fastest growing sector of the British economy, absorbing a quarter of all new industrial investment, this was an achievement of some magnitude.

Oil and the Debate on Britain's Future

Nevertheless, in the mid to late 1970s, with Benn and a Labour government in power, the oil companies saw themselves as on the defensive and under threat. They were only too well aware that the political situation had changed markedly since 1971. At that point, the alliance of forces involving the City of London, the British and US oil majors and the Conservative government, gave every appearance of permanence and effectiveness. Since then, there had been two very major changes.

First, there had been a significant degree of radicalization within the trade union movement, and to a lesser extent in the general population. The suc-cess of the trade union movement in thwarting the government's attempt to limit strike action legally, and to impose an incomes policy, had changed expectations within the workforce. The effectiveness of direct industrial action had been demonstrated. The balance of power within major unions shifted decisively to the Left. This, in turn, was being reflected in demands for constitutional change in the Labour Party. While the Labour governments of Wilson and Callaghan were doing their best to stabilize the situation, it was not clear how long the right wing could maintain dominance. The election manifesto of 1974 had talked of an 'irreversible shift in the balance of wealth and power in favour of working people'. The 1975 Petroleum Act conferred considerable reserve powers on the state, and BNOC itself had every appearance of being the thin end of a very dangerous wedge. In Norway, it was just this period that saw trade union recognition being made obligatory. Why not in Britain also? So far, the companies had maintained a separate production regime more by evasion and delay, than any firm agreement. Funkhouser's State Department telegrams are testimony to the concerns of the American multinationals about the future potential of the Labour Left (Harvie, 1994: 243).

Second, there was possibly an even bigger worry on the horizon. This concerned the stability of the alliance created at the top level of British capital during the early 1970s. The alliance was still effective in the mid-1970s and was what sustained the political influence of the oil majors; but the warning signs were already there. Those elements of regional and industrial capital which wanted a different path of development, elements hitherto contained, were beginning to gain important new allies. By 1976 a major debate had erupted among the strategists of both industry and banking about the impact of the oil industry on the rest of the productive economy. There were two sides to this concern. One immediate problem was the inflationary effect of fast UKCS development on the rest of the economy. The other was the long-term effect on the currency.

The North Sea Costs Escalation Study published in 1976 showed that expenditure costs were running far ahead of the original estimates. The Forties field, as a typical example, cost £750 million against the £350 million predicted. About 70 per cent of the cost overrun was because the work was technologically more demanding than original estimates. Thirty per cent was the result of a direct increase in costs. A wage premium of up to a quarter was fairly routinely paid to attract labour. It might also be surmised that contractors' profits had a role. The relatively tight ring of US supply companies seem to have been able to ensure high margins in circumstances where all development costs could be claimed back against tax by the operators. Given the relative size of UKCS investment, these were worrying conclusions. Fast development was clearly injecting a significantly inflationary element into the economy (DEn, 1976b: 2, 9, 18).

The other issue of concern was longer-term but even more fundamental. The fast development of the UKCS would by the end of the decade, or shortly after, bring oil self-sufficiency. The balance of payments would then swing into surplus and sterling rise sharply in value. In the early 1970s this had not been an immediate concern of industry; the main worry at time of the OPEC price hike was the supply of energy and its high cost. Now, in 1977 and 1978, a petrocurrency pound was within sight. Added to global competitive pressures, a strong and relatively permanent appreciation of sterling could lead to a radical decline in industrial exports and investment. The force of this concern was all the more far-reaching because it would not simply effect industry. Sections of banking and the academic community began to consider the long-term impact of the loss of a manufacturing base – once either the volume or price of UKCS oil began to decline. Thinking into the future, the consequences would be no less serious for the City of London than they were for industry.[17]

For the US and UK oil strategists confronting OPEC, this debate was most unwelcome. The most obvious remedy in terms of Britain's national economy was to follow Norway's example and slow the pace of development and extraction. And such demands would start to impact on policy at just that point when the terms of the 1975 Petroleum Act made it possible to trigger depletion controls on existing licences. The early 1980s would be the critical period. Other things being equal, the output from the UKCS would then equal 20 per cent of petrol-grade oil being exported on to the world market. As long as depletion controls were not imposed, it would be possible to start to destabilize the OPEC alliance and resume control of the much more lucrative sources of oil in traditional locales.

The issues at stake were clearly fundamental ones. The prospect of industrial decline had the potential to create a new alliance around the demand for slower UKCS development which would have backing within British capital – with the strategic interests of the oil majors, particularly the American oil majors, and the US government, being seen as openly divergent. This was the dilemma of the years 1977 and 1978. While in the early and mid-1970s the opponents of 'fast' development were relatively isolated, the imminence of a petrocurrency in the late 1970s had the potential to change the balance.

Oil and the Thatcher Experiment

It was in this context that the debate about oil became interlocked with others about the whole future of the Conservative Party and British society. These two years saw the emergence of what has been rather misleadingly described as Thatcherism. It is extremely difficult to distinguish cause and effect, or even sequence (the only certainty is that virtually none of the ideas can be attributed in origin to Thatcher herself). But within the emerging arguments of those urging a radical break with the corporatist policies of the past, the issue of what was now called the 'oil bonanza' was central.

The prospect of a long-term balance-of-payments surplus, and high oil revenues to the government, opened up strategic options which had previously been dismissed as unthinkable. It also, and crucially for the oil majors, reversed the terms of the debate about oil. The oil surpluses now became positive: a political as much as an economic opportunity. They made feasible the type of radical surgery on the body politic that could permanently change the balance of forces in Britain. The radicalization of the trade union movement, the cycle of rising expectations in wages and the Leftward shift of the Labour Party could be ended by one massive 'market clearing' operation. The oil money would provide the safety net while governments applied the shock therapy of mass unemployment. The temporary difficulties of some sections of industry would be of little significance besides the long-term gains for British capital as a whole.

These arguments emerged in the summer of 1977. At that point, the main bogey of the oil lobby was still depletion controls. The Trade Policy Research Centre, headed by Frank McFadzean, managing director of Shell, continued to denounce any such controls as violating the free market, and forcing the UK to miss out historically in the sale of high-price oil (Robinson and Morgan, 1978). But in terms of the overall debate, the arguments of the New Right were far more effective.

They directly addressed the concerns about the wider impact on the industrial economy. As articulated in *Daily Telegraph* editorials and features, an oil-driven high exchange rate became entirely beneficial and to be encouraged. Overseas it would provide the launch pad for a new era marked by the massive export of capital. At home it would create, in safety-netted conditions, the deflationary environment needed to break the wages cycle and implement the shock therapy being advocated by Milton Friedman and Sir Keith Joseph from 1975–76 (Friedman, 1975, 1977).[18] What had been, a year or two earlier, a purely theoretical construct was, by the later 1970s, converted into real politics by the prospective oil surpluses. The rebirth of a truly entrepreneurial capitalism was now possible.

It should be stressed that, at this stage, most sections of industry still remained totally unconvinced. During 1977 the CBI became increasingly alarmed by the prospects of the pound as a petrocurrency. In October 1977 it produced a manifesto, *Britain Means Business*, which urged a quite contrary response to oil surpluses. The government was to prevent the appreciation of sterling by expanding the economy and spending the tax revenues itself internally. The way forward was not tax cuts or the freeing of exchange controls for capital export. It was a massive programme of infrastructural investment. The CBI's programme was duly denounced as corporatist by the New Right, who had just launched a counterattack on the collaboration by big business leaders (the 'Keartons, Catherwoods, Parkers and Ryders') with the Labour Party. The structures of large-scale industry, it was argued, destroyed the entrepreneurial instinct no less effectively than the civil service. Re-education was needed. Shock therapy applied as much to business leaders as to the trade union movement.[19]

At this stage, it is extremely difficult to say which sections of British capital supported the ideas of the New Right. Some sections of the City clearly did. In the short term, at least, there were prospects of very lucrative overseas activity – using a high value pound to pick up cheap assets in a depressed global economy. On oil money, there is not much direct evidence – although the New Right publications and think-tanks had close links with the American Right, which did draw income from corporate sources of this kind (Ross, 1983; Overbeek, 1990: 201–3).[20] But in terms of the substance of the argument, oil did have a key role. And this was equally so for the tactical planning of the New Right. Nicholas Ridley's Final Report of the Conservative Policy Group on Nationalised Industries was leaked by the *Economist* in May 1978.[21] This outlined the detailed steps needed to break the power of the trade union movement. Oil did not just have the role of creating a shock-therapy environment of high unemployment. It was also the technical means by which the UK's power stations could be switched away from coal as the preliminary to breaking the miners' union. The New Right for the first time put forward a vision of a trade-union-free environment very similar to what already existed in parts of America – and which already existed in the UK just offshore in the North Sea. To this extent, the late 1970s saw a critical move: from the localized implantation of an American production regime to the creation of a more generalized political regime which in many respects matched it.

The Implantation of a Matching Political Regime

The story of Thatcher's rise to power, first within the Conservative Party and later electorally, has been told many times elsewhere and needs no repeating.

It is, however, important to stress one or two aspects. The first is that the rise of the new leadership group did mark a radical break for the Conservative Party and its traditional base within British capital. The new group was vigorously opposed within the Conservative Party itself. Its ideas met determined resistance within large-scale industry and the CBI. It was openly challenged in 1978 by the *Economist* and sections of City opinion.[22] Conversely, its champions tended to be publicists and ideologues. They saw their primary task as one of political education. A new type of base had to be created within industry and finance. In this sense, it did mark an implantation of new ideas that were external to the previous organic link between British capital and the Conservative Party. The unquestioned, natural convergence of view between businessmen and their party no longer held. Newspapers and journals, the *Daily Telegraph* and the *Spectator* especially, were central to the drive to transform attitudes. The Institute of Directors consciously presented itself as an ideological counter to the CBI, with formal programmes of political education for industrial leaders presented monthly in its journal.[23] It was only after some years of this work, by about 1982, that a substantial constituency was won for the new ideas. It was then that journals like the *Economist* reversed their previous position and began arguing for a radical assault on corporatism and the trade union movement.[24] The years 1981 and 1982 finally saw the union-free, flexible labour environment of the American sunbelt (and UK offshore) being posed generally as the accepted model for the future.

The second point is that the one consistent theme of the New Right was the internationalization of the British economy and the conviction that its future depended on the introduction of production methods from outside – both Japanese and American. Bromley and Overbeek, and to some extent Jessop, point to the correspondence between this development and the growth within the UK's corporate sector of overseas firms themselves. Taking the top 1000, the number grew from less than 100 in the early 1960s, to 400 in the early 1980s (Bromley, 1987: 134; Overbeek, 1990: Ch. 7; Jessop *et al.*, 1988). It was this issue of internationalisation, and the degree to which it provided a secure base for the future, that was the rationale for the final battle with the Conservative old guard over Westland Helicopters in 1987 which dislodged Heseltine from the Department of Trade and Industry (DTI).[25]

The final point is that the new ideas, though radical, were by no means particularly coherent or indeed well grounded in economic reality. The global objectives were posed – but not the means. Nor were the new ideas implemented at all consistently. The chosen vehicle, Mrs Thatcher, was a very astute career politician with an instinct for conviction politics. But she possessed little economic knowledge on which to base these convictions. The role of advisers was therefore both important and potentially disastrous. There were elements in Thatcher's entourage with direct links with the American Right. There were others who were patrician class warriors, like Ridley, or newly rich City speculators. There were still others who were populist street fighters, ever ready to urge the use of the race card in a crisis. So while there was a common adherence to 'freeing the market', there was little agreement about how this was to be done. As advisers changed, so did policies. This is particularly clear when it comes to the politics of oil.

The immediate target was BNOC. Thatcher's instinct was for peremptory destruction. But BNOC was still there five years later – surviving, in the style of the Arabian Nights, on a succession of plausible sophistries from the BNOC directors. Thatcher was initially persuaded to stay her hand on grounds of nationalism (Corti and Frazer, 1983).[26] Privatization would lay UK oil reserves open to control by the European Commission. BNOC's existence conversely enabled Britain to dominate EC energy politics. Once the issue of privatization had been conceded, BNOC was saved for another couple of years by a conflict between advisers over whether its assets should be sold off in bits or whether it should be privatized as an entity; and after that, over whether it was justifiable, on both ideological and political grounds, especially in Scotland, for its Scottish-based production arm, Britoil, to be sold to the second biggest British oil major, BP.

However, the most crucial decisions concerned the regulation and control of the UKCS as a whole, and it is here that the inconsistencies become most apparent. In a strange but predictable way, the UKCS represented the Achilles' heel for Thatcher and the policies she espoused.

If there was one common theme to these policies it was an internationalisation of the economy, to the immediate benefit of the City of London financial sector, on the back of the revenues from the UKCS. These revenues were real and massive. In 1982 they reached £20 billion – approximately 7 per cent of the UK GDP (*Bank of England Quarterly Bulletin*, 1986; DTI, 1995, II). The element of risk, or perhaps wish-fulfilment, was the belief that an accompanying transformation would occur within the productive base of the economy, and that the oil revenues would continue long enough for this to happen. Timing was critical. And this, as at least some advisers could see, was the central contradiction of the policies. The opening of the UKCS was financed by US money. It depended on the strategic importance attached to it by the US oil majors and the US government. Sooner or later, and most commentators thought it would be the early to mid-1980s, the chips would be called in. The OPEC cartel would be challenged. While the intention was not to knock the bottom out of the oil market, it was certainly to reduce the price and gain access to cheaper sources of oil for future investment. In the event, the fall in price began in 1983 and had become precipitate by 1985. By then the price of oil had fallen, in real terms, back to the level of the early 1970s.

Hence, the big policy question facing the government throughout the early 1980s was how to sustain the pace of investment in the UKCS once prices had started to fall and the UKCS had lost its strategic importance for the US government and the US oil majors. As with much other policy emanating from the Thatcher governments, the response was confused, contradictory, and bedevilled by successive changes of personnel at ministerial level. The first tactic, in 1981-82, was to attempt to draw in new investment ventures, independent of the US banks, and funded from the now cash-rich City of London. This was done both by using the discretion of new licensing rounds to favour new smaller British oil companies, the first wave of 'independents', and by pressing forward the privatization of state assets within the UKCS. Enterprise Oil was carved out of the oil interests of British Gas; somewhat later, Britoil emerged from BNOC. This policy had very uneven success. Many of the smaller independents either were taken over by the oil majors or took speculative profits by selling their licence holdings and becoming dormant. At their peak, in the early 1980s, there were over 40 of these companies. By the later 1980s their number had been cut to 15 and by the early 1990s to 5 (Harvie, 1994: 297, 315).[27]

The next tactic was to throw money at the oil majors themselves. In 1983 the level of the Petroleum Revenue Tax was reduced and additional allowances made to cover capital expenditure. The most fateful policy change came after the oil price crash of 1985. The Petroleum Revenue Tax was now further amended. This time companies were allowed to offset all exploration and development costs for new fields against PRT on oil flowing *anywhere* within the UKCS.

The magnitude of the change in 1986 is explained by severe effects of the fall in oil prices on activity in the UKCS. Within twelve months the level of drilling and new exploration work had dropped by 60 per cent. Two-thirds of the rig yards were idle. The overall work force fell by 20 per cent. A significant number of the US supply firms withdrew from what they now considered to be a very marginal province with little apparent prospect of growth. Among those firms that remained there was a significant degree of merger and takeover (Pike, 1993; Salmond and Walker, 1986).

It was the combined effects of these responses to this crisis of 1985–86 which underlay the much more far reaching structural crisis of 1989–92 and the breakdown of the established industrial relations regime which is the main subject of this study.

First, there was the direct impact on maintenance and health and safety spending. By 1986, most of the structures were from ten to fifteen years old. They had been built at an early stage in the development of deep sea technology. They were now corroding and often overloaded. The effect of the collapse in oil prices was to bring an immediate suspension of maintenance programmes and a postponement of more major refurbishment. In addition, and probably far more dangerously, there were the safety consequences of the cuts in staffing levels and the increases in effective working hours. In circumstances where, as will be explored in later chapters, there were no trade-union safety representatives and statutory safety inspection had become purely formal, this situation in itself was dangerous enough.[28] It was, however, compounded by the other unique feature of the UKCS: its disaggregated management structures.

Hallwood studied the industrial organization of the UKCS just before the final impact of the price collapse was felt in 1984–85. He found the structures introduced in the early 1970s still in place. Eighty per cent of the employees on any rig would be employed by supply and contract firms. Many of these themselves used subcontractors. The oil operators sought to contain costs by using the invited tender system, which in periods of slack trade or recession, like 1986, enabled them to push down contract prices sharply and unload risk and costs onto others. The consequences for safety were therefore dire. There were no clear lines of responsibility. Each contractor would seek to limit its own remit. Communication would be poor and sometimes non-existent.

The other aspect of industrial structure which was to impact on the crisis of 1989–92 was the degree to which it was still overwhelmingly dependent on American-owned subsidiaries. The predictions of the 1970s proved correct. Fast development had made it almost impossible for UK-owned firms to enter any of the high-value, high-technology areas. Seventy per cent of the value of all work was still, according to Hallwood, conducted by overseas-owned firms. The proportion was even larger for high-value work (Hallwood, 1990; Cairns and Harris, 1988).[29]

In 1986 this had a particularly detrimental effect on the viability and vigour of the infrastructure of UKCS. As the global pattern of new oil investment started to shift, so the overseas-owned firms either reduced the scale of local operations, or closed them altogether. In Norway, a locally owned infrastructure of supply firms had by then been created. In very many cases, these were firms with other pre-existing locally based activities in shipping, engineering and ship construction and who thereby remained on site despite a downturn in oil-related activity. In the UKCS this was much less the case. The consequence of the 1985–86 price downturn was therefore a sharp shrinkage in the supply base, and, even worse, a shrinkage that reduced the viability of the market in a number of key specialisms.[30]

The results were soon felt. Oil prices started to rise in 1988 and then, in the run up to the Iraq–Kuwait war, temporarily escalated to the levels of the early 1980s. This revival in the oil market stimulated a renewed burst of exploration and development activity. However, its scale, as a result of the change in the tax regime in 1986, was disproportionate. Under the new tax dispensation the expenses involved in exploration and development anywhere in the UKCS could now be written off against Petroleum Revenue Tax on any UKCS oil source – not just the particular field producing that stream of oil. In what was now a free market for licences and licence assets, this meant that oil firms could search for oil virtually free of charge and either develop the finds themselves or sell them off at very high profit; 83 per cent of exploration costs could now be recovered from the government. The result was a surge of speculative finance into the UKCS and the arrival of the 'second wave' of independent oil companies. This set off massive inflationary pressures within the shrunken infrastructure of the UKCS. According to the DTI, production costs per barrel of oil rose by 50 per cent between 1988 and 1991 (DTI, 1993a: 3 and 8). Capital costs rose even faster. By 1991, the UKCS had become the highest-cost oil province in the world. At the same time oil prices fell back to their 1985 level.

This, then, was the magnitude of the wider crisis, and it was this that formed the economic background to the actions of the workforce in 1989 and 1990. Finally, therefore, before going on to examine these actions, we need to sum up our argument so far.

Oil had been a key ingredient of Britain's wealth long before its discovery in the North Sea. It represented the biggest single element of income derived from empire and ex-empire territories from the 1920s to the 1960s. This wealth was controlled by Britain's two biggest companies, BP and Shell, was critical for the stability of sterling and created very close links between these firms, the government and the City of London. Oil had also been the basis of close commercial relations with the United States. Up to 1970 this alliance had been tactical and qualified. At times there was conflict – as during the closing stages of the Second World War and during Suez. More generally there was co-operation. The demands of the Cold War in particular brought the British and American governments together in joint stratagems for the control of the Middle East and for the dominance of the world oil market. It was OPEC's challenge to this dominance which led directly to the search for oil in the politically secure waters of the North Sea. This was also why the assumptions governing the opening of the UKCS were so different from those operating in the Norwegian sector. The British oil majors wanted safe oil for the same reasons as the US oil majors: as part of a wider strategy for reasserting market power over the sources of cheap oil in the Middle East and elsewhere.

It was this overriding and urgent strategic objective that gave the earlier tactical alliance a new character in the 1970s. There were still quite separate national agendas. What changed was the scale of joint commitment to a vast and highly risky investment programme designed to produce globally significant amounts of oil within ten years. The objective of the British government and oil majors was to ensure that this risk was shared and that the Americans were locked into long-term investments. The Americans for their part wanted to ensure that they got the best possible deal on tax and capital equipment purchase and that there was no hindrance whatsoever to the speed of extraction or to the utilization of the oil.

This was the settlement reached in the early 1970s. Quickly, however, it underwent critical modification. On the one side, a new and radical Labour government began to cut into the freedoms of the American oil majors. On the other, the approaching prospect of the pound as a petrocurrency caused increasing sections of British industry and banking to question the long-term wisdom of fast extraction. It was in this context that the politics of free-wheeling monetarism began to contend for dominance within the Conservative Party. These politics had a variety of origins: those within the state apparatus who had been traumatized by the collapse of the Heath government; those like Ridley who had been most closely identified with that government's failed offensive against corporatism; those like Joseph who had become infatuated with the grandiose schemes for social engineering propagated by Friedman and the American New Right. But there was one common assumption: a belief that the arrival of massive oil surpluses could somehow be used to effect a Friedmanite shock therapy on Britain's industrial base and transform the character of the economy.

It is unclear how much support the US oil majors or US interests in general gave to these politics – except that they were seriously alarmed at the threat of some sort of depletion policy emerging under Labour (and possibly under old-style Conservatism). What is clear is that the new politics profoundly divided the Conservative Party and the key institutions of British capital, and that their implementation in government quickly exposed their economic incoherence. Thatcher allowed the oil economy to go at full throttle. The pound shot up in value. Manufacturing was decimated. But there was little sign of industrial regeneration or the repatriation of capital. And this left the government with a problem: how to ensure the continuation of oil investment and income in order to make up the deficit. The logic of the 1970 settlement was that oil from the UKCS would be used quickly and effectively to break OPEC and restore control over cheap oil. Investment would then flow in the other direction and the investment in high-cost oil taper off – which was as much the objective of the UK oil majors as the Americans. Faced with an imminent fall in the price of oil in the mid-1980s the government's only solution was to direct massive subsidies at new oil investment, with the inflationary consequences we have just described. This policy did indeed sustain a significant element of US involvement. But at the same time it gravely endangered the operations of the two British oil majors, BP and Shell. These companies found themselves disproportionately locked into the UKCS and unable to generate the income needed to reinstate themselves elsewhere on the globe. We will examine this particular dilemma in a later chapter. For the moment we will quote the main strategist of BP, John Browne, speaking in 1991:

> In my view the future can only be assessed properly in the full context of the position of the industry as a whole. The mature areas cannot be discussed in isolation. In terms of investment in particular this is an indivisible business. Political change, the trend in oil prices and profit margins and the changing shape of the industry world-wide will all influence what happens here in the North Sea.
>
> In essence it means intense competition in attracting investment. That competition comes from the newly accessible regions of the world which offer the prospect of large volumes of additional reserves at low cost. And that competition is made all the more intensive by limited cash flows and by the extent to which at the margin the sector has become a relatively unattractive place for new investment. (Browne, 1991)

So to conclude. We have described the arrival of an American production regime in the UKCS. We have examined the implications of oil for UK politics, and the degree to which it temporarily resulted in a very specific modification of the policies of the Conservative Party and of its links with British capital. We ended with the outcome of these policies for the British oil majors. They now wished to resume their traditional role as oil producers overseas – and found existing government policies obstructing this.

Fittingly, however, it was not the realm of economics which precipitated the crisis itself. It was the workforce on the rigs and platforms – those most directly exposed to a production regime which Thatcher had seen as a model for the whole country. In 1988 Piper Alpha blew up. Outrage and militancy were the result. Within four years, the old production regime of the 1970s was being actively dismantled. To quote a joint working party report from the DTI and the oil employers:

> A profound change of culture is necessary for all parties involved in the offshore-related industry if the costs of UKCS development are to be controlled. This will call for a change of approach from all concerned: oil companies; government; contractors and suppliers. ... We need to move away from adversarial contractual relationships and nurture relationships wherein people learn to work together in a common direction and purpose. (DTI, 1993a: 4)

Notes

1. Edith Penrose also points out that by the 1960s the pattern of non-UK shareholding in Royal Dutch Shell had become dispersed. The UK still held just under 40 per cent. Dutch shareholdings amounted to 18 per cent, US to 19 per cent, French to 12 per cent and Swiss to 10 per cent (p. 41).

2. See also *The Times*, 11 June 1938 and Shell Trading Company Limited, Accounts for 1937.

3. *Stock Exchange Year-Book*, 1939: entries for Anglo-Persian Oil Company Ltd and Shell Transport and Trading Company Ltd.

4. Aaronovitch notes the close linkage of the two oil majors with the dominant finance capital groupings – with interlocking directorships particularly strong with Samuels and Rothschild, Morgan Grenfell and Jardine Matheson.

5. Richard Funkhouser's address to the National War College, Washington, 4 December 1951, gives the most explicit account of US national interests. It was reproduced verbatim in the US Senate Committee on Foreign Relations hearings of 1974, pp. 160 ff.

6. Cave-Brown reproduces verbatim the documents of the US Joint Chiefs of Staff approved for implementation by President Truman in 1949. The documents were released under the Freedom of Information Act in 1977.

7. It was also the case that the US government used its influence to promote the entry of new oil companies. In large part this was probably to offset the threat of US anti-trust legislation being triggered by the close links between the US government and the Standard Oil successors (as in Aramco). Yergin, 1991, provides the example of the establishment of Getty Oil in the neutral zone between Kuwait and Saudi Arabia in 1948.

8. The Cazenove & Co projection in 1972 was that it would take about ten

years for non-OPEC outputs to have effect. This projection proved quite accurate (see p. 94).

(see p. 94)

9. The Cazenove projections of 1972 were £5 billion over ten years or 15 per cent of annual industrial investment.

10. Bromley, 1987, notes the degree to which Shell and BP influenced policy in these years, as does Jessop, 1983.

11. Interview with Dr Burke, BP project manager for the Forties field, 1994: transcript held by Fine Art Productions, London, for Channel 4 *Wasted Windfall* series.

12. Interview with Norman Smith, 1994: note 11 *above*.

13. Interviews with Norman Smith and Tony MacKay, both 1994: note 11 *above*.

14. The first director of OSO, Norman Smith, gives this explanation: note 11 *above*.

15. Sir Peter Baxendall of Shell. Interview 1994: note 11 *above*.

16. Interviews with Sir David Steel of BP and Dickson Mabon, 1994: note 11 *above*.

17. Bromley, 1987, examines the development of this debate in Part 2.

18. See also *Daily Telegraph*, editorial 7 July 1977 (praising commentaries in *Greenwell's Monetary Bulletin*) and *Daily Telegraph*, 9 June 1976.

19. Feature by Anthony Lejeune on 'Why businessmen do not make good politicians' in *Daily Telegraph*, 26 July 1977.

20. Ross gives figures on donations to the Tory Party which show comparatively small donations from the oil sector.

21. See *Economist*, 27 May 1978.

22. The leaking of the Ridley Report in May 1978 to the *Economist* was part of this criticism – Chris Patten, Director of the Conservative Party Research Department, was sacked as secretary to the shadow cabinet the following week. Thatcher's maverick right-wing positions were attacked in features and editorials of the *Economist* on 15 January 1978, cf. 21, 28.

23. *The Director* began 1981 with an interview with Sir Keith Joseph in January and carried monthly educational study themes for use in its branches.

24. By 1982 the *Economist* was supporting Tebbit against Prior and calling for a hard line against the trade union movement. The issue for 30 January 1982 carried a long feature on the potential of the sunrise belt of the M4 as a haven for Japanese-style union-free electronics firms.

25. Interviews with Sir Leo Pliatsky (Treasury), Lord Gilmour and Lord Weinstock, 1994: note 11 *above*.

26. Interviews with Sir Alistair Morton, Managing Director of BNOC,

and David Howell, Secretary of State for Energy from 1979: note 11 *above*.

27. Interview with Colin Phipps, Managing Director of Clyde Petroleum, 1994: note 11 *above*. Harvie cites D. Lawson in the *Financial Times*, 17 January 1986.

28. Interviews with Glenda Hogarth, manufacturer of safety clothing and equipment, and Professor Colin MacFarlane, 1994: note 11 *above*.

29. Interview with John D'Ancona, Director OSO, 1994: note 11 *above*.

30. Interviews with Norman Smith, first Director of the Offshore Supplies Office; John D'Ancona, subsequent Director, Dr Peter Dunn, production manager of UIE Clydebank, on Norway's ability to capture platform market, and Professor Tony MacKay, 1994: note 11 *above*.

2 PROBLEMS OF UNION MOBILIZATION OFFSHORE: THE 1970s AND 1980s

The New Frontier

By the early 1970s the number of those working offshore had begun to build up significantly. The Department of Energy *Brown Book* of 1974 lists 3760 employed offshore and that for the following year 6000, compared with a mere 1000 in 1970 (DEn, 1968–91). These figures, as we shall have occasion to note elsewhere, are a vast underestimate. They refer only to those workers who actually worked on installations and exclude support workers. Following the first oil price hike of 1973, the level of offshore activity in the UK sector sharply increased. This attracted workers to move north to a new industry which provided the opportunity for 'big money'. These workers often came from the declining industrial heartlands of Clydeside, the Northeast and Merseyside, as well as the rural hinterlands of the North. Even humble roustabouts (general labourers), the lowest members of the drill-floor pecking order, had the prospect of rising up the industrial hierarchy within a matter of a few months, and earning what seemed enormous sums. In reality, for most of the workforce the premium for enduring the isolation, discomfort and danger of working offshore twelve- to sixteen-hour shifts on a rota of two weeks on, one week off, was fairly modest. By contrast, North Sea divers in the mid-1970s, working under saturation dive conditions, could earn as much as £1000 a week. Pipeline welders, by working a seven-day week, could earn perhaps half that amount, still a considerable wage for the time.

Many of the early North Sea divers were ex-naval personnel, salvage divers or scuba divers who had literally pestered and bluffed their way into the industry (Punchard, 1989). It was a new industry, recruiting a new workforce. Having worked previously in 40 feet of water, some men made the transition to doing dives at 400 feet, literally overnight. Early North Sea divers faced harsh demands. The physical pressures of saturation diving for up to 30 days at a time, were accompanied by pressure from the companies to get the job done quickly. Tony Jackson, a diver, recalls inspection diving when operators were desperate to bring oil production on-stream.

> North Sea diving demanded everything of you. You were only ever as good as your last dive. If you screwed up a dive, then by the time you got out of the chamber, that would be the last time you'd ever work for that company or that particular client.[1]

In terms of pressure, the diver was 'the point of an inverted pyramid' but the financial rewards were great.

> You would spend inside as long as you possibly could because the motivation was to earn money and you earn money when you're in saturation as against standing on deck …. Guys would do 'sats' for thirty, forty days, be out, decompress, be on deck for a couple of days and then get blown back into 'sat' again and do another twenty to thirty days.

Phil Robinson, an ex-naval diver, was equally candid.

> You'd stay offshore for as long as you could, because you were all freelance, you didn't know when more work was going to turn up, so that's where the expression came from – 'more days, more dollars' … I got involved in saturation diving and I earned as much in a month as I did in a year in the Royal Navy.

But if the rewards were enormous, so too were the risks. Early diving activity was largely unregulated. As Tony Jackson put it, 'We were writing the rules as we went along'. It was not until January 1975 that safety regulations were enacted which governed diving operations on the UK Continental Shelf. An earlier passage of these regulations would possibly have prevented many deaths. Divers were on call 24 hours a day and 'used like a commodity' by the companies. We analyse the high fatality and injury offshore in a future chapter. While the safety of diving was a growing concern, accidents were also frequent in other offshore occupations. Particularly on the drill floor and among the construction workforce employed to 'hook up' the giant offshore production installations, the risk of serious injury and even death was substantial.

For most of the offshore workforce average gross earnings were moderate. One report of the period (*Aberdeen People's Press*, 1976: 17) lists the normal average gross wages for rig workers as shown in Table 2.1.

Table 2.1 *Average Gross Wages of Offshore Rig Workers*

Position	Rate
Oil company engineer	£1000–£1500 per month
Driller (overseas contract, no tax)	£750 per month
Derrick man	£350 per month
Crane operator	£350 per month
Roughneck	£300 per month
Roustabout	£280 per month
Offshore cook	£34–£36 per week
Assistant steward	£29–£35 per week

Source: Aberdeen People's Press, 1976

For those working on the supply vessels shuttling back and forth between Aberdeen and the offshore installations, the wages were equally unimpressive, except for the very few at the top of the hierarchy.

Table 2.2 *Average Gross Wages of Supply Vessel Workers*

Position	Rate per month
Master	£580
1st Engineer and Mate	£490
Cook	£260–280
AB seaman	£260–£300

Source: Aberdeen People's Press, 1976

Offshore basic rates were actually the same, or even less, than union rates onshore. Gross earnings were higher because of long overtime and other 'fringe' benefits, such as travel allowances, etc. In the early to mid-1970s a skilled engineer in a car factory was earning somewhere between £240 and £270 per month for a basic 40-hour week. Offshore workers generally worked more than twice those hours per week for not all that much more reward. Thus, while for some groups of workers with specialized skills the 'offshore premium' was considerable, for the majority of the labour force, contrary to popular perceptions, this was not so.

If the hours were long and the work was dangerous, the conditions were worse. Cramped four- and even six-man cabins, minimal recreation facilities, often nothing more than a film in the installation 'cinema', the lack of privacy and the continuous noise on a rig, made rest – far less sleep – difficult for many. On the worst rigs a 'hot bunk' system of rotating beds between successive shifts was utilized. The one thing which the workforce did relish about offshore life was the food, which, in typical American style, was lavish to the point of excess.

The industrial relations regime which the US companies had brought to the North Sea was typically perceived as uncongenial by most UK workers. The Louisiana and Texas oilmen brought with them an individualistic, macho, 'kick-ass' and anti-union culture quickly embraced by home-grown 'plastic Yanks'. Women were not welcome in this male-dominated world and only rarely were allowed to work offshore. The companies exercised absolute power over who could and could not stay on the rigs. A man could be ordered back to shore on the next helicopter, simply because the foreman didn't like the look on his face, didn't like long hair and in one legendary case, didn't like any Frenchmen on the rig. For many Americans, the Scots were simply 'tartan coolies'. Attitudes to safety and occupational welfare of employees were casual, to say the least, as were general views on existing UK regulations on safety. An infamous quote from one US oilman, cited by W. G. Carson (1982: 238) in his pioneering study of offshore safety, sums up the attitude too often encountered, 'We break your fucking law, every fucking day'. In these early phases of North Sea development the priority was to get the oil out of the sea bed. Money was no object, and the drilling companies' and operators' men made the workforce 'jump to it' to get the job done. Safety considerations were very often secondary. In the words of one US toolpusher (drilling supervisor), 'There's only two can'ts – if you can't do it, you can't stay'.[2]

With men working in the industry drawn from every known walk of life, and some previously not known, working offshore acquired the mystique of a 'frontier' existence. The reality was far more brutal. Accidents and injuries were frequent. Management practices were capricious and authoritarian, utilizing bullying and victimization tactics. Any worker identified by the operator or client as a 'troublemaker', perhaps someone who had raised a safety concern, or a union activist, was likely to be immediately 'run off' the plat-form. In the early phases of North Sea oil exploration, legal protection for victimized workers was non-existent, while organized trade unionism had yet to establish any kind of foothold offshore.

Life Offshore

In the mid-1970s, Aberdeen began to assume the appearance of a boom town. According to the Nationwide Building Society (1975), house prices had risen by as much as 30 per cent compared to 12.5 per cent nationally. From a dour grey granite city in which all night life ceased at 10.30 p.m. when the pubs shut down, Aberdeen gradually acquired an almost cosmopolitan atmo-sphere with clubs and restaurants open until the small hours. By 1975 there were some 5000 Americans and their families living in the city. Smart new hotels in the city centre displayed Houston time as well as UK local time above the reception desk. Cowboy boots, Levis, check shirts and 'JR' stetsons were a common sight, as free-spending oilmen came back into town after their offshore 'hitch'. It was still possible for a complete novice to go offshore without survival training, or indeed any other kind of skill. The daily pester-ing of the various receptionists of the drilling company offices scattered around Aberdeen town and out at West Tullos, East Tullos and Torry could still pay off for those looking for work. The list of the companies having recently settled in and around Aberdeen indicated the huge growth of US and foreign contractors arriving to service the industry: Santa Fe, KCA, Westbourne Drilling, Penrod, Sedco, Odeco, Global Marine, Zapata, Wes-tern Oceanic, Bawden Drilling, International Drilling Company and Trans-world. Aberdeen's own Wood Group, which was mainly a trawler fishing company, began to move into the new industry developing on its doorstep. News of which companies were taking on men travelled quickly on the grapevine in hostels and city centre bars.

In Aberdeen itself, students in the Department of Sociology obtained work offshore during the long vacations. They were recruited by the depart-ment as 'participant observers' of life and work on the rigs under the direction of Professor Robert Moore. Their archive of diary reports provides a contem-porary account of many aspects of an industrial relations regime based upon 'management by fear'. Here are excerpts from the diary of Steven Day. They describe his first offshore hitch in July 1976 on the Forties Charlie, as a roust-about, a general labourer, employed by Reading and Bates (R&B), a North American drilling company. Steven Day reports that roustabouts (drill hands) were 'the lowest of the low' on drilling rigs. This he knew from the moment of arrival on the rig.

> The chopper flight lasts for an hour. When I stumbled off for the first time I made my way to the toolpushers' office. While I was standing there, the roustabout pusher (Trevor) came in and was told by the Texan toolpusher to 'get your ass to work' – then looking at me: 'Don't sound too encouraging, does it, boy?'[3]

After only a couple of days offshore, hearing a rumour that he would not be coming back next trip, Stephen Day approached the toolpusher.

> I found out that the rumour was true. He said he felt that I wasn't cut out for this business, that he had too many novices on his crew and that pressure was being put on him to get his job done and that he just wasn't doing it. He added that he'd seen me standing on the wrong side of swinging loads and that I was a danger to myself. I was unable to dispute what he'd said, but could only put it to him that after only five days, I had not had much of an opportunity to learn. I also added that I wanted to make a career in the oil industry, that it had taken me two and a half weeks to get the job and that I had told Bill Legg [R&B's onshore personnel manager] that I was completely inexperienced, etc., etc. We began to chat and he admitted that it had taken him two years to 'break in' some wharrams. [Wharram is the drilling industry's name for a novice.]
> He finally decided, after telling me about his nine children and his twenty-three years in the industry etc., etc. that he would probably give me a two-week trial. Two points that should be added. Firstly, he'd started off by saying that at 45 years of age (he looks more like 60), it would be easier for me to get a new job than it would for him. This is quite true – one of the other roustabouts told me that a toolpusher working for R&B had been run off simply for missing an entry in his drilling report. Secondly, running off people is one means by which a toolpusher can show his employers that he's doing his job. To run somebody off now and again, is probably a healthy state of affairs from his point of view, reinforcing his own position.

Being 'rig-wise', however, knowing the unspoken rules of the game, was essential to survival. John (L) the 'roughneck', a member of the drill-floor team, who had first relayed the rumour of impending dismissal to Steven

Day, was also newly appointed to this position. He was to be run off that trip, because of hostility from the other drill-floor hands. In the frantic atmosphere of the drill floor, where the slightest mistake could cost a man's fingers or worse, you had to be able to rely completely on your fellow worker. Anyone who it was felt was not able to play his part in the team was a liability to be ditched at once. It was a work environment of rough 'justice'. Men could be run off for any number of reasons, and as Steven Day found out, just before he landed his own job with R&B, sometimes it was the only way for a newcomer to break into an offshore job.

> On Bank Holiday Monday I went down to Zapata where I met Ron Maywell and inquired about their vacancy for a roustabout. Mr Maywell, an American, replied that they now had fourteen vacancies. An entire crew had refused to continue working and were being flown ashore the same day. They had been offered a three-month contract to drill off of the coast of Labrador, with a £200 bonus on completion. According to the Drilling Superintendent, the men were demanding that this bonus be tax-free and that they receive forty hours pay for each of their two weeks ashore. This, he said, was impossible.

Any challenge to the authority of the management, or indeed to anyone with more authority in the drilling hierarchy than you, could be grounds for instant dismissal. Orders were given to be instantly obeyed. The head toolpusher kicked the roustabout toolpusher who in turn kicked the roustabouts. Here is Steven Day describing 'skidding the rig', that is, manoeuvring the drilling part of the rig to centralize over the next hole on the subsea template.

> Skidding the rig, which is carried out by means of hydraulic jacks, is hectic, and although I didn't know what was going on most of the time, time went quickly. Do this, do that, go up there, get two wrenches, undo these bolts, drop what you're doing, start something else – and be quick! A long list of orders which are often as quickly rescinded. This toolpusher is one of those who likes the sound of his own voice, an exponent of the American mentality of get-up-and-go with a maximum of noise, mostly of his own creation. When you complete something, he wants to know what took you so long. Trevor [the roustabout pusher] is putty in his hands – if he told him to jump off the side of the rig he wouldn't think twice.

Steven Day's contract of employment as a roustabout with Reading and

Bates reflected the hire-and-fire nature of the contract worker's existence.[4] Basic pay was £1.10 an hour with time and a half for hours worked over eight: 'You will receive no pay for your days off'. 'No subs [advances] will be paid at any time'. 'Your work schedule is fourteen consecutive days on the rig followed by fourteen days off'. 'Your employment is on an hourly basis'. 'The company does not provide a pension scheme'. 'The company will not provide you with sick pay'. Apart from a standard payment of £17 for each crew change, irrespective of where the employee's home was, 'travel to the place designated by the company to catch the helicopter or boat from Aberdeen to the drilling rig is at your expense'. Protective clothing, helmet, boots, raincoat and overalls, were provided, but the 'cost of work clothes will be deducted if employee terminates of his own accord within three months'. Some companies even made employees pay for their own work gear by a deduction from the first wage packet.

Among the eleven listed grounds for summary dismissal was 'failure to follow reasonable orders issued by authorised personnel'. Nevertheless, the contract stated, 'You are entitled to belong to or not to belong to a registered trade union'. This was in line with the employment rights legislation which the Labour government introduced in the mid-1970s. However, its effectiveness can be judged against the company 'grievance procedure' in which trade unions had no part to play.

> If you have any grievance relating to your employment you should discuss it orally with the Driller in charge of your crew. If your grievance is not dealt with to your satisfaction at this stage, the Driller will give you permission to discuss the matter orally with the Toolpusher. If the matter is still unresolved at this stage, you may make a written request to the Area Administrator that it be brought to the attention of the Drilling Superintendent or Area Manager, who will deal with it.

A roustabout's contract with Bawden Drilling was marginally better.[5] Hourly rates included an extra ten pence on the basic rate, a 'radius allowance' of £6 for employees living over fifty miles away, life assurance, and accident and sickness benefit of some description. The grievance procedure included the provision for the employee to state his case against disciplinary measures in writing. Once again, though union membership was stated as a legal entitlement, unions had no place in the grievance procedure. Bawden's contract also stated that the company did not 'infer any form of recognition of such organizations by the Company'. Bawden's issued a 'Code of Disciplinary Procedure' to all employees under the provisions of the Employment Protection

Act 1975. Breaches of discipline were divided into 'those of a minor nature which do not warrant dismissal and those of a serious nature where dismissal is advised'.[6] Sanctions were listed in order of severity from 'verbal warning', 'final written warning', 'dismissal with notice', to 'summary dismissal'. What is interesting, is that dismissal power was vested in at least five of the offshore management on the rig: the platform superintendent, the drilling superintendent, the mechanical, the electrical, and rigging superintendents. This situation was, in part, comparable to the 'drive' system of intense labour supervision, characteristic of the beginnings of nineteenth-century US factory organization, when individual workers were closely supervised by a large number of foremen with authority to dismiss (Elbaum, 1984). Among the dozen 'offences' which could result in summary dismissal was 'Insubordination or Wilful Disobedience of Authority'. Not surprisingly, ex-forces personnel were favoured recruits to the industry, in which carrying out an order unquestioningly, no matter how pointless or wrongheaded, was the first requirement. Here Steven Day describes his encounter with this mentality.

> Clearing away surplus water can be an interminable job, especially if you are doing it in the rain. This was probably the most ridiculous thing I encountered while on the rigs. While clearing water from the pipe deck on one occasion, when the job was nearly finished I turned around to find the roustabout pusher following me up from behind, hosing down the deck yet again. I stopped what I was doing and looked at him.
>
> He told me to carry on, whereupon I asked him what was the point? I was told to carry on and that he would tell me when to stop. The crane operator came over shortly afterwards and asked me what I had done to annoy B (roustabout pusher). When I asked him what B had said to him he said B had complained that I wasn't working hard enough and that he had threatened to put me on the maintenance roustabout crew.
>
> I reminded myself not to lapse from golden rule No. 1 – that you're hired 'from the neck down'. Don't bother to reason why. It's a part of what is known as being 'rig-wise'.[7]

Rumours of an extra ten pence per hour or of 'bonanza' wages being paid in Canada, the Middle East or Far East, produced a workforce with permanently 'itchy feet'. Some men moved around, 'jacked the job' just for 'a change of scenery'. Others, like John (L), the roughneck run off the Forties Charlie, turned up a couple of weeks later on a Santa Fe rig. Some men simply disappeared from the industry altogether, blacklisted by the employers for the cardinal crime of fighting for better conditions, not simply on their own behalf, but for their fellow workers.

Another 'participant observer' of offshore life, Tony Murphy, was also employed as a roustabout, not on a production platform, but on an exploration drilling rig, the Chris Chenery, on charter to Shell. On these mobile rigs conditions were if anything even harsher. His diary gives some insight into the safety regime. Arriving on the rig, Tony Murphy found that no one had been informed that he was coming and he was assigned to assist the welders. The following evening after a twelve-hour shift there was a 'safety meeting' in the Mess at 7.00 p.m. addressed by the toolpusher.

> He tells us that coffee, peanuts and popcorn will be available from now on during the evening film, but he says there will be no quadraphonic sound system until we hit oil. We get no 'bread' till we find oil – this rig costs 34 grand a day to run and all it's doing is losing money.[8]

'Making hole' and avoiding 'down time' was all that mattered in this bottom-line industry. After a short pep talk to the men, the 'safety' message was given:

> Smoking is now banned on deck except for the crane houses because of gas (normally it's [permitted] anywhere more than fifty feet from the derrick). 'Any questions?' – dead silence – everybody wishes he would shut up so then we can watch the film.

On day three, there was a regular fire drill, but Tony Murphy's lack of proper rig orientation was obvious.

> When there's intermittent ringing of the alarm bells you go to your fire station and wait till the 'all-clear' sounds. I haven't a clue where my fire station is, although there are notices everywhere, including the cabins, giving this information. Dave says there's a fire drill most Saturdays, and the medic, who spends most of his time in the toolpusher's office, told him that there would definitely be one today. I find out that mine is fire station 38 – the transformer room – where is the transformer room?

On his fourth day offshore, a roughneck asked him if he'd like to 'have a go' at working on the drill floor despite his total absence of training.

> Being a mug I say yes.

I'm 'stabbing', i.e. as the derrickman swings the pipe string out of the rack I have a rope around the bottom which I hold to stop the pipe flying about. (There's a lot of flex in 90 feet of 4 inch piping.) Unfortunately, the only 'safe' place to stand where one can keep enough tension on the rope and still make sure you don't get clobbered by the pipe, is about a foot from the edge of the 'V' door with a 50 foot drop to the deck. The drill floor is a pool of mud. Everything is covered in mud. I play out the rope until the pipe is nearly over the hole. I leave the rope and help manhandle the string into the previous one. Dennis (about 32 years, ex-merchant navy, married, two kids, a complete loony) whips the chain. The driller (late twenties, New Zealander) operates the winch from the monkey house which spins the drill string, screwing it into the other string. Dave and Dennis run in with the tongs which tighten the joint a final couple of turns. Meanwhile, I'm 'stabbing' a new string. I've never been so scared in my life but I get a kick out of it. Like anything, no doubt, the thrill wears off. The driller wants to know if I have the crane op's [operator's] permission to be up here. I say, 'I'm only a welder's mate, mate, I've come to collect me grinder' – he looks put out.

Later that night the captain gave a brief talk on life-jackets and man-overboard procedures: 'If you fall in this time of year, you have 9 to 11 minutes survival if you don't drown'. Tony Murphy writes in his diary that there are signs everywhere, 'Observe safety rules, your life may be at stake'. However, sometimes elementary commonsense precautions are simply absent, despite the 'safety rules'. Whilst handling unused casing on the night shift, he says, 'I nearly got my head taken off by one of the crane hooks. They should have ties on them'. The diary entry for Sunday/Monday, the last spell of his first hitch, describes the rig fire drill. He had completed his twelve-hour night shift at midday and gone to his cabin to sleep, only to be rudely awakened in a state of total disorientation.

At 4.30 p.m. 'in the morning' the abandon ship alarm goes, fall out of my bunk. I'm not going up on deck to freeze in jeans and a shirt. Put on an anorak and scarf. Stagger on deck to find it's a baking afternoon!

At our life-boat station a wizened old Texan who is the sub-sea engineer gives us a short talk concerning life rafts. 'Any of you arseholes know how to use these sons o' bitches?' – silence – I'm probably the only one there who doesn't, but everybody is either too bored or knows that whoever speaks will be asked to explain. Apparently you just throw it over the side and the rip cord makes it self-inflate. 'There's only one fucking way you're gonna get to that fucking asshole of a son of a bitch, and that's to fucking jump, which is why your life-jackets (which we are all wearing) have got these stiff collars – to stop you breaking your goddammed neck!'

But the two weeks offshore ends with a savage reminder that whilst he had been lucky this trip, not everyone was so fortunate.

At 10 p.m. I'm hosing the deck – don't hear chopper land – see Frank my cabin mate, bandaged, climb aboard. He's lost three fingers and he'd only been on the [drill] floor four hours to replace Dennis – tough! The day drags – at last we finish. Watch 'Goldfinger' – can't sleep. The chopper comes at 1 p.m. Monday afternoon. Free at last.

During his second hitch, he and his mate both have a 'lucky escape'.

The pair of us are in the welder's room as a bushing [this is a semi-circular solid steel object weighing about three hundredweight which, with its partner, is used to reduce the diameter of the rotary table on the drill floor], slips out of its sling and crashes beside us, having dropped from the crane, through the hatch in the welder's room, bounced on the steel floor, ricocheted off the wall and eventually come to rest beside us. Jack appears through the hatch looking apologetic.

Such dangerous occurrences were routinely covered up. Company accident statistics, therefore, were widely regarded with scepticism. Scrutiny of the accident record aboard one rig produced the following exchange recorded by Tony Murphy:

It's a load of bollocks. According to it there hasn't been a lost time accident for 145 days. It doesn't mention that Stan nearly got wiped out, that a toolpusher blew himself up smoking in the mud pits.
  Was he killed?
  No, just badly burned – that I was knocked unconscious by a pipe a month ago.
  Yeah, well, what do you expect?

Among the incentives offered to those who appeared to have observed safety rules were £5 Marks and Spencer gift vouchers. More senior personnel who achieved a period of 210 or 500 days without a lost time accident recorded, would receive a gold watch presentation, and perhaps their picture in the company newsletter to mark the occasion.

Workers' injuries had as much to do with the way industrial relations were conducted offshore as with the inherent danger of their tasks. This last entry in Tony Murphy's offshore diary, this time on a Santa Fe rig, reflects on just how the authority system, far from assisting efficiency, actually creates 'wastage' in one form or another:

> I am now grinding subs [a shortened section of drillpipe] with an airpowered grinder, but it has no guard. When the wheel disintegrates as I knew it must, I count my blessings at not being hit, and go to see the crane-op. I say, 'John, I'd rather not use that grinder as it's dangerous'. 'Well, there's nothing else – just take it easy'. I was going to say that I can't control the air pressure but there's no point.
>
> Now, here is the main reason for a lot of accidents, jackings and sackings. If a roustabout is told to do something which he rightly, or wrongly, considers to be abnormally dangerous (considering his working environment), then there are several courses of action open to him. He can do it and hope for the best. He can ask not to do it: this will invoke ridicule (except where the person who does it is hurt; and then it will be he who is ridiculed for being so stupid as to do such a dangerous thing), or he can refuse to do it. Now, if I had said bluntly, 'I'm not using that grinder', this would have been questioning the crane-op's authority and he would have told me I had to do it whether I liked it or not. (The question of whether the task is dangerous is no longer under consideration – the crane-op's reputation is at risk.) If I still refused, he would go to the toolpusher explaining that I had refused to carry out an order and I would be sacked. Alternatively, I could have gone to the toolpusher, usually with the same result – dismissal.
>
> Occasionally, when something is overtly dangerous, even by the toolpusher's much lower 'somebody could get killed' threshold (he has been subjected to a rig environment for a far greater length of time and consequently sees things in a different light), then he may intervene, but by doing this the roustabout incurs the crane-op's wrath. He has been insulted and retribution is sure to follow. The end result of this ritualistic behaviour is an accident, a jacking, a sacking or at least open antagonism which will manifest itself in another way at another time. This confrontation situation obviously doesn't just occur between crane-op and roustabout, but also between roughneck and driller/assistant driller, derrickman and toolpusher, etc.

In my case, I continued to use the grinder but at such a slow pace that there was no danger, and a job that should have taken another hour took the rest of the shift. In this case John, the crane-op, was quite content because nobody would get hurt, and yet the job was being done, albeit slowly, thereby keeping the toolpusher off his back. In other cases the crane-op might either get another roustabout to do the job (but if he also 'goes slow' he will consider it open rebellion) or do it himself: here he will either do the task and then ridicule the roustabout, or he will do the task and get hurt; many consider the latter the ideal solution.

The confrontation situation occurs normally, when either or both of the parties are feeling belligerent, and/or are quitting anyway, and most of all with newcomers to oil rigs who are not, even unconsciously, aware of the unwritten and unsaid codes of behaviour which must be followed.

Calculating actual accident rates with any accuracy, especially during the first half of the 1970s, was highly problematic, for several reasons. Not least was the fluctuating offshore population. Table 2.3 gives the persons on board (POB) numbers for the Forties Alpha for a four-month period, at the time when Steven Day was on its sister platform, the Forties Charlie. The contractor workforce typically formed the majority throughout.

Table 2.3 *Forties Alpha: Persons on Board*

Date	Total Population	BP Personnel	BP/Total (%)
3.8.75	218	57	26
30.9.75	140	53	38
30.10.75	175	56	32
31.12.75	120	57	48

Source: BP unpublished report 1975

An internal BP report lists 216 gross accidents for the Forties Alpha, Bravo and Charlie, as well as for three drilling rigs belonging to or on charter to BP. Table 2.4 illustrates the differential exposure of contractors' personnel to accidents compared to BP's own staff, even assuming BP personnel are present on BP's own fixed installations at a 50 per cent maximum ratio. On the drilling rigs the number of oil company representatives would be limited to a few senior positions. The category 'Others' covers the contract workers, including catering, whose injury incidence is negligible compared to 'outside' workers.

Table 2.4   *BP Staff Accidents Compared to Contractor Personnel*

Name of Rig	Staff	Others	Staff/Others (%)	Period
Forties Alpha	19	80	19/81	Apr–Dec 75
Forties Bravo	2	9	18/82	Oct–Dec 75
Forties Charlie	1	12	8.3/91.7	Oct–Dec 75
SEDCO 'K'	6	23	21/79	Mar–Aug 75
SEDCO 703	2	30	6.25/93.75	12 months
Sea Quest	2	30	6.3/93.7	6 months
Average:			13.14/86.86	

Source: BP unpublished report 1975

While there is no estimate of the severity of the accidents, it is clear that even though the numbers may be underestimated, accidents involving contractor staff were considerably more frequent.

'Wastage rates', that is offshore turnover rates for drilling crews on BP's Sea Quest are provided for the years 1968 to 1973 (see Table 2.5).

Table 2.5   *BP Sea Quest: Turnover Among Drilling Crews*

Year	Rate (men per month)
1968	2.1
1969	2.1
1970	1.8
1971	1.1
1972	0.6
1973	1.3
Average:	1.5

Source: BP unpublished report 1975

With an average of 1.5 men per month or 18 men per annum, BP calculated an equivalent to a turnover rate of about 45 per cent per annum. However, some authoritative estimates put a similar turnover rate (40 per cent) as occurring every two weeks in certain drilling companies (IRRR, 1975). Skilled workers, such as mechanical and electrical fitters, appear to have had a turnover rate of about 15 per cent per annum. These skilled workers, often recruited in the marine industry, overseas oil, or onshore engineering, had a much more stable employment pattern compared to the less skilled. This was the case even within a drilling crew, as Table 2.6 suggests. As we descend the industrial hierarchy, the average length of service also decreases.

Table 2.6 *BP Sea Quest: Average Length of Service*

Work Type	Length of Service
Pumpmen	4 years 3 months
Rigmen	3 years 10 months
Derrickmen	3 years 6 months
Crane Drivers	2 years 11 months
Roustabouts	1 year 7 months
Average:	3 years 2 months

Source: BP unpublished report 1975

In the early to mid-1970s, drilling personnel operated on the two weeks on, one week off cycle for most of the period. Turnover was highest during the first four months of service, as adapting to the 'alien' environment was difficult for many. Securing a stable workforce became a matter of concern for operators such as BP, seeking to staff platform crews 'from scratch' and with oil due to come on-stream in the Forties field in the autumn of 1975. Writing in July 1974, W. David Nicholson of BP predicted, 'Wastage for junior engineering staff on the Forties Platforms will be between 75 per cent and 130 per cent during the first year of operation.'[9] We now explore how the workforce responded to these conditions.

First Attempts to Organize: The Inter Union Offshore Committee

Responses of organized labour to the situation offshore began to take shape by the early 1970s. Resolutions to the Scottish TUC 1972 Annual Conference and the Labour Party Conference of that year called for economic development related to the industry to be directed towards the Scottish economy (STUC, 1973: 667; Wybrow, 1982; Labour Party Scottish Council, 1973). At the Labour Party Conference a number of shop stewards formed a committee to press for the building of oil supply vessels in the east coast shipyards. These stewards, mainly from the shipbuilding industry, formed the North Sea Oil Action Committee in October 1972 under the auspices of the Confederation of Shipbuilding and Engineering Unions (CSEU), an inter-union body which co-ordinated trade union strategy in the industry.

In an attempt to create a political consensus around their demands for state participation in oil development, the Action Committee broadened its base to include public and media figures from across a wide political spectrum (Middleton, 1977: 3). In addition, the Action Committee started addressing issues about the living and working conditions on the drilling rigs. These issues were discussed at weekly press conferences which received both local and, increasingly, national publicity (Middleton, 1977: 3).[10] The Action Committee, prompted by anonymous calls from frightened workers, accused the rig companies of having, in the words of its secretary, Bob Middleton, 'employed management techniques and imposed working conditions, the likes of which had not been seen in Britain since the Industrial Revolution' (Middleton, 1977: 6). By 1973 the Action Committee was building up dossiers on most of the companies operating offshore (North Sea Oil Action Committee, 1973).

The 1973 STUC Annual Conference in Aberdeen also expressed concerns about the level of trade union organization and working conditions offshore (STUC, 1973: 70). Sympathetic MPs had made representations to the Secretary of State for Employment, Maurice Macmillan. A series of meetings between the members of the STUC Economic Committee and representatives of the Scottish Parliamentary Labour Group in 1973 had criticized the handicap being placed on the unions by the oil companies which were described as 'notoriously anti-trade union' (STUC, 1974: 102). Middleton suggests that some changes started to occur in 1974, primarily due to labour shortages. These resulted in improved pay and conditions, week on/week off rotas, some simple training schemes for roustabouts and a reduction in arbitrary dismissals. The diaries quoted in the previous section, which were written over the following years, suggest that these improvements tended to be only temporary.

The oil industry's temporarily modified tone was also influenced by the return of a Labour government in 1974, and the intensified and apparently successful lobbying by the North Sea Action Committee of Michael Foot. Foot, the new Minister of Employment, pressed for more stringent safety and employment rights measures. Both the Employment Protection Act 1975 and the Health and Safety at Work Act 1974 were now extended offshore by Order in Council over the next few years. Unfortunately, particularly with regard to the latter Act, the offshore application of this legislation was crucially deficient. The legislation failed to extend to North Sea oil workers the same rights for trade union involvement in health and safety as existed onshore. Protection against unfair dismissal offshore, moreover, was minimal.[11]

In November 1973, the trade unions, encouraged by the Action Committee, formed a group of full-time officers to co-ordinate the hitherto sporadic attempts to unionize the offshore workforce. Safety and offshore working conditions had been one of the key subjects of a conference of all unions involved in the North Sea, convened by the STUC in Glasgow in June 1973 (STUC, 1974: 112-3). That year's STUC Conference saw further discussions on how to begin to organize offshore. From these initiatives arose the first meeting of the Inter Union Offshore Oil Committee (IUOOC) in April 1974 at Aberdeen Trades Council. Once again, it was the Confederation of Shipbuilding and Engineering Unions, as an existing inter-union body, which convened the foundation meetings of this new inter-union forum. A circular to full-time officers, inviting them to set up an offshore committee, stressed the need for 'maximum co-operation between unions' and that the various 'spheres of influence ought to be decided regarding classes of labour organized by the respective unions'.[12] Achieving both of these objectives, however, proved difficult.

Union bodies, such as the Confederation of Shipbuilding and Engineering Unions, within the Scottish labour movement already perceived the necessity of fostering unionization in the offshore sector. Remarkable in this context was their anticipation of the potential damage which could be caused by an outbreak of uncontrolled sectionalism. The conscious attempt at preempting such a development, by forming an inter-union co-ordinating committee, was a mark of the maturity and the wider class perspective of those involved at this time. This perspective, in part, had emerged with the Left-led shop stewards' movement, which had only recently successfully forged an alliance of forces which compelled the Heath Conservative government to alter its course in the famous U-turn on economic policy in 1972. This alliance had compelled, through a popular campaign of resistance, the withdrawal of the threatened closure of the Upper Clyde shipbuilding yards (Foster and Woolfson, 1986). This and other class battles over the nature of employment legislation had produced, within the union movement, a broader and more radical 'class' perspective which went beyond the immediate boundaries of individual sectional union objectives.

The IUOOC was made up of the full-time officers representative of various unions with an interest in recruiting offshore. Central among these were the seafarers union (NUS), the Transport and General Workers Union (TGWU), the Boilermakers' union (ASB), the technicians' union (ASTMS), the engineers' union (AUEW), the electricians' union (EETPU) and the merchant navy officers' union (MNAOA). Much of what Carson (1982: 214) described as 'the fraught history of trade unionism in the British sector of the North Sea' revolves around the competitive relationships between these various unions. Each saw the advancement of their own position in the industry as being, to some extent, necessarily at the expense of rival unions. Sectionalism was in part conditioned by the emergence of this new industry whose occupational boundaries were still unclear.

Secretary of the new inter-union body the IUOOC was Bill Reid, district secretary of the TGWU, and chairman was the redoubtable Jimmy McCartney, Communist Party member and Boilermakers' full-time official in Aberdeen and former convener of shop stewards in the city's Hall Russell shipyard. As a first step the IUOOC invited all drilling companies to meet the committee on 14 May 1974. The committee warned the companies that 'a rejection of the proposed meeting would indicate that the drilling companies have rejected a settlement based on conciliation' and that the trade unions 'would immediately resort to their industrial power to establish recognition'.[13] The 'power' on which this threat was based, however, was predominantly rooted on the network trade unions had established onshore. With regard to those working offshore, this power was exogenous, as such foothold as the unions had established was at best tenuous. The credibility of a threat of a recognition drive was therefore limited. If a credible threat was to be made, this still depended on the willingness of the trade unions onshore to involve themselves in concerted action.

The drilling companies, perhaps not surprisingly, did not respond to this threat, although Shell, which along with BP professed not to be anti-union, claimed not to have received the original invitation letter. Shell at least was prepared to talk to the committee. Apart from Shell, only one company, Smedvig, replied. Smedvig operated with a Norwegian crew whose members were already part of the Norwegian seamen's union. The company, whilst not averse to attending could, therefore, not see the benefit from participating. US companies such as Sedco and Odeco thereafter became prime targets for union-organized industrial action. This action began with a twenty-four hour 'withdrawal of facilities' from Sedco by supply boat crews organized in the NUS. The company, which had previously proved reluctant to meet the unions, eventually was 'persuaded' to do so.

Eric Varley, then Labour's Energy Secretary, had asked the trade unions to refrain from further action, whilst the Department of Employment made approaches to the drilling contractors involved. By April 1975, the IUOOC nevertheless felt it necessary to organize a successful embargo on all supplies to three Odeco rigs, Ocean Victory, Ocean Kokuei and Ocean Rover. This required the co-operation and support of the east coast dockers in the TGWU who loaded supplies, and of the unionized crews of the supply vessels themselves. The previous year, the NUS had successfully negotiated an agreement with the seven major North Sea oil rig supply boat operators (IDS, 1975: 8). Such 'secondary action' was, therefore, highly potent. Actions of this kind proved forcibly that IUOOC's threat to use industrial action carried real weight, so long as it could mobilize the support of organized workers. By the following morning, Odeco had agreed to meet representatives of the IUOOC and arranged for two of its officials, Bill Reid the IUOOC secretary, and Harry Bygate, the local NUS official, to visit the rigs and talk to the men (*Aberdeen People's Press*, 1976: 21). Shortly after this visit, the assistant crane operator on the Ocean Victory, also a newly elected shop steward, was demoted to roustabout. In a fury, he demanded to be flown back immediately to 'the beach' (onshore) to consult with the IUOOC. Odeco deemed the man thereby to have dismissed himself. Under the threat of further union embargo, however, Odeco reinstated him six weeks later. In such day-to-day skirmishes each side tested the other's strength and determination. It was a period of ongoing low-intensity guerilla warfare between management and unions. In other industries such conflicts have served as the necessary prelude to the development of a more stable framework of collective bargaining. Offshore, this development was to be forestalled by continuing employer resistance, which created a deeper and ultimately much more disruptive set of tensions in offshore industrial relations.

Union recruitment took place on rigs such as Sedco's 702, Zapata's Ugland and on a number of Shell rigs. Two IUOOC officials were allowed offshore by Shell in January 1975 to visit the 30-strong crew of the Staflo for recruitment purposes. But despite Shell's formal declaration of tolerance towards unions, the company challenged union claims of 50 per cent membership with its own 'union membership audit'. This audit showed that out of the total crew of 60, 13 men were not fully paid up union members and 23 were non-union. Shell agreed to a second visit by officials to talk to the other back-up crew, after which there was an official union ballot on recognition. In all, it took two years from the start of talks to the granting of union recognition. Union officials as yet had no formal right of access to the two dozen or so offshore rigs in the North Sea. Companies were under no obligation to provide the means and facilities for such visits to take place (for example, places on heli- copter flights for officials), or to recognize trade unions even where a major- ity of the workforce had expressed a preference for collective representation. Without either of these rights, the progress towards unionizing the offshore workforce was necessarily slow.

Occasionally, more sustained confrontations occurred as the workforce became increasingly confident and combative and more willing to respond to high-handed arbitrary dismissals by management. The first real trial of strength occurred in November 1975 on the rig Venture One, sub-contracted by Conoco to Placid Oil.[14] The company owning the rig and carrying out the drilling on Venture One, paraded under the appropriately Southern-style name, Dixilyn. A trainee crane operator on the rig, Billy Cowan, was dis- missed causing the whole crew to stop work in sympathy. Cowan had been summarily dismissed, by the rig superintendent, for moving lengths of pipe without safety tag lines attached to them. The crew claimed that the rig 'super' had actually been present throughout the operation but had failed to stop it. On stepping down from the crane, Cowan was therefore astonished to be told: 'you're on tomorrow's chopper, in fact you can go to your cabin now'. Other workers tried to intercede on Cowan's behalf without success, and on hearing this, the rest of the crew decided to act upon the 'unfair dis- missal'. Further representations on Cowan's behalf were refused, causing work to be stopped for three hours in protest. Davie Robertson, the rig welder and an active member of the Boilermakers' union, who had tried to speak up for Cowan, was also dismissed, for 'incitement'. As the crew called for senior Placid personnel to be flown offshore to discuss the deteriorating situation, management reluctantly agreed to reinstate the two men. Initial threats to have the men forcibly removed by 'law enforcement officers' and of management preparedness 'to change out both crews', i.e. dismiss the entire rig workforce, were withdrawn.

The crew had taken action because it had felt that there would be 'no sense of job security left on the rig'.[15] They were assured that their grievances would be discussed with Dixilyn's onshore management in Dundee. As they returned onshore they found that all ten members of the crew were dismissed. Management claimed that there had been a 'mutiny' and that 'incidents of this nature can endanger lives'. Approaches by Bill Reid on behalf of the IUOOC and the officials of the government's Advisory, Conciliation and Arbitration Service (ACAS) to Dixilyn and to the rig charterers, Conoco, were rebuffed. An appeal to the International Transport Federation (which organizes the seafaring unions worldwide) and the willingness of Dundee dockers to 'black' supply ships to the Venture One, finally produced an agreement with the company. The dismissed crew were reinstated, re-employed on the sister rig Venture Two under construction in Finland, and reimbursed for 50 per cent of wages lost between November and the dispute settlement date of 6 February 1976.[16] It had taken three months and a huge local and international campaign by the unions to secure this victory. However, Dixilyn got their revenge. The crew were exiled to Finland, not for three months as originally anticipated, but for a year. The completed Venture Two rig was not contracted for North Sea work and the crew were dismissed without being offered the opportunity to be re-employed on Venture One again. Davie Robertson was to find it impossible to obtain employment thereafter on any drilling rig as a welder.

Tony Benn Lends a Hand

In June 1975 Tony Benn became the Secretary of State for Energy. His appointment coincided with the first landing of oil from the North Sea at the Isle of Grain refinery, from Hamilton's Argyll field. Benn had indicated his desire to consult with the trade unions on matters of North Sea oil policy.[17] The IUOOC requested and held a meeting with Benn in late July 1975 following his visit to BP's Graythorpe One platform, then under construction for the Forties (Benn, 1989: 419). Jack Jones, General Secretary of the TGWU, had expressed his anger to Benn at his union's precarious situation offshore, and indeed, at the march that the NUS appeared to have stolen on his own union in terms of recruitment (1989: 444). In an hour-and-a-half-long meeting with Benn, the major unions with offshore interests elaborated on their difficulties in organizing the workers on offshore installations, their concern over accident rates offshore and over the use of non-British ships in servicing offshore installations. In response, Benn agreed to convene a high-level meeting of the trade unions and the operators. He also suggested that the next round of licences would include a statement which would allow union access to the rigs.

The unions were given the task of drafting a 'Charter for the Unionisation' of the offshore industry, the first of what were to be several such documents over the following years. The Charter proposed the establishment of a National Board for the industry comprising employers and unions. It was to regulate terms and conditions, rights of access for trade union officials, recognition rights, reasonable facilities to keep in touch with the membership, collective bargaining arrangements, deduction of dues from the payroll, recognition for elected shop stewards and the full extension offshore of the Health and Safety at Work Act.[18] While Benn may have been personally sympathetic to the unions' cause, senior civil servants at the Departments of Energy, Employment and Trade who met with IUOOC and TUC officials to discuss the Charter were careful to preserve a non-committal stance so far as supportive government action was concerned.[19] Privately they had warned off Benn from making union recognition one of the criteria for the granting of new licences (Benn, 1989: 516). For its part, the IUOOC had tentatively agreed certain 'spheres of influence' for organizing oil rig workers into the appropriate unions. In most instances, these spheres replicated existing onshore arrangements. Thus mechanics, motormen and rig technicians were organized by the engineering union, the AUEW, the electricians by the EETPU, and the welders by the Boilermakers' union. Divers and catering crew were organized by the NUS, although the TGWU also had an interest from its onshore activities in this latter area. The TGWU, with existing interests in crews working on trawling vessels and waterways, sought to recruit the lower grades of drill crews, from roustabouts up to derrickmen, who could be otherwise classed as general labourers.

The technicians' union, ASTMS (later to become MSF) instructed its local officer to prioritize recruitment in the North Sea on production platforms, particularly among the technicians who were direct employees of the operator companies such as Shell. ASTMS had particular ambitions to organize the offshore workforce that went beyond the direct employees, seeing itself as 'the' offshore union. It duly established an office in Aberdeen. The ASTMS official, however, was not present when the IUOOC met in August 1975 to discuss, for the first time, the question of spheres of influence.[20] At this meeting it was agreed that the NUS, the TGWU, the Boilermakers' and the AUEW would seek to recruit those working on the mobile drilling rigs. Different arrangements would apply in future to employees on the increasing number of permanent fixed installations, such as the Forties and Brents, that were now coming to dominate the offshore scene. This attempt to delineate 'spheres of influence' addressed one of the central reasons proferred by the offshore employers, and by some of the men themselves, for resisting trade unions offshore – the fear of demarcation disputes. This bogey was erected and resurrected by the employers, who claimed that any work disruption could have hugely damaging financial and safety implications on an offshore oil rig.

Even as these complex inter-union discussions were evolving, throughout the autumn of 1975, a new threat emerged to the unity and potential viability of the locally based IUOOC. In early October 1975 trade union recognition and a closed shop agreement was negotiated nationally with Houlder Brothers, a subsidiary of Furness-Withy, the UK's only major drilling contractor. The seamen's union NUS, the naval officers' union (MNAOA), and the engineering union (AUEW), together with the radio engineers officers' union (REOU), were collectively members of a different, long-established national inter-union body, the British Seafarers Joint Council (BSJC). Since their successful agreement with the employers to organize crews on the supply boats in 1974, the NUS and the other specialized maritime unions affiliated to the BSJC, had continued to try to organize in the more central areas of the newly emerging industry. Shipping companies that moved into oil exploration and oil service industries became natural targets for the extension of the BSJC unions' traditional maritime bargaining areas.

The BSJC brokered an agreement on the Dundee Kingsnorth, and Kingsnorth UK rigs, operated for Conoco and Occidental respectively, which was an industry benchmark. Toolpushers received £10,332 per year, drillers £7812, crane operators £5832, roughnecks £4092 and roustabouts £3792, and even the lowest grade of laundrymen £3552. In addition, there was a bonus of £1000 a year, medical insurance, travel and clothing allowances (IDS, 1977a: 4). A BSJC agreement was also reached with Houlder Brothers for an entirely new oil industry semi-submersible surface support ship, the *Uncle John*, and the subsea service vessel *Oregis*, the following year. Agreement on flexibility between these two vessels took these unions 'still further into the heart of the oil exploration industry' (IDS, 1977a: 5). There was consternation among the local IUOOC officials, because the IUOOC had not been informed of these negotiations, nor of the intended outcome. From the perspective of the maritime BSJC, NUS had claimed the Dundee Kingsnorth rig was legitimately to be classed as 'a ship'. The IUOOC argued that as a 'semi-submersible' rig its primary function was to drill, and therefore representation of the workforce was more properly within its jurisdiction.[21] BP and Shell, among others, were quick to question the claim of the IUOOC to speak for all the trade unions in the industry and its ability to reach negotiated agreements, in the wake of this débâcle with the BSJC.

Lengthy discussions had been set in motion by Benn, to persuade the operators to grant access to union officials. The Houlder Brothers' agreement with the BSJC was used by the operators to suggest that any formal agreement reached with the IUOOC might fall victim to similar inter-union difficulties. The companies now demanded reassurance from national General Secretaries of the member unions of the IUOOC that this would not be so. To smooth out any future difficulties, John Smith, as Minister of State for Energy, Albert Booth for Employment and leading members of the TUC Fuel and Power Committee met together with local officials of the IUOOC. The Ministers spoke of the need to 'avoid a fragmented approach' towards offshore unionization and the TUC affirmed that it 'regarded the IUOOC as an appropriate body for these purposes'. Local officials meanwhile stressed that the inter-union committee 'enjoyed support from its constituent unions at local and national level'.[22] The minutes of this meeting, however, record John Liverman, the senior official at the Department of Energy, reiterating that: 'Operators were nervous of negotiating with the [IUOOC] Committee as they felt its constituent unions might break ranks and seek separate settlements. Individual cases of this had already occurred.'

The authority of the IUOOC was 'not accepted' by the operators. This was doubly disingenuous, since the operators, numbering 40 companies, were now grouped in their own association, the United Kingdom Offshore Operators Association (UKOOA). UKOOA, under its terms of association, specifically precluded negotiations in the sphere of industrial relations. UKOOA's Memorandum of Association laid this out explicitly: 'The objects of the Association shall not extend to . . . the regulation of relations between its members and their customers or between workers and employers or organisations of workers and organizations of employers'[23]

UKOOA claimed it had no authority to make decisions which might bind its individual constituent oil company members. As an association, it argued it could only act through persuasion. It could not instruct either its own members or the contractors who were employed by member companies on any matters concerning industrial relations. These issues remained the sole prerogative of the individual companies concerned. By means of this approach, UKOOA extricated itself from any commitment to engage in substantive discussions on issues of industrial relations or trade union recognition which the IUOOC was anxious to pursue.

The Memorandum of Understanding on Access

The first formal discussion between representatives of the oil industry and the trade unions took place at the House of Commons on 11 May 1976. The confidential background brief for senior staff at the Department of Energy described the meeting as having 'made surprisingly positive progress in an atmosphere which no one present saw fit to try to sour'.[24] UKOOA's Council recommended to its members that they should agree to the unions' request for reasonable access, 'provided this could be fitted in with normal operational requirements'.[25] The Department of Energy had already prepared a draft Memorandum of Understanding on this issue, aimed at assisting future direct discussions between the unions and the operators. Chairing the meeting was Tony Benn, supported by Dickson Mabon as Minister of State for Energy and Harold Walker for the Department of Employment. The TUC was represented by Frank Chapple of the EETPU and Harry Irwin of the TGWU, both for the General Council of the TUC. The IUOOC was represented by its local Aberdeen-based officers. The employers were represented by UKOOA's Director General, George Williams, and a phalanx of oil company representatives: Shell, Hamilton Brothers, BP, Union Oil, Amoco, Occidental and Mobil. Despite the employers' request that the national officials of individual unions should take part in these discussions, only the AUEW had sent its national organizer. The IUOOC was not formally a sub-committee of the TUC. The TUC Fuel and Power Industries Committee, within whose remit it might naturally have fallen, was formally responsible for all oil industry matters. In 1974, the TUC Congress had carried a resolution calling for a special TUC committee to lead the struggle for trade union recognition offshore. However, as the IUOOC was already in existence, it was felt that 'a separate committee would have proved superfluous and have given rise to duplication and overlap'.[26] The IUOOC hence was not an integrated sub-committee of either the TUC or the STUC. The STUC, uniquely compared with regional TUC organizations, possessed considerable devolved powers of its own but could not take the IUOOC under its wing. This would have been the prerogative of the TUC. Indeed, the STUC as a body was not even represented at the May Commons meeting between the unions and UKOOA. Its absence reflected ongoing political differences between the more moderate TUC organization and its more radical regional counterpart.

The upshot was that the IUOOC, a committee of local full-time trade union officials, found themselves sitting across the table from the most powerful group of multinationals on the globe, grouped together in UKOOA. In the evolving talks, the IUOOC lacked even a formal constitution and agenda. Its minutes were still handwritten notes recorded by its secretary. While the presence of Benn and the TUC support bolstered the IUOOC's position in the initial stages, it was left to find its own way thereafter.

The TUC at the Commons meeting had wished the ten-point 'Charter for Unionisation' in the offshore oil industry to be the agenda for discussion. But it was already clear that the major oil companies had no intention of addressing it seriously. To pursue the Charter with the employers would require further meetings, 'chaired and arranged by the Energy Minister, perhaps on a quarterly and more formal basis'.[27] While such meetings took place, the ten-point Charter slipped off the future agenda. It was replaced with a far more restricted set of concerns. Upon entering the Commons meeting, the trade union side had already agreed to narrow the remit of the IUOOC to the northern sector of the North Sea, in order 'to prevent operators from trying to throw doubts on the viability' of the committee.[28] Apparently, the Aberdeen-based committee feared that charges would be levied that the IUOOC would not be well placed to discuss the problems of the southern sector gas fields. The maritime unions, especially the NUS at national level, meanwhile were still committed to a strategy of exclusive agreements on the rigs under the auspices of the BSJC, which further undermined the IUOOC as the authoritative spokesperson for the trade unions in the North Sea.

Sectional tensions between the maritime unions and other constituent IUOOC member unions remained a key characteristic of trade union relations throughout the next decade of the offshore saga. Although the TUC had been happy to act as broker to trade unions seeking influence offshore, it failed to resolve the sectional differences between its affiliates. It also failed to provide the IUOOC with the resources, financial and technical, which could have enabled that body to present a serious challenge to the employers. This meant that the IUOOC as an inter-union body was in no position to press forward with the ten-point Charter demands. When Chapple for the TUC attempted to raise the issue of the Charter at the Commons meeting, he was roundly rebuffed by the Shell representative and by Williams for UKOOA, claiming 'legally, UKOOA cannot negotiate collectively'. Shell challenged the standing of the IUOOC as a trade union committee capable of representing workers offshore. It was countered by Irwin: 'The TUC has given support to the Aberdeen Committee and surely this is sufficient'. The IUOOC notes of this meeting do not record whether or not the oil companies were in any way impressed by this declaration.

By 1976 a Memorandum of Understanding on Trade Union Access to Offshore Installations was on offer to the unions.[29] It signalled the operators' agreement, in principle, to provide facilities for representatives from unions in membership of the IUOOC to visit the rigs and offshore platforms. The companies would provide transport and facilities for officials. 'Reasonable access' was to be granted 'provided this could be fitted in with normal operational requirements'.[30] On paper at least, the broad principle of union access offshore appeared to be accepted. In practice, it was to work out rather differently. Nothing was agreed on the vexed question of union recognition procedures, although Harold Walker was able to reassure the unions that the Employment Protection Act 1975 was about to have its provisions extended offshore. This was probably a sop to the unions, to make palatable what otherwise appeared as a limited set of assurances in the Memorandum on Access. In practice, it was to fail to meet union expectations. Progress with regard to access and recognition for trade unions offshore was to prove painfully slow.

The Memorandum on Access represented the oil industry's recognition that some limited voluntary accommodation on the question of trade unionism offshore was preferable to more stringent legislative compulsion. A Labour government committed to the furtherance of collective bargaining might otherwise have resorted to more drastic measures. The minutes of the IUOOC, however, record continual frustration at what was seen as a consistent delay by the companies in acceding to reasonable requests for access by union officials to offshore installations.[31] By the end of 1977, the DEn's *Brown Book* records only nine such visits to offshore installations (DEn, 1978: 12). By 1980, the number of visits arranged was still only nine, rising to twenty-one in 1981, as a result of IUOOC pressure, but thereafter falling again.[32] By the 1980s, with the arrival of a Conservative government, the oil operators reconsidered the Memorandum on Access. Union officials wishing to go offshore for recruitment purposes now found that they had to wait between four and nine months to arrange visits with certain operators.[33] Opportunities for officials to speak to the workforce as a collective body, once on the installation, were sometimes limited or even non-existent. Union officials had to approach the men as best they could, at meal breaks or in their cabins. Often no prior notice would be given of an official's arrival. Sometimes the union official would be placed in a cramped cabin next door to the office of the Offshore Installation Manager (OIM). Many men feared that to express open interest in trade unions might damage their career prospects, a not unreasonable feeling in view of the recent history of the industry. Tales of union recruitment forms being slipped under the cabin door of a visiting official were not unusual. Oil industry consent to the Memorandum of Access was a condition of the fifth and subsequent rounds of licensing. This probably did as much as anything to ensure continuing trade union visits offshore. On the trade union side, there were severe deficiencies, however, in organizing who should go offshore, with whom and when. More often than not, these difficulties were influenced by sectional rivalries between the IUOOC unions, as various unions strove to secure a competitive recruiting edge. Typically, at least two officials would be sent on a visit, to allay suspicions of unfair recruiting. Twelve months after the signing of the Memorandum on Access the IUOOC still had to achieve a breakthrough on union recognition on any of the fixed installations in the North Sea (IDS, 1977b: 5).

Union Avoidance

As part of a union-avoidance strategy, the companies put in place a series of 'consultative committees' to address employees' concerns without union involvement. The establishment of such consultative committees had traditionally served as a union-avoidance strategy in the US, especially in the post World War II period. Kochan, Katz and McKersie note with regard to US oil and chemical multinationals that consultative alternatives to unions, or to the presence of 'third parties' had been fostered since the 1950s. They report the philosophy of one large US oil company as 'The company does not feel that a third party bargaining unit is necessary and will deal with employees directly pursuant to the (our) human relations philosophy' (Kochan, Katz and McKersie, 1986: 58).

But hostility to 'interference' by third parties was by no means a new phenomenon. US managements had long experience in developing surrogate forms of employee representation 'in response to the threat of or as a direct substitute for unionisation' (Greenfield and Pleasure, 1993: 184). Brody describes the long tradition of 'unitarist' management philosophy in US industrial relations:

> Workers did not need a 'third party' such as a broad-based trade union and would naturally benefit from ... management-created structures because, as one observer contended in 1929, 'modern business acted on the "sincere belief that the interests of the employer and employee are mutual and at bottom identical"'. (Brody, 1980: 51 cited in Greenfield and Pleasure, 1993: 184)

Even at the earliest stages of the evolution of offshore industrial relations, trade unions voiced dissatisfaction with these types of management-dominated consultative committees, which they perceived as 'a device of employers to inhibit the development of trade unionism offshore'. The employers asserted that such consultative committees were 'a normal medium for communication between the company and its employees'.[34] Alix Thom quotes the definition of 'consultation' from one oil company handbook: 'Consultation is a process for communication between staff and management to enable the views of staff to be expressed, discussed and taken into account before management makes a decision on a matter' (Thom, 1989: 101).

The handbook states that the consultative committee is not 'a forum for negotiating terms and conditions' (Thom, 1989: 102). While Thom's study suggests some minor variations in the scope of such committees, their common function, at least in the words of offshore management was to act as a 'safety valve'. Indeed, one instance is reported when employees persisted in talking about negotiating terms and conditions, which led to the collapse of consultative arrangements. Management had made it clear that such issues were not open to discussion and removed them from the arena (Thom, 1989: 102). Where unionization threatened, management consultants were on hand to provide employers with supportive advice, which depicted the desire for collective representation as a form of neurotic response. A report, by Robert de Board of Henley Management College, found the workers on the platform were suffering from 'acute anxiety'. The workers were 'looking for the feminine mothering side of human nature which is being deliberately excluded in the macho management style'. The consultant concluded that the wish for union representation was 'a cry for help, "come and look after us"'.[35]

The use of management consultants was particularly important for companies such as Mobil, who were strongly opposed to unionization on their platforms. Mobil delayed a request for a visit by IUOOC representatives to the Beryl Alpha for over three months, ostensibly on the grounds that there had already been one such earlier visit and that two visits per year were a 'reasonable' number. Industrial relations problems that summer had led Mobil to bring in Henley Management College consultants.[36] Mobil denied that this was part of a 'union avoidance' strategy. The Mobil employee relations manager noted:

> Sensitive discussions were taking place with our employees to resolve the difficulties identified earlier. As we informed you, a union visit during these discussions would endanger proper focus on the actual problem at hand, and jeopardize our immediate objective to resolve the issues through direct consultation with our employees.[37]

If the presence of a 'third party' union official could be avoided until after management consultants had sorted out the problems and a consultative system was securely in place, so much the better. As Mobil put it:

It remains our aim to institute an employee relations environment offshore, which is second to none. Our employees have been fully involved in the review of future needs, and in-depth consultation with them will continue. An increasing number has indicated trade union representation is not wanted and expressed the desire to see formal internal consultative machinery established. The feeling is that further union visits should be suspended until our discussions are completed.

Devices such as consultative committees remained a continuing feature of oil company union-avoidance strategy. Against this, however, there was the reality of growing trade union and political pressure onshore to concede traditional forms of collective bargaining arrangements. The challenge facing the operators was how to prevent union pressure from undermining the anomalous industrial relations regime they were seeking to implement offshore. At this point two fundamentally different sets of expectations clashed. On a national union level there were expectations of the extension of collective bargaining to all sectors of the economy. On the oil multinational side, expectations persisted, often based on US experience, that unionization could be avoided in the long run. Quite possibly, the operators believed that business could be conducted offshore in the absence of comprehensive collective bargaining, without direct conflict with the contemporary British political economy. The strategy adopted, therefore, was not always one of explicit challenge to unionization, but rather one of delaying tactics and prevarication. In this sense, the oil industry's endorsement of the Memorandum of Understanding was probably a tactical concession rather than representing any real commitment. If any concession towards unionization was to become part of the oil companies' strategy, this was, as we shall see later on, often aimed at exploiting and enhancing inter-union rivalries.

The Relationship between IUOOC and UKOOA

Since conceding the Memorandum on Access in July 1976, the industry knew that it would only be a matter of time before the trade unions began pursuing recognition for bargaining purposes offshore. The industry now wanted to create a mechanism for monitoring trade union intentions, especially as the IUOOC now had both a TUC and a government seal of approval. In September 1976 UKOOA's Director General wrote to John Liverman, the responsible civil servant at the Department of Energy, that UKOOA's Council had approved the formation of a Liaison Panel 'whose function will be to act as a channel of communication for UKOOA on matters concerning employee relations offshore'.[38] This Liaison Panel would comprise six members of UKOOA's Employment Practices Committee on the employers' side who would meet with representatives of the IUOOC on a periodic basis. Predictably, the Liaison Panel would 'not have any power, express or implied, to negotiate, either on behalf of the Council or individual member companies'. By specifically refusing to perform a counterpart role on behalf of the employers, UKOOA again tried to preserve for itself and its constituents a maximum of autonomy and freedom of manoeuvre. The terms of reference for the Liaison Panel expressly limited the scope of the Panel 'on matters concerning employee relations' to items which 'can be discussed in general terms on an exchange of views basis'.[39] To this effect, the document itemizes in detail those issues around which there might be dialogue and those that UKOOA had ruled out on a prior basis. It is worth quoting these as they indicate graphically UKOOA's intention to prevent the emergence of anything that would be familiar to trade unions as a collective bargaining forum.

Subjects for Discussion

One of the purposes of the Panel will be to try, through the medium of discussion, to inform the unions of the differences between onshore industrial life and the offshore working environment, which, in the industry's view, justify a different approach by both employers and unions to offshore industrial relations. Approved subjects which can be discussed are:
1. Accommodation and recreation
2. Training
3. Safety and safety representation
4. Consultation with government on consultative documents dealing with proposed labour legislation or proposed Codes of Practice
5. General problems associated with new labour legislation
6. The practical application of Codes of Practice on grievance procedures and disciplinary procedures
7. The technical/safety problems of strikes offshore
8. Access to installations
9. Common interest groups

These subjects were selected because discussion of them can help to create more realistic attitudes in government and the IUOOC.

Subjects that Cannot be Discussed

1. Terms and conditions of employment: salaries, allowances, pensions, sick pay and sick leave, job grades, over-time, etc.
2. Recruitment of employees
3. Specific complaints about any individual company or its employees
4. Contractors
5. Manning levels and operating strengths

The UKOOA Liaison Panel was an attempt to replicate at industry level the kind of consultative arrangements the operators were attempting to sustain at company level, presumably with the similar 'safety valve' function. Since the Liaison Panel was given no express authority over its constituent member companies, there was no commitment to 'take into account' the views of the IUOOC. Hence, any issue of real contention, such as employer resistance to recognition, was adroitly fielded away as a matter to be taken up with the 'individual employer' (Thom, 1989: 195ff). Bottom of the list of subjects 'approved' for discussion, but probably top in terms of UKOOA's real concern, was the question of 'common interest groups'. UKOOA was anxious to know how the unions, having secured some form of access offshore, intended to deal with any subsequent claims for recognition which might arise on behalf of particular groups of workers. The Liaison Panel and the IUOOC exchanged draft proposals for a procedural agreement on recognition.[40]

After five months of discussion and several further exchanges, both sides arrived at the Memorandum of Understanding between UKOOA and the IUOOC as to how 'recognition may be achieved'.[41] The substance of this second Memorandum conferred on the IUOOC the role of processing and overseeing applications for recognition on behalf of individual trade unions. Any union seeking recognition would require to do so through the auspices of the IUOOC. The employer and unions would then determine what the 'common interest group' might be, and thereafter, under third party supervision, employees would be balloted. In discussions, the operators made it clear that, if possible, they would like to keep the Advisory, Conciliation and Arbitration Service (ACAS) out of any formal involvement in the recognition process.[42] The union would have to show 'significant' membership in the common interest group, a word that the unions succeeded in having inserted in place of UKOOA's preferred formulation of 'substantial' membership. This still left the employers with considerable say in which workers might comprise the target group. In fact, over the next few years, the unions acquiesced in the enlargement of the definition of the bargaining unit for negotiating rights, from single platforms, to whole fields or even groups of fields. The employers, for their part, often refused to reveal to the trade unions, or subsequently changed the boundaries of, those employee groups they were prepared to include within the common interest group.

While the IUOOC sought to have included 'extended facilities for both on- and offshore meetings for the purpose of consolidating membership', the employers did not approve.[43] In practice, UKOOA endorsed its view that consultations with employees should 'reflect the situation that prevails at that particular point in time and take into account the needs and values of all parties involved'.[44] With this, and the stress on the primarily 'representational' role of unions restricted to individual grievances and disciplinary procedures, the Memorandum on Recognition hardly resembled a trade union manifesto for securing collective bargaining rights. Demands by the IUOOC that there should be a 'requirement that new contracts should stipulate recognition of the unions, as was the case in Norway' brought reassurance from UKOOA of 'oil companies' willingness to grant recognition where their employees wanted it'.[45] However, soon thereafter the operators mounted a rearguard resistance. Benn's *Diaries* record:

> I had a long struggle today with Shell-Esso, who are being very difficult and trying to pull back from the Memorandum of Understanding which they have with us concerning their North Sea operations. I was courteous but Dick Mabon was much more aggressive, as we agreed he should be. I felt at the end we were losing. (1989: 166)

This diary entry was for 15 June 1977, two days after the signing of the Memorandum on Recognition.

In part, these problems reflected deficiencies in the recognition procedures and provisions of the relevant legislation, the Employment Protection Act of 1975. Faced with implacable employer hostility, the formal rights bestowed by the Act were wholly ineffective, both onshore and offshore, as a vehicle for obtaining trade union recognition. The Labour government sought to promote a climate and institutions conducive to the extension of orderly collective bargaining, but failed to provide the legislative means to compel it. The employers, by simple non-co-operation, could set the trade union organizers an almost impossible hurdle to surmount, since nothing in the Act compelled the granting of formal recognition and bargaining rights.

The role of ACAS in facilitating the process of recognition has already been referred to. After the acute labour unrest of the preceding years, ACAS's role in furthering orderly industrial relations was seen as central. Although no numerical threshold for recognition was stipulated, ACAS recommended recognition if employee support was near or above 50 per cent, and non-recognition, if below 40 per cent (IRRR, 1978). ACAS could prepare written reports where a recognition issue could not be resolved by voluntary settlement. But, as an analysis of the labour law of the period suggested: 'It [ACAS] did not have to recommend recognition and nor was there any kind of general legal obligation on employers to recognise or bargain' (Lewis and Simpson, 1981: 141).

There was an enforcement procedure of sorts, where an employer failed to comply with an ACAS recommendation. If a union complaint against an employer was not settled voluntarily at appeal, the union could ask for an arbitration award. This award could be statutorily incorporated into individual contracts of employment, giving individual employees the right in principle to sue a recalcitrant employer. But even that limited legal purchase on the issue of recognition was undermined by a series of hostile judicial decisions which 'classically illustrated the judges' inability to comprehend the realities and values of collective labour relations' (Lewis and Simpson, 1981: 142). The limited powers of ACAS were seen as highly inimical, for example, by Lord Salmon in the Grunwick case, a bitter dispute over recognition in which the employer had dismissed the unionized workforce. Referring to the role of ACAS in trying to resolve the dispute, Lord Salmon said, 'Such an interference with individual liberty could hardly be tolerated in a free society unless there were safeguards against abuse' (Lewis and Simpson, 1981: 142).

The judges provided such 'safeguards' by the most restrictive interpretation of ACAS's remit. By June 1979 the chairman of ACAS had informed the Secretary of State that ACAS could no longer 'satisfactorily operate the statutory recognition procedures as they stand' (quoted in Lewis and Simpson, 1981: 143). At Grunwick, the employer had refused to co-operate with ACAS, by preventing access to the non-striking workforce, as well as withholding their names and addresses for purposes of balloting. The courts had ruled that non-strikers as well as strikers had to have their opinions ascertained. Thus ACAS was caught in a legal Catch 22.

The impotence of ACAS was well illustrated in a dispute contemporaneous with that at Grunwick. This was between North Sea helicopter pilots, their union BALPA, and the Bristow Helicopter Company; a company which will re-appear in our story at several points, including the account of the Cormorant Alpha disaster. BALPA had been steadily recruiting at Bristow's Aberdeen base in the late autumn of 1976 and the following spring, so that by April 1977 it had 62 out of about 100 pilots in membership. Longstanding grievances over pay and hours had been allowed to fester by the strongly anti-union chairman of the company, Alan Bristow. Bristow had at first conceded the setting up of an internal consultative body to provide 'inputs' to company policy, but in reality aimed at avoiding claims for collective bargaining recognition from the union, BALPA. When the in-house forum began to assume a negotiating stance, it was effectively sidelined.

Bristow's attitude to trade unionism can be judged from an internal company memorandum to the chairman written by its operations manager four weeks before a major strike erupted. The memo observes, 'BALPA are mounting an all-out effort to gain sizeable support within Bristow's so that union recognition can be sought – and they are having some success.' Noting the matter was of 'grave concern', the memo continued:

[BALPA] will endeavour to expand the numbers and seek recognition as soon as possible. We must be prepared to fight … As confrontation on a large scale between Bristow's and BALPA is now inevitable I feel that it might be beneficial to have an all-out attack at the highest level on BALPA. (quoted in Department of Employment, 1977)

An early BALPA member at Bristow's, identified by management as an activist, was singled out for transfer to a posting abroad and was subsequently dismissed when he refused the company offer. Fifty-four fellow pilots took strike action in support and were also dismissed, including six pilots who were not even union members. BALPA had sought recognition with the company but the dispute now supervened. It quickly escalated to involve blacking by the NUS supply boat crews, TGWU dockers, tanker drivers and onshore refinery workers and pilots from the rival British International Helicopters. With TUC and STUC support for 'a dispute we cannot afford to lose' these actions virtually closed Aberdeen's Dyce Airport and threatened to seriously disrupt the activities of BP in the Forties, Mobil in the Beryl field, Hamilton's Argyll, and Amoco's Montrose fields. Behind the scenes, the government contacted BP, the major client, to pressure company chairman Alan Bristow into some form of ACAS involvement in resolving the problems, but the company remained obdurate. The situation became sufficiently intractable for the government to take the unusual step of appointing a Court of Inquiry which examined the circumstances of the dispute in some detail. Its report pulled few punches about the company's responsibility for provoking the dispute, and its 'intransigent attitude' (Department of Employment, 1977: 53). In the end, the strikers remained dismissed and Bristow 'union-free'. Benn's *Diaries* record his private support for the strikers, 'because the dispute doesn't involve pay policy, the Social Contract or anything like that – just the principle of trade union recognition' (1990: 119). But direct minister-ial intervention in this industrial dispute was neither favoured nor likely to have been able to alter the course of events.

The numbers of workers gaining recognition under the Employment Pro-tection Act had been relatively modest, given the judicial constraints. Under the 1980 Employment Act, the new Conservative administration repealed Sections 11–16 of the Employment Protection Act, those sections designed to encourage employers to grant union recognition. The removal of the recognition-facilitating sections of the Act, while probably of minimal stat-utory significance, signalled to employers that government pressure towards extending union recognition was effectively at an end. As with so much 'pro-tective' legislation meant to enhance workers' rights, however, it was not the formal juridical guarantees that were ultimately important, but the real bal-ance of power between labour and employer at the place of work. The Employment Protection Act failed decisively in its offshore application so far as recognition was concerned, because that balance of power was even more heavily weighted than onshore in the employers' favour.

One other major piece of legislation, also a product of the Labour govern-ment's Social Contract, was the Health and Safety at Work Act (HSWA) 1974. It too was extended offshore in 1977 by Order in Council, but in one critical respect, in an incomplete manner. The HSWA, in both its origins and imple-mentation, was a sister Act to the Employment Protection Act. Regulations which provided for trade union-appointed safety committees and safety repre-sentatives onshore were tied to expectations of the extension of orderly collect-ive bargaining between employers and recognized trade unions. The oil majors, as we have seen, were largely able to resist extensive union recognition offshore except on their own restricted terms. They also proved equally adept at preventing safety legislation, specifically union-appointed safety representa-tion, that could itself have been an important foothold for trade unionism off-shore. This is an important aspect of the North Sea story to which we will return. From the first, however, the trade unions did raise concerns about health and safety offshore. An early meeting of UKOOA Liaison Panel and IUOOC which discussed union recognition proposals heard a request from the unions to discuss the new Health and Safety at Work Act and 'the possibility of it being implemented offshore before this became a legal requirement'.[46] The ASTMS official recorded the operators' response. 'All the companies intimated that they felt they had fairly satisfactory safety committees and representatives, etc., but agreed there would still be room for improvement. However, they were not prepared to give any undertakings at this time.'[47]

At the subsequent meeting with the Liaison Panel, IUOOC representatives again argued that not enough was being done on safety matters. The training and election of safety representatives, said the unions, should include representatives from the contractors' workforces, where concerns had been raised about the number of accidents on platform construction work.[48] The operators responded that the Health and Safety Commission (HSC), the tripartite body bringing together employers, unions and government to oversee the effective functioning of the new safety legislation, had still to establish an industry advisory committee for the oil industry. Any proposals in advance of this would be premature. An Oil Industry Advisory Committee under HSC's aegis, on which the trade unions were to have a voice, eventually emerged. However, the TUC's proposal to have an exclusively offshore-oriented oil advisory committee was successfully opposed by the CBI on behalf of the oil operators.[49] The specific dangers to the workforce posed by the hazardous offshore environment were subsumed within more general discussions concerning the oil industry, onshore as well as offshore. More importantly, when offshore safety seemed likely to become a contentious issue, the employers successfully contained any threat to their right to manage the oilfields in whatever way they saw fit. One of the few mentions of a specific operating company being approached by concerned union officials on safety matters, was a request from the AUEW and the Boilermakers' union in 1980 to Occidental management regarding the Claymore and Piper Alpha platforms. The outcome of the meeting is not reported, except the comment that 'no further meetings' were planned.[50]

The Pursuit of Sectional Advantage

If the employers were able to deflect trade unionism offshore, the trade unions themselves must be apportioned some of the responsibility for this outcome. They had brought to the offshore world the perspectives, identities and institutional structures which they believed were serving them appropriately and effectively onshore. At the time, there was a supportive government in power and trade union membership was growing, particularly in the latter half of the 1970s. Yet the offshore world was a complex multi-faceted industry in a physically remote and hazardous environment. In many respects, the methods and approaches of onshore trade unionism were not adequate to the scale of the task which confronted the trade union movement.

The offshore oil industry, in this sense, provides an important case study of 'organized' trade union responses to a new industry and perhaps contains lessons for the future. Patterns of subcontracting which were well developed at the inception of the offshore industry have now become widespread within onshore production industries. Subcontracting, if strategically and consciously developed by industry, can place formidable obstacles to union organizing efforts, and in that sense, the experience offshore was to foreshadow more widespread developments onshore.

Given the multiplicity of unions involved in the North Sea oil industry, some degree of sectional competitiveness was perhaps inevitable. Given also that many of the jobs offshore were 'new', and did not necessarily fit within traditionally demarcated areas derived from onshore industry, some inter-union boundary disputes were inevitable. The further ingredient of 'grand designs' on the part of certain unions added new problems. An orderly approach to offshore unionization was doomed once these forces overcame the initial intentions, as voiced by the Confederation of Shipbuilding and Engineering Unions, for co-ordinated organizing efforts.

Such a 'grand design' was pursued by the ASTMS. It had seen little point in recruiting in the exploration drilling side of the industry. But there appeared to be new opportunities for recruitment on fixed-installation production platforms. Especial, but not exclusive targets, were the permanent operator staff and the workforce in general in the southern sector gas fields. The remit of the IUOOC did not run to the southern sector. Roger Spiller, the ASTMS divisional officer, requested access to Phillips platforms off the coast of East Anglia. This produced the standard oil company response:

> We have no direct request from our employees to be represented by a union and it would appear that everyone is quite satisfied with the existing machinery for consultation through the works committee. There would not appear to be any need, therefore, to change the present arrangements.[51]

Phillips went on to note that it was its understanding that all matters dealing with unionization offshore, were 'dealt with through the inter-union off-shore committee and not through individual unions'. By raising this jurisdictional question, Phillips had opened up an issue which went to the core of the IUOOC's ability to unionize offshore. As an inter-union body its purpose was to give all its constituent members an equitable chance to organize. The IUOOC would then consider and attempt to negotiate recognition agreements on individual unions' behalf. Most agreements would therefore be 'multi-union'. Where 'spheres of interest' might overlap between different unions, IUOOC would provide a forum for the resolution of competing claims. What the recruitment overture of ASTMS to Phillips made clear to other IUOOC unions, was that this union saw tightly defined spheres of interest as inimical to its wider aim of concluding single-union recognition agreements where possible.[52] In the southern sector, ASTMS could recruit all the various categories of offshore worker from catering stewards up to platform managers. Its participation in IUOOC was perhaps to that extent tactical, rather than a whole-hearted concurrence with the general objectives of the committee.[53]

This position aroused strong resentment from other union officials on the IUOOC, particularly as most of them represented manual-worker unions whose own 'staff sections' were weakly organized and, therefore, not well placed to compete with ASTMS. Eventually, a compromise deal was worked out, whereby if an individual union could show overwhelming membership on any installation, a single-union agreement could be accepted by the IUOOC, provided the rights of other unions were safeguarded. The IUOOC would have the power to vet any such recognition agreement.[54]

All of this was still hypothetical, as no union recognition agreement had been concluded under the auspices of the IUOOC. Partly based on miscalculations about the ease with which organization offshore was possible, the expectations of the IUOOC ran ahead of what was actually achievable offshore. By January 1977, with ASTMS claiming 60 per cent membership on the Phillips platforms, it appeared to be in a position to make a bid for recognition. The IUOOC finally gave ASTMS permission to pursue what were in effect sole negotiating rights, with the face-saving rider that 'the rights of other constituent members of the committee were unimpaired'.[55]

With this, the strategy of Phillips in using the supposed joint-union remit of the IUOOC as a screen against the sole-bargaining aspirations of ASTMS was effectively at an end. The company took until July 1978 to agree to an ACAS supervised ballot which secured ASTMS full negotiating rights on Phillips' Hewett gas field.[56] Phillips had attempted to introduce further delays by demanding that onshore staff also be included in the ballot. When the ballot could no longer be avoided, the company appealed by letter to individual members of its workforce to preserve the 'close working relationship . . . maintained over the years' and the 'mutually developed understanding and informality' which made the need for collective representation unnecessary.[57] Said the letter from Phillips' management, 'It is our belief that you would prefer to continue to deal directly with the company as in the past.' Only as a result of vigorous ASTMS protests was the union able to get references to 'outside third parties' removed. These responses, as so often in offshore industrial relations, demonstrated the company's expectation that a union-free environment could be maintained in the long run. Only when subject to sustained pressure, and after having used all available deflection strategies, did Phillips finally concede. Unions attempting to organize offshore not only had to reckon with reluctant employers, but also with ones which were willing to exploit inter-union tensions for their own purposes. This point is even more graphically illustrated in the next section.

The IUOOC/BSJC Breach

IUOOC's evolving breach with the maritime unions, first opened up over the BSJC agreement on Houlder Brothers drilling rigs, became a running sore in 1976. The BSJC unions, the NUS, the AUEW, the naval officers in MNAOA and the radio engineers in REOU, although also participants in the IUOOC, were seeking to consolidate the bridgehead provided by the Houlder Brothers agreement. Now they planned to extend their influence throughout the drilling side of the industry. While the IUOOC had been forced to concede that drilling rigs whilst in transit were 'ships', as covered by the Merchant Shipping Acts, once on station they were fixed 'environments of work' and thus could come under the remit of the IUOOC. Even if it were necessary to concede that in their basic design many drilling rigs did have more in common with ships, the same argument could not be necessarily extended to 'semi-submersible' drilling rigs; novel structures floating on huge subsea pontoons anchored to the sea-bed. The incursion of the BSJC unions into the semi-submersible sector was therefore viewed with alarm by the IUOOC.

The IUOOC received the endorsement of the TUC Fuel and Power Industries Committee for its view that 'unions in membership of the BSJC' were pursuing policies which 'run contrary to those of the IUOOC'.[58] A letter from Len Murray, TUC General Secretary, was sent to the relevant BSJC unions and the IUOOC, reiterating 'the TUC's continuing support' for the work of the Aberdeen inter-union committee.[59] When the BSJC unions appeared unhappy with this implied criticism, the Fuel and Power Industries Committee convened a meeting between the two bodies to discuss the issues in contention in March 1977. This discussion also included the question of the geographical remit of the IUOOC and whether it should extend to the southern sector of the North Sea. At this meeting, the national officers of the NUS and the AUEW engineering union, in particular, pressed for the BSJC view that 'national negotiations should be conducted by national officials', rather than by the committee of local officials in IUOOC.[60] The BSJC representatives were particularly keen to stake their claim to the semi-submersibles. The

NUS official pointed out that his union organized drilling crews because 'roustabouts were required to have Able Seamen's certificates before they could become drillers'. Were they to be recruited by the TGWU (that is, fall within the remit of the IUOOC), then that route to advancement from the drill floor to management would be closed to them. Other BSJC union representatives reiterated that these self-propelled rigs 'required certificated seamen to operate them'. Morever, it was pointed out that the BSJC unions had 'not sought to influence policy or organisation on the fixed platforms'. ASTMS, although not a BSJC union, supported this position, possibly because it sought to conclude agreements with the employers independently of the IUOOC, for its own reasons.

While the restricted remit of the IUOOC to the northern North Sea was reaffirmed, the TUC, like the operators, would have preferred the extension of the IUOOC to embrace both the southern and northern North Sea.[61] Although the possibility of establishing a separate southern-sector IUOOC committee was discussed, it was never to materialize. During the successful campaign for recognition in Phillips Hewett field, ASTMS effectively became proxy for the IUOOC in the south, covering all categories of the workforce. In addressing the Phillips employees in its pre-ballot appeal for support it described itself as 'ASTMS [acting] on behalf of the IUOOC'.[62]

The IUOOC had already demarcated a sphere of influence on the semi-submersibles which directly cut across that of the maritime NUS. The chief beneficiary was to be the TGWU, who supplied the secretary, Bill Reid, to the IUOOC. His appointment became a driving force in the dispute with the BSJC unions. The rivalry between the NUS and TGWU was then imported into the deliberations of the IUOOC. Faced with these intractable hostilities, the TUC Fuel and Power Industries Committee (FPIC) felt unable to resolve what it saw as a problem of demarcation.

> The FPIC could not adjudicate on the right of particular unions in the North Sea offshore area ... it was not the FPIC's job to judge between unions in this way. However, since all member unions of the BSJC were also represented on the Aberdeen IUOOC it should be possible for an accommodation to be reached.[63]

Such an 'accommodation' was eventually reached in February 1978, in which the IUOOC agreed to recognize the sphere of influence of the BSJC unions on semi-submersibles as well as on drillships and pipe-laying barges. However, those drilling rigs which were classed as permanent production platforms (and the semi-submersible Stadrill, where an IUOOC application on behalf of the TGWU to Shell for a recognition agreement already existed) would not come within the sphere of the BSJC unions. The TGWU had found itself in a minority of one on the issue of which union body should organize the semi-submersibles, with those unions represented both in the BSJC and IUOOC in favour of the proposed settlement. However, problems of inter-union sectionalism did not end there.

By 1978, the IUOOC was faced not simply with a crisis of credibility but its possible dissolution, brought to a head by a further claim by the AUEW engineering union for recognition on the BP semi-submersible rig Sea Conquest. The AUEW now insisted that the agreement should be negotiated under the auspices of the BSJC, since the staff it was seeking to represent were mainly redeployed marine engineers from BP's tanker fleet. BP, on the other hand, wished the IUOOC to be the vehicle for recognition.[64] The AUEW at national level seemed prepared to see the IUOOC disintegrate if it proved an obstacle to achieving recognition on the Sea Conquest. As a consequence, thereafter, all of the drilling side of the industry was effectively conceded to the BSJC 'maritime' unions.[65] The remit of the IUOOC from then onwards was to be confined primarily to fixed installations in the northern sector. Here recruitment had been proceeding steadily since the previous autumn, particularly in the Brent and Forties fields. On Occidental's Piper Alpha the first IUOOC-sponsored agreement in the northern sector was reached in late 1977, enabling company employees to be represented by the ASTMS union in grievance and disciplinary matters, though not for full collective bargaining purposes. This was the first toe-hold that the trade union movement had succeeded in establishing on a production platform in the northern sector of the North Sea. But it was to be some time before further limited encroachments (individual representational rights but excluding health and safety) were to be made on fixed installations, and then primarily restricted to the Shell platforms in the East Shetland Basin.

The BSJC unions, for their part, had only very limited subsequent success in organizing the drilling side of the industry, especially as many of the rigs were foreign-owned, operating under flags of convenience. This side of the industry was to remain 'union-free' with but few exceptions. A year later, in 1979, the BSJC unions were subject to 'severe criticism' by IUOOC for their 'non-activity in approaching or organising further rigs'. This led IUOOC to consider requesting visiting rights to the semi-submersibles.[66] Further conflict emerged in this area between the rival inter-union bodies, which now actually magnified the sectional tendencies of their constituent unions. Such was the strength of sectional antagonisms, that what were by now old wounds refused to heal.

UKOOA, through its Liaison Panel, viewed these developments with some concern. The chairman of the Liaison Panel wrote to the IUOOC noting 'the fragmentation of the union presence offshore'. Having successfully boxed-in the IUOOC unions, with two Memoranda which were of little use in securing collective bargaining rights, the last development the oil operators wished was the intrusion of a new inter-union body in the offshore scene. UKOOA's Liaison Panel complained:

> We can only view the incursion of a second Trade Union organisation, the British Seafarers' Joint Council, in seeking 'jurisdictional rights' over non-fixed structures or semi-submersibles, as a retrogressive step in the relationships the Industry and the Trade Union movement have been striving to develop.[67]

Benn had written to the IUOOC pointing out that he would not want to object to this new arrangement conceding semi-submersibles to the BSJC which modified the Memorandum of Access, provided it would 'ensure an orderly approach to industrial relations offshore'.[68] Nevertheless, the committee was gently reminded by Benn of the 'tripartite' nature of the original agreement, and that UKOOA's preparedness to accept the arrangement would also have to be taken into account. The IUOOC and BSJC unions, however, had failed to consult either the TUC, the government or the employers before reaching this new 'accord'. This was much to the embarrassment of Benn, leading him to write to UKOOA, 'I appreciate UKOOA's desire for all negotiations to be through one organisation, and had myself hoped that IUOOC would play that role, but now fear this is not possible'.[69]

Following the débâcle over the semi-submersibles, the IUOOC began to organize itself in a more concerted manner. A formal constitution was adopted and agreement was made to meet on a regular basis every two months.[70] Moreover, the committee began to push harder for the operators to arrange offshore visits for the officials, and to develop its own agenda of issues to be put before the joint meetings with UKOOA's Liaison Panel. Despite some valiant efforts, however, the IUOOC remained neutered as an effective force for developing offshore trade unionism. On the one hand, it was subject to the employers' carefully contrived strategy of union deflection and avoidance. On the other hand, its ability to act in a co-ordinated manner was undermined by sectionalist tendencies within the trade union movement itself, and by its lack of authoritative status within the established structures of the trade union movement. Given these obstacles, the spread of offshore unionization remained predictably slow. Nearly three years after the Memorandum on

Access had been put in place, the IUOOC belatedly complained to the TUC about 'the general lack of progress of unionisation in the North Sea'.[71] The major impetus towards trade unionism, such as it was, came from another direction.

Collective Bargaining Arrangements: The Hook-up Agreement

The IUOOC had concentrated most of its efforts initially on the oil companies' operatives. Here only limited representational agreements had been secured on some platforms, but they tended to deal with the exclusive concerns of this group. Even these agreements were a rarity. Over two-thirds to three-quarters of the offshore workforce were employed, not by the operators, but by various contractors and specialist service companies. These employees formed a growing army of itinerant workers, seen as 'temporary guests' on the platforms, although increasingly numerically dominant offshore. They were mainly involved in the gigantic tasks of 'hooking up' the production platforms, fitting the various modules for drilling, production, processing and accommodation, on top of the installation 'jacket'. In servicing the hundred and one different functions to be found on a production platform, there were also further groups of workers employed by numerous contractors and sub-contractors.

While the oil operators were largely successful in deflecting unionization among their own employees, they were prepared to contemplate at least a partial accommodation between the trade unions and the contractor employers when it served their purposes. The emergence of fragmentary collective bargaining arrangements, covering specific limited areas of the contractor workforce, occurred with tacit and sometimes active operator approval. It was driven by two principal forces, the threat of labour militancy and the possibility of labour shortages.

Any unanticipated labour stoppage, even though involving small groups of workers, could be highly disruptive. Nowhere was such disruption more acutely unwelcome than when the operators were still at the stage of platform assembly, the so-called 'hook-up' phase, prior to 'first oil' coming on stream. Prior to the completion of the hook-up phase, construction workers could inflict hugely expensive delays on the operators by engaging in official or unofficial action. In terms of economic theory this represented the classical case of hold-up: that is, a situation where technical circumstances permitted a small group of workers to exert temporary and 'disproportionate' pressure on the firm because it had made specific investments which would not reap any return unless the respective groups of workers contributed their part (Klein, 1984).

In the early and mid-1970s, it was in the interests of the operators to bring their platforms into production as quickly as possible. This was rooted in two factors: first, government pressure to accelerate oil production for wider economic imperatives; and second, the wish of oil companies themselves to recoup their enormous outlays. Under these circumstances, there were important advantages in having a trade union agreement, whereby procedures for resolving industrial relations problems existed without the threat of work stoppages. This threat of industrial action was by no means hypothetical. The engineering construction workforce recruited to carry out the hook-up work offshore was drawn from onshore workers with strong traditions of local bargaining over pay and conditions in the rig-building yards, power stations and petrochemical construction sites.

It was apparent that the 'chaos' of stoppages and wage demands which had characterized onshore construction engineering, if exported offshore, could squeeze the contractor employers and their clients the oil majors in a vice of labour militancy. In the 1960s only the docks and motor vehicle manufacture were more 'strike prone' (NEDO, 1970: 107). Industrial site level agreements could become benchmarks for pushing up wages at the next 'site' in an upward spiral of leap-frogging claims (IDS, 1980). The employers feared it would only be a matter of time before there was a spillover effect from onshore sites. Labour stoppages could have huge financial implications offshore. With the construction workforce bringing with them their onshore unionized identities as well as their tradition of unofficial action, the offshore contractors and, more critically, their clients, were resigned to some degree of union penetration in this sector. The key challenge was to contain the overall level of unionization and to prevent any outbreak of uncontrolled local-level bargaining, rather than seek outright union avoidance as such. For this to be achieved, an offshore national agreement with the unions was an immediate imperative.

The powerful construction unions, namely the AUEW and the EETPU, had already established a reputation as reliable partners in strike avoidance. In the late 1960s, the Isle of Grain power station project, one of several major UK construction projects was disrupted by unofficial stoppages, instigated by insulators organized in the TGWU and Boilermakers' Society. Eric Hammond, General Secretary of EETPU, and John Baldwin of the AUEW construction section, had ridden together on a bus through the picket lines to secure a resumption of work. Their commitment to restoring industrial order in the engineering construction industry could scarcely be questioned. Hammond stated explicitly 'the only way to restore [union] authority was for all site matters to be determined nationally' (Garfit, 1989: 6). In order to extend such national bargaining arrangements to offshore contract workers, union leadership had to solicit the support of the oil operators for any agreement which the contractor employers might be party to.

Another element added to the urgency of an agreement; namely the potential shortage of skilled men. For the engineering construction industry in oil-related activity, the early 1970s had been turbulent. The establishment of major rig-building yards at Nigg Bay, Loch Kishorn, Ardersier, Methil and Ardyne Point in Scotland and at Graythorpe on Teeside, together with the construction of pipeline terminals at Flotta in Orkney and Sullom Voe in Shetland, as well as the St Fergus gas terminal at Cruden Bay near Peterhead, produced a huge demand for skilled labour for oil-related work and a rash of industrial disputes. The growing demand for similar kinds of labour on offshore platform hook-up assembly work provided for the unions the potential springboard of a very tight labour market. The records of the Oil and Chemical Plant Constructors Association (OCPCA) reveal that these developments were kept under the closest scrutiny in a liaison committee of the contractors with UKOOA. A Note of the Client/OCPCA Liaison Committee for March 1974 suggests that the real dimensions of the labour shortage facing the offshore industry were considerable. Requirements of 3000 rigger/erectors, 2400 boilermakers and platers, 4800 pipefitters, 600 mechanical fitters and 1200 instrument fitters and electricians, a total of 12,000 skilled workers in all were estimated.[72] Thus the workforce was not without leverage. The Client/OCPCA Liaison Committee of May 1976 concluded that 'the probability was that in due course of time the work would become unionised. It would therefore be prudent to plan with this in mind'.[73]

Campbell of BP said 'the oil companies needed to know what terms and conditions the contractors proposed to offer'. BP, it appeared, had already been 'embarrassed' by one non-OCPCA contractor offering 'above the rate'. It was agreed, in turn, that BP would supply information to the OCPCA on the terms and conditions applying to oil company employees on production platforms. The OCPCA, for its part, would produce a 'Model Agreement', with earnings levels for contractor employees, for comment by the client operators. OCPCA proposed a standard Model Agreement which, in the first instance, could be applied by the individual contractor employers. Subsequently, it could be converted into a national agreement negotiated with the unions offshore 'if the work became unionised'.[74]

For the operators, part and parcel of containing offshore unionization was retaining the loyalty of their own staff. This meant that an agreed differential between operator personnel and contractor employees had to be maintained. The exchange of information with the contractors was, therefore, crucial. It was important for the client oil companies to preserve the perception of privilege among their own employees and hopefully, a consequent imperviousness to unionization. The oil companies had already adopted a two weeks on, two weeks off cycle for their own employees on the production platforms, at a time when the contractor workforce was still employed on a two weeks on, one week off basis. As a BP representative observed with regard to the company's own employees' terms and conditions, 'the same should not necessarily apply to construction employees'. In the short term, the tactic of divide and rule seemed sensible, especially if some limited concession towards the collective-bargaining pressure from the contractor workforce was now imminent.

The minutes of the Client/OCPCA Liaison Meeting of November 1976 record the OCPCA 'looking to the clients for support', if the contractors were to concede to a national offshore agreement. It was clear that the offshore situation now needed to be resolved. Linklater of Shell, speaking for the clients, agreed it was time to 'talk turkey'.[75] On 24 November 1976 the clients represented by the Capital Projects Clients Group, together with representatives from the Electrical Contractors Associations (of Scotland and of England), the Engineering Employers Federation and the OCPCA met the national officers of the craft unions in the engineering construction industry in London's Park Lane Hotel. On the union side, representatives of the onshore National Engineering Construction Committee led by Baldwin, and not the offshore-oriented IUOOC, brokered the Hook-up agreement. Indeed, the local official of the AUEW construction section at this time still had only temporary affiliate rather than full membership of the IUOOC, on the grounds that hook-up work would be 'a passing phase' in the industry.[76]

Baldwin, for the unions, pointed out the likely consequences of the absence of an offshore national agreement for the unions. Onshore, the national officials had lost authority to shop stewards at site level, who were able to negotiate very large bonus premiums. The threat of the onshore 'anarchy' being replicated offshore was sufficient to concentrate the minds of the employers and persuade the operators to allow the contractor employers to reach an agreement with the unions. A draft offshore agreement was proposed, which was in the end signed by the AUEW, Boilermakers' Society, EETPU and National Union of Sheetmetal Workers. The Hook-up agreement, formally known as the Northern Waters Offshore Construction Agreement (OCA), provided for full collective bargaining rights, the appointment of shop stewards and premium rates of pay to be reviewed on an annual basis. The package offered in the Hook-up agreement amounted to a single consolidated offshore rate, including all overtime premiums and condition payments, thereafter known as the 'platform rate'. There was a suggested standard working pattern of two weeks offshore followed by one week onshore as leave. The new agreement was initially applied to the Thistle, Ninians Central and Northern, and Brent hook-up contracts. Gradually it came to prevail throughout the northern North Sea sector. In due course, a more limited Southern Waters Agreement (SWA) was also put in place. The operators had conceded what they saw as inevitable, given their perceived vulnerability in the offshore context prior to first oil starting to flow.

The role of the operators in controlling and monitoring concessions by the contractors to trade unions remained constant throughout. The UKOOA–contractor relationship was regularized in the Employment Practices Committee of UKOOA, whose terms of reference were previously described. Section 13 of UKOOA's Employment Practices Information Booklet (UKOOA, 1988) actually defines UKOOA's role in relation to the contractors in regard to such matters as policies towards agreements with trade unions. This section is headed 'UKOOA Contractors' Liaison Sub-Committees'. There are two of these liaison sub-committees, one in London and the other in Aberdeen. Their purpose is stated as that of maintaining liaison between UKOOA and the contractors' associations. One of the most significant aspects of this liaison is described as allowing UKOOA to 'monitor the progress of contractors' negotiations with the unions, in line with its Terms of Reference, to promote orderly industrial relations and to ensure a reasonable degree of uniformity in terms and conditions of employment'. Far from terms and conditions being a matter simply for the contractor employees and the contractor companies, UKOOA itself had the guiding hand in any such negotiations.

Two types of challenges to the Hook-up agreement were made by the workforce. The first was industrial action of a localized nature by workers seeking to secure the kinds of concessions from management typical in onshore construction engineering. In the summer of 1977 a number of employees claimed a 'completion bonus' on BP's Thistle platform. The men had previously worked in the Graythorpe fabrication yard where the Thistle jacket had been built, and had received a 'float out bonus' and other redundancy payments. The national officers, however, agreed that existing Hook-up redundancy provisions should be strictly adhered to in order 'to prevent the floodgates being opened up'. Local officials were instructed to visit the platform and order a return to work, which in the event was secured. A similar fate befell a group of electricians working offshore on the East Shetland Basin Shell platforms in January 1978. The men, employed by Mather and Platt Alarms, were trying to negotiate severance pay and embarked on sit-ins on the Brent Alpha and Bravo, the Brent Spar and the Dunlin Alpha. The EETPU had ordered the men back to work, and when they refused they were dismissed by the company. After two weeks the offshore sit-ins ended and the men were flown off the platforms, to be disowned by their national official.

The second type of challenge had more important long-term consequences for the character of offshore industrial relations and unionization. It was directly related to the perceived inadequacies of the offshore agreement itself, and as such marked the evolution of new distinctive offshore demands, which stood largely independent of previous onshore agendas. Up until 1978 the Hook-up agreement had seemed to work to the satisfaction of both the contractors and the clients. A meeting of the Client/OCPCA Liaison Committee in the spring of 1978 commented, 'The real question was whether the North Sea was to be eventually unionised. If it was to be unionised, then the OCPCA [Hook-up] agreement seemed to be the only way to contain the situation.'[77]

During 1978, however, an offshore shop stewards committee had been formed by engineering construction union activists. An immediate grievance was the one-week-off leave cycle. In bad weather employees could be delayed and unable to return home for the full week, or even miss their leave entirely. The demand for two weeks on, two weeks off, on a par with the oil company employees, for increased wages and allowances, and for a renegotiation of the Hook-up agreement for 1979, was rejected by the contractor employers. Instead, they proposed a three-week-on, two-week-off cycle.

An unofficial strike of nine weeks, the longest and most widespread industrial action seen up to that point in the North Sea, duly began in January 1979. Discontent had been simmering since the previous autumn and had already resulted in a two-week unofficial stoppage of 500 men in the Ninian field, with dismissals followed by reinstatement. Subsequently, shop stewards from across the various northern sector oil fields had met in November 1978 to formulate their collective grievances. The contractor employers, with the backing of the client oil companies, refused to concede workforce demands. The leaderships of the signatory unions were committed to upholding the Hook-up agreement. Unofficial action which began was outwith the existing grievance procedures, and union officials saw their first responsibility as preserving the credibility of the only major national agreement they had succeeded in establishing in the offshore oil industry. The workforce, who had returned to 'the beach', were eventually induced to resume work by their

officials without having any gains to show for their prolonged action. There
had also been intervention at government level by Dickson Mabon, as Junior
Energy Minister.

A stormy mass meeting of 2000 strikers in Glasgow in February 1979
sealed the fate of this unhappy episode. It had seen local officials urge the
crossing of onshore picket lines, mounted by the offshore strikers in an
attempt to broaden the dispute, and workforce accusations of betrayal by
the officials. A wedge of bitterness was created which divided officials and
offshore workforce for the next ten years and was in great measure responsible for the cynicism and apathy towards trade unions among many construction workers. Such was the level of demoralization, that on subsequent hook-
ups in the early 1980s, such as the Brae Alpha, the number of elected shop
stewards never reached the agreed maximum permitted under the Hook-up
agreement. When the Brae Alpha shop stewards sought to have elected safety
representatives and a safety committee established, the contractors were to
advise them against 'attempts to over-organize' because of the probable dis-
favour of the client, Marathon Oil.[78] Not only was the campaign for
improved terms and conditions weakened by the failure of the 1979 strike,
but so too, therefore, was the ability of the cowed and defeated workforce
to press for improved safety.

The defeat of the offshore workforce's most serious challenge to the contractor employers had taken place at the supposed high-water mark of the
labour unrest of the 1970s, the so-called 'winter of discontent'. It was to be a
decade before the offshore workforce fully recovered its combativeness in
new seasons of discontent.

The Struggle for a Post-construction Agreement

Offshore, the Hook-up agreement was seen by the operators as relatively
'expensive' both in terms of wages and redundancy provisions. The oil companies, therefore, started letting their maintenance work go to non-Hook-
up-agreement contractors. While the Hook-up agreement seemed to be
working well, the Client/OCPCA Liaison Committee concluded that 'the
only concern expressed by the UKOOA representatives was the cost of this
agreement for subsequent maintenance and minor construction work on
platforms'.[79]

This illustrates the precise limits of the offshore oil companies' toleration
of collective bargaining with trade unions (IDS, 1981). Both maintenance and
repair work had begun to assume increasing proportions by the early 1980s,

as the number of hook-up projects declined and as more fields came onstream. New modules were being continuously added to existing installations as production processes were modified or, in some cases, as new accommodation units were added. The workforce desire for some form of 'post-construction' agreement grew, especially as it was often the same workers involved in 'maintenance', who had previously been employed under the Hook-up agreement. With the commencement of 'first oil' production, the Hook-up agreement lapsed. The trade unions were effectively 'derecognized', with the engineering construction worker having to accept lower rates of pay. Despite this anomalous situation, the trade unions failed to extend the limited collective bargaining arrangements covering hook-up work to the increasingly important 'post-construction' sector of maintenance and repair work over the following two decades.

The variable nature of the industry's requirements for repair, maintenance and installation services made the achievement of a comprehensive collective bargaining agreement difficult. The contracting companies, often operating both onshore and offshore, were, initially at least, fully trade union organized (IRRR, 1977).[80] The sector was dominated by around twelve large companies who employed perhaps three-quarters of the workforce, and a periphery of small to medium-sized companies. Of the top twelve maintenance contractor companies, around ten were signatory to the Hook-up agreement. Within the space of a few years, between the late 1970s and early 1980s, the trade unions claimed, 'The number of offshore maintenance companies with trade union agreements had decreased from 30 to less than 10, and the number of "cowboy" (non-unionised) companies had increased from 6 to 25' (Cited in Buchan, 1984: 361). The chairman of the IUOOC was reported in the local press as complaining, 'New [maintenance] contracts are being awarded to smaller companies who seek to avoid unionisation and pay terms and conditions of employment below that of the negotiated rates' (Cited in Buchan, 1984: 365). So concerned were union officials that they threatened to organize action to force the introduction of 'union only' clauses, tactics which were legally debarred by the Conservatives' Employment Act of 1982.

For offshore workers, the most tangible reminder of their increasingly invidious position in 'post-construction' was both lower wages and inferior terms and conditions to hook-up work and the absence of travel expenses, leave pay and severance payments. The numbers employed in post-construction work varied, according to the length of 'shutdowns' of the oil platforms for repairs and maintenance, during the brief summer 'weather window' in the harsh North Sea climate. In the mid-1980s, one estimate put the total post-construction workforce at around 3600 men (Carrigan, 1985).

The differential between a worker on hook-up rates and one on non-hook-up rates was calculated at 30 per cent in real terms (Carrigan, 1985: 10). With labour costs as the greatest single element, the contractors were vulnerable to client pressure in a competitive bidding 'free for all' situation. Strathclyde Process Engineering Ltd., for example, a company which did have a union agreement, was forced by the client operator in 1983 to cut wage rates from £5.49 per hour to £5.00 per hour in its contract with Occidental Petroleum on Piper Alpha (Carrigan, 1985: 12).[81] Another contractor, Offshore Platform Maintenance Ltd., in a letter to an official of the EETPU, put it bluntly: 'We have Hobson's choice in this matter – offer our Client the market rate and secure continuity of work or . . . let the contract be awarded to others who will certainly be offering rates which are the same or less . . .'.[82]

After a number of unsuccessful overtures to the operators at national level seeking a post-construction agreement, John Baldwin, for the National Engineering Construction Committee, wrote to UKOOA in June 1981. He asked for a meeting between national officers and senior representatives of the oil companies to negotiate 'the kind of agreements that would be most successful for repair and maintenance work offshore'. Baldwin conceded that the Hook-up agreement was 'not the kind of agreement the oil companies feel is ideal'.[83] However, he received a firm rebuff from UKOOA suggesting the matter could be discussed at a Liaison Panel meeting between the IUOOC unions and UKOOA.[84] An approach by Baldwin, this time to the OCPCA, produced a frank appraisal from the contractor employers as to the futility of pursuing discussions over an agreement on 'post-construction' or maintenance work. The OCPCA noted, 'The client oil companies had made it very clear to us that they could not support such an agreement.'[85]

There matters stood until the annual review of the Hook-up in January 1985, when the Hook-up unions went so far as to offer a standstill on wages, if agreement could be reached on post-construction maintenance work, but again to no avail (Carrigan, 1985). In January 1986, the unions had felt sufficiently confident to refuse to endorse the Hook-up agreement for two new major projects unless the contractors agreed to extend its provisions to maintenance work.[86] It appeared that the strategy had achieved success, when the contractors in the OCPCA looked set to concede an Offshore Construction Services Agreement, although probably as a shield for themselves against further operator pressure to cut costs. The 'post-construction' agreement was to be stillborn, as client refusal to endorse it once again brought the contractors to heel. The representative of Brown and Root UK spelled out to the unions:

> During the past weeks the contractors had held lengthy meetings ... with the operating companies to try to persuade them to give their support to such an agreement ... it would probably come as no surprise that the operating companies have not agreed to provide that support.[87]

Offshore, trade union activists, with encouragement from the local officials, had begun to regroup in 1984 and 1985 around the unofficial 'Bear Facts' committee. This was a rank-and-file group, producing an appropriately named agitational newsletter, *The Bear*, as the offshore engineering construction worker had come to be known.[88] Just at the moment when labour combativeness was beginning to re-emerge after the defeat of 1979, the oil price collapsed from just over $30 per barrel to under $10 within a few months. There were massive cutbacks in exploration, development and maintenance programmes. These were accompanied by even more savage wage reductions and redundancies of up to one-third of the contractor workforce. Twenty-five contractor firms went bankrupt or reduced a significant proportion of their workforce.[89] In all, job losses in oil-related firms in the period July to December 1986 were of the order of 10,000 employees.

Preparations by the unions, under rank-and-file pressure, for a strike ballot over the employers' failure to progress towards a post-construction agreement were abandoned. It was not until the aftermath of Piper Alpha that the struggle for more comprehensive union recognition and bargaining arrangements for engineering construction to embrace the post-construction workforce was to be resumed with renewed intensity.

The SJIB Agreement

One exception to employer resistance to union agreements in the post-construction sector, was the so-called Scottish Joint Industries Board (SJIB) agreement between the EETPU and the Electrical Contractors Associations. Although not providing the same rates as the Hook-up agreement, the SJIB Offshore Post-Construction Agreement had given electrical maintenance workers a collectively bargained agreement since it had come into being in 1982. The oil operators permitted this one tiny island of unionization in the post-construction area. In a hazardous environment, such as a 'live' platform, electrical work needed to be of the highest standard for safety reasons. The specialist contractors providing these services were grouped in the tight-knit Electrical Contractors Associations (of Scotland and of England) and were able to exercise some bargaining leverage against UKOOA (Garfit, 1989: 16;

Carrigan, 1985: 14). Nevertheless, contracts were also awarded to non-association contractor companies, such as Strathclyde Process Engineering Ltd. on Piper Alpha, in which electrical work was only one element within a 'multidisciplinary' contract. The SJIB agreement was not fully protected from downward pressure, and rates were significantly less than those awarded under Hook-up. Moreover, from a trade union point of view, whilst the EETPU argued that the SJIB agreement provided a benchmark for all post-construction workers to aim at, the reality was that perhaps only one-third of the EETPU's own membership in post-construction was covered by the agreement. The EETPU's collusive arrangements with employers had been the hallmark of the union's history. Onshore it had enabled the EETPU to secure a high level of unionization, often at the direct expense of other unions. In the context of the offshore world, the SJIB agreement delivered some limited temporary sectional advantage. The SJIB agreement apart, however, attempts to gain a comprehensive collective agreement for offshore engineering and construction workers covering *both* hook-up and post-construction maintenance work were to dominate the next ten years of offshore trade unionism, contributing to the massive labour upheavals at the end of the decade.

The COTA Arrangement

One final area where 'collective bargaining' arrangements were tolerated offshore was in the catering contracting side of the industry. Here collective arrangements were actually encouraged by the clients. As with the Hook-up agreement, client approval was a precondition. Competitive tendering between catering companies had forced down wages to such an extent that by the late 1970s this produced the unhappy combination of low morale, high labour turnover (one study reported 300 per cent) and periodic bouts of unofficial industrial action (Buchan, 1984). This situation led the operators to pressure the contractors into seeking some kind of understanding with the trade unions in order to secure reasonable standards of service for their own employees.

In June 1977, catering workers sat in for 48 hours on the Belford Dolphin 'flotel' adjoining the Thistle Alpha platform, seeking union recognition, travel and accommodation allowances, sickness benefit and wage increases. The company concerned, Offshore Catering Services, was the first catering contractor to concede union recognition in the North Sea.[90] Over the next twelve months both the TGWU and the NUS, under the aegis of the IUOOC, sought and obtained recognition from other major offshore contractors

ARA Offshore Services, Scot Catering and Kelvin Catering Camps Ltd. No industry-wide formal collective bargaining agreement was ever put in place, however. The unions met with a group of leading catering contractors, with the resulting 'understanding' setting a common wages structure. The nine key catering employers came together to form the Catering Offshore Traders Association (COTA). The oil operators, through UKOOA, had sanctioned the formation of such an association following the Offshore Catering Services dispute to provide a means of collective regulation of this sector of the industry (Buchan, 1984: 318). In addition, UKOOA informally agreed not to accept tenders for catering services from non-COTA companies, although it was an arrangement which was never placed in writing (Thom, 1989). Here the incentive to permit unionization was fundamentally different from that which was discussed earlier in the context of construction workers and 'hold-ups'. In the context of catering, at least for the operators, there was no economic imperative to resist unionization. Catering contributed only a small percentage to the overall expenses bill of the operators, and any increase in the cost of catering represented an insubstantial element in the operators' profit calculations. The cost of labour unrest and a general deterioration in the quality of catering services, by contrast, could be high, as such problems could aggravate already troubled labour relations with the rest of the offshore workforce.

Low wages continued to be a source of discontent in catering, leading to an official strike from late July to mid-August 1979, only a few months after the offshore construction workers' strike. Catering shop stewards demanded a minimum rate of £600 per month. This remained the target figure despite official union hesitation. While the support of the Dutch seamen's union was gained, the Aberdeen dockers refused to 'black' offshore oil-related supplies and transport. Out of a total workforce of 1100, the employers claimed only 500 had struck, as against union claims of 800. Picketing at Aberdeen airport met with some success, especially among sympathetic engineering construction workers, but the effect of the strike was circumvented by transporting workers offshore from smaller airports in the North East (Buchan, 1984: 326). Nevertheless, the NUS ensured that supply boats did not service the twenty to thirty rigs and platforms affected. The strike itself was defeated after three weeks due to the difficulty in effectively communicating with the workforce in scattered onshore locations. The catering workers began to trickle back offshore and, amid some considerable rancour from the Glasgow-based membership, the leadership settled, prematurely it was felt, for a basic figure nearer £400 per month. The lack of full solidarity among other IUOOC unions led the NUS official, Harry Bygate, to resign from secretaryship of the IUOOC in November 1979.

The longer-term effects of the dispute were considerable. Although the COTA arrangement applied only to fixed installations and not drilling rigs, and only to the northern sector of the North Sea, the employers recognized the need to secure some labour stability. An award of 31 per cent was made which, taken together with a previous 25 per cent mid-term award, meant that the basic pay of catering stewards actually increased by nearly 65 per cent over a twelve month period in 1979 (IDS, 1979: 7-8). The following year a further 20 per cent was conceded.

The catering employers were bound together by little more than a 'gentlemen's agreement'. This created a tendency amongst rival contractors to revert to cut-throat competitive bidding, given even modest pressure. With labour costs up to 50 per cent of overall costs, wages in this sector were the first target. During the oil price downturn in the mid-1980s, Occidental broke ranks with UKOOA, disrupting the COTA arrangement. It awarded a two-year 'housekeeping contract' to Phoenix Catering, a new company on the offshore scene. Under this contract catering stewards would receive £2000 per year less than the agreed COTA rate, claimed the unions.

It seemed, at first, as if other catering companies might follow Phoenix's lead, but union pressure succeeded in having the company excluded from COTA. The episode emerged at the time of the annual wage talks between the unions and COTA. It was important for both the COTA contractors and the unions, that UKOOA did not accept bids which undercut the COTA rate. The union side agreed to what was effectively a six-month wage freeze to ensure that the operators would continue to regard the COTA rate as competitive. In the Alice-in-Wonderland world of offshore collective bargaining, Phoenix was able to claim, with some justification, that as there was no formal written industry agreement, the COTA rate was a fiction and its exclusion from the caterers' association was therefore illegitimate.

Although COTA members subsequently drew up a written industry agreement with the TGWU, at the eleventh hour COTA member companies refused to sign it for fear of suffering client disapproval. The TGWU indicated to UKOOA informally via the Liaison Panel that should another operator accept a non-COTA bid, the union would ballot for strike action. Whether, with less than 50 per cent of the catering workforce organized, the union could have carried through such a threat, is doubtful. Subsequent contracts were, however, issued based on COTA rates. The immediate crisis passed, although UKOOA still refused to acknowledge publicly that it would sanction COTA-only based contract bids (Thom, 1989: 172-84, 206-10). The operators remained the controlling influence in shaping and monitoring the precarious viability of the COTA arrangement with the trade unions. From a trade union perspective, this understanding remained an unsatisfactory and incomplete form of collective bargaining. By its very existence it prevented the development of a more satisfactory bargaining forum.

The 1980s: A Decade of Frustration

Ten years after the first oil had been pumped ashore, the trade unions seemed to have achieved all that they were going to, in terms of unionizing the North Sea. There had been some limited progress by ASTMS (later MSF) in securing representational rights for direct employees of the oil companies. In particular, Shell employees on the Brent field sought and obtained limited union recognition on five and eventually seven installations, initially after industrial unrest over what was seen as management heavy-handedness in disciplining an operative on a safety matter.[91] Elsewhere, ASTMS preserved the earlier agreements it had obtained in 1978 in the southern sector with Phillips in the Hewett field and eventually, after a protracted campaign, obtained full recognition on Phillips' Maureen platform. The representational agreement continued up until the disaster on Occidental's Piper Alpha. But the limited advances in the Brent field left seven other Shell installations in the North Sea unorganized. It was not to prove the start of a 'domino effect'. Apart from these, operator resistance had if anything intensified, particularly among US companies such as Amoco, Mobil and Chevron. These companies created maximum obstacles and delay in any attempts to unionize their workforces.[92] Thus a request to Amoco for representational rights was denied on the grounds of insufficient union membership. However, the company refused to specify what was 'sufficient' when challenged. The original agreement by the oil companies to the terms of the Memorandum on Access implied that recognition would be granted in due course where employees wanted it. Specific procedures had been the subject of the separate Memorandum of Understanding on how recognition was to be obtained. A decade later, in the different climate of the 1980s, it was far easier to evade the spirit of any understandings with the unions that had been reached in the mid-1970s. The typical oil company response to union requests for recognition, not just that of US companies like Amoco, was now to deny evidence of any desire for such forms of representation. Britoil, the privatized portion of BNOC, typified the kind of response unions faced offshore.

We have to advise you that we do not propose to have any discussions

> with trade unions on recognition for our offshore fields unless we receive
> a clear indication from a significant proportion of our staff that they wish
> to discuss some form of representation. In the absence of such
> indication we do not believe a meeting with members of IUOOC would
> be appropriate.[93]

The downturn in the industry in the mid-1980s intensified this operator resistance, as massive job losses and widespread job insecurity made the task of membership recruitment, retention and recognition claims even harder.

So discouraged was the electricians' union, the EETPU, that their organizer proposed an alliance with ASTMS in early 1987 for purposes of recognition, under the umbrella of the IUOOC, utilizing the Memorandum of Understanding on Recognition. Within its terms, said the EETPU:

> there seems nothing to prohibit more than one union seeking
> recognition, just the reverse. The document seems to emphasise the role
> of the [IUOOC] committee. Perhaps the committee could form Common
> Interest Groups of two, three or even four unions in order to achieve
> recognition in a particular company or on a particular platform.[94]

In fact joint applications from the EETPU and ASTMS were made for Britoil's Beatrice and Thistle platforms.[95] Later that year, the EETPU again suggested a joint recognition attempt on Conoco's Hutton TLP.[96] However, it was an idea born out of desperation. Moreover it was largely ahead of its time. The trade union movement was not yet ready to consider pooling its collective resources in a non-competitive alliance to extend its influence offshore, never mind co-operate for purposes of full collective bargaining recognition.

So far as the contractor workforce was concerned, their second class status and treatment did not alter throughout the 1980s. The Hook-up agreement continued to fulfil its allotted purpose in securing industrial relations harmony for the engineering contracting employers and the clients. The contractors in the OCPCA with offshore interests had regrouped with the Electrical Contractors Associations to form themselves into the Offshore Contractors Council (OCC). Henceforth it was the OCC which was to be the key offshore contractors' negotiating body. In the southern sector, which had not hitherto seen hook-up type contracts, the major Easington-Rough project for British Gas in 1983–84 brought many of the northern construction workforce south but on much lower wages and inferior conditions. The resultant discontent led to a month-long sit-in which secured the Southern Waters Offshore Construction Agreement. Although paying lower rates than the northern sector

Hook-up agreement, this was seen as a small step forward for the trade unions.

On the IUOOC, the rumbling feud between the TGWU and the BSJC unions, specifically the NUS, erupted again in the early 1980s as the TGWU attempted to recruit on a Sedco drilling rig, the Sedco H. The TGWU claimed to have organized about half Sedco's employees. After much heated argument the BSJC agreed to accept that the TGWU could organize the Sedco rigs, but only if the BSJC were allowed to organize elsewhere on semi-submersible rigs. The issue again threatened to result in the break-up of the IUOOC and again required the informal intervention of the TUC.[97]

NUS, for its part, succeeded in procuring a union agreement for offshore divers with Comex Houlder, the first UK diving company to enter into such an agreement.[98] The divers remained numerically split about equally between the NUS and the non-TUC Professional Divers' Association. The latter was eventually to merge with the EETPU. A change in the tax status of North Sea divers from self-employed to Pay-As-You-Earn in the late 1970s had provoked fury among the divers and had caused many experienced men to leave for more lucrative work abroad. In the 1980s, continuing pressure from the diving companies to cut pay rates in order to win contracts, led to simmering unrest in this sector.[99] A five-day sit-in on the Ninian field occurred in 1983 and a wider 48-hour stoppage in 1984. Despite much talk of more concerted action, future planned strikes fizzled out. Following the Ninian sit-in in 1983, a Diving Contractors Association had been formed, which thereafter entered into negotiations with NUS. It reached an agreement in August 1984. The Professional Divers' Association, for its part, was certified as an independent trade union in 1985 and sought its own agreements with individual drilling companies. Throughout this period, until the Professional Divers' Association merger with the EETPU in 1988, ASTMS continued to provide technical services on a contractual basis for the association.[100] Competition between the divers' unions helped prevent co-operation on the pressing issue of safety for this sector of the industry.

Elsewhere in the North Sea, the NUS retained its grip on the crews of the supply boats servicing the rigs and installations. However, with the downturn in 1986, industry-level negotiations were abandoned by the employers for company-level settlements which, like the COTA arrangement, produced an industry 'norm' (IDS, 1988: 7). Following strike action in 1988, taken in sympathy with NUS members in dispute with P&O, all of the firms in the federated employers association, and several non-federated firms, de-recognized the NUS for bargaining purposes. Thereafter perhaps a dozen supply boat crews, out of the 120 which now serviced the offshore installations, were unionized. With a general decline in British-flagged vessels, the NUS influence in the North Sea sharply declined. Only with the arrival in Aberdeen in the late 1980s of two new local officials, of the NUS and TGWU, did these unions begin to work together in developing new strategies and burying old enmities.

For the IUOOC, the one body that was mainly concerned with advancing the cause of offshore trade unionism, the 1980s were years of disappointment and increasing frustration. This led to periodic bouts of soul-searching on the committee over the value of continuing meetings with UKOOA.[101] The need to prepare agenda items in advance, to meet as a committee in between formal meetings with UKOOA, and other proposals for conducting its business in a more effective manner, were discussed. The offer of a researcher to support the work of the committee, from the Labour Party Offshore Group of MPs, was refused on the grounds that each union already had a research department and it was unlikely that additional union funds would be found for such a post. For the most part, what one IUOOC official described as 'too cosy a relationship' continued with UKOOA.

The IUOOC was occasionally forced to question the value of the Memorandum on Access. At one meeting with the Liaison Panel of UKOOA, the IUOOC chairman went so far as to tear up a copy of the Memorandum in a symbolic gesture of disgust (Thom, 1989: 198). On safety-related issues, IUOOC met with a similar lack of progress. Offshore workers, especially in catering, were still being forced to pay for their own survival training, a scandal which led to malpractice and fraud. IUOOC attempts to have survival training costs excluded from the contract price, and therefore outside the competitive bidding process, met with UKOOA's stock response: such practices, although condemned by UKOOA, were best pursued with the contracting company concerned and were outside the remit of the Liaison Panel (Thom, 1989: 203). Reluctance of UKOOA to assume direct responsibility for the employment practices of their contractors worked powerfully to the advantage of its member companies and to the disadvantage of the trade unions. When it suited UKOOA, as in the case of the Phoenix catering débâcle, trade union concerns could be amplified in the decision-making councils of UKOOA. However, when it did not suit UKOOA to take on board the concerns of the unions, then the virtual impotence of the IUOOC was painfully apparent.

The Chinook Disaster

Nothing illustrated more clearly UKOOA's evasion of trade union representations than the operators' response to the unions arising out of the Chinook helicopter disaster. Forty-five men were killed. The only survivors were the pilot and one passenger. This particular aircraft, with its high passenger payload, had been subject to complaints by the offshore workforce on safety and comfort grounds over many years. Foxtrot Charlie was one of four Chinooks owned by British International Helicopters (BIH) on charter to Shell in the Brent field. On 6 November 1986 it ditched in the sea, two minutes from Sumburgh airport in Shetland. The crew of the MSV *Stadive* had the gruesome task of salvage and recovery operations.[102] As offshore workers, they wanted to know whether they would be forced to fly in the Chinooks, or could refuse to do so without fear of employer retribution. The owner of BIH, media tycoon Robert Maxwell, took to the air in a much-publicized demonstration of the aircraft's safety, and also no doubt with a pending contract with another major operator in mind. In fact, the Chinooks were responsible for well over half of BIH total revenue. But Shell agreed four weeks later to suspend use of the aircraft for three to six months while an inquiry was held. Its own employees on the Brent Charlie, whence the ill-fated flight had departed, had taken the unprecedented step of airing their determination never to travel in a Chinook again, even if it meant leaving the company's employ.[103] Letters in the local press from concerned wives of men who did not wish to be identified for fear of victimization added a further embarrassing twist.

The issue was raised by IUOOC at a meeting with UKOOA's Liaison Panel (Thom, 1989: 210-15). Shell 'declined outright' to meet IUOOC and 'reminded the Committee that the meeting was not at liberty to discuss individual companies' (Thom, 1989: 213).[104] ASTMS, which held representational agreements with Shell, was further reminded that these agreements specifically excluded discussion of health and safety matters. When IUOOC union officials attempted to ascertain future operator intentions regarding the Chinooks, they were informed that Shell's decision would be communicated to its employees through its internal domestic machinery. Trade union officials pointed out that while nine of the 45 fatalities were direct employees of the company, the rest were contractors. When one official argued that he had recognition agreements and sought to discuss this issue, he was directed to raise his concerns with the contractor employer rather than Shell (Thom, 1989: 214–5). As Thom observed, the operator concerned 'had no hesitation and no difficulty in keeping them [the unions] out of the matter completely'.

Thom's conclusion summed up the prospects facing the trade unions off-shore:

> It is reasonable to suggest that if the company with which the trade union movement has had most success can virtually ignore the individual [ASTMS] union and the Committee as a whole, then the IUOOC has a very long road ahead to fulfil its aspirations of organising the core labour force in the North Sea. (1989: 215)

The Chinook tragedy occurred at probably the lowest point of morale of the offshore workforce, coinciding with the 1986 slump in the oil industry. Its consequences, in terms of repercussions for industrial relations, could be easily contained by the employers. In fact, Shell abandoned the use of Chinooks thereafter. The Piper Alpha explosion, coming two years later, was an entirely different matter. Its repercussions were enormous, not merely because the scale of fatalities was nearly four times greater, but because of the nature of the disaster, a major conflagration on an offshore platform. This disaster, in the view of the offshore workforce, exemplified all that was wrong in the offshore safety set-up, and more particularly, in the repressive system of industrial relations which had allowed that set-up to be perpetuated.

Piper Alpha: A Survivor's Testimony

The Piper Alpha oil production platform was situated 110 miles north-east of Aberdeen. It started oil production in 1976, exporting oil to the onshore terminal at Flotta in the Orkneys, and gas to St Fergus in Grampian via the MCP–OI gas compression platform.

On the night of 6 July 1988 it was destroyed in a series of explosions. In the inferno, 165 of the 226 persons on board perished. In a selfless attempt to rescue Piper personnel, two crewmen of the emergency stand-by boat *Sandhaven* were also killed.

The Piper Alpha disaster was the nightmare every offshore worker feared: a hydrocarbon leak finding a source of ignition and developing into an uncontrolled inferno. Many expected just such a disaster; many expected it would be Piper.

What follows is the edited testimony of one of the men who survived. His harrowing story was relived before Lord Cullen at his public inquiry into the disaster. In clear and compelling language, the magnitude of the hell the men

Illustration 2 The Piper Alpha platform showing pipedeck and other features related to the escape from the platform

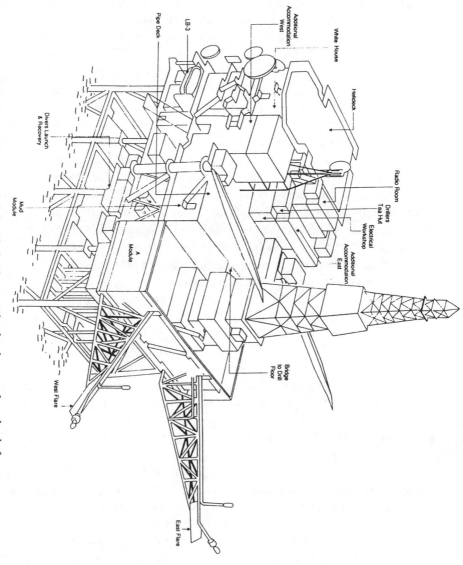

were trapped in is graphically revealed. At 22.00 hours the first explosion occurred, immediately knocking out the control room, electrical power and communications. Those in the accommodation block were at first unconcerned. People started to muster in the galley. As the minutes ticked by it became evident to many that they were in trouble. At 22.20 hours a massive fireball engulfed the already blazing platform, convincing some that if they did not get out they were going to die. Others, however, made no attempt to leave the accommodation and waited in hope of a helicopter coming. Still others remained because they simply did not know what else to do. There was no systematic attempt to lead the men to a means of escape.[105]

Andy Mochan had worked offshore for ten years. He worked for Wood Group as a supervisor and described his escape.

Q. Did you also go to try to find an exit from the accommodation block?
A. Yes.
Q. How many doors did you try to see if you could get out?
A. We tried them all, and that is all right down the deck of the accommodation.
Q. You tried all the doors?
A. Yes.
Q. Was it possible to get out of any of them?
A. No; it was pretty bad.
Q. I know that time is very difficult, but could you estimate how long you spent trying to find a door that you could get out of?
A. I would say that we spent at least an hour in the accommodation going along passages. We were looking into cabins where there was still water in the taps and wetting towels over our heads for the smoke. It was about an hour before we found we were able to get out just adjacent to my office. There was a door out there.
Q. Is that the little door I pointed out to you on the plan a while ago?
A. Yes. We had got to that door and I think the *Tharos* water cannon was spraying at the time, and that is what allowed us to get out. It may have been one of the other vessels, but whoever was spraying water allowed us to get onto the deck.
Q. Did that bring you out onto the pipedeck?
A. Yes.
Q. What was the situation like on the pipedeck?
A. It was pretty horrendous. We could not get moving to the edge of the platform to get an opportunity to get off by any means. The helicopters and the lifeboats had run out since the first ten minutes.

The only way to get off the platform was to get into the water; that was very evident. There was steelwork and burning debris everywhere and we could not get across the pipedeck.

Q. Was the heat bad?

A. Yes.

Q. Did you take shelter from the heat in a place known as the white house [drill store]?

A. Yes.

Q. That is just to the north of the pipedeck?

A. Yes.

Q. Do you know how many of you were taking shelter in the white house?

A. I would say maybe about 20 people.

Q. Did something pretty dramatic happen to the platform while you were in the white house?

A. Yes. There were two major explosions when we were in the white house. We were more or less taking shelter in the white house. It was complete darkness and in the first explosion I remember there was a chap who landed on top of me, one of the Bawden chaps called Bob Paterson. The drilling equipment, blocks of steel and drilling bits were being thrown about like matchsticks. You were more or less just huddled waiting to be hit and hoping it was not going to be too bad. That was the first one. I got trapped and hurt with my legs in that white house. That was when I first felt the platform starting to go very slightly.

Q. The platform started to tilt?

A. Yes; it went two or three degrees. There was another massive explosion and we managed to get out of the white house. The pipedeck had gone to 45 degrees by that time.

Q. Did everyone manage at this point to get out of the white house?

A. I do not think so, no. The numbers were thinned down by that time.

Q. Do you know what had happened to some of the people in the white house?

A. No.

Q. Did they just disappear?

A. They just disappeared, did not make it.

Q. When you came out of the white house, did you notice something had happened to one of the cranes on the platform?

A. I imagined it was a crane at the time anyway. As you can well imagine, by this time things were really traumatic. I remember, we were crouched on this deck which was at the 45 degree angle, with no way across the pipedeck. I remember, I think it was Ian Fowler, the joiner, was on top of what looked like the jib of a crane, and he beckoned us to come from the pipedeck up on to this debris, because he could obviously see a way over to the water.

Q. Did you manage to get up to this jib and to get along it?

A. Yes.

Q. How did you get along it? Did you walk or run?

A. With difficulty. It was burning.

Q. It was very hot, was it?

A. Yes. That was where I received the burns I got. I was burned on both hands and my backside and elbow. So it was not a very dignified exit.

Q. From there, could you actually see the water down below?

A. Yes.

Q. Did you, in fact, jump into the water?

A. Yes.

Q. Are you able to tell us, Mr Mochan, I know it is difficult, because the platform was in a bit of a mess at this stage, approximately what height it would be that you jumped from?

A. They reckoned it was 150 ft.

Q. But you managed to come to the surface again?

A. Yes. I came up coughing and spluttering. I do not know whether I was knocked out for a minute with the blow. Every bone in your body gets quite a shake up. But I think I came to fairly quickly.

Q. When you did come to on the surface, did you find others were in the water with you?

A. Yes.

Q. People whose names you could give us?

A. I remember Jim Russell being in the water fairly close to me, and I remember there was a lad from Score [valves]. He was in the water too, but I cannot remember his name. But there were not many.

Q. Are you able to estimate for us, Mr Mochan, of the men who had been in the white house, how many of them actually got into the water?

A. I would say probably eight or something like that.

Q. Roughly eight out of twenty then?

A. I would have thought so, something of that nature.

Q. And once you had surfaced, where did you go? In which direction did you go?

A. I headed towards the *Tharos*, lying on my back, but I spotted a piece of debris about half a mile out, and I managed to get on to that, so that the top half of my body was out of the water.

Q. Was the water cold?

A. Yes, it was bitterly cold.

Q. Could you see the platform as you were swimming out on your back?

A. Yes.

Q. What kind of state was it in by this stage?

A. I reckon that, on my back looking up at it, there was not a square inch of it that was not on fire by the time I got off.

Q. We know that the pipedeck tilted – you noticed that – and that there was a crane jib down. Could you see whether any other parts of the platform were disintegrating?

A. It was totally disintegrated, I reckon. The superstructure was still there. I do not think anything major had fallen into the water at that time. But, as I say, every part of the rig was an inferno.

Q. Can you tell us what injuries you suffered, Mr Mochan?

A. I was burned on both hands, my elbow, my backside; both feet were badly bruised. My bones in general were bruised, I know. I still get pain in my rib cage here, and I think that is partly due to the jump into the sea, into the water.

Q. I think your legs and feet were hurt while you were in the white house in the first explosion?

A. That is right, yes.

Q. Did you also have some pain as a result of inhaling smoke in your chest?

A. Yes, I was pretty badly damaged with smoke inhalation, and hypothermia of course.

Q. From being in the water?

A. Yes.

Q. Are you working just now, Mr Mochan?

A. No.

Q. Have you worked since 6 July?

A. No.

Q. Is there any indication as to when you will be fit for work?

A. No, none whatsoever at the moment.

Q. Would you work offshore again?

A. No, I do not think I would be able to.

The Renewal of Activism: The Offshore Industry Liaison Committee

The latter part of 1987, and the first part of 1988, saw a renewed upturn of activity offshore with major new projects announced, such as Shell Expro's Kittiwake, Tern and Eider projects and BP's Miller project. Together with this upturn, there was a revival of drilling exploration. The initial springboard for what became a gathering insurrection of the workforce was provided by the first major hook-up for a number of years – the Tern project. It was initiated on 1 July 1988, exactly five days before the Piper Alpha disaster. Ronnie McDonald, at that time a rigger on the Tern, and soon to emerge as a highly articulate mass leader of the offshore workforce, recalled the dreadful night of Piper Alpha. 'We heard what was happening on the radio on a platform a few miles away with horror and a degree of shame too, because we knew that by our silence we had contributed to that tragedy.'[106]

Everything which followed was coloured by that event. It forced the off-shore workforce to reappraise every aspect of its conditions and circumstances. Above all, it underscored the consequences of their lack of voice and powerlessness as offshore workers. The Tern project, however, was one of the few places in the North Sea where the workforce could actually do something about the situation prevailing offshore. The project was conducted under the Hook-up agreement and therefore provided for trade union recognition and the appointment of shop stewards. The Tern hook-up, however, was initially intended to be one of short duration only. Key contractor employers such as Press Offshore were keen to ensure that rather than shop stewards being appointed, the men should simply elect 'welfare representatives'.

Technical problems caused the Tern project to be extended well beyond the initially envisaged time frame. This provided some half-dozen experienced union activists who had joined the project with the time needed to persuade the men that they would be far more effectively represented by credentialled shop stewards than 'welfare reps'. A serious near-miss incident, involving the 'auto-lift' and break-up of the connecting bridge between the platform and the adjoining flotel, intensified the already latent anger over safety issues which Piper Alpha had created. Put simply, the workforce 'had had enough' with respect to the neglect by management of their safety concerns. A series of meetings organized by the activists on the flotel suggested that, for the first time in nearly a decade, the antipathy of many of the 'bears' to trade unionism could be overcome. At discussions onshore between the Tern shop stewards and full-time officials from the Hook-up unions, the need to develop this growing collectivism was agreed. What was required was some sort of 'go-between' organization between the 'bears' and the officials – a committee which could also bring offshore workers together in their onshore leave time in the main centres of Aberdeen and Glasgow and start to mobilize them in an effective manner.

Mass meetings convened throughout 1988 to formulate the men's claim for the annual review of the Hook-up agreement were used by the activists to debate these wider issues of representation and safety with the workforce. The immediate focus was on the absence of a maintenance or post-construction agreement and the complete lack of safety input. The workforce, on completion of the Tern project, would be transferring almost *en masse* to a major engineering project in the Forties field – the gas lift project – promising a further three years' work. The remainder of the workforce expected to go to other major projects in the East Shetland Basin. This situation epitomized for many the whole paradox of restricted union recognition. The gas lift project was to be classified as 'post-construction' work. Therefore, it would not be covered by the Hook-up agreement, so in departing the Tern, these workers would experience a substantial reduction in pay and conditions and the derecognition of their trade unions. The absurdity of separation of 'hook-up construction' from 'maintenance construction' and the need for comprehensive union recognition was increasingly transparent.

This rebirth of offshore activism led to the realization that a committee similar to the grass roots unofficial 'Bear Facts' committee of 1983–85 had to be reactivated. This new body was the Offshore Industry Liaison Committee (OILC) with the former Tern shop steward, Ronnie McDonald, now acting as its spokesperson. McDonald had been dismissed by Press Offshore and was fighting an industrial tribunal case. He was financed in his new role onshore as unofficial OILC organizer by the contributions of his offshore colleagues. The OILC was formed in February 1989 with the active encouragement of local union officials. In reactivating the unofficial committee, after it had been dormant for two and a half years, all the founders, local full-time officials and Tern activists, initially saw its primary purpose as that of 'cat's-paw' for the unions, a role which it was subsequently to carry out effectively. But it ultimately proved impossible to contain the objectives of the committee within such a narrow frame. In mobilizing the offshore workforce in a manner that demanded their direct involvement, the prescribed role envisaged for the OILC by the union officials inevitably widened. It soon became an open forum for all workers in the industry.

At onshore OILC mass meetings throughout 1989, years of pent-up frustration were vented against the trade unions and, in particular, against local full-time officials. Attendances at these meetings in the major urban centres where oil workers were concentrated rapidly climbed and spread from Aberdeen and Glasgow, to Middlesbrough and Liverpool.[107] In the early days, these unofficial mass gatherings served as an exorcism of the demons of the past. For many, it was their first opportunity to assemble in one place with their officials, to analyse the defeat of 1979, the repression of the 1980s, the Chinook and the trauma of Piper Alpha. Faced with their own history for the first time, and its tragic legacy, new and far more searching formulations of the problems began to emerge. At every mass meeting the same question was repeated: 'Why can't we have our own offshore workers' union?' It was a question which went to the heart of the offshore workers' dilemma.

While the offshore workforce rallied behind OILC, the official unions became entangled in rivalry. This point is illustrated by the EETPU's opportunistic intervention, in the week following Piper Alpha. Local union officials had embarked upon what appeared to be an unseemly internecine squabble. This had led to the exclusion of the EETPU from the IUOOC following its suspension from the TUC at national level for membership poaching. The IUOOC claimed that it was merely acting towards the EETPU as a consequence of its inter-union status, having 'always been accepted as a sub-committee of the Energy Committee of the TUC'.[108] During a meeting of union officials with the TUC-appointed Health and Safety Commissioner immediately following Piper Alpha, the EETPU official was to use the occasion to proclaim his union's grievances to the assembled press, much to the acute embarrassment of the rest of the IUOOC.[109] The EETPU also complained about its exclusion to the Department of Energy, which in turn sought clarification from the TUC as to the exact status of the IUOOC. David Lea replied for the TUC referring to its 'longstanding relationship with the IUOOC' and the TUC's involvement in meetings on trade union facilities offshore, including the May 1976 meeting with Benn on the Memorandum on Access. The TUC noted, however, 'Although we have therefore given material assistance to the IUOOC, it has never operated as a sub-committee of the Energy Committee of the TUC'.[110]

The Department of Energy duly faxed the TUC letter to the secretary of the IUOOC in Aberdeen, noting also the TUC's comment that until TUC Annual Congress in September had heard the EETPU's appeal against its suspension, 'there should be no change from previous practice'. Seen from the perspective of the EETPU, its exclusion from the IUOOC was 'not for any principle of being seen to support the TUC but for political and membership advantage'.[111] In early November 1988 the EETPU was duly reinstated to membership of the IUOOC. However, the acrimony among the unions in the immediate aftermath of the disaster was to remain a continuing feature of the trade unions' response to subsequent events. By contrast, at the base of the growing movement of resistance among the offshore workforce the new watchword was 'unity'.

The One Union Document

In May 1989, the 'One Union Discussion Document' was launched by resurgent activists, now forming OILC. It explored arguments for a single offshore union embracing all workers on the UK Continental Shelf (McDonald, 1989). But the activists did not immediately envisage such a development. Rather, the demand for a single offshore union expressed the rank-and-file aspiration for a new kind of unity. The knowledge that a process of union rationalization was already taking place in the Norwegian sector reinforced the logic of this argument. The document argued that the unions' own fragmentation was the biggest contributory factor in perpetuating the problems of the contract workers. As a further OILC (1989) discussion paper submitted to union officials at the TUC in Blackpool put it:

> The purpose of this document is not to castigate any union or its officials for defending the legitimate self-interest of their respective unions. It is merely to suggest that a suitable forum must be found to enable these, at times, conflicting interests to be reconciled in the cause of organising the North Sea effectively.

The discussion document was an attempt to analyse the conditions within which the unions, once united, would be in a position to demand full recognition for purposes of collective bargaining. The principal objectives of OILC were twofold and intimately linked: that every offshore member should have the right and opportunity to be represented by his or her trade union through a collective agreement, and that the status of the offshore contract worker as a second-class citizen, exemplified by the lack of protection of fundamental aspects of UK safety law, should be ended. Thus, the issues of safety and union recognition were seen as one and the same.

These demands were by no means incompatible with the ultimate aims of the official trade unions. The problem in taking industrial action in support of these aims was the nature of the Conservatives' industrial relations legislation and the refusal of the offshore employers, particularly the client oil companies, to contemplate any wider trade union agreements. This prevented the unions from pursuing a normal strategy of collective bargaining. It was from this impasse that the OILC emerged as an organization, operating at a purely unofficial level and outside the restrictions of Conservative trade union laws. In this capacity OILC was able to pursue the option, now made difficult for the official unions, of industrial action.

The Summer of 1989

In these early days of the post-Piper mobilization there was a degree of uncertainty in the ranks of the offshore workforce. The suggested tactics to be employed in the imminent industrial action were largely novel. They had been developed through a realization that the defeat of the 1979 action was in part due to giving up the territory offshore, rather than maintaining a physical presence at the place of work. This time, the workforce would have to stay on the platforms and occupy. Using the example of sit-ins previously staged in the northern sector in pursuit of relatively minor domestic issues, and the Easington-Rough sit-in of 1984, it had already been seen that there was considerable value in this tactic. Properly applied, it could embarrass the contractor in the eyes of the operator and, more importantly, take the workforce challenge directly into the heart of the operator's territory.

The key was the occupation of the production platforms. On the flotels a different set of constraints prevailed. The operator had the option of simply floating the adjoining accommodation barge away from the platform unless counter-measures were taken. During the run-up to the action of the summer of 1989, the OILC committee strenuously exhorted those workers resident on flotels to keep a presence on the platforms. If necessary, there should be a picket on the linking bridge between installation and flotel to prevent its disconnection. The failure of the Forties workforce to observe this central tactical requirement led to their isolation at the height of the industrial action. It allowed strike-breaking Dutch labour to be imported onto the production platforms.[112]

The summer of 1989 had arrived as the industry was half-way through its year of notice from the trade unions that change to existing agreements was required, otherwise the unions would refuse to re-sign the Hook-up agreement for 1990. When action was taken, the operators rode it out. Both they and the contractors were nevertheless severely shaken by the scale of the industrial action. It had begun in May with a sit-in by 300 men in the Forties field. The main contractor affected was Press Offshore, but others were Aberdeen Scaffolding, Atlantic Power & Gas (APG), an associate of the engineering giant Babcock, Salamis, Scott, SGB Scaffolding and Wood Group. Following the initial Forties sit-ins, a renewed wave of sit-ins took place over the next two and a half months. Rolling twenty-four hour stoppages occurred throughout the summer of 1989, affecting 37 platforms and involving about 4000 workers. In all, there were about two dozen sit-ins, each accompanied by varying degrees of support. The operators responded with a generally conciliatory approach. This was due in most part to the wish not to engender a further upsurge in public antipathy towards the oil industry after Piper Alpha and further exacerbate the labour problems offshore. The first anniversary of the disaster on 6 July was marked by a stoppage of 7000 offshore workers. In the onshore side of the industry, construction workers downed tools in sympathy at Highland Fabricators, at Davy Offshore Dundee, at the St Fergus terminal and at BP Grangemouth petrochemical plant. Safety concerns had been the spark which ignited the offshore industrial unrest but the resolution of these problems was seen as wholly bound up with settling long-standing grievances in industrial relations.

The dispute became focused on one central issue – the question of trade union recognition, itself a precondition for any wider collective agreement. The offshore workforce sought union recognition, to be determined in a secret ballot. This was a demand Shell Expro appeared to endorse publicly. In a 'Situation Report' released to the media on 13 July 1989, Shell stated, 'So far as the question of union recognition is concerned, we believe that such a key question should be decided by an independent secret ballot, so that the employees can make their own decision.'[113]

Seeking to head off further industrial unrest, four leading contracting companies gave written undertakings to their workforce that, on return to normal working, the issue of union recognition would be considered. At the height of the action, Aberdeen Scaffolding, one of the leading scaffolding companies in the offshore industry, wrote to the local engineering union official, Tommy Lafferty, saying:

> Owing to the current circumstances, and after discussions internally, and with some of our client customers, we are of the opinion, that the only way forward is to have a local union recognised agreement for our workforce. To this end we would welcome a meeting with you at the earliest opportunity ... We are of a mind that the inclusion of Trade Union Recognition would further the possibility of acceptance.[114]

Three other OCC member contracting companies gave written undertakings to their workforces. APG wrote to their employees on Shell contracts,

'We will be seeking talks with your local full-time Trade Union official to assist in bringing the full company agreement into being within the next three months.'[115] A month later on 20 July, and after talks with representatives of the workforce, the company issued an undertaking to their employees on Shell's Cormorant Alpha:

> Atlantic Power & Gas Limited thereby agree to engage ACAS to undertake an independent separate platform ballot, in order to establish the overall consensus from all the employees as to their wishes for Union Representation or vice versa.[116]

In that same week, Press Offshore, a subsidiary of the conglomerate AMEC, gave a written assurance to the occupying workforce on the Brent platforms 'to hold a secret ballot of its employees in the Shell Northern and Brent fields to clarify the workforce's opinion on the matter of trade union recognition.'[117] It was signed in front of the shop stewards by Alan MacPherson, Press Offshore Operations Manager. Only a month before, Press Offshore had written to its employees stating that the present industrial unrest was 'causing the company severe anxiety over the future of its contracts'.[118] These undertakings, accepted in good faith by the striking workers, were subsequently reneged upon after the industrial action had been terminated. Indeed, when the local ACAS official sought to initiate the ballots promised by the contracting companies, he was politely shown the door.

In a memo addressed to their workforce on the Brent Delta, Dick Hogg of Wood Group had written:

> In order to clarify the way ahead and ensure there is no misunderstanding, I must make the following points clear .... Our position is that we have no objection in principle to you being represented by an appropriate Trade Union in discussion on terms and conditions of employment for your platform if this is the wish of the majority of our employees on the platform.[119]

This matter was then to be progressed through procedures laid out in the workforce's contract of employment. The company thereafter showed no inclination to institute a secret ballot. In frustration, the workforce on the Brent Charlie and Delta conducted their own ballots. The results were presented to Wood Group's senior management at a meeting at their headquarters in Aberdeen on 9 August 1989. On the Brent Delta, the ballot for 'a North Sea Agreement' was 56 for, 2 against and 3 don't knows, while on the Brent

Charlie it was 42 for, 3 don't knows and none against. The ballot was based on 75 per cent of the workforce. It was acknowledged by the company 'as an apparent feeling among the workforce'. The minute of this meeting goes on to record:

> the Company could not share the view that Trade Union recognition was in the best interests of the workforce .... Over the past months the Company had stepped up its communication with the workforce through platform visits and meetings on the beach and it was the Company's view that its rapport with its employees had been improved, as instanced by the current round table frank discussions. The Company could not share the Representatives' view on secret ballots and Trade Union recognition. Both parties agreed to differ.[120]

Notwithstanding this, the company managing director, Sir Ian Wood, was to declare in a broadcast discussion on BBC Radio, over a year later and following a further round of industrial action:

> We do recognise trade unions. All our agreements cover the right of any of our employees who are in trade unions to be represented by the trade union in any dispute that takes place. There really is a lot of distortion in this whole case.[121]

In the autumn of 1989, the operators intervened to make clear to the contracting companies that they would not put contracts out to tender on the basis of a wider 'post-construction agreement'. The trade unions at national level accordingly served notice of their intention to terminate the Hook-up agreement.[122]

Concessions of a major nature were won by the sit-ins of 1989 despite the failure of the ultimate objectives of the workforce. A pay rise of approximately £2 per hour was implemented, bringing tradesmen's rates up to about £7.05 per hour. This was the first of a series over a period of a year and a half, and amounting to an overall increase in excess of 40 per cent, which were imposed in an attempt to deflect further demands for union recognition. Under 'Model Terms and Conditions' imposed by the contractors, there was now a unified pay and conditions structure. A system of arbitration for individual employee grievances, with joint panels of hearings, was also instituted. This embodied an undertaking that the rules of 'natural justice' would prevail, and the findings of the panel be binding on all parties. These were seen at the time as indirect gains of substance. There were other lessons for the future of a more tangible nature. During the sit-ins of 1989 the self-confidence of a hitherto cowed and disorganized workforce had re-emerged. The necessity for much greater co-ordination and organization was obvious. The operators and contractors were exposed as neither invincible nor as omnipotent as had previously been assumed. But next time around, and there would be a next time, the workforce would have to be much better prepared.[123]

Between Solidarity and Sectionalism

In 1959, Clark Kerr argued that in a newly emerging industry where job recruitment was booming, unions were likely to adopt a sectionalist bargaining stance. Individual unions, trying to recruit as many members as possible, would ignore the broader impact of their actions, and stress narrow workplace and occupation-wide concerns in order to appeal to prospective members.

To a casual observer, the offshore oil industry would seem to fit precisely with Kerr's paradigm. In the late 1960s, it was expanding rapidly and occupational boundaries were fluid. Yet, in certain crucial respects, our examination of trade unionism in the UK offshore oil industry contradicts Kerr's assumptions. Offshore unionism, as we have explained earlier, started with an anti-sectionalist impetus in which individual unions perceived themselves in Kerr's terms as 'class bargainers'. Organizing the offshore workforce, in the early days of the industry, was seen as a joint effort, rather than a competitive arena for trade unions. At this time, the UK labour movement as a whole, particularly in Scotland, had achieved a level of cohesion which had enabled it to address wider issues of class and corporate power. This broader perspective was conditioned by the experiences of mass labour unrest and protest in the late 1960s and early 1970s, previously referred to. The 'class bargaining' view was reinforced by the specific nature of offshore employment: the blatantly autocratic nature of industrial relations, the lack of job security, and the relatively low pay in what were essentially high-risk occupations.

One thing that the early offshore trade unionists did not foresee was that the multinational oil corporations, including the British ones, were to adopt a persistent union-avoidance and explicitly anti-union stance. In the context of a Labour government, attempting to foster a pro-union environment, there was no reason to expect the offshore oil industry to be difficult to organize. Achieving union recognition presumably would not require any measures which went beyond those adopted in onshore production industries. But with one important exception. The offshore industry was geographically and physically remote from the organizing centres of trade unionism.

Remoteness and access, however, were not to be the principal obstacles to union recognition. Companies involved in offshore construction and production agreed to provide access to unionists early on, even though their commitment to this promise was often half-hearted. The hostile attitude of large-scale construction contracting companies towards unionization was well known to the unions. What the unions did not expect was that such views would be actively shared and underwritten by both domestic and US oil multinationals. Difficulties in unionization experienced in the early period of the making of the offshore industry, contrary to the expectations of the unions, were therefore not transitory.

Anti-union philosophies were part and parcel, not just of the construction industry, but also of the oil multinationals' approach to industrial relations. They had been developed in the US refineries and chemical industry, as well as in BP's and Shell's overseas facilities. Kochan *et al.* (1986) note that as early as 1946, the US chemical and refinery giant, Du Pont (whose subsidiaries include Conoco), had established a rule that all new plants would be started up and 'maintained' on a non-union basis. At that time, 94 per cent of Du Pont's blue collar workers were represented by unions, but by the late 1980s only about 35 per cent were covered by union contracts. This non-union approach was perfected by another oil-chemical giant, Procter & Gamble. During the 1950s and 1960s, P&G had established several production facilities near urban centres, which were successively organized by unions in the chemical field, such as the Oil, Chemical and Atomic Workers and the International Chemical Workers. Starting in the mid 1960s, P&G entered into an ambitious programme of expansion, now establishing factory sites only where it expected that union recognition was unlikely to occur. Tyre companies such as Goodyear, Firestone, General and Uniroyal, all located their new facilities in southern states where anti-union animus was strong, and had kept them 'union-free' ever since. Mobil Oil opened one of its largest refineries in the rural Illinois hinterland in the early 1970s – not on Lake Michigan as geographical proximity to tanker unloading facilities would lead one to expect – and had maintained it as a union-free plant ever since.

If many of the US oil companies were experts in establishing and maintaining 'union-free environments', the unions still had hopes that the Labour government would intervene on their behalf, ideally to compel the companies to grant recognition as a condition of future licensing. Such expectations were a miscalculation, since, as we have discussed in Chapter 1, the need for rapid exploitation of the oil resources and the requirement for the resulting flow of oil-revenue taxes compromised Labour's ability to explicitly oppose anti-union company practices.

Unions trying to organize offshore underestimated the cohesion between client operator and contractor, which was to become the hallmark of offshore industrial organization. While onshore the relationship between, say, a building or maintenance contractor and a chemical plant operator was typically short lived, and small scale, offshore work involved subcontracting on a grand scale (NEDO, 1970; Mills, 1972; Bresnen, 1990). For the client operators, this meant that communication concerning, and control over, contractors' labour policies was essential. This is eloquently borne witness to by the OCPCA/Client Liaison Committee deliberations. For the unions, it meant that operators and contractors would, if necessary, present a united front, typically with the operators dictating how contractors should conduct their industrial relations with the unions. Even when the contractors saw it to be in their interests to concede the extension of collective bargaining beyond the narrowly defined remit permitted by the operators, they were quickly whipped back into line. This control, without doubt, gave the operators considerable leeway in implementing their anti-union strategies, particularly when, as we have suggested in Chapter 1, that contractor was itself US-based and had a previous longstanding relationship with the client.

A final aspect which the unions had not expected, was the high degree of concerted and strategic action by the operators themselves. Here, UKOOA provided the principal vehicle, not just for the deflection of union demands, but also for the rebuff of the Labour government's interventions on behalf of unions. UKOOA's statutes were premised on such a strategic perspective. Any discussion about matters of industrial relations could be rejected by UKOOA as outside its remit, while the association could effectively voice its demands to government.

With hindsight, it is not difficult to see why the progress of union recognition offshore was slow. For the unions at the time, however, lack of progress could become a source of sectional strife. If an inter-union organization like IUOOC could not make major inroads into the industry, maybe individual unions could and should. Sectionalism always loomed over the offshore sector. Offshore workers were employed in this new industry where boundary lines between union spheres of influence had yet to be clearly drawn. What brought sectionalism to the fore time and again – against the initial intentions of those participating in early offshore organizing efforts – was the unexpectedly persistent and successful anti-union stance of the oil multinationals.

But there was more to come. If sectionalism provided a means of thwarting concerted union action, the oil multinationals were ready to use it consciously for their own purposes. By granting limited agreements to small sections of the labour force or even sections of the labour process (in the case of the Hook-up agreement but excluding maintenance work), the oil operators could shield themselves from on-site militancy. In addition, through these limited agreements, they were also to able play upon growing sectional tensions to their own advantage. Participation in partial, and in some sense unacceptable agreements, such as the Hook-up, was programmed to evoke protests from other parts of the workforce. Unions, in the view of the oil companies, were not parties to be negotiated with in good faith; rather they were objects in a grand strategy – a strategy whose ultimate goal was an environment in which unionization only existed when the benefits (namely the securing of a policing structure to deflect militancy) outweighed the costs.

For offshore workers and the unions there were several possible responses to this situation. First, an agreement could be struck establishing uncompromising inter-union solidarity, potentially by penalizing those who fell out of line. This strategy was hardly feasible, given that some unions had already achieved definite benefit from sectional agreements, and neither the UK level nor the Scottish TUC would have been able to exercise such control. Alternatively, each union could maximize its own sectional agenda, by trying to make the most of its bargaining ability. Given the employers' leverage, such a policy would have been likely to result in few gains. Finally, one possible response was to discard existing union affiliation and form a new offshore union from scratch. This was difficult, because it would undermine long-standing established union structures and loyalties, particularly among skilled craftworkers in construction, whose union card was a necessary ticket for future possible employment onshore.

The possibility of a new, more all-embracing industrial union, in which old sectionalist divides had no place, could however be attractive, given the offshore workers' increasingly ambivalent relationship to established union structures as the 1980s unfolded. For this to happen, however, there needed to be a more substantial dislocation of existing sectional identities. The defeat of the 1979 offshore strike had begun this process, but it was the explosion on Piper Alpha which finally disintegrated previous loyalties, assumptions and goals. In doing so, it created the space for the emergence of a nascent, more homogeneous, anti-sectionalist labour identity. Underpinning such an identity would be the common experience of danger and risk, as well as a rejection of the inequitable hierarchy of power which had precluded workforce safety inputs. In the end, it was this path which offshore workers adopted: a result of their particular legacy. How this path came to be chosen, and what it meant for offshore unionism will stand at the centre of the next chapters in Part II.

Notes

1. Interview with Tony Jackson, 1994. Transcripts for the *Wasted Windfall* Channel 4 TV production, held by Fine Art Productions, London.

2. Interview with Fred Busby, 1994, note 1 *above*.

3. Steven Day, 1976, offshore diaries, Department of Sociology, Aberdeen, currently held by the authors by kind permission of Robert Moore.

4. Reading and Bates, 1976, Terms of Employment for Offshore Hourly Employees.

5. Bawden Drilling Company, 1976, Statement of Terms and Conditions of Employment.

6. Bawden Drilling Company, 1976, Code of Disciplinary Procedure.

7. Day, offshore diaries, note 3 *above*.

8. Tony Murphy, 1976, offshore diaries, commissioned by Department of Sociology, Aberdeen, currently held by the authors.

9. BP unpublished report into Staffing, 1975: accidents, turnover and average length of service.

10. R. Middleton, 1977, provides a full account of the developments upon which Wybrow's 1982 account draws verbatim. See also papers of North Sea Oil Action Committee, 1973, currently held by the authors.

11. The legislation on dismissal was the Employment Protection (Offshore Employment) Order SI No. 266, 1976. The mere presence of this legislation did little to enhance the precarious position of the contract workforce.

12. CSEU Circular, Aberdeen No. 41 District Committee, 5 April 1974.

13. IUOOC letter from W. P. Reid, Secretary, to Drilling Companies, April 1974, contained in IUOOC Minutes, held by the authors.

14. This account is based on the report of the *Aberdeen People's Press* (1976) together with contemporary documents provided by Davie Robertson, plus interview with Davie Robertson, note 1 *above*.

15. Venture One crew's statement concerning incident on board rig, 3 November 1975; letter to Operations Manager (Europe) from crew of Venture One.

16. Record of Agreement between Dixilyn (International) AG and Mr Bill Reid of the IUOOC, 6 February 1976.

17. TUC Fuel and Power Industries Committee, summary report of a meeting with the Secretary of State for Energy, 12 June 1975.

18. IUOOC, Charter for Establishing Trade Union Organisation and Recognition on Offshore Installations (Rigs and Platforms), Aberdeen, 1975.

19. Note of a meeting to discuss offshore unionization held at the DEn, 17 November 1975.

20. IUOOC minutes and discussion of 'spheres of interest', August 1975.

21. Letter from W. B. Reid, Secretary, IUOOC, to General Secretary of AUEW (Engineering Section), 8 October 1975.

22. Note of a meeting between Ministers, the TUC and IUOOC to discuss offshore unionization, 30 March 1976.

23. Extract from UKOOA Memorandum of Association, cited in minutes of evidence of Energy Select Committee, Seventh Report, Offshore Safety Management, HC343, 17 July 1991, London: HMSO, 22.

24. Department of Energy, *Onstream*, Issue 35, 12 May 1976.

25. Note 23 *above*, p.3

26. TUC document, Trade union organisation in the North Sea offshore area, 26 January 1977.

27. TUC, Trade union recognition in the offshore area, TUC points for discussion, Meeting note, 11 May 1976.

28. IUOOC minutes and notes of meeting between Ministers, the TUC and UKOOA, 11 May 1976.

29. Memorandum of Understanding on Trade Union Access to Offshore Installations, 11 May 1976.

30. Note 29 *above*, p.3

31. IUOOC minutes, various 1976-77.

32. Letter from G. Williams, UKOOA to L. Murray, General Secretary TUC, 18 November 1982.

33. Letter from Campbell Reid, Secretary of IUOOC, to Hamish Gray, Minister of State, Department of Energy, 26 May 1982.

34. Record of discussion, UKOOA Liaison Panel and IUOOC, Edinburgh, 18 January 1977; Letter from Bill Reid to Tony Benn, 14 January 1977.

35. From typescript of article by A. Dalton, 'The tragic legacy of the oil boom', *Labour Research*, November 1988.

36. *Sunday Times*, 22 August 1982.

37. Letter from T. P. Boston, Employee Relations Manager, Mobil North Sea Limited, to Campbell Reid, IUOOC, 26 July 1982.

38. Letter from G. Williams, UKOOA, to J. Liverman, 3 September 1976.

39. UKOOA, Employment Practices Committee, Information Booklet, 1988, p. 4.

40. IUOOC Minutes, 18 January 1977.

41. Memorandum of Understanding between UKOOA and IUOOC: Recognition May Be Achieved, 13 June 1977.

42. Notes of IUOOC/UKOOA meeting, Campbell Reid, ASTMS, 15 February 1977.

43. Draft of IUOOC, Proposed guidelines through which recognition may be achieved, n.d.

44. Note 41 *above*, Memorandum on Recognition, point 6.

45. Note of a meeting between the Secretary of State for Energy, representatives of offshore operating companies and UKOOA, and representatives of the Inter-Union Committee and the TUC Fuel and Power Committee, July 1977.

46. IUOOC Minutes, 18 January 1977.

47. Report of Campbell Reid, ASTMS, to Head Office, 16 February 1977.

48. UKOOA/IUOOC Minutes, 15 February 1977.

49. Telegram from D. Lea, Secretary of TUC Economic Department to W. Reid, Secretary of IUOOC, 20 July 1977.

50. *Financial Times North Sea Newsletter*, No. 258, 1 October 1980.

51. Letter from Phillips Petroleum to Roger Spiller, ASTMS, 23 July 1976.

52. IUOOC Minutes, 26 January 1977.

53. Memo from Campbell Reid to R. Lyons, 7 December 1976.

54. IUOOC Minutes, 25 January 1977.

55. Letter from W. Reid, IUOOC to R. D. Young, Phillips Petroleum Company Europe-Africa, 5 August 1977.

56. Agreement between Phillips Petroleum Company UK Branch and the Association of Scientific, Technical and Managerial Staffs on behalf of the Inter-Union Offshore Oil Committee, 21 July 1978.

57. Phillips Petroleum (Hewett Field) Trade Union Recognition, letter to employees, 7 April 1978.

58. IUOOC Minutes, 7 September 1976.

59. Letter from Len Murray, TUC General Secretary, to trade unions, 1 December 1976.

60. TUC Fuel and Power Industries Committee, Trade Union Organisation in the North Sea Offshore Area, 23 March 1977.

61. Letter from D. Lea, TUC Economic Department to S. Davidson, ASTMS Head Office, 24 May 1977.

62. Letter to Phillips Employees from R. Spiller, 7 April 1978.

63. Note 61 *above* p.3.

64. Letter from Bill Reid, IUOOC, to affiliates, 10 February 1978.

65. IUOOC Resolution, 17 February 1978.

66. IUOOC Minutes, 6 February 1979.

67. Letter from G. P. Hoverkamp, Chairman UKOOA Liaison Panel to B.

Reid, IUOOC, 6 February 1978.

68. Letter from T. Benn to B. Reid, IUOOC, 8 March 1978.

69. Tony Benn to G. Williams, Director General of UKOOA, 30 May 1978.

70. IUOOC Minutes, 10 April 1978.

71. TUC Fuel and Power Industries Committee, Minutes, 24 January 1979.

72. Notes of the Client/OCPCA Liaison Committee, March 1974, OCPCA deposit, Modern Records Centre, University of Warwick. The following account draws extensively on the OCPCA deposit together with Garfit's 1989 University of Warwick Working Paper. Tim Garfit was the first Secretary of the OCPCA.

73. Notes of the Client/OCPCA Liaison Committee, 6 May 1976, OCPCA deposit, note 72 *above*.

74. ibid.

75. Notes of the Client/OCPCA Liaison Committee, 11 November 1976, OCPCA deposit, note 72 *above*.

76. IUOOC Minutes, 7 September 1976.

77. Notes of Client/OCPCA Liaison Committee, 9 March 1978, OCPCA deposit, note 72 *above*.

78. See Minutes of Evidence of Energy Select Committee, Seventh Report, p. 49, note 23 *above*; notes of a meeting between J. McCartney (Boilermakers) and T. Lafferty (AUEW Construction Section) with shop stewards from the Brae 'A' contract, 6 June 1983.

79. Notes of Client/OCPCA Liaison Committee, 16 June 1978, OCPCA deposit, note 72 *above*.

80. See also *Press and Journal*, 15 September 1981.

81. See Strathclyde Process Engineering Ltd. letter to all employees on Occidental, Piper and Claymore Platforms from D. Reid, Personnel Manager, 20 January 1983, cited in Carrigan, 1985.

82. Letter from J. Lawson, Offshore Platform Maintenance Ltd., to D. Carrigan, 12 May 1983, cited in Carrigan, 1985.

83. Letter from J. Baldwin, Secretary, NECC to G. Williams, Director General of UKOOA, 12 June 1981.

84. Letter from G. Williams, UKOOA to J. Baldwin, NECC, 18 June 1981.

85. Letter from T. Garfit, OCPCA to J. Baldwin, General Secretary, AUEW (Construction Section), 14 March 1983.

86. Offshore Contractors Council, Offshore Construction Agreement, Minutes of the Stage IV Meeting, London, 23 January 1986.

87. OCC Minutes of meeting to discuss the draft Offshore Construction Services Agreement, London, 7 May 1986.

88. *The Bear*, Issue No. 3, December 1984.

89. *Glasgow Herald*, 15 January 1987.

90. IUOOC Minutes, 5 June 1978; Offshore Catering Services steward's strike diary, June 1977, commissioned by the Department of Sociology, Aberdeen, currently held by the authors.

91. In an ACAS-conducted ballot, held after ASTMS had demonstrated at least 40 per cent membership, Shell technicians voted for recognition on the Auk (83 per cent), Brent Bravo (81 per cent), Brent Delta (91 per cent), Cormorant Alpha (85 per cent) and Fulmar (90 per cent). This totalled 370 workers out of a total of 3000 Shell employees. See *Financial Times*, 10 October 1985; *Press and Journal*, 10 October 1985.

92. Letter from C. Reid to Alick Buchanan-Smith, Minister of State for Energy, 10 April 1987.

93. Letter from B. C. Clark, Manager, Britoil, to C. Reid, IUOOC, 7 May 1987.

94. Letter from R. W. Eadie, EETPU, to C. Reid, 23 February 1987.

95. *Offshore*, Journal of EETPU, Issue No. 2, Summer 1987.

96. Letter from R. W. Eadie, EETPU, to C. Reid, 9 October 1987.

97. TUC, FPIC North Sea Oil: Note for a meeting with BSJC and IUOOC representatives, 24 January 1979; TUC, North Sea Oil Issues: Summary report of an informal meeting with the IUOOC held at Congress House, 4 June 1981; Minute of Special Meeting of the IUOOC held in the TGWU offices, King Street, Aberdeen, 16 September 1980; TUC meeting with IUOOC, 3 July 1981; Joint Statement of Intent regarding spheres of influence of IUOOC unions regarding personnel employed on Sedco semi-submersible drilling rigs, 8 October 1981.

98. *Financial Times North Sea Newsletter*, No. 308, 5 August 1981, p.13.

99. *Financial Times North Sea Newsletter*, No. 413, 24 August 1983, p.12.

100. A. Miller, The history of the Association of Professional Divers, March 1990 (unpublished ms).

101. IUOOC Minutes, 13 January 1982.

102. Letter to MPs from the crew of MSV *Stadive*, November 1986.

103. Minutes of Shell Staff Consultative Committee, Brent Charlie, 12 December 1986.

104. Minute of Special Meeting of IUOOC, 4 February 1987; Note of a meeting of the UKOOA and the IUOOC, 4 March 1987.

105. Piper Alpha Public Inquiry, 13 March 1989, Day 34: 32H–39H.

106. Ronnie McDonald, speech to Aberdeen Trades Council rally in support of the offshore workers, Aberdeen, 2 September 1990.

107. *Bear Facts,* May 1989.

108. Letter from W. Reid, IUOOC, to B. Eadie, EETPU, 27 July 1988.

109. Minute of Extraordinary Meeting of IUOOC, 15 July 1988.

110. Letter from David Lea, Assistant General Secretary of the TUC to W. C. F. Butler, Department of Energy, 5 August 1988.

111. Letter from B. Eadie, EETPU to T. Lafferty, AUEW, 8 September 1988.

112. *Press and Journal*, 31 July 1989.

113. D. O'Dell, Shell Expro Situation Report, 13 July 1989.

114. Letter from J. M. McDonald, Managing Director, Aberdeen Scaffolding to T. Lafferty, AEU, 9 July 1989.

115. Letter from G. Beattie, Operations Director, Atlantic Power & Gas to employees, 23 June 1989.

116. Letter from G. Beattie, Atlantic Power & Gas to all employees on Shell Cormorant Alpha, 20 July 1989.

117. Document of Press Offshore, signatory Alan McPherson, Operations Manager, 19 July 1989.

118. Letter from Press Offshore to employees, 22 June 1989.

119. Letter from R. Hogg, Wood Group, to employees on Brent 'D' platform, 21 July 1989.

120. Minute of Stage II Discussion to review points of concern raised by Brent 'C' and 'D' workforce, Wood Group Engineering Contractors Ltd., 9 August 1989.

121. Sir Ian Wood recorded BBC Radio Scotland, 'Headlines', with Ruth Wishart, September 1990, tape in the authors' possession.

122. OCC, Minutes of a meeting to renegotiate the Offshore Construction Agreement, London, 15 December 1989.

123. As this volume was going to press a somewhat brief unreferenced parallel account of these two decades of offshore unionism was provided by Sewel and Penn, 1996. Sewel and Penn suggest that UK operating companies were less hostile and more circumspect in their dealings with trade unions. Our analysis finds no support for this view, and indeed largely contradicts it. We suggest that UK operators participated with alacrity in the implantation of a US-type production regime, and equally embraced union-avoidance strategies.

PART 2 INDUSTRIAL ACTION

The following two chapters are based primarily on intensive participant observation conducted over a period of ten months. The views of the workforce at each stage of the dispute, and the sometimes fierce debates over tactics and strategy, are drawn from over 250 hours of tape recordings of mass meetings. These recordings were made in Aberdeen, Glasgow, Hull and on the offshore installations themselves. They provide a unique window into the growing consciousness and determination of the offshore workforce. Numerous interviews were also conducted and several offshore diaries were compiled or recorded by some of those most involved in the dispute. Included here also is material which is drawn from recordings of the inner deliberations of the strike leadership as it sought to sustain the cohesion of the workforce and at the same time outflank the employers on a day-by-day basis.

Chapter 3 discusses the mounting of a second wave of unofficial industrial action during the spring and summer of 1990. We review the strategy of the employers, ranging from initial efforts to bribe the workforce, to an attempt to provoke premature action, to the wholesale dismissals of those engaged in the dispute. We discuss the growing unity amongst established trade unions in support of unofficial activists. The chapter highlights the particular difficulties of mounting industrial action in the offshore context.

Chapter 4 chronicles the successive stoppages and offshore sit-ins organized by the unofficial Offshore Industry Liaison Committe. We discuss the escalation and de-escalation of the conflict, highlighting the limited range of options available to the dispute organizers. Our analysis concludes with a discussion of the failure of the official trade movement to take the campaign goals of the offshore movement further.

3 PRELUDE TO ACTION

The 1990 Summer Shutdowns

> *As always in a cyclical uptick in an industry, the labour force sees their bargaining position helped by their growing indispensability.* In cyclical troughs the workforce is too scared about job stability to complain too much. So as the oil price rises, the workforce is feeling more militant and pushing hard for a whole set of stored-up grievances to be redressed. At the heart of the matter is the desire for a solid unionized labour structure that replaces the poorly represented short-term contract labour force that has prevailed for so long – in other words a shift in the balance of power from mighty 'Big Oil' to the workforce. *But other entirely justifiable requests such as a better safety policy are also being demanded.*
>
> We predict a worsening labour situation in the North Sea ... if the [OILC] does not get its way of 'unionising' the whole North Sea. And if it succeeds the cost structure in the North Sea will again see upward pressure. (*UK North Sea – Union Problems*, Kleinwort Benson Securities, 1990: 29, original emphases)

The year 1990 saw the biggest planned maintenance shutdown in the history of the North Sea. It involved 27 platforms. OILC had already led a campaign of industrial action that had rocked the oil companies on their heels. As an unofficial body of activists, it was now to renew its campaign for safety improvements and for comprehensive union recognition in this 'window of vulnerability'. The cost to the operators of the summer shutdown was estimated to be a staggering £1.65 billion. Any slippage in the work programme could only add to those costs. The stakes on both sides of the industry could hardly have been higher. In the Shell field alone, which was responsible for about a quarter of the total UK oil production, the Cormorant Alpha platform had only just resumed production at the end of February after a tenmonth shutdown following a gas leak and explosion the previous April. The Cormorant Alpha platform acted as the linchpin of the Brent pipeline system. Oil from thirteen fields was pumped to the Cormorant Alpha and from there to Sullom Voe in Shetland, 176 km away. But it was on the ageing Brent installations that Shell's problems assumed their most serious form. Bad weather in February and March had delayed maintenance schedules which carried over from the previous year. In 1990, the Brent Charlie had already been shut down for a year for maintenance. Hopes of recovery to a UK output level of two million barrels per day now looked extremely unlikely. In real terms, the price of oil was lower than at any time since 1972, with only brief exceptions in 1986 and 1988.[1]

The key target of OILC action was the Far-North Liquids and Gas System (FLAGS) line to St Fergus which was due to be purged and decommissioned. The OILC intended to strike at the point of maximum vulnerability when the system had been dismantled, requiring the contractor labour force to put it together again. Any delay in start-up would be enormously costly for the operators. The problem was that the 'pig' to purge the FLAGS pipeline to St Fergus could not be sent down the pipeline until the diesel fire pump system on the Brent Charlie was operational and working at full capacity again. A previous attempt at a start up of the pumps had to be abandoned. The precise date of this year's summer shutdown, originally planned for May, was becoming increasingly difficult to predict. It was a matter that Shell was keen to keep a closely guarded secret. Its offshore personnel were ordered to institute a 'clear desk policy' with respect to sensitive documentation, albeit to little avail in the final event.

Even without unanticipated problems, Shell had already estimated that the Brent field would be operating at little better than half capacity for much of the year.[2] At its peak the Brent system had a throughput of 960,000 barrels per day, but current production by the end of April was already less than 500,000 barrels per day.[3] Cuts in output in 1989 had already caused Shell's profits from oil production to fall by £45 million to £195 million. Any further delays in the recovery of production to former levels had serious financial implications. Shell correctly guessed that their installations were likely to be a prime target for OILC.

Another target for OILC was the Ninian pipeline system running direct from Ninian Central to Sullom Voe. Oil from BP's Heather, Alwyn North and Magnus platforms was piped to the Ninian Central and from there to the terminal in Shetland. Further shutdowns were also anticipated in the Forties system and in Texaco-operated fields. The combination of these shutdowns, together with the Brent system, was expected to reduce UK production to 1.49 million barrels per day during October 1990. If the Ninian and Brent shutdowns were to overlap, production might drop as low as 1.37 million barrels per day, with the Brent–Sullom Voe pipeline scheduled to shut down for some six weeks from late September and the Ninian pipeline for three to four weeks during September.[4] The shutdown of the FLAGS system in the Shell field as such was, therefore, merely the first of a series of rolling shutdowns.

The Amoco Montrose Incident

Amoco, which was described by trade unionists as a 'typical hardnosed American operator', provided renewed impetus for safety demands. Amoco's platform, the Montrose, had already acquired a degree of notoriety among the offshore workforce. A near-disaster on the platform had many elements that bore an uncanny resemblance to those that led to Piper Alpha. Both Piper Alpha and the Montrose were part of the first generation of offshore installations which were installed in the summer of 1975. The Montrose was characterized by one worker at an OILC meeting as 'a rust-bucket waiting to blow up'.[5] In offshore incidents, whether fatalities or injuries result is owed more to good luck than anything else. The Montrose experienced a massive gas leak in February 1990. The scenario of events was recounted by investigative journalist Callum Macrae after a briefing by OILC:

> Tuesday 13 February was a typical day for the men on the Montrose oil platform. For the previous five months they had been working against the clock to refurbish the installation and bring into operation a new pipeline linking it with the neighbouring Arbroath platform.
>
> In production modules 2 and 3 riggers were working to remove a large pressure safety valve from a six-inch gas pipeline. They removed it … but it is not clear what happened next. It seems that the following morning, after a gas leak, it was found disconnected. Above the riggers … although the platform owners Amoco deny any knowledge of it … work was being carried out to connect new cables to the electricity station in module 9.
>
> Unknown to both sets of workers, a decision had been taken to bring the platform on-stream that night. The scene was set for what most

people on the platform appear to regard as a near disaster.

When, on 16 February, Amoco issued its acknowledgement that there had been a 'leak of gas' on the Montrose two days earlier, it concluded: 'All construction work on the platform had been stopped before the production restart process'.

Last week, a spokesman insisted that 'all the construction work permits were withdrawn at 03.00 on 14 February'. But he admitted later that two 'cold work' permits were in operation at the time of the incident. 'One was for work on the ventilation trunking on the number one turbine, which was shut down and in any case is distant from modules 2 and 3,' he said. However, a worker told *Observer Scotland* that work on the ventilation trunking system had involved the use of chisels, and so far as he understood, that should be classified as 'hot work' because of the danger of sparks.

When the alarm sounded at 8.03 a.m. [on 14 February] there were 273 men on the 'flotel' alongside the Montrose, and 88 on the platform itself. The emergency was over quickly. Such was the apparent speed of the leak that the entire area of modules 2 and 3 ... covering an area more than 100 feet long, 80 feet wide and 22 feet high ... became sufficiently filled with gas to trigger over 20 gas sensors.[6]

If there were sparks it could have triggered a massive explosion which could have resulted in a disaster comparable to that on Piper Alpha. That it did not do so was perhaps fortuitous rather than the result of responsible actions by management. Like Piper Alpha, it is in the detail of the incident that the breakdown of proper managerial control and communication is revealed. Just as the operator of Piper Alpha, Occidental, was already known for safety violations, this was by no means the first time that Amoco had been accused of deficiencies in the management of its permit-to-work system. Only ten days before the incident, Frank Doran, MP, had listed what was described as 'a catalogue of safety mismanagement' on the Mr Mac drilling rig, adjacent to the Montrose. This included an incorrectly validated 'hot work' permit, among a total of fourteen serious defects identified during a Department of Transport rig inspection.[7]

On the Montrose itself, modules 2 and 3, where the gas is gathered, were directly below module 9, the electricity station. Members of the workforce claimed this was itself a potential source of ignition, whether or not the use of chisels required a 'hot work' permit. It was alleged that in the course of connecting the new cables to module 9 the 'transit blocks' which normally close off the conduits through which the cables pass from module to module had been left open. Normally, the electricity station would be sealed and positively pressurized, precisely to prevent any spark from a switch igniting an ingress of gas which could result in an explosion. Open transits were sufficient grounds for concern. It further transpired that the accommodation block on the Montrose, a supposedly 'safe area', had been constructed before the 1974 regulations prohibiting the use of combustible building materials had come into force. These 'temporary living quarters', adjacent to modules 2 and 3, had subsequently remained in place for the next fourteen years. In 1988, in the aftermath of Piper Alpha, the Department of Energy (DEn) granted further exemption from current regulations for the Montrose accommodation despite its now demonstrable deficiencies.

Temporary units of the kind used on the Montrose were first put in place in the North Sea to house construction workers during the hook-up phase of platform construction. An architect involved in the design of similar offshore living quarters in the mid-1970s described their features as 'unrestricted by the use of non-combustible materials'. Such accommodation modules

> ... were mainly constructed of timber. This did not overly matter, as they were temporary work camps, the platforms were not 'live' and the certifying authorities happily allowed them to be installed on the platforms. They had a design life of five years, although they were only intended to remain in place for up to 18 months. (Hardie, 1991)

The workforce put it rather more graphically, describing the Montrose accommodation as, 'built in Louisiana – out of second-hand railway sleepers'. What they did not know was that these accommodation units were part of a 'job lot' of USAF surplus. Similar units were also supplied to Piper Alpha.

Under parliamentary questioning from Frank Doran, Peter Morrison, the Energy Minister, conceded that the accommodation module on the Montrose was to be replaced by April 1991 and, in the interim, additional safety measures were to be implemented.[8] Amoco had been ordered by DEn safety inspectors to begin an 'immediate programme of instruction' for all platform personnel on permit-to-work procedures. A delegation of OILC and union representatives had failed to win assurances from the DEn that production on the Montrose would be halted pending further investigation into the company's safety regime. Even as the union side pleaded its case, unbeknown to them, the Montrose had come back on-stream the previous evening, with the necessary approval from the Department of Energy. While the accommodation module been lacking in requisite safety standards throughout its operational life, the helideck above the accommodation module, one of the main designated escape routes in the event of fire, was also, at least partially, made of wood. It too, failed to meet current safety standards and had been erected with a 'temporary exemption' from the DEn.[9] The restarting of Montrose production was a vital precondition for bringing its new sister platform, the Arbroath, to the urgently awaited point of first oil. In the view of trade unionists, this represented yet more evidence of the fatally compromised role of the regulatory body, the DEn, with regard to safety. Roger Spiller of the MSF union (formerly ASTMS) summed up the frustration felt by the unions at the DEn's attitude: 'It's not a question of the operator having to prove to the DEn that the platform is safe. It's a question of *us* having to prove it's *unsafe*.'

The 1990 Campaign Commences

At OILC mass meetings in Glasgow and other centres, continuing breaches of safety by the employers provided a backcloth of resentment as preparations for the coming summer confrontation were hammered out. Discussions in the smoke-filled hall of the engineering union in Glasgow's West Regent Street were remarkable both in intensity and quality of argument. Here were ordinary offshore riggers, mechanical fitters, catering workers, scaffolders, drillers, electricians and pipefitters locked into a fierce debate which involved exploring the finer intricacies of the union-avoidance strategy of multinational capital, governmental policy, Conservative employment law, economic forecasting, as well as the only slightly more mundane subjects of offshore oil and gas engineering, safety systems and industrial relations. Into this crucible of collective scrutiny were thrown the results of literally hundreds of daily offshore tea-shack, cabin and canteen conversations, arguments and observations. Each of these discussions was a microcosm of the growing workforce awareness of the need for change. Here among the offshore 'bears', a collective movement of rank and file workers was stirring.

The OILC, as an organization for ordinary offshore workers, as yet did not have a formal existence. Since October 1989, OILC had opened an office in Aberdeen. But OILC was still an *ad hoc* body without formal rules, governed by the most simple and direct form of democracy which involved weekly mass meetings that every and any offshore worker could attend and voice his or her opinion. The membership of the Standing Committee of OILC, the collective leadership body, was drawn from these mass meetings. Structurally, OILC was the antithesis of the bureaucratic trade unionism which was said to have failed many offshore workers so badly in the past. But OILC was also the child of that trade unionism. Although the legacy of defeat of the 1979 strike still soured the view of many towards the established unions, OILC was not in general opposed to official union bodies. One of the key functions of the unofficial commitee was to persuade offshore workers who had never joined unions before to become members, or if they had allowed their membership to lapse, to rejoin. In terms of developing strategy and tactics, at each stage, local union officials worked closely with OILC activists during the spring and summer of 1990. Nevertheless, a tension between the official unions and OILC, always latent, eventually re-emerged. What ensued was a long and tangled interrelationship, the twists and turns of which provide an insight into the wider problems facing contemporary trade unionism in a hostile legal and industrial environment.

The Official Trade Unions

For the official movement, the immediate difficulty was achieving unity at national level. This required an organizational structure that supported a common goal which each of the unions with an interest offshore could share. Achieving such unity was no simple matter.

When OILC activists met the national union officials in Blackpool during TUC week in September 1989, it had been agreed that the proposal for 'one offshore union' was not acceptable. Instead, the relevant unions intended to meet and formulate a single-table approach, or, as it had become known, a 'one-table approach'. Single-table bargaining had been one of the issues which preoccupied the TUC Special Review Body during 1989. The review body had been set up to reform and modernize the bargaining agenda of the trade unions. The intention of this strategy was to reduce some of the supposed problems of multi-unionism. Single-table bargaining was thought to be one possible way of making trade unionism acceptable to employers. Single-table arrangements would apply where more than one union was recognised, but for negotiating purposes, all unions would bargain as a single unit. Ideally, such bargaining would cover both manual and non-manual employees. As the authoritative *Industrial Relations Review and Report* (1989: 3) put it: 'Single-table bargaining is an alternative to single union deals, allowing a multi-union environment, without running the risk of a fragmented bargaining structure.' However, research commissioned by the TUC from Warwick University suggested that where such moves to single-table bargaining occurred, it was management which was often the driving force. Such bargaining, moreover, often occurred as part of major changes of terms of employment. Where no changes in employment were considered, management tended to favour the status quo, especially where it was able to play one union off against another. The TUC gave the notion of single-table bargaining a cautious welcome, noting that this could possibly increase inter-union solidarity (TUC, 1989). In the offshore context, it was clear that inter-union cooperation was a vital precondition to any successful challenge to the employers.

The following spring, some seven months after the OILC had met the union officials at Blackpool, a one-table group of national officers concerned with the North Sea had still not been formed. The delay was a source of growing irritation at OILC mass meetings. In defence of the failure of the officers in 'getting their act together', local engineering union official Tommy Lafferty tried to shift the responsibility for the lack of progress back on to the workforce. 'If there was an upfront show of strength from the men the national officials would have given it more priority.'[10]

With characteristic bluntness, Lafferty expressed his view that OILC now realized it 'couldn't deliver' and was 'trying to put the blame on someone else'. It was a view strongly echoed by Eddie Bree, the local Boilermakers' official. Putting in place a one-table approach among the unions required two preconditions. First, the existing fragmented agreements that different unions had negotiated with the various sets of employers had to be suspended. Second, a common programme, or comprehensive agreement, that would still satisfy the aspirations of each of the constituent unions with an interest offshore had to be agreed upon. Achieving a comprehensive agreement, the Continental Shelf Agreement as it became known, would be the ultimate objective of the campaign of industrial action.

There were varying degrees of union reluctance, so far as suspending existing agreements was concerned. The signatory unions to the Hook-up agreement led the way. They had warned that they would terminate their participation in the Hook-up agreement, if the 1989 dispute did not succeed in forcing the employers to concede a broader post-construction recognition agreement. On 24 January 1990, the signatory unions, the AEU, the Boilermakers' union (GMB) and the MSF formally terminated the Hook-up agreement in both the northern and southern sectors. This voluntary abandonment of what little recognition they had achieved over the years was a source of anguish to some. Greg Douglas, AEU local official with offshore responsibilities in the southern sector, referred back to the victorious Easington-Rough dispute in the mid-eighties:

The only thing I had to show for eight years of activity as an official was the southern sector Hook-up agreement. There Ronnie McDonald in his wisdom is having the balls to ask me to cancel it. It took nearly a three-week sit-in and six weeks of negotiation to win.[11]

The situation with the TGWU and NUS with respect to the COTA arrangements was even more fraught and complex. There was some doubt as to whether the Hook-up signatory unions, in particular the engineering union, the AEU, actually wanted the TGWU and NUS to be participants in the proposed one-table approach. Under pressure from the OILC mass meetings, the local officials of the AEU had agreed to ensure that the TGWU and NUS were to be formally involved at national level in any future one-table approach. Yet, as late as the third week in March, neither the TGWU nor NUS had received an invitation to a national officers' meeting which had been convened for 18 April by the Hook-up unions.

Since the arrival of John Taylor, the new local TGWU official in Aberdeen, in the autumn of 1989, the destructive rivalry between the TGWU and NUS in the offshore industry had been overcome. The two unions now worked together to recruit catering workers and had 'negotiated' jointly with the COTA employers. Their collective efforts had produced a degree of success, not least of which was the election of 70 shop stewards offshore, and the creation of an unprecedented level of offshore organization. Over a period of about a year, the combined registered membership of NUS and TGWU had increased from about 780 to over 1500, with the TGWU predominating by a factor of two to one. In January 1990, after protracted negotiations with the COTA employers, an agreement had been reached which gave a significant wage increase to catering workers of between 16 and 18 per cent. It was still one of the worst paid sectors of the offshore workforce. This increase was intended to blunt the edge of militancy among this section of the workforce. Since December 1988, the NUS and TGWU had made an attempt to negotiate a more comprehensive agreement for catering workers covering both northern and southern sectors including Morecambe Bay. As it stood, the COTA rises still only applied to the northern sector and exclusively to fixed installations, not drilling rigs.

In mid-March, the TGWU and NUS proposed a joint campaign to recruit members from within the drilling industry. This public proclamation of unity perhaps also indicated a degree of reservation about the possibility of a broader unity between all the unions. On the basis of the 1989 industrial action offshore, such reservations were understandable. There had been considerable confusion as to the role that the catering workers were being asked to play in that dispute. In the past, very little consultation with them or their officials had taken place when crucial decisions were taken by the construction engineering workforce. In the 1989 dispute, the 'bears' had to admit to striking catering workers that if a deal providing post-construction recognition for the engineering construction workers emerged, it would be accepted, whether or not their supporters among other sectors such as catering would benefit. The advice given to the catering workers was to secure whatever gains were on offer through the COTA arrangements. But as Norrie McVicar, local official of NUS, now put it, 'This year we are all singing the same song'. If the national officers agreed that nothing would be signed unless it covered *all* offshore workers, then, said John Taylor, 'we will recommend that catering workers walk away from COTA'.[12]

The other major participant in any one-table approach was the electricians' union, the EETPU. Their sectionally exclusive collective bargaining agreement in the offshore industry was the SJIB. In the 1989 dispute, the EETPU broke ranks by resigning the SJIB agreement, while the rest of the organized engineering construction workforce was still in dispute. Bob Eadie, as the local EETPU official, had to endure considerable criticism at OILC mass meetings for this previous 'betrayal'. The penance for the sin of 1989 was to be in the public commitment of the EETPU to the one-table approach for the proposed Continental Shelf Agreement. Yet the EETPU was the most reluctant to abandon the SJIB agreement, which it described as a 'role model'. In more candid moments, Eadie admitted that this much vaunted 'post-construction' SJIB agreement held by the EETPU had its 'deficiencies'. It was by any reckoning a highly sectionalist agreement. Half of the pipefitters were employed by 'mechanical companies' rather than electrical contractors and, therefore, were not covered by the SJIB agreement. Only about one-third of the union's total offshore membership was covered. The long-term future of the SJIB agreement was also in doubt, as employers were increasingly recruiting adult trainees to replace skilled tradesmen. The EETPU position was, that it would defer the re-signing of the SJIB agreement, but that the time scale was not unlimited. Even though the agreement was not due for renegotiation until September, Eadie warned, referring to the forthcoming campaign of industrial action, 'if by July we are not achieving anything we will not allow this agreement to wither on the vine.'[13]

The Continental Shelf Agreement

The goal of a one-table approach, a comprehensive agreement embracing *all* the major unions, was not easy to formulate. A series of intense discussions beginning in early March 1990, between OILC and local officials in the IUOOC, hammered out the details for the proposed Continental Shelf Agreement. Included in its terms were union recognition, the right to elect shop stewards, rights to receive proper training, facilities to perform their duties, holiday entitlements, and a reduction in working excessive hours. It was modelled on the Hook-up agreement, but with many of the provisions which had been eroded over the previous years restored. Significantly, it was not 'a claim about money'. No target figures for wages increases were mentioned. Rather, it was argued that once the basic issue of union recognition could be resolved, 'the money would look after itself'. McDonald observed, perhaps correctly, that the twenty or so closely-typed pages of the Continental Shelf Agreement document, were not designed to 'electrify the workforce'.[14] There was no 'magic target figure' of £10 per hour to inspire militancy. To some degree, there was a danger that the men would not see the relevance of the proposal or feel 'it's worth going for'. Its significance lay elsewhere, said McDonald:

> We've got to demonstrate to the employers that this agreement is in their own interests. Quite simply, without it there will continue to be industrial mayhem. We must convince them that gone forever are the days when they can run this industry by fear, intimidation and the NRB.

The term NRB (Not Required Back) had come to signify for the workforce much of what was wrong in the North Sea. Any worker identified by the operator or client as a 'troublemaker', perhaps because he had raised a safety concern, or was a union activist, stood the risk of being 'NRB'd'. The contracting company which had hired the man would be told by the client that the individual concerned was no longer welcome, 'Not Required Back', on that installation. At the end of his trip he would be returned to shore and suddenly discover himself 'down-manned' or 'surplus to contract requirements'. Getting 'picked up' on any future contract often proved difficult, whether the contractor was working for the same operator or not. Proving victimization through the NRB system was extremely difficult, and such nominal legal recourse as existed was ineffective. Formal recognition of trade unions through collective bargaining would do much to redress the balance of power between individual worker and employer, while curbing these employer excesses and victimization.

The Bribe

The Continental Shelf Agreement document provided a set of demands around which to educate and mobilize the workforce for the coming summer campaign of industrial action. The employers, however, had one very powerful card to play which could potentially blunt any eagerness to take industrial action. On 2 March 1990, a substantial 11.7 per cent wage rise for contractors' employees on BP and Shell Expro installations was announced. This was to take effect on 1 April 1990 and was in addition to a previous imposed annual wage increase of 8.9 per cent. The main beneficiaries were those engineering construction workers employed by the contractors Wood Group and Press Offshore, affecting, in all, more than 1600 men. The employers claimed that the new package provided earnings as high as £22,000 per year for craftsmen, and closed the wage gap between the contractor employees and those of the operators. OILC denounced the imposed increase as a crude attempt to bribe the men in the hope it would 'buy off trouble' during the summer.[15] *Blowout*, OILC's lively monthly tabloid for offshore workers, reminded the workforce that Wood Group had been amongst the most vigorous enforcers of wage cuts during the 1986 downturn.[16] What had been given now, in the absence of a properly negotiated agreement, could just as easily be taken away later on. The wage cuts of up to one-third in 1986 had proved that. The timing of the increase, falling well outside the normal period of annual wage review of the so-called Model Terms and Conditions, could be construed as a classic 'buy-off' attempt. More concrete evidence that this was part of the employers' game-plan was later to emerge. Contractors on other operators' installations now came under pressure from their own employees to match the award on Shell and BP installations. There was fertile ground for shifting of attention away from the central issues of union recognition in an industry-wide agreement and from the issue of the workforce's safety concerns.

The Overtime Ban

The issue of working hours, spelled out in the Continental Shelf Agreement document, had an additional offshore specific dimension – safety. Studies of major disasters such as the Clapham rail crash and the Zeebrugge ferry sinking had suggested that fatigue, due to excessive working hours, could be a major contributory factor in a number of cases. The Department of Energy had issued a Safety Notice on 5 January 1990, reminding the companies that the 'normal' working day should not exceed twelve hours, and that 'only in very exceptional circumstances' should a maximum of sixteen hours in any one day be exceeded. In any event, an uninterrupted rest break of eight hours should follow any period of work of more than twelve hours.[17] So far, only two operating companies had implemented this. With major shutdowns approaching on 27 platforms, operators such as Shell were seeking to postpone the implementation of the DEn notice until after the summer period of intensive work.

For OILC, the DEn Safety Notice provided an appropriate launch platform for the start of its 1990 campaign – the call for the overtime ban across the whole North Sea. The campaign for the overtime ban was a way of putting economic pressure on the contractors and the clients whilst doing least damage to those taking the industrial action, the workers themselves. In implementing the ban, the workforce would be doing no more than working to their existing contract of employment.

In early 1990 it had been the view of Tommy Lafferty, endorsed by the OILC committee, that a successfully organized overtime ban, sustained over a six-month period, could have produced a result in terms of recognition that would have satisfied the objectives of the trade unions at that time. The post-Piper refurbishment work had begun in earnest by this time. The operators were legally obliged to install or resite emergency shutdown valves at the platform–pipeline interface by the end of that year. The immediate target of an overtime ban would be the contractor employers. Industrial action, in the form of the overtime ban, would deprive the contractors of the enhanced profits which they were now securing after several lean years. Tenders had been submitted by the contractors at inflated rates, exploiting a temporary leverage over the operators anxious to complete the Piper-related safety work. These tenders were based on costings relating to twelve-hour days and covered agreed profits and overheads. By depriving the contractors of an extra three hours' work per man each day, the overtime ban could potentially cut contractors' profits by 25 per cent or more in a situation in which they wished to maximize the number of hours worked on each contract. The ultimate target of the overtime ban, the operators, would thus also come under pressure as their planned schedules would be disrupted. In a situation where bed spaces for personnel offshore were already at a premium, every hour that could be worked and was not, added to the pressures.

Since the downturn of the mid-1980s, the fifteen-hour day had become part of the way of life of the offshore contracting workforce. Many had come to depend upon it to sustain their individual financial commitments. Over the previous ten months preceding the campaign, at least three offshore workers had been NRB'd simply for refusing to work overtime. There was an unacceptable element of compulsion and coercion in overtime working which summed up much of what was wrong with the offshore industrial relations regime. Paradoxically, many of the workforce, while ready to follow the OILC and 'have a go' in full-scale strike action, were reluctant to lose what amounted to between a quarter and a third of their wages, through refusing regular overtime working. In the Forties field in 1989 there had been the seemingly contradictory situation of men being prepared to take strike action one day, but working all the overtime they could thereafter to make up for lost wages. The issue of overtime working posed the OILC with a sharp dilemma which impinged on its ability to organize and orchestrate industrial unrest offshore.

OILC's original intention had been to announce the overtime ban to coincide with the 1 April imposed wage rise. The 'work to contract' was an integral part of a phased escalation of protest action. Ultimately, the workforce intended to confront the contractor employers, and more particularly the operators, with strategically timed sit-ins at the point of their maximum vulnerability. These sit-ins would take place on the platforms, and at the moment when decommissioning work during shutdowns had passed the point of no return. The costs to the operators, the real target of the industrial action, in terms of delayed start-ups after the completion of maintenance work, could be enormous. OILC had to demonstrate itself capable of leading and controlling the industrial action, in a disciplined and co-ordinated way, until that point of open confrontation had been reached. This strategy would build on the successful overtime ban of the previous year and mark a contrast to the spontaneous and haphazard sit-in actions of 1989. Phased escalation would signal to the employers the potential strength of OILC's organization, its ability to 'call the shots'.

The original proposal for an overtime ban did not meet with an immediate positive workforce response. In key areas such as BP platforms in the Forties field, OILC organization had been almost completely dormant over the winter. But even on the Shell installations, a stronghold of OILC support, there appeared to be some reluctance among the workforce, when it came to refusing overtime. From Tommy Brady, a boilermaker with Press on the Brent Charlie, came warning of 'serious reservations' about the overtime ban. The view offshore was, said Brady, that 'OILC is taking money out of our pockets'.[18] Other key activists, such as Gordon Douglas, a painter from Shell's Dunlin, echoed the feeling that OILC should 'leave well alone'. Among a vociferous minority of the committee, it was felt that since industrial stoppages were anyway inevitable, the men should be left to build up as much financial reserves from overtime working as possible. But from Rab Kemp, an electrician with Press on the Beryl Alpha, came a different view:

> *We* must take the initiative ... we've lost it to some extent with the 11.7 per cent [imposed wage rise]. It has to be *us*, the workers in the North Sea, not the oil companies or the Department of Energy, that stops the overtime.

Jamie Jamieson, a leading OILC activist on the Claymore, also called for a ban on working more than twelve hours. Another worker derisively remarked, 'Twelve hours ... for fuck's sake, I thought eight hours was enough for anybody!' With this division of opinion, it was clear that implementing the overtime ban on 1 April would be premature. The acute dilemma this posed for the OILC was articulated by Ronnie McDonald at a subsequent mass meeting. Said McDonald, 'If we do set a date and the men don't respond, we expose our weakness. But we're getting to that stage of the campaign where we can't fudge issues any more.'[19]

In the midst of this uncertainty, a sinister episode intruded which had the potential of undermining the credibility of the OILC's safety-oriented campaign. Jamie Jamieson, who had been a vocal critic of poor safety procedures, was taken off the Claymore in handcuffs by the Grampian police, accused of a serious act of attempted sabotage. A bolt had been found left in a gas compression unit. The operator of the Claymore, Occidental, now facing intense public scrutiny in the ongoing Cullen inquiry into the Piper Alpha disaster, decided to call in the police. All those working on the module were interviewed, including Jamieson, a mechanical fitter and safety representative, who had previously been NRB'd as a 'troublemaker'. No evidence could be found against Jamieson. Occidental, in the interim, issued a press statement suggesting 'the presence of someone on board the platform who has no respect for the safety of his fellow workers' and speaking of 'a deliberate act'.[20] The following day, the Scottish tabloid press carried the headline 'Sabotage Bid by Rig Maniac'.[21] Next day, Jamieson was released without charge from gaol in Aberdeen, and Occidental were unable to prevent him being allowed back offshore. Even before Jamieson had been physically removed by the police, a spontaneous sit-in in his support had begun among the men offshore.

Elsewhere across the North Sea, low level harassment of OILC activists continued. Joe Morran, a credentialled engineering union shop steward with Press on the Beryl Bravo, was removed from the contract for collecting money for OILC. On Sedco drilling rigs, the *Blowout* itself was banned. Any activists 'caught' selling it were threatened with being 'run off' the platform. Yet, if the North Sea was in a state of undeclared war, the problem of when to begin hostilities lay as much with the OILC. Attendances at mass meetings were still noticeably down when compared with the build-up to industrial action during the spring of 1989. The leadership among the key activists, meanwhile, remained divided over the pace of escalation.

The unease offshore caused by the overtime ban led to the issue being left in abeyance. Now even experienced offshore activists like Willie Stevenson on the Brent Charlie were conceding that 'the guys didn't want to know'. Rab Kemp reiterated the view that 'it's only a hard core that wants to work the [contractual minimum] twelve hours to get things kicked off'.[22] Gordon Douglas pointed out that some men were still working 'three-weekers' and more if they could get it – people who ought to be regarded as 'job thieves'. The majority of the workforce had yet to be won over to participate in the overtime ban through patient argument and explanation. It was to take several months in the spring of 1990, of continuous shuttling between weekly OILC mass meetings in Aberdeen, Glasgow, Newcastle and Liverpool, before Ronnie McDonald's and the majority view of the committee on the necessity of the implementation of the overtime ban was to prevail among the offshore workforce. By the late spring the decision over when to act on the question of overtime simply could not be postponed any longer if OILC was to retain any credibility as an organizing force.

The National Offshore Committee

It was in the midst of this ongoing debate that the door of the Glasgow AEU hall opened and Bill Morris, then assistant general secretary of the powerful TGWU, mounted the platform to address the unofficial OILC mass meeting. His arrival was something of a surprise, as this was the first time a national officer of such standing had appeared at an OILC meeting. Morris was in Glasgow attending the annual conference of the STUC, and had taken time out to convey the support of his union for the offshore workers' struggle. A meeting of the national officials of all the unions with an offshore interest had taken place in London the previous day, resulting in the formation of a National Offshore Committee. Jim Airlie, Scottish executive councilman of the AEU, Tom MacLean, national secretary of the AEU's construction section (after Baldwin), Paul Bevis and Hector Barlow, national officials of the EETPU, Jim McFall of the GMB, Fred Higgs from the TGWU, Keith Sneddon of MSF, together with the local union officials and OILC representatives, had met and endorsed the final draft of the Continental Shelf Agreement. A 'one-table approach' had at last been put in place. When the national officials met again on 8 May, all levels of the trade union movement seemed to be heading in the same direction – national officials, local officials, the unofficial OILC and the offshore workers. At the meeting on 8 May, a press statement was issued:

> The National Officials reaffirm support for an objective of a Continental Shelf Agreement to cover terms and conditions of all employees engaged in offshore work. To this end we will not conclude any agreement that does not encompass these principles.[23]

No individual union would negotiate an agreement which did not encompass the principle of a Continental Shelf Agreement unless approved by the National Offshore Committee. This position was endorsed by the six major unions involved – the AEU, GMB, MSF, EETPU, TGWU and NUS. This meeting had seen some tough talking by seasoned campaigners such as Jimmy Airlie. Airlie, ever the realist, outlined what might be a possible 'fall-back position'. 'There will come a time', Airlie reportedly said, 'when you can't hold it together; we have got to know so that something can be salvaged out of it'. There was to be no 'bullshit'. The national officers were to be kept fully informed. Tom MacLean, as secretary of the National Offshore Committee, would liaise daily with local officials and OILC. The National Offshore Committee would now meet on a regular basis, if necessary at short notice. The officials had now delivered their side of the bargain. The rest was up to the OILC; it had to deliver industrial action offshore.

Unity and Disunity in the Ranks

Among the national officers who had endorsed the Continental Shelf Agreement, there had been a surprising degree of unanimity. The same could not be said of the OILC. An impromptu meeting of some half-dozen leading members of the Standing Committee took place as various individuals were waiting to go offshore at Sumburgh airport in Shetland. What was thereafter known as the 'Sumburgh Convention' decided to reverse the overtime ban decision of the previous OILC Standing Committee. Confusion reigned offshore as a result. OILC, as an acitivist organization, was failing to provide a clear lead to the workforce, and it showed in the lack of unity offshore. A worker from the Beryl Bravo described events on his platform: 'They voted to implement the ban and [yet] guys were running up to the foremen asking for a transfer. This was immediately *after* they had voted in a meeting for the overtime ban!'[24]

From the Brent Charlie came another disturbing report from a worker who had just returned onshore that day:

> The night shift had an overtime ban but the day shift shop stewards wouldn't even come to a joint meeting. They're making excuses. The way to get action out there, is to have a show of hands – a lot of people are going to have to be embarrassed into this action.

One platform, the Tern, had had a meeting and voted unanimously to implement the ban on overtime. But it was the only one, out of 42 fixed installations in the northern sector, to have done so. For the first time, there were heated disagreements at OILC mass meetings. It was graphically summed up by one worker, an old-timer from the shipyards:

> I come up to a lot of these meetings and I've heard a lot of boys talking ... 'Wood Group ... the union ... You're not fighting Wood Group or the union. It's the men you're fighting against because half of them buggers don't want to know nothing, or the first thing they say is, 'Where's the ham?' [overtime][25]

In the last week of April and early May, however, the ban on overtime began to be instituted on a more widespread basis, particularly on Shell's Eider, Tern, North Cormorant and Dunlin platforms. Differences in the OILC committee, which had impeded the implementation of the overtime ban, were finally resolved. Conflicting messages were no longer being taken offshore. Yet resistance to OILC's proposed action, and even to regular financial levies, still existed among small groups such as the Brent Delta Wood Group electricians, although on the whole support in the northern sector was becoming increasingly solid. Paradoxically, the Brent Delta electricians with Wood Group were outside the SJIB and thus had much to gain in the longer term from the proposed Continental Shelf Agreement. There was an absence of shop stewards and a lack of leadership among that group. Where there was united and effective offshore leadership, the potential for action could at last be seen, and this was reflected in steadily rising numbers of workers at OILC mass meetings during the month of May. An index of growing support for OILC was the increasing level of financial contributions coming in on a daily basis from offshore. By April 1990, in the sixteen months since OILC had been formed, £63,000 had been donated to the OILC fighting fund. Platforms which had lain dormant over the winter now began organizing regular collections and distributing *Blowout* football cards and issues of *Blowout*. On an increasing number of installations, men were pre-pared to allow themselves to be elected as 'spokespersons', although they were not willing to act as fully credentialled shop stewards. The reluctance to make the extra step from informal to formal lay union representative, was a matter of concern, since it would be easier to protect activists who were also *bona fide* union shop stewards. This remained a weakness in trade union workplace level organization offshore. Even among TGWU and NUS shop stewards in catering, there was a considerable turnover among those who were elected. While 60 or 70 men and women could be assembled for a shop stewards' mass meeting, it was clear that a good many of them had only the briefest acquain-tance with organized trade unionism. None of the other unions had devel-oped a durable offshore shop steward structure.

The War of Words

By the end of May, the contractors faced some form of workforce overtime restriction on over two dozen platforms. On behalf of the Offshore Contrac-tors Council (OCC), the body representing the contractor employers, David Odling issued the first of many press statements: 'The majority of offshore employees are well-satisfied with their new terms and conditions of employ-ment, but are being misled by false statements being circulated by a minority.'[26]

The war of words began in earnest. For the past three weeks, the contrac-tor employers had seen the OILC overtime ban spread across the North Sea from platform to platform. In the Brent field, Shell's Cormorant Alpha, North Cormorant, Eider, Tern and Dunlin were affected within the first week. By the end of the second week, Conoco's Murchison, Chevron's Ninian South, BP's Thistle and Arbroath, the Amoco Montrose and Mobil's Beryl Alpha were hit. By the third week in May, support for the ban was coming from BP's Forties field and the overtime action was beginning to take on a comprehensive character. Industry analysts started to speak of the action as being 'more than an insignificant local dispute'.[27] Predictions were that the overtime ban could actually help to firm up oil prices, which were already expected to rise in the later part of the year. Therefore it was expected that higher revenues would be generated from the oil still being produced. It was noted with respect to future start-ups, 'the gain is unlikely to offset the addi-tional cost incurred by any delays'. Claims by BP and Shell Expro that 'the action had not had any effect on operations', while technically correct, did not reflect the real gravity of the long-term situation they faced in complet-ing maintenance work and bringing the oil back on-stream.[28]

There were still minor pockets of resistance to the overtime ban until well into May. The discussion offshore on the Safe Felicia's flotel in the Forties had been lengthy and acrimonious before industrial action was agreed. While the Ninian Southern had a united contractor workforce, on the Southern and Central Ninians, electricians working for APG and Lassalles, and catering workers in the Ninian field, had been reluctant to take action. Again, the Brent Delta electricians remained unwilling to participate in a dispute which they thought might erode their differentials. On the Claymore, the workforce spokesmen were coming under pressure from the contract foremen, warning that the contract was due for renegotiation and would be endangered by the overtime ban. Only on one platform, BP's Maureen, had a meeting rejected the call for a ban on overtime outright. On the Kittiwake, the Tartan, the Magnus, the Braes, Hutton TLP and perhaps half a dozen others, however, no meetings whatsoever had been held to discuss taking action. Nevertheless, by the beginning of June, 27 platforms had implemented the overtime ban, covering the majority of the key northern North Sea installations.

Despite these local difficulties, industrial action slowly gathered momentum. Good attendances at the OILC mass meetings were now reported, not just in Glasgow, where the majority of the workforce were concentrated, but also in Hull, Aberdeen and Liverpool, which remained important regional centres throughout the dispute. In the words of Jim Fleming, one of the previous doubters, 'There are vibrations from the "bears" that they're keen to get back offshore and "do the business". We're on the right track now.'

Among the workforce there was growing unity which was reflected in improved co-ordination between official and unofficial levels. Jake Boyle from the Cormorant Alpha summed up the change of mood among activists in the workforce, particularly those previously disenchanted with the established unions – 'We need to bury the hatchet with the officials'. Others remained bitterly hostile to the union officials, including such influential figures on the OILC Standing Committee as Neil Rothnie, editor of *Blowout*. Rothnie, a graduate in sociology from the University of Aberdeen, had worked offshore as a mud engineer on drilling rigs. Rothnie's abiding suspicion of union officials was primarily based on his far-Left political convictions. The officials were an obstacle to industrial action. Hostility towards the unions still resonated with the views of many offshore workers, who found easy identification with OILC as the most immediate vehicle for their aspirations. OILC, for many, was all the 'union' they needed. Time and again, the pro-union loyalists on the Standing Committee, like John Padden of the pro-TUC breakaway electricians' union, the EPIU, had to protest about the 'union-bashing syndrome' which seemed to characterize many OILC meetings. In the eyes of the offshore workers, for the time being, the established unions were 'on probation'. Should they be seen to fail again, then the demand for a single offshore industrial union, always just below the surface, would be quickly resurrected.

The IUOOC Changes its Constitution

Official and unofficial union movements were now working in tandem. Strategy and tactics were worked out in common. The official union movement had even made an attempt to involve the OILC in its structures. In December 1989 the IUOOC changed its constitution, for the first time, to make provision for unofficial (lay) union representatives. One co-option was Ronnie McDonald in his role as manager of the Offshore Information Centre, OILC's research arm. This put the OILC on the IUOOC in all but name. Two days later, UKOOA cancelled the scheduled regular quarterly meeting between its Employment Practices Committee Liaison Panel and the IUOOC, on the grounds that they were not prepared to accept the presence of lay delegates or co-opted members. The introduction of lay and co-opted delegates to the existing consultative arrangements was unacceptable to UKOOA, because it could have been understood as a tacit form of recognition of OILC as a legitimate union organization.

While there was some resentment at what was seen as an attempt by UKOOA to 'interfere in our constitution', the view of Tommy Lafferty as the IUOOC secretary was brutally frank as he turned to his colleague Eddie Bree of the Boilermakers: 'I think it's absolutely true, Eddie, that neither your union or my union would be greatly upset if these meetings that take place four times a year are cancelled.'[29] Eddie Bree was even more forthright: 'I've said it before, we should not be going because all we ever get out of it is a free meal and a free drink, and that's all we've ever had out of fifteen years of meeting UKOOA.' As Bree put it, these meetings were elaborate 'window dressing'. It allowed UKOOA to go to the government and argue that a formal trade union agreement was not necessary, as 'we've talked to the trade unions in Aberdeen'. Other unions, however, were much more cautious in their appraisal. For the EETPU, the issue went to the heart of their membership of the IUOOC. Following their forced withdrawal from the TUC for membership poaching, the EETPU were excluded from all other joint forums. Therefore the EETPU fought to preserve their right to participate with the other unions in the offshore industry, both on the Health and Safety Executive's (HSE) Oil Industry Advisory Committee (OIAC) concerned with safety matters, and on the IUOOC.

A specially convened sub-committee of UKOOA and IUOOC failed to resolve the issue to the satisfaction of either side. This posed a dilemma for the IUOOC. UKOOA had already cancelled the scheduled May 1990 meeting and was now threatening to terminate all future meetings. Some members of IUOOC argued that there had been benefits from the contacts in the past. Campbell Reid, former MSF organizer in Aberdeen, pointed out that trade union representation on the Offshore Petroleum Industry Training Board (OPITB) was increased from one to four, with UKOOA's agreement, through their joint contacts. Bob Eadie of the EETPU recalled the previous help the IUOOC had obtained from UKOOA over the Phoenix catering episode. Individual unions, such as his own, said Eadie, would retain links with UKOOA, if necessary on a separate basis. Roger Spiller of MSF, was equally adamant that participation in joint discussions with UKOOA was useful. At the last meeting of the HSE's OIAC, for example, IUOOC representatives had succeeded in forcing UKOOA to admit publicly their view that one standby vessel per installation was not necessary. This was a highly contentious safety issue. Moreover, said Spiller, the joint meetings provided an opportunity to talk to the oil companies collectively about the contractors. Operators such as Conoco and Amoco, who had refused to meet MSF as an individual union, could be faced with applications for recognition via the IUOOC through the Memorandum of Understanding. There would be even more severe difficulties, in terms of both recognition claims and offshore visits, if joint discussions with UKOOA were terminated. Even though UKOOA always claimed they could not speak on behalf of individual companies, Spiller argued, this had usually 'been got around' at their joint meetings.

UKOOA's position was that they would only meet full-time officers of *bona fide* trade unions in any future discussions. IUOOC had to decide whether or not to exclude the lay delegates. The motion 'for', was moved by MSF and seconded by the EETPU. These two unions voted to concede to UKOOA, while the rest, including the AEU and TGWU, voted against. The EETPU official, Bob Eddie, made a hasty and dramatic exit from the meeting.[30] Roger Spiller commented sadly, 'I think frankly we have a problem. This committee has disintegrated'. Spiller's irritation summed up the disarray in the affairs of IUOOC at the very moment when it should have been operating at a high level of organization, including acting as a key link between the offshore workforce and the National Offshore Committee in the developing industrial dispute.

The COTA Ingredient

Tommy Lafferty, the local official of the engineering union, had attempted to increase pressure on the operators. He had refused to negotiate a new site agreement with Mobil and Shell, covering onshore construction work at the St Fergus terminal and the Mossmorran refinery, until the 'offshore problem' was resolved. From the NUS, however, there was a continuing note of caution. The COTA employers had told the workforce offshore that a wage rise was in the offing. All that was required was for the officials 'to come in and negotiate'. This was an attempt by the employers to encourage union members to pressure union officials to settle grievances on an individual sectional level, thereby detaching this part of the workforce from the escalating broader campaign. Local TGWU and NUS officials restated their fears that the employers 'could trump us with an agreement which divides us'.[31] While there was consensus on the broad strategy of the Continental Shelf Agreement at national level, local officials still had to clarify the tactical issues involved. Was the Continental Shelf Agreement simply a long-term objective for two or three years hence, or the immediate goal? How far should the various unions' approach be 'incremental'? Would a COTA deal with 'nearly everything that was in the Continental Shelf Agreement' be acceptable? What ensued was a fierce argument between John Taylor of NUS and Ronnie McDonald of OILC, representing polar positions. All the diplomatic skills of Roger Spiller of MSF were deployed to smooth over rather deep cracks of mutual suspicion which had appeared. As Spiller put it:

> There's no problem negotiating with COTA providing it is on the basis of the Continental Shelf Agreement. If I were negotiating with COTA I would say, 'We want to talk to you about an agreement that covers all catering staff. Are you able to talk about that?' If they say 'No', you can go back to your members and say they're not prepared to talk about the members on other platforms. That seems to me to generate solidarity. If they say they can negotiate an agreement that will be used in all the tendering processes and only companies party to this agreement will be permitted to tender to the oil companies, then great![32]

When the TGWU and NUS finally met with COTA, the employers professed they had no mandate to discuss the Continental Shelf Agreement with the unions. Union recognition, they said, could only be given on a company-by-company basis. The COTA arrangement was, therefore, not signed by the unions, although the talks dragged on until July before they were finally suspended. To have met the objectives of the Continental Shelf Agreement, COTA rates would have had to be extended to the southern sector and would have had to include the drilling sector, both demands which had long been resisted by the employers. The eventual COTA offer to increase wages on certain clients' platforms only, was seen by the unions as a divisive attempt to create a 'two-tier' wage structure. This was firmly rejected. Some observers suspected, however, that the COTA talks dragged on as long as they did because the TGWU and NUS were pursuing their own strategy of maximizing their bargaining leverage in a period of general industrial unrest offshore. Whether the TGWU and NUS were really committed to the Continental Shelf Agreement remained to be seen.

The Employers

The 11.7 per cent pay rise imposed by the employers in April on the engineering construction workforce had been the first evidence that the employers were responding to the threat of future industrial action. Among the operators BP and Shell led the way in underwriting the pay rise for contractor employees on their platforms. UKOOA's formal position, and the view of individual operators, was that the issue of union recognition was a matter for contractors to sort out with their own employees. The contractors' organization repeated their claim 'to be under pressure from the clients not to conclude national deals'.[33] Clem Cooke, the chairman of OCPCA, the parent body of the Offshore Contractors Council, pleaded for the offshore clients to 'get their act together'. Cooke, the construction director of contracting giant Kellog, had suggested that 'anarchy' could prevail if there was not a single agreement covering both North Sea hook-up and post-construction maintenance work. Such breaking of ranks, however, was only momentary and nothing more was heard of the proposal for such a comprehensive agreement. The client oil operators ensured that both they and the contractors maintained a united front, in public at least, for the duration of the 1990 dispute. In private, the situation was different.

A letter from John R. Milligan, Managing Director of the major offshore contractor Atlantic Power & Gas (APG), to I. J. Hardy, BP's field group manager of northern operations, spelled out the resentment of the contractors towards the operators. This resulted from the decision by Shell and BP to sanction the 11.7 per cent increase.[34] The letter from APG described a meeting attended along with other maintenance contractors at BP's Dyce office in Aberdeen at which ongoing discussions between Shell and BP and a number of contractors were discussed. It stated:

> The net result was that the assembled gathering were presented with a proposal whereby Shell and BP agreed to underwrite substantial increases to the hourly rates and benefits packages of offshore labour force and chargehands ... to pre-empt and extinguish foreseen industrial unrest which was being mooted by the OILC for the 1990 summer shutdown period ...
>
> Unfortunately, having taken on-board the rates payment to the men and honoured our commitment in good faith, we now find that the initial indications given by BP covering reimbursement would appear to have been retracted ...

APG complained of 'an erosion in our net return as a percentage of our turnover, and this has adversely affected our performance and trading power with our banks'. The final section concluded:

> We would also, with the benefit of hindsight, question the wisdom of the decision to award free *gratis* substantial increases to the workforce, since it appears to have strengthened their resolve for unionisation rather than to quash a dispute as was envisaged at the time.

This resentment of contractors, at having to bear the costs of the pre-emptive increase, was heightened by the fact that it seemed merely to have worsened the developing industrial unrest. It indicated a sharp divergence of interest between client and contractor, when a real threat of union pressure was exerted.

The Operators

It was Shell's intention to discredit the OILC campaign through the sensitive issue of safety. Shell would argue that industrial action threatened refurbishment and safety upgrading work, in particular the installation of platform emergency shutdown valves. OILC turned this argument back on Shell. These platform safety valves, OILC noted, were not being fitted at the recommendation of the Cullen Inquiry, which at that time had not yet presented its final report. The issue of subsea safety valves was an entirely different one from Shell's installation of platform emergency shutdown valves. The platform shutdown valves in question were those to be located topside, at the pipeline–platform interface above the waterline. The need for these valves had been identified by the Burgoyne Committee back in the late 1970s. For cost reasons, for the rest of the decade this recommendation was not implemented by the operators. Because of the absence of such platform safety valves, the Tartan platform fed the Piper Alpha inferno on the night of the disaster. Now the operators had until 31 December to install them but in fact they had already had ten years in which remedial measures could have been taken.

Shell not only conducted its war of words in the media. In addition, it battled against the unions on the installations where the workforce's opinions were critical. A typical memo from the Tern Installation Manager, headed 'Unofficial Overtime Ban', made the following points.[35] First, it was pointed out that although management had permitted a mass meeting to take place on the platform 'this was in no way a recognition of OILC as a negotiating body on your behalf'. Second, it stated that OILC was not recognized by the company 'since it is not a *bona fide* union' and that the company, therefore, had no agreement with it. Third, workers were told that the vote for the overtime ban which was taken on a show of hands, 'cannot be considered to be democratic or to represent the total Contract Staff'. Accordingly, said the memo, contractor employees 'may not wish to participate in any action', particularly those coming onto the platform as part of a crew change. Should anyone wish to work 'reasonable overtime', there must be 'no intimidation or pressure put on him not to work'. This, the memo said, was agreed to by the OILC spokesperson who 'would not wish to be part of any form of intimidation'. For those who wished to work 'within the Department of Energy Guidelines', overtime would be available. Finally, 'where work is safety related' Shell expected 'no-one would object to working additional hours'. A number of other installation managers likewise attempted to pressurize the men into working overtime on the grounds that the work required was 'safety-related'.

In order to isolate OILC influence from the workers, the operators tried to appear receptive to workforce concerns. Ian Henderson, the Aberdeen-based head of Shell, embarked on two extended three-day trips to assess the mood offshore. Henderson had held face-to-face discussions with some of the 'bears' in the tea-shacks, which had resulted in what could diplomatically be described as 'a frank exchange of views'. In one session, the men were asked to put their grievances to him. What followed was a series of sharp questions and exchanges. Why was Shell against the Continental Shelf Agreement when onshore they were party to industry-wide agreements covering engineering construction work? Why could contractors' personnel not have the same security of employment and conditions of work as Shell's own employees?

Why did the operators prevent the contractors signing a post-construction agreement with the unions in 1989? Were the employers planning the use of cheap foreign labour to undercut existing terms and conditions? Why was the Health and Safety at Work Act not fully implemented offshore? Why were safety representatives not permitted to attend STUC-run training courses? Was there any truth in the assertion that Shell would apply for a government 'dispensation' on any uncompleted safety work, particularly on the shutdown valves, allegedly resulting from industrial action? The 'bears' remained unconvinced by this exercise in 'dialogue'. The constant schooling of the OILC mass meetings had produced an educated, conscious and combative workforce. The growing confidence of the workforce, and their ability to challenge management arguments, became a new element in the confrontation which management had not expected. Such day-to-day challenges were the chisel edge of the campaign.

A One-day Stoppage?

Having initiated the overtime ban, against some resistance, the OILC committee now faced the prospect of having to sustain it over a much longer period than had originally been anticipated. This posed difficulties for several reasons. Overtime payments for helicopter shuttling time for some individuals could amount to an additional twenty hours per week. If the 'shuttlers' were to 'lose money' they wanted assurance that 'everyone else is also losing money'.[36] For this reason, on some platforms the overtime ban was becoming a matter of dissension. Activists on the OILC Standing Committee began to call for an early day of action, a stoppage, as a 'show of strength'. Construction and catering workers would strike together and their new-found unity could consolidate. Tom Brady estimated that the overtime ban would only hold perhaps another two weeks. During the discussion, Jim Fleming had a cautious estimate of the impact of a stoppage: 'This one day stoppage is a gamble – they [the operators] might ride it out, but they might say "let's get it over and done with now and then get on with the shutdown".' McDonald argued that the workers had certain tactical strengths in a stoppage despite the danger of an employer lock-out:

> The lock-out is their most effective weapon. That's where the catering workers come in, from our point of view. If they use the big stick and go for a wipe-out [mass dismissals] they've immediately got the catering workers on their back. So platforms that would otherwise be producing will be shut down.

May 23 was mooted as a new Shell pipeline maintenance shutdown date. Hence, any earlier stoppage was unwelcome. The message to the mass meetings was clear: 'Don't jump the gun. Don't do your own thing without consulting [the committee]. They'll try to make us shoot our bolt.'[37] Such warnings were not sufficient to prevent a spate of rumours sweeping the North Sea that a stoppage was imminent. OILC had to counter rumours which, more often than not, operated in a disruptive manner. The men had to be persuaded to look to the OILC as the source of authoritative information, to telephone the office in Aberdeen, 'if they wanted to find out what was really going on'. The mass meetings were the most important channel of communication with the workforce. The *Blowout* was another. The discipline and cohesion of the industrial action was to be sustained by direct daily telephone contact between the OILC office in Aberdeen and the activists out on the offshore installations. As early as the second week in May, BP had already put in place the means to automatically block certain telephone numbers and had isolated the Safe Felicia accommodation barge or 'flotel' from contact with the OILC office. In these circumstances, rumour tended to do much damage to the workers' co-ordinated action. Rumours, however, also caused a degree of havoc among the employers. Tommy Lafferty reported receiving calls from three major contractors during the last week of May asking about 'the strike called for tomorrow'.[38] The contractors were becoming jumpy and the men were getting impatient. Then suddenly the phoney war was over. On the Beryl Alpha, Press Offshore dismissed 107 employees in a 'wipe-out' of the entire contractor workforce.

The Beryl Alpha 'Wipe-out' Incident

The Beryl Alpha episode typified the daily problems that arose in offshore industrial relations. A night-shift worker had 'knocked off' early and retired to his cabin to sleep. When discovered by a chargehand, not the man's own supervisor, the individual in question had been issued with a written disciplinary warning, or 'white-lettered'. The worker admitted his offence but the men on his shift, among whom this particular chargehand was already unpopular, felt there had been a 'dig out', an element of victimization. The men downed tools in a two-hour protest. They were immediately suspended and then dismissed by the contractor, Press Offshore, and flown off the platform. The operator, Mobil, subsequently suspended the contract with Press Offshore. The next day, Press Offshore sacked those on leave, the 'back-to-backs', on the grounds that 'custom and practice is that decisions taken by workers offshore apply to the men onshore'.[39] There was much ribald speculation as to what the back-to-backs might have been doing onshore at the precise moment of their dismissal. In addition, seventeen men were sacked who were fog-bound in Stavanger and could not reach the installation. The punitive element in the action of the contractor caused shock and anger among the workforce. Such a move by an employer was unprecedented, even in North Sea industrial relations. Subsequently, the dismissals of the back-to-backs were withdrawn. The men were to be transferred to a new contractor on the Beryl Alpha, APG, or be made redundant. This was small comfort to the men, some of whom had accumulated as much as ten years continuous service with Press Offshore.

Bewildered and slightly embarrassed members of the dismissed Beryl Alpha workforce trooped into the OILC Aberdeen office. They recognized that they had been victims of an employer provocation which could well have escalated prematurely into a wider North Sea confrontation. OILC characterized the incident as a local dispute. It did not require the mobilization of widespread sympathetic action. For OILC, it was a matter of 'keeping the powder dry'.

The Beryl Alpha dispute typified the growing combativeness of the employers. The situation on the Beryl Alpha had been tense for some time, especially over safety issues. The workforce had complained that the continuation of oil and gas production while welding and other 'hot jobs' were being carried out jeopardized safety. There had been a number of incidents, including at least one fire, during which workers alleged the platform alarm systems had failed to function.[40] The 'white-letter' incident seems to have been the last straw. The failure on the part of the platform workforce leadership was in not consulting with OILC leadership before taking action. In part this was due to inexperience, something for which the Beryl workforce could not be held entirely to blame. There had been a history of union activists being removed from that installation as soon as they became known to the management. Mick Gibbons, a prominent OILC activist, was the most recent to have been 'fingered' on Beryl Alpha. He had successfully taken his case for wrongful dismissal to an Industrial Tribunal.

What had occurred on the Beryl Alpha was a spontaneous reaction to managerial high-handedness. The response of Press Offshore was a clear indication that the employers intended to take a tough line against any future industrial unrest. A letter issued to the workforce by the company, urged the majority to stand up against the 'intimidation' and 'misrepresentations' of 'the small minority of militants'.[41] All contract supervision on Shell's Brent Delta, Brent Charlie, Dunlin Alpha and Cormorant Alpha received an urgent and confidential briefing from Press Offshore head office detailing the events on the Beryl Alpha. The briefing observed that 'it is our intention to apply the same approach to any withdrawal of labour for whatever reason on any other installation'.[42] Supervisors were asked to 'emphasise the futility of any similar action' and to remind the workforce 'that the overtime ban is now losing support', and that their earnings 'are being affected by a minority influence'. Briefing notes for Press Offshore supervisors had spelled out the 'consequences of escalation of industrial action'.[43]

> Contractors and Operators are not prepared to tolerate disruption, particularly the type which occurred in 1989. Employees considering this type of action should be advised to consider the possibility that the Company, if forced to carry through dismissals, cannot be selective and will not re-engage within three months to comply with the legislation.

By dismissing the entire workforce for a twelve-week period, without selectively re-employing any of their number, an employer could avoid claims for unfair dismissal at an Industrial Tribunal. It was a provocative tactic, seeking to exploit a loophole in the employment protection legislation only rarely resorted to by employers in the UK industrial relations scene. Such action was drastic and would necessitate the recruitment of an entirely new 'replacement' workforce (should the employer wish to resume activity prior to the expiry of the twelve-week period). Any replacement workforce would, in all likelihood, have to be non-union. With this strategy for the suppression of industrial action, a determined employer could create havoc merely by exploiting existing employment law. This was graphically illustrated a few years later, during the bitter Timex strike in Dundee (Miller and Woolfson, 1994). This threat confirmed a hardening of employer attitudes which extended to the onshore fabrication side of the industry as well. The company had dismissed the entire shop stewards committee at Press's Tyneside yard earlier in the spring. The workforce, preparing for the Kittiwake 'skid-out', had been involved in a local dispute. After the removal of the stewards, a strike ensued. The company proceeded to import strike-breakers to the yard. Apparently, the existence of a 'Manpower Services Manager' at Press Offshore did not signify any greater sophistication in their employee relations techniques. The dismissed Beryl Alpha men, meanwhile, were able to pick up work with other contractors, eager to employ them because of the shortage of skilled labour.

The final twist to the saga of the Beryl Alpha came a few days later, when a 'deep throat' within the company organization contacted OILC. Press Offshore, it was alleged, was using a labour-recruitment agency, Petrology, to supply workers for the Ravenspurn hook-up in the southern sector. It was operating a selective blacklist on men from the Beryl Alpha. The informant was appalled by the actions of his own employer in victimizing men who, he felt, had done nothing wrong. Not for the first time, the blacklist featured as the secret weapon of the employers. It contradicted assurances from the client, Mobil, to the responsible national union official that the ex-Press men would be given 'preferential treatment' in hiring by the new contractor on the Beryl Alpha. In fact, APG took on a number of 'new-starts', some of whom, it was claimed, did not possess offshore survival certificates. They had been hired with the supposed tacit approval of the operator Mobil. Although not a legal requirement, the survival certificate, in line with UKOOA's own guidelines since Piper Alpha, had become a precondition for a job offshore. What Mobil now were allegedly sanctioning was a throwback to pre-Piper practices when forged survival certificates changed hands in Aberdeen pubs. APG, however, had an ingenious explanation for its practices. A survival certificate was not a normal requirement for APG personnel working offshore fewer than fifteen days per annum. One of APG's senior employees with responsibility for 'quality assessment' produced an internal memorandum noting that:

> We cannot honestly represent that anyone we send offshore is intended to do less than 15 days per annum, even with one client … The management team supported the decision to send operatives offshore without survival courses. On the basis of the above I believe this decision to be wrong.[44]

Incidents such as this seemed to confirm the credibility of OILC's view that safety offshore was still a secondary consideration.

The Media Battle: Shell under the Spotlight

Informed accessibility to journalists enabled OILC to succeed in wrongfooting the employers time after time, with seemingly disconcerting ease. For the media, OILC was the underdog, the David, facing an overbearing industrial Goliath, the multinational oil industry.

In June 1990 once again, courtesy of OILC, an embarrassing press exposé enraged the operators.[45] Under the headline 'Shell may ask for Piper safety delay', a 'disturbing new move over North Sea unrest' was detailed:

> The great Shell Oil Company is poised to ask the Government to allow delays in safety work ... including the installation of emergency shut-down valves ordered after the Piper disaster ... in order to help defeat industrial action in the North Sea this summer.

The source of the story was seven pages of confidential memoranda prepared by the Central Controller of British Gas, R. F. Francis, which had mysteriously arrived at OILC's office.[46] The subject of the memoranda was 'Potential Industrial Action Summer 1990'. That dated 8 May 1990 was from Mr Francis to his Director of Operations, one B. Heywood. British Gas was worried about the impact of industrial action on their supplies which 'might make the return of some fields from maintenance later than planned'. Shell's Brent field was identified as a 'primary target', along with the Leman and Indefatigable fields in the southern sector. Delay in restarting oil production would have an immediate effect on levels of gas production. British Gas were considering whether the completion of their own shutdown in the Rough field could be brought forward. The attached file recorded comments from the various operator suppliers to British Gas which reveal the operators' thinking. Francis reported a conversation with Tony Jarvis (TJ) of Shell management on the Brent situation:

> Shell had already offered some money to contractors and some other benefits to try and disarm the potential trouble, but the reaction had been that the topic was about safety not money. What the unions really want is safety representatives to be union representatives which would of course give the unions power to shut down platforms etc. TJ assured me that Shell were working on contingency plans to overcome any problems but would not give any commitment on the risks of action.

For Shell, the perception of the OILC campaign was not about money, but about trade union power, using safety as a pretext. Norwegian suppliers to British Gas in the Frigg field had suggested to British Gas that:

> the Shell delay on their Brent system shutdown could be strategic rather than technical, i.e. they hope that someone else will take the brunt of the industrial action and they hope that it will be settled before the Brent shutdown.

This seemed to confirm a growing suspicion among offshore activists that Shell were actually delaying the Brent shutdown, in the hope that when industrial action came, the company would not be in the front line. Hamilton Brothers, the operator of the Ravenspurn North in the southern sector, claimed to British Gas to 'have spent considerable sums refurbishing accommodation, paying particular attention to catering and entertaining facilities to keep the workforce sweet'.

This hook-up was being run by Press Offshore from Aberdeen, with a mainly northern contractor labour force. One of the 'bears', upon reading this company claim, remarked with disbelief, 'I must be on a different hook-up'.[47]

Two weeks later, an internal British Gas memorandum from Mr Francis to a Mr Dixon, the British Gas Plant Operation Engineer, was definite that the Rough field shutdown must be brought forward in order to secure future continuity of gas supplies in case industrial action took place.[48] A further confidential note from Mr Francis to Mr Heywood, Director of Operations, reported on his annual meeting with Shell's industrial relations specialist in May.[49] It carried a résumé of Shell's views on the background to the current dispute:

> Late in 1989 the OCC (Offshore Contractors Council) agreed to embrace a 'post production' agreement. This agreement had been drafted to extend the present Hook-up and construction agreement into maintenance and modification work. In January 1990 UKOOA decided not to support this agreement.

Here, at last, was firm proof that what had prevented the contractors from endorsing a post-construction agreement was direct pressure from the operators. It confirmed that a comprehensive agreement for 'post construction' had been within the workforce's grasp in the previous year. The British Gas note revealed the company's hopes that the April 1990 imposed wage increase, in Shell's words, 'might drive a wedge between the men and the unions, if the unions attempted to press further'. Shell's forecast for the rest of the summer of 1990 was for 'sporadic guerilla type action' rather than 'all-out strikes'. The company, however, had taken precautions in arranging its programme of work:

> to ensure that major items of plant are taken out of action in such a way that should there be overall strike action, they can put that plant back to work and still produce after the summer. However, this might involve asking the Department of Energy to defer some of the post-Piper Alpha work. Shell believe that the Department of Energy might be more sympathetic to this than perhaps they have indicated in the past.

Shell were also taking steps 'to ensure that key offshore personnel such as helideck attendants are if possible isolated from the situation'. Thus, strategically important sections of the workforce were, if possible, to be insulated from the activists.

In the context of the threatened industrial action, operators such as Shell now expected that deferral of safety work be relatively easily solicited from a sympathetic Department of Energy. The storm of unfavourable publicity which these revelations raised provoked the installation manager on Shell's Dunlin Alpha to issue his own statement to platform personnel. He explicitly denied that the deferral of safety work was being used by the company as a tactic to paint the workforce in a bad light:

> It would be irresponsible for Shell not to take account of the various scenarios, technical and otherwise, that might unfold over the summer, and perfectly understandable that British Gas and the Department of Energy should both be interested.[50]

The British Gas memorandum of 22 May, by contrast, indicated 'real concern on gas production in the autumn'. Industrial action could contribute to problems in this respect, together with complex interrelated technical problems the operators faced in the Brent field.

By the autumn of 1990 the Brent Charlie would have been out of action for eighteen months. Bringing it back on stream would be 'virtually recommissioning a new platform', said the British Gas memorandum. In addition, Brent Bravo had 'commissioning' difficulties. Brent Alpha, which collects gas from the Bravo, Charlie and Delta, pumps it on to the Cormorant Alpha from where it is piped to the Sullom Voe terminal. The Brent Alpha was subject to shut down, as was the Cormorant Alpha, thus cutting off this major export route to the mainland. With the Ninian system feeding oil to Sullom Voe also due to close, this meant that by the autumn, the bulk of UK oil would have to be tanker loaded rather than piped ashore directly. Crucial would be the Brent Spar tanker loading facility linked to the Brent Bravo and the Auk. As Shell indicated in the British Gas memorandum, the problem was

> that during October and November gas production to some extent depends on being able to take oil from the Spar system by tanker as the oil pipeline would still be shut down. This is very weather-dependent and bad weather could limit gas production.[51]

The interdependence of gas supplies on the vagaries of oil production was one major uncertainty. In this context the prospect of industrial action further delaying recommissioning on the Brents could only exacerbate an already difficult situation for British Gas. What the documents revealed was the sheer scope of strategic planning to minimize operator vulnerability to the impact of industrial action that summer.

The Norwegian Frigg suppliers had been apportioned a critical role in emergency measures aimed at combating shortages in the UK sector. Gas from the Frigg field was exported from Norway to the UK sector, via the MCP-O1 installation, and from there to the St Fergus terminal. The Norwegian sector had already been hit by industrial action that summer. While NOPEF, the Norwegian petrochemical workers' union, had settled, OFS, the rival breakaway offshore workers' union, was still pursuing militant action until forced to suspend it by compulsory arbitration. In return for guarantees to reinstate its sacked members on Phillips' Norwegian installations, a promise had been given by the Norwegian union that the export of gas supplies to the UK would be unimpeded and, if necessary, increased over the following period to make up for any shortfall in the UK supply. Had OILC been aware of this then it could have taken steps to forge cross-national solidarity with the Norwegian offshore workers much earlier.

The Overtime Ban Runs On

Towards the end of June the overtime ban had been in place for a full month. The shutdown in the Brents, decommissioning the FLAGS line, was now delayed until the last days of July. With at least another month to go, the issue facing OILC was whether or not they could continue the overtime ban. Once again, discussion was intense inside the OILC Standing Committee and at the mass meetings. Tom Brady observed, 'a lot of the lads are either chafing at the bit and wanting all-out action or wanting back on the "ham" [overtime]'.[52] There was no doubt that however unpopular among the men, the overtime ban was causing problems for the operators. Shell had now arranged a conference with its contractors to express its concern. On the Tern it became necessary to put on a night-shift to try to circumvent the impact of the overtime action. On the North Cormorant, there was an 'up-manning' of five or six electricians for a similar reason. On the Brent Bravo, the installation manager sought permission from the OILC spokesperson, Davie Robertson, a long-time offshore activist who previously featured in the Dixilyn episode, for two men to work overtime. This request was 'regretfully' denied.

While the overtime ban had disproportionate impact on the work schedules of perhaps three or four platforms, it was having virtually no impact
on certain others. The longer the action dragged on the more it became
'frayed around the edges'. On the Brent Bravo, the scaffolders returned to
fifteen-hour working for a period. On certain key platforms, for example
both the Brae A and Brae B, the Magnus and the Beryl Bravo, there was still
no support for the ban. A signed editorial by Ronnie McDonald in the July
issue of *Blowout* conceded 'some dissatisfaction' among the 'bears' over the
'work to contract' but spelled out the implications of not maintaining support for the unofficial action:

> Those who are not participating in the 'work to contract' must be made
> aware of the potential harm they are doing to the rest of the men. They
> are signalling to management that the workforce has no backbone ...
> The issue is clear cut. If the loss of some overtime hours is deemed to be
> too high a price to pay, our fight is over now ... Did we get this far in so
> short a time, just to see it slip through our fingers on the issue of a
> couple of hours of 'ham'?[53]

One recent encouraging development was the spread of the overtime ban
to the southern sector, with contract workers on the Ravenspurn South now
voting in support.

At OILC meetings renewed discussion focused on the desirability of an
early 'day of action' in which catering and construction workers would strike
together. Several of the leading activists now voiced the fear that the strength
of the campaign was ebbing. Tommy Lafferty was particularly vociferous in
calling for early strike action. Catering workers, whose own discussions with
COTA had now reached impasse, relayed to the OILC committee that a day
of action was favoured that coming Saturday, 23 June. This added a new note
of urgency to the debate. But in the end caution prevailed and a one-day
stoppage was not called.

But within a week OILC had both called and then abandoned a further
industrial stoppage. Within the leadership, the internal pressure for industrial
action was producing vacillation. Although the earlier call for a one-day
stoppage had been resisted, details emerged of the official inauguration of
the oil industry chapel, St Nicholas in Aberdeen, at which all the operators
would be present as would HRH Princess Anne. The opening of the chapel
was intended to mark 25 years of North Sea activity. Such a jamboree seemed
too good an opportunity to miss. Late on Thursday night, 21 June, OILC
began to mobilize for a half-day stoppage on the following Sunday afternoon

to coincide with the opening ceremony. By 11.30 p.m. on Friday, thirteen platforms were ready to take action. The main problem was the Forties. Some five key activists were not offshore at that time but home on leave, which created severe problems of communication with the workforce. Faced with the prospect of staggered action, the decision was taken to call the strike off late on Friday night. OILC spokesmen offshore had to face the embarrassment of informing their platform offshore installation managers (OIMs) that previously announced stoppages would not take place after all. Widespread support from other platforms was phoned in on Saturday morning, but by that time it was too late to proceed. Press Offshore gleefully noted that it was 'heartening' that the offshore workforce 'rejected the call, which could have resulted in another futile stoppage such as occurred recently on Beryl "A" and which resulted in over 200 people being dismissed and losing their jobs'.[54] Had OILC persisted it would have had support from over eighteen platforms, an indication that when a call for industrial action was eventually issued, support would be forthcoming, even from installations which up until then had been reluctant. What was needed was the nerve and self-discipline to 'hold fire' until the right moment came for full-scale confrontation.

One further encouraging feature was the degree to which expressions of support were forthcoming from the southern sector workforce, which had been quiescent over much of the preceding four months. OILC meetings had been held in Hull, Liverpool, Lowestoft and Great Yarmouth on a regular basis, with local officials supporting and, in the case of Hull, even acting as committee secretary. Now in July, half a dozen southern platforms were preparing to join in industrial action. Strong support came from the West Sole and Indefatigable fields and from the Safe Lancelot accommodation flotel. Reports from OILC activists in the south indicated that major operators such as Amoco were now seriously worried by the industrial action.

At mass meetings in Glasgow and Aberdeen final briefings were given to the offshore workforce. Faced with the possibility of lock-outs, it was going to be difficult to find sufficient workers with enough determination to stay on the installations and, if necessary, occupy them. The lesson of the Forties events of the previous year was that it was a mistake to restrict action to sit-ins on the accommodation barges. This risked the connecting bridge to the platforms being lifted and the occupation being detached and isolated by management from the main installation. The occupations were to be peaceful. But 'if the employers come against us with intimidation and a heavy hand . . . we will be as bloody-minded and pig-headed as them', one meeting concluded.[55] Norwegian offshore workers, during their strikes, had put containers on the helideck to prevent management landing helicopters to clear the installations of occupying workers. Such an escalation was one possible scenario in the British sector.

This year, the workforce would have to act together to ensure that the implementation of industrial action would be unified. In 1989, platforms where maintenance work had required a shutdown, held two-day stoppages, while those where production continued struck for only one day. This had created divisions in the workforce. This year everyone would take one day of industrial action together. If certain platforms could not follow, then it was preferable for them to 'stay out of the action altogether' and remain at work.

Although the strikes led by the OILC would be unofficial, it had been agreed at the National Offshore Committee meeting in London on 17 July that where possible, on selected platforms, ballots would be held for official industrial action. Organizing such ballots in the absence of employer co-operation was a task of almost insuperable difficulty. Existing employment legislation attached no penalties to a company for refusing to co-operate on union balloting. By contrast, severe penalties were imposed on unions who called stoppages without first adhering to the prescribed balloting procedures. If there were to be ballots offshore, it was unclear whether they should be by installation, by contracting company, or throughout a particular field. It was, therefore, anticipated that any union ballot would take about five or six weeks to complete. Such were the difficulties the unions faced should they wished to embark on official legally-sanctioned industrial action.

Local officials of the GMB, AEU, EETPU, MSF, TGWU and NUS had attended most OILC mass meetings on a regular basis to emphasize, at least tacitly, the official unions' support. Publicly they were more guarded in their pronouncements. One possibility that the trade unions had to consider was that employers would seek injunctions, demanding that the officials produce a 'letter of repudiation' of any unofficial industrial action. There was the ultimate threat of legal sequestration of union funds should they fail to do so. As Bob Eadie of the EETPU, perhaps the most 'moderate' of all the North Sea local union officials, put it:

What I'm saying now, before any lawyer does arrive on the doorstep, is bear in mind and weigh up anything you may see like that [letter of repudiation] in the next few weeks, weigh up everything *we've* said in the past year, and I think it will be quite clear where the real sympathies and the real balance of union support lies in this matter.[56]

On the eve of industrial stoppages the opinion of local officials such as

Tommy Lafferty was that the coming strike action was going to be 'very bloody', a prediction which was to come true.

The Brent Spar

July 6 1990 marked the second anniversary of Piper Alpha. It was accompanied by mass stoppages offshore as each shift took one hour to reflect on the fate of their former colleagues. Management pressure to limit lost time was considerable. The industrial chaplain for the offshore workforce provided a special ten-minute video to be shown offshore at the end of shift. Within less than three weeks, the workforce were yet again to be tragically reminded of the hazardous nature of offshore work.

At 11 a.m. on 25 July 1990 a Sikorsky S–61, owned by Robert Maxwell's British International Helicopters, call sign G–BEWL, crashed into the North Sea with the loss of six men's lives. The Sikorsky S–61, known as the 'workhorse of the North Sea', had nineteen persons on board. It had been carrying out a normal crew change in fine weather, one of the literally dozens of daily in-field flights, in the Shell and Forties fields. This particular flight was a shuttle hop from the Polycastle accommodation barge moored alongside the Brent Alpha, where six men had disembarked, to the nearby Brent Spar tanker loading facility. As the Sikorsky approached the Brent Spar, its rear rotor blade struck the Brent Spar crane jib. The helicopter spiralled onto the helideck where it hung on the edge for a few seconds before toppling 100 feet into the sea. The crash survivors spoke of momentary relief that they were not going to tip over into the sea below.

The offshore contractor workforce immediately downed tools and stopped all work as news of the disaster came through. At Sumburgh airport in Shetland 150 workers waiting to fly out to their installations refused to board waiting helicopters. Rumours of the accident had swept the airport but Shell personnel had spoken only of 'operational delays'. Men telephoning home were told by anxious wives of news reports confirming the crash. Some forty minutes later, the workers at Sumburgh were officially informed of the situation. By this time open revolt had broken out and OILC spokespersons had taken charge of an impromptu airport mass meeting. Of those assembled at Sumburgh, only twenty direct employees of Shell continued their onward journey by helicopter. Ian Henderson, Shell's troubleshooter, had flown post-haste from Aberdeen to allay the men's fears. Severely chastened by the angry workers, he later conceded to the press, 'I take the personal blame . . . We failed miserably to keep our people informed'.[57]

Since the Chinook disaster, helicopter travel had been regarded as a particularly dangerous aspect of working offshore. Although the Brent workforce in the East Shetland Basin now travelled by safer fixed-wing aircraft from Aberdeen to Sumburgh, the necessity for onward shuttling to the platforms was unavoidable. There had been ditchings of Sikorsky helicopters in July and November 1988, fortunately without loss of life. The S–61 had been flying for almost 30 years and about 130 of them were in civil use world-wide. Built under licence by Westlands as the Sea King, it was also used extensively for Search and Rescue (SAR) work and other military operations. The issue of helicopter safety offshore had been subject to occasional scrutiny by the Civil Aviation Authority for some time. Regular low-level routes over the North Sea, sometimes with extremely tight landings, as on the Brent Spar, exposed helicopters to particularly demanding operational conditions. A sister aircraft to the ill-fated BIH S–61 was fitted with an advanced safety monitoring apparatus known as Health and Usage Monitoring System (HUMS). This simultaneously monitors the condition of the engine, gearbox and transmission, detecting signs of unusual vibration or metal fatigue through fibre-optic sensors. Unfortunately, the fitting of HUMS was not mandatory on all aircraft, although it is debatable whether it would have altered events in this case.

While the Brent Spar accident was seen as a tragedy for which no direct blame could be attached to the operator, it underscored wider concerns over offshore safety. It heightened the issue of safety at precisely the moment when OILC was poised on the brink of escalating the overtime ban into full-scale industrial stoppages and occupations of the offshore installations.

From Latent Unrest to Open Confrontation

From the inception of the offshore industry its labour relations were characterized by latent unrest. These brush fires, while often reaching considerable intensity, rarely mobilized the workforce across occupational boundaries. After Piper Alpha this situation changed radically. What used to be a 'hidden constituency' of offshore employee interests, now became a full fledged mass movement (Bem, 1970).

Like all forms of hidden constituency, that of the offshore worker was created by joint experience. This included the blatantly authoritarian management structure, the risks and dangers involved in offshore work, the dislocated life style of two weeks on, two weeks off, and the common background of previous onshore work, with which offshore experiences were contrasted and assessed. In some respects these experiences matched those of existing onshore constituencies, namely the occupational and industrial identities represented in established trade unions. In other respects, however, the offshore experience was radically different. The recognition of workforce demands was, if anything, more difficult to achieve offshore than it was onshore. Yet, in the high risk environment of the offshore workplace, the ability to communicate grievances about health and safety matters was of particular urgency.

The experience of risk and danger came to the fore in several incidents such as the Chinook and Brent Spar helicopter disasters, but also in the ongoing daily toll of injury and death. The latent resentment at inability to impact on the ever-present hostile and threatening managerially-dominated environment finally asserted itself powerfully, with the tragedy of Piper Alpha. Safety, which had for too long been a sole managerial prerogative, had visibly broken down. Any managerial claims about ensuring a safe environment for offshore workers were now thoroughly discredited. Abelson (1959) identified several strategies which individuals apply in dealing with deep shock and grief: *denial, bolstering,* and *transcendency.*

Denial of the troublesome belief that offshore work was unsafe was not a credible prospect for most, if not all, offshore workers. The notion that Piper Alpha was a freak accident, brought about by an unlikely combination of circumstances, might have consoled much of the public, but for the offshore workforce it was simply not acceptable. The Piper Alpha disaster, for the offshore worker, was a direct consequence of the faulty managerial and regulatory regime that had been haphazardly erected offshore. The subsequent near-disaster on the Amoco Montrose simply reaffirmed this perception.

Bolstering, the seeking of supportive beliefs within the disruptive experience, was an equally inadequate strategy. Statements such as 'offshore work is dangerous but, then again, it's well-paying', while part of popular mythology, did not make sense to the offshore worker. He knew full well that his income was as much a result of the sheer number of hours worked offshore – often double the normal onshore number – as the result of any special 'compensatory premium'.

The path chosen by much of the offshore workforce was *transcendency,* that is, a process in which troubling realization is integrated into a larger concept of political understanding implying the need for change. Much of the offshore workforce contextualized Piper Alpha and other safety incidents in a wider problem-set of an industry which had been created without appropriate safety provisions for those who had to work in it; and an industry in which the safety agenda had been surrendered to those who managed. The workforce, therefore, had now to seize the initiative and had to do so collectively. The brush fires of the past had to be transformed through a concerted, planned strategy.

In 1989, and again in 1990, the hidden constituency of the offshore workforce became an open political force. After the initial action of 1989, re-gathering strength for the offshore workforce was at first a painfully slow process. There were considerable obstacles to overcome. They included: the residual reluctance among workers to sacrifice overtime payments, Shell's strategic delay of the maintenance programme in order to wear down the patience of the workforce, the occasional vacillation among the activists as at the 'Sumburgh convention', and the potential vulnerability of the workforce to be provoked into premature action as in the Beryl Alpha 'wipe-out'. Moreover, in this hire-and-fire industry workers knew that any challenge would be responded to with the utmost vigour by management; in most cases the outright dismissal of all those directly or indirectly involved. An additional obstacle was created by the key contractors' attempts to bribe workforce, at the behest of the operators, with an imposed pay rise. It was a manoeuvre which paradoxically backfired, as it underscored the arbitrariness of employer benevolence which, in the absence of collective recognition, could be revoked just as quickly as it was granted.

Yet, despite all of these barriers, by the mid-summer of 1990 the offshore workforce was poised to launch the most significant industrial action in two decades of North Sea industrial relations. The common perception among the workforce was that nothing had changed, nor would it until the workforce itself became active on its own behalf. Now, offshore activists had succeeded in bringing official union leaderships into some semblance of a unified one-table approach for a comprehensive offshore agreement. This would overcome the previous disabling divisions. Causing union leaderships to strategically suspend those limited agreements they had so painfully acquired was, in itself, no small matter. The action that ensued, showed that the lessons of the previous summer had been learnt. The workforce now creatively used the constraints on the employers, facing a complex programme of necessary refurbishment, to amplify the impact of co-ordinated industrial disruption. In the period between the workforce challenges of 1989 and 1990 an unparalleled system of communication, and a network of activists, had been built up which would enable the workforce to cope with the sheer difficulty and audacity of organizing industrial action in the improbable environment of offshore oil installations. The moment of *transcendency* had arrived.

Notes

1. *Glasgow Herald*, 28 March 1990.
2. *Financial Times*, 23 March 1990.
3. County NatWest Wood/Mac, North Sea Report, No. 204, 30 April 1990.
4. Country NatWest Wood/Mac, North Sea Supplement, August 1990.
5. OILC mass meeting, 8 March 1990.
6. *Observer Scotland*, 25 February 1990.
7. *Morning Star*, 17 February 1990.
8. *Scotsman*, 6 March 1990.
9. *Observer*, 18 March 1990.
10. OILC Standing Committee, 8 March 1990.
11. ibid.
12. OILC mass meeting, 13 March 1990.
13. OILC mass meeting, 22 March 1990.
14. OILC mass meeting, 29 March 1990.
15. *Scotsman*, 3 March 1990.
16. *Blowout*, No. 6, April 1990.
17. DEn, Petroleum Engineering Division Safety Notice S1/90, 10 January 1990.
18. OILC mass meeting, 22 March 1990.
19. OILC mass meeting, 29 March 1990.
20. *Scotsman*, 30 March 1990.
21. *Daily Record*, 30 March 1990.
22. OILC mass meeting, 19 April 1990.
23. Press statement following meeting of national and local officials concerned with the offshore oil industry, 8 May 1990.
24. OILC mass meeting, 26 April 1990.
25. OILC mass meeting, 1 May 1990.
26. Offshore Contractors Council (OCC) News Release, 25 May 1990.
27. *Scotland on Sunday*, 13 May 1990.
28. OILC Standing Committee, 8 March 1990.
29. IUOOC meeting, Aberdeen, 6 June 1990.
30. IUOOC meeting, Aberdeen, 5 May 1990.
31. IUOOC reconvened meeting, Aberdeen, 5 May 1990.
32. IUOOC meeting, Aberdeen, 5 May 1990.
33. Clem Cooke, article in *Contract Journal*, 26 April 1990.
34. Letter from John R. Milligan, Managing Director, Atlantic Power and Gas to I. J. Hardy, Field Group Manager, BP Northern Operations, 27 June 1990.

35. Memo, Unofficial overtime ban, from L. Coote, Tern OIM, Shell, to all Contract Staff, 11 May 1990.

36. OILC Standing Committee, 10 May 1990.

37. OILC mass meeting, 15 May 1990.

38. OILC mass meeting, 31 May 1990.

39. *Scotsman*, 6 June 1990.

40. *Scotland on Sunday,* 13 May 1990.

41. Letter from W. Murray, Manpower Services Manager, Press Offshore, Termination of employment, n.d.

42. Press Offshore Briefing Note, N. Christie, 4 June 1990.

43. Press Communiqué 1, 8 May 1990.

44. APG memorandum from Eric J. Rossiter to C. A. Nichol, 18 June 1990.

45. *Observer*, 17 June 1990.

46. Memorandum: Potential Industrial Action Summer 1990, R. F. Francis, Central Controller British Gas, 8 May 1990 to B. Heywood, Director of Operations; Report of Conversation with Tony Jarvis, Shell; Hamilton Brothers to British Gas.

47. OILC mass meeting, 21 June 1990.

48. Note 46 *above*; memorandum from R. F. Francis to P. H. Dixon, Plant Operation Engineer, British Gas, 22 May 1990.

49. Note 46 *above*, R. F. Francis to B. Heywood, 16 May 1990.

50. Dunlin 'A' Public Affairs, OIM Statement, 19 May 1990.

51. Note 46 *above*, report of conversation with Tony Jarvis, Shell.

52. OILC mass meeting, 21 June 1990.

53. *Blowout*, No. 9, 6 July 1990.

54. Press Offshore, Employee Newsletter, June 1990.

55. OILC mass meeting, 31 July 1990.

56. ibid.

57. *Scotsman*, 26 July 1990.

4 THE SUMMER OF DISCONTENT

The First Day

As offshore workers began their industrial action, 100,000 Iraqi troops massed on the border, crossed over into Kuwait, setting in motion the inexorable chain of events that led to the Gulf War. In the North Sea another oil war had broken out.

After days of anxiety in the OILC office, it was almost an anti-climax as the

Illustration 3   *Ronnie McDonald of OILC*

first platforms phoned in on Thursday 2 August to confirm the 24-hour stop-pages. In the last week of July, sympathetic informants inside the Shell organ-ization informed OILC that the FLAGS system was down at last. The final cut in the line to St Fergus, crossing the decommissioning threshold would be made on 30 July. After that, it would simply be a question of choosing which day in early August to commence the industrial action. The stoppage had taken place three or four days too soon. The gas line from the Bravo was not actually cut, but the decommissioning work overall was effectively 'past the point of no return'. When the appointed time arrived, 7 a.m. the start of the day shift, all the telephones in the OILC office in Aberdeen began ring-ing simultaneously. They were to ring continuously, day and night, for the next six weeks.

Offshore, the first potential point of confrontation had occurred the pre-vious evening on the Brent Alpha. With the stoppage impending, the instal-lation manager had begun trying to clear the platform of contractors' workforce. From Shell's point of view, it was particularly disturbing that key service personnel involved in the shutdown work on the Brent Bravo, employed by the specialist company Furmanite, had voted to join the indus-trial action. Particular attempts had been made by Shell to avoid the 'contam-ination' of this group and other key groups of workers by OILC. This had included Shell personnel chaperoning the Furmanite men around the plat-form to limit contact with the activists. Drillers employed by KCA on the Bravo, who normally stood aloof from the rest of the 'bears', had also joined the dispute.

By 7.50 that Thursday morning, it was confirmed that contract workers were on strike on every Shell platform in the East Shetland Basin except the Fulmar, on all the Forties platforms, and on at least ten installations in the southern sector. Some platforms, such as BP's Magnus, which had previously ignored the overtime ban were now taking part. By 8.30 that morning it was apparent that the Brent Alpha workers were going to be locked out rather than being allowed to return to work at the end of the day of the 24-hour stoppage. Shell were going to take a hard line. Bob Strick, Aberdeen-based public relations spokesman for Shell, was reported as saying, 'I'm going to nip this in the bud right now. These men will be on the beach by tomorrow morn-ing'.[1]

What was not in dispute as the day unfolded was that OILC had put on an impressive 'show'. By 9.15 a.m. the tally of striking platforms had risen to thirty-three. Offshore, striking workers saw their own spokesmen being interviewed at length on TV news. Satellite broadcasts throughout the North Sea, taking place at half-hourly intervals, were an instant morale booster. By mid-morning, reports of management retaliation had reached OILC office from Shell's North Cormorant. The workforce was being given a deadline of one hour to return to work or face dismissal. By lunchtime, estimates of the scale of action pointed to its widespread nature both in the northern sector and in the southern sector, including the Indefatigable and Leman gas fields. Among the engineering construction workforce in the Shell field, there were stoppages on all of the Brents, the Eider, Dunlin, Tern, North Cormorant, Cormorant Alpha and the Auk. In the BP Forties field, the response was also almost 100 per cent. BP's Thistle, Clyde and Magnus were also affected, but not the Buchan, Cyrus and Beatrice. But on Marathon's Brae A and Brae B there were no stoppages. All three of Chevron's Ninian platforms were on strike, as were, to varying degrees, Occidental's Claymore and the *Tharos*, Amoco's Montrose and North West Hutton, Conoco's Murchison and the Hutton TLP, Mobil's Beryl Alpha and Bravo, Total's North Alwyn and the Amerada Hess. On some of these platforms, such as the small installations in the southern sector, the numbers taking part in the action were relatively few. One important feature, however, was that support was coming from the catering workers, despite trepidation of the officials of the NUS and TGWU concerning the possible legal implications of unofficial action. On the Brent Alpha, the catering workers' resolve was hardened by what was seen as the provocative stance of the Kelvin Catering Company's 'camp boss' in threatening a lock-out. Individual catering workers were to provide some of the most determined leadership offshore in the dispute.

The euphoria which accompanied the first hours of the campaign was dented by the news from the Brent Delta that the leading activist on that installation, himself a foreman, was preparing to 'cut and run'. Management had made the telephone lines available for the Delta contract workforce representative to contact the rest of the field so that he could communicate his doubts. Other seasoned Brent Delta activists were at home on leave. As the day unfolded it was confirmed that the strikers in the Shell field were now officially suspended rather than dismissed. The workers were invited to board helicopters to return to the beach, so that the dispute could be resolved 'in discussions with local management'. There were assurances of 'no reprisals', and the added inducement of half rig-rate pay until normal working could be resumed, for those prepared to co-operate by leaving the platforms.

In the OILC office the ceaseless cacophony of telephones had reached fever pitch as platforms continued to call in. A deluge of press inquiries ranging from Reuters to the *Shetland Times* flooded in, while camera crews of local and national TV stations trundled their equipment and cables through the jam-packed outer office. Nearly lost in the seeming chaos was a discreet but significant inquiry from the US Consul General in Scotland. Could he meet with OILC to discuss the background to the current industrial action? As if the tension, noise, hyperactivity and heat within the OILC office were not enough, at that moment a sustained programme of major road excavations began outside the building, providing a mind-numbing background of heavy pneumatic drills, morning, noon and night for the entire dispute.

The regular weekly OILC mass meeting in Glasgow, packed with offshore workers home on leave, heard up-to-the-minute reports of the progress of the dispute. As an impromptu show of solidarity with their striking compatriots offshore, more than 100 'bears' marched on BP's impressive smoked-glass tower-block headquarters, fomerly that of the state-owned Britoil, in Glasgow's city centre. Security men panicked as noisy and exuberant oil workers invaded the cool, opulently marbled lobby. The event was a publicity stunt, but nevertheless it enabled the workers onshore to feel that they were part of the action too.

By mid-afternoon it was now clear that there would be retaliatory lockouts of the striking workforce on most, or all, of the Shell platforms which had joined the action. Platform managements had issued final ultimatums to the strikers to return to work or be flown off. At Sumburgh, Shell had assembled a fleet of Sikorsky S-61 helicopters to take the men to the beach. As if to add to the company's woes, the pilots now briefly struck in protest against the requirement to fly in immersion suits, hot, bulky and uncomfortable at the best of times, but unbearable in the current spell of sweltering weather. The pilots at Sumburgh had taken advantage of the disruption offshore to pursue a few grievances of their own.

That evening the main ITN television news carried the dispute as its third headline item after the Gulf Crisis and an IRA assassination.[2] UKOOA and the Offshore Contractors Council (OCC), it was reported, had both issued statements alleging 'substantial intimidation' by the strikers. OILC claims of 4000 to 5000 taking part in the action, perhaps half the engineering construction and catering workforce, were put at nearer 2000 by the oil companies. Nevertheless, OILC's declaration that the strike was 'primarily about safety' was broadcast. For the first time the campaign was receiving national exposure.

As the first 24-hour stoppage drew to a close, the OILC advice to those offshore was, 'dig in', and resist management pressure to leave the platforms, at least over the weekend until the following Monday morning.[3] It was recognized that not all the workforce would have the stomach to sit in. There was to be no harassment of those who wished to board the choppers and leave the platforms. On the other hand, the message to those remaining offshore was blunt: 'If you're going for it, you've got to stick it out'. Meetings were to be held on the installations that night so that those taking part in the sit-ins would be aware of the implications, including the possibility of eventual dismissal. On other platforms, where there was no lock-out by management, it was anticipated that the men would be allowed to return to work following the stoppage without any subsequent reprisals. Amoco, Conoco, Chevron, Mobil and Total seemed to be prepared to 'ride out' the day of action and allow normal work to resume.

Shell appeared to be the prime mover in terms of a hardline response to the strikes on its platforms. BP, by contrast, seemed to adjust its reactions according to the contractors' wishes on its individual platforms. On BP's Magnus, Thistle and Clyde, return-to-work ultimatums were individually issued to the workforce. No such threats were made by the contractors on the Forties, where it now appeared that the men would be allowed to return to work as normal in the morning. These varied operator and contractor responses were something OILC had not fully anticipated. It added a further layer of complexity to the ongoing tactical discussions of the Standing Committee, now meeting in virtually permanent session, in the boardroom of the AEU headquarters in Glasgow.

By the end of the first day of action, the tally was impressive. In the northern sector, 35 installations had been affected and as many as 30 in the southern sector.

The Moment of Truth

At the start of the day shift on the next morning, Friday 3 August, the moment of truth arrived. Would those workers who were locked out now commence occupying the installations as had been planned? Most of the main operators had simply allowed a resumption of normal work. A partial exception was BP, on the Clyde, Thistle and Magnus, where the workforce was not permitted to resume work. But on BP's Forties, men were being shuttled to the platforms as normal. The main operator retaliation, however, was conducted by Shell. Offshore management began clearing the platforms of contract personnel. A quick assessment had to be made on each of the installations where lock-outs were being imposed. The OILC's message to the activists was simple:

> If you have the organisation and 'bottle' and can hold it until next week, go for it, but if the men can't take the punishment tell them to come ashore. They're still on our side and they can fight another day.[4]

In OILC's estimate, on BP's Clyde, Thistle and Magnus and Shell's North Cormorant platforms, the strikers did not possess sufficient strength to sit in, an act which entailed direct and open defiance of management. However, in the Shell field, on the Brent Alpha, Bravo and Charlie, on the Tern, on the Dunlin and on the Cormorant Alpha, the majority of the workforce were determined to occupy immediately.

In the East Shetland Basin, Shell's Brent field was now in a state of siege. Internal communications between installations had already been cut. Telephone communication from the OILC office to Shell platforms was becoming increasingly difficult, although at this stage, workers could still telephone in from offshore. On individual platforms where occupations had begun, the numbers of workers involved varied considerably. On the Brent Bravo there were 118 occupiers, on the Charlie 130, and on its adjoining flotel, the Safe Gothia, as many as 400 had joined the sit-in. On the Safe Supporter, bridge-linked to the Cormorant Alpha, a further 260 were sitting in. On the Dunlin there were about 80 occupying. On Shell's North Cormorant, there was only a brief sit-in, and on the BP field about 45 men also sat in on the Clyde platform. In all, that weekend there were about 1000 workers sitting in on Shell platforms. The instruction from the OILC office to those telephoning in from the sit-ins, was 'hold it until at least the middle of next week, by which time we'll have the whole North Sea out again'.[5] The necessary time frame for the occupations had begun to be stretched from a few days, over a weekend, to a full week ahead.

The 'hard core' of activists began to organize themselves for what would be long days and nights. The remainder of the contractor workforce from Shell installations, about 400 in all, and the Wood Group and APG contractor workforce cleared from BP installations, were beginning to arrive back at Aberdeen Airport. Most of the men were still supporters of the dispute, although they had reservations about joining the sit-ins. Only one worker, eagerly seized upon by the waiting media, could be found to support the increasingly aggressive claims by both the UKOOA and the OCC of widespread intimidation offshore.[6] Shell, in particular, pointed to alleged intimidation on the Safe Gothia and Safe Supporter accommodation flotels. The charge in the local Aberdeen newspaper that women catering workers were being harassed was particularly ugly; a charge the women themselves were vigorously to rebut.[7] BBC news broadcasts reported that two men had complained of 'being sworn at'.[8] There was much ironic laughter among the activists at the thought of North Sea 'bears' being 'intimidated' by bad language.

But the extensive coverage on television and radio was not uniformly hostile. From the sit-in on the Tern, John Whyte, a member of OILC's Standing

Committee, gave the view of the ordinary offshore worker in a telephone interview during the ten o'clock national television news.[9] Derek McGillivray, OILC spokesperson on the Brent Alpha, became something of a regular television news feature. In all the media, the issues underlying the dispute, in particular the question of safety offshore, were receiving serious consideration. In an editorial the *Scotsman* commented on 4 August 1990:

> The firms' reaction to the stoppage was more bluster than reasoned response. It will occur to many onlookers that it is irresponsible, even unacceptable, that the North Sea industry is not covered by an all-embracing safety code that is backed by an independent inspectorate. If the companies have good and sound reasons for conducting their business in that fashion, they have not made them clear so far. Their employees' representatives, therefore, are quite right to seek answers from them and are entitled to bring what pressure they can to bear to support their search.[10]

Shell, meanwhile, confirmed that the thousand workers sitting-in on its installations were now formally dismissed by their employers. After two days of rumours, 'usually reliable sources' in the media indicated that Shell were about to call in the police.[11] The much-heralded arrival of the forces of law and order, however, did not materialize. Grampian police 'let it be known' that, providing there were no breaches of the criminal law, they were reluctant to intervene in the problems of North Sea industrial relations.

Subsequently, Shell asked the police to investigate a forced locker on the Safe Gothia. After a one-day investigation the police departed and no charges were laid. Occupying workers overheard the comments of police officers who were none too pleased to be investigating this trivial affair. A measure of where police sympathies lay can be judged from the fact that they slipped a donation into the strike fund before departing. In an attempt to isolate the occupiers on the Safe Supporter, Shell next tried to lift the bridge connecting the flotel to the Cormorant Alpha. The plan was thwarted when about 200 angry 'bears' rushed onto the bridge to prevent disconnection. Like the locker incident, this was later construed by Shell's lawyers as evidence of illegal actions and threatening the safety of the installation.

While Shell reconsidered its tactics, the contractors came up with a time-honoured form of intimidation of their own: the 'document'. As soon as the workforce returned onshore, they were bussed to the contractors' headquarters to be given a 'no-strike' undertaking to sign. This pledged no further participation in unofficial industrial action upon threat of dismissal. OILC advice to the men was, 'sign the paper and take the first available opportunity to get back offshore, and be ready to "do the business" again'.

Having failed in their initial attempts to physically dislodge the sit-ins, Shell now resorted to psychological tactics. First, occupiers were warned that unless they ended the sit-in by noon on Saturday, they would be held to have 'effectively dismissed themselves'. For some, this was the third notification of dismissal since the action began. Occupiers on the Dunlin were invited by the installation manager to individually sign faxed copies of their P45 dismissal forms. As noon on Saturday came and went, the offshore sit-ins remained solid. Over the Tannoy system, the installation manager began broadcasting a statement warning the occupiers that they were committing trespass and were in violation of section 22 of the Conspiracy and Protection of Property Act of 1875. They were ordered to take their private possessions and proceed at once to the waiting helicopters. This proved to be a piece of not-very-inspired bluff. OILC's lawyer quickly ascertained that section 22 of the Conspiracy and Protection of Property Act did not in fact exist. Legal advisers suggested that only sections 5 and 7 of the 1875 Act might be of relevance. Section 5, concerned with attempted sabotage, was hardly relevant to these peaceful and orderly sit-ins. Section 7, concerned with intimidation, required substantiated evidence, which despite repeated allegations from the employers remained unforthcoming. The penalties for breach of the Act were allegedly a fine of £500 and/or three months 'hard labour'. Offshore oilworkers, it was wryly observed, were anyway more than accustomed to 'hard labour'. On the bridge connecting the Safe Gothia flotel to the Brent Charlie, now patrolled by rotas of the workers on a 24-hour basis, the occupation unfurled its banner of defiance. It read, in ironic reference to a then popular movie, 'Shell – A Bridge Too Far'.

With the first day's stoppage over and the sit-ins now firmly in place offshore, it was time to take a step back from the past 48 hours of frenetic activity and reconsider tactics. The Standing Committee had now arrived in Aberdeen and immediately went into emergency session to consider the next moves in the dispute.[12] One important feature was apparent. Whereas in 1989 the dispute had mainly been confined to the northern sector, this year there was workforce support across the entire UK Continental Shelf. Future support for a further day of industrial action was growing. The southern sector was apparently 'raring to go'. In the northern sector too, enthusiasm was intensifying. On Marathon's Brae Alpha, which had not previously participated in industrial action, news came in that the workforce had held a meeting. They had elected six shop stewards in order to 'get themselves organized'. The following day, 90 men on the Brae Alpha occupied the platform.

The question facing the Standing Committee was not if, but when, to call out the workforce again. Sunday 5 August was agreed as the date for the next one-day stoppage. For those sitting-in in the East Shetland Basin, this would provide a show of solidarity, and would keep the maximum pressure on the employers to resolve the dispute as quickly as possible. What the activists sought to create was a dramatic and intense escalation of the dispute. This time, it was anticipated that there could be a response to the strike call in both the northern and southern sectors, on as many as 100 installations. It would be 'the biggest show in the history of the North Sea'. Platforms were already telephoning in to indicate support, especially from the southern sector. The members of the Standing Committee had never even heard of the names some of these installations before. The OILC office now moved onto a 24-hour footing. Its centre was dominated by an 'operations board' on which the status and readiness for action of each platform was continuously updated.

The Second Day of Action

Day two of strike action, Sunday 5 August, produced a full quota of drama and humour. On the Dunlin, the installation manager had addressed the men, pointing out that, as they were no longer contractor employees, Shell would now be responsible for their insurance cover. 'Does that mean we're also on three weeks off, two weeks on?' piped up one of the men, implying that some of the other conditions of Shell personnel would also be quite welcome. Mass meetings on the Safe Gothia flotel were, according to one account, 'more fun than Sunday Night at the Palladium'. Those sitting-in were entertained with quizzes and bingo competitions to raise money for the strike. From the Safe Supporter came tales of the men 'dancing a conga' around the helideck. The flotel master publicly commended the men for their good behaviour and the cleanliness of the accommodation.

But the dispute had its darker side. From Shell, and from David Odling of the OCC, came renewed charges of 'widespread intimidation', 'football hooligan tactics' and 'the manipulation by a minority for disruptive ends'.[13] Shell accused strikers of throwing kit-bags of departing workers, who had decided to come ashore, over the side of the helideck. Just over a third of those sitting-in on the Safe Gothia and Safe Supporter flotels in the Brent field, had returned to the beach, but a solid core of over 400 remained. After four days of occupation, some of the workforce were beginning to feel the strain of isolation. It was no accident that the theme song of the Safe Gothia occupiers, which caught the mood of both desperation and determination, was the classic Beatles song 'Help!'. For many workers, there were intense domestic pressures to return home, especially from wives worried about the prospect of their husbands permanently losing their employment. On several platforms, when helicopter flights were made available, the men took advantage of the contractors' offer to return onshore on standby pay or half rig-rate.

For OILC, this was disappointing. It had hoped that once the workforce voted to join the action, they would remain offshore at least for the full 24 hours of each one-day stoppage. Those returning to the beach arrived at the OILC Aberdeen office in their scores, to 'apologise' for not staying on the rigs. Nevertheless, on some installations, such as the Forties Bravo, Charlie and Delta and the Safe Holmia flotel in the southern sector, the sit-ins spread during the second day of action. BP conceded that about 650 contractors' personnel had taken part in the second stoppage in the Forties field. BP quickly followed Shell's example, blacking out all satellite televisions news coverage of the dispute, cutting intra-field communication between platforms, and telephone communications to the beach. In the southern sector, on the Safe Holmia, about 270 workers were now sitting in, while in total about 1500 had joined the stoppage across the North Sea.

The situation, with regard to precise numbers, was confused by a lack of accurate information due to the problems of communicating directly with the workforce. Shell claimed that response to the call for the second day of action had been 'patchy', with little if any escalation in the numbers taking part. OILC pointed to the fact that, this time, as many as 80 platforms, from Shetland to East Anglia, were affected. But it did not have the accurate figures to be able to rebut the operators' estimates. The media had drawn OILC into a 'numbers game' which it was almost impossible to win. Many of OILC's supporters were still 'on the beach' after the previous day's stoppage, not yet having been recalled for platform 'up-manning'. As many as 6000 workers were now waiting onshore to return offshore. The real level of support was not adequately reflected by the absolute numbers of workers involved in sit-ins offshore. On the Dunlin, OILC activists daily posted counter-estimates to Shell's statements which suggested that the numbers occupying were declining. What was certain was that the number of workers now dismissed had risen to over 1000. This was denounced by OILC as an example of the employers' 'industrial thuggery'.[14]

Once again, during the second day of action offshore, it was the bridges between platforms and flotels which were the point of confrontation with management. On the Safe Gothia, a management request to raise the connecting bridge to the Brent Charlie in order to conduct 'an emergency drill', was refused. Shell immediately reported this 'violation of safety procedures' to the Department of Energy. On the Safe Felicia, bridge-linked to the Forties Charlie, management did succeed in lifting the bridge, most gallingly, while the men were holding a mass meeting to allocate bridge-guarding rotas. The number of installations where sit-ins were still continuing had risen from six to thirteen, but with perhaps an equal number cleared altogether of contractors' personnel. Of the thirteen installations occupied, nine were platforms and four were flotels: the Brents Alpha, Bravo, Charlie; Cormorant Alpha; Dunlin; Tern; Forties Bravo, Charlie, Delta; Safe Gothia, Safe Supporter, Safe Holmia and Safe Felicia.

The second day of action ensured continuing national prominence in news coverage of the dispute, despite the slower-than-expected spread of sit-ins. BBC and ITV film crews flew out over occupied installations and brought back dramatic news footage of strikers defiantly waving from the helidecks of the Safe Gothia and the Dunlin.[15] The ultimate mark of media newsworthiness came with a prime-time Radio 2 extended interview with Ronnie McDonald, as OILC spokesperson, on the mid-morning Jimmy Young programme. This was a forum in which public figures from the Prime Minister downwards vied to air their views. Now not even Surbiton housewives could be unaware of the bitter grievances of the offshore workers.

Sustaining the Sit-ins

While the offshore contractors' representatives had declined an offer to put forward the employers' point of view on the Jimmy Young programme, the OCC did hold their first press conference in an Aberdeen hotel. It quickly became clear that the employers' position had hardened. The official trade unions had formally requested a ballot for union recognition. The companies now responded, in a significant change of tone, that they could not co-operate with the unions under the 'duress of unofficial strike action'.[16] The editorial column of Lloyd's List next day commented that the Offshore Contractors' Council seemed 'ill-equipped to deal with a dispute on this scale'.[17]

Important as the media war was, the real battle was taking place offshore. It was becoming apparent that, although the sit-ins had spread to other fields, they could not be sustained. It was only in the East Shetland Basin that there appeared to be the necessary organizational strength and determination. In the Forties field, one man remained defiantly in occupation on the Safe Felicia, refusing to end his protest unless instructed to do so by OILC. The question was, whether the Shell sit-ins could be maintained until the following weekend, by which time the occupiers would have been sitting-in for ten days or more. Once again, the time frame was for the sit-in being expanded. What was needed was a morale boost for those sitting-in offshore.

Behind the scenes, the trade unions searched for ways to mobilize support for the dispute, although impeded by the severe limitations imposed by recent Conservative employment legislation. There had been talk of an emergency resolution from the TUC, of a union boycott of Shell and BP, and of a nationwide financial appeal. The need for demonstrative support in the form of sympathetic industrial action was paramount. One key area where that support might be expected was from the onshore rig-building yards at Methil, Ardersier and Nigg Bay. The construction workers there had a close affinity with the offshore workers. Indeed, since 1981 they had agreed to pursue their aims in tandem. Many of the onshore workers had worked offshore at various times and vice versa. However, there were intense rivalries between the individual yards, conditioned by the boom-and-bust nature of the industry, which prevented them from acting cohesively. An early one-day sympathetic stoppage would be a significant gesture of support if it could be achieved.

Sympathetic action that involved the supply boat crews servicing the offshore rigs could cause the operators more serious problems. Due to the defeat and sequestration of the NUS in the P&O strike of 1988, however, the supply boat crews were in no position to offer support without being open to severe employer retaliation. Little help could be expected from the dockers who loaded the supply boats at Aberdeen. These men had been the first in the whole country to abandon the campaign of the TGWU to defend the National Dock Labour Scheme when abolished by the Conservative government in 1989 (Turnbull et al., 1992). In any event, support from such groups would, under current employment legislation, constitute illegal secondary action.

That left the personnel directly employed by the operators themselves, the Shell and BP men out on the platforms. Individual company employees were discreetly quite supportive to the occupiers, but there was no possibility of direct organized solidarity action here. Inspired by the OILC, Shell employees on the Brent Bravo were conducting their own 'ballot' on whether they too wished union recognition. The results indicated that many were unsatisfied with the existing company consultative machinery and would have preferred full collective bargaining rights. On the Brent Charlie, 'C' shift conducted a secret ballot on whether or not to remain in Shell's in-house staff association. Three voted for, and 25 voted to pull out on the grounds that they had 'lost faith' in the company-based system of consultative committees. Significantly, 24 Shell employees voted for some form of union representation and only four against. Attached to a memo to Shell management was a list of grievances, including accusations of 'unsafe practices by Shell management'.

As a result of OILC's action, Shell was beginning to see stirrings of unrest among its own employees. Shell operatives began holding collections for the men and women on strike and passing over sweets, cigarettes and other gestures of support. On the Dunlin, Shell employees handed over a collection of £150 with the message, 'stick in and beat these bastards'. On the Brent Bravo, £270 was collected by the operator's personnel for the strikers. From up and down the country, financial and moral support from ordinary workplaces and from other trade unionists had been pouring into OILC's office. In terms of solidarity, the newly established contact between OILC and the Norwegian offshore workers was of great importance. The Norwegian workers were closely following the progress of their UK counterparts.

Nevertheless, at the end of the day, the offshore contractor workforce would have to win this dispute for themselves. This would have to be accomplished by increasing the pressure on the employers through yet more unofficial stoppages and action. The oil operators were adamant that, so far, production had not been directly affected. Yet all parties to the dispute knew that with each day the action continued, shutdown overlap on the Brent and Ninian fields became more likely. The delay of the start-up dates for the completion of the shutdowns was likely to have substantial financial implications for the operators. If the contractor workforce was now being harmed by mass dismissals, so too were the operators by the continuing labour uncertainty. The government too was worried. Senior Ministers were reportedly now taking 'a keen interest' in the development of the dispute.[18]

In Aberdeen, to a packed meeting of 500 offshore workers in the city's famous Music Hall, with officials from all the IUOOC unions present, Ronnie McDonald explained to rapturous applause 'We are entering the seventh day of occupation in the East Shetland Basin – and there's no way they're coming off.'[19]

From the Music Hall, coachloads of workers proceeded to Shell's ultramodern headquarters at Altens, on the outskirts of Aberdeen, where a mass picket was mounted at the entrance barrier. An OILC delegation was invited inside to meet Bob Strick, Shell's head of public relations. For the assembled media, which now included foreign as well as UK television film crews, the OILC saga was providing some excellent material. Those occupying offshore were unaware of the increasing coverage of the dispute. They were now subject to a total news blackout, not just of satellite television but of BBC and ITN news.

OILC hosted a twice-daily press conference, providing up-to-the-minute coverage of the dispute, and line-by-line rebuttals of the employers' arguments. Ronnie McDonald expounded the case for union recognition and safety with conviction and skill. The basic demand of the workforce – a comprehensive collective bargaining arrangement – was characterized by OILC as 'arguably so moderate, as to sit happily with current Conservative employment legislation'. It effectively defused the operators' charge that the dispute was being orchestrated by wild-eyed militants, using the issue of safety as a 'cover' for the pursuit of 'other ends'. Operator attempts to portray the dispute as holding up vital safety work had also largely failed to gain credibility with the media. Far from forcing OILC onto the defensive, the issue of safety provided new ammunition to attack the employers on an almost daily basis.

From the Beryl Alpha came disturbing reports of a purported breakdown in safety procedures in the absence of safety permits and safety precautions. Sparks were allegedly landing on parts of live plant during oxy-acetylene burning, but those who protested, including contract supervision, either walked or were taken off the platform. It was alleged that no fire blankets or gas monitors were being used during this operation. The captain of the bridge-linked accommodation flotel, the Polycastle, had stopped personnel transfers when it appeared that there were breaches of safety procedures.

As concerned workers from the Beryl Alpha relayed the details to OILC, it was felt that the information merited an immediate alert to the Department of Energy in London via its emergency 'hotline'. This hotline number, displayed on every cabin door offshore, is a 24-hour facility, meant to provide workers who have serious safety concerns with a direct and immediate recourse to the authorities. A call from the OILC office at 5.38 p.m. to the listed Department of Energy London emergency number 071–276–5999 was answered by a tape-recorded message:

> The Department of Transport, Energy and Environment duty officer is not here at the moment to take your call. If you'll please leave your name and telephone number after the tone, I will get back to you shortly.

A second call, placed two minutes later, to the alternative Department of Energy emergency hotline number in Aberdeen, was also answered by a tape-recorded message:

> The number you have dialled is unavailable. If you wish, you may leave a message after the tone. If you wish to report an incident or an emergency, please dial 071–276–5999.

First Signs of Movement

The offshore dispute appeared increasingly intractable, with the ongoing sit-ins continuing and further one-day stoppages being planned. The employers appeared to be immovable, on the surface at least, while the workforce occupying the installations remained equally resolute. Tommy Lafferty, as local AEU official, summoned members of the OILC Standing Committee to a private meeting in a hotel outside Aberdeen. The Offshore Contractors Council had been in contact with the trade unions to initiate behind-the-scenes discussions. They had met earlier for two hours with local officials from the Hook-up signatory unions, to discuss terms for settling the dispute. When the other unions, the TGWU and NUS, discovered they had been excluded, they were furious. Within 24 hours following the public display of unity among the union officials at the Aberdeen Music Hall rally, there was serious disarray. The contractors had asked for a period of time without further industrial action – a 'cooling off period' of two weeks. David Odling, on behalf of the contractors, had issued a conciliatory press statement calling for a 'halt to the mudslinging that had crept into the dispute'.[20] It appeared that the dismissals of those who had briefly occupied the BP installations during the previous one-day stoppages were now 'not final', although the situation remained unaltered for those dismissed in the East Shetland Basin. Offers by the contractors of reinstatement were only partial. For those thousand or so who had been dismissed, said the contractors, there was 'an appeal procedure and that would be adhered to by the employers'. This was an undertaking that was later to be reneged upon.

Two questions needed to be resolved before OILC could offer a guarantee of no further disruption. Would all the sacked workers be reinstated and would the employers now sit down with the unions to hold discussions about the Continental Shelf Agreement? Tempting as the prospect of a cessation of hostilities might have been, particularly if the contractors were to agree to these terms, OILC still felt it had punches to deliver. In the words of one activist: 'So far we've only taken the legs away. I want to kick the head in.'[21] From Tommy Lafferty came a word of warning: 'We've already got them. I don't want to end up with 1200 martyrs.' Bob Eadie, full-time official of the electricians' union, had publicly speculated on an early resolution of the dispute, much to the annoyance of fellow Hook-up union officials who had thought that the discussions with the contractors were to remain confidential. As long as dismissed members were reinstated, said Eadie, everything else was 'negotiable'.[22] There was now a further division among the union officials.

To smother any speculation of a resolution of the dispute, OILC announced its third 24-hour stopppage in the space of seven days for Thursday 9 August. With this new escalation, external political forces sought to become involved. Labour's employment spokesperson, Tony Worthington, straying dangerously on to the patch of local MP Frank Doran, Labour's oil and gas spokesperson, appealed for both sides to get round the table. But it was senior Tory grandee Sir Albert McQuarrie who provided the predictable note of Gulf War hysteria. 'Saddam Hussein, the newly-activated Hitler of Iraq, would do the Highland fling if he learned of the threatened disruption to our oil supplies.'[23]

The geopolitics of oil were certainly an increasingly important element in the dispute. A more accurate reflection of the patriotic motives, or otherwise, of the offshore workforce was given by one worker, shaking his head in incomprehension at a media interrogator on the 'strategic implications' of the dispute: 'Ah well, you see . . . I'm just an ordinary mechi fitter.' But ordinary mechanical fitters, and caterers and electricians and roustabouts, were now doing something extraordinary. For the first time, they were effectively challenging the oil multinationals, most of whom cared little, or nothing at all, for Britain's interests. Oil workers felt they had already paid too high a price for serving the 'national interest'. Ronnie McDonald had the last ironical word on that subject: 'Depriving citizens of your own country of the full protection of UK safety legislation is not exactly patriotic either. I think we can see the Falklands spirit is alive in the North Sea at the moment.'[24]

The Third Day of Action

With a third day of industrial action now imminent, communication by telephone from offshore to the OILC office and to the local office of the engineering union in Aberdeen became impossible. Wives called the OILC office to get the latest information to relay to their husbands offshore. Even these 'domestic' calls were abruptly terminated as soon as the words 'strike' or 'union' were mentioned, much to the amazement of one Gaelic-speaking worker in conversation with his girlfriend. The line went dead when the dreaded initials 'OILC' were spoken. The marine radio at Wick, on the northern tip of the Scottish mainland, was used to relay messages to the sit-ins via the rig radio operators. In the railway station car park, outside OILC's Aberdeen office, a car telephone became an important temporary communications link to offshore. Local MPs Alex Salmond and Frank Doran made their constituency office telephones available to relay messages between OILC and offshore, warning the operators that any interference with these 'communications with constituents' might constitute a breach of parliamentary privilege. One activist using the OILC car telephone was interrupted by a voice. 'Look out of the window and see if they're still using the car phone'. The line crackled. As he looked up he caught a reflected glint from an upper window in the Post Office tower opposite the car park.

Shell maintained that on the installations, the telephone 'hardware' was the property of the company, and they therefore they could impose 'certain restrictions' if they so wished.[25] The OILC office quickly became littered with mobile vodaphones, with activists using alternative telephone numbers which were periodically rotated. In this war of communication, such logistics were all-important.

In the midst of this hectic atmosphere, the US Consul now arrived in person at the OILC office for a briefing on the various issues involved in the dispute. An affable, diminutive and unassuming man in an open-necked shirt, he had at first been mistaken for a striking pipe-fitter. After a courteous but chaotic discussion of the merits of the offshore workers' case, punctuated by yet more telephone calls, he left somewhat bemused, retreating to the relative peace and sanity of the street outside. Inside the OILC office, the level of activity reached a new and even more frenetic crescendo. In due course, a crisp little brief would doubtless be sent to the State Department in Washington indicating that in one sector at least, British trade unionists still posed a threat to corporate US interests despite over ten years of Mrs Thatcher's rule.

The third day of action, Thursday 9 August, again involved workers in both the northern and southern sectors. On fourteen offshore installations contract workers downed tools. Twenty other platforms had already been cleared of contractors' personnel. With most of the troops 'confined to barracks' onshore as a result of previous actions, the numbers taking part in stoppages offshore were relatively small. The contractors claimed a figure of 754 and OILC about twice that number. In total, both offshore and on, about 6000 workers were directly or indirectly involved. Only two installations in the northern and central North Sea remained unaffected, the Beatrice and the Maureen.

In one respect, there was an escalation. For the first time, onshore workers took solidarity action. At McDermott's rig-construction yard at Ardersier near Inverness, 2000 workers began a token sympathy stoppage at 4 p.m., despite management threats of retaliation. At Davy Offshore in Dundee, 1000 workers began a twenty-four hour stoppage, while 200 contractors carrying out refurbishment work at the St Fergus terminal near Peterhead also came out in sympathy. For the 450 workers still entrenched in the East

Shetland Basin sit-ins, this was an important demonstration of support.

OILC now chartered a scallop trawler, the good ship *Unison*, which was to set sail for the East Shetland Basin from Lerwick in Shetland that evening. It would tour the vicinity of those installations where the workforce was sitting in and act as a 'mobile communications centre', linking OILC to the occupations via ship radio telephone. A more graphic description of the *Unison* was – 'the world's first floating picket'.[26] All was not plain sailing for OILC's banner-festooned trawler in its tour of the choppy seas of the East Shetland Basin. Oil-rig standby vessels chased the *Unison* as soon as it appeared anywhere within range of the 500-metre exclusion zone surrounding the offshore installations. As one standby boat cut across their bows, an OILC acitivist aboard the *Unison* commented, 'It's like the bloody Cod War!' On the Dunlin, the occupiers 'mooned' contemptuously at the standby vessel. On the Brent platforms, Shell management confiscated all hand-portable radios to prevent direct communication with the *Unison*. After brief contact with the men on the Safe Gothia, Shell cut off the flotel and installation radio telephones. Nevertheless, there was much waving and cheering and hoisting of 'hands across the sea' banners as the *Unison* sailed defiantly by. Although it boosted

Illustration 4   *Safe Gothia occupied (Photograph courtesy of Spindrift)*

the morale of those on the sit-ins, spirits sank as the vessel turned back for the shore. As one of the occupiers commented, 'it was like being in prison at the end of visiting time'.

The voyage of the *Unison* was a bold, although at a £1500-a-day charter an expensive, gesture. It once again captured the attention of the media. Even the staid and respectable Glasgow *Herald* ran an editorial endorsing the unions' demand for the transfer of responsibility for offshore safety regulation from the Department of Energy to the Health and Safety Executive.[27] At lunchtime on the third day of action, the Offshore Contractors Council issued a press statement which appeared to confirm that they were 'willing to co-operate' with the unions in organizing a ballot once 'normal working conditions had been resumed'.[28] Some evidence had begun to appear that a split was emerging among the employers. Reports from men employed by smaller contractors suggested that assurances were given that if they abandoned the occupations now, there would be full reinstatement for those dismissed and a guarantee of a ballot on union recognition. Aberdeen Scaffolding, for instance, appears to have had ballot papers already printed in anticipation of a recognition vote. Such concessions by smaller contractors, however, were opposed by the 'inner circle' of larger contractors which included Press Offshore (now AMEC), Wood Group, AKER and AOC. However, such assurances had also been given during the previous year's industrial action.

Offshore, the sit-ins were increasingly well entrenched, with a measure of real power in the hands of the workforce. Only after a management pledge that it would be replaced once a mechanical defect had been completed, could the lifting of the bridge from the Safe Supporter be permitted. OILC spokesperson Gordon Douglas was allowed to cross over to the Cormorant Alpha while the repair work was being carried out, to ensure management's compliance. If the bridge had been 'lost', it would have been a powerful psychological blow to the occupation. The determination of those in the sit-ins could be gauged from the Dunlin occupation, which had volunteered to conduct a hunger-strike. On the Brent Bravo, one young man due to be married intimated to his intended partner that arrangements would have to be postponed. His fellow occupiers arranged a 'marriage' on the installation, complete with appropriate ceremonials. The 'dearly beloved gathered together' in the cinema 'in the sight of OILC'. The groom's black morning suit was fashioned from a plastic bin bag, while the 'bride', who obligingly volunteered her services as a stand-in, for the purposes of the ceremony only, was one of the stewardesses in the occupation.

Far from the action crumbling, as the contractors were claiming, the dispute had now increasingly taken hold throughout the southern sector. As OILC prepared to open regional offices in Hull and Lowestoft to co-ordinate activity in the southern sector, it was confirmed that on both the Safe Lancelot and the DB101 barges, servicing numerous satellite platforms, somewhere in the region of 300 men were on indefinite sit-in. The action had encompassed the key Sole, Leman and Clipper fields in the south. Now it appeared that some of the workforce were prepared for 'all-out' indefinite strike action.

Reassessing Tactics

For OILC this raised an acute question. After three separate days of strike action, some thought the moment was coming when tactics should change from guerrilla stoppages to indefinite strike. 'All-out' action, encompassing the southern sector as well, would certainly escalate the dispute. The danger in escalating, however, was that there could be uneven support from the workforce. Any divisions would be easy for the employers to exploit. It was clear, for example, that the Safe Lancelot in the southern sector was not yet at the same level of militancy as the DB101. Not only was there a lack of precise information on the southern sector, but there was some confusion in OILC's Aberdeen office. This resulted in the southern sector being told prematurely by one committee member to go 'all-out'. These workers had to be ordered back to work by OILC at the end of the day's stoppage. The premature action had partially spilled over into the following day in the southern sector, allowing the OCC to claim that OILC was losing control of the dispute.[29] Apart from this 'communications hiccup', the third day of action ended without any lock-outs or further dismissals. If the enthusiasm of those in the southern sector could now be channelled in a co-ordinated manner, then further industrial action was an immediate possibility.

The problem was that the sit-ins on the Brent field, now entering their second week, were beginning to show signs of battle-weariness, with more and more workers coming off the installations each day. This posed the dilemma as to how this key point of pressure on Shell could be sustained. The Standing Committee of OILC met to consider the options facing them. The following excerpts from the committee's internal discussions illustrate the intense cross-pressures which existed, as Ronnie McDonald and the leading activists attempted to take stock of the available options.[30]

Tam   How about we 'up the ante' to a 48-hour shot?

Ronnie   No, let's go for a Monday stoppage in the southern sector and obviously also in the northern sector. But if the men leave the platforms we're done for. They must stay out there for 24-hours and not come back.

Tam   Ideally the northern platforms should be crewed up more. We want the men back out there, yet we're calling strike action and not letting them time to get out there.

Jake   It's important that we give the Brent sit-ins a lift, the numbers are diminishing and diminishing.

Ronnie   But if you call for 'all-out action' a lot of the men will run to the beach. They'll send out 'scabs' as soon as we vacate the platforms.

Frank   There's a big squad [of scabs] sitting onshore just waiting for a telephone call. They know there's nobody out there to annoy them or stop them from scabbing.

Sammy   But the vibes from the Brent sit-ins are for 'all-out' [indefinite strike].

Ronnie   What does that mean? Words are meaningless – practical results are what counts. 'All-out' – so what? So the men come to the beach. The contractors can do the work at their leisure there and let us stew.

Frank   Even with 24-hour stoppages, the men are running for the beach.

Ronnie   There's two things we need to do simultaneously. First of all continue action and allow, even encourage, the upmanning. ... We've always said 'all-out' is not in our vocabulary. It's the last resort, back against the wall stuff.

Jake   So why not step up to 48 hours and let the guys on the Brent see an escalation in it?

Ronnie   Look, if the men in the Brent field feel that they want to come ashore, they'll come ashore regardless. The fact of the matter is, as soon as you mention 'all-out' you'll get a mass exodus. It's that simple. These platforms will be upmanning during the week and that'll be our credibility down the tubes. We've got to be in a position to say 'these men are getting in the choppers to go back out because we're telling them to.'

Jake   But why not take the 48 hours, something that the guys on the Brent can see ...

Ronnie   Those guys on the Brent know the score ...

Jake	Ronnie, are they not going to be listened to? Are we not going to listen to the vibes coming down the line?
Ronnie	Are you giving us a good reason why we should change the tactics we've had in place for a year?
Jake	It's not *that* we want, but a bit stronger action from 'the [OILC] office'.
Ronnie	What stronger action? What can we deliver?
Jake	We can deliver a 48 ...
Ronnie	It's utterly meaningless. What is the point of it?
Jake	The point is 'psychologically' for the guys ...
Frank	Yes, but we can't lose the whole thing just to support the Brents. If we lose the Brents ...
Jake	... we've lost the whole thing.
Frank	Jake, we've not lost anything. The boys will sit there. We've had a telephone call from Jamie. They'll sit there for three months. That's not the vibes that I'm getting, 'that they're ready to come off'.
Ronnie	Wait a minute – we're making a mistake here. This committee has a strict policy followed month after month of 24-hour stoppages. Policy changes occur here, not in telephone conversations with people offshore or onshore. Twenty-four hours. Give us a good reason why we've got to have 48 hours? If the only reason is that we've got to flag up support for the men in the Brent field, we can't deliver. The men will get in the choppers – it's that simple. We hope the men will get sacked for taking the 24 hours and then they'll sit-in, but unfortunately 90 per cent of the offshore workforce have come ashore.
Tam	We don't want them on 'all-out' strike, we want them locked out.

The Fourth Day of Action

With the original tactics reaffirmed, the weekend was given over to organizing a fourth day of action for the following Monday, 13 August. The Sunday tabloids condemned the 'taproom wildcats' and Sir Albert McQuarrie gave further vent to his fury at this return to the 'bad old days of union triumphalism'.[31] Even the more sober of the Sunday press spoke of 'heightened fears of an irretrievable breakdown in relations between the unions and employers'.[32] One national Sunday newspaper reported that the oil companies, increasingly conscious that there might only be a few weeks of good weather left in the North Sea, had called on the TUC to intervene.[33] What was now obvious was that both sides were deeply entrenched and any prospect of an early resolution to the dispute was fast receding. The editorial writer on the *Herald* endorsed the OILC demand for a ballot on union recognition as 'a fundamental democratic right' and called for 'a more enlightened approach by the employers'.[34]

Such expressions of support needed to be seen against a background of increasingly hostile publicity for the oil majors in general, viewed by many as shamelessly profiteering from rapid price rises in the cost of petrol, imposed ostensibly as a result of the Gulf crisis.[35] Even Mrs Thatcher appealed for only 'strictly necessary' price rises, while some Conservative backbenchers, including the Chairman of the Commons Trade and Industry Committee, went so far as to call for the Office of Fair Trading to intervene and 'grab the oil companies by the throat'.[36] During the Gulf War, 7 per cent of the world's oil supplies were cut off by the crisis. But it was known that official reserves of one billion barrels existed, not to mention huge potential production increases among OPEC suppliers. Every $1 increase on the price of a barrel of oil created £107.5 million of extra after-tax profits for BP alone.[37] With the last tanker-loads of Kuwaiti or Iraqi oil due to reach western ports in the coming week, there was every expectation that North Sea Brent crude could reach $28 a barrel compared with an average for the second quarter of the year of $16 a barrel. The pressure was now on the oil companies in the North Sea. For the first time, UKOOA's spokesman, Chris Ryan, admitted that the strikes might cost 'millions' due to delays in start-ups. Dr Jim Walker, the leading oil economist with the Royal Bank of Scotland, confirmed that the industrial unrest had surfaced 'at the worst possible time', comparing the government's response to this potential disruption of non-OPEC oil production to 'Nero fiddling while Rome burned'.[38]

Britain's 'other oil war' began its fourth set-piece battle in the North Sea on Monday 13 August. This time both sides were to claim victory. The OCC had issued a last-minute plea to the men to ignore the strike call and instead use existing grievance procedures. It was claimed that almost 80 per cent of the workforce had heeded their call for calm.[39] The picture presented by OILC at its daily press conference was rather different.[40] Seventy-four platforms out of about 105 installations in the North Sea were taking action, including men who were 'back-to-backs' with the first contingent of strikers and others previously down-manned. Texaco's Tartan platform had been hit for the first time in the dispute, while the Amoco Montrose, which had not participated in the last action, was also involved.

In the southern sector where support was particularly strong, there was retaliation. Jimmy Ashcroft, an activist on the Safe Lancelot, was informed by management that his cabin had been locked and he would not be allowed to return to it. Photographs had been taken of the cabin smoke-detector covered with a plastic bag and of 'dog-ends' found in a cup, evidence of smoking in a forbidden area. Ashcroft and his room-mate were flown off at once. According to OILC, this 'blatant set-up' only reinforced the determination of the men on the Lancelot to take action. Ashcroft immediately devoted his energies to organizing from the OILC's Lowestoft office.

With the fourth one-day stoppage, there was a perceptible hardening of Shell management's attitudes. On the Tern, the installation manager informed the occupiers that they would no longer be allowed to eat with the rest and could only enter the galley in the last twenty minutes of meal-times. They would be permitted to obtain only one clean towel per week. Cigarettes and toiletries would no longer be available from the 'bond' shop. The occupiers' spirit remained as determined as ever. On the Dunlin, OILC spokesperson Brian Dell had now completed 28 days offshore, the sit-in having started the day he was due to go off the platform. Shell management were informed that the occupiers had worked out voluntary cleaning rotas up until Christmas. The spirit of the sit-ins was captured on a tape circulating offshore from the Dunlin comprising occupation 'hit-tunes': 'O-I-L-C' performed by a ragged chorus of occupiers to the tune of the Village People's chart-topper 'Y-M-C-A', and 'We'll stop the oil', borrowing heavily from the old-time favourite 'Roll out the barrel'. On a more serious note, Shell now intimated that the company was contemplating court action which might involve the repossession of workers' houses. In the Brent field over 300 workers were still sitting-in. On the Brent Charlie, they now painted 'prisoners' arrows' onto their OILC T-shirts.

OILC maintained 'thousands' had taken action during the fourth one-day stoppage, with 24 platforms already cleared of contractors, keeping 3500–4000 men on the beach. Shell claimed that only 250 contract employees out of 2000 offshore had taken part, while BP gave figures of 'less than 5 per cent', some 76 workers out of 1435.[41] Whatever the actual figures, the deadlocked dispute now had an extremely high national profile. Once again, there was support from onshore workers, this time among contract workers at the British nuclear submarine base at Coulport and US Faslane base on the Clyde, where 200 contractor employees of Press Engineering, a sister company to Press Offshore, stopped work. In Aberdeen a newly formed women's support group staged a protest outside BP's northern headquarters. Also in Aberdeen, IUOOC union officials held a press conference to reiterate union support for the overall objectives of the dispute, regretting only that the current trade union laws prevented them from directly supporting the industrial action. A meeting of local and national officials was to take place at Transport House in London later that week to discuss the dispute. Meanwhile, UKOOA publicly condemned the action as interfering with the current £750 million safety programme. It called for the national leadership of the unions to become involved in the dispute and 'get off the fence and face up to their responsibilities'. OILC's response was summed up in the phrase, 'utterly surreal'. 'We agree with UKOOA in this instance. If the proper collective bargaining procedures were in place, the trade unions *would* be able to become involved. But for twenty years, UKOOA has been trying to keep the unions out of offshore industrial relations.'[42]

Illustration 5   *OILC Wives Support Group*

The Stalemate Continues

As the third week of the dispute commenced, it was apparent to observers on all sides that the stalemate between the employers and the offshore workforce was set to continue. The first hints of impending legal action were a measure of Shell's growing impatience. The OILC Standing Committee was not optimistic about holding the occupations in place for much longer. This was the case despite the growing support that OILC was receiving from the organized onshore trade union and labour movement. Ambulance workers, who had been given assistance by OILC during their own recent bitter dispute, now returned that support with a donation of £1000. A widow of one of the victims of Piper Alpha sent a personal donation of £200, while the Piper Alpha Families and Survivors Association issued a public declaration of support. In Stornoway a mass meeting of 50 oilworkers had set up a branch of the OILC, while a new OILC office had opened up in Liverpool. An offshore worker and family hardship fund had been established by the STUC, which had called a major conference of Scottish shop stewards to mobilize support for the dispute. Workers at Govan Shipbuilders were instituting a levy to provide financial assistance. The onshore oil refinery conveners, representing 8000 workers, called a meeting in Aberdeen to organize moral and financial assistance. In Aberdeen itself, the Trades Council emergency executive called for a demonstration and march in the city on 1 September.

The difficulty for OILC was maintaining the momentum of the dispute and the focus on the key issues. There were reports about the low state of morale on some of the flotels such as the Safe Supporter, where something of a 'siege mentality' was developing. Once again, the Standing Committee grappled with the problem.[43]

Ronnie   We're bogged down. There's no debate any more. The next watershed is obviously the National Officers meeting on Thursday. We'll get some mileage out of this on Friday and then we're into the weekend again. What can we do to sustain the struggle?

Frank   All we've got is 'action', and if we're going to lose the [Safe] Supporter tomorrow ...

Ronnie   Well, we're not sure about that. The men feel there's nothing happening ... We've got to decide what to do about the men on the sit-ins. Are we asking them to stay, and if so, what are we supporting them with, or are we asking them to come ashore and if so, when? We've got to sustain them with *issues*, we've got to sustain them with issues.

Tam   Come Thursday they'll have been sitting there for fifteen days. Come Monday that's nineteen days. They'll have had six days of fuck-all. Can they sustain six days of inactivity?

Jimmy   There's still guys coming off today and the activity [the fourth day of action] was yesterday. There's some guys who just can't hold out any more.

Tam   Can we ask the guys to sit there till Monday and nothing's happening?

Frank   Can we ask them to come off? They'll go fucking bonkers when they've got nothing to show for it. You can't ask them to come off, it'll break their hearts. It broke my heart last year.

Ronnie   We've got everyone in a hole and no-one is moving. Do we go for more action and dig them out of those holes? … Look, we've got a stark choice. Do we continue the campaign in the manner we've been doing, with continuing sporadic sit-ins and telling the men in the East Shetland Basin to sit rock solid? Or do we consider a change of tactics – withdrawal and regroup?

Frank   If you withdraw and regroup, who do you regroup with, because you certainly won't get any of the stewards or the hardliners back out there.

Jimmy   Yes, all the spokesmen … they [the employers] will pick and choose. They'll never get back out onto the platforms.

'Regrouping' as an option would probably not only mean that the activists would be excluded from any future up-manning offshore, but send entirely the wrong signal to the offshore workforce. The sit-ins were to be held in place, until at least the meeting of national officers. Then, if possible, OILC could represent any withdrawal as 'handing over the baton to the official movement'. The strategy of the OILC had been based on the assumption that with industrial relations havoc created offshore, the OCC would be 'knocking on the door' of the national officials. This had not happened. If anything, the contractors' position was more intractable now than at the start of the dispute.

The OCC had placed a full half-page advert in regional and national newspapers outlining the employers' side of the dispute. It called on the workforce to open up personal channels of communication with the employers to end what it termed 'these damaging and unnecessary strikes'.[44] The OCC accused the union officials of failing to negotiate within existing agreements and of failing to instruct their members to resist calls for unofficial strikes. Jimmy Hay, the managing director of BP, had also written to each national official demanding that they formally repudiate unofficial action. Chris Ryan of UKOOA warned that it would be difficult to complete the outstanding safety work before the 31 December 1990 statutory deadline if the dispute continued.[45] The various contractor employers also began telephoning workers individually at home, asking if they would agree to work normally, promise not to strike, and be prepared to work overtime, if returned offshore.

The final decision on whether or not to embark on further action could not be made until Thursday evening, after the national officers had met in London. It was seen as imperative that the national officials conclude their meeting with 'something to deliver', perhaps some kind of 'statement of intent' that would break the deadlocked dispute. If Shell were to seek court action to end the occupations, OILC would have 'scored a jackpot'. It would refocus media attention while at the same time providing motivation for the men in the East Shetland Basin to continue to sit it out. So far, however, there was only rumour of such impending legal moves.

The national officers' meeting in London had been a somewhat disorganized affair with over 35 local and national officials present. Senior union officials had met the OCC that afternoon, and it was clear that the contractors were determined to end the dispute on their own terms. There would be no co-operation with the unions over balloting for recognition. The national officers accordingly announced the initiation of their own balloting procedures. They did so in the full knowledge that without the employers' co-operation, and with less than half the contractor workforce unionized, any such ballot would be open to legal challenge. It would take up to five weeks to organize an official dispute that was properly balloted, due to the nature of the offshore work pattern for contractors' employees. Tom MacLean, the secretary of the National Offshore Committee, had called for direct talks with the oil companies rather than the contractors. In the inimitable words of his fellow officer, Jimmy Airlie, it was time to talk to 'the organ grinders ... not the monkey'.[46] The involvement of the official unions in the industrial action was viewed by industry analysts as posing a 'significant threat' to maintenance and construction programmes.[47] UK offshore oil production had already dipped 12.6 per cent in July and it was now probable that Britain would become a net importer of oil in September and October.

The Standing Committee went into emergency session late that night to consider its next moves, as platform representatives telephoned in for further instructions.[48] Many had been hoping to end the sit-ins after the national officers meeting, but now were faced with a Standing Committee request to 'hold on', at least for a few days more. OILC was calling for renewed unofficial action over the weekend as a last bold act of defiance. It was now certain that the timescale for success or any victory was shortening.

On the Brent field, the occupiers had received notification that Shell

Expro were planning legal action against those 240 still remaining in occupation. Shell were seeking a petition for an interim interdict (injunction) at the High Court in Edinburgh, the petition to be lodged early the following week. The prospect of being brought before the courts produced some consternation among the men offshore. OILC reassured them that providing any interdict granted was immediately complied with, then no criminal or civil offence could be held to have been committed. To ignore such an interdict, however, would be to risk proceedings for contempt of court. It was, of course, by no means certain that Shell's application for an interim interdict would be any more successful than it was the previous year. OILC had taken the precaution of securing the services of one of Scotland's top advocates who should be equal to any of the legal counsel that Shell could field.

An ex-Caterpillar worker telephoned the OILC office to offer some words of encouragement: 'Tell the men to ignore the interdict. We did, and nothing happened'. In the three-month occupation of the Caterpillar tractor plant at Uddingston near Glasgow in 1987, the workforce had fought on, despite legal threats, against plans by the company to close the 'plant with a future' (Woolfson and Foster, 1988). The Caterpillar occupation had provided a moment of resistance for the Scottish working class in what had appeared to be the darkest days of Thatcher's rule. North Sea oil workers had now inherited that mantle.

The Fifth Day of Action

Saturday 18 August, 7 a.m., saw the start of the fifth unofficial offshore stoppage in seventeen days. The contractors described the call for further strike action as 'provocative in the extreme'. Again, they estimated that up to 80 per cent of the workforce continued working normally.[49] The OCC claimed only 600 stopped work. OILC estimates were somewhat higher: 1000 striking offshore, and 3000 still held on the beach as part of an 'enforced demobilization'. Up to 35 platforms had been affected. For the first time, the disruption had spread to the gas fields in Morecambe Bay off the west coast; 250 workers had struck. On two of Conoco's platforms, the Murchison and the Hutton TLP, and on Amoco's North West Hutton, it appeared at one stage that workers would defy return-to-work deadlines and embark upon sit-ins. Communications offshore were cut off and it emerged that the platforms had been cleared of strikers. Once again, the sit-ins had failed to spread. On the other hand, on the Shell installations such as the Brent Delta and the Kittiwake, up-manned after previous days of action, the men responded to the call for a 24 hour stoppage and were taken off the platform yet again. Shell conceded that there were still 185 contractors occupying its installations. Those asking to return to shore, said Shell, would no longer have transport laid on for them on request, but would only be taken off as and when routine helicopter seats became available.

Within a few days of the fifth day of action, three oil majors, Shell, Chevron and BP, separately announced that the fitting of emergency safety valves would be delayed beyond the end of the year. The statutory deadline for fitting the topside shutdown valves remained 31 December, and indeed Chevron already had its topside valves in place. The oil companies were installing subsea valves voluntarily in order to pre-empt a legal requirement to do so. Prior to Piper Alpha, ten such subsea isolation systems had been installed in the British sector of the North Sea. After the disaster around 60 were to be put in place at an estimated cost of over £250 million. While Chevron blamed the continuing industrial unrest for the postponement of its £20 million subsea safety programme, OILC pointed to commercial considerations. With UK production targeted to rise as quickly as possible from the current output of 1.6 million to 2 million barrels per day, a shutdown of Chevron's Ninian pipeline would have involved a complete halt to production not only in the Ninian field, but also for the BP Magnus, Total North Alwyn and Unical Heather, amounting to a further loss of production of over 400,000 barrels per day. With oil prices now 50 per cent higher since the invasion of Kuwait, it was charged that once again, the oil companies were profiteering. Piper Alpha survivor Bob Ballantyne commented:

> They could have installed these valves eight years ago and I wouldn't have been blown up. Suddenly after just three weeks of industrial action, they are claiming the programme has been put back. I find that hard to believe.

Energy Minister, Colin Moynihan had a different interpretation: 'It is to be regretted ... that the current industrial action has impacted on further work to improve offshore safety which appears to be one of the concerns of those taking industrial action'.[50]

Court of Session

The Court of Session in Parliament Square, Edinburgh, provided an incongruous setting for the final moves of the offshore dispute, far removed in every sense from the drama being played out on the rigs.[51] On 21 August, Shell sought application for an interim interdict before Lord Cameron of Lochbroom. When Shell had sought interdict on an interim basis during the 1989 offshore dispute the motion had been refused.

This year, the hearing, lasting six hours in all, stretched over three days and was largely taken up by dry-as-dust legal argument. Court No. 1 is high-walled, so that the voices of the litigants all but disappear into the heavily-corniced roof far above. Cathy Arnott, whose husband was in the Shell Brent sit-ins, remarked, 'They're just reading to each other out of books, aren't they? Nobody's saying why the men are where they are, and what they're doing it all for. Their case isn't being put over at all, really.'

Shell appeared to lose the first round on Tuesday, 21 August. The company needed more time to re-write their inaccurately-worded petitions. OILC's lawyers needed more time – and access to the platforms and the occupiers – so as to be able, amongst other matters, to 'lodge answers' to Shell's 'averments' (replies to their claims) concerning alleged acts of disobedience and alleged intimidation of personnel. Lord Cameron granted a two-day adjournment.

Two days later, both sides were back in the Court of Session. The last two stewardesses from the Brent Bravo sit-in had meanwhile reluctantly returned ashore, to be greeted by a blaze of media publicity. They provided public refutation of Shell's claims that they had been harassed or intimidated.

For Shell, Mr Andrew Hardie QC had opened by stating that 626 people were sitting in on platforms on eight Brent field installations on 4 August. (Brent Alpha 46, Brent Bravo 58, Tern Alpha 18, Dunlin Alpha 57, Brent Charlie 29, Safe Gothia 218, Cormorant Alpha 8, Safe Supporter 192). Hardie later added that other installations which were also initially affected by sit-ins included Brent Delta, Brent Spar, North Cormorant, Eider and Auk. Of about 2500 contracted employees, about 1500 took part in the first 24-hour stoppage, according to Shell. At 7.30 a.m. on 24 August, the numbers in the sit-ins had fallen to 127 (Brent Alpha 3, Brent Bravo 32, Tern Alpha 4, Dunlin Alpha 31, Brent Charlie and Safe Gothia 41, Cormorant Alpha and Safe Supporter 16). Interdict was sought for the removal of 112 persons, a further 15 having left their installations before the hearing ended.

Hardie said that there had been 'unrest' for some considerable time between offshore workers and their contract companies. He emphasized that the petitioners (Shell) were not the employers. The unofficial 24-hour stoppage of 2 August was 'called by a body which is not a recognized trade union'. The stoppage had started at 7 p.m. the previous night, on Brent Alpha and Brent Bravo, when a number of contract employees refused to go on shift.

They were given an hour's moratorium to reconsider their position, relayed by tannoy message, said Hardie. The strikers had been told that, if they had a grievance with their employers, facilities would be available for them to return onshore to take these up with their employers, in accordance with the procedures laid down in their contracts of employment.

Mr Donald Mackay QC (for OILC) argued that these 'procedures' provided for little more than settling differences over pay packets – they provided no framework at all for negotiating trade union recognition, representation, or safety measures. When other platforms became involved, said Hardie, the same moratorium was offered, and a considerable number availed themselves of the opportunity to fly ashore, 'but equally a large number remained and sat in . . .' On 3 August, the Offshore Contractors Council had issued an ultimatum, warning that those refusing to go ashore would be dismissed. More than 400 helicopter seats were made available to employees to return within the deadline. Many went ashore, but again, an equal number remained on board their installations. They were dismissed. The suggestion that Shell prompted these dismissals had no foundation – 'quite untrue', said Hardie for Shell.

Shell decided to take action to remove these persons because they were occupying the company's installations without their employers' authority, and no longer had any business there. The platform installation managers, in each case, had decided that their continued presence was 'not consistent with the health, safety and welfare' of those on board. They issued orders to those sitting in to leave. By Sunday 5 August a large number of Shell installations were completely 'cleared of the dispute' (Brent Delta, Brent Spar, North Cormorant, Eider and Auk), because employees had 'availed themselves of the opportunity to go ashore and negotiate with their employers'. By Monday evening, total numbers sitting in on Shell installations had fallen to just under 500. On 8 August the figure had reduced to about 450, and there were further reductions as time went on. After this brisk introduction of 'background', Hardie built up several 'tiers' of argument.

He made great issue of the lawful authority of the offshore installation manager (OIM), who should be obeyed without question at all times. Hardie duly rehearsed all the statutes empowering OIMs. He went on to read out all Shell's 'averments' – complaints about the misdemeanours of the sitters-in. They had 'occupied' flotel bridges, refused to attend a muster drill, stolen a log book, damaged instruments and equipment, hoisted flags and banners, occupied a helideck, harassed personnel employed by Furmanite. 'Mr Hardie, when you say "occupation", said Lord Cameron, 'you surely don't mean that your clients' property has been seized, taken over. They are taking up space, are they not?' 'No, your lordship', said Shell's advocate. He was not using the word in that sense. He merely meant the workers were 'in occupation' of certain parts of the installations. The *'Phestos* case' was cited as a precedent for an 'occupation' of a place of work during an industrial dispute. It involved seamen who had held a sit-in in 1983 aboard a vessel owned by a shipping company of that name while it was docked at Leith.

The debate between the advocates took on a surreal character to those listening on the public benches. Was an offshore platform, or a flotel, 'heritable property', like land, or was it movable, and did the laws of trespass apply? In Scots law, trespass is an intrusion on 'heritage' without the owner's permission. Whether structures such as offshore installations could be regarded as 'heritage' was just the kind of issue to captivate legal minds. Lord Cameron seemed to suggest that the onshore equivalent of a flotel might be a caravan parked in a lay-by. Would a tramp who jumped aboard a moving caravan as it pulled out of a lay-by be guilty of trespass? Shell considered an oil rig pretty well fixed, since, for example, it would take £78 million to shift Cormorant Alpha from its seabed position.

Hardie for Shell suggested to Lord Cameron that so long as he was satisfied those sitting-in had no entitlement to be there, then the only course open would be to grant the interdict forthwith. To proceed with the 'balance of convenience' arguments, which would establish Shell's disadvantages if the sit-ins continued, would therefore not be necessary, Hardie said hopefully. Lord Cameron showed no inclination to bring such a contested interdict to such an abrupt conclusion. The proceedings went into the history of the *Phestos* case, and the issue of whether the offshore industrial action was covered by immunity under the now amended 1974 Trades Union and Labour Relations Act.

Shell's advocate finally rehearsed the 'balance of convenience' debate. He contended that the sacked workers had a remedy onshore – at industrial tribunals. It was also claimed that the occupying workers could effectively continue their industrial action onshore. The respondents, he said, were 'the authors of their own misfortunes'. The sit-ins had prevented essential safety-related maintenance and repair work. Refusals to accept an OIM's orders would result in loss of confidence and undermine authority. If the occupations continued, loss of production would result, with substantial costs to the company, and a significant effect on the British economy. The company might not be able to fulfil its statutory duty to complete the fitting of topside shutdown valves by 31 December. If production start-up was delayed, revenue receipts would be pushed back, said Hardie. Brent Charlie was a transfer point for piping oil ashore, so that if it was held up, other platforms would be affected. Brent Alpha was a gas point, so if it was inoperative, no gas could go to the St Fergus terminal at Peterhead. There was an aspect of international interest. Apart from a drop in oil revenues to the UK government, 'there is the added complication of the situation in the Middle East'. The longer the oil was delayed, the more adverse the effect on the balance of payments. If Brent oil was not available, to make up the deficit, Britain would have to either export less oil, or import. Either way, it would have an adverse economic effect.

All ears were pinned back in the public gallery, as Hardie went on to say that on 1989 figures, Brent revenues were £2.6 million a day, of which the government received £2.2 million in petroleum tax. As an example, the Dunlin Alpha produced £500,000 a day, of which the government's share was £400,000. Tern and Cormorant's output was worth £1 million a day, out of which the Exchequer received 35 per cent. 'What we are talking about in terms of these figures, is a total production of £4 million a day, of which the government receives £2.95 million', said Hardie, adding, somewhat apologetically, that these were 'very rough' figures.

Mackay, for OILC, contested Shell's claims. There could be no suggestion that disobeying an OIM's order was by itself a 'delict', he said. Shell's petition that men had 'acted in concert' together, he said, was irrelevant 'unless you can go into a civil conspiracy'. On 'trespass', he said the company had offered 'no factual basis' to show that the sitters-in had unlawfully interfered with Shell's business. Their aim was to advance a trade dispute, not to damage the economic interests of Shell or the coffers of the Exchequer. Mackay pointed out that the goal was to gain certain rights as individuals, and for 'the officials of certain trades unions, the right to represent them on matters of safety, pay and other topics'. As for undermining the authority of OIMs, he said that contract workers would obey any legitimate orders of an OIM in an emergency. After all, their whole campaign was directed at gaining measures to increase their safety. The men had failed to clear a bridge when an OIM ordered them to do so for the stated purpose of repairs, because they feared this was 'just a ruse' to have them confined to their flotel, from where they could be towed to shore. Allegations of threatening the safety of a helideck, and of harassing individual personnel were vigorously denied. Mackay stressed that his clients' chances of pursuing effective industrial action for their claims while onshore would be 'extremely limited, if not completely eliminated'.

A key part of the legal debate in this case hinged upon an interpretation of section 13 (2) of the 1974 Trades Union and Labour Relations Act. Repeal of this section had removed the legal defence for sit-ins, which brought a victory for the 'Plessey women' in 1982. Lord Kincraig had told 117 women and ten men occupying the Plessey factory in February that year that he was recalling his own previous interdict against them, because he accepted their defence on the basis of furthering a trade dispute. Since then, the law had been altered to favour employers' interests in ending an occupation of their premises (Miller, 1982).

Shell did not achieve all it sought, although Lord Cameron did effectively order the sit-ins to end.[52] The decision was taken on the 'balance of convenience'. While some of Shell's allegations had been clearly discounted, Lord Cameron appeared to accept that having unauthorized personnel on board compromized safety. The sit-ins by their very nature had had an effect which was detrimental to Shell. The balance of convenience in Lord Cameron's view was tilted in favour of Shell, and the interdict to remove the occupying workers, requested by Shell, was granted.[53] Nevertheless, it was accepted that the offshore workers were involved in a genuine trade dispute. Therefore, OILC was protected from claims for damages against it by Shell.

As the proceedings concluded there was an unreal emptiness in the Court of Session building. Security guards, Shell executives and their counsel, Ronnie McDonald and the OILC's counsel, three women supporters, and about a dozen media-men were the only people remaining late on Friday afternoon. The human drama offshore, which had largely failed to emerge from under the law books, seemed to belong to a different, far more remote world.

The Watchword – 'Defiance'

In Parliament Square, outside the High Court, McDonald held an impromptu press conference. OILC had only just been 'pipped at the post'. There were between 3000 and 4000 workers who had been 'held on the beach' for the last two to three weeks, waiting to go offshore. When they got out there, said McDonald, they would be participating in the OILC campaign. There was every likelihood of more occupations. The court had recognized that this was a legitimate trade dispute and therefore, that the sit-ins as such were not illegal. If Shell or any other operator came back to court seeking further interdicts, OILC would contest them. The media pressed him – would there be more sit-ins, in spite of the court decision? McDonald confirmed that 'further action is guaranteed'.

OILC's lawyer, not Shell's OIMs, had been given the task of advising the men to leave the platforms. For some OIMs this was a bitter pill to swallow.

Those who had remained on the Cormorant Alpha platform had been summoned to the OIM's office to be informed of the terms of Shell's interdict application. In an act of petty humiliation they were ordered to remain standing as they were read the interdict. With the interdict granted, the OIM wished the satisfaction of personally ordering the men off his installation. As news of the court's decision reached offshore, the last man on the Brent Alpha sent a message to Ronnie McDonald, 'Does that mean I can now stop picketing the bridge?' The watchword remained 'defiance'. The men complied with the court order, but they were returning to the beach unbowed.

At Aberdeen airport, OILC supporters and wives gathered to welcome home the men from the East Shetland Basin. There were clenched fists of defiance and victory signs as those returning, each in the distinctive OILC T-shirt, filed through the barrier to be greeted by applause and embraces. The OILC logo, emblazoned in red, was an ironic reference to the emblem of the Polish Solidarity movement, an unofficial 'trade union' which Mrs Thatcher was so eager to support. The young man who had postponed his wedding was reunited with his fiancée and the happy moment recorded for posterity. Outside the terminal, stalwarts proudly unfurled their banners – *OILC Gothia* – *Frontline*. The bus back to town from the airport rocked with hearty choruses of occupation songs. In the bar of Aberdeen's Station Hotel, with the first taste of drink for over a month, lost time was quickly made up for. A slightly bemused wedding party was caught up in the general festivities as exuberant 'bears' recounted tales of the occupations. One youngster, an electrician from Cumbernauld, had been on his first trip offshore. He had completed only 24 hours' work on the Brent Bravo when the sit-ins commenced. He remained in the Safe Gothia occupation for the entire period of over three weeks.

> To start with I didn't even know what the strike was about but the longer I stayed there, the more I realized I had to stay. And every time I picked up the *Aberdeen Press and Journal* it made me more determined to stay – the amount of lies they were telling about intimidation.[54]

As in the case of perhaps half of the occupiers, he was not even a member of any union. The experience of the occupation had been an intensive political education. Now he intended to join his union in order to be able to participate in any future ballot for official industrial action. On another rig, the occupation was something of a family affair, with a father and two sons sitting-in together. These men had grown in self-respect and dignity, not just because they had endured weeks of isolation and pressure, but because they

Illustration 6 *Aberdeen Airport, 'OILC Gothia Frontline' August 1990*

had stood up to management. They had demonstrated that they were no longer a subservient workforce.

The occupiers related how management authority was successfully challenged and undermined on a day-to-day basis until mutual respect was established. It had been a 'war of nerves'. For some Shell management, used to being 'lords of all they surveyed', the collective empowerment of the occupations was simply too much to handle. Other management tried to establish some kind of a working relationship with the OILC spokespersons on their installations. For the activists, the occupations were 'meetings, meetings, meetings'. Communication was what held the workforce together, and kept morale high when time hung heavily. It was only by constantly talking to the men that daily management 'misinformation', in the form of company bulletins detailing declining numbers on the sit-ins and diminishing support for strike days, could be countered. Cut off from contact with other platforms, and deprived of information, it was easy to make the occupiers feel isolated. The activists had to work hard to fight feelings of boredom and unease in the face of continuing management pressure. Those who had kept daily diaries offshore provided a fascinating and often hilarious glimpse of the kind of tenacity and resourcefulness which enabled them to remain in occupation, in some cases for a period totalling over five weeks.[55] Returning offshore veterans looked relaxed as they swapped 'war stories'. For some, the weeks of inactivity had produced a noticeable increase in girth. By contrast, those who had been staffing the Aberdeen office during the last few hectic weeks, looked lean and haggard. To triumphant cries of 'No surrender!', Ronnie McDonald announced to what was by now a very merry gathering, 'The court has said sit-ins are not illegal, and just to prove the point, we are going to have a few more of them'.

Reassessment of the Campaign

Despite the rhetoric of defiance, it became clear that the court decision had marked a watershed in the campaign. Over the next few days, a fundamental reassessment of the dispute began to take place. As the Standing Committee met to consider their options, it became clear that the scope for further action in the immediate future was severely limited. There had been a temporary suspension of strike calls during the Court of Session hearings, but it was now nine days since the last stoppage. In terms of future action in the northern sector, the outlook was bleak. OILC now had practically no organized presence on any of the Shell platforms. On the Fulmar, some men were working 'three-weekers' again and had already voted not to participate in any future action at a meeting the previous week. Apart from the Brent field, the three Ninian platforms, the Magnus, the North West Hutton, the Murchison and the TLP were now empty of contract personnel, while only 150 contractor employees remained on the Forties, and even less on the Claymore. In the southern sector, the picture was rather different, but still confused. On the Safe Lancelot and DB101 flotel, the workforces were ready for more action, but the key contractor on Shell platforms had signed a deal with the official unions, including AEU, EETPU and MSF, based on onshore arrangements. It effectively meant that the main workforce in the south would not participate in future action offshore. Although these contractor employees had refused to cross picket lines in the southern sector during the second and third days of action, their convener and key local official had repudiated the unofficial offshore action from the start. On the other coast, the Morecambe Bay workforce was calling for immediate all-out sit-ins on the platforms.

In addition to this unevenness of militancy, OILC now faced profound financial pressure. Having a senior barrister represent the occupiers at the Court of Session had cost £12,000 over the period of three days. The trade unions had contributed nothing towards these costs. The *Unison* voyage had also drained away a large chunk of the funds. Those returning from the sit-ins had to be given travel fares, since they had been dumped on the beach, in most cases without a penny to their name. There had also been hardship payments to the occupiers' families. In addition to the Aberdeen office, there were OILC offices functioning in England, not to speak of the huge telephone and other bills. Contributions from sympathetic trade unionists continued to come in, albeit slowly. Funds from the offshore workforce itself would only really start to grow again once the men returned offshore and were earning a wage. The 'war chest' of OILC, which once amounted to £100,000, was practically empty.

One almost unnoticed development, whose profound impact became apparent only later, was a carefully-timed initiative by the operators to radically alter the whole offshore production environment; an issue which we explore in greater detail in a later chapter. From now on, Shell indicated that instead of employing a variety of contractors on its installations to carry out various construction and maintenance jobs, it would offer exclusive four-year contracts to selected contractor companies on specific platforms or groups of platforms. This move towards 'turn-key' contracting would, it was claimed, alter the whole offshore environment. It would mark an end to the competitive bidding system between contractors which had been the dominant method contract allocation. It was claimed that the stability which longer-term contracts would provide could be passed on to the contract workforce in the form of greater job security through longer individual contracts of employment and regular index-linked reviews of wages and conditions. The contracting companies acknowledged publicly the importance of this initiative in underwriting the terms and conditions they offered to their employees. In this instance it would mean a 'big extension', according to OCC's David Odling, in progress towards more secure contracts and uniform rates of pay. In exchange for this, oil operators such as Shell would be seeking productivity improvements and the ending of job demarcation among the workforce.

For Shell this was an opportunity to refocus public attention from health and safety and union recognition and onto matters of job security and, in the words of one Shell spokesman, the creation of a 'stable and well-motivated workforce'.[56] The trade unions seemed to welcome the development, as implying that the operators had somehow tacitly acknowledged that the contractors should now negotiate a recognition agreement with the unions.[57] Certainly, single contractor platforms could, in the longer term, make such installations easier targets for industrial action, but as events were to show, the contractors were a long way from conceding recognition, tacitly or otherwise. Within days, major contractors such as Wood Group, Press Offshore and AOC International, had placed half-page adverts in the popular and 'quality' press for every known category of offshore worker, from project engineer to cleaner, offering 'job security' to 'suitably experienced candidates'.[58] Wood Group would now be the key contractor in the Brent Charlie and Brent Delta, Press Offshore were awarded the Dunlin and the Cormorant Alpha, and AOC International, the Fulmar, Auk, FSU and Kittiwake. Job security would certainly be an issue exercising the minds of the hundreds of workers who had now been dismissed as a result of their participation in the offshore dispute.

The most important question facing OILC, was how to secure the reinstatement of these dismissed. Would all of them be re-employed when the contractors up-manned again, or would the employers pick and choose those who would be allowed back out? Unless the dismissed workers were reinstated, OILC would be unable to regroup offshore. For the Standing Committee, the simple choice was between more action now, albeit on a limited basis, or calling a truce in the hope that the activists returning to the platforms could, in time, regenerate some of the previous militancy. At the TUC annual conference in Blackpool on 6 September, in ten days time, there was to be a meeting of national officials concerned with offshore affairs. OILC could declare a ten-day moratorium to allow the official trade unions to take an initiative with the contractors. But there was little real hope that the union officials were in a position to achieve anything significant by way of reinstatement.

Tom MacLean, as secretary of the National Offshore Committee, had already had an exchange of letters with the contractors' organization the previous week, a fact which was not known to OILC. The unions had asked the companies to co-operate in the preparation of a ballot. This ballot was to assess whether the workforce wished to take action to secure union recognition in an agreement to cover all engineering and construction work.[59] The OCC had responded by saying that, before such a request for co-operation could be considered, the national officials should 'publicly repudiate the unofficial strikes and instruct the workforce to resume normal working with no further disruptive action'.[60] The unions, said Odling, if they were to have 'any future role at all', must 'emerge from the shadows and declare their hand'. Before agreeing to assist in a ballot, the OCC would be seeking 'clarification' on points raised by the unions. In particular, the OCC wished to know what the unions sought concerning conditions of employment and safety that was not 'already covered by the OCC's existing Model Terms and Conditions of employment'. The OCC, Odling claimed, had 'definitely not refused to co-operate in a ballot'. Jimmy Airlie was quick to denounce the OCC request for 'clarification' as 'playing games'. He considered their demand that the unofficial action be repudiated as an 'utter impertinence'. The unions had not overtly supported the strikes, but neither would they repudiate them.[61]

Both sides were jostling for the bargaining initiative. For OILC, the resumption of 'normal working' had to be accompanied by an end to the victimization of the dismissed workforce. Somewhat ominously, the OCC warned that 'as a result of the dispute and the postponement of "non-essential" maintenance work, many of the jobs of the dismissed workers were no longer available'.[62] In any event, workers who felt they had been unfairly treated could utilize the appeals procedure, in which 'each case would be considered on its individual merits'. The OCC would differentiate between those workers who had, it claimed, 'breached safety requirements', and those who had simply been 'swept along by the tide'. This unsupported claim that workers had indeed breached safety requirements, alone, signalled the lack of sincerity with which future negotiations would be conducted. It was a none-too-subtle indication that the employers intended to weed out the activists. The situation had all the hallmarks of employer retribution. This view was reinforced when the OCC refused to accept what it referred to as the 'imposition of an arbitrary deadline' (meaning OILC's requirement that all workers be reinstated) by what it called, 'an unofficial body whose activities, they [the unions] appear to be reluctant to control'.

The impression that the employers were in anything but a conciliatory mood was reinforced by two further developments. The offshore catering company *SAS* announced the dismissal of their entire crew of 60 who had taken part in sit-ins on Conoco's Murchison and Hutton platforms. On the Murchison, militant catering workers had actually provided the lead for the 'bears' in taking action. Now they were receiving their payback. In the Brent field, Shell's OPRIS (Offshore Personnel Records and Information System), an identity card system for monitoring personnel safety status, was now being employed as a means of identifying and then blacklisting those who had taken part in the action.

The stakes were as high as they had ever been, as the OILC delegation travelled to the TUC conference. A rearguard defeat for the offshore workforce by wide-scale victimization could destroy effective resistance for another decade.

The Shift in Mood

The TUC conference in September 1990 provided the occasion for rousing speeches and enthusiastic applause for the offshore workers' cause; particularly as an emergency resolution in their support was debated. Moving the resolution on offshore health and safety and trade union recognition, Jimmy Airlie pledged, 'If we don't get a negotiated settlement then we will stop every installation throughout the Continental Shelf. That is a guarantee'.[63]

Airlie had assured the OILC delegation that there would be no settlement until all the dismissed workers had been reinstated. Now the union officials pledged that they would press ahead with arrangements for a ballot. Advertisements would appear in national newspapers on 19 September urging offshore workers to use freefone numbers in order to register for the ballot before the membership register closed on 28 September. Thereafter, ballot papers would be sent out, with a view to initiating official industrial action sometime in November.

Lack of employer co-operation made the legal situation very complex. Local officials could not simply visit the workplace and site ballot boxes in the appropriate place, nor could a postal ballot be carried out without detailed information on a workforce which, in any event, changed from week to week.[64] It would be necessary for the unions to prove that there was a trade dispute with each contractor employer, and that the ballot had been open to all members, who might be called upon to take action (Bowers, Brown and Gibbons, 1993: 116; Hendy, 1993: 61). With up to 300 employers in 168 different locations and as many as twenty employers on a single rig, the task was formidable. In order to persuade those who were union members or those who had allowed their membership to lapse, to register, the GMB was to simplify its rejoining procedures, while the AEU was considering a membership amnesty by waiving the £30 fine and rejoin fee.

To OILC, it initially appeared that the official movement had embraced their cause. From the delegates in general at the TUC, offshore workers had received a rapturous welcome. *Blowout* was selling fast from an OILC stall in the foyer, and campaign collecting buckets were circulating. The offshore dispute was a welcome reminder to many delegates that workers could still defy injustices at their place of work. It had been a TUC conference that was otherwise dominated by political manoeuvring, as reluctant unions such as the TGWU were dragooned into accepting the TUC line that the union movement would not call on a future Labour government to repeal wholesale all previous Conservative employment laws.

Despite the moratorium on unofficial action offshore, the dismissals continued. The OCC and trade unions remained as far apart as ever. OILC reaffirmed its intention to utilize whatever remaining potential for action it still had, particularly as the result from the union ballot would take at least another six or seven weeks to materialize. Shell was now crewing up rapidly in the northern sector. But on the Fulmar and Auk, mass meetings had already indicated that there would be no support for further stoppages. Five workers on the Fulmar who argued for industrial action were removed by management from the platform within an hour and a half. In the northern sector, these were the first indications of a shift in mood among the workforce. On the North Cormorant, contractors' personnel working for Salamis and Cape Scaffolding were now working overtime. On the Brent Alpha, one man had been run off the platform for collecting for OILC. Here, and on the Dunlin, about half the workforce were totally new to the offshore scene. One seasoned activist commented, 'They're walking round the platform in wide-eyed wonder'. Elsewhere, on the Cormorant Alpha, the up-manning contained only 6 out of the original crew of 40. The rest of the workforce were 'Press heavies', loyal company men with favoured long-term status with the company. While the participants in the dispute were being held on the beach, there were reports that the offshore contractors were advertising in the Irish press for new recruits.

With the possible exception of the Forties field, where relatively strong unofficial organization remained partially intact, the main potential for OILC support was confined to the southern sector, where activists had been leafleting at the heliports from which workers went offshore. There were perhaps three weeks left before extensive down-manning commenced in the southern sector. As the summer weather window for maintenance came to an end, OILC called for one further sixth day of action for 12 September.

Outside of the Forties and the Montrose, in the north only a handful of workers supported the action, although in the south both Morecambe Bay and Humberside gas fields were to the fore. Once again, the Lancelot and DB101 gave 100 per cent support, as well as the Ravenspurn South. From the Brents, however, there was no response. On the Brent Bravo, the men had taken part in a 'ballot' organized by management and had voted 90 per cent against taking action. They ignored the stoppage call, but claimed that they were 'still with the OILC'. The Forties had held mass meetings and stopped work, rejecting management offers of a return to work without retaliation. When choppers were sent out, the men threatened to sit-in, but by the following day they had come off the platforms as requested by management. On the Montrose, the workforce also took action, but on former OILC strongholds such as the Claymore and a number of other platforms, the workforce had not even held mass meetings to consider support. On the Tern, two contract workers from a crew of five remained on the installation in a defiant sit-in. Most of the northern workforce had either been without a wage for five or six weeks, or seen what had happened to their fellow workers. They now feared dismissal and wished 'to keep their heads down'. In total, perhaps 500 workers took part in what was to be the last day of action, in both the northern and southern sectors. The relatively weak response in the northern sector confirmed the ebbing of previous militancy.

According to OCC's own figures, a total of 534 workers had now been dismissed, and a further 500 from among member companies had been 'made redundant due to a reduction in the maintenance workload off-shore'.[65] The contractors reminded the workforce that as a result of the dispute, the workers had already lost more than £3 million worth of wages. On the other hand, the relatively strong support in the south during the last day of action had damaged AOC International in particular, David Odling's firm and the main contractor on the Amoco installations. This had previously been seen as 'OILC proof'. It undoubtedly sent a signal to the OCC that even yet, OILC was far from being a completely spent force.

In England, OILC now had offices in Newcastle, Hull, Liverpool and Lowestoft. Most of these, at least initially, had been largely staffed by activists from the north. In certain areas like Hull and Lowestoft, it had proved difficult to get local offshore workers involved. Now, offices in Liverpool and Hull seemed to be developing a life of their own, with separate fund-raising initiatives and their own organizational infrastructure. As a rank-and-file body, OILC still lacked a formal structure. Its very informality was seen as one of its virtues, particularly the 'absence of the bureaucracy', seen as a feature of the official trade union movement. With local areas developing their own independent activities, there was now a need for some kind of accountability to the OILC centre in Aberdeen. The purely *ad hoc* nature of the organization needed to be complemented by a more formal mechanism which would ensure that the various regional committees would report directly to the OILC, represented by its Standing Committee. In particular, the temptation which existed for local activists to assume a 'full-time' role as 'paid officials', had to be resisted. In addition to facing a decline in combativeness among the workforce, OILC now had to grapple with internal organizational problems.

Achieving the balance between democratic accountability and the desire to 'minimize bureaucracy', while retaining flexibility, was to remain a continuing problem for OILC. In some local areas, individuals in the organization began to see possible 'career opportunities' opening up, and had begun to organize local fund-raising efforts in the name of the OILC to finance these careers. At one stage, three separate 'OILC appeals' were circulating in the trade union and labour movement, a situation which created considerable confusion, as well as undermining the credibility of OILC as a whole. Since the official unions could not fund OILC, for fear of legal repercussions, it was important for OILC to appeal directly for assistance from other trade unionists up and down the country. Setting its affairs in order, therefore, became an urgent task.

The sixth one-day stoppage had not been a wholesale disaster for OILC, but neither was it a resounding success. It had proved that OILC had not completely 'shot its bolt' as the OCC had surmized. Where there were supporters offshore, OILC still had the potential to create problems for the employers. The official unions had written to the OCC again requesting further talks. Bill Jordan, president of the AEU, had entreated 'ours is the voice of sanity'.[66] For its part, the OCC now seemed to be adopting a more conciliatory tone. David Odling argued that, if the unions could persuade OILC to accept 'the error of its ways', then the OCC would 'reconsider the position'.[67] Yet for all the manoeuvring between unions and employers, OILC had not succeeded in the primary objective of its campaign. This had been to force the contractors to seek an accommodation with the official trade unions in order to forestall the disruption created offshore by unofficial stoppages and sit-ins.

Now, particularly in the northern sector, the activists felt that the men were to some extent 'hiding behind the ballot' which the unions were attempting to organize. OILC had also directed its energies to supporting that ballot. At the railway stations in Glasgow and Aberdeen, as the workforce travelled to and from the rigs, OILC activists distributed union membership registration forms on a nightly basis. If a ballot were to be held for industrial action, it was important that as many workers as possible were paid-up union members.

Yet OILC seemed reluctant to concede that its ability to organize stoppages had been weakened. This would have meant conceding the leadership of the campaign to union officialdom. But, with some men on such former strongholds of militancy as the Brent Bravo now doing 'three-weekers' and fifteen-hour shifts, the prospects for further OILC-led unofficial action looked slim. Even on the Tern, where one stalwart, Billy Kennedy, remained defiantly in occupation, some contract workers were doing 'three-weekers'. Others had refused to return offshore, while 'the occupation' still continued. In the end, Billy Kennedy found himself sharing a room with a pipe-fitter who was not only working overtime, but was also regularly working a fifteen-hour shift. On the Brent Charlie, some men were actually working sixteen hours. The unwritten trade union rule that workers in dispute do not work over-time, particularly when colleagues were dismissed, was being largely ignored. Those men who continued to refuse overtime were being put under severe pressure by management, some having to agree to work overtime as a condition of being allowed back offshore.

The Standing Committee oscillated between a desire to condemn such people outright as 'job thieves' and 'scabs', and the realization that to do so would simply alienate the workforce further. It would make it harder to 're-educate' and 'remotivate' them in the longer run.[68] Those few OILC activists who were able to continue working offshore, quickly found themselves 'fin-gered' for the not-required-back (NRB) treatment by management. Rigblast had Les Peel run off the platform when he was overheard in the tea-shack trying to 'noise the men up'. Les Peel had his own personalized OILC T-shirt. It listed the five NRBs he had so far acquired in his career offshore. The letter from Rigblast stated simply, 'We are not prepared to allow you to continue your activities unchallenged.'[69] An activist on the Brent Bravo, a Piper Alpha survivor, was put on the next chopper when he tried to start a collection for OILC. The previous infrastructure of OILC leadership offshore had been decimated by the mass dismissals. As the up-manning continued in the northern sector, the frustration at the 'lack of response' from the back-to-back crew changes was voiced in the Standing Committee. Some dismissed activists wished to issue a call or 'all-out action' as much to confront and embarrass the men themselves, as the employers.[70] As one worker put it, 'We're fighting our own members now – it's fallen flat on its arse'. Another commented sadly, 'They're not even prepared to sit down and discuss any-thing. If you start talking about OILC or the boys that have been sacked, they don't want to know. You're left sitting by yourself.'[71]

The call for an indefinite all-out strike was echoed by a minority within the Standing Committee. It was argued, while there would be no response in the northern sector, the southern sector was still 'raring to go'. A call for a seventh day of action in the southern sector was, therefore, made in the third week of September, but it came after a lull of almost two weeks. Preparations for a stoppage of 48 hours duly made were cancelled at the very last moment, much to the embarrassment of the committee. By the late evening prior to the planned action, with a down-manning of 400 about to take place, work-ers on the DB101 had voted almost unanimously not to take action. The absence of workers from the DB101 left the Morecambe Bay workforce on its own. The Liverpool OILC office issued a press statement that morning, announcing the imminent action. This had to be later repudiated by OILC headquarters in Aberdeen. Now the OCC was able to point to the 'lack of co-ordination and control' by OILC. 'We hope the offshore workforce realize that whatever credibility OILC had, has now gone', said the OCC statement.[72] Based in Aberdeen, the OILC Standing Committee had been listening to the voice of the activists in the south, unable to monitor the often mercurial mood of the workforce as they had done so effectively in the northern sector. From that point on, the potential for further OILC-led unofficial industrial action was exhausted.

The day after this débâcle, a long-rumoured government intervention shifted the balance of forces decisively in favour of the employers. Energy Minister Colin Moynihan announced that the government would be willing to consider requests for exemptions beyond the mandatory date of 31 December for the completion of safety work. Where it could be shown that such delays had been suffered as a 'direct result of recent industrial action', the Department of Energy would be prepared to show flexibility.[73] Thus, at a stroke, any impact of future industrial action was stymied. By the end of September 1990, it was clear that the 'summer of discontent' was over. The future lay, for the time being, with the official trade union movement.

The Registration Campaign

The first sign of problems with the official-led union campaign for a ballot was the decision to extend the registration date for potential members, by first one and then two weeks, into mid-October. It was clear that the 'membership amnesty' to persuade workers to join or rejoin had produced little more than 500 new names in the three major construction unions, the AEU, EETPU and GMB. In addition, those workers who had been dismissed as a result of the dispute were regarded as ineligible to vote in the ballot, for fear of running foul of the employment legislation. Engineering construction and catering had between them a potential constituency of between 7000 and 10,000 members. The unions would be lucky if even half that number was legally eligible to vote on industrial action. So far, it was claimed, a maximum of 4500 had registered in total.[74] The total figure for the three construction unions was probably around the 3000 mark.

The TGWU and NUS catering unions had already balloted their combined memberships for separate strike action in early September. The attempt by the COTA employers to impose a pay differential of 12 per cent between those working on platforms and those on semi-submersibles was rejected by the union officials as undermining the previous unified arrangement with

PAYING FOR THE PIPER

COTA in the northern sector. The results of the COTA unions' ballot had showed the workforce split over industrial action. Out of 1273 papers distributed, 758 were returned of which 615 favoured industrial action. The unions called off the action in the third week in September. As a group, catering workers were even more exploited than the rest of the contract workforce. Among many of them, including the activists, there was now the feeling of 'Why should we sacrifice ourselves in this fight?' Up to 100 of their number had in fact been dismissed for supporting the engineering construction workers.

Even if voting papers were to be immediately distributed to the 10,000 members that it was now claimed were registered by the time the joint union register had closed, any result would not be available until well into late November. The chances of securing an affirmative vote for industrial action in the weeks before Christmas, from a workforce most of whom had already come through a sustained period of industrial action and loss of wages, looked negligible. The offshore dispute provided a textbook case study of how the Conservative employment legislation in respect of balloting could make it extremely difficult to mobilize timely official industrial action while still remaining within the law. There was frustration among the activists over the fact that the official union register had been compiled too late in the campaign. The press adverts encouraging offshore workers to register had only appeared in a few papers. For example, the joint union advert encouraging workers to register appeared only in the northern edition of the Scottish tabloid, the *Daily Record*, which went to Aberdeen, thereby missing the central belt readership.[75] Elsewhere, local newspapers in Hull and Middlesbrough, and the *Lancashire Evening Press, East Anglian Times* and *Eastern Daily News*, carried adverts with local union office contact numbers for workers to call. *Blowout* had carried the unions' advert free of charge, and probably reached more of the offshore workforce.

The National Offshore Committee met again at the end of October to review the final results of the registration campaign. Although it was claimed that approximately 7000 workers had now registered, the figures were far from encouraging in terms of the numbers who could actually be approved for balloting purposes. The decision to postpone the implementation of the ballot until at least the following spring was a foregone conclusion. For the activists it represented a deep disappointment. But realistically the chances of calling for a strike were remote. Even with the best of intentions and the most efficient organization which could have been mustered, the official movement's strategy might well have failed, given the complexities of the industry, the employers' persistent hostility, and the obstacles recently erected by the law.

Table 4.1 *Joint Union Register of Offshore Memberships*

Union	Nos. Registered	Nos. Approved for Ballot
EETPU	1111	600
AEU	1650	1400
TGWU	1500	1500
MSF	1300*	–
GMB		759
RMT	1300–1500†	–
TOTAL		4259

*subject to examination †still to be approved
Source: *National Offshore Committee Minutes.*[76]

The Aftermath: Counting the Cost

Until OILC publicly conceded that its campaign of action was at an end, the OCC had stipulated that it would not set in motion arbitration panels to hear cases of the dismissed workers. The total number of dismissals, around 1000 workers, at that time was staggering. In addition to more than 100 catering workers dismissed from the COTA companies, Press Offshore had dismissed nearly 200, Vauldale 100 and Aberdeen Scaffolding 74, to name only three main employers. In the 1989 dispute, just eight offshore workers were dismissed, all of whom were eventually reinstated. The joint employer–union arbitration panels had been established by OCC companies in the aftermath of the 1989 action. Since then, the majority of contested dismissals had been successfully fought by the unions. It remained to be seen how far that record could be maintained in the new situation of mass dismissals. As it stood, the fate of the dismissed workers remained in limbo.

OILC advised the workers to submit Industrial Tribunal or IT(1) applications, in addition to their joint employer–union arbitration panel applications. Under the Employment Protection Act they were entitled to claim reinstatement on the grounds of 'unfair dismissal for trade union activities'. By citing dismissal for union activities, many of the workforce, who had lacked the statutory two years' employment qualification period with their employer, were at least ensured their right to an industrial tribunal hearing.

The priority was to get as many of these workers as possible back offshore as quickly as possible, and not just with a view to rebuilding organization offshore. Most had experienced several months of severe financial hardship, denied social security payments, and, because the industrial action was unofficial, had been without strike pay from the unions.

OILC finally conceded to the media that unofficial industrial action, although not the actual dispute, was over.[77] The Standing Committee had agreed this after several weeks of agonizing debate which for the first time had begun to split its members in formal votes. Only persistence from the committee's leading members had finally won round the reluctant majority to face the new reality. A small consolation was that many of those workers listed in Shell's OPRIS bar, as 'temporarily not acceptable' on its installations, were beginning to filter back offshore. Many more, however, remained 'sacked and blacked', with the most prominent activists in the sit-ins standing little chance of ever working offshore again. Some men, among them Wood Group employees, had even got as far as Sumburgh airport in Shetland, only to be turned back at the Shell check-in desk. Shell's 'OPRIS bar' differentiated between those occupying workers who had complied with requests to come ashore during the one-day stoppages and those 'who had repeatedly disobeyed the "lawful" instructions of the OIMs' by joining the sit-ins.[78] One inexplicable exception was former OILC spokesperson on the Brent Charlie, John Goddard. Goddard had been allowed back offshore as far back as early September, despite the fact that he was one of the Wood Group employees who had participated in the sit-ins. The name of John Goddard was to feature again in the saga of the North Sea.

But if the dispute had cost the offshore workers dearly, it had cost the industry even more than had been conceded during the Court of Session hearing for Shell's interim interdict. Frank Doran, Labour's shadow spokesperson on oil, a local MP in Aberdeen with his ear very close to the ground, revealed private industry estimates of the costs of the action to be in the region of £120 to £140 million in total. This was roughly £500,000 per day, in addition to a sum of between £50 million and £70 million lost in delays in starting new offshore projects.[79] Before the end of October, Energy Minister Moynihan's earlier offer of extended deadlines for valve installation was taken up by Shell in the Brent field and BP in the Forties. Both companies' applications for extensions beyond the 31 December date were accepted by the Department of Energy.[80] Coincidentally or otherwise, this postponement enabled the previous increase in September UK oil output, to 1.7 million barrels per day, to be sustained until the end of the year. Four-star petrol was to remain below £2 per gallon for the first time since the beginning of the Gulf crisis, which would bring the oil companies some much-needed good publicity.

The Conflict and its Aftermath

The summer of discontent was characterized by all the elements of an industrial dispute (Hiller, 1928; Karsh, 1958; Pondy, 1967). A latent conflict, emerging from discontent over working conditions and safety, was translated into a perceived conflict, in which workers realized that their demands stood in clear and unrelenting opposition to management goals. This perceived, cognitive conflict in turn was transformed into manifest conflict: that is, the adoption of conflictual behaviour by employees and mangement, which we have described in some detail in this chapter. Finally, following the escalation of this labour dispute, a phase of de-escalation was entered.[81] This de-escalation, as so often in recent labour disputes, was characterized not by conflict resolution, but by a mere suppression of existing grievances and a reassertion of raw managerial power (Miller and Woolfson, 1994; Turnbull, Woolfson and Kelly, 1992). This suppression reinternalized latent discontent among the offshore workforce, including resentment against those who were perceived as having given inadequate support towards their cause. The dynamics of organic growth and decay of worker combativeness were interrupted, turning criticism inwards against fellow workers. Even longer overtime hours, conflicts between those who had upheld the strike and the 'back-to-backs' who did not do so, as well as a growing distancing between strike leadership and the offshore workforce, were characteristic of the post-dispute period.

Within this dispute, there were also some rather untypical features. By contrast to a typical labour dispute, there was no established continuing organizational structure which could have provided adequate material, political and psychological support for the workers involved. What organization existed was unofficial, with only indirect links to the established players of industrial conflict. More importantly, the organizational structure of the conflict – OILC and its *ad hoc* Standing Committee – was to a large degree the product of the conflict itself. Its strength and ability to organize, bargain, and negotiate fluctuated with the fate of the workers offshore. It acquired potential bargaining leverage with the gathering wave of strike activity offshore, and conversely, its immediate significance as bargaining agent all but collapsed when stoppages were terminated. In the end, the employers calibrated the threat posed by OILC only against the strength of support for its last stoppage. Gradual attrition of numbers in the sit-ins was taken to signal a trajectory of decline. For the unofficial movement, the possibility of learning new methods of self-defence and of mobilizing new resources against employer strategies was severely limited, not least because those who carried the conflict were now systematically victimized and excluded from the work-force.

Unusual, also, was the position of the employers. Whereas the classical industrial relations literature assumes that employers, at some point in time, will engage in *bona fide* direct bargaining, evidence for the willingness of the contractors to engage in negotiations is at best tenuous (Kochan, 1980). Even if the contractors had wanted to reach an accommodation, they themselves were ultimately constrained by the hidden hand of the operators. The cost–benefit calculus which is attributed to strike action in much conventional literature (Edwards, 1992: 384-5), therefore, played little role in our context.[82] Workers could not and did not immediately aim at any direct material gains; rather they questioned the totality of the assumptions upon which the entire offshore production system had hitherto been based, most fundamentally its managerial authority and legitimacy.

The summer of discontent, in that sense, was reminiscent of earlier types of industrial action which characterized the pre-World War II and early post-war period. It was more akin to an upsurge of social unrest than an attempt at securing incremental bargaining gains. Karsh (1958) notes with respect to collective action in these conditions:

> Situations of social unrest are crucibles in which new shared perspectives are forged out of old ones. … Old loyalties, allegiances, and identifications are at least partially challenged, their efficacy comes under question and the practices which stem from them come under attack.

In this context of a 'social unrest-type' industrial action, the socio-psychological component dominates over the direct economic dimension of the dispute.[83] Collective action is aimed at the re-empowerment of a disenfranchised workforce, rather than short term gains. Such action is by no means rare. In many respects, the offshore workers' dispute was part of a series of industrial disputes aimed at systemic rather than incremental issues. Examples of such actions include the miners' strike of 1984–85, the docks strike of 1989 and the Timex dispute of 1993, to name just a few.[84] In part, these industrial actions reflect a generative collectivism which the most macho management has not been able to extinguish.

The outcome of the summer of discontent was an impasse. On the surface, the causes of this impasse appear obvious. The structures of unofficial labour organizations are said to be inherently weak. Unofficial movements are often too radical, while lacking the professionalism to engage in effective bargaining (Kochan, 1980). Employers, therefore, are likely to ignore or ride out unofficial challenges, anticipating that in the long-run the labour dispute, and possibly the organization behind it, will collapse. In conventional analyses, unofficial labour organizations, therefore, are typically viewed unfavourably. It is postulated that they should be integrated into established bargaining structures (Donovan, 1968). Unofficial movements are viewed as deriving their strength from establishing new sections within the working class, which weaken the prowess of the labour movement as a whole (Turner, 1963). Typically, so the argument goes, they lack solidarity with the needs of others in the labour movement (Turner *et al.*, 1967).

Our analysis suggests that many of the assumptions underlying this conventional view of unofficial action are anachronistic. Particularly in the 1980s and 1990s, employers have challenged the role of established unions as 'accepted' bargaining partners. Establishing recognition and bargaining agreements for existing unions has become by no means automatic. Employer obduracy, combined with unsympathetic legislation, now makes it almost impossible to force recognition through legally balloted official industrial action. One response is for workers to commit themselves to an unofficial forum, which can become a surrogate vehicle for the pursuit of legitimate grievances.

In our analysis, the unofficial movement had overcome rather than reasserted sectional boundaries in this process of challenge. In order to rally the established unions behind OILC, the committee had initially adopted a broad set of goals, namely the aspiration for a North Sea Continental Shelf Agreement. This proposed an industry-wide collective bargaining agreement encompassing all offshore employees. This goal was the ultimate aim. Although providing a convenient rallying point for the one-table approach of the trade unions, it is less clear whether their leaderships regarded it as realistic or even attainable in the short term. After all, no matter how deep the crisis of labour control, a shift from a virtually union-free environment to one of comprehensive union recognition implied a transformation of employer attitudes on a significant, and perhaps unrealistic scale. More realistic, and perhaps more attainable, was the extension of existing collective bargaining arrangements such as the Hook-up to 'post-Hook-up' engineering and maintenance work. At one stage, it looked as if, as in 1989, certain contractors might have been prepared to accept such an agreement. This time around, however, the OILC pursued an 'all or nothing' outcome strategy, raising the stakes to an industry-wide agreement. Therefore, the logic of the campaign prohibited bargaining when there was a limited opportunity to compromise on a sectional basis. In the end, neither an industry-wide agreement, nor a limited 'post-Hook-up' concession was achieved. The established unions, who were unable to openly support the unofficial action, were now given the initiative. Seeking the conventional channel of a legally organized ballot at a time when workforce combativeness was already ebbing away meant that the employers easily regained the upper hand. Employer obduracy, combined with organizational failures on the part of the established union movement, now made impossible the attainment of even this limited objective of the ballot. The balance of forces, as 1990 drew to a close, had shifted decisively in favour of the employers.

In this sense, our story highlights the particular weaknesses and problems a workforce encounters in pursuing an exclusive strategy of unofficial action, particularly in the context of new forms of industrial organization where the immediate bargaining partner – in our case the contractor – is not necessarily the dominant employer. OILC, once the campaign started, had available only very limited choices. Essentially, the only option open to it was successive one-day stoppages. To attempt to involve the mass of the workforce in more, was to risk everything. The sit-ins provided the moral weight for the action, but in a sense they isolated the hard core activists from the rest. The decision to sit in meant confronting management and making personal sacrifices on a wholly unprecedented scale. As one worker commented, 'doing a normal two-week stint is hard enough, I just don't have the stomach to stay out there indefinitely'. Once the strategy of one-day stoppages was itself exhausted, little was left of the unofficial movement's bargaining power.

The next four chapters take us first to the cataclysmic event of the offshore saga, Piper Alpha. We will then assess the impact of the Cullen report on offshore safety and the responses of the employers and the trade union movement to Lord Cullen's recommendations. For the industry, its response to Cullen was driven and constrained by a new set of strategic priorities, Cost Reduction Initiative in the New Era, the so-called CRINE programme. This is the context within which we seek to provide a preliminary appraisal of whether the offshore industry today is any safer than it was at the time of Piper Alpha.

Notes

1. Press information relayed to OILC office, Aberdeen, 2 August 1990.
2. ITN News, 2 August 1990.

3. OILC office telephone communication, 2 August 1990.
4. OILC office telephone communication, 3 August 1990.
5. OILC office telephone communication, 3 August 1990.
6. *Scotsman*, 3 August 1990.
7. *Press and Journal*, 4 August 1990.
8. BBC Radio Scotland News, 4 August 1990.
9. John Whyte, STV Interview, News, 4 August 1990.
10. *Scotsman*, editorial, 4 August 1990.
11. Credence is given to this by later events during the Greenpeace occupation of the Brent Spar installation in 1995. Shell made representations for police and military assistance. In the event, special forces were reportedly available on standby.
12. OILC Emergency Standing Committee, 3 August 1990.
13. *Scotsman*, 6 August 1990.
14. OILC Press Conference, 5 August 1990.
15. BBC and ITV News, 5 August 1990.
16. OCC Press Conference, 7 August 1990.
17. *Lloyd's List*, 8 August 1990.
18. BBC Radio Scotland, 7 August 1990.
19. OILC Dispute Meeting, Music Hall, Aberdeen, 7 August 1990.
20. *Press and Journal*, 8 August 1990.
21. OILC meeting with T. Lafferty, Stonehaven Hotel, 7 August 1990.
22. *Herald*, 9 August 1990.
23. *Scotsman*, 9 August 1990.
24. OILC Press Conference, 9 August 1990.
25. *Press and Journal*, 9 August 1990.
26. *Morning Star*, 9 August 1990.
27. *Herald*, 9 August 1990.
28. OCC Press Release, 9 August 1990.
29. *Herald*, 11 August 1990.
30. OILC Standing Committee, Aberdeen, 11 August 1990.
31. *Sunday Express*, 12 August 1990.
32. *Scotland on Sunday*, 12 August 1990.
33. *Sunday Times*, 12 August 1990.
34. *Herald*, 13 August 1990.
35. *Financial Times*, 10 August 1990.
36. *Independent*, 22 August 1990.
37. *Observer*, Business Supplement, 12 August 1990.
38. See Note 32, *above*.
39. *Scotsman*, 14 August 1990.

40. OILC Press Conference, 13 August 1990.
41. Note 25 *above*.
42. OILC Press Conference, 13 August 1990.
43. OILC Standing Committee, 14 August 1990.
44. *Press and Journal*, 17 August 1990.
45. *Scotsman*, 17 August 1990.
46. ibid.
47. County NatWest Wood Mac, North Sea Supplement, 1990.
48. OILC Standing Committee, 16 August 1990.
49. *Financial Times*, 18 August 1990.
50. *Financial Times*, 22 August 1990.
51. The following account is based on the detailed notes of Martin Gostwick, Scottish Correspondent of the *Morning Star*.
52. ibid.
53. For Lord Cameron's opinion see Shell UK Ltd. v. McGillivray, *Scots Law Times*, Reports, 1991, pp. 667–73.
54. Interview with authors.
55. Occupation diaries 1990, held by the authors.
56. *Scotsman*, 25 August 1990.
57. *Daily Record*, 25 August 1990.
58. *Daily Record*, 27 August 1990.
59. Letter from Tom MacLean, AEU, to Les Balcombe, OCC, 21 August 1990.
60. Letter from Les Balcombe, OCC, to Tom MacLean, AEU, 24 August 1990.
61. *Financial Times*, 31 August 1990.
62. OCC Press Statement, 30 August 1990.
63. *Herald*, 7 September 1990.
64. See Tom MacLean, National Secretary's Report, AEU Journal, September 1990.
65. OCC Press Statement, 12 September 1990.
66. AEU News Release, 11 September 1990.
67. *Scotsman*, 13 September 1990.
68. OILC Standing Committee, 13 September 1990.
69. Letter from Rigblast to Les Peel, 26 September 1990.
70. OILC Standing Committee, 20 September 1990.
71. OILC Mass Meeting, 27 September 1990.
72. OCC Press Statement, 25 September 1990.
73. DEn News Release, 26 September 1990.
74. *Financial Times*, 5 October 1990.

75. *Daily Record*, 19 September 1990.

76. National Offshore Committee Minutes, 29 October 1990.

77. OILC Standing Committee, 11 October 1990.

78. Shell Press Statement, 30 October 1990.

79. *Press and Journal*, 17 October 1990.

80. *Financial Times*, 24 October 1990.

81. There are several models of the stages of strike action. One of the most recent, by Meredeen, 1988, borrows heavily from Hiller, 1928. These models rely on the pre-existing presence of a union and are not applicable to our situation.

82. The classical cost–benefit model of industrial conflict greatly over-simplifies reality. Workers are assumed to engage in industrial action if the expected gains – typically wage gains – from such action substantially exceed the potential costs of the strike. The presence of a union, which articulates these demands, is presupposed. Any wider dimensions of the conflict, beyond immediate wage gains, are usually ignored.

83. This again reflects the narrow dimensions of the conventional industrial relations literature. Conflicts which might have a deep material base are reduced to narrow 'economistic' demands, which are equated to the profit-seeking of the employer.

84. The theoretical literature on strike mobilization has, as Edwards' 1992 survey exemplifies, hitherto largely failed to address the nature of industrial disputes driven by such wider agendas.

PART 3 OCCUPATIONAL SAFETY

Chapters 5 to 8 explore the characteristics of the post-Cullen offshore regime. Chapter 5 investigates Lord Cullen's analysis of the Piper Alpha disaster. We highlight the debate revolving around workforce and union involvement as a means of enhancing offshore safety. In Chapter 6, we lay out the principal elements of economic restructuring in the North Sea. Here we discuss the shifts that have occurred in the relationship between oil majors and supply contractors. Chapter 7 explores the post-Cullen regulatory reconstruction of the offshore health and safety regime, analysing the resistance by the operators, who have deployed a strategy of containment which has led to a gradual erosion of regulatory reform. Chapter 8 complements this analysis with a quantitative investigation of enforcement and accident indicators. We pose the question of whether the criminalization of corporate behaviour might produce more effective compliance than the primary reliance on regulatory reform.

5 LORD CULLEN'S REPORT

So, remember the Piper
You who are to blame
(from *Death of a Piper*, John Fyvie)

On 12 November, Lord Cullen's 800-page report, *An Inquiry into the Piper Alpha Disaster* (Cullen, 1990) was published. This followed a public inquiry lasting thirteen months, between January 1989 and February 1990, during which evidence from 260 witnesses amounting to six million words was considered. At the outset of the inquiry Lord Cullen had explicitly rejected the reported comment of one trade union official who had claimed its remit would be confined to 'the narrow technical question of whether a valve worked or did not work'. Cullen reiterated what he had said at the preliminary hearing:

> On that occasion, I pointed out that my remit was wide, especially in regard to the opportunity which I have to make observations and recommendations with a view to the preservation of life and the avoidance of similar accidents in the future. I said, of course, that my remit does not entitle me to embark on a roving excursion into every aspect of safety at work in the North Sea or into every grievance, however sincere or well founded, that is entertained. But I went on to say that, when considering whether a particular line of evidence should be explored, whoever raises it, the question for me will be whether there is any tenable connection between that line of evidence and the events that occurred. (1990: Ch. 2.15)

Lord Cullen indeed considered issues that went to the heart of how the whole offshore oil industry was managed and run. These issues were part of two key questions the final report sought to answer: what caused the disaster and what could prevent a repeat of such an event in the future? (1990: Ch. 2.7)

The Causes of the Disaster

As regards the immediate causes of the disaster, Lord Cullen broadly confirmed what had already been established by the DEn's own interim technical inquiry. The initial explosion on Piper was a result of the ignition of a low-lying cloud of gas condensate. A pressure safety valve in the gas compression module (C Module) had been removed from a condensate pump for maintenance work and a blank flange had been fitted in its place. This modification was unbeknown to the nightshift. Due to lack of proper communication at shift handovers and a failure to rigorously apply the system of permits-to-work, this maintenance work was still incomplete and the original valve had not been replaced. When one of the pumps for the injection of gas condensate into the main oil export line broke down at 21.45 on the evening of 6 July 1988, the nightshift started up what they presumed to be the relief pump. In so doing they initiated the chain of events that led to an uncontrolled gas emission, leading to an initial explosion which caused extensive damage as the escaping gas found a source of ignition.

The initial explosion at around 22.00 led to a large crude oil fire in B Module which engulfed the north end of the platform in dense black smoke. The fire was spread and sustained by oil leaking from the main oil pipeline to the shore and also from pipelines carrying oil and gas from the connected Claymore and Tartan platforms. Following the explosion and fire in B Module virtually every emergency system was rendered ineffective from the start. A second major explosion occurred some twenty minutes later. This second explosion, which massively intensified the fire, was a result of the rupture of the riser on the high-pressure gas pipeline from the Tartan platform. This was followed at 22.50 by a further rupture of the riser on the export gas pipeline from the MCP–01 compression platform, which was a pumping station from the Norwegian Frigg field to St Fergus. At 23.20, the final gas pipeline to the sister Claymore platform ruptured. At about this time, large sections of Piper Alpha's topsides began to disintegrate and fall into the sea. Despite the visible conflagration on Piper Alpha, described by the Offshore Installation Manager (OIM) on the Tartan as 'a red envelope of flame' (1990: Ch. 7.41), neither the Tartan nor the Claymore platforms were shut down. They continued feeding the inferno that Piper had become.

The sequence of events on the Claymore and the Tartan gives some indication of the unpreparedness of senior personnel for a major emergency, as well as their inability to take an independent initiative with regard to shutting down production. The OIM on the Claymore, 22 miles away from Piper, was told of the fire and explosion on Piper at 22.15 but decided, in spite of the advice of his deputy, to continue production, even though it was known by then that Piper Alpha had shut down oil production. The Claymore continued production until 23.10 after a period of controlled shutdown. An emergency shutdown would have had immediate effect, but the installation manager awaited a direct instruction from Occidental's land-based headquarters before taking any action of a drastic nature, despite the entreaties of his second-in-command. The installation manager on the Tartan, twelve miles away from Piper Alpha, had realized that the situation was serious, but also maintained production in the belief that Piper was doing so. The full shutdown of the gas pipeline took 45 minutes, and the main export valve on the oil pipeline was not closed until 23.52 hours. It was apparent to Lord Cullen that the Tartan's OIM 'was reluctant to take responsibility for shutting down oil production' (1990: Ch. 7.49). Neither the responsible manager on the Tartan, nor his counterpart on the Claymore, appeared capable of reacting to these events by immediately shutting down production on their own installations. If they had done so earlier the rupture of the gas riser from the Tartan platform would probably have been delayed. In the graphic words of one survivor quoted in Lord Cullen's report: 'The Piper did not burn us; it was the other rigs that burnt us' (1990: Ch. 19.4).

The initial explosion knocked out the Control Room and disabled power supplies and communications. Survivors have spoken of the eerie silence that descended on the platform as the background noise of generators and plant abruptly ceased. The fire-water deluge system had been out of commission for several months and was inoperable. At the time of the explosion two of the diesel fire pumps which sucked in water for the fire hydrants were on manual mode. Others were switched off altogether to prevent divers working in the vicinity being sucked into the intake. Had they been operational, it would still have required manual intervention to restart the operation of the pumps, as they could not be switched on again from the Control Room, a crucial deficiency in Piper Alpha's safety system. What sprinklers did operate used the remnants of the water left in the system (Punchard, 1989:126).

Most of the persons on board the installation were in the accommodation area, many in the cinema watching the movie *Carrie*. Others, who were on duty, made their way there in accordance with installation procedures in the event of major emergency. However, smoke and flames outside the accommodation module made the anticipated mode of evacuation by helicopter or lifeboat impossible. Faced with this situation and the virtual disablement or failure of all emergency systems, including the emergency lighting, which had failed after some ten minutes, the situation in the galley area of the accommodation module began to deteriorate into one of panic.

Within another fifteen minutes of the lights failing, dense smoke began to penetrate the galley. The installation manager, whose responsibility it was to assume command and control of the situation, failed to provide any kind of leadership. Inside the accommodation area, the men were forced to crawl along the floor to escape the smoke, using wet towels to assist in breathing. Others were quickly overcome.

According to Ed Punchard (1989), with the rupture of the gas riser from the Tartan at 22.20, 'the conflagration was multiplied tenfold'. Punchard, a diver on Piper Alpha, who provides an account of the unfolding of these terrible events. Says Punchard:

> As there'd been no fire-water deluge either to contain further leaks or cool the massive quantities of machinery, the heat from the fires had compounded the severe failures resulting from the first blast. At the centre of the cellar deck, just above the dive skid, the Tartan gas-import riser blew – eleven and a half miles of eighteen-inch-diameter gas pipeline started to release hydrocarbon gas at a pressure of 1,800 p.s.i. The effects were devastating. A fireball shot out from below the centre of the jacket, enveloped the platform and rose to a height of some 700 feet. The roar was blood-curdling and it was not to stop for the next four hours. (1989:130)

The gas escaped at about three tonnes per second, a rate which is of the same order as that at which the entire UK consumes energy. Following the rupture of the Tartan riser, some of the men decided individually or in groups to ignore advice to wait in the accommodation area for assistance to arrive and to seek their own way out. The Cullen report states:

> Some left the galley because there was no point in staying there. Others realised that if they did not get out they were going to die there. Others took the view that they had nothing to lose by at least attempting to save themselves (Cullen, 1990: Ch. 8.19)

There was no 'systematic attempt to lead men to escape from the accommodation', yet to remain there meant certain death. Those who survived did so either because of sheer luck or because of their familiarity with the platform layout. The entire catering crew of eighteen employed by Kelvin Catering, whose knowledge of the platform outside of the accommodation module was minimal, perished to a man. At least 81 personnel remained in the accommodation. Of those who left the area 28 survived. Among the total of 61 survivors were 5 who jumped off the helideck at the 175 ft level, 15 who jumped off at the pipe deck, 133 ft level, and the remainder who either jumped or climbed down ropes or hoses from various heights, or in one case descended by stairway to the 20 ft level. Many of those who escaped were already horribly injured with burns to their hands and feet. Many of those who jumped from the higher levels did so in the expectation that it was likely to prove fatal, which in at least three cases it was. This firm expectation was a result of the information given during offshore survival training which the men had received. There was no mandatory requirement for personnel to have survival certificates but companies generally insisted upon it. Three of those who died on Piper were found to have had false survival certificates, while eighteen had none at all. A lucrative black market in forged certificates had been created by the practice of even reputable contractors of making employees pay for the costs of their own survival training, sometimes by weekly wage deductions. Nearly two-thirds (63 per cent) of those who had been on night shift duty survived the disaster, whereas only 13 per cent of those off duty did so (1990: Ch. 8.23). Of the bodies which were recovered, eleven of the deceased died by drowning and an equivalent number from injuries, including burns. The main cause of death in the case of 109 victims was inhalation of smoke and gas (1990: Ch. 10.19).

For the lucky ones, once in the water, the grim battle for survival was by no means over. With the platform disintegrating above them and the sea on fire around them, their only hope lay in being plucked from the water as quickly as possible. Regulations required that within five nautical miles of every off-shore manned installation there should be a standby vessel, ready to give assistance in the event of an emergency. On the evening of the disaster the standby vessel for Piper was the *Silver Pit*, a converted trawler, having the capacity for 250 survivors and a fast rescue craft ready to be put into action. In addition, fortuitously or otherwise, the *Tharos*, a semi-submersible vessel owned by Occidental, with fire-fighting capabilities and a helicopter, designated as a support vessel for major emergencies, was stationed close to Piper. It was carrying out tasks in connection with pipeline installation work. Various other vessels were in the vicinity of Piper, including the *Maersk Cutter*, the *Lowland Cavalier* and the *Sandhaven*, the latter being on standby duty for a Santa Fe drilling rig which was four and a half miles from Piper. The *Sandhaven* was equipped with its own fast rescue craft.

Within two minutes of the initial explosion the *Silver Pit* had launched its own fast rescue craft and within a further three minutes had picked up its first survivor, who had walked down stairways to the 20 ft level. Thereafter, it continued to ferry survivors to its parent vessel. Within five minutes of the initial explosion the *Tharos* started moving towards the platform, a process which took about half an hour before close range was reached. Within eleven minutes the helicopter from the *Tharos* was airborne but the pilot reported the helideck on Piper was obscured by smoke. When the Tartan riser ruptured at 22.20, so great was the intensity of the heat that it blistered the paintwork on the *Silver Pit*. At one stage the crew of the work-boat of the *Lowland Cavalier* had to get into the water to escape a fireball whilst attempting to pick up survivors. In the air, RAF Kinloss scrambled a Nimrod and the coastguard brought in Sea King rescue helicopters. Aboard one of these was a television crew making a documentary about the search and rescue services. The cameras meticulously recorded the ghastly unfolding of the events of that night.

The sky was illuminated by flames which roared into the air. The sheer intensity of the blaze was such that effective fire-fighting was an all-but-hopeless task. Nevertheless the *Maersk Cutter* managed to deploy 7500 tons of water per hour through her fire monitors, as well as using her searchlight to point out survivors in the water. The *Tharos* decided to deploy her fire monitors to cascade the platform rather than aim jets of water which might injure the survivors. However, it took half an hour before it began to discharge water under the correct pressure and 50 minutes before all the fire pumps were opened. The delay had been created by pressure problems arising from opening too many monitors simultaneously. By the time the *Tharos* had begun extending her gangway towards the platform, the landing position on Piper was already obscured by smoke and flames. As it was, the fire boom supporting the gangway would have taken 75 minutes to reach the minimum usable length of 30 metres. But at 22.33 the Tharos had received a radio message from Piper: 'People majority in galley area. *Tharos* come. Gangway. Hoses. Getting bad' (1990: Ch. 9.20). The best that could be said of the *Tharos* was that a number of the survivors felt 'the benefit of the spray from her monitors, in particular in giving some alleviation of the intense heat and dense smoke . . . also some cooling to fast rescue craft'.

As the conflagration intensified with the rupture of the MCP–01 riser at 22.50, and a third even more powerful explosion shook Piper Alpha, the *Tharos* had to move away again. In the hype for the capabilities of the *Tharos*, Occidental had quoted 'Red Adair', who was described as having helped in the design of the vessel, saying 'the *Tharos* is the best solution to date'. The editor of *Oil and Gas Journal* was similarly quoted saying that 'the people on the Claymore and Piper fields can certainly now sleep a little bit more safely at night' (1990: Ch. 9.51). Among the survivors the vessel was referred to as 'the most expensive white elephant in the North Sea'. Had they known that the *Tharos* could not get in close, claimed one survivor, some of the men in the accommodation might well have sought their own way out. Lord Cullen considered these and other criticisms of the capabilities and role of the *Tharos* on the night of the disaster, but chose in his wisdom to take a more generous view (1990: Ch. 9.52–58).

The last explosion, which had threatened to partially engulf the *Tharos*, destroyed the fast rescue craft of the *Sandhaven* which had turned back to pick up two additional men, with the immediate loss of the boat's occupants including four survivors and two of its crew of three. The bravery of the crew of the fast rescue craft in returning time after time to the very bowels of the blaze was recognized posthumously by an award to the sole crew member to survive, Ian Letham, no doubt as a result of Lord Cullen's commendation (1990: Ch. 9.34). The crew of the fast rescue craft of the *Silver Pit* were also commended for their 'cool courage in the face of extreme hazard'. Of the 61 survivors, 45 were recovered by these means. Nevertheless, here again the survivors had criticisms, not so much of the crew members, but more specifically of their parent crafts, in particular, of the *Silver Pit* (Punchard, 1989). Badly injured survivors had to endure indescribable agonies as they were first dragged out of the water onto the rescue craft and subsequently transferred to the parent vessels. Some survivors with badly burned hands had to use scrambling nets cast over the side of the *Silver Pit* to climb aboard. Once on board, narrow passageways made manoeuvring stretchers a nightmare. In some respects the crew were ill-prepared and ill-equipped for their tasks, it was claimed, no matter how well intentioned.

What was certainly undeniable were the gross inadequacies of the *Silver Pit* for the job in hand. Just under 90 per cent of the standby vessels, including the *Silver Pit*, were former trawlers, some 40 over 50 years old, and nearly half more than 25 years old. Critics of the industry have pointed out that standby vessels had long been an area where there was clear evidence that the oil operators had sought to minimize costs. The crew of the *Silver Pit* were 'seriously undermanned' and 'should have been better trained', said Cullen. But the actual vessel had been the real failure. Trawlers have limited manoeuvrability and even with the addition of thrusters, as in the case of the *Silver Pit* it was necessary to approach survivors by drifting down-wind, beam on; a necessarily slow process. Hand steering was normal but on the night of the disaster the bow thruster broke down after five minutes. Moreover, the vessel's searchlight was not working, there being no replacement bulbs on the vessel, and the wiring may also have been defective. In any event the lighting would not have covered 360 degrees around the vessel. There were other problems. When an attempt was made to open a gate in the side of the vessel it fell off. An inflatable craft was found to be unserviceable. There were no adequate supplies for treatment of burns such as bandages, no saline drip, no pain killers except the personal supply of the medic and only enough morphine for a few injections. The latter was locked in the master's cabin and only the master could administer it, but he could not leave the bridge. There were insufficient warm clothes, blankets and hot drinks. Men being moved by stretcher to the *Tharos* experienced distress which could have been lessened by the use of a more suitable type of stretcher stowed in the forward area of the vessel but the medic (also the second engineer) was unaware of that. The most seriously injured men had been put in cabins in which it was difficult to manoeuvre (Cullen, 1990: Ch. 9.44–9.46). Of his final 106 recommendations, Lord Cullen was to make nine separate recommendations regarding standby vessels, a number only exceeded by the thirteen recommendations relating to the Safety Case (1990: Vol. 2, Recommendations 88–96).

As dawn broke on the morning of 7 July most of the superstructure of what had been Piper Alpha had either incinerated or collapsed into the sea. What was left of the platform was a smouldering tangled heap of metal and the still burning remains of a gas flare. Of the 167 who died that night, 30 persons from Piper remained missing presumed dead. One of the demands of the Piper Alpha Families and Survivors Association, emblazoned, on their banner, was that the bodies of those who died should be recovered from what was left of Piper. Another of their demands was that Occidental Petroleum be prosecuted and those responsible brought before the courts. It was a demand not only echoed by the trade unions but given banner headline support by the tabloid Scottish *Daily Record* of 13 November on the morning after the report's publication, in two succinct and bold words, 'Charge Them!' The reasons for such anger could be found in Lord Cullen's indictment of Occidental's haphazard and irresponsible attitude to the safety of those who worked on Piper.

The Indictment of Occidental

In his report, Lord Cullen devoted a whole chapter to the organization of work on Piper Alpha, in particular the permit-to-work system and shift handovers (1990: Ch.11). The exact circumstances of the permit concerning the work on the pressure release valve and the shift handover on the evening of 6 July had already been meticulously described in Chapter 6 of the Cullen report (1990: Ch. 6.81–6.109). Now Cullen turned his attention to the general 'way in which Occidental management discharged their safety responsibilities' (1990: Ch. 11.1). Clearly an effective permit-to-work system was central to this as 'an essential part of a procedure to ensure that the work is done safely' (1990: Ch. 11.2). An examination of Occidental's system over a 'substantial period' showed 'numerous errors in completion of various details' (1990: Ch. 11.3). Cullen listed altogether ten examples which, in his own words, 'serve to demonstrate that the operating staff had no commitment to working to the written procedure', and that the procedure was 'knowingly and flagrantly disregarded'. Occidental's system relied on 'informal communication' between personnel rather than on the strict observance of laid-down procedures. Indeed, for many of those who had to work with the procedures, Occidental provided 'no formal training in the permit to work system' (1990: Ch. 11.6). The operator placed the responsibility of ensuring that contractors' employees were familiar with the system on the contractors themselves. Safety inductions for newcomers to the platform made only slight reference to the system, and the small *Safety Handbook* distributed at the heliport by Occidental, while containing three pages on the permit-to-work system for Claymore and Piper, was incorrect , indeed, 'dangerously misleading' as regards the latter platform in several important instances (1990: Ch. 11.8). The handbook contained the injunction that the possessor should 'study it well – it may be your passport to survival'. At induction sessions on the platform, workers were told it was their duty to read it.

Inaccuracies regarding the permit-to-work procedures were compounded by other faulty information. A method of throwing life-raft capsules over the rail – which did not apply to Piper – was shown, and advice on boarding life rafts via scrambling-nets was given. Scrambling-nets had been removed from both platforms in the early 1980s. A number of Piper survivors claimed that they had received no, or at best perfunctory, safety induction on arrival on the platform. Several had never even been shown the location of the liferafts nor how to launch or inflate them. The monitoring and auditing of the permit-to-work system required checking its effectiveness on a routine basis to see if it was operating safely. The safety officer on the platform had not conducted such a review in the twelve months before the disaster. In addition, even the written procedures themselves were in certain respects inadequate and imprecise (1990: Ch. 11.12). Concerns about the permit-to-work system had been raised by the maintenance lead hand at a head office seminar with Occidental in early 1988 but by July 'nothing had really come from this' (1990: Ch. 11.4). 'Everybody had their own idea of how the permit to work system should be applied and it sort of changed week to week and crew to crew.' Lord Cullen regarded these and other similar comments as 'well-founded' and viewed them as underlining 'the grave shortcomings in Occidental's approach to potentially dangerous jobs'.

That the problem with permits-to-work and handover procedures was not new to Piper was illustrated by the so-called 'Sutherland fatality'. Frank Sutherland, a rigger employed by a contractor, was killed on 7 September 1987. He died as a result of injuries sustained from a fall while attempting to attach lifting-gear to overhead beams. The only permit issued for the job was to 'check and repair the thrust bearing'. Lifting operations were not mentioned and a fresh permit, which might have ensured the safe conduct of the work, had not been applied for. Occidental was prosecuted under the HSWA and pleaded guilty to a complaint specifically pinpointing the absence of a 'new permit' to work and 'inadequate communication of information' between shifts (1990: Ch. 11.16). 'Inadequate communication of information', it may be suggested, was one of the hallmarks of the industry since its inception. Its basis often lay in the wider atmosphere of fear, secrecy and intimidation which inhibited the free flow of communication throughout the offshore world. Perhaps typically, although two memorandums were issued concerning Piper Alpha, one of them specifically encouraging more detailed job descriptions in the permits-to-work, such action 'did not have a lasting effect on practice', said Cullen (1990: Ch. 11.16).

Piper Alpha had been one of the few platforms in the North Sea which actually had a functioning safety committee, although made up of contractors' employees only. In March 1984, there had been a near-disaster on Piper Alpha involving an explosion, gas release and fire which resulted in a full-scale and fortunately successful rig evacuation by helicopters which, unlike the situation in 1988, were able to land on the platform. As in 1988, it was apparent that the *Tharos* had problems in extending her gangway onto the platform. The results of an internal Occidental board of inquiry into the 1984 incident, rubber-stamped by the DEn at the time, were not made available for discussion to the safety committee or to the trade unions, who requested a copy of the report. The Occidental employee safety representatives resigned in protest. At the time of the Piper disaster supervisors from the various departments effectively dominated the remaining contractor workforce representatives.

In 1984, the DEn had concluded that prosecution of Occidental would not be appropriate. The 'dangerous occurrence' of that time was ascribed to a 'design fault', probably attributable to the work of non-United Kingdom bodies. Further, according to the Energy Minister, 'prompt corrective action had voluntarily been taken by the operator'.[1] Occidental's report on this earlier near-disaster was only revealed on the same day as the DEn released its interim technical report into the Piper Alpha disaster, and could only be read in the DEn's library. One of the Occidental employee representatives who resigned in protest from the safety committee after the 1984 episode, George Fowler, was himself to die when Piper exploded in July 1988.

Occidental's attitude towards communicating the results of its own board of inquiry into the Sutherland fatality can be gauged from the fact that 'the result of the investigation was not passed to senior onshore personnel, let alone senior personnel on the platform' (1990: Ch. 14.32). The platform installation manager heard some of the conclusions 'on the grapevine' but did not see a copy of the report. A memorandum concerning the fatality from the Legal Department to the Vice-President Engineering, one Mr G. E. Grogan, submitted a few days after Frank Sutherland was killed, perhaps illustrates the prevailing attitude most forcefully. It is quoted in Lord Cullen's report:

> I would confirm that there is significant exposure here and that prosecution is possible. I would therefore respectfully suggest that we proceed with care, particularly in our dealings with the Department of Energy. I would suggest that staff be reminded not to discuss the detail of the incident itself or follow-up investigation. (1990: Ch. 14.32).

What had resulted from the review of the earlier 1984 incident was an increased emphasis on helicopters as 'the favoured means of evacuation' in the event of a major emergency and an improvement in the radio communications from Piper (1990: Ch. 14.13). A memorandum prepared by the onshore Safety Superintendent significantly entitled 'How It Was vs How It Could Have Been' pointed out that the actual incident had occurred under extremely favourable weather conditions in which all systems of containment and emergency support had been effective. In particular, doubts were raised about the ready availability and efficacy of a rapid intervention vessel in fighting a prolonged fire fed from a ruptured gas riser. This is precisely the scenario that the *Tharos* faced four years later, even though by pure chance it was already on the scene. The 1984 memorandum, however, was felt by Occidental's senior staff to be 'painting the worst case situation'. Although a number of additional measures were considered such as re-siting an alternative helideck, re-siting lifeboats and providing an in-field helicopter, these were rejected as the platform was thought self-sufficient in catering for any types of emergency (1990: Ch. 14.15).

When Piper Alpha blew up under far better than the 'worst case' conditions, the assumption that internal fire-fighting equipment would be an effective means of controlling the situation proved hopelessly wrong. The diesel fire pumps were kept on a manual mode while divers were in the water to prevent accidents around the pump intakes. There was no switch in the Control Room which would have enabled them to be immediately transferred to automatic mode. The need to keep the fire-water system in peak operating condition at all times was increased by the fact that on Piper, unlike the Claymore, there was no fireproofing of the structure or the gas risers. Yet during the diving season, the pumps were routinely kept on manual mode between 6 p.m. and 6 a.m. the following morning; a practice endorsed by the installation manager, and described by Cullen as having 'inhibited the operability of the pumps in an unnecessary and dangerous way' (1990: Ch. 12.11). Worse, however, was that the deluge systems in the critical area of the gas compression module had been discovered to be 50 per cent blocked by scale in a routine test in May 1988. This was a well-known and longstanding problem. The disaster occurred before the planned replacement of pipework in the deluge system could take place.

A further instance of what can perhaps best be described as senior management complacency, was Occidental's attitude to the 1987 Saldana consultant's report which specifically addressed the problem of the rupture of a gas riser and a prolonged high pressure gas fire (1990: Ch. 14.19–24). In Lord Cullen's own words:

> I must make every effort to avoid being influenced by hindsight, but making all allowances for that I consider that management were remiss in not enquiring further into the risks of a rupture of one of the gas risers and in such an event the risk of structural damage and injury to personnel. (1990: Ch. 14.23)

Occidental's attitude to the assessment of risk was deemed to be unsatisfactory, and the quality of their management lacking, in reviewing and monitoring safety procedures. In addition the company was found to be deficient in investigating past incidents and learning the lessons from them. It had failed to recognize the safety implications of changes in equipment and activities. As regards this last point, Lord Cullen found it 'puzzling' that with so much ongoing construction and maintenance work on Piper Alpha, the decision had been made to allow production to continue (1990: Ch. 14.43). Others, perhaps not as even-handed and restrained in their comments as Lord Cullen, were in no sense puzzled by Occidental's failure to order a shutdown. They pointed instead to the imperatives imposed by the 'bottom line'. Despite the measured tones of his report, however, Lord Cullen's evaluation of Occidental's conduct is not far from utterly damning:

> It appears to me that there were significant flaws in the quality of Occidental's management of safety which affected the circumstances of the events of the disaster. Senior management were too easily satisfied

that the PTW (permit to work) system was being operated correctly, relying on the absence of any feedback of problems as indicating that all was well. They failed to provide the training required to ensure that an effective PTW system was operated in practice. In the face of a known problem with the deluge system they did not become personally involved in probing the extent of the problem and what should be done to resolve it as soon as possible. They adopted a superficial response when issues of safety were raised by others, as for example at the time of Mr Saldana's report and the Sutherland prosecution. They failed to ensure that emergency training was being provided as they intended. Platform personnel and management were not prepared for a major emergency as they should have been. (1990: Ch. 14.52)

Trenchant as these criticisms were, they were surpassed by those laid at the door of the regulatory body, the Department of Energy, which had failed to reveal these deficiencies on Piper Alpha documented by Lord Cullen.

The Offshore Regulatory Regime

The problems of Occidental's safety management can in part be traced to a faulty regulatory system which had evolved in an utterly haphazard way. The UK government ratified the Convention on the Law of the Sea of 1958 and incorporated it into UK law in the Continental Shelf Act of 1964. The Act vested in the Crown entitlement to dispose of the hydrocarbon reserves of the Continental Shelf. Exploration and production licences were subject to model clauses prescribed by regulations under the Petroleum (Production) Act 1934. The system of licensing was extended offshore by the Continental Shelf Act of 1964. So far as safety issues were concerned, the main focus of this Act was on minimizing the risk of a well 'blowout' (1990: Ch. 16.20). The regulations required the identification and approval of an 'operator' discharging the responsibilities of the licensees. Effectively, however, short of shutting down a drilling operation, which occurred on a couple of occasions, the only means of securing safe practices offshore was to revoke the operator's licence. In Department of Energy parlance this 'would have been using a sledgehammer to crack a nut, even if it had been politically acceptable'.[2] Attempts in Parliament to secure amendments that would make the offshore application of the Factories Acts quite explicit were 'stiffly resisted' by the offshore industry (Carson, 1982: 146). The inadequacies of these arrangements were revealed in 1965 when the jack-up rig, the Sea Gem, collapsed with the loss of thirteen lives. The Ministry of Power, the predecessor of the Department of Energy, set up a Tribunal to investigate the disaster, but the Tribunal was forced to operate without statutory authority and without the power to compel the attendance of witnesses or to administer oaths (Carson, 1982: 148; Ministry of Power, 1967: 1).

It was recognized that safety legislation was required, since the only sanction available to ensure proper safety procedures was licence revocation. The procedures relating to the safety of employees were put into operation in theory through the voluntary Model Code of Safe Practice in the Petroleum Industry issued by the Institute of Petroleum in 1964. There were no penal sanctions which could be invoked (Ministry of Power, 1967: 2). The Tribunal therefore identified the need for a statutory code supported by 'credible sanctions' (Ministry of Power, 1967: 24). In consequence, the Mineral Workings (Offshore Installations) Act 1971 (MWA) was passed, although after a considerable delay. It was not until 1969, two years after the Tribunal had reported, that the Labour government announced its intention to legislate, but it had left office without finding sufficient parliamentary time for a Bill to be presented. Reviewing this sequence of events, Carson concluded:

> It would not perhaps be too unkind to take the legislative alacrity of the Conservatives in 1964 and the subsequent tardiness of their Labour successors as indexing something akin to bi-partisan neglect with regard to safety. (1982: 150)

The MWA empowered the Secretary of State to require the offshore installations to be certified as fit for purpose and for regulations to be made 'for the safety, health and welfare of persons on offshore installations' (Cullen, 1990: Ch.16.3). In practice the MWA had both positive and negative features. Said Peter Selwood, a senior DEn official with responsibility for offshore safety:

> The advantages of the legislation are powers of prosecution based on detailed specific regulations. The *disadvantage* is that the more detailed the regulations, the more resistance there is by Company personnel to our enforcing items that are not *specifically* mentioned.[3]

The prescriptive nature of the MWA, leading to compliance with the letter rather than the spirit of the law, characterized so much subsequent offshore legislation; compliance, however, was never rigorously pursued by the regulator. In the early 1970s the government was anxious to reassure the industry that it intended to proceed by 'benevolent enforcement . . . generally advisory in nature' (Carson, 1982: 152). The Minister responsible for shepherding the original Bill through Parliament was Nicholas Ridley MP. It was his mission to convince the industry that the new regulatory system was 'fair, reasonable, effective and practicable' (1982: 152). The MWA came onto the statute book just as exploration was moving into 'more northerly and much more expensive areas' of the North Sea (1982: 152). The government was preparing to embark on the fourth round of licensing to stimulate the rapid development of oil extraction. It was therefore necessary not to discourage this new spirit of activity by a 'hostile' regulatory framework. In Carson's words, the industry was to be offered

> effective guarantees that the rules of the game would not be radically altered in such a way as to compromise cost profiles or timescales, and this is arguably what heavy-handed legislation might well have appeared to be doing. (1982: 153)

In some sense the MWA was 'tailor-made' to the needs of the industry (1982: 153). Effectively, the DEn presided over a regulatory set-up characterized by Carson as the 'institutionalised tolerance' of non-compliance (1982: 231).

At the same time, onshore, a comprehensive re-examination of health and safety legislation was taking place under the Robens committee, which reported in 1972 (Robens, 1972). Robens found that the existing legislation, including 30 Acts and some 500 sets of regulations, was too complex and that there was 'too much law'. Furthermore, Robens felt that existing safety law was too preoccupied with the physical circumstances of work rather than the safest way of organizing it. He sought to address what he saw as the underlying defective attitudes encouraged by the existing prescriptive legislation which made for superficial compliance with the detailed letter of the law, at the expense of a more fundamental appraisal of safety as a system. Robens called for legislation which would promote effective 'self-regulation' by those who created the risks, rather than reliance on punitive sanctions as a means of securing compliance. In addressing underlying attitudes to safety and the proper management of safety systems, Robens promoted what is generally described as the move towards more modern goal-setting regulations. What ensued was the single comprehensive unifying Health and Safety at Work Act 1974 (HSWA), essentially based on Robens' philosophy of self-regulation and goal-setting legislation. It was an approach, both at the time and since, which has been criticized as having certain intrinsic weaknesses (Woolf, 1973; Dawson et al., 1988; Nichols and Armstrong, 1973; Woolfson and Beck, 1996). Robens' flawed and simplistic view of accident causation, the downgrading of the role of external regulatory control and of legal sanction, and the over-estimation of a 'natural consensus' between employers and employees on safety limited the efficiency of Robens' and the HSWA approach to safety. Perhaps equally importantly, it separated safety concerns from issues of industrial relations. In comparison to the detailed prescriptive legislation which had preceded it, the HSWA with its new emphasis on first principles, was an advance. As such, it stood in sharp contrast to the slow and reactive evolution of offshore safety regulation under the more prescriptive MWA. In Carson's telling phrase, the MWA 'was in a sense almost an anachronism before it came into effect' (1982: 153).

The HSWA imposed wide-ranging general duties on employers to ensure the health and safety of their employees, 'so far as reasonably practicable'. From early 1975, the onshore regulatory body, the Health and Safety Commission (HSC) had indicated its desire to assume responsibility for occupational safety offshore (Carson, 1982: 193). In Parliament, itself, there was political pressure building up to extend the HSWA to the Continental Shelf, partly because of concerns over safety and partly in the hope that the provisions of the Act for the appointment of trade union safety representatives would assist unionization offshore. In July 1976 it was announced that the HSWA would be extended offshore, although responsibility for structural safety and blowout risks was to remain with the DEn. What followed was peculiar administrative fudge and delay: the two signal characteristics of offshore safety. Even this is to oversimplify, since while the HSE was also to assume direct responsibility for occupational safety in connection with pipelaying operations and crane ships, the structural safety of these vessels remained with the Department of Trade, which it implemented under the Merchant Shipping Acts. Helicopter travel, the responsibility of the Civil Aviation Authority, however, remained a further administrative 'loose end', until continuing concerns over safety and a series of further disasters were to bring its regulatory practices under scrutiny.

The HSWA had eventually been extended offshore over a year later by Order in Council on 1 September 1977, although various individual sets of regulations under the HSWA required a separate offshore extension which in crucial cases never took place, e.g. regarding the control of hazardous substances, and on safety representatives and safety committees, of which more below. The responsibility for the front-line offshore safety administration was not given to HSE inspectors, however, but transferred after some further delay of fourteen months to the DEn under what was known as the 'agency agreement', dated 1 November 1978. The 'agency agreement' between the Health and Safety Commission and the DEn empowered the Secretary of

State for Energy to enforce legal safety requirements offshore. This work was in the main carried out by the Safety Directorate of the Petroleum Engineering Division (PED) of the DEn. Lord Cullen sought to examine the effectiveness of the system of offshore inspection and investigation by the PED that was then in place. The DEn's own statement of objectives produced at the inquiry reflects the attitude that had persisted among regulators.

> The purpose of inspection is not exclusively to seek out cases of non-compliance with the regulations, but more to assess the adequacy of the safety of the installation as a whole. This is an essentially selective procedure. Neither in this, or in any other area of industrial safety, would it be possible or right to provide total supervision of the operator's activity, which he carries out in pursuance of his own primary responsibility for safety. The purpose of inspection, supported as necessary by enforcement, is to provide stimulus and support to that eventual activity and to ensure that standards are maintained. (1990: Ch. 15.4)

Inspection by the Petroleum Engineering Division

At the time of the disaster there were 139 fixed installations and 76 active mobile ones in the UKCS. The average period between inspections was between 12 and 18 months. According to Jim Petrie, Director of Safety of the PED since 1987, such inspections were 'essentially a sampling exercise' aimed at obtaining an overall picture of the installations' operation, rather than a detailed checklist. They would normally take two days and could cover any aspect of the installation. The inspector for Piper was a certain Mr R. D. Jenkins who had joined the PED in March 1987. Offshore inspections were not surprise visits, due to the need to obtain the operator's permission to secure a helicopter place and the problems of providing visitors' accommodation offshore, lack of which required advanced notice to be given.

The inspection could cover any aspect of installation activity and the view of Mr Petrie was that during visits the inspector would 'ensure he was available to discuss any points which personnel wished to raise with him' (1990: Ch. 15.10). This, it should be said, was not a view shared by the contractor workforce, most of whom had never seen an inspector, far less been consulted by one, a situation which appears to have persisted since Carson had reported a similar observation at the time of his research, a decade previously (1982: 222). Mr Jenkins, however, envisaged a further point of employee contact in meeting with workforce safety representatives. Since the representatives on Piper Alpha were non-elected supervisors, 'a formal meeting was not held with them'. After the inspection, the inspector would discuss any concerns with the OIM and give him a note of any matters requiring attention. There would also be a letter to the company. If the inspector remained dissatisfied he could (i) indicate improvements to be made; (ii) enforce these by use of improvement or prohibition notices under the HSWA; or (iii) recommend prosecution, the latter being the very last resort, and as the record shows, almost never resorted to (1982: 230 ff). Subsequent reports prepared after an inspection visit would be consulted by the next visiting inspector.

Another aspect of the PED Safety Directorate's work examined by Lord Cullen was the investigation of accidents and dangerous occurrences, from which it was supposed 'lessons . . . can be learnt' (1990: Ch. 15.14). Any serious accident offshore was to be immediately reported to the DEn and was then supposed to be subject to investigation, especially if the accident had proved or was likely to prove fatal. Mr Petrie said that all fatalities and accidents involving extensive injuries were investigated to see if there were any major lessons to be learnt (1990: Ch. 15.15). The DEn also claimed that 'so also were the larger explosions and any "near misses", having regard to their potential severity'. In fact, only 40 per cent of the total of fatal and serious accidents reported to the Department were investigated, while many 'near-misses' were grossly under-reported. The 40 per cent figure was regarded by Mr Petrie as an acceptable, 'indeed quite high' level of investigation. Limitations on manpower were cited as the reason for this state of affairs.

Turning to the inspection of Piper and the activities of Mr Jenkins, Lord Cullen had the results of two visits to consider, the first in June 1987 and again in June 1988, a mere eleven days before the disaster. There was, in addition, a further visit in September 1987, the day after the death of Frank Sutherland. The visit in June 1988 was not merely routine but also a 'check visit' consequential on Occidental's prosecution following the Sutherland fatality and the issues of permit procedures which that had raised. In the event, ten hours were devoted to the inspection of Piper in June 1988 during which time Mr Jenkins took 'a comprehensive walk' round all the production and drilling areas and the 68 ft level (1990: Ch. 15.23). The inspector appeared satisfied that the handover between shifts, another aspect of the Sutherland fatality, had been 'tidied up' (1990: Ch. 15.24). It appeared that there had been no time to witness an actual handover, and what the inspector had received were merely verbal assurances. Some examination was also made of the permits in the Control Room but 'nothing abnormal was found' and since the permit-to-work 'was not regarded as a key factor in the Sutherland fatality' he did not concentrate on it any further. There was no attempt made to assess the overall quality of the permit system in the light of that fatality (1990: Ch. 15.25). The inspector's report suggested that lessons appeared to have been learnt from that fatality and that a routine inspection in one year's time would be appropriate (1990: Ch. 15.26).

Lord Cullen was moved to comment on what he called the 'striking contrast' between the above and 'what was revealed by the evidence in the inquiry'. Lord Cullen also examined the qualification and training of inspectors, the guidance given to them, the monitoring of their work and the manning of the Inspectorate itself, which over the previous decade had remained persistently understaffed. Offers of secondments of HSE staff to the PED to assist in the shortfall in their inspectorate were resisted even though at times the PED was 50 per cent under strength. In his final observations on the inspection system the full force of criticism was directed at the regulatory regime overseen by the DEn both with respect to Piper and in the wider sense.

> Even after making allowances for the fact that the inspection in June 1988 proceeded on the basis of sampling it is clear to me that it was superficial to the point of being of little use as a test of safety on the platform. It did not reveal any one of a number of clear-cut and readily ascertainable deficiencies. The visit failed to follow up the investigation into the Sutherland fatality in an effective way, in that Mr Jenkins failed to grasp the importance of the weakness in the permit to work system and misunderstood the position in regard to the procedure for handovers. (1990: Ch. 15.48)

> It would be easy to place responsibility for these criticisms on Mr Jenkins but I do not consider that this would be fair, having regard to his relative inexperience and the limited guidance which he was given. Further this would not address the shortcomings in the inspection system itself. In my view the inspectors were and are inadequately trained, guided and led. Persistent under-manning has affected not only the frequency but also the depth of their inspections. These shortcomings affected the quality of the inspections on Piper, and in particular the inspection in June 1988. Apart from any other consideration, the length of the visit at that time was manifestly inadequate having regard to the size of the installation, the activities then taking place and the recent fatality. (1990: Ch. 15.49)

Finally, in questioning the inspection system 'in a more fundamental sense', as exemplified by the 'sampling' approach to offshore inspections, Cullen noted:

> the limitations of sampling, especially on the basis of 'what catches the eye' within a relatively short visit to an installation runs a plain risk of missing what lies deeper than a surface inspection and of failing to reach a true assessment of the installation as a whole. (1990: Ch. 15.50)

Only five inspectors policed the entire North Sea oil industry and routine inspections had been reduced from once every six months to once a year or more.

Yet for all the incisive nature of Lord Cullen's criticisms of the DEn's inspection regime, he specifically rejected the view that the regulatory procedures of the DEn had been compromised in the area of safety, either by the closeness of the department's connections with the industry or by the DEn's desire as sponsoring ministry to facilitate the maximum rate of oil extraction by the industry. Said Cullen, 'I am not convinced that the Safety Directorate actually lacks independence or that its actions had been affected by considerations relating to the exploitation of resources' (1990: Ch. 22.38).

Writing in the early 1980s, Carson observed that the inspection processes carried out by the PED tended 'to revolve around a central preoccupation with major hazards' (1982: 241). This led to a neglect of 'the detail of more mundane issues' which related to general occupational safety. This created some resentment on the part of professional offshore safety personnel who felt their efforts were being wasted, as well as on the part of the HSE. One official who is quoted by Carson underscored the difference in approach between the two authorities.

> Quite often they [the DEn] get the big things right – the big things are more dangerous for an enforcing authority ... But, you know, you've got to get the little things right. That's where you make the biggest impact on accidents. (quoted in 1982: 241)

Even in the 'big things' the PED got it drastically wrong. As Carson said, 'the role of law in the protracted business of raising the standard of routine, everyday operations was undervalued' (1982: 242).

Carson documented the case history 'of one of the most important North Sea platforms'. This is important because it demonstrates that the regulatory tolerance which the Piper Alpha inquiry revealed was by no means unique.

The case history relates to the erection in late 1974 of temporary living accommodation described as 'portacabins' during the phase of platform construction. Before oil production had started up, the DEn had granted an exemption from the requirement for a Certificate of Fitness under the Construction and Survey Regulations 1974. The deadline for a certificate specifying appropriate levels of fire protection and escape routes was August 1975. In June 1975 an inspector had noted potential problems in safe evacuation should an emergency arise. By this time drilling activity had already begun. A second visit, three weeks before the August deadline, noted that production was due to begin before the end of the month. Some tentative concerns were raised at the overlap of construction and production phases. However, the platform received its Certificate of Fitness some ten days after the prescribed date. Carson quotes DEn correspondence with the company, that 'concurrent construction, drilling and production had not been contemplated when the regulations were drafted', so Certifying Authorities were advised 'to virtually ignore construction quarters and activities and [to] give partial certificates to "drilling"' (1982: 243). This had subsequently been extended to include production. One month after the Certificate of Fitness had been issued, another inspector visited the platform and confirmed that production had indeed commenced although there were still some months to platform completion. This inspector expressed doubts as to the 'efficacy of the Certificate of Fitness', given that 55 of the 199 persons on board were construction workers. While acknowledging 'the economic plight of the country and the political significance of producing oil yesterday', the DEn inspector suggested that the 'start-up' had been three months too soon and went on, 'I state this so that no-one is in any doubt that corners are being cut and calculated risks are being taken to obtain objectives' (1982: 244).

While on this occasion it was felt that the risks were 'valid', after a visit some six months later the same inspector felt compelled to write to the company's safety officer to the effect that, notwithstanding the Certificate of Fitness, 'many disturbing features are still evident'. Guidance Notes issued by the department in May 1977 attempted to rectify some of these issues although it appears the company made one additional, possibly successful, attempt to secure a further exemption in regard to the 'temporary' accommodation. Carson is unclear as to the final outcome of these events.

With regard to the accommodation block on Piper Alpha, there is no lack of clarity as to the outcome. In its submissions to the inquiry, the Trade Union Legal Group presented the Bechtel Design Specification (OXY/DAI–1), in which the temporary nature of the Piper Alpha accommodation block is identified.[4] The Piper Alpha accommodation was, in fact, part of a job-lot of ex-US Air Force base modules originally located in Alaska and purchased by the oil industry. Four of these, owned by Arco, had burnt out while still in Alaska and one, owned by Bawdens, had also suffered a similar fate while in store. Nevertheless, two of these modules had subsequently been placed on the Piper Alpha platform, one remaining at the time of the disaster. It was in this module that many of the Piper victims met their appalling end.

Official doubts about the fire protection capabilities of such modules were first raised in correspondence between the DEn and Occidental on 19 March 1975.[5] Inquiry Production 341 by the Trade Union Legal Group was the DEn's exemption for the accommodation module on Piper, dated 1 July 1975. This exemption overruled concerns expressed by Lloyd's Register, the Certifying Authority. The DEn granted permission to use the accommodation module three months later, on 4 October 1975. It was to remain in place for the next thirteen years. Amoco had also used identical accommodation to this on its Rough platform in the southern gas fields. As previously pointed out, the temporary living quarters on its Montrose platform in the northern sector remained in use, with exemption from the DEn, given *after* Piper Alpha.

Lord Cullen was much exercised by the lack of adequacy of the accommodation block on Piper which was the designated key muster and control point for evacuation in the event of an emergency. Indeed, Cullen's key recommendations, examined in the following section, detail specific measures in terms of the location of accommodation areas and the blast and fire-proofing construction requirements for such modules. Cullen suggested that they might constitute 'temporary safe refuges' for platform personnel. He saw them as intrinsic to the new Safety Case regime he would propose. Yet, in view of the evidence of systematic non-application of regulatory controls on the industry by the DEn, it is perhaps surprising that Lord Cullen was not more forthright. The oil companies had successfully sustained an offshore fief virtually unconstrained by regulatory interference up until Piper Alpha. The power of the oil majors was exemplified in a *de facto* 'zone of exclusion' which embraced the entire UK Continental Shelf and enabled them to conduct their operations unmolested by officialdom. In essence, the DEn had been subject to 'regulatory capture' by the very industry over whose conduct it was charged with regulatory oversight. John Rimington, Director General of the HSE, tellingly depicted the essence of regulatory capture to Lord Cullen's inquiry: 'When we ourselves bring forward some fresh regulation, the first thing that many of those whom we regulate think of doing is to poach one of our experts who has been busy developing it.'

The Prevention of Future Disasters

The second volume of Lord Cullen's report concentrated on the prevention of disasters similar to Piper Alpha. The main concern was to make specific recommendations with regard to what sort of system of safety management and form of regulation should replace that which had so obviously failed. Two crucial comparators existed which had to be considered: the onshore safety regime administered by the HSE under the HSWA and the Norwegian offshore model. Both were in key respects superior to what Cullen had found in the British offshore sector. What the comparators provided, was a comprehensive system of safety assessment and its management based on a completely different conceptual approach.

The concept of 'Formal Safety Assessment' (FSA) highlighted by Cullen involved 'the identification and assessment of hazards over the whole life cycle of a project' through all its stages of development to final decommissioning and abandonment. Included in the concept of FSA were certain analytical techniques of risk assessment. Such techniques include hazard and operability studies (HAZOP); quantitative risk assessment (QRA); fault tree analysis; human factor analysis; and safety audits (1990: Ch. 17.13). Formal Safety Assessment results in what is known as a 'Safety Case', a systematic documented review of all hazards potentially existing on an installation, and the safety management systems put in place to deal with them. The notion of the Safety Case became the centrepiece of Lord Cullen's proposals for the new offshore regime.

Onshore, the Safety Case approach had been an important aspect of the regulation of major hazard installations such as petro-chemical establishments. In fact the regulations which governed the conduct of such establishments, the CIMAH (Control of Industrial Major Accident Hazards) Regulations 1984, had their origins in the Flixborough disaster in 1974 and in the Seveso disaster in Italy in 1976. This had resulted in an EC Directive on Major Accident Hazards, known as the 'Seveso' Directive (Directive 82/501/EEC). Both these pieces of legislation imply or utilize the concept of a Safety Case. The Safety Case, then, is 'a means by which an operator demonstrates to itself the safety of its activities' (1990: Ch. 17.11). It also 'serves as the basis for the regulation of major hazard activities' by the regulatory authority, which in the case of CIMAH is via an inspector of the HSE who would check and evaluate the contents of the Safety Case (1990: Ch. 17.12). This could include both the hardware aspects of the establishment and its procedural and safety management systems. The requirement that the operator produce such a Safety Case was seen in itself as a 'valuable exercise' since the assessment of risk engendered awareness of potential hazards. The Norwegian model, Cullen observed, had 'developed in the same general direction' (1990: Ch. 17.7). Indeed, this kind of approach had been in place in the Norwegian sector since the mid to late 1970s with attempts to apply numerical criteria of risk assessment and analysis since the early 1980s. The latest version, the 1990 Norwegian regulations, no longer contained numerical acceptance criteria but placed the major emphasis on general goal-setting rather than more prescriptive regulations which underlay the whole approach to safety in the British offshore sector (1990: Ch. 17.19–20).

By contrast, the British offshore regime overseen by the DEn, had in Lord Cullen's view moved in this direction only slowly and with considerable hesitation (1990: Ch. 17.25). There seemed little understanding of the possible relevance of the CIMAH Regulations in the DEn. None of the existing offshore regulations had as yet been amended from the detailed prescriptive approach towards a more goal-setting form (1990: Ch. 17.27). The operators' association UKOOA, in their evidence to Cullen, now favoured Formal Safety Assessment, which was equivalent to a CIMAH Safety Case. It was to be carried out by individual operators. This was something of a latter-day conversion. Although Cullen did not choose to comment upon it, evidence by the Certifying Authorities had been presented to the previous inquiry into offshore safety under Burgoyne, criticizing the offshore industry for its failure to learn from the experiences in safety engineering of other technologically sophisticated industries (Burgoyne, 1980: 154). The Trade Union Group argued that the Safety Case should be implemented by the immediate extension of the CIMAH Regulations offshore. Lord Cullen accepted that the Safety Case goal-setting approach should become an intrinsic part of the new offshore regime. He said:

> The offshore Safety Case, like that onshore, should be a demonstration that the hazards of the installation have been identified and assessed, and are under control and that the exposure of personnel to these hazards has been minimized. (1990: Ch. 17.37)

Central to the Safety Case would be the demonstration that an installation possessed a 'temporary safe refuge' (TSR), an area with specified durability in the event of a major incident in which employees could shelter for sufficient time to permit their safe evacuation. Quantitative Risk Assessment (QRA) was seen as an important tool in this respect whose purpose it was 'to assess the risks, to identify and assess potential safety improvements, and to ensure that the TSR meets the standard set' (1990: Ch. 17.61). But Lord Cullen did not consider FSA and the Safety Case, as UKOOA had argued, sufficient in themselves as a system of safety management. In Cullen's view, FSA and the Safety Case required the complement of a system of goal-setting regulations 'setting intermediate goals [which] would give the regime a solidity it might otherwise lack', for example in construction, fire and explosion protection, evacuation, escape and rescue (1990: Ch. 17.63). This transition to a new offshore regime would not 'take place overnight' (1990: Ch. 17.67). Cullen's proposal to assign a central role to FSA and the Safety Case led him to consider what would be the appropriate body to evaluate the operator's Safety Case. This was perhaps the single most important question dominating the reconstruction of offshore safety after Piper Alpha: which agency would have the future regulatory responsibility for offshore safety?

The Burgoyne Report 1980

Lord Cullen reviewed the whole history of safety legislation, its philosophy and its administration both offshore and on. A key starting point of this review was the inquiry into offshore safety in the late 1970s under Dr J. H. Burgoyne. Burgoyne, a consultant scientist and engineer specializing in fire and explosion hazards, sought to examine the safety regulatory arrangements put in place during the earlier phases of Britain's oil industry. The Burgoyne inquiry was a response to growing public concern over offshore fatalities, particularly, although by no means exclusively, in the diving sector of the industry.

Between 1971 and 1978, 29 divers had been killed offshore out of a total of 53 recorded fatalities (DEn *Brown Book* 1976, 1977, 1978 and 1980). Although this was a somewhat unreliable index because of reporting inaccuracies (non-inclusion of fatalities in connection with pipelaying barges), and the variable numbers employed offshore, the offshore divers' fatality rate appears to have peaked in 1974 at 11.1 per 1000 (DEn *Brown Book* 1975). This compares with an aggregate offshore fatality rate of 2.3 per 1000 employees for the same year. As Carson commented, 'there is no doubt about the price which Britain's oil has extracted from divers in the past'. Taking the workforce as a whole, he noted:

> by the mid-1970s, the likelihood of being killed in the course of employment on offshore installations operating in the British sector of the North Sea had risen to around eleven times that of accidental death in the construction industry, to nearly nine times that of becoming a fatal casualty in mining, and to nearly six times that of being killed as a quarryman. (1982: 21)

Mishaps in diving typically resulted in fatalities rather than serious accidents. Serious accidents occurred particularly during drilling activity and accidents involving cranes (being struck by moving equipment), closely followed by offshore construction (falls). Of the 268 recorded serious accidents between 1971 and 1978, 112 were in the drilling sector alone (DEn *Brown Book*, 1980: 45). These figures are substantial underestimates and only establish the relative orders of magnitude.

By the late 1970s, the dangers of working offshore were threatening to become a national scandal, and an embarrassment to the Labour government. Benn recalls a meeting with a key official, John Archer of the Department of Trade Marine Division, and with Frank Kearton of BNOC, to discuss offshore safety. Kearton had warned, said Benn, that, 'the rigs were desperately dangerous installations . . . and that a leak would cause a massive explosion killing up to 200 people' (1990: 265). Kearton, as an outsider who had come into the offshore industry from synthetic fibre manufacturing, heavily dependent on chemical feedstocks, was not merely prescient, but, coming from onshore, well placed to judge the backward realities of the industry. An inquiry into offshore safety seemed the sensible way forward, but civil servants were resistant. Benn records in his *Diaries* of 19 December 1977:

> John Archer, who is chairman of the Marine Safety Committee – an interdepartmental committee – said there were uncompleted reports on fire, the safety of cranes, rigs and platforms under construction, and divers and standby vessels, and he hoped to have these reports in six months. He didn't want anything superimposed. (1990: 265)

The Marine Safety Committee (of which Archer was in charge) was probably the only body which would have been capable of sorting out the interdepartmental confusions, overlaps and inconsistencies in offshore safety at a day-to-day operational level. Its terms of reference were 'to co-ordinate the development and implementation of policy relating to safety at sea'.[6] Yet there was a greater priority in the political arena, namely to prevent government meddling in offshore affairs if at all possible. It took a further nine months for the Burgoyne Committee to be set up and it was to be over a year later on 11 January 1979 before it met for the first time.

Burgoyne's inquiry recommended that, in the allocation of regulatory responsibility for safety, there should be 'a single Government agency whose task it was to set standards and ensure their achievement' (1980: Ch. 6.5). The government department considered by Burgoyne as 'capable of discharging this responsibility effectively' was the DEn, with the caveat 'provided it is suitably strengthened and seeks advice from other bodies on matters of common concern' (1980: Ch. 6.6). Among these 'other bodies' referred to by Burgoyne as 'principal sources of advice' was the HSE, with its remit of issues of occupational safety.

The agency agreement between the HSE and DEn whereby the latter exercised front-line responsibility for occupational safety, extended only to the activities of the Petroleum Engineering Division inspectorate in relation to offshore enactments under the HSWA. As regards a more general audit of the PED's inspection and enforcement procedures, the HSE had no desire to trespass over departmental boundaries by questioning the competence of the DEn's inspectors. The Burgoyne Committee, in looking at the overlapping of departmental responsibilities offshore and recommending its streamlining, had established the pre-eminence of the DEn in offshore affairs. Since then, the HSE, aware of the DEn's 'sensitivity', had respected the demarcation of responsibilities which Burgoyne had suggested. The problem of overlapping authority was solved by the *de facto* exclusion of the HSE offshore by the PED, under the terms of the agency agreement. This agreement itself was subsequently revised and strengthened in the light of Burgoyne's recommendations.

That the Burgoyne report envisaged any role for the HSE at all was something of a surprise. In the first chapter of the Burgoyne report the committee listed thirteen organizations invited to meet the committee to amplify or clarify their written evidence. The HSE is listed among them, but with the bracketed information 'did not submit written evidence' (1980: Ch. 1.8). This seems indicative of the essentially peripheral role of the HSE in offshore safety matters, and appears to confirm Burgoyne's recommended allocation of major responsibility to the DEn. In fact, the HSE was effectively 'ambushed' by the oil industry and the DEn. A glance at the remit of the committee gives a clue as to how this happened.

> The terms of reference are designed to cover primarily the Department of Energy's areas of responsibility in the United Kingdom sector offshore ... occupational ... safety ... the present concerns of the Health and Safety Executive are not included. (1980: Appendix 2.1)

When it became clear that Burgoyne's committee exceeded its terms of reference by examining the role of the HSE, a written submission was then made. This the committee chose not to reproduce in the final report.[7] Reproduced in full was a 'Selection of Evidence' covering 29 organizations and amounting to 177 pages, that is, more than half the total length of Burgoyne's 300-page final report. Included also were two supplementary submissions each by Shell and BP, produced months after the original submission dates, but not that of HSE. An examination of the submissions by UKOOA, Shell and BP shows that together with the DEn, they mounted a sustained attack on any extension of the HSE's already limited role offshore.

UKOOA, a member of the HSC's Oil Industry Advisory Committee (OIAC) since its foundation meeting in October 1978, and a regular partici-pant since, had given no warning to OIAC that it would launch an attack on the HSE. When the oil industry was challenged to explain why its complaints regarding the HSE had not been brought before OIAC, UKOOA responded disingenuously that OIAC was 'a very new organization which had only met two or three times and had had little time so far to get into details' (Carson, 1982: 197). UKOOA complained of the 'degree of confusion created by the Health and Safety Executive having some of their laws applicable offshore' (Burgoyne, 1980: Submission 43, para. 2.1.7). Citing examples of overlap, a bewildering dichotomy between departments, and delay, UKOOA con-cluded:

> UKOOA believes the Mineral Workings Act and its offshore Regulations already give an adequate and comprehensive package of law for its Members and that additional legislation by the Health and Safety Executive will only cause confusion. (1980: Submission 43, para. 2.1.7)

Shell UK Exploration and Production were equally forthright:

> We also consider the Department of Energy is the correct organisation for the administration and enforcement job in respect of offshore installations. The Department of Energy Inspectorate has grown up with the offshore industry and has acquired valuable knowledge and experience. In our view this level of expertise is not to be found in other Government Departments involved in offshore work. It would be of benefit to all parties if the Department of Energy's role were to grow. (1980: Submission 11, para. 2.1.B)

Similar sentiments were expressed by BP, BNOC, the Institute of Petroleum and, not surprisingly, by the DEn itself:

> While it is appreciated that one Goverment body cannot and should not act in isolation from another interested organisation, the very broad

scope of the HSC's activities and their policy of attempting to standardise regulations, codes of practice etc. across all work activities means that any proposals they make take a long time to come to fruition. Long time-scales are particularly wasteful in what we have already said is a relatively short-lived industry. (1980: Submission 37, para. 15)

The argument concerning the 'special expertise' of the DEn, and its safety arm, the PED, was one which was to weigh heavily with the Burgoyne Committee. It was a view, however, which was contested by academic experts on health and safety (Drake and Wright, 1983). In a scrupulously impartial text they pointed out at the time that the 'expertise of the PED could have been retained even though transferred to the HSE' (1983: 38). The argument concerning the need to preserve specialist expertise within sponsoring Ministries had been fought and lost with the mines and quarries inspectorate (formerly DEn) and the agricultural inspectorate (formerly Ministry of Agriculture) and even with respect to nuclear installations. Indeed, Robens himself had explicitly rejected the 'specialised industries' case for exclusion (1972: 33). He envisaged that the offshore industry would in due course come under the unified remit of the HSE, that is, it would 'fall naturally within the ambit of the unified system we propose' (1972: 35). Robens had suggested that the MWA was among legislation which should ultimately be brought within the new unified framework of health and safety legislation 'unless very sound reasons can be adduced for leaving these outside'.

The 'special expertise' argument for the offshore marginalization of the HSC and HSE did not bear scrutiny when subject to parliamentary attack during the debate on the Burgoyne report.[8] The very constitution of HSC/E as a consensus-seeking body preoccupied with harmonizing regulations across the whole range of industries resulted in slowness in framing regulatory responses. This was construed by the oil industry as an inappropriate encumbrance when what was required was fast reaction in a frontier industry (Carson, 1982: 201–2). Yet, it was precisely this careful consultative approach by the HSE, as exemplified by the discussions on OIAC between all interested parties, which John Rimington was to commend to Cullen as a 'process . . . sometimes protracted . . . which . . . produces a wide respect for the standards'.[9]

The 'special relationship' built up over the preceding years between the DEn and the offshore industry, was meanwhile regarded as almost sacrosanct (Carson, 1982: 204). It was sustained by frequent exchanges of personnel, guaranteeing a common outlook on the priorities to be addressed within an industry-set agenda. This was exemplified when Jim Petrie's predecessor as head of operational safety in PED resigned his post on taking up a new appointment as the permanent technical director of UKOOA. Petrie himself was to depart for the same destination after a decent interval elapsed. Such recruitment of former civil servant regulators by industry has been referred to as a system of 'deferred bribery' (Spiller, 1990). The minority report of the Burgoyne Committee authored by the two trade unionists on the Committee, Roger Lyons of MSF and J. Miller of the TGWU, already expressed concern over this relationship. This 'Note of Dissent to Burgoyne' had argued for the transfer of regulatory authority from the DEn to the HSE in order to overcome 'the conflicting pressure emanating from the exigencies of production on the one hand and the requirements of safety on the other' (1980: Note of Dissent, para 6). In Carson's words, the HSC/E

> threatened the Department of Energy's special relationship at its most vulnerable if crucial point – the fact that it encompassed not only the issue of safety, but also other vital matters such as licensing, the encouragement of exploration and the maintenance of progress towards self-sufficiency in oil. (1982: 206–7)

In asserting the pre-eminence of the DEn over the HSE in offshore matters, Burgoyne effectively ignored the entire thrust of Robens' report, that no Ministry which acts as a sponsoring department should simultaneously be responsible for the occupational welfare and safety of the employees of that industry. In so doing, he confirmed that the institutionalized tolerance of regulatory non-compliance would continue as before. As Carson commented, writing only shortly after Burgoyne reported, 'it is difficult to overcome the impression that, by 1980, even the limited and short-lived intrusions of the HSE into the affairs of the North Sea had touched some very raw nerves indeed' (1982: 197). The Burgoyne report was a missed opportunity to harmonize the onshore and offshore regulatory regimes concerning health and safety.

Applying Kay and Vickers' (1990) definition of regulatory capture, as a process where 'a regulatory agency comes to equate the public good with the interests of the industry it regulates', the Burgoyne Committee's affirmation of the hegemony of the DEn marked the final step in the regulatory capture of offshore regulation by the oil industry. The dominance by oil capital manifested itself thereafter in policies of minimum regulatory interference, free from the contamination of trade unionism and from constraining health and safety legislation. The 'gamekeepers' of the regulatory authority turned 'poachers' on behalf of those they were supposed to regulate. The subordination of offshore regulation to the operators' interests seemed uncontestable until the unthinkable happened: a major disaster involving enormous loss of life.

Regulation from Burgoyne to Piper Alpha

After Piper Alpha, the question was whether the 'single governmental agency' responsible for offshore safety that Burgoyne had talked of, could continue to be the DEn or whether the HSE should take over. The oil operators at the Piper Alpha inquiry claimed to be 'agnostic' on this matter. This stood in contrast to their previous hostility to the HSE at the time of Burgoyne. Mr Ferrow of Conoco spoke to UKOOA's position paper at the Cullen inquiry, emphasizing that it was

> essential that the outside authority is competent in assessing both the engineering and management control aspects. Due to the integrated nature of FSA [formal safety assessment] there should be a single body responsible for overall assessment. (1990: Ch. 21.35)

According to Ferrow, the operators did not wish to be encumbered by a complex regime 'which requires us to interface with several bodies on specific matters' but rather they wished to 'deal with one single body'. The operators correctly anticipated the possibility of sweeping change which might give the HSE a much more direct role in offshore affairs. The UK Offshore Operators Association would have had some difficulty in attempting to defend the status quo in which the DEn had served their interests so faithfully in the past. Their position therefore was one of neutrality as to whether it should be the DEn or HSE which took responsibility for offshore safety in the future, providing only that the body chosen should have 'sufficient competence and expertise'.[10]

Lord Cullen was led to examine the philosophy of safety which lay beneath the competing regulatory alternatives of DEn and HSE. The evidence he had heard suggested that all sides wished for a future regime which was controlled by regulations of a goal-setting rather than prescriptive variety. In this respect the previous record of the DEn did not commend itself. Said Cullen:

> The movement towards goal-setting regulations would be in full accordance with the philosophy adopted by the Robens Committee for Safety and Health legislation. However, despite the statements of attitude made by witnesses from the DEn there has been virtually no

progress towards the creation of new goal-setting regulations since the publication of the report of the Burgoyne Committee in 1980. (1990: Ch. 21.40)

Most of the sets of regulations under the MWA had been made prior to Burgoyne and, said Cullen, 'are different in their general approach from the type of goal-setting regulations which have been produced by HSC on the basis of HSWA' (1990: Ch. 21.40). While the Petroleum Engineering Division claimed it intended to update regulations under the MWA in a goal-setting direction, this simply had not happened.

Burgoyne had recommended that future regulations should 'avoid overlap' between the MWA and HSWA (1980: 6.15). The HSE had seconded four officers to the Petroleum Engineering Division in the expectation that new regulations would be put forward under the HSWA. Reviewing the history of the 1980s regulations, Cullen observed:

In the event no legislation under the HSWA has been promoted by the PED apart from the Offshore Installations and Pipeline Works (First Aid) Regulations 1989 ... the offshore application of sets of regulations prepared by the HSE in the modern form which is in line with the views of the Robens Committee and the policy of the HSWA has occurred in only a limited number of cases. (1990: Ch. 21.46)

This was a state of affairs which had continued up to 1990 even though the HSWA, extended by Order in Council, in theory at least, applied to the UK offshore scene since 1977. The only explanation which the evidence suggested was quite simply one of continuing resistance to offshore extensions of the HSWA within the PED. Under the agency agreement, the Petroleum Engineering Division advised the Health and Safety Executive regarding future extension of regulations offshore under the HSWA. 'Out of 27 occasions in which the PED's advice had been solicited the answer on 7 occasions was in favour of, and on 20 occasions against, offshore application' (1990: Ch. 21.47).

Among the key regulations that the PED advised against offshore application were the Control of Industrial Major Accident Hazards (CIMAH) Regulations in 1983, governing the control of hazardous installations, and the Control of Substances Hazardous to Health (COSHH) Regulations in 1988. The latter were described by Rimington of the HSE as 'the most important reform for thirteen years'. A version of the COSHH Regulations was only subsequently introduced offshore in 1991. Another very important set of regulations under the HSWA, the Safety Representatives and Safety Committees

Regulations 1977 (SI 1977 No. 500) were also not applied offshore. The tangled history of these regulations is discussed below. In fact, even under the MWA, few new regulations were introduced after the Burgoyne report until Piper Alpha blew up eight years later. Those regulations under the HSWA that the Petroleum Engineering Division *were* prepared to endorse, related to asbestos, lead, ionizing radiations, freight containers, diving and first aid. Without exception, none of these sets of regulations could be seen as disturbing the essential character of the prescriptive regulatory regime predominantly determined by the MWA.

During the 1980s the Health and Safety Commission itself had eventually invited the PED to produce a view on the 'relative operation in the future of the HSWA and the MWA' because clearly there was a 'tension' between the two and there was obviously some 'general factor' at work in the PED's responses to proposed offshore extensions of the HSWA.[11] Among the reasons given by the Petroleum Engineering Division for rejecting the offshore application of the CIMAH regulations was the claim that existing regulations under the MWA were 'far in advance'. In fact, the DEn had only the most limited understanding and appreciation of the importance of CIMAH (1990: Ch. 2.15–16). The Petroleum Engineering Division's policy of principal reliance on the MWA had twofold consequences. The existing regulations under the MWA 'stagnated' and the effect of PED policy was 'to distance offshore regulations from the influence of the mainstream of practice in modern regulations on health and safety' (1990: Ch. 21.51). For example, with respect to CIMAH, the DEn had revealed a 'serious failure' to address 'the regulatory requirements for dealing with ... major hazards ...' (1990: Ch. 22.18). In short, said Cullen:

> The approach of the DEn seemed to me to tend towards over-conservatism, insularity and a lack of ability to look at the regime and themselves in a critical way. From this certain practical results have followed: the introduction of improvements in safety has been hampered; and the development of legislation on the basis of the HSWA has been kept back. (1990: Ch. 22.20)

As regards developments in the Norwegian sector, where more modern goal-setting regulation had been put in place offshore, 'Nothing appears to have been learnt from the experience of the NPD with which the DEn were in regular contact' (1990: Ch. 22.21).

The result was that the offshore management of safety seemed to Cullen to be 'a number of years behind the approach onshore' (1990: Ch. 22.21). In his final report, Lord Cullen consequently recommended the transfer of responsibility for offshore safety from the DEn to the HSE and suggested that a new division of the HSE be formed, exclusively devoted to offshore safety (1990, Vol. 2, Recommendation 25). This was to become known as the Offshore Safety Division. Henceforth it would have the primary responsibility for overseeing the new regime which Cullen envisaged.

Union Exclusion from Workforce Involvement in Safety

A change in the regulatory authority, from the DEn to the HSE, the adoption of Formal Safety Assessment and the Safety Case, together with the numerous other recommendations made by Lord Cullen on improving aspects of offshore health and safety marked a serious attempt at regulatory renovation offshore. But these could all be rendered ineffective without one further essential ingredient. Lord Cullen called for the 'involvement of the workforce' in the reconstruction of offshore safety (1990, Vol. 2, Recommendation 27).

> It is essential that the whole workforce is committed to and involved in safe operations. The first-line supervisors are a key link in achieving that, as each is personally responsible for ensuring that all employees, whether the company's own or contractors, are trained to and do work safely and that they not only know how to perform their jobs safely but are convinced that they have a responsibility to do so. Possibly the most visible instrument for the involvement of the workforce in safety is a safety committee system. (1990: Ch. 18.48)

Pre-Piper such safety committees as existed did so on a purely voluntary basis. The Burgoyne Committee had supported the view that on each installation there should be a safety committee 'the members of which are elected, appointed or co-opted to represent those employed for the time being on the installation, including the employees of contractors' (1980: 5.96.3). Burgoyne did not, however, recommend mandatory regulations. He was also prepared to contemplate a variety of forms of representation on such committees (1980: 5.97). Prior to Burgoyne, as the PED itself confirmed in its evidence to the committee, there were 'virtually no Safety Committees offshore'. After Burgoyne, the situation did not substantially alter.

The demand for the offshore extension of the 1977 HSWA Safety Representatives and Safety Committees Regulations, enabling the establishment of trade-union-nominated safety representatives and safety committees, was one of the principal issues raised in the 'Note of Dissent' by the two trade union members of the Burgoyne Committee. Lyons and Miller contrasted the almost complete absence of functioning safety committees, the lack of trade union recognition and involvement in safety, and the absence under law of a right to halt dangerous work in the British sector, with existing provisions in the Norwegian sector (1980: 62). The position in the UK sector, they said, was 'really quite scandalous' when the rights of Norwegian employees were considered. The terms of their objection are important for much of the subsequent debate on this issue.

> The token non-union committees that have been set up by employers, often with appointed memberships, are no real answer to the need for genuine employee involvement. Until well-trained, union-appointed Health and Safety representatives are operating on all offshore installations, and effective trade union based Health and Safety Committees monitor events within each company and across the North Sea as a whole, there will be a quite inadequate offshore safety machinery. Unionisation and recognition is an important element in proper monitoring of accidents and full reporting of incidents. At the moment lack of union protection leaves employees totally exposed. (1980: Note of Dissent, para 26)

The oil industry's resistance to safety committees was based on the view that these might become a 'Trojan horse' for unionization. It explains much, if not all, of the industry's hostility to the offshore extension of the 1977 onshore regulations. Burgoyne's report landed on the desk of a newly elected Conservative government which had little inclination towards furthering the aims of trade unionism. In fact, there had been apparent agreement on this question at a meeting on 21 November 1979 of the tripartite Oil Industry Advisory Committee (OIAC) established to advise the HSC. After a year's objection by UKOOA, the 1977 onshore safety regulations would now be extended offshore.[12] At a subsequent OIAC meeting in March 1980, Jim Renton of HSE reported that draft regulations were to be put before parliament in December 1980 but there had been a 'two month slippage'. OIAC minutes suggest that what further contention was expected on the issues involved which could be left to the TUC and CBI representatives to sort out during a further three month consultation period.[13] Questioned in November 1980 during the debate on the Burgoyne report, Hamish Gray MP, Minister of State for Energy, explained:

> The draft extending these regulations offshore is being considered by the Health and Safety Executive's legal advisers. The consultations over the draft have been protracted because of the complex employment practices in the offshore oil industry.[14]

As late as December 1981, Gray, in reply to a parliamentary question from Bob Hughes, MP for Aberdeen North, was still claiming:

> It has been agreed in principle that the requirements of the Safety Representation and Safety Committee Regulations 1977 (SI 1977 No. 500) which provide for the nomination of safety representatives by Trade Unions should be applied offshore. This is proceeding.[15]

However, with the change of government, the resistance of the operators to union involvement had stiffened once again. Following Burgoyne, there were three positions. The first, which the industry reverted to, was that individual companies develop their own systems of representation, with the assistance of DEn 'Guidance', of a non-mandatory character. This was essentially what the Burgoyne majority had recommended (1980: 5.97). The second position was that of the unions articulated in the 'Note of Dissent', calling for the extension of the 1977 onshore regulations. A third position favoured by the DEn was to draft an entirely new set of regulations which would deal specifically with the offshore situation. The sorry record of progress of these discussions thereafter is itself an indictment, especially of the industry and the regulator.

Trade union representatives on OIAC raised the issue of the offshore application of the regulations in July 1983. B. W. Hindley, Principal Inspector, Health and Safety, replied 'that due to other work and a lack of manpower these regulations had been ignored, but PED are to tackle them in the near future'.[16] In November 1983 reassurance was given at OIAC that a paper from the DEn setting out the proposals for extending the regulations offshore, would be placed before OIAC by mid-1984, as a matter which 'will be treated urgently and not subjected to further delay'.[17]

In November 1984, Hindley eventually circulated a five-page letter 'on an *informal* basis for initial consultation'.[18] It pointed to a series of 'practical difficulties' in attempting to simply apply the 1977 Regulations offshore. These regulations placed duties on the employer, but offshore there might be several different employers at one place of work. Some employers might be transient only with respect to a particular installation. Thus it 'would appear inappropriate, and possibly unmanageable' for each set of employees to elect safety representatives. Moreover, the onshore regulations permitted the appointment of safety representatives 'only by recognised trade unions' (original emphases). Such a requirement offshore might result in limited application of the regulations 'due to the organisation of labour in the industry at the present time'. In view of these difficulties it appeared to the DEn 'to be necessary to proceed along different lines'.

There were several possible options with respect to arrangements for safety committees. The 'installation owner' could be made responsible for setting up a safety committee and appointing representatives 'from among all those persons working on the installation'. Again, the owner could be responsible for setting up a safety committee and appointing representatives from any persons on the installation who were trade union members, whether recognized or not. Lastly, each employer on the installation could be made responsible for the appointment of safety representatives from his employees, subject to the overriding control of the installation owner. Union officials on the IUOOC were clearly unhappy with these management-driven options. The TGWU felt that they left 'control very firmly either with the owner of the installation or the several employers'.[19] An internal NUS memo to head office from Warren Duncan, the union's North Sea Organiser, recalled an OIAC debate some six months before, in mid-1984, in which 'the employers stated categorically that under no circumstances would they entertain the idea of trade union representation on safety matters'. The discussion was described as being 'pretty irate'. Duncan's closing observations were pessimistic: 'I am not very optimistic and I believe we will get bogged down with consultation and discussions and consensus seeking'.[20]

In October 1985 a DEn discussion document was finally presented to OIAC, 'Arrangements for safety representatives and safety committees in the offshore petroleum industry'.[21] In response to the informal consultative letter, the unions had reiterated the view that mandatory, union-appointed safety representatives were required and that the difficulties of 'multi-employer' workplaces could be as easily overcome as they had been onshore, for example, on construction sites. The employers repeated their view that, if it were necessary to follow through Burgoyne's recommendations, even though 'existing arrangements appeared to be satisfactory', then it should be on the basis of 'flexible guidance' produced by the DEn.[22] UKOOA wished the owners of the installations to retain the power to set up safety committees and appoint representatives.

In its consideration of the views expressed on OIAC, the DEn accepted that the workforce, even with the difficulties of a multi-employer site, should be able to choose their own representatives 'if the spirit of [onshore regulations] is to be carried offshore'.[23] However, it did not accept that the right to elect representatives was the sole prerogative of recognized trade unions. Moreover, while the proportion of employees in multi-employer work sites was a minority of the total onshore workforce, the offshore employment structure was 'more complex, and multi-employer work sites are the norm'. Some of these employees were on shorter-term contracts where their employer 'has a more limited ability to take care of their health and safety than exists onshore'. Such an employer was unlikely to have a major physical presence on the installation. The onshore regulations 'would create widespread operational difficulties which would render such regulations largely ineffective'. Thus the DEn sought to introduce non-union safety committees offshore 'on the basis of flexible guidance' from the Department, much in line with industry preferences of the employers. Such guidance, however, would not require statutory backing, since the Department's view was 'that the offshore petroleum industry responds positively to guidance'.[24] A review of the effectiveness of such arrangements could take place after two years by a working party representing all interested parties, and if necessary, legislation could be put in place.

In the absence of consensus on OIAC, it was agreed in 1986 that the DEn should set up a working party comprising TUC, CBI and departmental representatives 'to pursue this subject vigorously' (DEn, 1986: 51). Hindley, as convener of the working party, wrote to Roger Lyons requesting confirmation that a TUC position paper would *not* be forthcoming before fixing a date for the first meeting of the group. According to Hindley, 'it seemed that the TUC side were in the process of reconsidering whether there was a need for such a paper'.[25] Delays, it seemed, were not all on the employers' side.

As late as December 1986 Roger Lyons, as a nominated member of the working party, was still seeking advice from the TUC Social, Industrial and Welfare Department as to its views on the DEn proposals. The DEn-sponsored working party finally met on 5 June 1987. The *Brown Book* for 1987 notes that, 'as a result, the employers' side agreed to produce a paper on the way forward' which was to be 'expected shortly' (DEn, 1987: 55). The working party met again on 19 January 1988 at which considerable frustration was voiced by the trade union members over the failure to move forward after nearly a decade of discussions. While the unions were now willing to modify their position, UKOOA, however, remained unenthusiastic. This second meeting of the DEn working party was a mere six months before Piper Alpha exploded.

Draft regulations were circulated outlining safety-representative provisions specifically applicable to offshore conditions.[26] The final preparation of a draft guidance note and regulations was given 'a low priority' in the DEn's programme and no further progress was made until after Piper Alpha. The impact of Piper Alpha was to prioritize the drafting of new offshore regulations requiring the setting up of workforce safety committees on every offshore installation. They were to be put in place within a twelve-month period. Minister of Energy Cecil Parkinson was given the job of carrying through this exercise with all due haste. The second impact of the disaster was that the trade unions announced their intention to withdraw from the DEn working party and reasserted their original demand that there should be trade-union-appointed safety representatives offshore. UKOOA for its part remained implacably opposed to the importation of the onshore regulations. 'The operating companies believed that the existing arrangements offshore were by and large satisfactory and that there was no need to extend the regulations to the offshore industry.'[27] There matters stood until Lord Cullen considered the vexed issue of workforce involvement in safety.

The Offshore SI 971 Regulations

The regulations hurriedly drafted by Parkinson were enacted as the Offshore Installations (Safety Representatives and Safety Committees) Regulations 1989, SI 971 (DEn, 1989). Initially, they were to be in place for two years, after which time their effectiveness would be subject to review by the regulatory authority. In a letter to Bob Hughes MP, Parkinson spelled out the government's approach in framing the regulations:

> Our aim is to protect the interests of all on the installation whether they are members of trade unions or not and to ensure that their representatives are elected because they are the best men for the job, not because they happen to be trade unionists. We have been working towards this through a working party, chaired by my Department, on the possibility of regulations being made under the Mineral Workings (Offshore Installations) Act 1971 ...[28]

The SI 971 regulations were enacted under the MWA and not HSWA. They established the entitlement of the whole workforce to elect safety representatives. Where safety representatives were elected, a safety committee would be established. Although 'clearly a step forward', said Lord Cullen, it still left as 'the bone of contention' the issue whether safety representatives should be appointed by trade unions, as was the case onshore. The government and operators argued, the new offshore regulations allowing the election of representatives from the entire workforce, both union and non-union, were 'more representative' (1990: Ch. 21.77). Lord Cullen observed that there was 'a clear controversy ... as to the *form* which the requirements in the offshore safety regime should take' (1990: Ch. 21.74, emphasis added). As to 'the need for such requirements' he was in no doubt, both for the safe conduct of installation affairs and for the wider effect it would have on 'the morale of the workforce'. It would enable their views to be taken into account and ensure that they could make thereby a 'worthwhile contribution' to their own safety. Section 2(4) of the HSWA under which safety committees were established onshore, provided for the appointment of safety representatives by 'recognised trade unions', that is by independent trade unions which the employer *recognized for the purposes of collective bargaining* on terms and conditions of employment. Section 2(5) of the preceding Conservative Bill, which had made provision for the election of safety representatives by the workforce as a whole as an alternative to trade union appointment, was removed by the incoming 1974 Labour government. Thereafter, the HSWA onshore regulations had become bound up with the legitimation of trade unions as the means of employee representation at the workplace on safety issues. The attempt to give unions the key role in safety representation was a part of the package of measures of the Social Contract of the Labour government of the 1970s, promoting corporatist-style industrial relations (Dawson *et al.*, 1988).

The trade union movement itself had responded to the opportunities provided by the onshore legislation by providing training and support for safety representatives on a nationwide scale through TUC-sponsored shop stewards' health and safety training courses. Since the Safety Representatives and Safety Committees Regulations came into effect in 1977, over 100,000 safety representatives had been given basic training by the TUC, not to mention the many thousands who had attended individual trade union courses. It was this experience which led Rimington to comment in his evidence to the Cullen inquiry on the valuable part played by safety representatives in the promotion of safety onshore and in relation to inspections. It was, he said, 'a very great strength' that these were appointed by the unions. As Rimington put it, 'The unions train them in quite a sophisticated way. They have the means of putting a great deal of power at the elbow of safety representatives where they care to do so' (1990: Ch. 21.75).

The problem arose, however, where unions were weakly organized or not recognized at the place of work. This was the prevailing position in the North Sea. There was perhaps a maximum of 30 per cent of the total workforce who were unionized, and this was largely concentrated among contractors' personnel. The difficulties in securing collective bargaining arrangements, in the face of employer hostility, have been documented. It had enabled UKOOA to object to the offshore application of the 1977 regulations 'on the ground that there were very few installations where there was a "recognised trade union"' (1990: Ch. 21.76). The fact that the operators themselves had a large measure of responsibility in this regard, through their resistance to collective bargaining, was not an issue Lord Cullen commented upon. He recognized, however, in his summary of the trade unions' evidence, 'the background . . .of . . .a long-standing frustration as to the limited extent to which trade unions had been "recognised" offshore', whereas the unions had been recognised by many of the operating companies in relation to their operations onshore' (1990: Ch. 21.79). Roger Lyons of MSF had reviewed for Cullen those limited representational agreements which MSF had secured offshore. With the partial exception of the Phillips Hewett field, they specifically excluded union involvement in health and safety as, for example, in the Shell representation agreements. Lyons had 'castigated' Parkinson's SI 971 Regulations as 'contrary to the spirit' of the HSWA (1990: Ch. 21.80). He pointed to the reluctance of the workforce to stand for previous Shell safety committees. Lyons instanced the 'fear factor' for workers who raised a safety issue 'that might be seen as embarrassing to management' and the 'Not-Required-Back' policies, from which contractors' employees in particular suffered. All this Cullen noted, as well as UKOOA's stated opposition to the application offshore of the trade union-based 1977 regulations. However, in his observations on the matter he declined to be drawn or to come down on one side or the other.

> My remit does not extend to matters of industrial relations, whether or not the point at issue is a controversial one, as it is in the case of the offshore workforce. Accordingly I am not concerned with the merits of the recognition of trade unions offshore or with the means by which support for such recognition should be ascertained. I have to concern myself with the question of safety, and in doing so take account of the existing situation in the North Sea. (1990: Ch. 21.83)

Lord Cullen was only prepared to consider matters of safety separate from questions of industrial relations. Yet the interconnection between the two was an intrinsic feature of the Norwegian set-up so central to other aspects of the inquiry.

Explicit comparisons on the role of Norwegian trade unions offshore, first made by Miller and Lyons at Burgoyne, were difficult to ignore. Hugh

Campbell, as counsel for the Piper Alpha Trade Union Group elicited from
Magne Ognedal, head of safety at NPD, a positive view of the trade union
situation in the Norwegian sector. This provoked an immediate intervention
from Hardie QC for the employers. Campbell sought to ascertain whether the
Norwegian operators were required to discuss 'terms and conditions' with
employees' representatives. Hardie interrupted to remind Campbell of 'the
undertaking that my learned friend gave that he would not be seeking a
recommendation for recognition of trade unions'.[29] Lord Cullen agreed with
Hardie, permitting Campbell to continue only 'as long as he is not directing
questions to the end that I involve myself directly in the question of recognition'. Not only did Cullen not wish to be drawn on the issue of recognition for
unions in the UK offshore sector, but he had a prior specific agreement with
counsel that he would not be asked to give an opinion on the issue. Yet, while
not fully endorsing the unions' case for trade union-appointed safety representatives, Cullen left the door slightly ajar, conceding

> that the appointment of offshore safety representatives by trade unions
> *could* be of some benefit in making the work of safety representatives
> and safety committees effective, mainly through the *credibility and
> resistance to pressures* which trade union backing would provide.
> (1990: Ch. 21.84, emphasis added)

The position offshore, he noted, was complicated by a number of factors.
These included not only the relatively limited level of trade union membership and the limited extent of their 'recognition' offshore, but also the fragmentation of employment between a number of different employers, with a
high proportion of workers being employed by contractors on a temporary
basis. In one of the most contested paragraphs of the report, Lord Cullen
observed:

> As matters stand it does not seem to me to be appropriate to replace the
> 1989 Regulations with the offshore extension of the 1977 Regulations.
> This would remove safety representatives from a very large part of the
> workforce and would undo the limited progress which was achieved in
> difficult circumstances by the making of the 1989 Regulations. Further
> those regulations have been in force for only a short period. Experience
> will show whether or not representatives elected under those
> regulations lack adequate credibility or resistance to pressures. (1990:
> Ch. 21.85)

Lord Cullen felt the issue of the effectiveness of the SI 971 regulations and of how representatives are to be chosen should be left to the review process, scheduled to be conducted by the regulatory body after there had been two years' experience of these regulations in operation.

> When carrying out that review the regulatory body may consider there is room for improving the effectiveness of safety representatives; and *putting the trade unions' contentions to the test* for that purpose. For example, it may consider that it is appropriate to modify the existing scheme so as to require that safety representatives are appointed by trade unions in certain cases, *such as where a trade union has achieved recognition in relation to a substantial aspect of labour relations* and had *substantial membership on the installation in question*. (1990: Ch. 21.85, emphasis added)

In these remarks Lord Cullen effectively presented the trade unions with a challenge. Their claims would be examined and the system of appointing safety representatives could be altered under two conditions: first, where a union had achieved some substantial degree of recognition, and second, where it had a substantial membership on the individual installation. As matters stood the trade union movement was not in a strong position with respect to either of these conditions. The question therefore was this: could the trade unions with interests offshore sufficiently organize themselves so as to allow them to have their claims for involvement in offshore safety 'put to the test'? In grappling with an answer to this question much of the subsequent history of offshore trade unionism was shaped.

Lord Cullen conceded that the issue of victimization of those who raised issues of safety needed to be urgently addressed. To that end he recommended that safety representatives should have enhanced legal protection (1990, Vol. 2, Recommendation 30). Cullen suggested that 'the type of protection provided in the case of trade union activities under Sec 58(1)(b) of the Employment Protection (Consolidation) Act 1978[30] should also be afforded to the activities of an employee as a safety representative' (1990: Ch. 21.86). Without getting enmeshed in thorny issues of industrial relations, Lord Cullen sought to increase the ability of individual safety representatives, whether or not appointed by a trade union, to resist management pressure. The use of the model of the Employment Protection Act meant that an individual safety representative would have the right to seek redress before an Industrial Tribunal for any employment discrimination suffered as a result of his or her activities as a representative, up to and including actual dismissal. There would be no requirement for that representative to serve any qualifying period before a claim for unfair dismissal could be made. Normally an employee would require a two-year period of service before compensation for unfair dismissal could be sought at an Industrial Tribunal, except where the individual had reason to believe that dismissal was by reason of trade union activities. In that case, as with Lord Cullen's recommendation for offshore safety representatives, early access to a tribunal could be permitted. Even a favourable tribunal decision, however, would not, under existing law, require an employer to reinstate a dismissed worker (or safety representative), although if the employer failed to do so, more severe financial penalties would attach. For some employers such a price could be well worth paying.

Reactions to the Cullen Report: The Government

Lord Cullen's report came out in 1990. A total of 106 Recommendations were made which the government of the day accepted in full.[31] Opposition speakers were quick to seize upon the criticism of Occidental and the DEn and to call for prosecution. The Secretary of State for Energy, John Wakeham MP, indicated that a copy of the report had been passed to the Lord Advocate for consideration. Thereafter, however, Wakeham seemed more concerned to defend the record of his department, noting that Lord Cullen had rejected the view that the DEn had put production before safety. Wakeham implied that Lord Cullen's decision to recommend transfer of responsibility for offshore safety from the DEn was a finely drawn one. 'Lord Cullen has recommended that, on balance – again it is a question of balance – the best case would be for transferring responsibility to the Health and Safety Commission.'[32] Lord Cullen had used the well-known judicial phrase 'the balance of advantage' (1990: Ch. 22.34). It was an estimate which was by no means narrowly made, however. It arose, said Cullen, from 'decisive considerations ... from considering the differences in approach between these two bodies to the development and enforcement of regulatory control'. These differences had been 'plain for some years' and flowed 'from differences in the way in which the bodies are directed and managed'. As such his 'major changes' recommended were 'in line with the philos-ophy the HSE has followed. This alternative is clearly preferable to the PED ...' (1990: Ch. 22.34).

When pressed by Labour MP Stan Orme to consider the extension of the 1977 Safety Representatives and Safety Committees Regulations offshore, 'Lord Cullen', said Wakeham, 'rejects the simplistic equation of union recognition

and safety, and endorses the Government's approach'.[33] In fact, an intervention from Sir Trevor Skeet (Conservative MP for Bedfordshire North) suggested that the oil industry's response to Burgoyne had been 'rather
reasonable' and that Piper Alpha was 'a unique case'. Sir Trevor was a long-
standing exponent of oil industry political objectives since the 1950s, and as
Vice-Chairman of the Conservative Energy Committee an opponent of Benn
in the 1970s during the era of the British National Oil Corporation (BNOC).
In December 1984 he had urged the abolition of BNOC. Sir Trevor is
described in Andrew Roth's *Parliamentary Profiles* as an 'assiduous right-wing
energy specialist' with a brother who was a BP executive (Roth, 1984: 741).
Sir Trevor Skeet's helpful contribution allowed Wakeham to agree with his
Hon. Friend 'that this great disaster was not symptomatic of a badly run
industry'.[34] Moreover, Lord Cullen's recommendations, said the Minister,
were 'based on existing best practice in the industry'.

Michael Colvin MP (Romsey and Waterside), representing another rural
Conservative constituency (in deepest Hampshire) asked Wakeham to
acknowledge that Cullen's inquiry had mainly dealt with fixed production
installations which are 'fundamentally different' from mobile drilling rigs
and requested 'my Right Hon. Friend bear that difference in mind when
deciding how to implement the Cullen recommendations'.[35] He, like Sir
Trevor Skeet, was a member of the Commons Energy Select Committee, having joined the committee some nine months previously. Colvin, a Lloyd's
Name, was one of a number of Conservative MPs to feature prominently as
a tide of sleaze allegations engulfed the government in late 1994. In Colvin's
case, it was the failure to register a paid consultancy with a pro-apartheid
public relations firm. In the Members' Register of Interests, Colvin is
described as a 'self-employed landowner and farmer' with properties including 600 acres of land and a 'stately home', as well as proprietorship of Tangley
village's *Cricketers Arms* (Roth, 1984: 133). Neither he nor Sir Trevor Skeet had
any declared financial remuneration that could be directly linked to the oil
industry. The Conservative MP whose downfall attracted the most public
attention, Neil Hamilton, Minister for Corporate Affairs, who shared with
Colvin an undeclared interest in the pro-apartheid public relations firm,
had actually declared a previous financial consultancy with the oil industry.
The years of and following Piper Alpha, he had been paid by Mobil Oil,
although it was denied by Hamilton that he had made any parliamentary
interventions on Mobil's behalf. How many other MPs were recruited by
the oil industry at that time is not known, as entries in the Members' Register
of Interests remained voluntary.

Perhaps the most astonishing intervention in the debate came from Alick

Buchanan-Smith, former Minister of State for Energy during the period 1983–87. Many of the victims of Piper Alpha came from his Kincardine constituency. Welcoming the 'new approach to safety' and 'the intention to put safety under the Health and Safety Executive', Buchanan-Smith nevertheless saw fit to defend the record of the PED during these years. He said:

> I pay tribute to those who work in the [DEn's] safety directorate. Having spent time working with them, I pay tribute to their integrity and independence of mind in dealing with safety matters. I hope we do not forget that.[36]

Buchanan-Smith's integrity and independence were not forgotten by the oil industry on his demitting ministerial office. He was to be consultant to and then director of Texas Eastern North Sea, of Davy Offshore Ltd, and in the year following this parliamentary debate, consultant to Amoco (UK).[37] Buchanan-Smith's successor at the Department of Energy as Under-Secretary of State for Energy, Peter Morrison (1987–90), was likewise to be rewarded with an oil directorship on demitting office, becoming a director of Ranger Oil,[38] as did, in turn, his successor, Colin Moynihan (1990–92).[39]

It was perhaps John Wakeham's unruffled patrician air which allowed him to deflect Opposition criticism from his own Department as he responded to the debate on Lord Cullen's report. Oil workers and their families listening to this debate in the public gallery of the House of Commons realized that while the Cullen report represented a turning point, the future shape of the offshore safety regime would still be a matter of contest.

UKOOA

The operators were by no means unhappy with the Cullen report. After years of complacency, recognizing that they were dangerously exposed in the aftermath of Piper, they decided to 'put their house in order'. UKOOA was anxious to show to Lord Cullen that since the 'shock' of Piper Alpha, they were 'proactively' reforming themselves. Indeed, in advocating such concepts as Formal Safety Assessment (FSA) and the Safety Case they argued that they had anticipated the main thrust of Cullen's recommendations. For the operators, dealing with the cost implications of Cullen's recommendations now became a priority. The industry needed to develop a cohesive policy approach. Above all, UKOOA wanted to avoid identification of the industry as being systematically out of line with British onshore safety practice. UKOOA strategy was to show, firstly, that it had analysed and absorbed the lessons of Piper Alpha; and secondly, that it was now in the vanguard of advanced safety philosophy and engineering. In this way it hoped, in the longer term, to be able to limit potentially expensive future regulatory interference in the affairs of the industry. Its success in doing so is analysed in more detail in a following chapter.

A key player among the operators, in carrying through UKOOA's immediate objectives at the Cullen inquiry, was Conoco. As part of the Du Pont Group, it had developed an elaborate and sophisticated safety-management regime within which 'safety' was the centre-piece of a corporate gospel. Senior personnel from Conoco were seconded to assist UKOOA's Director of Technical Affairs. Their job was to co-ordinate and provide expert witnesses in support of a legal team fielded by UKOOA to the Cullen inquiry, independently of Occidental's own legal team. The UKOOA group carefully monitored the evidence of Part 1 of the inquiry, the circumstances and causes of the accident. UKOOA's team did not present evidence to this part of the proceedings. The second part of the inquiry was concerned with the avoidance of similar accidents and recommendations for the future. Now 'UKOOA wanted to make sure', in the words of J. N. Hall of Conoco, that the 'inquiry has the most thorough information' at its disposal (Hall, 1991: 111.5). UKOOA reviewed more than 100 people in the industry as possible expert witnesses. Some 80 papers were commissioned, 43 witnesses were eventually proposed to the inquiry, and 34 gave evidence. UKOOA provided more than half of the total of 63 witnesses who gave evidence to Part 2 of the inquiry (Taylor, 1991). UKOOA's objective was to retain as much discretion and flexibility over the shape of the post-Piper safety set-up as they could. Conoco provided four key witnesses, including R. E. McKee, their safety-evangelizing UK chairman and managing director, who played the pivotal role in the inquiry.

The Cullen inquiry also sent several delegations to Norway to examine the Norwegian Petroleum Directorate, since clearly any public scrutiny of the industry's practices would draw immediate unfavourable comparison with Norway. The NPD had a much more prominent regulatory profile in the industry than the DEn. The essence of the Norwegian system is what is described as 'internal control'. The operators are responsible for organizing the safety of their installations within the general goal-setting framework laid down by the NPD, rather than through a mass of externally-policed detailed prescriptive regulations. UKOOA seized upon the Norwegian system because it allowed maximum latitude to retain control over all aspects of installation safety. A Safety-Case-based 'goal-setting' regime, said UKOOA, was entirely in line with Robens' rejection of detailed regulations, going back to 'first principles' of safety management.[40]

UKOOA's advocacy of Formal Safety Assessment and the Safety Case at the Cullen inquiry was precisely based on the flexibility such an approach would offer to the operators. This was spelled out in UKOOA's internal briefing document prepared to present the best possible face for the industry to the media following the publication of the Cullen report.[41] A paper entitled 'Off-shore Safety – The Way Forward' noted that FSA has 'many advantages' in that it is 'flexible' and can take account of the different types of installation in the UK offshore environment. It was an issue with cost implications of a major kind, already raised by UKOOA's parliamentary allies. FSA had the advantage in that it 'does not *dictate* to the operator *how* safety should be achieved' (Taylor, 1991: 6, emphasis added). Once FSA had been completed for an installation, UKOOA recommended that existing regulations should no longer be applied, a position, as noted, which Cullen rejected as going too far too quickly.

UKOOA's 'strategy' in dealing with media on the publication of the report was also outlined in the briefing document.

> We should use the media opportunities presented to us to state UKOOA's aims and objectives and where possible show how they have been advocated by Lord Cullen ... The advantages of FSA can be used to answer any detailed question ... Using this strategy we should be able to avoid being dragged into detailed argument about specific proposals. If Lord Cullen makes a specific recommendation, which is counter to the actions already under way in the industry, we should embrace it objectively, and agree that it seems sensible and promise to look at it.[42]

Among the 'useful phrases' which UKOOA had ready for media 'sound-bites' in bold type were the following: 'Safety is our Number 1 Priority' and, 'A Safe Platform is a Profitable One'. UKOOA claimed that in the two years since Piper Alpha, the operators had spent £750 million on safety improvements, roughly £1 million a day. £230 million of this expenditure was on the fitting or relocation of topside emergency shutdown valves on risers at the interface with the platforms. These were required by the Emergency Pipe-Line Valve Regulations, passed in July 1989 in the wake of Piper Alpha. A further £230 million was spent on subsea isolation systems, and a further £300 million on other safety measures. In any event, up to 80 per cent of this total expenditure could be offset against petroleum revenue tax. Although difficult to quantify, probably the greatest bulk of this expenditure was occasioned by the postponed maintenance work which was left over from the oil price downturn of 1986. Enhanced safety work was almost impossible to separate out in cost terms from essential maintenance, a point we return to. Nevertheless, UKOOA's figures of huge safety expenditure went largely uncontested. Shell Expro and BP, as we noted previously, used the opportunity of the publication of the Cullen report to make public their request to the DEn for an extension to the deadline for completing work on topside emergency shutdown valves which it was claimed arose directly from delays caused by the summer's wildcat strikes.[43]

Occidental's Response to the Cullen Report

If the industry had sought to salvage its own reputation, there was little it could do for Occidental in the light of Cullen's report. As Brian Taylor put it on the day of the publication of the report, Part 1 of which examined the causes of the disaster, 'UKOOA has decided as a matter of policy to offer no comment on the content of Part I ... of the report, believing this to be a matter for Occidental to deal with as it thinks fit.'[44]

Even though a member company of UKOOA, Occidental was effectively left alone to face the storm of criticism raised by the report and the vigorous public demands for the prosecution of the company.

Responsibility for conveying Occidental's response to the report was given to Glenn Shurtz, president of Occidental Petroleum (Caledonia). Said Shurtz, 'We have always practised the management of safety. Offshore it's our number one priority.'[45] Much more than this, however, was impossible to draw out of the company spokesperson. Shurtz refused to take part in a live Scottish TV debate on the report's findings. Agreeing to a prior taped interview, Shurtz observed that the report was 'bulky' and that he would need time to review it with his technical staff before making any direct comment.[46] Shurtz also attempted to fend off criticisms of the company at a press conference, in much the same terms: 'We have just received Lord Cullen's report, and it is a little unfair for me to accept criticism which I haven't had a chance to look at.'[47]

Occidental was less reticent about claiming it had already spent in excess of £50 million on improving safety, including £28 million on emergency shutdown valves in the Claymore field. Over three-quarters of the cost of the disaster had been borne by the public purse. Only 10 per cent fell directly on the Occidental group. A report by the stockbroker Kleinwort Benson revealed that of the £2.02 billion cost of the disaster, petroleum revenue and corporation tax relief amounted to £1.96 billion and savings in royalty payments to a further £180 million.[48] In any event, the construction of a brand-new £780 million replacement installation, Piper Bravo, was now well under way, again at one-third of its replacement cost to the company due to the generous structure of petroleum tax incentives. Occidental remained reticent about its views on the Cullen report: 'Despite media pressure to do so, Occidental does not believe that it is constructive to respond piece by piece to criticism.'[49] Specific criticism was brought against one of its own employees, Colin Seaton, the installation manager on Piper on the night of the disaster. Occidental's spokesman was 'saddened by and disagrees with the interpretation placed by Lord Cullen upon the actions during the disaster of the Piper Alpha OIM'.

On the day after the disaster, Occidental's legendary chairman, Armand Hammer, 'the man who knew Lenin', had arrived in Aberdeen by his private jet from Los Angeles and accompanied by his ever-present personal film crew. To the grieving families he had promised £100,000 each and pensions for life. It was not to materialize. The offer was to the families of the directly employed only, 31 out of the 167 who had been killed. As Ed Punchard commented, 'Once again, it proved to me that the majority of North Sea workers, who were employed by contractors, were in every way – even in death – treated as second class people.' (1989: 174). The families of contractors' employees and survivors were subsequently to receive compensation from Occidental, although at a lesser rate and after considerable delay. Occidental were in this way able to avoid contested claims for restitution in either the British or US courts.

Punchard commented in the preface to his account of the disaster, that what had happened on Piper Alpha, whilst no surprise, could have happened on many other rigs in the North Sea (Punchard, 1989). This raises the question as to whether there were particular features about Occidental's operations as a company which made it 'disaster-prone'. As a company, 'Oxy' was not one of the oil majors, but an 'independent' and as such regarded as an outsider. Its entry into the oil business came in 1956. Hammer, the president of Occidental, was already 58 years of age, with a considerable fortune already amassed from, among other ventures, ten years of residence in early post-revolutionary Russia, during which he secured lucrative trade concessions from the Bolshevik government. Whilst much of Hammer's remarkable biography was designed for posterity, there is no doubt that so far as the oil and gas business was concerned, Hammer's facility for risk-taking and perseverance paid off handsomely, first in California, then Libya, Venezuela, Iran, Colombia and, spectacularly, in the North Sea. This did not exclude other ventures into real estate, coal, tanker fleets, cattle, agricultural fertilizers and art dealing. Hammer's attempts at international power-broking between the Communist and non-Communist world leaders were accompanied by megalomaniacal philanthropic gestures, intended to immortalize his name and resulting in a highly personal style of corporate management which bordered on the erratic.

Wherever Occidental sought to extend its operations, the path was smoothed by the wooing of officials, legislators and politicians. The original consortium which sought entry to the North Sea was comprised of J. Paul Getty, Lord Roy Thomson, Allied Chemical Corporation and Occidental. The threat of nationalization in Libya, where Occidental was a major player with three billion barrels of recoverable reserves, was the major impetus for the move into the North Sea. Now the world's sixth largest producer, by 1970 Hammer was determined to find alternative sources of oil for Occidental. The biography written by Hammer's long-time PR assistant, Carl Blumay, suggests that Occidental's initial difficulties in dealing with the British government over drilling concessions were overcome by providing senior officials with prostitutes, personally vetted by Hammer himself, at his suite in Claridges (Blumay and Edwards, 1993: 153).

The first oil landed from the hugely productive Piper field had come ashore at the Flotta terminal on Orkney on 27 December 1976. Since then, Piper Alpha had become the world's most prolific producer of oil from a single offshore platform, pumping out 284,000 barrels per day. Its centrality as a revenue earner in Occidental's otherwise somewhat fluctuating fortunes, was heightened by the vulnerability of operations elsewhere. The company had just emerged from an extremely expensive $3 billion acquisition deal and an uncomfortable profits squeeze in 1986, which had coincided with the global downturn in oil prices. This had reduced Occidental's net income by $515 million and increased its debt to a staggering $5.6 billion. Blumay and Edwards note Occidental's response to the crisis in 1986:

> Occidental was not only forced to slash its capital budget twice, but also initiated a cost-cutting programme involving the consolidation of operations and the elimination of two thousand jobs, and sold half its Columbian interests to Royal Dutch/Shell for $1 billion. (1993: 429)

The impact of this 'cost-cutting programme' on the operations of Occidental is described by Punchard. Having identified a crack in weld No. 3 on the main oil line to the Flotta terminal, the dive team requested mastic cast material to effect the necessary repairs. Only after the failure of the first compound provided and 'much whining about cost' from Occidental management, was the necessary quality of repair product purchased. Punchard comments,

> It provided a perfect example of how budget conscious oil companies
> were, even though in this case we were dealing with the most serious
> defect in the most serious location I'd ever seen. If the pipeline failed, not
> only would there be a loss of 12 per cent of the UK's oil production, but
> there would be major pollution in the North Sea. (1989: 114)

Similar testimony was provided by another Piper Alpha survivor, Andy
Mochan, the maintenance superintendent for Wood Group, whose account
of escape on the night of 6 July has been previously cited. He saw, first hand,
the postponing of maintenance work which was thought by Occidental not
to be essential:

> We were going to carry out a maintenance programme and somebody
> in their wisdom decided it could be postponed for another year. That
> was something that was already on stream ... but they decided to cut
> and say, 'No, we'll not do that for another year. We'll wait and see how
> the oil price goes before we decide just how much maintenance we're
> going to do'.[50]

The fact that maintenance work had been deliberately shelved and was then
reinstated at a later date while production continued, might be thought to be
material in the attribution of blame and the due process of law which could
have been expected to follow the disaster.

Lord Cullen's report was placed in the hands of the Lord Advocate, Scotland's highest legal officer, with a view to possible future criminal prosecution.
Lord Cullen himself did not address the issue of liability for compensation.
Occidental, as a US-based company, would potentially be liable to higher
compensation payments if pursued in the American courts rather than in
the UK. The issue of prosecution was to leave a bitter taste in the mouths of
the bereaved relatives and those who survived.

Since the death in 1990 of Armand Hammer at the age of 92, the new chairman, Ray Irani, had quickly entered a massive restructuring exercise involving the sale of $3 billion worth of assets, a reduction of share dividend from
$2.50 to $1.0 a share, and the write-off of $2 billion against anticipated losses
from the sale of unprofitable businesses (Blumay and Edwards, 1993: 464). In
early May 1991, the long-rumoured sale of its North Sea assets, worth $1.36
billion, to the French state-owned group Elf-Aquitaine, was announced.[51]
There had been some doubt as to whether the acquisition would go ahead or
be referred to the Monopolies and Mergers Commission. Peter Lilley, Minister
for Trade and Industry, had previously complained about 'nationalisation by

the backdoor'. Elf was then a state-owned enterprise, but as it was foreign and not UK-owned, the sale was allowed to go ahead.

Occidental was pulling out of the North Sea although not the oil business. Its withdrawal raised new doubts as to whether charges would ever be brought against the company. The Lord Advocate had had the evidence compiled in the Cullen report before him since November 1990. In late July 1991 it was finally announced that there would be no criminal proceedings against Occidental on the basis that there was 'insufficient evidence'.[52] It was unusual for the Lord Advocate to give any detailed reasons for such decisions. In this instance it was pointed out that a successful criminal prosecution would require proof 'beyond reasonable doubt' in Scots law. Lord Cullen's report was based on 'inference' in so far as much of the crucial evidence and many of the key witnesses had been annihilated by the disaster itself. The decision not to prosecute Occidental not surprisingly provoked much outrage. Whatever the deficiencies in the existing criminal negligence law might have been, the Piper Alpha Families and Survivors Association felt there surely had been clear breaches of health and safety legislation. Offshore, or onshore for that matter, a criminal charge had still to be brought against any operator or employer under relevant health and safety legislation which would result in imprisonment. Occidental was to be no exception. The only avenue now open lay in bringing a private criminal prosecution against Occidental, a legal move only once before permitted by the Crown Office in the Scottish courts. Given those difficulties and the potential costs involved, such a course was eventually reluctantly conceded as being beyond the relatives' financial resources. The scales of justice were heavily tilted against individual citizens securing legal redress against powerful corporate concerns such as Occidental.

The real financial fall-guys for Piper Alpha appear to have been not Occidental Petroleum but syndicates in Lloyd's Insurance, the so-called 'Names', whose individual £0.25 million entrance stake formerly provided them with potentially unlimited profits but also made them personally liable to unlimited losses. The Names were sufficiently outraged at their treatment as to resort to legal action. Their underwriter colleagues at Lloyd's, chasing lucrative reinsurance commissions, appeared to have unloaded upon them the attendant liabilities for a number of major disasters. For Piper Alpha alone, this amounted to an estimated $1.8 billion in 'direct' claims plus a further $9.9 billion in reinsurance claims (Riches, 1991). Occidental was to suffer the subsequent minor indignity of being forced to lodge the sum of £500,000 with the Scottish courts, pending the awarding of costs of legal action mounted by the company against the 23 contracting companies on Piper Alpha at the time of the disaster. It was Occidental's intention to recover the £110 million in compensation payments it had disbursed to bereaved families and survivors. Occidental were challenging Lord Cullen's findings, in order to place the full burden of blame, and therefore financial responsibility, onto the shoulders of the contractors.[53] Occidental's attempt to minimize its liability extended also to a lengthy and ultimately successful appeal against a claim for £300,000 compensation from a worker based on the *Tharos* who had witnessed the horror of the night of 6 July at close quarters and was thereafter unable to work again.[54] Ultimately, it appears, for Occidental the Piper Alpha tragedy and its aftermath was primarily a matter for the company's balance sheet.

The Trade Unions

The response of the trade unions to Lord Cullen's report was as disorganized as their approach to the whole inquiry had been. Different unions held their own press conferences variously in London and Aberdeen. For Tom MacLean, acting as spokesperson for the National Offshore Committee, the report was to be 'unreservedly welcomed'. There was no hint of disappointment that Lord Cullen had declined to comment on the contested issues of industrial relations offshore. Indeed, said MacLean,

> Lord Cullen doesn't actually state that the trade unions should have recognition, nor should he do so. The Minister [John Wakeham] has said today that he would be discussing the various aspects of the way we go from here with the parties, including the trade unions.[55]

The prospect of a meeting with the Minister for Energy seemed an invitation to come in from the cold. It could still hardly be regarded as a great step forward in the campaign for trade unionism offshore. Yet for MacLean the fact that safety would now be under the control of the tripartite HSC meant that trade unions could become 'involved' in health and safety offshore in a new way.[56] This was undoubtedly true at a higher level; it was far away from the goal of trade union-appointed safety representatives. MacLean commented that the Cullen report now made it 'much less likely that a strike ballot would be held among the offshore contract workforce on the issue of union recognition'. Thus for some trade union leaders the publication of the report signalled a 'new era' which allowed them to step back from the campaign for effective trade unionism offshore.

While MacLean spoke to the press in London, in Aberdeen, Roger Lyons of MSF was holding a separate press conference. Thirty-seven of those who had died on Piper worked directly for Occidental and were personnel whom MSF in the normal course of events would have sought to recruit and represent. For Lyons, as joint author of the 'Note of Dissent' to the Burgoyne Committee's report, the findings of Lord Cullen were a vindication of arguments put forward a decade previously. Lord Cullen did concede, in the final paragraph of his report, that there was a 'perception' that the DEn lacked independence 'at least among some trade unionists' (1990: Ch. 22.38). As Lyons put it at his press conference, 'The credibility of the Department of Energy is in shreds and the sooner they are removed from the safety scene the better.'[57]

Lord Cullen recognized the Trade Union Group's contribution to the proceedings of the inquiry. The Piper Alpha Trade Union Legal Group led by Hugh Campbell QC and Ian Truscott, advocate, acted for two firms of solicitors representing 23 of the deceased and 8 survivors. It had been responsible for some of the most searching cross-questioning and the forensic exposure of the evidence influencing Lord Cullen's final recommendations. The Trade Union Legal Group was separate from the Piper Alpha Disaster Group which comprised 154 firms of solicitors representing 142 deceased and 49 survivors. This latter group also represented the EETPU electricians' union, and was paid for by Occidental itself. The Trade Union Legal Group, on the other hand, was financed for the entire inquiry by the TGWU and MSF who had rejected Occidental's 'blood money' in order to provide independent union representation. It had at first been discussed at the TUC's Offshore Safety Group that there would be a co-ordinated legal effort among the offshore unions. However, following the National Union of Seamen's near-bankruptcy, and the EETPU's acceptance of Occidental's offer of financial support, the other unions also withdrew, leaving MSF and the TGWU to finance their own legal representation. NUMAST, the ship's officers' union, separately represented one of its own members, the captain of the *Silver Pit*. As a tribute to the input of the Trade Union Legal Group, Lord Cullen awarded to MSF and the TGWU 40 per cent of the costs of their participation in the inquiry. In recognition of the valuable work of Campbell and Truscott, Cullen commented that while not all the points which they sought to explore proved to be of assistance, 'in regard to the opening up of matters of possible criticism . . . the burden of exploring such matters fell to a large extent to the trade unions'. (1990: Appendix A, para 11).

The OILC, whose industrial action had focused a powerful spotlight on the issues of North Sea safety and generated a heightened atmosphere in which Lord Cullen's report would be closely scrutinized in the public media, also welcomed the report. A fresh start could now be made in the industry, but first those remaining 726 dismissed and victimized workers who had taken part in the action would have to be reinstated. Shell would have to lift its OPRIS exclusion bar. Within a week, a parliamentary Select Committee on offshore employment practices was to be established with the issue of black-listing as one of its central preoccupations. But, in a wider sense, the publication of the report was the beginning of a much deeper strategic reassessment of the way forward for offshore trade unionism.

In the context of the growing disarray among the official unions' one-table approach, the Cullen report was the occasion for some backtracking. The lack of any co-ordinated future long-term strategy let it fall to the unofficial movement to explore the implications of Cullen for the trade unions. Twice before, OILC had issued keynote documents which attempted to set the agenda for the official trade unions. It was now clear that a third document was required which could draw the lessons of the immediate past and provide a focus for debate within the trade union movement as to the way forward.

The Survivors

It had been with incredulity that the Piper Alpha Families and Survivors Association had learned that Occidental Caledonia had 'earned a special pat on the back by Britain's health and safety watchdog', the Royal Society for the Prevention of Accidents, in association with washroom product manufacturer Kimberley-Clark. Occidental had received a 'silver sword for making the working environment safer for employees'. Said 'awards manager', David Walker:

> We hear a lot about safety at work when there is an accident and people are either hurt or killed. The awards give the opportunity to redress the balance by giving people the chance to hear about safety when it's successful.[58]

Amidst the outpouring of analysis and commentary on offshore safety consequent on the Cullen report, some of it, as above, quite simply bizarre, it was salutary to be reminded of the human dimension of the disaster. Bob Ballantyne, as a Piper survivor, had been an outspoken critic of Occidental at the inquiry and after. On the night of the disaster Bob had just finished his shift and was relaxing in the television room when the first explosion shook the rig. He made his way back to his cabin to find his mate, Ian Gillanders, and then went to the galley area. Seeing the seriousness of the situation, he had returned to his cabin to collect his survival suit and lifejacket. A second attempt to go back up to the galley area was abandoned.

> We tried to get up the stairwell. It was rather crowded. Also, we could hear people shouting in the confusion about being afraid, about it being hard to breathe, about difficulties with breathing. I heard some of the chaps say that if you lie on the floor or sit on the floor, it's easier to breathe. We heard someone from the lower decks tell us that the air was fresher down there, so we went down there.[59]

Returning to his cabin with his colleague a third time, they wrapped wet towels round their faces and distributed their spare towels to others. In one of those oddly normal actions which people perform under acute stress, Bob collected his spectacles and the copy of Voltaire's *Candide* that he had been reading, 'because I thought if I was rescued, I would need something to read that night'.[60] They checked other cabins to see if people were still in them and to see if there was any escape route. Eventually they found their way to the pipe deck at the 133 ft level, where there were about twenty men by this time. An attempt to get to lifeboats proved futile. After a tortuous journey, beaten back by flames and falling embers, now separated from his colleagues, Bob finally found a way down a platform leg via ladders and a rope to sea level. Tragedy and farce often come uncomfortably close together. Shortness of leg almost defeated his escape over the side of the platform. Finding a rope, Bob tied it to a handrail, allowing him to scale over the final obstruction. Once in the water, the second explosion engulfed the platform in a fireball. With the sea on fire all around him he was fortunate that the current pulled him away from the platform to eventual rescue. For Occidental, Bob had nothing but contempt.

> They have had two years to think about what happened and it is time they started to accept their responsibility for what happened. All those men were working unaware that they were sitting on a time bomb. But Occidental made the decision to carry on despite all the dangers.[61]

Ballantyne had a welcome tinged with the renewed pain of recollection for Cullen's report. 'People ask me if I have come to terms with what happened. But how can I come to terms with 167 of my mates dying? The Cullen Report is for public consumption but the nightmare images are mine.' Piper Alpha's 168th victim was to die by his own hand in 1994. Dick Common was finally overwhelmed by the burden of having survived while others close to him had died. For the members of the Piper Alpha Families and Survivors Association the desire for justice remained an unfulfilled legacy.

One man for whom it became a personal crusade was Gavin Cleland. Gavin had used every opportunity to demand that Occidental be brought before the courts for manslaughter and that those responsible be given prison sentences. Fierce determination had taken Gavin the length and breadth of Britain, speaking at meetings, lobbying MPs, organizing petitions and letter-writing campaigns. Wherever the banner of the Families and Survivors Association was unfurled, it would be Gavin who would be there. Emblazoned on the Piper banner was the demand: 'Government must bring the men up now!' It had been argued by government that the expense of recovering the wreckage of the rig, in which were the remains of many of the deceased, was too great. Gavin's son Robert, who had died aged 33, remained unaccounted for, alongside 29 others. Gavin brought those who would listen face to face with Piper Alpha's tragic waste of human life. He would reach into his jacket and produce the photograph of Robert he carried everywhere with him.

Illustration 7   *Gavin Cleland with the Piper banner (Photograph courtesy of Spindrift)*

His granite face and rasping ex-miner's voice gave Gavin a stature and authority which more than compensated for his diminutive frame. As one oilworker remarked after listening respectfully to yet another impassioned plea, 'Aye, Occidental made a bad mistake the day they blew up wee Gavin's boy'.

Capture and Containment

In political terms, Lord Cullen's inquiry into the Piper Alpha disaster represented a paradoxical effort. At the time the inquiry took place, deregulation had become an article of faith for the UK government. The Conservatives saw their political mandate as getting the government 'off the backs' of business. Yet here, in the context of the offshore industry, a Scottish High Court judge was appointed with the explicit task of identifying deficiencies in the existing governance of the offshore industry, and to recommend new rules and regulations which would make it safer.

With regard to the first task, Lord Cullen's inquiry delivered what was one of the most compromising pictures of the interaction of government and industry. Cullen unmasked a level of complicity between regulator and business which ran counter to most popular assumptions. Public officials, in the classical, benevolent view, are assumed to further some kind of vision of the public good. They act either according to their own vision of the public interest, or their superiors' view of what that public interest is. In pursuing such agendas, they are assumed to be immune to special interests, as well as to temptations to accept personal gains (Davis, 1970).

This model of the public official hardly applied to the DEn officials whose conduct Lord Cullen investigated. On the whole, officials followed another, more sinister trajectory, namely that of 'regulatory capture', which Downs had identified as early as 1957, and Olson elaborated on in 1965. Downs and Olson used economic models of individual profit maximization to understand and predict the political actions of regulators and regulated businesses. For them, regulators and the regulated were each driven by self-interest, rather than a vision of the public good. In Downs' view, private interests, particularly powerful business interests, were willing to expend resources, in the form of persuasion, campaign contributions, or promises of future employment, in order to see policies put into effect which would enhance their wealth or profit. If public officials, and in particular those assigned to regulate an industry, could invent policies or modify existing policies which enhanced the profits of these businesses, a relationship of mutual sponsorship and support would emerge between the two groups. Over time even closer ties between the regulator and the regulated would evolve in which the regulator would be gradually 'captured' by business interests. Common agendas, of the regulator and the regulated, would then be stressed, whereas potential sources of conflict would take a back seat. The regulator would neither seek nor pursue compliance, and would provide increasingly for the institutionalized tolerance of non-compliance.

As a consequence, the state and its officials lose authority, allowing the respective business to act in a 'state-like' manner, where it imposes its own rules over itself and those subject to its authority. Downs argues that this authority is often exercised in a 'deviant' way, as corporate power lacks the checks and balances of the state. Deviant practices may include an ignoring of or a failure to communicate important findings about safety to lower management and the workforce, as was the case when the DEn rubber-stamped Occidental's inquiry into the 1984 fire and explosion on Piper, and the Saldana report into danger attached to ruptured risers, or the results or the Board of Inquiry into the Sutherland fatality, the circumstances of which were subject to active cover-up. Even where prosecutions take place, they may have little or no effect on the long-term safety management practices of companies like Occidental.

Regulatory capture on many levels described what had happened to the DEn and the oil industry. Rather than acting as an independent agent with the mission to oversee the industry, the DEn had effectively come to shield the industry from scrutiny. This position culminated in the systematic exclusion of other agencies, such as the HSE, whose remit would logically have extended to offshore matters. In formulating policy, public officials came to consider the costs and benefits of forming and maintaining coalitions, while their sponsors – the oil industry – weighed the costs and benefits of influencing the government and its bureaucrats to act in its favour.

This process was helped by what modern political science would refer to as 'slack' (Kalt and Zupan, 1984, 1990). Slack between the general polity and the regulator is created by high information, monitoring and organization costs. In the context of offshore regulation it emerges from the industry's remoteness, its operation at the frontiers of technology, and by its venturist nature which often requires secrecy in the planning and securing of investment and exploration opportunities. These transaction barriers shield officials from accounting to the general public and can be used by a regulator and its business sponsor to pursue regulatory policies which benefit special interests.

What then are the limits of such policy collusion? The model of the captured regulator would suggest that there are very few. One possibility is that a powerful dislocation occurs when regulation becomes so ineffective that it results in a 'regulatory breakdown', which focuses the attention of the public and the media.[62] Such was the case with Piper Alpha. Far less certain, however, is the outcome of such a dislocation. One possibility, particularly relevant in the US context, is the criminalization and punishment of the business involved. Another, seemingly more rational alternative, is that of lesson drawing, in which an independent public official is assigned not to prosecute wrongdoing, but to recommend steps which will reduce the risk of a similar incident in the future. Lord Cullen's inquiry derived its legitimacy from the notion of impartial scrutiny. Cullen was expected to recommend steps which would re-legitimize the industry and its regulatory framework. The scale of dislocation which had occurred had to be matched with a complete regulatory overhaul, which specifically included the replacement of the DEn's authority with that of the HSE. Despite this regulatory overhaul, Lord Cullen's endeavour faced several problems.

Firstly, in embarking on such an inquiry, the newly-appointed investigator faced many of the 'information' and 'monitoring' problems of the old regulator. This informational asymmetry was exacerbated by the unwillingness to give full and truthful information by the old regulator, as well as its complicity with the regulated business. Secondly, just as before, the industry had every incentive not just to mask its previous misconduct, but also to start on a new, perhaps more intensive campaign on behalf of its own special interests. This extended to the careful grooming of witnesses to the inquiry by UKOOA, as well as a systematic effort to persuade the inquiry that the industry had already 'anticipated' future regulatory demands. It culminated in the industry attempt to push the new goal-setting regime in the direction of unilateral self-regulation, creating for itself new leeway where the regulator played only a peripheral role. Finally, the concrete implementation of the new regulatory regime, where new opportunities and incentives for collusion might occur, was beyond the remit of the inquiry.

To what degree Lord Cullen's inquiry was able to cope with these problems, and to what degree its recommendations were tainted by these forces, will be the subject of a following chapter. There we will examine in some detail whether the post-Cullen regime was first contained and then perhaps recaptured by the industry.

Notes

1. *Hansard*, 21 September 1990, Vol. 181, col. 148.
2. DEn, *Onstream*, No. 76, 26 May 1978, p. 15.
3. ibid.
4. Piper Alpha Public Inquiry, 25 January 1989, Day 6: 107.
5. See Piper Alpha Public Inquiry 1989, and Piper Alpha Trade Union Legal Group Submission Ch. 3, p.23.
6. DEn, *Onstream*, No. 41, 10 September 1976, p. 27.
7. Minutes of 6th Meeting of OIAC, 19th March 1980, para. 14.
8. *Hansard*, 6 November 1980, Vol. 991, cols. 1489ff.
9. Piper Alpha Public Inquiry, 11 December 1989, Day 157: 7.
10. Piper Alpha Public Inquiry, 14 February 1990, Day 179: 41F.
11. Piper Alpha Public Inquiry, 11 December 1989, Day 157: 65H–66A.
12. Minutes of 5th Meeting of OIAC, 21 November 1979, para. 25.
13. Note 5 *above*, paras 5–6.
14. *Hansard*, 6 November 1980, Vol. 991, col. 1536.
15. *Hansard*, 1 December 1981, Parliamentary Question No. 199.
16. Minutes of 16th Meeting of OIAC, 20 July 1983, para. 32.
17. Minutes of 17th Meeting of OIAC, 2 November 1983, para. 10.
18. Letter from B.W. Hindley to C. Reid, IUOOC, 'The implementation of the recommendations of the Burgoyne Committee in relation to safety committees and safety representatives in the offshore oil and gas industry', 8 November 1984 (original emphasis).
19. Letter from Melvin Keenan, District Officer TGWU, to C. Reid, IUOOC, 23 November 1984.
20. Warren Duncan to Jack Kinaham, NUS, Internal Memo, 6 December 1984.
21. OIAC (1985) 'Arrangements for safety representatives and safety committees in the offshore petroleum industry', Discussion Document 85/23.
22. ibid, pp. 1–2.
23. ibid, p. 2.
24. ibid, p. 5.
25. Letter from B.W. Hindley to R. Lyons, 12 June 1986.
26. Proposed Regulations on Offshore Safety Representatives and Committees, enclosed with letter from W. J. McL. Marshall, Principal Inspector PED, to J. P. Hamilton, TUC, 27 December 1987.
27. Minutes of IUOOC/UKOOA meeting, 24 August 1988.
28. Letter from C. Parkinson, Minister of Energy to Bob Hughes MP, 18 October 1988.

29. Piper Alpha Public Inquiry, 10 January 1990, Day 169: 53E.

30. Incorporated in the Trade Union and Labour Relations (Consolidation) Act 1992.

31. *Hansard*, 12 November 1990, col.330.

32. ibid, col. 333.

33. ibid, col. 335.

34. ibid.

35. ibid, col. 338.

36. ibid, col. 334

37. Members' Register of Interests, 8 January 1990, HC 115; 14 January 1991, HC 140.

38. Members' Register of Interests, 13 January 1992, HC 170.

39. Peter Walker, Secretary of State for Energy (1983–87), who was responsible for the privatization of British Gas, became a £20,000-a-year director of the utility on his retirement.

40. Piper Alpha Public Inquiry, 14 February 1990, Day 179: 9B.

41. 'Lord Cullen's Report – UKOOA responses.' Briefing document prepared by Brian Taylor, 7 June 1990.

42. ibid.

43. *Scotsman*, 14 November 1990.

44. *Financial Times*, 13 November 1990.

45. ibid.

46. *Piper Alpha – The Aftermath*, BBC Scotland, 12 November 1990.

47. *Herald*, 13 November 1990.

48. Kleinwort Benson, Report 1990.

49. *Scotsman*, 14 November 1990.

50. Interview with Andy Mochan, Fine Art Productions, 1994, cf. ch.2, pp. 108–11.

51. *Press and Journal*, 9 May 1991.

52. *Press and Journal*, 25 July 1991.

53. *Scotsman*, 22 January 1993.

54. *Scotsman*, 17 November 1995.

55. ITV *World In Action*, 'The Cullen Report', 12 November 1990.

56. *Financial Times*, 13 November 1990.

57. *Press and Journal*, 13 November 1990.

58. Piper Alpha Bulletin, Families and Survivors Association, Autumn 1990.

59. Piper Alpha Public Inquiry, 16 March 1989, Day 37: 32E.

60. ibid.

61. ibid.

62. Industrial accidents, according to Wraith and Lamb, 1971, have been a 'principal source' of public inquiries. The state is historically described as 'increasingly compelled' to intervene via such procedures in the sphere of private interests in circumstances where there is conflict 'between the public and private good' (see p. 27 and pp. 146–53). Lord Cullen's appointment by the Secretary of State for Energy under the Public Inquiries Regulations occurred within a week of the disaster. In 1996 Lord Cullen was to perform a similar role at the inquiry into the mass killing of Dunblane schoolchildren, in which deficiencies in the regulatory control over firearms became a major issue of public contention.

Lord Cullen himself was an appropriate choice in both instances, being very much a product of the distinctive Scottish educational and legal systems. He was educated at Dundee High School, St Andrews University and Edinburgh University, where he obtained an LL B. He was called to the Scottish Bar in 1960 and became a Queen's Counsel in 1973. He served as an Advocate-Depute (prosecutor in the High Court) from 1978 to 1981, and in 1986 was elevated to the bench of the Court of Session and High Court of Justiciary (see Cullen, 1996, p. 5).

6 'A PROFOUND CHANGE OF CULTURE'

A profound change of culture is necessary for all parties in the offshore related industry if the costs of the UKCS are to be controlled. Change on the scale that is needed will require the development of a high degree of trust and confidence between all parties ... We must move away from adversarial contractual relationships and nurture changes in attitude wherein people learn to work together in a common·direction and purpose. (DTI Report of the Working Group on UKCS Competitiveness, 1993a: 3.1)

The Cullen Report signified a formal legal condemnation of the type of production regime which had characterized the UK Continental Shelf (UKCS) since the 1970s: decentralized, highly competitive, based on a multi-plicity of supply firms, short-term contracts, domineering managements, weak or non-existent unions and compliant state regulation. The report might easily be read as reflecting the widespread anger and concern over Piper Alpha and even endorsing the practical action of the workforce in demanding a new structure of industrial relations.

But Cullen also had a different context. It appeared at a key turning-point in the organization of production in the UKCS. Within a couple of years the UKCS was witnessing one of the most dramatic and far-reaching processes of industrial restructuring in recent British history. The report did not cause this restructuring. But significant parts of its critique were informed by exactly the same trends of thinking. By 1992 these had crystallized into the blueprints for the massive project of industrial reorganization known as the Cost Reduction Initiative for the New Era (CRINE). Our opening quotation comes from the DTI Report of the Working Group on UKCS Competitiveness, presented to Michael Heseltine as President of the Board of Trade in February 1993 in one of the founding documents of this initiative. This report takes a similar position on industrial structure as Cullen. Competitive, adversarial relations had to end. The future depended on an entirely new ethos: on co-operation and partnership within the industry and between different contractors and suppliers.

This brief chapter seeks to outline the logic behind this restructuring, and does so in order to provide the necessary background for our further analysis of industrial relations and changes in health and safety compliance between 1991 and 1995. We begin by examining the economic crisis which erupted within the UKCS and the UK oil and gas industry as a whole between 1990 and 1992. We will then look at the response – and argue that it was fundamentally determined by the character of worker resistance analysed earlier.

A Crisis of Profitability – and Direction

Let us begin by recapitulating our earlier review of the very special political economy of the British oil industry. First of all, the industry was old. It had been of key importance for British capital long before the opening of the UKCS. It provided 5 per cent of the UK's profit income by the late 1930s and up to 14 per cent by the early 1950s. This income gave Britain's two great oil majors, BP and Shell, a special place within the governing institutions of the City of London and within the policy formation of successive governments. After 1945 the exigencies of world politics added a further factor: a close alliance with the United States in which the joint control of international oil reserves played an important part.

Following the discovery of oil on the UKCS this strategic alliance with the United States underwent a profound change. In the 1950s and 1960s the American alliance was limited and external. It was based in a general but definitely not complete convergence of foreign policy interests. It had virtually no purchase on internal industrial policies. It was, conversely, in terms of industrial structure that the biggest change came after 1970. Britain's two largest multinational firms became locked into joint investment strategies with their US partners that shifted a very major part of their production activities back into Britain – and did so on the basis of a production regime that was imported virtually wholesale with the United States multinational supply companies that controlled the technology. This pattern of development was in strong contrast to the Norwegian sector. In Norway slow, gradual expansion gave local firms the time to build up skills in oil supply in the knowledge that the key phases of investment would not take place for a decade. In the UK the priority was fast development. This was so because of the wider politico–

economic goals of UKCS development: to bring market pressure on OPEC. It was for this reason that the initial investment in the UKCS was so massive – consuming between 1972 and 1982 a quarter of the country's industrial investment.

The speed and smoothness with which this very special path of development was adopted in the UK between 1970 and 1972 can only be explained in terms of the prior links between UK and US governments and the centrality of the UK's oil majors to strategic decision-making in both government and the City. The joint investment in the UKCS did, however, transform the existing relationship and take the practices of US industry to the productive core of the UK economy. It was, we argued, this experience which decisively influenced debates on the UK's economic and political strategy in the late 1970s. The attempt to create the environment for a new type of entrepreneurial capitalism – and bury corporatism – was founded on the apparent success of the UKCS as a production regime, the presumption of continuing oil revenues and the possibility of safety-netting during the required period of severe industrial deflation for the economy as a whole. Even the detailed tactics for the defeat of the trade union movement depended on the availability of oil and gas as alternative energy sources to coal.

It was the unravelling of these assumptions, including in part at least those sustaining the US alliance within the UKCS, which characterized the 1990s and explains the nature of the restructuring of the oil industry from 1992. This crisis was not just one of profitability. It involved a decisive change of direction.

The onset of the crisis was apparent from the mid-1980s. Its origins resided, as we have already noted, in the quasi-political character of UKCS oil production as a long-term bargaining counter to regain control over OPEC-sourced oil. This international strategy had an inevitable domestic sequel. This was the need to find ways of sustaining investment in the UKCS once this objective had been achieved and the price of oil brought down – and after investment access had been restored to much more cheaply produced oil in the Middle East.

The answers of the 1980s did not involve any basic change of direction. They relied mainly on fiscal incentives to make investment more attractive. In the early 1980s the licensing rounds were used to draw in investment from new smaller independent British and American oil companies. In the mid-1980s the Petroleum Revenue Tax (PRT) was first reduced and then, in face of the oil price crash of 1985–86, offset against exploration and development work anywhere in the UKCS. It was precisely this expedient that then interacted with the deepening contradictions within the industrial structure of the UKCS. When oil prices rose sharply in the late 1980s, the result was a new and much deeper crisis that inflated UKCS costs way beyond those of comparable oil provinces. The shrinkage in the industry's local employment base by 20 per cent after 1985–86, the loss of a range of externally-owned supply firms and the absence of a significant presence of local firms in high-technology areas, combined to create a seller's market. Previously the industry's outsourced and highly competitive structure had worked in the oil companies' favour. Now it worked decisively against them.

The changes in PRT gave an immediate incentive for speculative oil ventures. These tended to be funded through the cheap finance available during the final stages of the inflationary Lawson boom between 1987 and 1989 in order to undertake exploration and development activity that could be directly discounted for tax purposes and, in the case of smaller concerns, sold off as exploration assets to the bigger oil companies. It was this that provided the main drive for the inflationary pressures that increased the production costs of UKCS oil by 50 per cent between 1989 and 1991. Within this process, the collapse of management control over labour had a critical role. The tight labour market was compounded with the psychological shock of Piper Alpha to create the first effective basis for trade union organization. The outcome was a direct and detailed challenge to management authority. Because of the previous exclusion of collective bargaining this challenge was potentially much more far-reaching than anything onshore. By 1990 this labour revolt was threatening to become irreversible. In addition to large-scale victimization, managements ultimately had to use to head off demands for trade union rights. Cumulatively, selective wage increases amounting to 40 per cent were made to contract staff between 1989 and the end of 1990. Then, from late summer 1990, the oil price started to tumble and continued to fall through 1991 and 1992 back to the lowest levels of the 1980s.

This was the crisis faced by the oil companies in 1991. To understand how it was resolved, and the particular direction in which this outcome took the industry, it is essential to appreciate three things. First, there were major conflicts of interest between different sections within the industry itself over future development. Second, the international environment for oil production and marketing shifted dramatically between 1990 and 1991. Third, the crisis coincided with a change of government.

The Economic Geography of the Economic Sea

Highlighting prospects for a third wave of independent oil company activity in the North Sea, managing director of Enterprise Oil, John Walmesly, told a UKCS oil and gas tax conference in London that only a third of the oil found in the UKCS is being produced and only a fifth of the gas. He said a question yet to be determined was whether profits of oil developments went through into transport systems through pipeline dominance, or would competition for tariff income among pipeline owners facilitate many cheap developments. (*Aberdeen Petroleum Review*, 4 November 1992)

Three great arteries take oil from the British sector of the North Sea and land it for further transport and refining. The biggest, in terms of oil carried, is the pipeline system running from BP's Forties field to Cruden Bay near Aberdeen. This takes up to 40 per cent of UKCS oil. The second biggest (the FLAGS line) is to the north and runs from the Shell-Esso Brent field to Sullom Voe in the Shetlands. This takes about 25 per cent. The third is midway between the other two and takes oil from the Piper field. It was built by Occidental and runs into Flotta in the Orkneys. This carries around 10 per cent.

These pipelines form the infrastructure of the UKCS. They were built in the 1970s to service the biggest of the original fields, and took a significant part of the start-up investment. In time a whole series of smaller and subsidiary fields were hooked into them as new discoveries were made. The two big pipelines are owned and operated by the two UK oil majors, BP and Shell, and their US partners.

By the late 1980s these pipeline systems faced a very specific crisis of their own. They were old, required increasing levels of maintenance and, very soon, would need systematic refurbishment. As we saw, problems with pipeline design and control played a major part in the Piper Alpha disaster, and in 1989 and 1990 the summer maintenance programmes presented serious challenges for managements across the UKCS. Secondly, these pipeline structures were handling a decreasing amount of oil from the companies that originally built them. They serviced the original fields along the eastern and central troughs of the UKCS which were now producing at substantially lower levels. They tended to be remote from the newer fields being brought on stream as new licensing rounds opened up the north and west of the UKCS. Both here, and in the new fields in the central and eastern troughs, finds were generally smaller and often more effectively exploited by surface loading direct on to tanker. In addition, these new discoveries were principally in the hands of companies that had arrived more recently, and which were in the forefront of the burst of speculative exploration and development in the late 1980s. So the owners of the UKCS infrastructure, mainly BP and Shell, were in 1990 faced with a very difficult strategic problem. They needed to refurbish the pipelines which took the oil from their own flagship fields to the shore. If they were going to be able to overcome their depletion problems, had to enhance collection by hooking-in an array of smaller feeder wells. Yet the exploration frontier for new discoveries was moving elsewhere in the North Sea and, if this trend continued, it was clear that a sharply declining proportion of UKCS oil would go through the original pipelines. The cost of maintenance, therefore, would become an increasingly heavy burden on their own oil revenue. Then, to add insult to injury, BP and Shell had to contend with a fiscal regime which rewarded precisely those companies whose activity had seriously inflated the supply market. These relatively new arrivals in the UKCS effectively got their exploration and development free by offsetting it against tax. BP and Shell, with a quite different gearing between exploration and production from mature fields, continued to pay very substantial amounts of PRT.

When the managing director of Enterprise Oil, as quoted at the beginning of this section, spoke of an 'undecided question', he was referring to precisely this dilemma. If the existing fiscal regime continued, there would indeed be a third wave of independents able to exploit the UKCS market of the early 1990s – following on the first two waves of independent investment at the beginning and end of the 1980s. Given the tax write-off, it was still profitable to open up new fields, and such development work was scheduled to peak in 1992 despite the fall in the oil price. On the other hand, such expansion was certainly not a possibility for Britain's oil majors. Already by late 1991 and early 1992 the cash squeeze on BP was so severe that the second quarter dividend had to be cut. City opinion was uncertain about the company's long-run ability to service its massive debts. Shell was better cushioned by external income but was still under pressure. In 1991–92 it was quite feasible that one or other of the companies would soon have to start divesting themselves of some of their UKCS assets and surrendering control of the pipelines.[1]

These, then, were the concerns of the management strategists of BP and Shell as they read the Cullen Report and contemplated how they could meet its demands – and do so, what is more, in face of a workforce that in 1990 remained dangerously intransigent.

These problems might seem quite sufficient to depress the leaders of the UK's two top companies. But there was in fact an additional one. It was not as immediate; yet in its long-term implications it was even more dangerous. It concerned the international role of the two UK companies which still stood at the centre of banking and finance in the City of London. The nine months between autumn 1990 and summer 1991 had transformed the geopolitical map for global energy production. US-led forces had regained control of the Middle East and left a massive army of occupation in Saudi Arabia and Kuwait. Then in August 1991 the USSR disintegrated. The USSR had been the world's biggest oil and gas producer. It had also been a political counterweight to the US, and provided support to movements and states that rendered large parts of the world potentially dangerous places for commercial oil firms. From 1991 previously undreamed-of possibilities opened up for access to cheap oil and gas. There was the Middle East itself. There were the oil-bearing territories of the former Soviet Union – commanding the pipelines into energy-hungry Europe. In the Far East, in Vietnam and China, there were fields immediately adjacent to the even hungrier Japanese market.

BP and Shell had grown as world oil companies on the basis of colonial and ex-colonial oil. Their future as major players in the world market depended on access to the cheapest oil in a variety of strategic locations. But, at the very moment when such opportunities had finally opened up, they lacked the cash flow to exploit them. They would have to watch as rival oil majors moved in, while they themselves, and especially BP, remained locked into the North Sea producing oil at a cost base that was rapidly making it unprofitable.

Michael Heseltine and the European Dimension

Mrs Thatcher was replaced as Prime Minister by John Major in Summer 1990. Michael Heseltine simultaneously became President of the Board of Trade and took charge of the Department of Trade and Industry.[2]

It is not unduly fanciful to suggest that among the first callers on Michael Heseltine, either separately or together, would have been senior managers from BP and Shell. These executives would have been very anxious to brief him on the Thatcherite policy disaster in the oil industry. They would have pointed out that the poll tax or even the destruction of the housing and property markets were strategically of small consequence compared with the ineptitude of government policy for oil. Heseltine's visitors would also have been quite clear about the first essential step on the road to recovery: the scrapping of the Petroleum Revenue Tax. Ending PRT would restore the income flow for BP and Shell and screw off the inflationary pressures deriving from speculative exploration and development funded from the tax claw-back. Heseltine's visitors would no doubt have acknowledged that the step would be highly controversial. It would be damned by the smaller independent oil companies and their investors. It would infuriate those major oil companies, mainly American, who had bought up large acreages of the UKCS in the last licensing round and now needed to develop them. It would anger the big US multinationals like Brown and Root and MacDermott which dominated the construction market. There would also be consequential effects for the viability of Aberdeen as a supply base which would need to be addressed with some urgency.

On the other hand, Heseltine's interlocutors would have been able to offer him, and themselves, a highly attractive prize in return: the consolidation of the UK's industrial base within the European Union (EU).

Britain had few world-class companies and even fewer industries which might enjoy a competitive edge in Europe. A significant exception, possibly the only one, was petrochemicals. Other EU countries had large oil and gas companies. Some, like France, also possessed sophisticated petrochemical supply industries. But none had companies as large as Shell or BP and, more important, possessing a global control of oil and gas production – both in Europe and outside – which enabled them to be net energy exporters. In 1991 the extra-European reserves of BP and Shell required buttressing. But if they had the cash to exploit their new discoveries in Colombia and the Gulf, and for Europe to penetrate the oil and gas bearing territories of the former Soviet Union, then their European dominance would be assured.

The EU market was potentially very lucrative. Energy was one of the very few areas that had not yet been subordinated to competition policy. Most EC states had sought to protect their internal markets to safeguard against energy shortages like those of the 1970s, and had brokered deals with extra-EC suppliers of oil and gas to fuel their industries. In almost all cases both domestic and industrial energy prices were between 10 per cent and 40 per cent higher than those pertaining in the UK (DTI, 1995: 113). Correspondingly, the creation of a single energy market appeared to be much to the advantage of the two UK oil majors.

If asked to sum up, the representatives of BP and Shell might have put their position as follows. The strength of Britain's petrochemical industry had traditionally resided in its grip over oil reserves on an international basis. The time had now come for the balance of UK activity to be shifted back in this direction. The UKCS would certainly remain vital for a very long time to come because of the scale of investment and the importance of its output, particularly of gas, in commanding the EU market. Yet its role from now on was basically to be that of a revenue stream that would meet investment requirements elsewhere in the world. In an era when cheaply-produced oil was once more available overseas and prices were likely to remain low for at least the next decade, it was vital that the bulk of oil was derived from such overseas sources if the UK was to secure the EU energy market. This was why it was essential to solve the problem of the UKCS. It was from here that the new investment had to come, and radical measures would be necessary to reduce costs and stabilize labour relations. What was required was a production environment that was geographically clustered around the existing pipeline infrastructure and which maximized production from existing fields. The stress had to be on maintenance rather than development. Cheap, basic systems, with the maximum of commonality, were the pattern of the future – servicing non-staffed production facilities and seabed wellheads that fed directly into pipelines. How this transformation might be achieved would at this stage be a little unclear. But it would require something very different from the existing structures. Establishing the new production regime would involve detailed government support as well as some conflict with the US supply industry. On the other hand, the biggest of the US oil majors also had considerable investment locked up in the UKCS and had a common interest in finding a solution.

Precisely whether such exchanges took place directly with Heseltine, whether they occurred before or after Thatcher's fall from power, or whether they occurred at a much more remote level, is somewhat immaterial. Such perspectives did exist at senior management level in the UK oil majors, and it is clear that the period 1990 to 1992 saw a critical change of course in UK energy policy.[3] It was signalled by a decisive move towards Europe. It irrevocably changed the character of the production regime in the UKCS. It heralded a much looser and more contradictory relationship with the US oil industry. And it matched very closely the particular needs of BP and Shell.

The policy outcomes can be enumerated as follows. 1991 saw the UK government securing agreement to a European Energy Charter Treaty aimed at establishing 'open, liberal and non-discriminatory energy markets' in Eastern and Central Europe and 'protecting foreign investors against political risk' (DTI, 1994). It also saw the initial agreements on Phase I in the establishment of the Internal Energy Market for the EU. 1992 saw the first phase of the deregulation of the UK gas market, the lifting of the 60 per cent ceiling on the generation of electricity from oil and gas and Heseltine's proposals for the virtual elimination of the main competing UK energy source: coal. 1992 also saw the unveiling of the Cost Reduction Initiative for the New Era with joint sponsorship from the oil operators and the DTI, and the development of plans – mainly through the DTI and Scottish Enterprise (Oil and Gas) – for a consolidated 'home base' for the oil industry in North East Scotland. February 1993 saw the publication of the DTI-sponsored Report of the Working Party on the Competitiveness of the UKCS, and March 1993 saw the scrapping of PRT and the tax clawback for all new fields. For existing fields PRT was reduced from 75 per cent to 50 per cent. Shell-Esso gained an additional £1 billion revenue from one field (Brent) as a result of the tax change over the following three years.

Partnership and Co-operation in the New Era: The Blueprints

In the late 1970s when new flexible, market-led, competitive systems of industrial organization were being pioneered, theory always stood a little to one side of practice. It provided an effective public rationale. It bore more than a passing resemblance to what was happening, and gave coherence to a number of otherwise disparate activities. But it certainly did not explain the wider politico-economic processes which brought about the implantation of this industrial structure.

Exactly the same points can be made about the processes of industrial reorganization which occurred in the UKCS from 1992. The DTI Report of the Working Group on Competitiveness in the UKCS and the first Report of the Cost Reduction Initiative for the New Era produced by UKOOA are both highly illuminating documents and deserve to be quoted at some length – as much as anything because they closely inform our subsequent discussions of health and safety and industrial relations. But, as we will see, they do not explain the wider political and economic processes by which change was to be effected (DTI, 1993a; CRINE Secretariat, 1993).

The informal discussions which led to the Cost Reduction Initiative were underway by the beginning of 1992. In October 1992 the oil operators' association, UKOOA, formally announced their sponsorship of the initiative. It was essential, it was said, in order to overcome the 'doubling of UKCS costs'. A week later the Energy Minister at the DTI, Timothy Eggar, announced the establishment of the Working Group on UKCS Competitiveness headed by John D'Ancona of the Offshore Supplies Office and including representatives from across the industry.

The first formal UKOOA document on CRINE, published in 1993, set out the context and objectives (CRINE Secretariat, 1993: 2–4).

The UK oil and gas industry is facing a number of fundamental challenges to its future prosperity. Real oil prices are expected to continue to remain at historically low levels in the short to medium term … Against this background, capital and operating costs have continued to escalate. Unless urgent action is taken to reverse this trend, the future of oil and gas development in the UK North Sea will be in serious jeopardy.

There are individual and multi-company initiatives underway but only with a truly industry-wide, collaborative effort can the full potential for reducing costs be realised. The DTI, recognising the same pattern of falling revenue and rising costs, launched its own study of UKCS competitiveness. It is the industry itself, however, that must lead the transformation in North Sea development culture that is required. The oil companies, through the commitment of their management, must be the drivers of the process.

The document goes on to specify the problem which has to be tackled:

North Sea development costs can be in the order of 4–6 times greater than their lower cost counterparts in other oil and gas provinces, such as the Gulf of Mexico and the Pacific Rim … In contrast with engineering practice in other areas, North Sea projects are founded on highly complex specification and use non-standard materials, equipment and procedures … CRINE has identified 'industry culture and business practice' as the root cause of the distrust and adversarial relationships which are commonplace. These basic problems lead to technical complexity; adversarial management; unnecessary and unbalanced risk of financial exposure; and inadequate communications, education and development.

The remedy, in UKOOA's view, was 'a fundamental change in culture':

A shift is required, not only in the way the industry conceives, designs and builds hardware, but just as importantly in the way the industry interacts and relates as a whole … The culture envisioned by CRINE is one characterised by teamwork and openness. It is one where the full potential of people working together towards common objectives can be realised and all parties have the opportunity to prosper.

The specific outcome was, above all, to be standardization:

Maximize standardisation and repeatability in design, procurement and construction.

Introduce fit-for-purpose functionality into codes, specification, contracting and procurement documentation.

The diagnosis of the DTI Working Group on Competitiveness in the UKCS, published a few months earlier, was almost exactly the same. This paper also called for a profound change of culture (DTI, 1993a: 3.1, 3.2, 3.5):

Following the peak in activity during 1991–92, it is clear that the UK North Sea market is entering a period of significant change. Over the past few months the extent and nature of this change has been the subject of much discussion within the industry.

It would be natural to ask why this current dip is judged to have greater long-term significance than those previously and why, when activity picks up again in a year or two, the Group believe that the market will be significantly different ... In the Working Group's view there are a number of factors, any one of which individually would affect the market to a considerable degree, but which, taken together bring a dramatic step change with implications for all parties – oil companies, suppliers, contractors and Government.

These factors in themselves are sufficient to lead to the conclusion that the future North Sea market will be significantly different ... but there is one further factor which emphasises the need for a changed response from the industry – that of increased world wide opportunity. Over the past few years new oil and gas provinces have opened up: there are new deep water prospects in the Gulf of Mexico and off West Africa, there are new opportunities arising in the more traditional markets e.g. in the Middle East, and new provinces are opening up as a result of the break up of the Soviet Union and the change of approach in countries such as Vietnam ... the international oil companies will give priority to those prospects which offer the best overall return.

The recommendations of the DTI-sponsored document were, in essence, the same as those of the UKOOA document: co-operation between operators and contractors to overcome adversarial relations and to produce standardized procedures and equipment. The Working Group report was, however, somewhat more comprehensive and strategic. It included representation from the trade union movement (in the form of the General Secretary of the STUC) and received formal presentations from the Health and Safety

Executive, local authorities and the Offshore Contractors Council. The report addressed in considerably more detail the issues of health and safety, 'human resources' and the precise forms of relationship between operators and contractors.

On health and safety the DTI Working Group report welcomed the rethinking of the processes of statutory supervision as an opportunity for both reducing accident rates and for cutting the costs of health and safety compliance. It recommended that:

> The HSE should expedite the establishment of a new safety regime based on goal-setting rather than prescription.
>
> UKOOA should urgently provide HSE with its priorities for the repeal or adjustment of existing prescriptive legislation.
>
> HSE's review of the Certifying Authorities should be undertaken without delay and should take account of the opportunities for cost reduction.

The Working Group identified the 'large proportion of contractor and agency staff' as the major cause of the industry's past difficulties in developing 'a structured approach to training and career development'. The DTI report noted that the current stress on out-sourcing non-core functions would, other things being equal, tended to exacerbate these problems. Its answer was to call for stable core workforces which could make possible long-term staff development. This programme was to include 'the training and motivation of staff, the development of enhanced competencies and consideration of career structures for core staff retention'. Such sweeping changes 'emphasize the importance of involving the workforce in the formulation and development of new approaches. For an effective outcome the workforce and, where appropriate, their representatives, have an essential role to play and particularly in times of significant change, the need for effective channels of communication *up* through a management chain is of equal importance to the more obvious top-down approach'. The report specifically recommended that 'employers and unions consult' but included an important caveat. This consultation should be at 'national level'. The objective, 'if UK contractors are to compete effectively,' had to be 'increased workforce flexibility'. This was not described as 'multi-skilling'. The concept chosen by the Working Group was 'multi-tasking with the emphasis on the retention of core skills but the flexibility to perform peripheral tasks outwith the core area' (DTI, 1993a: section 4.5).

The approach of the Working Group to the role of contractors and suppliers complemented this stress on long-term staffing policies. The report noted the degree to which operators were already experimenting with the concept of 'partnering' whereby 'one contractor is given long-term responsibility for a significant area of platform operations instead of the traditional award of annual contracts to a multiplicity of contractors. This, it noted, reduces the cost of managing such contracts and increases the stability of contractors' workforces, enhancing efficiency and safety and improving the effectiveness of training.' In platform construction the report commended the introduction of the 'alliance' concept. In the alliance scheme the operator, design engineer and fabricator agreed to work towards a common objective and to share any savings or losses on a predetermined basis. (DTI, 1993a: section 4.6).

Partnership and Co-operation: The Sanctions

In many respects the recommendations of the two reports run exactly parallel, and mark a significant move towards the establishment of a new partnership of an essentially corporatist character between government and industry. The DTI joint Working Group with the industry set the overall perspectives. The employer bodies then co-operated to establish sector working parties with specific technical remits. Even the trade unions were to be involved in strategic planning of human resource requirements – although the specification of 'national' makes it quite clear that this involvement was at the level of traditional trade union structures and would bypass the new unofficial movement. In terms of the scale of reorganization, and the industry-wide character of the process, it was without parallel in recent British history. Government was to be brought in in a way that would have been anathema under Thatcher. The stress was on long-term co-ordinated planning of technological change – with partnership, co-operation and trust being the hallmark of the new era.

The practice was, however, significantly different. In the circumstances it was bound to be. The immediate objective was a 30 per cent reduction in absolute costs over a three-year period. This had to be at the expense of some of the existing players. The rules of the game meant that the oil companies themselves were excluded. It was the costs *to* the operators that had to be cut. The labour force was also ruled out in any direct way. The fragility of management control in 1991 and 1992 still precluded any absolute reductions in wages or conditions. It was this, above all, that made the resolution of this crisis structurally so different to that of 1986. Then the main solution was direct cuts in wages and conditions. This time it was the supply industry itself that had to absorb the costs. For the contract and supply companies this could only mean smaller profit margins on smaller workforces and, most of all, fewer contract and supply firms sharing in the industry's revenue stream.

The CRINE objectives also had another implication. If the new technological drive was towards simplified, standard equipment, then the focus of activity on the UKCS had to change. The main work of contractors had to shift away from producing the inherently non-standard 'frontier technology' required to break out new areas of oil and gas development. Instead, the industry had to be focused on the much less challenging work of servicing and refurbishing what existed, and enhancing recovery in developed fields. It was this area of work which required, and permitted, the development of cheap, standardized and semi-automatic systems.

This was why the change in tax regime was central to the reorganization of the UKCS. The phasing out of PRT announced in March 1993 immediately changed the balance of market power. It meant less activity in total, and it shifted the type of activity away from exploration and development. Most significant of all, it took market power out of the hands of one section of the industry and placed it in the hands of another. Previously, it had been the newer oil companies involved in exploration who drove the market. After March 1993 it was the small group of established companies servicing the original UKCS infrastructure.

For the first phase of the CRINE programme, between November 1992 and July 1994, 70 per cent of all major contracts awarded in the UKCS were commissioned by just three companies: BP, Shell-Expro and Amerada Hess.[4] Amerada Hess was now the fourth biggest producer on the UKCS and the company which supplied the chairman of the CRINE Steering Committee. The contracts awarded were overwhelmingly those for the refurbishment and redevelopment of existing fields in the eastern and central troughs of the UKCS and the existing pipeline infrastructure. The biggest programme was that actioned by Shell-Expro for the refurbishment of the Brent field in March 1993. This was to employ 3000 for two years at the cost of £0.7 billion.[5] BP announced a similar series of giant contracts for the refurbishment of the Forties field and associated pipelines between April and June 1993. When the CRINE document noted that it would be the oil operators who would drive the process, this is what it meant. The operators were now in a position to tell contract firms precisely what they had to do: to form alliances, use low cost methods, co-operate in the development of standardized systems and above all cut their own costs. If suppliers were not willing to work on these terms, they would be out of the ring.

It was because the new tax regime altered power relations in this way that the announcement of the changes, when it came, proved so controversial. The March 1993 budget, phasing out PRT, provoked the first major public split among members of UKOOA since the organization's formation. It enraged the representatives of the supply companies, and created great annoyance among those responsible for the economic development of the North East and the Aberdeen area in particular. The main defence of the changes was put up by BP. John Browne, head of exploration for BP, presented the tax change as essential for the long-term stability of the UKCS as an oil province and the only way of ensuring the full utilization of reserves in existing fields. Esso supported them as 'directionally correct'. So did the other big US company who had been in the UKCS from the beginning, Mobil.[6]

Opposition came from the newer entrants among the oil operators. Ranger Oil threatened to switch all new investment elsewhere. Amerada Hess, as the recent purchaser of large areas of unexplored territory, expressed its unhappiness. Thirteen past chairmen of the Petroleum Exploration Society of Great Britain united to lobby the Treasury against the change. Within the supply industry the International Association of Drilling Contractors denounced the new tax policy as leading to a 'collapse of Aberdeen as a centre of excellence for drilling technology'. From a wider perspective the Royal Bank of Scotland condemned the effects of the tax changes on the Scottish economy as a whole. This bank, which financed many of the local suppliers, joined with the Aberdeen Chamber of Commerce in writing to the government to demand a change of policy. The oil industry finance specialists Wood MacKenzie and Arthur Andersen were also opposed. These firms, which had secured good business from the industry as speculative money flowed during the late 1980s, estimated that the tax changes would reduce liquidity within the industry by approximately £750 million – although BP would be a net financial beneficiary to roughly the same extent. A couple of weeks later Wood MacKenzie strengthened its attack. It claimed the real cost of exploration would be increased fourfold and that many of the smaller oil operators would be forced out of the UKCS. It added that those larger companies benefiting from the tax changes would not invest their new revenues in the UKCS but would use them for overseas work.

The dispute came to a head in a public confrontation at an Offshore Technology Conference in Houston, Texas. Len Ironside, the Chief Executive of Grampian Initiative, challenged the Energy Minister, Tim Eggar. Together with the Economic Development Officer for Grampian Region, Ironside denounced the tax changes as directly detrimental to the supply industry. He then called on Eggar to 'join with me in supporting continued American investment in the North Sea'. Eggar evaded the question and attacked Ironside for being inaccurate and irresponsible. By May 1993 BP and Shell were becoming seriously alarmed at the level of resistance. Their opponents had come together to back some form of transitional relief that would retain the tax clawback for a limited period. In a joint statement BP and Shell said such an arrangement would be seriously inflationary. The following week Mobil condemned any phasing of the change as likely to lead to 'overheating'.[7]

This episode well illustrates the different interests which divided the industry at this point. In terms of numbers, the balance was strongly against the tax change. The bulk of the operators were opposed. Almost all the supply and contract firms saw the tax changes as detrimental. So also did the quasi-governmental and business-led bodies with responsibility for regional economic development. Only the two big UK oil majors were openly in support – together with Esso and Mobil. However, these companies controlled over 60 per cent of the output, and appeared to have the ear of government. In the end there was a slight amendment to the phasing of the new arrangements. But overall it was the biggest of the oil companies, led by BP and Shell, who won the day.

Partnership and Co-operation: Implementation

The implementation of CRINE got underway at the end of 1992. Some parts of the scheme, such as experiments with partnership and alliances, had been initiated by one or two of the leading oil companies over the previous couple of years. But essentially it was in 1993 that the programme was beginning to bite. It involved a fundamental reorganization of the industry and formed the immediate background to the adoption of new health and safety measures flowing from Cullen and the simultaneous attempt to stabilize industrial relations. The practicalities of its implementation are therefore an important part of our story.

Two surveys of supply and contract firms have been undertaken to throw light on these changes. One was carried out in 1992 and provides a snapshot of the industry before the introduction of CRINE and the change in PRT (Foster *et al.*, 1993). The other was conducted at the end of 1993 (Foster *et al.*, 1994). This was fifteen months into CRINE and after the new patterns of market demand were beginning to come into effect.

The 1992 survey was on the same lines as that carried out at Aberdeen University in 1984 and focused on who owned the supply firms in terms of the national base of the ultimate holding company. Ownership was then tracked across all sectors of the industry. It revealed two major changes. First, it found that there was a sharp drop in the number of US-owned firms. From this it was clear that the exodus of US firms after the collapse of the oil price in 1985 had not been reversed in the late 1980s. In some technologically key areas such as well management and electrical and mechanical engineering the number of US firms had halved. Only for the highly mobile area of drilling and diving did the 1992 survey show a slight increase of US firms. On the other hand, there had been a very significant cohort of new entrants to the industry in the late 1980s. Of the 46 new firms which responded to the survey only one was US-owned. Eighteen were owned from within Scotland. Most of the rest came from Norway, Holland and France, with a scattering from England. The bulk of the Scottish entrants were small firms in low value areas – although a few had penetrated technologically more demanding sectors such as surveying and the design and supply of drilling equipment. The continental firms tended to be larger and, especially the Norwegian, technologically advanced.

So the years between 1984 and 1992 had seen some significant shifts. Even though the remaining US subsidiaries were massive conglomerates and continued to dominate in most areas, the loss of a significant number of US firms (and the concentration of ownership among those that remained) had left something of a vacuum. During the five years of speculative expansion after 1987 this had enabled some big European multinationals to enter the UKCS and created conditions for the emergence of a significant number of new locally-controlled supply firms.

The 1993 survey showed this last trend being speedily reversed.[8] In the new circumstances the entry of new Scottish-owned firms was unlikely to be sustained. The second survey focused on the experience of supply firms within the new contract structures. It asked whether suppliers were experiencing pressure on pricing; how many of their contracts involved partnering; whether they had difficulty getting access to tendering and whether their contracts were longer or shorter than previously. The firms surveyed covered four sectors ranging from the very labour-intensive (catering and labour contracting) through non-destructive testing (using small-scale technology), to engineering construction and maintenance (large-scale) and well management and drilling (high technology). The results reproduced in Table 6.1 show a sharply divergent experience for smaller and bigger firms.

Most of the firms were finding difficulties with pricing, but it is clear that only the bigger firms were being drawn into the partnership arrangements. The smaller firms were finding themselves increasingly excluded from the tendering process. A significant number of the contracts secured by the smaller firms were actually of shorter duration than before.

Table 6.1   *1993 Survey of Supply Firms (All Sectors)*

	Employ less than 100 (%)	Employ 100 or more (%)	All (%)
Pricing: some or great difficulty	76	81	77
Partnering: more than a quarter of contracts	12	52	31
Access to tender: some or great difficulty	81	48	67
Contract period shorter than it was 3 years before	41	17	30
Number of responses	27	23	50

Source: Foster et al., 1994.

These findings, though based on a limited number of responses, are confirmed by contemporary reportage. The big operating companies had been slashing their lists of tender companies. BP had already cut its portfolio of contractors by a third and in August 1993 stated its intention to reduce the number of its major contractors from 300 to 100. Under the new system it was to be the bigger contractors who had the responsibility for forming alliances that would permit the supply of the maximum range of specialisms. The head of the energy division of Scottish Enterprise noted that the only way smaller firms could survive would be if they were themselves assisted to form alliances: 'the major thrust of restructuring is cost-driven and reliant on economies of scale'.[9]

This effectively meant that contract firms had to be big enough to develop standard techniques that could be copied on many installations for the same operator. Anthony Smith, director of the oil consultancy firm Smith Rea, pointed out that the consequences of this could be highly adverse. Instancing well management and drilling technology, he claimed that the insistence that one contract should cover all relevant specialisms had meant that single firms or hastily formed alliances had sought to deal with areas for which they had no expertise. This was resulting in the abandonment of some of the best technologies, and serious mistakes in the evaluation of data.[10]

This picture of a radical shake-out of smaller firms in the context of severe cost-cutting is further borne out by the survey of contracts to which we referred earlier. We previously noted that three major oil companies controlled over 70 per cent of the 225 major contracts awarded during the first eighteen months of the CRINE programme. Concentration was just as marked in the other direction. Of the 225 contracts 74 per cent were awarded to just 17 companies. The most successful company, with 30 contracts, was the US-based Haliburton group (which included Brown and Root and Rock-water). Four of the other firms were also American, seven European (of which two were Norwegian) and five British. Most of these firms had themselves formed alliances or consortiums in the course of the previous three years. This was so for three of the five British firms and five of the seven European firms. Scale seems to have been crucial (see Table 6.2).

So when the CRINE documents speak of a new culture of sharing, trust and partnership, it has to be understood in a certain way. Partnership depended on the concentration of market power in the hands of a small group of operators with a very clear idea of what they wanted, and the crea-tion of a small number of super-contractors who either themselves covered all specialisms or in turn controlled the sphere of activity for the small spe-cialists. This level of concentration was the necessary counterpart, in terms of industrial organization, of what was happening on the employment front: the drive for the creation of smaller, relatively permanent core workforces with individuals performing a much wider variety of tasks. The same concen-tration of control was also essential for safety in the new era. The credibility of claims to self-regulation depended on the creation of clear, stable lines of responsibility that ran down from senior management. The operator had to present a Safety Case for the whole installation. Contractors had to be seen as a cohesive part of its implementation.

The bottom line was, however, the issue of costs: the aim of a 30 per cent absolute cut within a historically very short time, three years.

Home Bases and the Paradoxes of Michael Porter

Michael Porter published his *The Competitive Advantage of Nations* in 1990 just before Heseltine arrived at the Department of Trade and Industry. Porter, an American academic economist, had been a consultant to US governments through the 1980s. His 1990 book was the compilation of work by research teams in each of the leading industrial nations: that in the UK was based at the *Economist* (Porter, 1990).

His key thesis was that the economic well-being of nations was dependent on the aggregate strength of individual industries. And the competitive advantage of each industry depended on the robustness of its 'home base'. On an international scale, for each industry, Porter sought to identify which

Table 6.2 *Allocation of Major Contracts, December 1992–July 1994*

Name of Firm	Nationality of Ultimate Owner	Numbers of Contracts
Haliburton (Brown and Root; Rockwater)	US	30
Schlumberger	French–US	13
Stena Offshore	Swedish	13
Stolt Comex Seaway	Norwegian–French	13
Trafalgar House	UK	13
Weir Group	UK	10
Kvaerner	Norwegian	9
AMEC	UK	9
Heerema	Netherlands	8
ABB	Swedish–Swiss	8
Wood Group	UK	7
AOC	UK	6
Baker Hughes	US	6
ENI	Italian	6
McDermott	US	6
Cooper Oil Tools	US	5
Foster Wheeler	US	5

Source: Foster et al., 1994.

nation had secured primacy and how it had been achieved. The section on Britain was particularly unflattering. Its competitive advantage was now limited to biscuits.

By the early 1990s, Porter's ideas had considerable influence in the Department of Trade and Industry. They provided sustenance to the growing view that industry, rather than just services, was critical to national survival, and that the question of who owned that industry was not irrelevant to national competitiveness. In Scotland, Scottish Enterprise hosted a series of very expensive seminars to enable Porter to air his views – including one seminar specifically organized for the oil and gas industry.

Rather like Friedman's ideas in the 1970s, Porter's arguments provided theoretical authority to a new set of priorities within government. They legitimized relationships between state and industry that were very different from those of the Thatcher era. They focused attention on the internal dynamics of an industry. They stressed the link between the breadth and sophistication of 'home' markets and the competitive strength of the industry abroad. Two key elements were identified for the maintenance of this strength. One was the vigour and depth of the supply infrastructure. The other was the creation of an environment of competitive emulation among core producers. In both cases the issue of ownership was central. If the main stimulus for innovation was the vigour of competition *within* the home base – both for supply firms and core producers – then causally it would be firms who were locally-based that would respond most readily. Firms whose principal base was elsewhere would be less likely to do so. While it was certainly conceivable that externally owned firms might make their home base in another country, it would still require a nucleus of nationally owned firms to achieve a critical mass of competitive interaction. National control of industry was once more important.

These were the ideas. Critics of Porter have argued that the governmental practice of his theory has been significantly different, and that its attractiveness was precisely that it supplied a rhetoric by which close governmental company links could be justified (Lazonick, 1991; 1993). Porter pays full deference to the key role of competition. He stresses the need for a critical mass of competing firms in order to generate and sustain product innovation. Yet the practical outcomes were often quite different. This, it is argued, was the reality of the industrial policies adopted by the Reagan and Bush governments in the 1980s. Their implementation depended on partnership between government and the biggest of the big corporations. Innovation in such key areas as information technology and aerospace was sustained by massive federal contracts and research subsidies and enforced by the corporate power of these companies. These corporations wanted a highly competitive local base of supply firms but it was to be run on terms which they set. 'Home base', in this guise, was at best a code for a drastic top-down restructuring of industries. At worst it was a cover for protectionism and discrimination in favour of the biggest existing home firms.

On these terms, Porter's rhetoric was uncannily relevant to the transformation of the UKCS in the early nineties. It matched precisely the agendas of the UK oil majors and their friends in government. The concept of the 'home base', in particular, made it possible to address one of the difficult contradictions in the cost reduction initiative – a contradiction which brings us back to the heart of relations between capital and labour in the UKCS.

The industrial restructuring of the UKCS in 1992 was different in kind from that which occurred in 1986. When the oil price fell in 1985, the operators cut back on all budgets: maintenance, development and exploration. Major supply firms saw the writing on the wall and left. The consequences for industrial structure were left to the anarchic wisdom of market forces. The biggest cost savings for the operators were in the areas that affected safety, the postponement of maintenance programmes, and, even more, labour. Wages and conditions were cut across the board. In 1991–92 these options were not so readily available. On the contrary, the only way of heading off a direct challenge to management prerogatives, and isolating the influence of OILC in the future, was to convince workers that they also were entering a new era. It might even require some kind of understanding with the established unions. A smaller workforce was possible and necessary. But it would need to be relatively well paid and have better conditions.

It was this that gave the industrial restructuring of 1992 its special character and which created its biggest single contradiction. Restructuring under CRINE had to be at the expense of the supply industry itself. BP's head of procurement directly addressed this issue at an offshore conference in August 1993. He spoke of the 'tremendous fears' which existed among suppliers, and then went on to reassure them that 'what we attack is not profits but costs'. For many suppliers this distinction between costs and profits was an exceptionally fine one. As we have seen, the logic of CRINE was to downgrade and exclude a whole range of smaller firms, and to require a process of merger, or at least alliance, among the bigger firms who were to be chosen as 'turn-key' contractors.

It was this that created the contradiction. The oil operators were only too well aware that it was the shrinkage of the supply base after 1985 that had been the biggest single factor in the subsequent escalation of costs. Yet the cure for inflation in 1992 involved a new and further reduction in the size of the local supply base. Operators were also aware that the relative competitiveness of the Norwegian sector was in part dependent on the creation of its own home base of supply firms. Over the previous few years the bigger Norwegian firms, such as Kvaerner and Stolt Comex Seaway, had proved competitive enough to move into a number of market niches in the UKCS. Most analyses of the Norwegian sector explained this success in terms of the preferential award of contracts by Norwegian state firms to national suppliers (Andersen, 1993; Howie and Lipka, 1993).

In these circumstances, the term 'home base' was of critical significance at both corporate and governmental level. During the bitter conflicts over the tax regime in March 1993 the energy minister Tim Eggar sought to reassure Aberdeen Chamber of Commerce by announcing a commitment to make Aberdeen the 'centre of the oil industry'. The concept of a home base provided the rhetoric to reassure nervous suppliers and to appease angry local authorities about the long-term future of Aberdeen as a supply base. It also provided an economic rationale for policy interventions to do this and to regroup what was left of the UK supply base in a much more focused way around Aberdeen. While this aspect of industrial restructuring receives no explicit mention in either the UKOOA or DTI documents, it had clear support from government, from quasi-governmental bodies such as Scottish Enterprise, from BP and Shell and also, it would seem, from those sections of the banking system with closest links to the oil industry.

Ian Wood, owner of one of the biggest UK supply firms, claims that he was finally making headway in government circles in favour of indigenous industry at the very end of the Thatcher government in 1989–90.[11] By early 1991 the term 'home base' was making itself felt. In May 1991 the Energy Select Committee endorsed Scottish Enterprise calls for the government to relocate the Exploration and Appraisal branch of the Department of Energy away from London to Aberdeen – on the grounds that this would force oil firms to relocate HQ personnel as well.

The big moves came in 1993 in the same month as the changes in Petroleum Revenue Tax. It was finally agreed that the Petroleum Engineering Division of the DEn would relocate to Aberdeen. The moves were justified in an advisory report from Ernst and Young which presented them as setting in motion a process of local agglomeration that would make Aberdeen a 'UK and international centre for the oil and gas industry'. 1993–94 saw Total, Chevron and Conoco all shifting their headquarters from London to Aberdeen, while BP moved its Britoil staff up from Glasgow.[12] Suppliers followed. One of the biggest US supply firms, Foster Wheeler, relocated its UK headquarters from Newcastle to Aberdeen, and formed a joint venture between its oil-related activities and those of the UK-owned Wood Group. The result was a massive combined workforce of 2000. Brown and Root (Design and Management) and the UK-owned AOC International also merged operations over the same period to create a 4000 strong workforce based in the Aberdeen area. More detailed moves signalled that a major motive behind this geographical relocation was directly to effect cost reductions in the supply environment. In March 1993, BP signed an agreement with the Wood Group, Trafalgar House, AMEC and Brown and Root that they would collectively retain sufficient chartered engineers in the Aberdeen area to effect a 30 per cent reduction in the premium then being paid to agency engineers.[13]

Within this combined process of contraction and geographical concentration, another trend became apparent by 1993. This was an attempt to stabilize within the Aberdeen supply base a significant core of firms that were, in part at least, nationally owned. In May 1993 Scottish Enterprise announced 'a new strategy to assist smaller companies' in the oil and gas industry, and over the following months acted as broker to bring together a number of consortiums of small, mainly UK-owned firms and to assist their penetration of new European markets such as that opening up in the former Soviet Union. BP also made a practice of highlighting, in its award of contracts, the presence of UK supply companies within larger alliances and consortia.[14] This national bias also appears to show up in the survey results for the autumn of 1993. In the area of drilling and well management three out of the four UK firms responding had more than a quarter of their contracts on a partnership basis. Of the non-UK firms only three out of nine were in this favoured position. It would also seem significant that two of the big UK supply firms were refinanced through the Stock Exchange in 1992–93 and emerged with past or present BP personnel on their boards.

We will examine later the success of these policies. What is important here is the scale of change in policy effected between the late 1980s and the early 1990s. The depth of the crisis in 1990–92 was, we have argued, a direct consequence of the flaws in the preceding industrial regime. So also was the character of the resolution. It could not be at the direct expense of labour. The political imperatives of the new era demanded a structured, strategically-driven reorganization that imposed the costs on the supply industry and the previously dominant independent oil sector. Although justified on quite different terms, its practical implementation required a very close level of co-ordination between government and the biggest of the oil majors. It also penetrated to the heart of wider decision-making. In particular, it demanded a new assessment of relations with the European Union. If the UK was to start to determine agendas on such critical issues such as energy policy for the EU as a whole, then new alliances had to be formed inside Europe. In the following years, as we will see, this realignment was to prove no less fraught and contradictory than the US alliance that preceded it. In the meantime it provided the context for the profound change of culture within the UKCS that would underlie subsequent attempts to stabilize safety provision and industrial relations.

Notes

1. *Financial Times*, 7 and 8 August 1992, discusses the implications of BP's dividend cut and the reactions of US investors. Earlier, BP's chief executive, Robert Horton, had been removed in a boardroom coup by non-executive directors representing City of London institutions and led by Sir John Baring (later Lord Ashburton): *Financial Times*, 8 May and 26 June 1992.

2. The following analysis draws on Bonefeld, Brown and Burnham, 1995, for its analysis for the Major administration – although the authors appear relatively unaware of some of the specific drives towards a new relationship with the European Union deriving from the needs of Britain's oil industry.

3. Many of the points discussed here can be found in the BP mimeo transcript entitled Speech by J. Browne, Chief Executive Officer, BP Exploration at the 5th International Offshore Northern Seas Petroleum Conference, Stavanger, Norway, 19 November 1991.

4. This is based on an analysis of 225 major contracts listed on a weekly basis in the *Aberdeen Petroleum Review*. Fuller details are given in the unpublished paper by Foster, Lipka, Maguiness and Munro, 'Competition and cooperation in the UK offshore oil industry', Department of Applied Social Studies, University of Paisley, 1994.

5. *Aberdeen Petroleum Review*, 7 April 1993.

6. The main sources are the *Aberdeen Petroleum Review*, 24 March, 31 March and 7 April 1993, for statements of position by Laidlaw of Amerada Hess, Jeremy Peat of the Royal Bank of Scotland, Ranger Oil, Aberdeen Chamber of Commerce and Esso; *Observer*, 28 March 1993 for statements by John Browne and David Simon of BP, Arthur Andersen and Wood MacKenzie; *Herald*, 13 April 1993 for further Wood MacKenzie analysis.

7. *Herald*, 3, 4, 5 May 1993 for the dispute in Houston; *Aberdeen Petroleum Review* for 6, 12 May 1993 for statements by BP, Shell and Mobil; *Scotsman*, 18 June 1993 for further call from BP for the government to stand firm.

8. The 1993 survey secured only 50 usable responses (within a more focused range of specialisms) as against the 158 responses to the 1992 survey.

9. *Aberdeen Petroleum Review*, (Nos. 32 and 33, 11 and 18 August 1993) for statement of BP contract policies from George Bain and Roger Wells; *Herald*, 6 May 1993, for statement by Mike Fleming of Scottish Enterprise Oil and Gas.

10. *Offshore Commentary*, December 1993.

11. Interview with Ian Wood, Fine Art Productions, London, 1994.

12. *Aberdeen Petroleum Review*, 3, 17 March 1993, for the relocation of PED staff. It is clear that this move inflicted heavy costs on the smaller independent oil companies who relied on partnerships with the oil majors, and by

March 1994 the Non-Operators Forum was calling for assistance with the redundancy costs arising from the relocation of the operators (*Aberdeen Petroleum Review*, 30 March 1994).

13. *Aberdeen Petroleum Review*, 24 March for the BP-brokered agreement on agency engineers; *Herald*, 9 July 1993 for the Brown and Root and AOC joint venture; *Aberdeen Petroleum Review*, 30 March 1994 for Foster Wheeler and Wood Group.

14. An example would be the award of the contracts for well stimulation in the Forties field to Baker Hughes Inteq and to CDP, a new consortium including Progenitive Services Ltd, 'a young innovative local company': *Aberdeen Petroleum Review*, 23 June 1993.

7 THE STRATEGY OF CONTAINMENT

The New Regime

Regulatory regimes are vulnerable to annexation by an industry group. This applies to offshore regulation under the DEn when there was a progressive capture of the regulator by the offshore operators. But regulatory regimes are also vulnerable to more subtle forms of undermining, when regulatory perspectives and practices become susceptible to industry-driven realignment and containment. This latter *strategy of containment* has been deployed by the operators since Piper Alpha, in part because the former strategy of outright capture was simply no longer appropriate. This chapter examines in some detail the oil industry resistance to the attempted reconstruction of the offshore regulatory framework in the period after Piper Alpha, which has led to a gradual erosion of regulatory reform.

The new Offshore Safety Division (OSD) of the HSE, specifically responsible for offshore safety, came into being in April 1991. The transfer of regulatory responsibility to HSC/E was confirmed by the Offshore Safety Act 1992 which marked the first phase of the post-Cullen reconstruction. The second phase was concerned with putting in place the regulations requiring 'Safety Cases' for offshore installations. The Safety Case regulations became operational for new installations on 31 May 1993 and for existing installations on 30 November 1993, thereafter allowing a two-year transitional period until 30 November 1995. Beyond this date it is an offence to operate an offshore installation in UK waters without a Safety Case accepted by HSE. For existing installations the two-year transitional period was thought to permit discussions with individual operators before granting final Safety Case 'acceptance'. All the required Safety Cases, bar one, were submitted to the HSE before the final deadline in November 1993, some 216 in all, 118 for fixed installations and 98 for mobile installations. Over half were submitted in the final month and some 15 per cent on the final day. The new regime therefore was not fully in place until some five to seven years after Piper Alpha. The lead-in period across the whole industry, given the scale of the regime transition proposed, was relatively short. It placed the OSD under a tight timetable. By contrast, the lead-in period for the comparable onshore CIMAH Regulations had been much longer. Tony Barrell of OSD commented 'The faster timetable reflected the magnitude of the catastrophe at Piper Alpha and the desire to secure needed improvements in standards as quickly as possible' (1994a).

The first two Safety Cases were formally accepted in January 1994 with a further six scheduled for the following month. By June of 1994, nineteen Safety Cases had been accepted, ten for fixed installations and nine for mobile ones, but not as many as the fifty OSD had at first anticipated. Not only did the OSD underestimate the resources necessary for the task, but each Safety Case, especially for the older fixed platforms, took longer to assess than planned, while the poor quality of some submissions was also a problem. This was particularly so in the drilling sector where the need to apply modern principles of risk assessment, as against reliance on prescriptive compliance with existing certification requirements, according to Barrell (1994b), 'has taken a lot of time to resolve with the industry'. In 1994 Barrell (1994b) diplomatically spoke of a learning process that 'has proved very difficult, both for the HSE and the industry'. While the OSD appeared confident of the eventual outcome, others were less so.

The Safety Case, by requiring the systematic analysis of all hazards and the assessment of related risk, sought to reduce hazards and guard against the escalation of an accident into a major disaster. A central plank of the Safety Case was the provision of a temporary safe refuge (TSR) on each installation, which would provide employees with a safe haven, and enhanced means of escape and survival, in the event of a major incident. After Piper Alpha the operators portrayed the industry as the dynamic engine of change in this process. This impression was promulgated by UKOOA at the Cullen inquiry (Hughes, 1991) and since. It is a selective and partial reading of events. Evidence of the operators' reluctance to take on board the full implications of Lord Cullen's recommendations has frequently emerged. The notion of goal-setting, as against a prescriptive regime, has resulted in UKOOA seeking to exploit ambiguities in the new language of safety management, as part of an overall strategy of containment. The dangers of a catch-all deployment of the broad 'goal-setting' concept of safety regulation were identified by the Trade Union Group during the Cullen Inquiry. In his final submission on behalf of the group, Hugh Campbell QC specifically warned that goal-setting regulations may not be enough: 'Not only must the objective be set, but specific, albeit minimum, standards must be imposed by legislation, *so that there is no doubt as to the minimum standard for compliance*[1] (emphasis added). The concern has since been echoed by technical consultants in the industry. To quote but one, 'There will undoubtedly be some attempt to underplay goals for commercial expediency unless they (the operators) utilise independent reputable consultants for this purpose' (Hardie, 1991).

Evidence for such an underplaying of goals can be found in a paper by Dr Harold Hughes (1992), Director General of UKOOA, to an HSE-sponsored conference on offshore safety. Here UKOOA's response to the draft Safety Case regulations was three-pronged (HSE, 1992a). It argued, first, that there were a large number of mobile installations unlike Piper Alpha, a northern-waters fixed installation, and asserted that the draft regulations assumed there was a uniformity. Second, the requirement for each installation to have a temporary safe refuge, was criticized as overly 'prescriptive'. Third, UKOOA was hostile to the requirement that the new regulatory authority would have formally to 'accept' the installation's Safety Case, a requirement which went well beyond the existing onshore CIMAH regulations. Hughes pointed out that the cost and time-scale for the preparation of Safety Cases would itself be a considerable burden on the industry. The crux of UKOOA's objection was stated by Hughes:

> The concept of acceptance places a great deal of power and discretion in the hands of the HSE without any of the safeguards often brought into such legislation to cover instances where real issues of difference arise between the regulatory body and industry. (1992: 4)

These 'real issues of difference' already existed with respect to expensive 'bottom line' requirements of which the temporary safe refuge was the main one.

The technical arguments are complex and have to do with the application of advanced safety engineering concepts such as Quantitative Risk Assessment (QRA) and the ALARP principle discussed below. UKOOA was concerned, said Hughes, that the Department of Employment, to which the HSE at that time ultimately reported, was 'non-technical' and, therefore, not well equipped to judge 'quite arcane technical issues' such as QRA (1992: 5). This was almost an exact replay of 'specialist expertise' arguments deployed against HSE by UKOOA a decade before at the time of Burgoyne. There was also the issue of an 'appeals structure' where disagreements remained over Safety Cases. The basic objection to the new regulations, as articulated by Hughes, had a familiar ring:

We find them too prescriptive, particularly in that they do not recognise the wide variety of installations which already are in place or in use in UK waters, each of which demands its own set of safety solutions to its particular configuration and operating mode. (1992: 6)

The substantive objection concerned the issue of temporary safe refuges. Cullen recommended that every installation have a temporary safe refuge or safe haven of specified durability to enhance the survival of installation personnel in the event of a major incident such as fire or explosion and systems failure (1990: Ch. 17.38). The first draft of the Safety Case regulations was published in December 1991 and in March 1992, as a consultative document (HSE, 1992a). The HSE had indicated, in response to representations from UKOOA, that the TSR requirements might be modified where *a satisfactory alternative* could be demonstrated. It was conceded that TSR requirements might be relaxed with respect to certain, not normally manned, installations or mobile drilling rigs. Nevertheless, this concession did not go far enough for UKOOA. Said Hughes:

Although the HSE have already signalled that exemptions will be available for such cases, it is a fact that over half of current UKCS installations are likely under this proposed legislation to be the subject of applications for exemptions ... It does not seem to us, to put it mildly, to be good law that demands, *ab initio*, the exemption of over half the installations to which that law is supposed to apply. (1992: 6)

The cost of each TSR was expected to amount to about half the total costs of the installation Safety Case. HSE estimated the outlay on TSRs alone as between £1.3 billion and £1.7 billion for the industry as a whole (HSE, 1992b: 8). Viewed from this angle, UKOOA's sensitivity to what it regarded as 'prescriptivity' was perhaps understandable.

Between the March 1992 publication of the consultative document on the draft Safety Case regulations and the final November 1992 publication of the regulations and accompanying guide to the Safety Case (HSE, 1992c), the HSE met with UKOOA on a regular basis. It also met the International Association of Drilling Contractors (IADC) and British Rig Owners Association (BROA) representing the drilling-rig owners. During the course of the consultation over TSRs, the very concept of a TSR was successively redefined by the substitution of the term 'temporary refuge' for temporary safe refuge, stressing the functional rather than the structural dimension of survivability (Pape, 1992). As the HSE guide to the Safety Case regulations described this:

... measures to protect the workforce should include arrangements for temporary refuge from fire, explosion and associated hazards during the period for which they may need to remain on an installation following an uncontrolled incident, and for enabling their evacuation, escape and rescue. (1992c: vii)

Thus, it was argued, simplistic notions of a refuge in terms of a 'protected box' or physical entity, normally the accommodation block, needed to be replaced by a more 'sophisticated' concept of a processual 'flow'. Personnel could be removed from the hazard source in a series of protected access or escape routes to evacuation points. In this redefinition it was even suggested that in certain circumstances a lifeboat could fulfil the function of temporary refuge.[2] In terms of safety engineering, it was argued, this had much to commend it. It offered flexibility in adapting to different installation requirements. However, as with the concept of 'goal-setting' itself, such flexibility also created space within which the operators could redefine safety parameters more freely and interpret regulatory objectives with greater discretion as to their cost implications. There, as elsewhere, what UKOOA was effectively seeking was the creation of a zone of compliance discretion within the new regulatory regime.

Quantitative Risk Assessment/Risk Valuation from Below

Hazards at work, especially in a 'dangerous' industry such as oil and gas exploration and extraction, are ever-present. Indeed, writers such as Perrow (1984) have argued that under certain circumstances in high risk industries with high catastrophic potential, accidents can become 'normal'. The evidence presented to the Cullen inquiry illustrated the potentiality for catastrophic safety system failure created by the 'interactive complexity' and 'tight coupling' of petrochemical extraction and processing in a contained offshore environment (1984: 62–122). In a continuous production processing system, the amount of 'slack' that exists in the system to accommodate error may necessarily be very limited. Even small errors or failures can quickly produce unmanageable consequences. In terms of disaster prevention, safety technology offers the possibility of risk reduction although the costs may be considerable, even 'prohibitive'.

Since Robens, it has been generally accepted that in achieving a safe working environment, a point will be reached where any further outlay would be 'disproportionate' and do little to reduce the further level of risk; the notion of 'reasonable practicability'. The question remains one of *how* that calculation is arrived at. Proponents of this view typically argue that some form of cost-benefit analysis provides a guideline; but cost-benefit analysis itself is not without its critics (Ball, 1979). Apparently objective criteria for safety expenditure decision-making can disguise assumptions that are essentially socially-based value judgements about practicable benefits to be weighed against costs. The same considerations are true with respect to the concept of risk.

Lord Cullen, in his report, considered recent advances in the measurement and control of risk. He endorsed the techniques of Quantitative Risk Assessment (QRA) which provide a more sophisticated cost-benefit analysis based on statistical probabilities. He saw this as a useful way of enabling the limits of what is 'reasonably practicable' in terms of risk management offshore to be accurately assessed (1990: Ch. 17.61). As a methodology, QRA itself had been 'a matter of some controversy'. Even the HSE at the Cullen inquiry was 'only cautiously enthusiastic' (1990: Ch. 17.53). Cullen felt, nevertheless, that QRA was an important tool which had an educative role for the operators, making them more rigorously define and monitor their procedures for risk control (1990: Ch. 17.49). Placing the final onus for risk management on the operator as duty holder was held to be fully in line with the philosophy of self-regulation underpinning Robens' approach. Cullen said that the specialized techniques of QRA were to be understood by the operators themselves, applied specifically to the endurance capability of the TSRs and more generally, to the Safety Cases themselves. Hence, the general thrust of the Cullen report was that acceptance standards for QRA should be proposed by the operator. The single exception, the acceptance standards for the TSR, Cullen said, should be 'one fixed point in the regime' where standards of endurance should be specified by the regulatory authority (1990: Ch. 17.57).

A central concept of QRA is the ALARP principle. ALARP seeks to specify the boundary of 'tolerable risk' at a level that is 'as low as reasonably practicable'. It involves a cost-benefit analysis compatible with a notion of reasonable practicability, albeit one that is statistically arrived at. However, what is considered by management as reasonably practicable and what workers may consider to be tolerable risk, on the basis of their on-the-job experience, may not necessarily coincide. The seemingly 'scientific' nature of the ALARP calculations and QRA are harder to challenge by the workforce. Judgements of acceptable risk hence are largely determined by management, but when presented in the guise of probabilistic theory, this remains obscured. Thus the power to decide what constitutes acceptable risk is shifted upwards, and in the final event rests with management. Moore, a critic of QRA, has commented:

> There exist no available economic or statistical techniques which can
> readily provide 'quick fixes' as far as improvements in health and safety
> at work are concerned. Safety is about effective workplace risk control
> and public accountability, not pliable mathematical exercises in statistics
> or economics. (1991: 13)

In developing a safe working environment it is not simply specialized
quantitative 'expertise' exclusively concentrated in the hands (or heads) of
management, but also what is described as 'low level safety intelligence',
which counts (1991: 11). Hazards are often identified and controlled most
effectively by those most immediately involved in the work-tasks, through a
process of constant monitoring or 'risk valuation from below' (1991: 11).

An example of such risk valuation from below is provided by an offshore
incident previously referred to. A pipefitter on the Amoco Montrose was
given a 'hot-work permit' and instructed to cut into a length of pipe. The pipe
contained potentially lethal explosive gases, but the worker did not proceed
with the job using oxy-acetylene cutting gear and thereby forestalled what
could have been a major accident. In this instance, on-the-job monitoring
of safety saved the day. It did so only because the worker was prepared to
exercise his initiative and adopt what he felt to be a safe work practice. The
individual worker contested an already managerially approved task assignment on the basis of his 'own tacit knowledge'. That contest indicates how
unequally valued are the relative risk valuations emanating from the bottom
as opposed to the higher levels of the authority structure.

There is an additional dimension to risk valuation from below which is
illustrated by the pipefitter incident. The individual concerned was an experienced craftsman with a knowledge of the job built up over many years. The
offshore employers, however, by recruiting large numbers of 'green labour',
are seeking to create maximum labour flexibility through new forms of
training so that workers would be 'multi-skilled' (OIAC, 1992). This attack
on craft boundaries enables operators to reduce the number of workers
required. But it also brings with it a reduction in the 'quality assurance',
and therefore safe working practices, that are an in-built part of the trades-
man's traditional training. Multi-skilling or, more accurately, multi-tasking,
is attractive to employers because it means that each worker can perform a
wider range of functionally related tasks and thus progress the job more
quickly. The pressure not to question management orders is thus even
greater, particularly where there is ambiguity about, or blurring of, task
demarcations, especially amongst inexperienced employees. While the
employer gets on with the pressing business of meeting client deadlines,

the workforce safety concerns are too often simply secondary considerations.

The pipefitter case was one that derived from the pre-Cullen context, that is, before the new goal-setting Safety Cases and attendant risk-assessment procedures had been put in place in the industry. Yet where there has been an attempt to apply risk valuation from below, the newly applied QRA techniques have been found wanting. In the voluntary Safety Case for Cormorant Alpha submitted by Shell to the HSE, a risk measure called the Individual Risk Per Annum or IRPA was utilized. Shell's own literature described IRPA:

> The frequency per annum of potential loss of life of an individual from all work-related hazards taking into account the fact that he is not always on the installation or at work and will, if given sufficient warning, try to escape from the hazardous event. (Shell Expro, 1993)

This measure combines the risk from travelling offshore, being offshore and working offshore with the probability of escaping from any incidents. IRPA, says Shell, 'is one of the most important risk measures from a quantitative risk assessment' (Shell Expro, 1993). Given the importance to Shell of IRPA measures, it could reasonably have been expected that great care would be taken in their calculation and use. Similarly, it could be expected that HSE as regulator would subject these calculations to the closest scrutiny.

Yet this most critical measure revealed certain basic mistakes. First, Shell calculated the IRPA using the time spent offshore of Shell staff, for example, at an average value of 1.5×10^{-3}. This ignored the fact that about 80 per cent of those on board the installation are not Shell staff. They are contractors' personnel who work a two weeks on, two weeks off shift pattern, making a working year of twenty-six weeks offshore, as opposed to twenty-one weeks for Shell staff. The effect is to underestimate the 'average' IRPA by about 29 per cent for an installation with a 150 roster of 'Personnel on Board'. Shell even presented the contract catering staff IRPA based on staff tours of duty. Second, Shell noted that the risks from travel and actual employment on board were relatively small, at around 3×10^{-4} as an IRPA. But these figures too will depend on risk exposure, and contractors' staff make about 25 per cent more flights and generally work longer hours in higher-risk occupations. Eleven offshore workers on a helicopter flight to Shell's Cormorant Alpha had only recently been killed. As OILC commented:

> It appears to be astonishingly inept and insensitive to make such a mistake in respect of the very installation that was to sustain a tragic loss

> of life in March 1992 when contractors' men in a shuttle flight were
> exposed to a risk not borne by Shell staff. (1993: 3)

This basic mistake Shell would correct, but it is revealing for the glimpse of
the mistaken assumptions that underlay seemingly rigorous risk calculations.
It illustrates the corporate mental block which ignores workers who make up
the majority of the offshore population. Hierarchical organizations tend to
concentrate power and therefore 'expertise' as a part of managerial control.
Moore's comments are especially pertinent to the offshore industry:

> For it is a fact that companies and managers remain reluctant to divest
> themselves of organisational or administrative power, leaving workers
> thereby poorly informed. The result of which is that, despite legislation,
> the power to decide or determine what constitutes a risk – and how risky
> a process might be – shifts upwards, always finally resting with
> management, technical experts and administrators. Therefore this
> acceptable risk approach is in truth about managers holding power and
> workers facing risks. (1991: 11)

For 'risk valuation from below' to be effective, the workforce need to be
informed. Much more than this, they need to be involved in the process of
risk assessment as fully legitimate active participants able to articulate their
collective concerns without constraint (Molloy, 1993).

Safety Cases and Workforce Involvement

The HSE has attempted to evolve formal procedures of its own to ensure
workforce participation in the new Safety Case regime (Emmott, 1993; Hall,
1995). The Safety Case regulations require consultation with the workforce
safety representatives, from initial presentation through to revisions necessary for the final decommissioning stage of a platform's life (HSE: 1992c). An
initial screening takes place to determine whether the Safety Case proposed
by the operator is suitable for assessment, to be completed by the OSD within
a 33-day period. Then, a second detailed assessment or Stage 2, with a proposed assessment timetable, would be set out. Where the OSD considers a
submission to be unsatisfactory or incomplete, it was intended that the Safety
Case or the relevant parts of it would be returned to the duty holder with a
written explanation, and a deadline for resubmission would be agreed. In any
event, that review would be completed before the statutory deadline of 30
November 1995. At Stage 2, detailed assessment of the Safety Case against

the prepared work plan would be conducted in an 'interactive' manner between the OSD's 'Case Manager' and the operator (duty holder). This is the stage at which issues would be identified, clarified and prioritized and outstanding differences and necessary improvements sorted out. 'Issue Notes' were to be sent to operators, raising specific matters of concern or 'targeted' questions with a prioritized 'severity rating', identifying which unresolved issues either would or could lead to rejection. These Issue Notes were, according to Barrell (1994b), 'taken very seriously'. Just how seriously, is indicated by certain companies putting both the Issue Notes and their responses to them through their legal departments. Thereafter, with the operator having been given time to respond to the Issue Note, the Safety Case would either be accepted or rejected on the recommendation of the OSD Case Manager. Where a Safety Case was rejected, the written notification would explain the reasons for rejection and invite discussion as to the way forward. The operator at this stage could apply to the HSE within 21 days seeking review of the rejection decision and, thereafter, could choose to attend a review meeting consisting of two members of the HSE and its solicitor (HSE: 1993b).

Throughout both stages of the assessment procedures, provision was made for informing and consulting workforce or safety representatives and for inviting their views. At Stage 1, where OSD might consider the Safety Case unsatisfactory or incomplete, representatives of the workforce (or installation safety representatives) would be informed of the OSD's decision in writing (1993b: para 9). At Stage 2 workforce representatives would also be informed of the acceptance decision (1993b: para 24). Where a rejection decision was challenged by a review, the operator had to include, along with the application for review, 'any views submitted by the installation safety representatives' (1993b: para 26). The HSE would in addition (a) inform representatives of the workforce of the duty holder's request and reasons for seeking a review; (b) invite representatives to make any points they consider relevant to the review at least ten working days prior to the review meeting, a summary of any such points to be sent to the duty holder; (c) invite representatives to nominate two of their number to attend the review meeting (1993b: para 29). Where there was no already existing workforce or appointed safety representatives, the HSE 'may make alternative arrangements as appear appropriate' to enable views to be heard, 'representative of those whose health and safety may be affected' by the matters under review.

Given the extensive formal provisions for workforce involvement in the Safety Cases, and the centrality of the Safety Case regulations to the new offshore safety regime, some assessment of these regulations in practice was deemed to be in order.

The HSE Interim Report

Initially, it was envisaged that a full evaluation of the Safety Case regulations would be undertaken two years after the end of the transition period between 1993 and 1995. A report was thus scheduled for 1997 or 1998. The Health and Safety Commission, however, expressed 'some disappointment' at the delay in feedback on the regulations. It was therefore decided to bring forward the main evaluation to 1996 and undertake an interim evaluation before the transitional period had ended. Five separate studies were undertaken, three of which were external, carried out by the University of Aberdeen, and two of which were in-house. These studies are reported by the HSE in *An Interim Evaluation of the Offshore Installation (Safety Case) Regulations 1992*, which was released in November 1995, coinciding with the official end of the transition period (HSE, 1995a). The following section will explore some of the key points made in this document, hereafter also referred to as the interim report.

In our view, the interim report marks a further stage in the progressive containment of the HSE as a regulatory agency by the industry. In this report the HSE adopts an accommodatory stance towards industry-driven priorities, and is modifying its goals accordingly. Overall, there appears to be a retrenchment of regulatory stringency, as both industry and HSE embrace shared underlying assumptions about necessary cost-cutting in the CRINE programme. While acknowledging the provisional nature of the report, the HSE makes positive claims regarding improvements resultant from the Safety Case regime, even in its early implementation; claims which have been immediately taken up by the industry (see Hughes and Taylor, 1995).

In summary, the HSE argues that 'the Safety Case regulations are having a positive impact on the offshore industry's approach to the management of safety'; that there is 'a more focused awareness of risk, better targeting of safety-related expenditure and improvements in safety management systems.' HSE claims that 'workers feel more confident about offshore safety', now that the Safety Case system is in place. It suggests 'managers in general support the Safety Case concept', and that there is evidence of a 'substantial reduction in risk' (HSE, 1995a: 1). In addition, the HSE makes promises regarding future deregulation in which it 'will discuss with the industry ways of improving the regime and minimising Safety Case preparation and assessment burdens' (1995a: 1).

Much of the evidence presented in the interim report is subjective in nature and open to alternative interpretations. In some instances, evidence is presented of a flawed regulatory system which is suffering from persistent communication problems between workforce and management, suggesting that workforce involvement is often incomplete. The following points are of greatest interest in our context:

Firstly, with regard to *regulation vs voluntary compliance*, the HSE attempts to distinguish the effects of Safety Case regulations from 'other factors bearing on safety management change', such as the impact of Piper Alpha and the Cullen report. The report indicates that 'just under half of the surveyed companies acknowledged a direct influence of the Safety Case regulations on their safety management systems' (1995a: para 21). In other words nearly 50 per cent of the companies surveyed needed to be forced to comply with new safety thinking. This must underscore doubts by critics of the industry about the appropriateness of reliance on a purely goal-setting regime based on self-regulation as the central path to reforming offshore safety practices.

Secondly, in *accommodating management cost-cutting demands*, the HSE reports that management has identified various benefits deriving from the Safety Case approach. The Safety Case accordingly results in more 'structured thinking' with regard to safety decisions. These observations are tied to the statement that the Safety Case approach is seen 'as a path to greater efficiency in safety related spending, through targeting resources more effectively' (1995a: para 17). In linking safety and efficiency in this way, the HSE appears to be implicitly endorsing the assumptions and objectives of the more recent CRINE programme. It remains to be seen how far the cost-cutting agenda can be pursued before the regulator feels compelled to question its programmatic content. What is of greatest concern is that regulatory reform is being set within an industry-determined agenda of cost control.

Thirdly, the report indicates that *industry estimates of safety spending* have been inflated. In its interim report, the HSE tries to separate out various costs incurred in complying with the Safety Case regulations. Attempts are made to distinguish these from other expenditures incurred in the aftermath of the Piper Alpha disaster, from costs incurred in complying with unrelated regulations, and from costs incurred as a result of non-Safety-Case-related recommendations in the Cullen report. To this purpose a survey of 16 oil companies and 5 drilling companies was undertaken. In this survey 'many respondents pointed out that it was difficult to distinguish expenditures associated with the Safety Case regulations from those arising from the Cullen report and from companies' own initiatives following Piper Alpha, and indeed, to separate these from spending on normal business activities' (1995a: para. 32). According to the HSE estimates, the total cost of safety expenditures from Piper Alpha up until 1995 amounts to between £2.3 billion and £2.6 billion (1995a: para. 26). These figures raise doubts about the industry's claims that it has 'expended millions of skilled man-hours on safety improvements in the last 6–7 years and has spent or committed nearly £5 billion over that period'.[3] Given that the industry has incurred, or is likely to incur substantial savings arising from the 'deregulatory effect of some of the [new regulations such as] PFEER (Prevention of Fire, Explosion and Emergency Response) provisions' (1995a: para. 34), it is obvious that industry claims of a safety spend must be read with the greatest caution. The industry, today, appears to be masking routine maintenance expenditures with safety claims. As an effect, it not only achieves undue publicity gains, but also confers a false picture of financial pressures resulting from planned or actual safety expenditures. Yet the HSE seems to be primarily concerned with demonstrating that the 'burden' of its Safety Case regulations falls into the lower range of previous estimates (1995a: 30–37). Such attempts to 'talk up' safety spending and conciliate industry complaints about the scale of expenditures implied in new regulations might potentially compromise necessary expenditures in the future. The distorted assumptions of previous cost-benefit analyses are in danger of being magnified still further by the need for the HSE to genuflect to current deregulatory imperatives of the wider political agenda set by government.

Fourthly, the report points to substantive *industry opposition to regulatory and procedural stringency.* According to the HSE interim report, the industry has identified a number of 'problem areas within the new regime'. These include 'bureaucracy/paper work burden, legislative overload, fears of return to prescription, inappropriateness of the regulations to certain sectors, and the extent of reliance on QRA, and the credence to be attached to it' (1995a: paras. 24–26). The HSE notes 'a widespread feeling' amongst operators that the Safety Case implementation was 'unduly bureaucratic'. Both the regulations and their administration were said to be 'too inflexible' (1995a: 25). The report comments that drilling company managers felt that Safety Case regulations, framed as a 'response to major explosion and fire in a large production platform involved wasted time and effort for no real benefit', and 'doubted their relevance to drilling operations' (1995a: 27). Such complaints are surprising, particularly in view of the fact that the International Association of Drilling Contractors (IADC) has produced a generic Safety Case providing industry-level guidance. It would appear that members of the IADC were experiencing difficulties even with the implementation of the industry-devised pre-arranged scheme. IADC has maintained the oppositional stance it has adopted from the very time the Cullen recommendations were first publicized. This opposition, together with Barrell's (1994b) previous comments on the difficulty of the drilling industry in adapting to the new regime, should have been of concern to the regulators, but now appear a matter of equanimity.

Fifthly, in its report, the HSE is unable to provide *meaningful assessment* of the effects of the Safety Case regime. In compiling its evidence on the success of the Safety Case regime, the interim report has relied heavily on surveys which sample a small fraction of the workforce, managerial staff or installation units available. In several instances the sampling techniques are inadequate, resulting in information which is either too subjective to provide a meaningful assessment or too unreliable to do so. In its Senior Management and Interim Compliance Cost Survey, the HSE included a sample of a total of 21 Safety Case duty-holding companies. While the HSE report asserts that selection was applied which 'incorporates a range of attributes', the actual selection process is not described in any meaningful way (1995a: 19). Critical readers will not be able to exclude the possibility of a selection bias, say in favour of companies which were more willing to discuss the issues at hand.

The report's assessment of the effects of the Safety Case regime on risks to persons sampled 13 out of a total of 216 installations which sought Safety Case acceptance. This represents a total population on board of 2254, which according to HSE estimates represents about 8 per cent of the offshore workforce. Apart from choosing such a dubiously small sample, the report gives little or no indication as to which selection criteria (if any) were applied. Although the report states reservations, it ventures into an examination of the 'quantified benefits envisaged' in the cost-benefit analysis, with regard to the risk to persons offshore (1995a: 62–3). Again providing less than clear statements about the process and parameters of its calculations, the interim report concludes:

> The evidence available from *some* of the offshore installation safety cases assessed to date indicates that there is *a potential* for a reduction in the risk of fatalities, *when planned remedial measures have been implemented*, of around 70 per cent … These findings are broadly compatible with the view expressed in the original CBA [Cost Benefit Analysis] that a 90 per cent risk reduction *might be achieved over a period of time* across the industry as a whole. (1995a: 47) (emphasis added)

These carefully qualified estimates, based on a very restricted sample and on an admittedly disputed methodology, have been seized upon by the industry and used in a rather different way. Thus, in a press release claiming that the latest HSE accident statistics 'confirm' industry claims to an 'improving safety performance', it is categorically stated: 'the HSE has estimated that the risk of a major disaster offshore has been reduced by 90 per cent'.[4]

The tendency towards a use of subjective information is most evident in the case of the workforce survey included in the interim report. In this survey, 1100 workers were surveyed on a self-selection basis, with questionnaires being distributed at heliports. The report notes that 'over 80 per cent of respondents said they thought that both management and workers now paid greater attention to safety issues than they did before 1988' (para. 48). 'The great majority (72 per cent) said they are more confident that risks are being managed/reduced' (1995a: 49). The usefulness of such attitudinal surveys may be doubted, but there are additional problems in this study. Firstly, the report does not discuss how many of the surveyed workers worked continuously since 1988 and/or how it deals with the responses of workers with shorter tenure. No significance can be attributed to statements about improvements in offshore safety since 1988 made by workers whose employment postdates this period. Secondly, the report itself gives indications about problems with regard to the validity of the subjective information evaluated. The appendix to the report notes, 'that those workers with the most offshore experience were less likely to perceive management and workers as paying more attention to safety matters now, than was the case for workers with less offshore experience' (1995a: 32). In analytical terms, the responses of long-term employees with greater experience should be of greater relevance to an analysis which would attempt to be more than purely subjective. The response differential between the two groups, as identified by the survey, might well reflect a process of self-deception amongst newer workers, whose fear of accidents translates into a distorted perception of offshore safety. In short, the surveys on management, risk and workforce appear to be based on assessments which are insufficiently *robust* to give any more than a very subjective and very tentative evaluation. In many aspects the interim report would seem to point in more than one direction.

Sixthly, the interim report raises methodological questions regarding Quantitative Risk Assessment. The report relies heavily on QRA procedures, and indeed, ties much of its claim of improved safety to such assessment (1995a: 63). The industry itself, while endorsing the 'central role of QRA' in formalizing and systematizing company approaches to risk assessment and control, also expresses 'doubts' and 'scepticism about the extent of reliance on QRA and about the value of the effort required to carry out such studies' (1995a: 28). Hughes of UKOOA has conceded that 'without the solid foundation of a good data base, QRA can become a self-delusion, a mere refinement on non-knowledge' (1994b: 9).

Such ambivalence is perhaps understandable, given the fact that over 50 per cent of QRA work on the Safety Cases was conducted by outside consultants. Apart from posing doubts about such methodology, this also raises concerns previously discussed about the shift in the management of safety in an overly technical direction to the exclusion of the workforce safety representatives. Again, the report makes some interesting statements on this question.

The issue of *communication and workforce participation* is also addressed. The interim report cites management observation that 'the technical nature of QRA was also seen as a potential obstacle to workforce involvement in the Safety Case process' (1995a: 28). A general workforce survey conducted by Whyte *et al.* (1996) provides documentary evidence, admittedly from a small sample, of a range of attitudes indicating inadequate participation and dissatisfaction on the part of the workforce with consultation over the Safety Case. The current technocratic approach appears to exclude workers to a degree which runs counter to Lord Cullen's explicit recommendations of increased workforce participation (see Cullen, Vol. 2, Recommendation 27). This situation is worsened by informational deficits on the part of the workforce and safety representatives. Interestingly, the interim report states that one-fifth of safety representatives 'appear to be unaware that management has a statutory duty to consult' in the preparation of the Safety Case (1995a: 43). One third of safety representatives meanwhile 'felt inadequately informed about the Safety Case' and a 'slightly higher proportion believed that their constituents were not adequately informed' (1995a: 33).

The interim report also notes there was confusion 'as to the respective roles of companies and HSE in the Safety Case process, with almost one in four of the sample believing that Safety Cases were HSE instructions to companies to carry out safety improvements and one in five believing that the HSE was responsible for producing Safety Cases' (1995a: 43). More generally, the HSE report stated that 'over a quarter of the sample said they required additional information: summary information and information tailored to particular worksites' (1995a: 45).

The workforce survey noted that 'formal training specifically relating to the Safety Case regulation or process, is rare among the general workforce' (1995a: 47). 'Over 25 per cent of the workforce indicated that they wanted additional information on the Safety Case regulations, and in particular, how the regulations would affect their work task in a day-to-day sense.' Given this evidence, there is a strong suggestion of persistent communication problems offshore, which is systematically related to the way the new safety system was set up and is currently being implemented on a day-to-day basis. It is clear that a significant portion of the workforce feel unable to use the Safety Case as an immediate orientation or safety barometer, when assessing the safety conditions of their workplace. Even senior management admits to the only mixed success in involving the workforce in the Safety Case (1995a: 46). Such statements should perhaps have led the HSE to show greater concern rather than painting the complacent picture implicit in the interim report.

Identifiable communication problems are particularly alarming when it comes to safety representatives. The report's conclusions note that a 'surprising number of safety representatives showed a lack of understanding in some areas' (1995a: 31). The HSE's analysis echoes statements reported from the Brent Charlie, in which a worker stated that 'The safety rep's training consists of a compulsory one-week course which is of little or no use. Why don't the HSE insist on in-depth training for safety reps?'[5] In the post-Cullen reconstruction, many observers expected widespread and high levels of workforce involvement in the safety management system, as well as comparable levels of comprehension. That this is not the case points to deficiencies in the reality of workforce participation.

In our view these deficiencies are attributable to the systematic exclusion of trade unions offshore as a countervailing element to management. Onshore trade unions have provided extensive training for safety representatives, collective support and an independent source of expertise in safety matters. We doubt that individualized offshore safety representatives are capable of acting as effectively in matters of safety (Fairbrother, 1996). We particularly doubt this, given the context of a longstanding deeply authoritarian system of industrial relations in this industry. In short there would appear to remain problems in the creation of effective participation in Safety Cases. The interim report notes that '45 per cent of Issue Notes' (through which the HSE signals dissatisfaction with operators' Safety Case proposals) 'related specifically to engineering matters.' A further 40 per cent were raised with respect to hazards analysis and risk assessment, and the remaining 15 per cent dealt with management system matters (1995a: para. 53). This distribution seems to reflect firstly the uncertain manner in which the industry applies hazard and QRA analysis. One would expect 'hard' errors related to 'engineering matters' also to be fairly easily spotted by the regulators. The fact that a significant proportion of Issue Notes (15 per cent) were raised exclusively with regard to management systems, which in the normal course of an evaluation would be less apparent, suggests that the wrongs identified were of a gross nature. This indicates that Lord Cullen's concern with revamping the managerial culture of safety is still an area where considerable improvement needs to be sought.

The importance of changes in managerial attitudes is emphasized in the interim report itself. The majority of the respondents in the manager survey held 'that the most significant changes were not in hardware but in attitudes, awareness, procedures and safety management systems, which are at the heart of Safety Case Regulations' (1995a: para. 22). Some managers of the 21 companies surveyed, moreover, conceded that 'whereas technical measures are designed to preserve and to mitigate rare extreme events, improved safety management systems have an impact on day-to-day operations' (1995a: para. 22). There appears to be a contradiction in managerial goals. On the one hand, there is a perception of the benefits of workforce involvement, while on the other hand, traditional concepts of managerial prerogative are stressed. Offshore managers are eager to reap the benefits of workforce involvement with regard to ongoing but costly day-to-day incidents, but are typically unwilling to allow for trade union back-up to safety representatives which could enhance such involvement.

While the formal provisions for consultation appear to be extensive, reservations about the ability of the safety representatives to make a constructive or even challenging contribution to the process remain. There are also doubts about the practicalities of the new arrangements. Consultation does not necessarily imply that safety representatives gain access to the full Safety Case detailed documentation, even assuming they have the necessary technical competence to conduct independent scrutiny. More often it is summary documents which are presented for endorsement. One study reports:

> The usual format for such a meeting was to gather together all of the safety representatives on a platform and supply each with a copy of the Safety Case. They would then be given a period of time (usually between an hour and half a day) to read selected sections of the Safety Case, and asked for comments at the end of the period of time. It was made clear that this would be their only chance to have an input into the Safety Case. This type of consultation exercise has understandably generated scepticism of the authenticity of operators' commitment to workforce involvement in safety. (Whyte *et al.*, 1996)

While safety representatives have in theory the right to seek assistance in assessing the Safety Case (the auditing expertise which a trade union safety department would normally provide), this right has yet to be tested in law. Finally, the question remains as to whether the processes of consultation with workforce representatives actually result in effective change. The proud boast by one operator that their Safety Case submission was endorsed by a safety representative's signature, actually begs more questions than it answers. Operators are currently under no legal obligation to provide such endorsement of the Safety Case. They are also not required to seek approval when they are seeking prior *exemptions* from specific Safety Case requirements. This last weakness in the consultation procedures has provoked the OSD to attempt to reassure the workforce that an opportunity to express a view will be provided where exemptions are sought (Barrell, 1993).

To sum up then. First, Safety Case procedures place the major burden of responsibility on line management and do so in a highly technocratic way. Safety Cases, produced largely by consultants, are extremely technical documents involving a range of both engineering and risk analysis skills such as QRA. Only a very small segment of the workforce (including management) understand how and why they specify certain procedures – only that these *are* the procedures. Second, compliance would also tend to be handled in a technocratic way. The HSE audits the processes set down in the Safety Case. It is no longer the case of inspectors coming to see if 'their' regulations are being observed. Prescriptive statutory regulations are being removed, but goal-setting self-regulation can only be an effective substitute if anchored in genuine workforce involvement. Third, the existing system of safety representatives, lacks a trade-union-based system of support. This means that direct workforce involvement would remain individualized, weak and ambivalent – and moreover without the technical knowledge or support needed to question management interpretation of Safety Case requirements. A safety regime of this character would be a cause for concern in any industry. It must be particularly so in the offshore oil industry.

There is a real danger that some of the misconceptions of the interim report will become conventional wisdom about the Safety Case system, while newly emerging problems will remain hidden. The publication of the interim report has been used by the HSE to signal a shift in emphasis away from major accident prevention to a more general concern with overall occupational welfare. Yet it is far from clear that the basic cornerstone of the new safety regime is securely in place. As this book went to press, disturbing allegations concerning lack of proper refurbishment of the passive fire protection system on Piper Alpha's sister platform, the Claymore, threw doubt on the Safety Case as an effective regulatory device.[6] Workers' testimony, and subsequent restricted access by concerned trade unionists to Elf's records, suggested necessary upgrading work during 1989/90 did not meet specification. The HSE argued that this did not constitute an enforcement issue. The presence of a new accommodation installation alongside the platform now provided a means of safe evacuation. Thus the passive fire protection was deemed adequate within the wider assessment of acceptable risk calculations of the Safety Case. Here would appear to be a possible example of how goal-setting, without the 'minimum standard for compliance' Hugh Campbell QC called for at the Piper inquiry, can enable the moving of regulatory goal posts.

The Third Phase of Regulatory Reconstruction

Interventions by UKOOA designed to contain Cullen recommendations, were also to be launched as the third and ongoing phase of post-Cullen safety legislation was initiated. The first phase had been the passing of the Offshore Safety Act and the second, the Safety Case regulations. In the third phase, existing offshore health and safety legislation was to be modernized and revised to a less prescriptive style that would complement the new Safety Case regime. Offshore-specific regulations on evacuation, escape and rescue, fire and explosion protection, design and construction, and on management and administration were to be proposed. Certain key existing onshore regulations under the HSWA, such as the Control of Substances Hazardous to Health (COSHH) Regulations 1988, were also at last to be extended offshore. New across-the-board safety regulations were proposed in addition to implement EU health and safety Directives.

Offshore-specific regulations

Offshore-specific regulations, goal-setting rather than prescriptive in nature, were typified by the Offshore Installations (Prevention of Fire, Explosion, and Emergency Response [PFEER]) Regulations and Approved Code of Practice (ACOP) (HSE, 1993a). These were implemented in the latest phase of regulatory reconstruction (HSE, 1995b). They were intended to simplify, rationalize and replace existing prescriptive regulations governing the prevention of fire and explosions, and emergency response on offshore installations. Coming into effect in June 1995, the PFEER regulations implemented, fully or in part, 38 of the 106 recommendations made by Lord Cullen (Todd, 1995). Lord Cullen himself recognized the need for a degree of regulatory 'solidity' in the Safety Case goal-setting regime:

> The regime should not rely solely on the Safety Case ... the regulation requiring the Safety Case should be complemented by other regulations dealing with specific features ... These regulations would complement the Safety Case by setting intermediate goals and would give the regime a solidity which it might otherwise lack. (1990: Ch. 17.63)

The operators tried to establish a false opposition between goal-setting and prescription in the minds of the regulators. In a speech to the Offshore Engineering Society in Aberdeen, Harold Hughes was explicit that UKOOA 'wants to ensure that all elements of prescription are done away with'.[7] Today operators seem content to embrace a goal-setting regime, but only insofar as it is denuded of any regulatory demands or controls of a more specified nature.

The PFEER regulations are important because they provide the kind of 'intermediate' regulations Lord Cullen called for, complementary to the more general goal-setting regulations of the Safety Case. OSD officials have conceded that 'PFEER does contain more detailed and more specific primary duties with which duty holders need to comply' (Patterson, 1995: 9). Yet there is some evidence that in this first attempt to provide operational specificity to the goal-setting Safety Case regulations, there was an inability on the part of the operators to relate the more general Safety Case requirements to the more specific. Another OSD official has commented, 'Even in the four months since PFEER came into force, inspectors are realising that there are some duty holders who do not understand the relationship, nor why it is necessary to have PFEER at all' (Todd, 1995: 7). The OSD also noted that some duty holders have put forward arguments that once they have an accepted Safety Case, they should not have to reassess fire and explosion and emergency response matters 'merely because PFEER comes into force' (Patterson, 1995: 9).

Approved Codes of Practice

Accompanying the PFEER regulations is an Approved Code of Practice. ACOPs prescribe the particular means of compliance with the legal requirements of the regulations, which if not followed, oblige the operator to demonstrate that an equally effective system has been devised. The normal burden of proof is then reversed and it is up to the 'duty holder' (the employer) to satisfy the default requirement in any legal proceedings. As such, ACOPs can be a powerful instrument in the auditing and enforcement in an effective system of self-regulation. From a strictly legal point of view, however, an ACOP has a less binding legal status than the regulations, although more so than non-mandatory Guidance. The attractiveness of ACOPs to the HSE has been that they can be issued with ministerial approval and without the necessity of complex parliamentary procedures for amendment. Far from being vehicles for the reintroduction of outdated prescriptiveness, as Rimington pointed out to Lord Cullen, ACOPs are 'an ideal vehicle for incorporating the results of changing technology' in developing modern health and safety standards.[8]

ACOPs address the need for that basic minimum specification of compliance required to meet a particular function, for example, a 'rescue from the sea' system under the PFEER regulations, but in a way that still leaves some flexibility. In the PFEER regulations, the twin functions of controlling fire and explosion and responding to an emergency are put forward. There can be little argument that these are necessary functions. The ACOP requires analyses to be performed and procedures and training to be adopted to meet the functions as minimal compliance. Within the main functions there are other sub-functions, for example, 'rescue from the sea', where a specification of compliance is also required. This could be an imprecise goal to be met by a variety of means, incorporating engineering standards or Guidance, or it might be a more precisely defined system or mechanism.

Predictably, UKOOA wishes all ACOPs to be reshaped as more general non-mandatory 'Guidance Notes', arguing that the Approved Codes of Practice are 'too prescriptive', because they carry potential 'legal implications'.[9] Said Harold Hughes of UKOOA, 'By supporting goal-setting Regulations with ACOPs rather than non-mandatory Guidance, the flexibility provided by goal-setting Regulations is greatly reduced' (1994a: 49). It is the reiteration of a line of argument, seeking to minimize regulatory oversight that the operators had consistently put forward since Burgoyne (1980: 134, para E).

The Mineral Workings Act regulations prescribed the presence within five nautical miles of a standby vessel (with the standard get-out clause of 'equivalent effectiveness') for each offshore installation.[10] OILC's submission on the draft regulations argued against UKOOA's attempt to secure the removal of any prescriptive requirement for a standby vessel:

> The discussion should therefore be about the need for a standby vessel –
> that is, on a detailed, item-by-item basis – rather than any scatter-gun
> condemnation of 'prescription'. There is always prescription, and UKOOA
> should try to discuss at a rational level the needs for any particular safety
> function. (OILC, 1993: 3)

The requirement that a standby vessel be present in the vicinity of five nautical miles from each normally manned offshore installation has historically always been resisted by UKOOA (1990: Ch. 20.39). Under the new goal-setting regime this prescriptive statutory requirement for dedicated standby-vessel recovery and rescue arrangements could finally be removed (HSE, 1995b: 33). According to regulation 17 of PFEER the standby vessel will now be part of a total package of facilities and arrangements for evacuation, escape and rescue within the Safety Case, which can include the demonstration of a satisfactory alternative.

However, Cullen specifically noted that 'some prescriptive regulations on standards and quality of equipment, crewing and training would be required' for standby vessels (1990: Ch. 20.39). Commenting that the cost of operating standby vessels had 'not necessarily enjoyed a high priority in the operating budgets of oil companies in recent years', Lord Cullen strongly urged that 'Basic standards should be introduced for existing vessels and a tight but realistic deadline for compliance set' (1990: Ch. 20.41).

Cullen went further in asserting that 'there is a strong case for setting *specific* standards' for standby vessels (emphasis added). This was in the light of the manifest deficiencies of the *Silver Pit*, a vessel which was in no way untypical. The Cullen report, therefore, set out those standards in detail (1990: Ch. 20.42). Indeed, such standards, said Cullen, 'should apply independently of what may be shown by the Safety Case to be required: and accordingly should be prescribed by regulations which would otherwise be goal-oriented with regard to rescue facilities' (1990: Ch. 20.42). Purpose-built vessels which meet the more rigorous requirements Lord Cullen recommended in the equipping and performance of such vessels can cost up to £3 million each. New requirements for the OPITO training of crews have brought a further £3.25 million expense. In 1990, Cullen noted that of the 187 standby vessels in the North Sea, 162 (87 per cent) were converted trawlers. There were only seven purpose-built vessels and eighteen multi-functional vessels in operation (1990: Ch. 20.40). By 1995 as a result of the 1991 revision of the Standby Vessel Code, 104 vessels were withdrawn from the UK fleet and 155 others were upgraded at a cost of some £200 million. Yet concerns about the suitability of North Sea standby vessels remained. Many were regarded by their crews as too small to fulfil their allotted tasks in the harsh winters of the northern North Sea. The use of 'Mississippi mud boats' was a particular source of criticism. These vessels, imported from the calmer waters of the Gulf of Mexico, were essentially built as day boats, to be tied up alongside the rigs and returning to port at night. They were not built to remain on station in the North Sea for 28 days at a time. Their cramped conditions are said to be detrimental to crew morale and their manning levels were regarded by those who worked on them as not 'sufficient to respond to a disaster on the scale of Piper Alpha'.[11] By 1995 there were still only a handful of purpose-built vessels in the North Sea, with thirteen vessels being added to the fleet in total. There was evidence that certification was being refused for the most inadequate of the older vessels. Yet there was also evidence to suggest that the operators were trying to force down charter rates of between £2000 and £5000 a day, and that available new purpose-built vessels were lying idle or being transferred to more lucrative contracts elsewhere in the world.[12]

Under a 'goal-setting' regime, a rationale is being exploited for ridding the industry of burdensome add-on costs which are seen as contributing nothing to the profitability of oil and gas extraction. The operators reflect the logic of the pressure of market forces which encourages them to adopt strategies which make safety provision a matter of economic calculation. The view of one serving standby-vessel ship's officer sums this up: 'It appears that the whole industry is trying to paper over the cracks with the cheapest possible options, and hope that another large-scale disaster does not happen.'[13]

Lord Cullen had strongly urged that the standard of the existing standby-vessel fleet be improved 'with dispatch' (1990: 20.41). The code covering such vessels had first been proposed in 1974, its 'binding force . . . based on a voluntary agreement whereby members of UKOOA undertook to abide by the standards set out in the code' (1990: 20.37). The Department of Transport felt that the voluntary agreement had been honoured. Lord Cullen, however, in an observation deemed worthy of repetition, expressed his concern at the time taken to update the voluntary code for standby vessels. The third edition had first been proposed in 1986 but was not published in draft form until 1989 and had still not been agreed at the date of his report's completion at the end of 1990. It finally came into effect in July 1991. The relative slowness in revising the industry code regarding standby vessels can be contrasted with the contemporary eagerness of the industry in setting its own standards in order to minimize regulatory interference and maximize 'self-regulation'.

Deregulating ACOPs and the Certifying Authorities

The whole purpose and function of HSE codes of practice, ACOPs, have been subject to a comprehensive review within health and safety law as part of the government's overall drive towards deregulation (HSC, 1995a; Woolfson and Beck, 1996). Although their legal status has been preserved, in the future ACOPs will be adopted 'on a more selective basis' (HSC, 1996a). This is part of a general review of UK health and safety law so as to reduce the 'burden' of regulation on business. So far as the offshore industry is concerned, the removal of ACOPs and any other form of 'prescription' is seen as central to the containment of regulatory interference. ACOPs are under direct attack, and an attempt both at government and industry level is being made to secure their long-term removal from the 'architecture' of safety legislation. Offshore operators, in the name of self-regulation, implement a strategy of containment in parallel with pre-emptive attempts to persuade the regulators that the imposition of ACOPs and non-mandatory HSE Guidance is unnecessary and ill-conceived. In the words of UKOOA:

> The danger is that the Safety Case will be diluted – if not lost altogether – because of the sheer weight of underpinning regulations, ACOPs and Guidance. The focus of compliance will be on the underpinning regulations rather than on the Safety Case itself and the concept of self-regulation based on the Safety Case would be strangled at birth. (Hughes and Taylor, 1995: 3)

What UKOOA has proposed as an alternative, is industry-created 'guidelines' to replace ACOPs and HSE Guidance. These would assist operators in setting their own standards of performance. Such guidelines would be based on 'good practice' (note not 'best practice') as defined by the industry itself (1995: 3). By late 1995, UKOOA had prepared 28 such guidelines and a further 13 were in preparation. Taylor and Hughes have claimed that although such guidelines are wholly non-mandatory, 'compliance with them is usually accepted by HSE Inspectors as evidence that safe working practices are being followed' (1995: 4). They have spoken of 'the willingness of HSE to recognise and accommodate an increasing role for industry-created guidelines' (1995: 4). Their intention seems to be to minimize the need for ACOPs and HSE Guidance 'which in effect can be viewed as pseudo-regulations'. Industry-devised guidelines, by contrast, are said to allow the industry to police its own practices. Because they are created by the industry, the industry itself is able to embrace such guidelines in a proprietorial manner, or take 'possession' of them (1995: 5).

A leading Certifying Authority observed in its comments on the draft PFEER with regard to the stance adopted by the operators:

> more and more, that the larger operators emphasize the *challenging* of all standards and in particular non-mandatory guidances ... This challenging is not always as the purist would have it, namely by virtue of improving the level of safety. Rather it is usually a challenge to find a cheaper alternative or equivalent solution, and not to set goals from that solution. Current experience with regard to this challenging shows that it extends to critical features related to availability of equipment during an emergency. (Det Norske Veritas, 1993, emphasis added)

Such an extraordinarily candid appraisal was not meant for public consumption, but as a private warning to the HSE. In part, no doubt, it was provoked by the increasing threat to the role of the Certifying Authorities as agencies of ultimate assurance within the offshore regime. Lord Cullen had placed something of a question mark over their future role, suggesting that their functions should in future be 'reappraised' (1990: Ch. 21. 63). Cullen felt that once the Safety Case requirements were securely in place, and safety management systems and audit compliance could be verified as being effectively carried out by the operators, it would be a matter for consideration 'whether and to what extent it will be appropriate to retain the present system of certification' (1990: Ch. 21. 64). Notwithstanding Cullen's cautionary note, that the new regime needed to be properly evaluated first, UKOOA argued at the Piper Alpha inquiry for a marginalization of the role of the Certifying Authorities, chief amongst which are Det NorskeVeritas, Lloyd's Register of Shipping and the American Bureau of Shipping. The 'certificate of fitness', said UKOOA, should in future be granted by the regulatory body on the basis of a survey and report by one of the existing Certifying Authorities *'or any other satisfactory body, subject to the inclusion of the operators themselves'* (1990: Ch. 21. 63, emphasis added).

The positing of 'the operators themselves' as having a direct role in the certification process represents a new twist in the spiral of unilateral self-reg-ulation, effectively *de*regulation, proposed by UKOOA. The specified list of Certifying Authorities endorsed by HSE as competent to approve design and construction fitness-for-purpose has again been attacked by UKOOA. In its submissions on the draft Design and Construction Regulations for offshore installations currently being developed in this area, UKOOA claimed that the specified list of six Certifying Authorities secures 'those bodies as providing such services with a largely captive market' (Hughes, 1994b). UKOOA has argued:

> that proof of fitness-for-purpose should be a duty of the operator under his Safety Case and that scope for appointment of a suitable authority should be much wider, *extending for instance to another expert branch of his own organisation* provided he could show to HSE's satisfaction its competence and that independence of judgement was still being achieved. (Hughes, 1994b: 4–5, emphasis added)

Cullen had cautioned that it 'would be going too far and too fast' for him to make recommendations regarding the future of the Certifying Authorities and that this was a matter for the regulatory body (1990: Ch. 21. 64). Only in its earliest phases, predating the Mineral Workings Act, did certification play a predominant regulatory role in the offshore scene. Since the early 1970s the Certifying Authorities had, if anything, moderated the prescriptiveness of the Mineral Workings Act, in providing a more systematic and comprehen-sive overview of installation safety. At the current stage of the evolution of the offshore safety regime, Cullen was reluctant to let the accumulated expertise of the Certifying Authorities simply be ditched. Cullen's caution has not inhibited UKOOA from successfully pressing its case against Certifying Authorities.[14] Under the Design and Construction Regulations their role is removed, to be replaced by a 'scheme of verification' of safety-critical elements of installations in which the operator (duty holder) will make 'verification arrangements' appropriate to each installation in accordance with the Safety Case.[15] These regulations then, effectively complete the major elements of the HSE's reform of offshore legislation. Given that the new regime is anything but secured, the undermining of Certifying Authorities, a relatively independent element within the overall regulatory set-up offshore, cannot be seen as other than detrimental to safety in the longer run (OILC, 1995).

The Outer Limits of Regulatory Resistance: The European Dimension

The other arena of regulatory resistance derives from the extension of European legislation. While the Social Charter in itself creates no enforceable rights, the resulting Social Action Programme and the Directives on worker protection which flow from it have the potential to do so. Under the Single European Act (1986) which introduced Article 118A into the Treaty of Rome, the Commission was given the authority to adopt Directives laying down 'minimum requirements'. The system of qualified majority voting now applies to working environment issues. This prevents any single government, such as a British Conservative administration, from blocking legislation by veto in respect of health and safety matters. However, the 'doctrine of subsidiarity' implied that individual national governments could retain the power to enact 'strong' or 'weak' versions of EU proposals.

The European Framework Directive (89/391/EEC) of 1989, which sought to encourage improvements in the safety and health of workers, and the various 'daughter' Directives which have been promulgated, hence impact on British domestic legislation whatever the UK Government might wish (DTI, 1993b). The passing into UK law of the so-called 'six-pack' of daughter Directives concerning work equipment, manual handling, personnel protective equipment, VDU-screen regulations and workplace risk assessment have been a particular focus of business hostility, with the Confederation of British Industry (CBI) calling for cost benefit analysis of all new European legislation.[16] It was no accident that the government's deregulation initiative took place at the same time, when Rimington of HSE referred to such

European-derived legislation as 'the biggest development in health and safety law since the 1974 Act' (HSC, 1993: xiii). Some way had to be found to halt what was seen as a 'tide' of European safety law. The European Framework Directive places broad general duties on employers and employees, but the primary responsibility for ensuring health and safety is put on employers. Employers are now obliged to assess the risks at work and take measures to prevent or reduce them.

What the Conservative government found objectionable was the widening of the scope of the new proposals brought forward since the adoption of article 118A. Since 1988, this created 'the potential for these directives to go beyond pure health and safety considerations and to venture into industrial relations issues' (DTI, 1993b: 88). The DTI claimed that the HSE itself supported the government's opposition to qualified majority voting applying to Article 118A, because of the fear 'that health and safety could be used as a Trojan horse by the EU Commission to legislate on industrial issues' (DTI, 1993b: 88). In 1994 the Conservative government eventually secured assurances that such a stratagem would not be resorted to. This was its sole 'success' in the UK climbdown over the extension of qualified majority voting as part of the process of enlargement of the EU.[17] A leaked internal document of HSE's Management Board suggests that the HSE's attitude to European legislation was at best ambiguous. HSE stated that it would do its best to secure a bare minimum of compliance and, on occasion, deliberately water down the objectives of Directives, where Directives are held to go further than existing UK law (James, 1993b: 66).

Within the CBI, UKOOA has been particularly active in seeking to secure 'derogations' and support 'opt-outs'. It has been sensitive to any areas where EU Directives might impinge on offshore interests. Harold Hughes of UKOOA stated: 'We have to be even more alert and ensure that directives are challenged at an early draft if they can damage the industry. We are trying to get early intelligence.'[18]

The 'Piper Directive'

The determination of the employers to limit the impact of European legislation on the offshore scene can be illustrated by their response to the Extractive Industries (Boreholes) Directive (92/91/EEC). Of all the Directives on health and safety, this is the one most directly generated in reaction to the Piper Alpha tragedy, giving it the name 'Piper Directive' (Rother, 1992). Within a mere six weeks during 1991, UKOOA had not only joined the CBI, but had used its membership of that body to leap-frog into a key position within the European employers' association. This ensured that UKOOA, among the employers' groups, led discussions on the future shape of the Directive. As R. E. McKee, Chairman and Managing Director of Conoco, put it to the House of Commons Energy Select Committee regarding the draft Safety Directive,

> There is no question that it is very prescriptive in nature and ... is diametrically opposed to what Lord Cullen recommended ... I have hopes personally that in the end the safety directive they propose will just go away and we do not have to contend with the differences. (1991: para 196)

Despite UKOOA opposition, in March 1994 a consultative document was eventually issued, Draft Offshore Installations and Pipe-line Works (Management and Administration) Regulations (HSC, 1994a). These draft regulations were intended to complement the requirements of the Safety Case regulations and implement relevant provisions of the 'Piper Directive'. The main features of the draft regulations were entirely unexceptionable, dealing with notification to the HSE of changes in the owners or operators of installations, movements into or out of the UK waters and the intention to commence pipeline works. Also covered were the appointment and powers of offshore installation managers, the need for co-operation among duty holders, the keeping of records of persons on board, permit-to-work systems, various operational and communication matters and the provision of suitable food and water supplies. Finally, proposals were made to tighten up the definition of an 'offshore installation' and clarify that the HSWA would apply to all activities carried out in connection with an offshore installation, for example, the provision of accommodation, even if the vessel concerned was not itself an offshore installation. The Application Outside Great Britain Order 1989 of HSWA would now also be extended to pipelines and the regulations covering their safety. The definition of 'pipeline works' was to cover pipelaying crews, the safety of wells not linked to an installation, and activities such as the servicing and testing of such wells. Diving operations carried out in connection with the survey and preparation of the seabed for an installation were also covered (HSC, 1994b).

In revoking relevant sections of the Mineral Workings Act and its various statutory instruments, the proposed regulations undoubtedly contributed to a necessary legislative overhaul, bringing much offshore-related work, hitherto excluded, within the remit of the Health and Safety at Work Act. The trade unions were concerned whether, in converting the 'Piper Directive' into UK law, these proposals still reflected the European Council's desire to secure not merely the maintenance but, in the words of the Directive, the 'improvement of workers' safety, hygiene and health at work' (HSC, 1994a, Appendix 4, emphasis added). Suspicions that the safety-enhancing implications of European Directives were being watered down remained strong (OILC, 1994). In particular, questions were raised over the revocation of regulations covering the general duty to provide safe access and a safe worksite, controls on the employment of young people, the recording of working hours and the continuing lack of interface between marine legislation and offshore regulations, especially covering mobile units and support vessels.

From a trade union viewpoint, the key concern related to proposed changes to the regulations governing the funding of safety representative training. Lord Cullen had specifically recommended that the operator as 'duty holder' bear the costs of such training (Recommendation 31). Cullen's recommendation had been based on the assumption that smaller contractors with few personnel working on an installation might have difficulty in providing training for any of their employees elected as safety representatives. The view of the HSC in its consultative document was that this did not take account of 'changing work patterns offshore, with more large contractors involved, who will already have trained safety representatives' (HSC, 1994a: 12). The proposed regulation change made it a matter of agreement between the operator and the employer of the safety representative as to who would pay for training, rather than specifying the operator as duty holder under law. Issues of choice of suitable courses and, in particular, support for safety representatives wishing to choose trade union courses, meanwhile remained unresolved. The Extractive Industries Directive, however, brought a much closer specification of the facilities, circumstances and conditions under which safety representatives were to be consulted regarding such matters as safety auditing, Safety Case preparation, the appointment of 'competent persons' and the introduction of new technologies (HSC, 1994a: 51–4). Paradoxically, the requirement to consult in these areas was to lead UKOOA to adopt some strange postures, as we shall show below.

UKOOA, maintaining the services of a full-time consultancy in Brussels to hold a watching brief on its behalf, was poised to lobby effectively against this and other proposed European safety legislation. UKOOA is also part of the world-wide upstream industry organization, the Exploration and Production (E&P) Forum, which set up its own Brussels operation to ensure the protection of European-level interests on behalf of the operators. Although part of the E&P Forum, UKOOA continues to maintain its separate political liaison work at European Commission level. As producer of 80 per cent of the Community's oil, it has vital interests of its own to preserve.

The Working Time Directive

In a remarkably frank article, Chris Ryan, the external affairs director of UKOOA, spelled out the trepidation with which the oil operators' association viewed the 'increasing deluge of European legislation ... threatening to swamp UK industry, including firms involved in the North Sea offshore oil and gas industry'.[19] Two proposed Directives were singled out for special attention. The first of these was the Directive which sought to establish Community-wide fair bidding opportunities on all major contracts. Of direct importance for the offshore workforce was UKOOA's opposition to the proposed 'Directive Concerning Certain Aspects of the Organisation of Working Time', the so-called 'Working Time Directive' (93/104/EC) limiting the maximum working week to 48 hours. The Directive was adopted on 23 November 1993, its provisions to be implemented by member states within three years. This too was formulated by the EU under Article 118A 'to preserve the health and safety of workers'.[20] The UK secured an additional 7-year opt-out period during which employees can work longer than 48 hours a week on a voluntary basis. Several recent studies in Britain had begun to explore a possible link between fatigue caused by excessive working hours and the compromising of safe working practices, although without firm conclusion (Harrington, 1994). In 1996 the government, with the operators' support, sought to challenge the legal basis of this Directive as a health and safety measure in the European Court of Justice. It did so precisely on the grounds of the alleged lack of evidence of a link between working hours and accidents and, moreover, that the proposal related to working conditions and employment matters and, therefore, required unanimous approval (Bercusson, 1994). The European Court seems likely to decide against the UK government.

The following gives some indication of the issues at stake in the Working Time Directive. The Commission intended that no worker would work more than 1680 hours per year. The average annual hours worked in UK manufacturing lie within the 1600 hour to 1800 band. An offshore contract worker in the British North Sea, excluding travelling time to and from shore and time spent in shore-based training, works 2184 hours per annum, an additional 400–500 hours of exposure to risk. Implementation of the Directive would reduce the working year by approximately one-third. In negotiating work patterns to cover round-the-clock shift working, a fundamental principle underpinning the Directive is that of 'equivalence'. Within the reference period, the maximum hours worked should not exceed those hours which would be worked in normal circumstances (i.e. day shift five days a week). UKOOA's argument was, that to comply with the Directive, the employers offshore would have had to install more accommodation and more beds and employ more people. For the Directive to be complied with, workers' time offshore would have had to be reduced, with the work cycle altered to two weeks on and three weeks off. UKOOA argued that the proposals could add up to 40 per cent to North Sea oil costs.[21]

UKOOA launched a campaign to oppose limitations on offshore working hours when it appeared that the European Commission might attempt to reclassify oil and gas production as a 'continuous industrial process'. This would have meant that the operators would be subject to the same regulations setting the maximum working hours per shift, or over a week, as governed onshore activities. Such a development would have been particularly unwelcome, since in 1993, as part of the cost-reduction exercise (CRINE), shift patterns had been altered by key operators to three-week tours offshore, from the previous two-on, two-off pattern, increasing actual hours worked. The new rotas, as Eric Brandie of Chevron revealed, saved his company alone £20 million per annum in helicopter charges (Brandie, 1994).

In mid-1994, UKOOA learned that the Exclusion which had been granted from the Working Time Directive for 'Work at Sea' was to be reviewed and that a special review group had been established. Renewed representations were made by UKOOA's Employment Practices Committee to the Commissioner for Social Affairs, Padraig Flynn. The industry has attempted to argue not only that its safety record was improving, but also that it was safer than a number of hazardous onshore industries. These claims we examine fully in the following chapter. Removal of the exclusion, it was argued, would lead to more shifts offshore, requiring more changeovers and more helicopter flights per individual, thus increasing the risk to personnel.[22] UKOOA's campaign was accelerated on all fronts. The chairman of Esso warned the UK government that if the Directive was implemented 'energy-intensive industries ... will simply migrate to other, less foolish parts of the world'.[23] The issue was to be tackled at the forthcoming inter-governmental conference in Turin in the spring of 1996. This conference would be of key importance in determining the future evolution of the European Union as a whole and held the prospect of an energy chapter being included in the final treaty.

In order to make the case for continued exclusion from the Working Time Directive, UKOOA sought the support of the HSE and, for the first time in the history of the industry, also actively consulted some trade union interests. As an alternative to the Directive, UKOOA proposed its own industry-devised guidelines on working time. UKOOA had to convince the Commission that the 'social partners', that is the unions, had been consulted and had voluntarily reached agreement on the guidelines, otherwise the industry could have legislation imposed upon it. The necessity to consult with trade

unions at UK level, even though they had been comprehensively marginalized by the industry, was the final irony in UKOOA's strategy of regulatory
containment.

Enforcement in a deregulated environment

So far as the question of enforcement of EU legislation is concerned, member
states are required to ensure that the legal provisions necessary for implementation are put in place. However, major difficulties confront any attempt to
raise non-compliance by a government at a European level (James, 1993a: 69).
The European Court has made no significant rulings in the field of workplace safety and health. While the UK record on enforcement may be open
to major criticism, it nevertheless remains in advance of a number of other
member states. The UK government was not under any pressure from Europe
to improve resources available to the HSE for enforcement. Whilst embarking on a programme of domestic deregulation, the government had used its
spell in the Presidency of the European Commission in the second half of
1992 to encourage initiatives to improve enforcement in *other* member states
as a means of ensuring that its own industry was not placed at a competitive
disadvantage (1993a: 70). Thereafter, it campaigned openly for its deregulation initiative to be replicated at a European-wide level.

While the European Trades Union Congress began to consider specific criteria for enforcement, it faced strong employer opposition to any proposal for a
future Directive on Enforcement. Today there is a definite formal enhancement of employee information, consultation rights, training and job protection in respect of safety at work in the European Directives which has
strengthened the existing UK regulations. Yet it is important that these reluctantly and unevenly applied advances should not be overestimated (James,
1993b). The emphasis in European Directives is for participation in decision-
making processes, not through organized trade unions, but rather through the
workforce in general. European law enhances the rights of the individual or
disaggregated employees rather than those of organized collectivities, such as
trade unions. In this regard it poses no challenge to the anti-trade union stance
of a Conservative administration. Although a Labour government might
acquiesce to the implementation of European Directives and the obligations
of the Maastricht Social Chapter, such statutes by themselves are not the most
effective measure to secure workforce rights. A principal role is played by
employees' ability to organize at the place of work. As James has put it,
'improvements in occupational health and safety can only be secured where
the financial interests of employers are adequately counterbalanced by pressures from their workforces and external enforcement agencies' (1993a: 37).

In sum, despite the appearance of greater regulation in the UK Continental Shelf, what in fact has occurred amounts to a creeping containment. There have been wider political developments which chime with UKOOA's strategy of containment so far as the reconstruction of offshore safety is concerned, in particular the CRINE programme. Far from offshore safety legislation being 'ring fenced', industry resistance to new goal-setting legislation and general regulatory interference is now being replicated by UKOOA's deregulatory initiatives at European as well as the British domestic level. With the approach of the 1996 European inter-governmental conference, the chairman of Esso spoke for the industry: 'I hope efforts to restore competitiveness will be the touchstone for change and policy priorities rather than more chapters, charters, regulations and directives.'[24]

At the same time, an attempt has been made to re-insulate the industry from all but the most sympathetic public gaze. Saturation of offshore news has been reached and safety as an issue, for the moment, has been put on the 'back burner' as production volumes of oil and gas reach record levels and the prospect of new oil and gas fields west of the Shetland Isles opens up. The industry is reported on the nine o'clock television news as having 'put Piper Alpha behind it', while its own formidable public-relations machine has been in top gear to reassure the public and dispel lingering doubts.[25] Any criticism of the industry has been met with vigorous rebuttal by representatives of UKOOA. As each new field is inaugurated, in one instance by Lord Cullen himself, it has been celebrated with a snowstorm of publicity about its state-of-the-art safety features (Chevron, 1994). Generous oil company sponsorship has been made available for studentships and research into aspects of risk and safety management at sympathetic institutions of higher education. Enormous technical and financial efforts have been deployed to ensure the 'normalization' of a previously sensitive issue. The public mood has again been conditioned to be tolerant of what is seen as a 'reasonable' level of accidents. Meanwhile the everyday steady human attrition – a rigger here, a welder there – has been relegated to a brief half-inch column at the very margin of the front page news, soon to slip off it altogether.

Exploring the 'Gradual Erosion Scenario'

The effective creation and implementation of major programmes of regulatory reconstruction, aimed at appreciably altering the status quo, is generally difficult. It is difficult under 'normal' conditions when there is agreement about the need for change, but it is much more so if the party to be regulated pursues its own concerted agenda – what we have described as a strategy of containment (Pressman, 1978; Pressman and Wildavsky, 1974). The planned *re*regulation of the offshore safety regime faced severe impediments from its beginning. Above all, it was undermined by UKOOA's challenges to the integrity of the proposed framework; the consistent and continuing attempt to extend notions of goal-setting and self-regulation so as to eliminate purported elements of regulatory 'rigidity'. In the post-Cullen era any element that could be construed as implying regulatory stringency was condemned out of hand by UKOOA as a 'return to outmoded prescriptivity'. The powers of 'acceptance' of the new Safety Case regime, bestowed upon the regulator, for instance, were immediately drawn into contest.

Due to the adoption of this oppositional stance by UKOOA, and the often implicit acquiescence to these views by the regulator, the remaking of the offshore regulatory regime was flawed from its inception. The HSE's interim evaluation of the Safety Case represented the final re-coalescence of the industry and its regulator. This process was strengthened by additional external factors. These included the more general deregulatory drive of the Conservative government, and the historical pattern of industrial relations offshore, which rendered difficult, if not impossible, the mounting of effective opposition by the workforce. Longstanding government–business contacts, and the new partnering network between operators and favoured contractors, meanwhile allowed UKOOA to organize opposition to proposed legislative changes seen to impinge too far on the industry's need to reassert some form of 'compliance discretion' under the new regime.

Yet in the post-Cullen debate arguments were not confronted directly. They were delivered in a coded form and focused on issues such as the relevance of further tranches of safety regulation, which were depicted as diluting rather than underpinning the Safety Case regime; the attempt by the industry to substitute its own guidelines for official regulatory codes of practice which would carry legal weight; and finally the squeezing-out of external audit by the Certifying Authorities in favour of in-house certification. In Europe, the same policies focused on the so-called Piper Directive, the Working Time Directive, and workforce consultation requirements.

Implementation theory suggests that there are several conditions for effective implementation (see, for example, Mazmanian and Sabatier, 1983). First, the enabling legislation should mandate policy objectives which are clear and consistent and provide some criteria for resolving goal conflicts. Second, the enabling legislation should incorporate a sound theory which identifies the principal factors and causal linkages affecting policy objectives, and should give implementing officials sufficient jurisdiction over target groups. Third, the enabling legislation should structure the implementation process so as to maximize the probability that officials and target groups act in accordance with set goals. This involves the assignment of regulatory tasks to sympathetic agencies with sufficient financial resources. Fourth, the programme should be actively supported by organized constituency groups, as well as by key legislators. Fifth, the relative priority of statutory objectives should not be undermined over time by conflicting public policies.

Unfortunately none of the above criteria fully apply to the context of the post-Cullen reconstruction of offshore regulation. From its inception, the policy objectives of offshore regulation were muddled. While on the one hand Lord Cullen sought to preserve some elements of regulatory stringency, on the other he conceded the advantages of self-regulation, which he saw as exemplified in the Norwegian context, which at the time was developing towards a goal-setting regime. In terms of its underlying theory, the post-Cullen regime was equally problematic. While the Cullen inquiry acknowledged difficulties in management–workforce communication as a cause of the disaster, and recognized the potential benefits of union-appointed safety representatives, it was unwilling to address and remedy the broken link between the fraught offshore industrial relations system and offshore safety. In terms of our third point, the issue of resourcing the new regulator, the post-Cullen regime also showed major deficiencies. The HSE as an organization had been weakened by budget cuts as well as constant appeals by the Conservative cabinet to adopt a 'softly softly' approach. Although supposedly 'ring fenced', the new Offshore Safety Division, as we show in the next chapter, was increasingly to share these constraints.

As far as active support by constituent groups was concerned, the key constituent, the operators, had ostensibly announced their co-operation in regulatory reform. In reality their actions were often marked by delay, as well as a strategic re- or misinterpretation of the goals of the legislator. Self-regulation via the Safety Case, which Cullen intended to be underpinned by workforce participation, for UKOOA became a weapon to oppose prescriptive legislation. Finally, and perhaps most importantly, even as the Cullen report underwent legislative implementation with the passing of the Offshore Safety Act, the offshore operators in collaboration with the government had begun to develop the conflicting policy agenda of CRINE, which focused on cost-cutting objectives rather than safety improvements.

What were the consequences of these implementation problems? In our view, the flaws in the post-Cullen reconstruction have resulted in what is best characterized as the 'gradual erosion scenario' (Wildavsky, 1979). The gradual erosion scenario describes a situation where a legislative agenda, which clearly mandates a behaviour change, gradually deteriorates as it faces a host of 'veto points'. These veto points emerge when concrete regulations are negotiated. In our context, the negotiation of these regulations allowed UKOOA, after an initial spell of seeming acquiescence, to reaffirm its opposition to regulatory interference both at a national and European level. Hence, the guise of self-regulation provided a convenient camouflage for what was in essence outright opposition to any costly safety requirement. In these veto points, resistance to legislative proposals such as Safety Case 'acceptance' by the regulator, the requirement for temporary safe refuges, the PFEER regulations and Approved Codes of Practice, and the removal of the requirement for independent certifying authorities, allowed the operators gradually to reassert their hegemony.

This erosion process can be graphically illustrated (see Figure 7.1). It started essentially following the publication of Lord Cullen's report and the establishment of the OSD. With the end of Lord Cullen's inquiry, the enforcement of a new offshore regime had become the responsibility of the HSE.

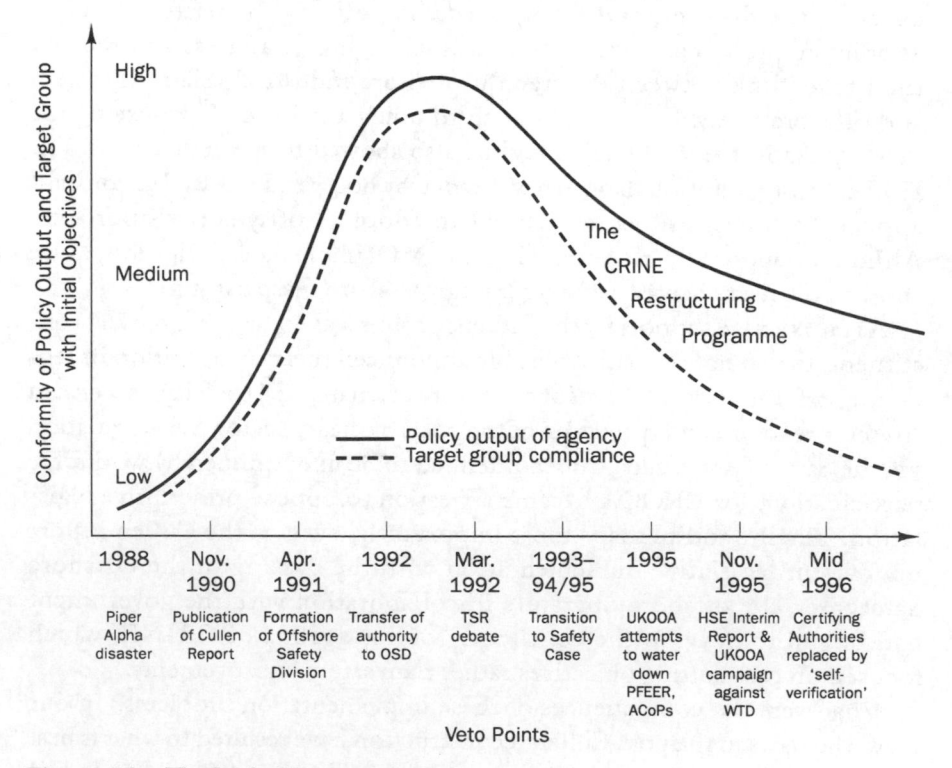

Figure 7.1 *The Gradual Erosion Scenario*

Initially, HSE staff involved in this effort were perhaps enthusiastic. However, this commitment wore off as more managerial staff, anxious to reduce conflict, were added or gained the upper hand. Meanwhile, the agency's supporting constituency, the media, and in part the offshore workers, has withered away, while the opposition, organized under UKOOA, has become increasingly demanding and vociferous. This weakening of the regulator, in turn, has encouraged the regulated business to make less effort in complying with the newly established rules, further reducing the credibility of the regulator.

Chapter 8 will look in some detail at the quantitative evidence for this deterioration which can be derived from accident rates and enforcement indicators. The combination of this quantitative analysis with the qualitative analysis of this chapter will hopefully give a realistic picture of the strengths and weaknesses of the post-Cullen regime.

Notes

1. Piper Alpha Public Inquiry, 24 January 1990, Day 177: 47C.
2. *Scotsman*, 25 February 1992.
3. H. Hughes, letter to editor of *Press and Journal*, 25 October 1995.
4. UKOOA Press Statement, 'Official statistics confirm offshore industry's improving safety performance', 18 March 1996.
5. Written testimony in the authors' possession.
6. BBC *Frontline Scotland*, 'Paying for the Piper', 16 May 1996.
7. *Financial Times, North Sea Newsletter*, Vol. 931, 24 November 93, p.18.
8. Piper Alpha Public Inquiry, 11 December 1990, Day 157: 13C.
9. *Euroil*, September 1993: 9; *Press and Journal*, 18 November 1993.
10. The relevant law is regulation 10 of the Statutory Instrument No. 1542 (1976): Offshore Installations (Emergency Procedures) Regulations.
11. 'Asking the impossible', *Telegraph*, journal of NUMAST, November 1994, p. 16.
12. *Aberdeen Petroleum Report*, 5 February 1992.
13. 'Offshore sector just papering over cracks', *Telegraph*, journal of NUMAST, January 1995, p. 6.
14. Notes of UKOOA submission on draft Design and Construction Regulations to HSE/OSD made by C. MacFarlane (personal communication). The DCR regulations came into force on 30 June 1996 as the Offshore Installations and Wells (Design and Construction, etc.) Regulations, S.I. (1996) No. 913.

15. See D. Michos, 'Brief overview of UK offshore safety legislation (1991–1996) following Lord Cullen's report on the Piper Alpha disaster.' Paper presented to American Bureau of Shipping Verification Seminar, Great Yarmouth, 11 June 1996.

16. *Safety Management*, Vol. 4, April 1994, p. 10.

17. *Financial Times*, 17 March 1994.

18. *Scotsman*, 9 March 1991.

19. *Press and Journal*, 25 February 1991.

20. European Parliament, Session Document A 3–0378/90/B, p. 7.

21. *Scotsman*, 14 October 1992. The figure of 40 per cent probably grossly overestimates costs occurring due to the implementation of the Directive.

22. *Scotsman*, 13 January 1996.

23. ibid.

24. Speech to the Edinburgh and Leith Petroleum Club, reported in the *Scotsman*, 13 January 1996.

25. BBC TV News, 7 March 1994.

8 PAYING FOR THE PIPER?

Offshore Incident Reporting

The human cost of North Sea oil has been very high. Assessing the cost has remained difficult because of problems of statistical reporting. Carson's pioneering, but cautious, analysis highlights the connection of statistical deficiencies to gaps in industrial safety legislation. Says Carson:

> Statistics, it should not be forgotten, always carry some political potential, and North Sea oil is not only a physically volatile substance but also a politically volatile issue. Added to that, the very deficiencies of the statistics themselves attest to important features of the North Sea safety regime. Inadequately co-ordinated with analogous figures for onshore industries, they point to the fact that for economic and political reasons ... industrial safety legislation has been substantially permitted to plough its own administrative furrow; incomplete in their coverage, they reflect the ad hoc nature of a regulatory approach ... always overshadowed by the other urgent considerations associated with North Sea oil. (1982: 16–17)

The Department of Energy's *Brown Book* figures for 1981 list a total of 106 offshore fatalities up to the end of 1980 (DEn, 1981: 45). The total of serious injuries at 1981 is given at 450. Fatalities and serious injuries are generally regarded as 'hard' accident statistics. The figure for 'dangerous occurrences' reported since 1974 corresponded to a total of 528, undoubtedly a huge underestimate, as are figures for minor injuries (Carson, 1982: 18). These figures only take account of incidents on or around an installation *within* a zone of 500 metres, but are in any event a gross underestimate of the actual incident level. Up to one-third of fatalities occurred in activities surrounding the installations, such as in diving, or on pipelaying barges, standby vessels, supply vessels, etc. but *outwith* the 500 metre zone. The incidents were not registered in the totals of the *Brown Book* accident statistics. For example, the Chinook helicopter disaster in which 45 men were killed was not recorded as an offshore incident. While UK-flagged vessels under the Merchant Shipping Acts reported incidents to the Department of Trade, these incidents were not added to the DEn's figures, as no separate record was kept of those originating in the offshore oil industry. As for foreign-flagged vessels operating in UK waters in the offshore industry, no legal obligation to report accidents to British authorities existed. In 1973, reporting procedures changed with the Inspectors and Casualties Regulations, which rendered figures before and after that date incompatible and made comparison difficult.

The incomplete and inadequate coverage of accident reporting regulations can be directly attributed to the exigencies of politically driven haste. The UK ratified an agreement with Norway for the exploitation of the Frigg gas field in May 1976. But the agreement could not be brought into force until both governments had taken all necessary powers to implement it. With planned commercial operations due to start the following October, the Submarine Pipelines (Inspectors etc.) Regulations had to be pushed through parliament before the summer adjournment. The timetable was met, but 'only just' according to a senior DEn official, who commented:

> ... but to achieve it, it was necessary to compress the consultation stage rigorously and to drop certain published proposals. These included those aimed at placing an obligation on masters of pipe-laying barges and other vessels engaged in pipe-line works, to report accidents to the pipe-line owner and to refrain from disturbing the site of an accident.[1]

The official noted in this account that anyway there would be a problem with enforcing these 'novel concepts in marine law' in relation to foreign vessels. Although 'regrettable' that these areas could not be covered in the regulations, it was observed that they *related primarily to occupational safety matters*, responsibility for which was about to pass to the HSC. As we know, formal responsibility was assumed by the offshore extension of the Health and Safety at Work Act (HSWA) in 1977 but the reporting procedures already established by the DEn remained unaltered.

Later attempts in the mid-1980s to introduce new procedures for the reporting of accidents and dangerous occurrences foundered. The *Brown Book* for 1987 notes that by the end of 1986 a first draft of outline proposals for new reporting procedures had been completed, 'but it will be some time before a consultative document can be circulated to the industry' (DEn, 1987: 55). Subsequent *Brown Books* were to remain conspicuously silent on the issue.

These difficulties were compounded by the absence of such elementary data as reliable estimates of numbers employed offshore for this period. As from 1980, the inclusive total of offshore employees was changed to incorporate mobile rigs, service vessels, support barges and survey teams as well as installations. After 1980 it is difficult, if not impossible, to calculate incidence rates for the installations themselves which are consistent with previous data. Even today, the total of estimated employees is derived from employer returns to the Inland Revenue for tax purposes and is, to say the least, uncertain. The current report on offshore accident statistics notes:

> This is usually the number of persons on board at a chosen date, and is scaled to account for offshore shift patterns. As these figures show, the offshore population varies depending on the level of activity in the North Sea, and *hence it is difficult to obtain an accurate figure for the workforce.* (HSE, 1996: 4, emphasis added)

The particularly hazardous nature of diving has been previously discussed. Here, we simply note that after 1978 no separate estimate of the numbers of divers employed was given by the DEn. In any event, figures for diving accidents did not include fatalities occurring in the course of activities undertaken from pipelaying barges. Carson's (1982: 39, n.13) comment that 'the published statistics . . . seem to be becoming more, rather than less opaque as time goes on' holds as true today as it did over a decade before.

In the early years the industry's 'frontier' image and its inherently hazardous operations provided a superficial rationale for the high number of accidents as being somehow 'necessary sacrifices' (Carson, 1982: 44). The unique exigencies of the industry, operating at the outer limits of existing technology and in appalling climatic conditions, were stressed. Yet, as Carson pointed out, these 'images of danger' obscured the more basic recognition that 'most offshore injuries result from comparatively conventional causes' (1982: 50). An analysis of drilling accidents suggested 'there was nothing involved in any of these accidents which would have fallen outside the competence and comprehension of a factory inspector.' (1982: 54).

Fatigue, cold, hunger and boredom, not to mention a working day nearly 50 per cent longer than the norm, could be seen as the major contributing factors. Accidents also tended to cluster around the beginning and end of shift changes and tours of duty. To these contributory factors we might add pressure to produce results, intensified by the increasing need to control cost margins.

As the industry moved from the hazardous exploration and construction

phases to the 'more stable phase of production itself' in the mid-1970s, Carson
suggested that the overall picture 'lends some credence to the common belief
that, whatever its record in the past, the industry is becoming safer' (1982: 19).
Carson observed, however, that increasing maintenance work could reintro-
duce 'construction type hazards'. He also cautioned that 'the statistical impact
which a major production incident could have' must be borne in mind. A 1978
Norwegian report on risk assessment offshore stated on this issue:

> The fact that potential hazards within the production phase, fortunately,
> have not yet led to any multi-death accident, calls for caution to take this
> as a true statement. If an accident such as the explosion at Flixborough,
> England, where twenty-eight persons were killed and over a hundred
> others injured, should occur to a North Sea installation, such an event
> would dramatically change our figures. (Carson, 1982: 20)

In the minds of the regulators in the Norwegian sector, the alleged improvement in safety accompanying the industry's move from the construction to
the production phase was always provisional.

A revised incident reporting form was eventually introduced in January
1991 in the wake of Piper Alpha (HSE, 1991b). This allowed for more detailed
analysis of incident types. But considerable doubts about the adequacy of the
existing reporting scheme remained. As late as 1996 the reporting form
remains non-mandatory, that is, the return of report forms by the operators
to the regulatory authority is essentially voluntary. The actual layout of the
form permits only the most perfunctory account of incidents to be rendered
and certainly not the kind of reporting that would enable a systematic analysis
of accident causation. Some indication of this may be gained from the fact
that the questions eliciting the principal operation, the actual activity and the
broad accident type involved in the incident rely heavily on the residual
'other' category. The Principal Inspector of the Nuclear Industry Inspectorate,
drafted in to assist the OSD to try and bring some order to the offshore statistics, has suggested overall that 'there are severe limitations on the value of the
data'.[2] Proper analysis of the risks attached to various offshore activities
would require not merely the listing of broad incident types but an analysis
of the distribution of risk by occupational group which takes account of the
number of hours' exposure to risk. However, obtaining such information is
by no means straightforward. Again the Principal Inspector conceded:

> This is not in hand. It is in fact what we would like to do, but
> implementation will ultimately depend on whether the industry wishes

to have information on how risk is distributed amongst the various occupations and is willing to supply the population data.[3]

One improvement in the further revised incident reporting form, introduced in August 1992, which is likely to result in improved reporting, is the requirement to include details of accidents on attendant vessels both inside and *outside* the 500-metre zone 'in the course of an operation undertaken on or in connection with an offshore installation' (HSE, 1992c: para (iv)). The preparation of a comprehensive incident database, however, remains to be undertaken. It requires industry co-operation at a level of detail so far not forthcoming on a voluntary basis or even required in law.

Concern still remains about the accuracy of reporting, particularly by contract management. The sources and incentives for distortion are still numerous. Evidence presented to the Energy Select Committee illustrated one consequence of Shell's 'Target Zero' scheme in operation – a safety incentive programme aimed at eliminating offshore accidents:

> As regards the reporting and the concern with regards contracting companies, there are constraints on them which prevent them reporting too many lost time incidents and minor incidents that lead to a bad safety regime on a particular installation. Some contractors, particularly one of the leading engineering contractors at the moment, Press Offshore, have a scheme where there is a reward if there is a decline in reported incidents and accidents. I do know from my own experience – I have worked with that company three times – that there is a desire on the part of offshore management, contract management, to minimise the statistics. I have actually witnessed that. There was a joke on the last major contract I was on, the Tern platform constructed by Shell. You went to the store to get a spanner or a widget or whatever and you were immediately confronted by several invalids hopping all over the place. These were offshore workers, welders and riggers and all the rest of it, being kept off the contract – throw them in the store, get the trip finished, they go ashore not as an accident statistic but as someone going on leave. The current scheme where there is reward for minimising accidents leads to an inclination not to report accidents. I have got personal experience of that. It is jokingly referred to as 'Don't Report an Accident Scheme'. (1991: para 266)

Such evidence is, of course, anecdotal. Both before and after Piper Alpha, the oil companies have embarked upon such campaigns to minimize 'lost time incidents'. The unfortunate winner of one of the coveted Target Zero type awards offered by Shell for an accident-free workplace, received a Swiss army knife. The individual promptly cut himself with this and had to be 'medivac'd' ashore. Carson (1982) reported that during an offshore visit he witnessed a safety officer reassuring a squad of highly concerned roustabouts that they would not forfeit their entitlement to the anorak being shown around simply because the crane driver had lost the top of one of his fingers a few days earlier. Carson also noted an immediate 'incentive to minimisation', namely the statutory requirement to call a halt to work following a serious accident to allow an investigation of the undisturbed scene to be carried out. In remote offshore locations the opportunity and the temptation to cover up clearly exist. Up until Piper Alpha less than half of offshore fatalities and serious injuries were properly investigated.

The absence of the offshore application of the Reporting of Injuries, Diseases and Dangerous Occurrences Regulations (RIDDOR) 1985, has made any comparisons with onshore industries very difficult. Onshore regulations differ considerably from the Offshore Installations (Inspectors and Casualties) Regulations 1973. For example, the definition of a 'casualty' in the 1973 offshore regulations is vague in comparison with the RIDDOR definition of 'major injury' and is also very limited in respect of 'dangerous occurrences' (HSC, 1994c). The industry agreed to make reports which largely conform to the standards and definitions used in RIDDOR on a purely voluntary basis (HSC, 1994c: para 10). Faced with the need to bring some coherence into offshore accident and incident statistics, revised RIDDOR requirements were extended offshore in April 1996. While this provides some prospect of systematic appraisal of the real state of offshore safety, it is to some extent undermined by the removal in 1997 of the legal obligation of employers to keep a record of the number of hours worked offshore by their workforces.

The proposed application of the revised RIDDOR to enhance the reporting provisions on occupational and communicable diseases is particularly overdue. Relevant public health legislation has not been applied offshore hitherto. As a consequence the dangers posed by dust from deposits of radioactive LSA (Low Specific Activity [so-called]) scale in pipework and valves have not been addressed. Concerns remain about the adequacy of protective procedures for industrial radiographers, the 'bombers', who test pipework welds. Up until 1995 occupational health offshore in general was an area which had previously been neglected by regulatory authorities. With the new Offshore Safety Division on their doorstep, the informal view was that the substantial under-reporting of incidents offshore by operators should begin to diminish. In testimony given to the Energy Select Committee by Shell's managing director, Chris Fay, it was conceded to the committee that 'the reporting of incidents has improved out of all recognition, and in particular in the last couple of years' (Energy Select Committee, 1991: 30, para 143). The significant rise in the reported number of 'dangerous occurrences' since Piper Alpha was at least partly a function of this factor. In 1992/93, for example, the number of reported dangerous occurrences rose by 40 per cent. These were mainly as a result of hydrocarbon leaks being more fully reported; again, it should be noted that the arrangements for doing so remained on a voluntary basis here too (HSC, 1994c: para. 22). Carson, a decade previously, identified problems with regard to the reporting of structural and other failures which could have been potentially dangerous occurrences (1982: 36–8). In 1991, the operators indicated to the Energy Select Committee that they still regarded the classification of dangerous occurrences as 'a subjective area' (Energy Select Committee, 1991: 29, para 141). The revised reporting form OIR/9A contained a fairly comprehensive list of such dangerous occurrences covering everything from the blowout of a well to a person falling more than two metres. Since near-misses could provide lessons to be learned in safety management, reporting in this area could in theory substantially contribute to offshore safety. Rimington conceded in his evidence to the Energy Select Committee that here too was a possibility of substantial under-reporting. 'The difficulty', Rimington said, 'arises not just with dangerous occurrences but when you start talking about things like near-misses, because what is one man's near-miss is another man's providential escape or "never heard of it, thank you"' (1991: 101, para 436). We return to the issue of under-reporting in the next section.

Inspection and Enforcement Offshore pre-Piper Alpha

The resourcing, enforcement procedures and philosophy of the pre-Piper Alpha DEn regime merits closer examination. One key question is whether the formal regulatory regime shift from DEn to OSD has produced an effective culture of compliance and enforcement which impacts positively on accidents and injuries in the offshore industry.

The rather fragile nature of the DEn's compliance and enforcement culture was revealed in the exchange during the Cullen inquiry between Hugh Campbell QC and Jim Petrie, Director of Safety of the Petroleum Engineering Division:

> *Campbell:* Can I ask you whether you are aware of any prohibition or improvement notices ever having been issued?
>
> *Petrie:* I believe two improvement notices were issued many years ago, but I was not involved with them. It was just before I became Director of Safety .
>
> *Campbell:* Do you see any value in the power of prohibition or improvement notices being more widely used?
>
> *Petrie:* No.[4]

Prohibition and improvement notices were routinely used as part of the graduated enforcement procedures under the HSWA onshore. Petrie's argument at the Piper Alpha inquiry, was that much the same powers to require improvements or to stop work under the HSWA onshore, were in any event available to inspectors under the Mineral Workings Act. These powers, claimed John Wakeham, Secretary of State for Energy in 1990, were 'designed specifically for offshore operations and are extensively used'.[5] Further questioning from Frank Dobson MP, Opposition spokesperson on Energy, failed to elicit how many times the inspectors had used such powers since 1978 as a result of accidents, as against conducting routine inspections. Wakeham produced the following stock answer, provided by civil servants for Ministers faced with awkward parliamentary questions: 'A detailed breakdown of the kind requested could only be provided at disproportionate cost'.[6] Wakeham's further observation that 'action to effect improvements is a feature of almost every inspection' gives little reassurance when examined against the objective accident record of this period. A grand total of thirteen prohibition and improvement notices were served under the HSWA between its first offshore application on 1 September 1977 and 1990.[7] None of those were issued before 1980 (Burgoyne, 1980: 60). In 1980, six improvement notices were issued and a further four in 1981 (DEn, 1981, 1982). Thereafter, the procedure fell into almost total disuse until 1990 when one further notice was issued, giving a total of eleven notices. Two unaccounted-for notices cannot be traced in the DEn's annual *Brown Books* for the 1980s. No improvement notices or prohibition notices were outstanding when the HSE took over responsibility for offshore safety in 1991.[8]

The number of successful prosecutions each year under the DEn's regime was also very low. Indeed, in some years no prosecutions at all were undertaken. This was particularly so in the period between 1971 and 1977, the formative years of the offshore oil industry, when the Mineral Workings Act was the primary safety statute. The DEn's Petroleum Engineering Division was faced with the equally unpalatable alternatives of either prosecuting the companies or 'the much more onerous and continuing sanction' of shutting down operations altogether. Prosecution in the courts might cost a company a £200 fine, as in the case of Shell, following a fatality in 1978, whereas shutting down a drilling operation could cost a hundred times that amount each day. The low level of prosecutions offshore was recognized as a potential embarrassment. The deputy director of the PED summed up the public relations problem facing the offshore inspectorate:

> In this respect I believe the Inspectorate is liable to suffer the same adverse publicity as came to the Alkali Inspectorate following the asbestosis uproar a few years ago. The Alkali Inspectorate was inferred to have done very little because the number of prosecutions it had conducted were virtually zero. Like us, the Inspectorate tends to work more through both discussion with the industry on the errors of their ways and the ultimate sanction of stopping them completely. With this route you do not have to go to Court, and you do not have to present evidence, and it hurts companies a damn sight more.[9]

The problem with the approach of persuasion as against prosecution was, that while resort to the court to secure compliance was avoided, so also was the 'ultimate sanction' of shutting down operations. Thus Carson's contention was that there was high-level institutionalized tolerance of non-compliance, rooted in the philosophy of the regulatory agency. By posing enforcement as an 'all-or-nothing' choice, the DEn neatly sidestepped its responsibilities for the effective regulation of safety, in favour of the greater imperative of securing uninterrupted oil flows.

Up until 1980, Carson could trace only 13 cases of prosecutions involving 23 charges under either the MWA or HSWA; 10 were under the MWA, and 13 were under the HSWA. Carson notes that the extension of the HSWA to the Continental Shelf in the late 1970s affected prosecution activity. This finding, however, was primarily due to the contrast of previous inactivity (1982: 250). Of thirteen cases prosecuted under the HSWA, the maximum fine of £400 on summary conviction was imposed in two instances. In another five cases which were partially or wholly successful, the fines ranged from £25 to £250 and, in all but one case, were imposed under the MWA. In no case did the penalties imposed constitute an economic deterrent to the oil companies or their contractors. Seven cases under the HSWA were either entirely or mainly unsuccessful, resulting from admonishment in a test case, dismissal of charges as incompetent or irrelevant, or simple not guilty findings (1982: 268–80). Carson's view was that the DEn showed neither the inclination to initiate prosecution, nor even knowledge of the relevant legal procedures (1982: 247–9). Lack of willingness on the part of the DEn to provide relevant information which might enable routine prosecution under the HSWA also characterizes DEn policies of the following decade.

Since Carson's analysis, the basic situation did not change substantially. During the period from 1979/80 to 1988 when the Piper Alpha disaster took place, not more than three dozen successful prosecutions took place. The outer limit of penalization by the courts is illustrated by two fines recorded in the mid-1980s. These fines, amounting to £10,000 and £5000 in 1984, both resulted from a bridge failure between an installation and an adjacent facility in which there were three fatalities. The installation in question was Piper Alpha and the adjacent facility was the *Tharos*. The DEn *Brown Book* for 1985 records that the fines on Occidental and on Strathclyde Process Engineering, the contracting company, were 'among the highest ever imposed for offences under the Health and Safety at Work Act' (DEn, 1985: 24). The incident had occurred on 24 October 1982 and the fine was levied on 6 March 1984. In 1985, BP was fined £15,000 as a result of an incident on the Forties Delta on 1 August 1983. Here a well blowout and fire caused eleven men to receive burns. This fire burned out of control for nine hours, and is described in DEn case files as being of such a magnitude 'that the safety of the installation was put in jeopardy' (OSD case files, Aberdeen; see Table 8.1).

From 1980 onwards, until Piper Alpha, the total of fines administered offshore was under £58,000. Questioned specifically on this issue, John Rimington, the HSE's Director-General, observed at the Cullen Inquiry that 'our powers are enormous', but the level of fines imposed by magistrates is 'regrettably low'.[10]

Inspection and Enforcement Offshore post-Piper Alpha

This section explores the quantitative indicators of changes in the offshore safety regime. As such it complements our qualitative analysis in Chapter 7. The qualitative evidence would suggest that we should not expect major improvements in enforcement and safety. This section investigates data on enforcement, whereas the next section takes a closer look at accident statistics.

The Offshore Safety Division was created as a new department of the HSE. Following Lord Cullen's recommendation, its mission was to carry through the regulatory reconstruction of offshore safety. Where such regulatory regime shifts have occurred in the past, as for example following the implementation of the HSWA 1974 onshore, the expectation has been that there

Table 8.1 *Successful Prosecutions for Breaches of Health and Safety Legislation Offshore 1980–88 (January to January each year)*

Date	No.	Amounts	Total Fines
1980	1	£100	£100
1981	3	£100, £100, £1000	£1200
1982	8	1 Admonished, £400, £500, £750, £100, £150, £750, £550, £200	£3400
1983	4	£350, £250, £500, £5000	£6,100
1984	3	£10,000, £5000, £500, £500	£16000
1985	8	£15,000, £1000, £750, £1750, £800, £900, £900, £350	£21450
1986	1	£1000	£1000
1987	3	1 Conditional Discharge 2 yrs, 1 Admonished, £3500, £1000	£4500
1988	6	£500, £400, £250, £1700, £500, £500	£3850

Source: HSE/OSD.

would be significant positive start-up effects on safety (Dawson *et al.*, 1988; Nichols, 1986). We suggest that the shift of regime offshore has not yet been accompanied by a significant fall in accident rates. There are two possible explanations for this. Either the new offshore regime is not yet sufficiently securely in place, or the regime itself, despite appearances to the contrary, is intrinsically flawed.

The first head of OSD, Tony Barrell, promised the industry 'a tough regime but one that is fair and workable' (1991: col. 388). While claiming that 'very often . . . some harsh words are spoken behind the scenes', the emphasis of OSD was to remain on 'constructive dialogue' with the operators. Legal theorists such as Braithwaite (1985) suggest that in such dialogues an inevitable blurring of regulatory scrutiny takes place. According to his view, over time inspectors tend to move toward a more sympathetic stance toward business. This process of mutual accommodation means that regulators will continually adjust their demands in the light of the responses they receive from business (Hawkins and Hutter, 1993).

Aware that Lord Cullen's report presented a potentially poisoned chalice, where a task was posed without the provision of sufficient funds, the HSC made it clear at an early date that adequate resources would need to be made available for the new Offshore Safety Division to carry out the task. Otherwise, as Rimington (1991) put it to the Energy Select Committee, 'they would be unwilling to take responsibility over'. The running costs of the PED Safety Directorate for 1989/90 were £7.2 million and for 1990/91 immediately prior to the takeover by OSD some £12 million.[11] In gross terms, OSD funding levels were projected to rise from £20 million for the financial year 1991/92, an increase of £8 million on the previous year, to a promised £35 million for the financial year 1994/95 (Energy Select Committee, 1991).

Given the sheer scale of the tasks facing the new OSD, the initial difficulties experienced in recruiting suitably qualified personnel were not surprising (Energy Select Committee, 1991: col. 413). The OSD inherited a safety inspectorate from the DEn that was severely depleted by 1990, with 43 inspectors in post and 18 vacancies.[12] Some gaps in the OSD administration were filled by transferring inspectors from other parts of the HSE, in particular key staff involved in major hazards work to assist with the Safety Cases. There were even some temporary secondments to the OSD from the oil industry itself, although not for front-line inspection duties. The HSC *Annual Report* for 1992/93 noted a significant decrease in the number of applications for vacant posts, despite a grading review and enhanced salaries. As a result, total staffing was 12 below the target of 332 at the start of the 1993 financial year. In particular, there was a shortfall of seventeen in the number of offshore inspectors, although a further seven joined the division early in 1993/94 (HSC, 1993: 75). The figure of 374.5 for staff in post was 8 per cent lower than the 407 target in the 1993/94 *Plan of Work* (HSC, 1994d: 72), while the figure of 342 for 31 March 1995 was 7.5 per cent lower than the target of 369.5 in the 1994/95 *Plan of Work* (HSC, 1994e: 66; see Table 8.2). However, 1995/96 saw a reduction of eleven in the number of inspectors, the first such since OSD took over responsibility for offshore safety.

Table 8.2 *Offshore Safety Division Staff 1991–96*

	1.4.91[1]	1.4.92[2]	1.4.93[2]	1.4.94[2]	31.3.95[3]	31.3.96[4]
Staff in Post	88	226	319.5	374.5	342	309
No. of Inspectors	41	82	166.5	192.5	197[5]	186[5]

Sources: (1) HSC Annual Report 1992/93: 122; (2) HSC Plan of Work 1994/95: 66; (3) HSC, Annual Report 1994/95: 123; (4) HSC Annual Report 1995/96:101; (5) Provisional figure informally supplied by HSE.

The budgetary cuts which the HSE as a whole was undergoing during this period also suggested that the OSD as a department could find it increasingly difficult to maintain its 'ring-fenced' position in the long run. In 1994/95 the total budget of OSD was £21.5 million, well below the initially projected figure of £35 million. In 1995/96 this was further reduced to £21 million.[13] Indeed, by late 1995, OSD was experiencing managerial 'de-layering' as the Safety Cases were finally put in place. It was accompanied by a reduction in the number of jobs related to Safety Case acceptance, while that section of OSD concerned with Safety Cases was itself relocated from Aberdeen to the HSE division in Bootle, Merseyside. There is some evidence that these organizational changes have had a negative impact on employee morale. In a letter of an OSD section head to the chief executive of the department, complaints were voiced about the failure of HSE to implement a planned long-term pay review. The letter concludes:

> I cannot impress on you enough the level of bad feeling in OSD on this issue. The very staff upon which the establishment of OSD and its successful operation during its formative years and in times of very high workload depended, have been treated abysmally instead of being rewarded for their flexibility, commitment and motivation (and in fact competencies as inspectors in the offshore industry at the highest level).[14]

This deterioraton of employee morale accompanying the adoption of primarily managerialist concerns by the regulator is part of what we have previously referred to as the gradual erosion scenario, in which an initially enthusiastic stance of the regulator is gradually replaced by a degree of indifference and alienation.

The inspection regime of OSD appears to have improved substantially when compared to the DEn, especially with regard to accident investigation, responses to individual workers' complaints, the frequency of offshore visits and contact between inspectors and the workforce. With the takeover by OSD, there was a steady increase in the number of planned inspections offshore although this is set to fall (see Table 8.3). The frequency of inspections is two or three times per year for each installation by 1994, as against one per year or even every two years at the time of the Piper Alpha disaster. HSE inspectors now routinely meet with the safety representatives in order to discuss safety concerns. Members of management were not to be present during these meetings with the workforce (Sefton, 1994).

In his evidence to the Piper Alpha public inquiry, Jim Petrie claimed that

Table 8.3 *Offshore Inspection Visits 1987–94*

1987	1988	1989	1990	1991	1992	1993	1994	1995	1996[1]
147	141	258	232	359	405	467	414	488	400

Source: DEn Brown Books,1988,1989,1990; HSC Annual Reports 1993/94,1994/95,1995/6; (1) 1996/97 Plan.

the DEn had received about 30 complaints from the workforce in 1988, and 45 in 1989.[15] The DEn investigated 42 accidents in 1988, 51 in 1989 and 36 in 1990 (DEn, 1989, 1990, 1991). Under the new OSD regime the total number of investigations of accidents and complaints increased from 89 for the year 1991/92, to 170 for 1992/93 (HSC, 1993: 117), to 328 for 1993/94 (HSC, 1994d). Of this total of 328 investigations for 1993/94, 119 were accident investigations, 147 were of dangerous occurrences and 62 were responses to individual workers' complaints. The following year 1994/95 saw a total of 680 investigations of which a roughly comparable 54 were responses to individual workers' complaints.[16]

The OSD's enforcement strategy also appears to have become more rigorous than that of its predecessor. Between April 1991, when OSD assumed responsibility for offshore safety, and March 1995, that is, in four years, there were 69 improvement and 17 prohibition notices served, compared to the negligible number in the whole previous decade (see Table 8.4).

Table 8.4 *Offshore Prohibition and Improvement Notices Issued 1991–95*

	Prohibition Notices	**Improvement Notices**
April 91 – Mar 92	2	0
April 92 – Mar 93	6	20
April 93 – Mar 94	4	15
April 94 – Mar 95	5	34*

*Provisional figure informally supplied by HSE.
Source: HSE/OSD.

Health and safety legal experts have observed that improvement notices requiring remedial action within a specified period effectively turn a 'blind eye' to current or past contraventions (Drake and Wright, 1983: 138). This removes the expectation of culpability from offences. In 1996, under the Deregulation and Contracting Out Act, and in response to political pressure from Conservative MPs, the terms of enforcement of improvement notices were diluted.[17] Employers could now appeal directly to an inspector's line manager and were to be given two weeks to make such representations. There was also an existing right of appeal to an Industrial Tribunal should the new delay option prove unsuccessful. Prohibition notices are tied to the risk of 'serious personal injury' and can require that an activity cease. While for this type of notice there is also a right of appeal to an Industrial Tribunal, a prohibition notice would normally remain in force in the interim. Usually, only in the event of a serious injury or a fatality would an actual prosecution be contemplated by the regulator. Rimington's evidence to Lord Cullen spelled out the HSE's enforcement philosophy with its bias against prosecution.

> Both forms of notice (improvement and prohibition) ... are extremely effective, and are more commonly applied than prosecution. They do not punish, except in the sense that compliance with them can be expensive, but they secure early or immediate remedy. As representing an unmistakeable exercise of the inspectors' authority, they provide the same kind of stimulus as prosecution.[18]

Owing to the expense of prosecuting companies in the Crown Courts, most prosecutions initiated by the HSE take place in magistrates' courts where the maximum fine available has historically been low. With the passing of the Offshore Safety Act on 6 March 1992, the level of maximum fines rose to £20,000 for more serious offences (breaches of sections 2–6 of the HSWA and failure to comply with a notice or court order). Higher courts meanwhile have remained free to impose unlimited fines and up to two years' imprisonment. From 1 October 1992 the maximum fine in the magistrates' courts was increased from £2000 to £5000 for other offences under HSWA.

From April 1991 to March 1994 under the first three years of the new OSD regime there were over 20 prosecutions instigated by the Procurator Fiscal in Scotland, following receipt of a report from the HSE. Of these, 18 were successful and only two prosecutions were unsuccessful. One was abandoned, as no registered UK office or place of business could be found at which to serve papers on the company concerned. That company was Sai Pol, a major Italian construction firm involved in the Tiffany project, a major new installation for Agip.[19] Similar difficulties led the procurator to abandon a case against Heerema in 1993. This was in spite of the huge Dutch-based contracting company's longstanding involvement in the UK offshore industry. These cases once again highlighted the jurisdictional anomaly of the UK courts with regard to foreign-owned companies and their personnel, which makes prosecution impossible unless a company has a registered office in the UK. It is 'a matter of continuing concern' to the Scottish legal authorities that this is the case even with respect to companies within the European Union.[20]

The preparedness to prosecute seems to be greater under the OSD than it was under the DEn, with the total level of fines imposed initially showing a substantial increase. A number of individual 'exemplary' fines were imposed, two in the six-figure region. However, the last two years have seen the total of fines imposed drop from £38,500 for 1994/95 to £14,500 the following year, an average of only £2400 (see Table 8.5). These fines must be assessed in terms of the deterrence effect which they exert on a company. Only when this is done can there be any realistic notion of economic deterrence and any proper expectation of corporate compliance.

Table 8.5 *Fines for Breaches of Health and Safety Legislation Offshore 1989–96**

Date	No.	Amounts	Total Fines
1989	3	£10,000, £5000, £7000	£22,000
1990	4	£2000, £2000, £800, £200	£5000
1991	1	£850	£850
1992	9	£1000, £30,000, £1000, £5000, £100,000, £1000, £5000, £10,000, £20,000	£173,000
1993	7	£1000, £25,000, £4000, £250,000, £25,000, £30,000, £75,000	£410,000
1994	7	£10,000, £2000, £3000, £2500, £10,000, £10,000, £1000	£38,500
1995	4	£12,500, £3000, £2500, £5000	£23,000
1996	5	£10,000, £500, £500, £2500	£23,500‡

*January to January each year. ‡March-April.
Source: HSE/OSD.

The level of individual fines for breaches of health and safety law still remains extremely low overall for the most part. In this respect the offshore pattern simply mirrors that onshore. The average UK fine imposed by the courts following HSE prosecutions fell in 1994/95 to £2645 from £3061 in 1993/94 (HSC, 1994d: 62; HSC, 1995b: 76). This latter figure was itself a doubling on the previous year's level of fines. However, when the largest fines are taken out, the average level of fines remained steady at approximately £2400 over the two years 1993/94 and 1994/95. The current average offshore fine for 1996 of £4700 is larger than the £2500 UK-wide figure. However, neither onshore nor offshore are there proportionate or meaningful levels of economic deterrence as measured against company profits. Recent decreases in the level and totals of fines suggest that here also the previously described process of 'gradual erosion' has affected the OSD's enforcement regime.

Offshore Safety: An Empirical Analysis

The ultimate question is whether the safety record of the industry has improved under the post-Piper Alpha regulatory reconstruction. The answer given by the industry itself is a clear 'yes'. In a letter to European Union Commissioner for Social Affairs, Padraig Flynn, Harold Hughes of UKOOA has argued that 'the frequency of lost-time accidents and fatalities has been steadily dropping since the early '80s, a record marred only by the Piper Alpha disaster itself.'[21] Using HSE figures, UKOOA has argued that the offshore industry is 'considerably safer already than a number of on-shore industries whose public profile in this regard has been much lower'.[22] UKOOA has claimed that the incidence of lost time accidents/fatalities is 'just a quarter of the highest risk industries'. On the basis of such arguments UKOOA has attempted to secure the continued exclusion of the offshore industry as 'Other Work at Sea' (OWS) under the provisions of the European Working Time Directive. During 1995/96 this exclusion became subject to scrutiny by a review group of the European Commission, much to UKOOA's concern as the dominant force within Europe's oil and gas industry.[23]

UKOOA has suggested that injury rates of those employed in oil and gas extraction are generally in the low range, falling, amongst others, below *Postal Services and Telecommunications* (rank order 10) and *Construction* (rank order 15). This is illustrated in Table 8.6 which is reproduced from a paper by Harold Hughes (1994b) to the Offshore Northern Seas Conference 1994. It is similar in content to others presented to oil industry forums (Hughes and Taylor, 1995). In 1992/93, accordingly, *Extraction of Mineral Oil and Natural Gas*, according to UKOOA, could be placed at a rank order of 22nd most dangerous industry. According to UKOOA's analysis, in 1993/94 the rank order using all-injury data had further improved to position 34th (UKOOA, 1995a). For the period from 1988/89 to 1994/95 UKOOA claimed an overall 48 per cent reduction in injury frequency.

Table 8.6 *Injury Rates by Industry (All Reported Injuries, including fatalities. List in order of rate per 100,000 Employees – 1992/93)*

1.	Coke ovens	5571.4
2.	Open cast coal workings	4142.9
3.	COAL MINES	**3957.8**
4.	RAILWAYS	**3151.6**
5.	Non-energy mineral extraction	2786.3
6.	Food, drink and tobacco manufacturing	2767.0
7.	Forestry	2026.9
8.	METAL MANUFACTURING	**1993.6**
9.	Manufacture of non-metallic mineral products	1831.3
10.	Postal services and telecommunications	1709.3
11.	WATER SUPPLY INDUSTRY	**1693.8**
12.	Processing of rubber and plastics	1655.8
13.	Repair of consumer goods and vehicles	1646.2
14.	Manufacture of metal goods not elsewhere specified	1611.8
15.	CONSTRUCTION	**1602.8**
16.	Manufacture of motor vehicles and parts	1538.3
17.	Production and distribution of energy (gas etc.)	1533.8
18.	Supporting services to transport	1526.0
19.	Production of man-made fibres	1500.0
20.	Timber and wooden furniture industries	1277.4
21.	Manufacture of other transport equipment	1263.4
22.	EXTRACTION OF MINERAL OILS AND NATURAL GAS	**1196.0**

Source: HSC, Annual Report 1992/93

Such claims, however, are based on a misreading and misrepresentation of HSE accident data. UKOOA's analysis has been severely criticised on methodological grounds (Parry and MacFarlane, 1994; Beck and Woolfson, 1995; Woolfson and Beck, 1995). First, much of the data presented by the operators have been calculated on the basis of inflated *counts* of the offshore workforce. The denominators of the working population have included employees who are predominantly stationed onshore and who may never, or only very infrequently, work offshore. In addition, the inclusion of support staff offshore, such as caterers, whose occupations are significantly less risky than those of construction, maintenance, transport and production workers, again distorts the estimate of incident rates when key risk groups are being examined. Third, and most importantly, UKOOA has relied on combined incident rates which include minor or 'over three-day' injuries. These minor injuries tend to be systematically under-reported in the offshore industry primarily because there are strong counter-incentives to absenteeism once a worker is on a platform. For an individual worker, the perception by management that absenteeism may not be fully justified, will necessarily lead to reduced future employment prospects. Medical evacuation by helicopter routinely involves unwelcome administrative procedures, disruptive to contract manning requirements as well as necessitating the registering of lost-time incidents. Previous research has indicated a strong relationship between job security and the reporting of minor injuries. Minor injuries tend to be *over*-reported in industries where there is high job security, such as the public sector, so that aggregate comparisons of offshore rates are heavily distorted. Even within the offshore sector, differential job security is reflected in reporting minor illnesses which result in absence from work. Sutherland and Cooper (1991) note that three times as many operators' personnel register absence due to illness, as against contractors' employees (21 per cent as against 7 per cent). The inclusion of minor injuries which are systematically under-reported offshore results in a dramatic distortion of overall aggregate accident figures and rates when comparing different industries. Comparative assessments of the offshore safety record with other industries, therefore, must exclude data which include minor injuries; a fact which appears to have been recently acknowledged by the Offshore Safety Division of the HSE. For the first time, tables are produced which concentrate exclusively on fatalities and serious injury rates (HSE, 1996).

Our analysis of the offshore safety record starts with hard data on fatalities and serious injuries, which are less subject to the vagaries of reporting. The definition of a fatality is obvious and there appears to be no space for reporting error. Nevertheless even in the context of this – the hardest data of all –

there are questions as to whether, say, a death resulting from a heart attack offshore, or a suicide, should be recorded as offshore work-related fatalities. Serious injuries are defined as bone fractures, amputations, injuries involving loss of consciousness and the like.[24] Again there is some, although limited, room for 'error'. If the stakes involved in accident records increase, there is some incentive for companies to compensate workers for such injuries informally and avoid an official report. Offshore contractors may be substantially rewarded by clients for eliminating lost time incidents and penalized for incurring them. Accounts circulate in the industry of men with injuries which would qualify as lost time incidents being reassigned to office 'functions' onshore and being pressured by management not to report injuries. Safety representatives have argued that 'lack of fitness for duty' should qualify such injuries for recorded lost time incidents, a request that has apparently fallen on deaf ears in the industry.[25] The BBC television documentary programme *Frontline Scotland* obtained testimony from one worker who although injured was persuaded to return to onshore work whilst accommodated in a luxury hotel in Aberdeen. If a lost-time incident had been recorded the contracting company concerned stood to lose a reported £200,000 bonus.[26] It is not just the contractors, but the operators too who have a stake in minimizing reported incidents. The view of one HSE inspector with first-hand experience of the offshore scene is cautionary.

> The icon offshore is the LTA (lost time accident). They all want to have an LTA rate at zero for 350 days. They will go to extraordinary lengths to get their LTA rate down. But from our point of view, the LTA is not a good measure at all. Companies I know will move heaven and earth to stop people being medivac'd and they will go to great lengths to stop recording an LTA. The duty holder is reporting in such a way to keep their own nose clean.[27]

With these caveats in mind, our own analysis is necessarily provisional.

Data on serious injuries and fatalities are reported in the HSC *Annual Reports* and, specifically for the offshore oil industry, in the DEn's *Brown Books* for the years until 1991, and thereafter in OIAC (1993) and the Offshore Safety Division *Accident and Incident Statistics Report* (HSE, 1994; HSE, 1995c; HSE, 1996) for the years 1991/92 to 1994/5. Again, some complications arise in these reports. Reported serious injuries for the most recent years can underestimate the actual number of serious injuries. This can be seen by comparing provisional and final HSE estimates which show consistently higher final totals after a time lapse. There are several possible explanations for this. What were initially reported as minor injuries may in the longer run turn out to be of a more serious nature, although not at first evident: for example, a back injury at first reported in the minor category may turn out to be a severe disabling injury. Evidence from the Health and Safety Executive suggests that onshore, one third of major injuries had to be reclassified from 'over three-day injuries', reported under RIDDOR (HSC, 1994d). Nichols (1994: 107) is categoric in regard to onshore manufacturing that 'the validity of the major [injury] rate as an index of temporal change in safety... must now be in doubt.' We would expect this to apply even more, offshore. Further, the drive to cost-cutting has created additional incentives to minimization of reported serious injuries.

Having considerably less confidence in the most recent injury data, our analysis focuses on the reporting year of 1992/93 (31 March to 1 April) and the period before, although references to the 1993/94 period will be made. We start by re-examining the comparative accident record of the offshore industry. In 1992/93, combined rates for fatalities and serious injuries alone place *Extraction of Mineral Oil and Natural Gas* at a level similar to *Non Energy Mineral Extraction*, at a rank order of 16. (Compare Figure 8.1 to Figure 8.2.) These data on the *Extraction of Mineral Oil and Natural Gas* do not however reflect the safety record of the offshore industry, as they include the separate gas extraction industry onshore as well as a large number of onshore employees of the offshore industry. Since 1991 the OSD has reported fatalities and serious injuries for *offshore* employees at a detailed level. For 1992/93, the OSD reported a combined incident rate of 284.7 per 100,000 employees (see Figure 8.3). Considering only the *offshore* figures, this gives *Extraction of Mineral Oil and Natural Gas* a rank order of 5, coming below (1) *Open Cast Coal Workings* (approximately 3500 workers), (2) *Coal Mines* (25,600 employees), (3) *Forestry* (approximately 1700 workers), and (4) *Coke Ovens* (approximately 500 workers).

The OSD's estimate of a combined incident rate of 284.7 per 100,000 employees is based on an assumed workforce of 29,500 workers. There are indications, as previously suggested, that this workforce figure (based on returns to the Inland Revenue) is an inflated estimate. Grampian Regional Council's Economic Development Unit has conducted successive annual surveys of persons on board 200 installations in the northern and central North Sea, based on the maximum summer-time period of employment. These estimates, arrived at by contacting individual operators for returns, provides the most reliable year-by-year time series available, for the period from 1980 onwards. The totals include a 'guestimate' for the total number of employees in the southern gas fields (which are in any event mainly unmanned) and the Morecombe Bay area.[28] Grampian workforce estimates are considerably more accurate than the Inland Revenue returns. Recently the OSD has

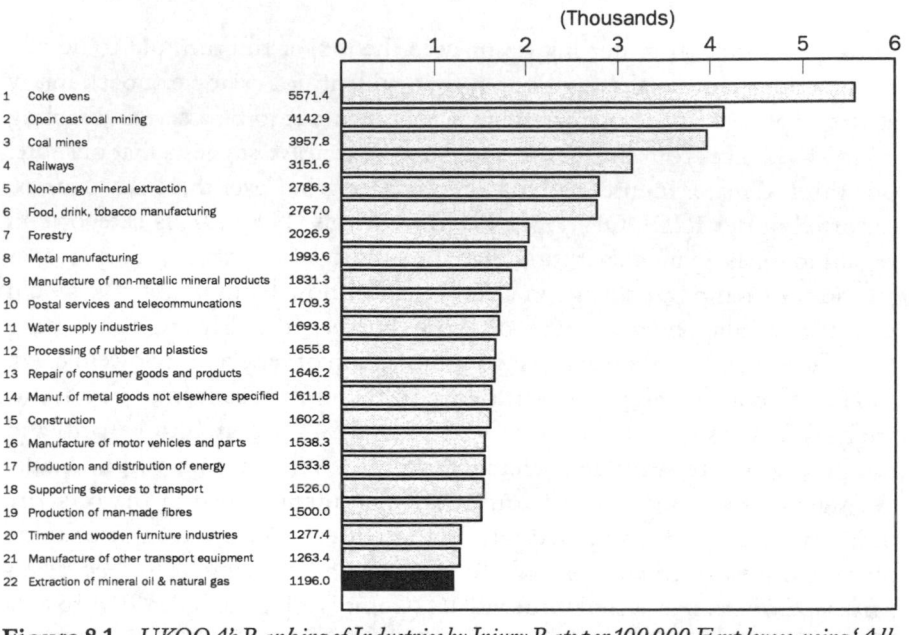

Figure 8.1 *UKOOA's Ranking of Industries by Injury Rate per 100,000 Employees, using 'All Reported Injuries' (including over three-day injuries) 1992/93*
Source: UKOOA

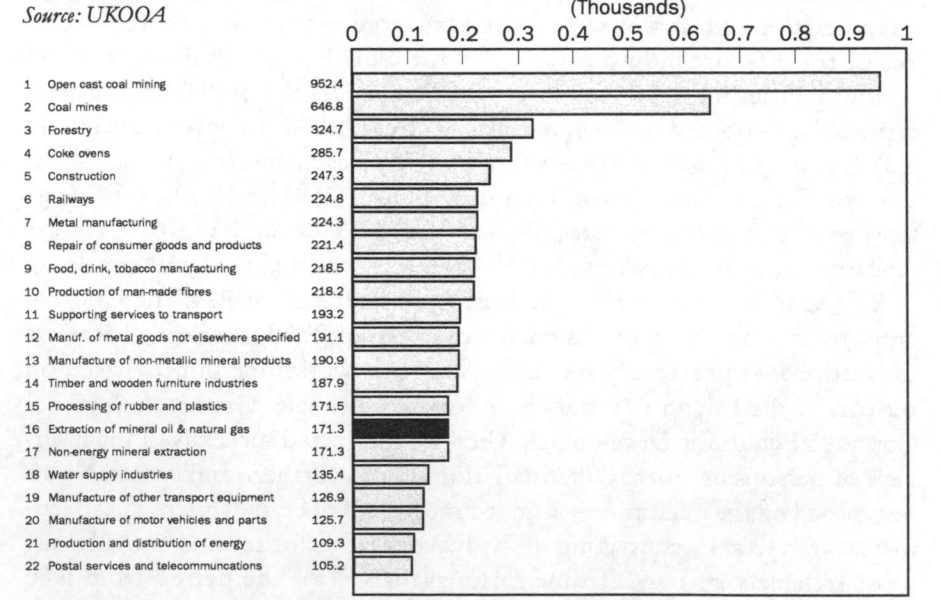

Figure 8.2 *Ranking of Industries by Injury Rate per 100,000 Employees, using Combined Incident Rates (fatalities and serious injuries) 1992/93: aggregate rate for onshore and offshore hydrocarbon extraction*
Source: HSE.

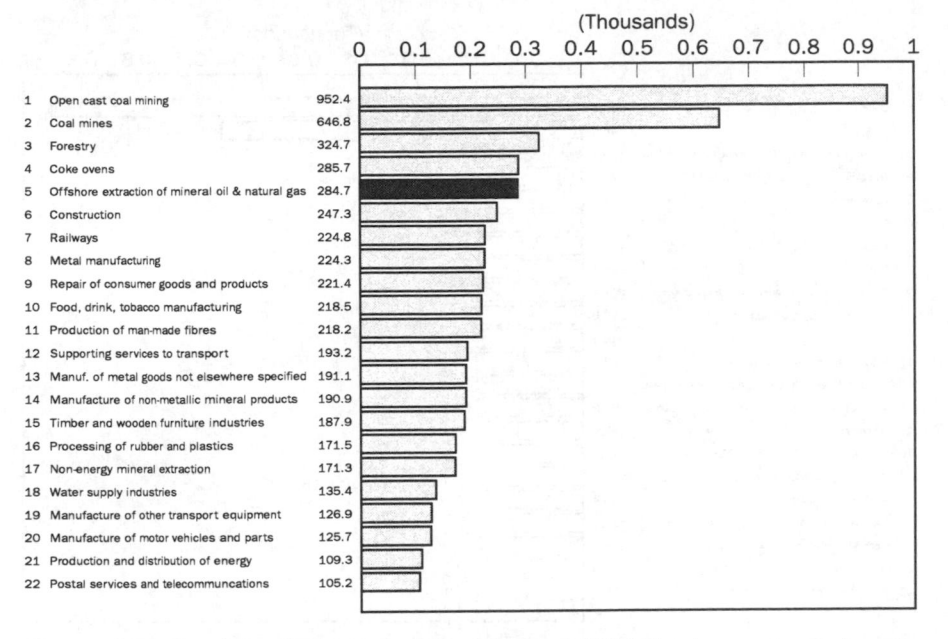

Figure 8.3 *Ranking of Industries by Injury Rate per 100,000 Employees, using Combined Incident Rates (fatalities and serious injuries) 1992/93: offshore rate only (excluding onshore incidents), using HSE employment figures*
Source: HSE/OSD.

acknowledged the need to establish a database which estimates the offshore workforce on the basis of accurate persons on board figures (HSE, 1996). Grampian Regional Council estimates the full-time equivalent offshore workforce in 1992/93 at 25,500 (Grampian Regional Council, 1993). Using this figure as a denominator, the combined rate of fatalities and serious injuries per 100,000 workers is 329.4, roughly 44.7 incidents higher than the OSD figure (see Figure 8.4). This ranks *Offshore Extraction of Mineral Oil and Natural Gas* as the third most dangerous industry overall, coming behind (1) *Open Cast Coal Workings* and (2) underground *Coal Mines*.

Although this figure more realistically reflects safety ranking, it could be argued that some of the onshore management of the offshore oil industry should be included in order to make the data more fully comparable to that of other industries. Grampian Regional Council estimates total management employment in the oil and gas extraction industries at 3400 approximately. If this figure were added to the actual offshore employment figure, the combined injury rate per 100,000 employees would stand at 290.7. This would put the injury rate of offshore workers behind that of (1) *Open Cast Coal Workings,*

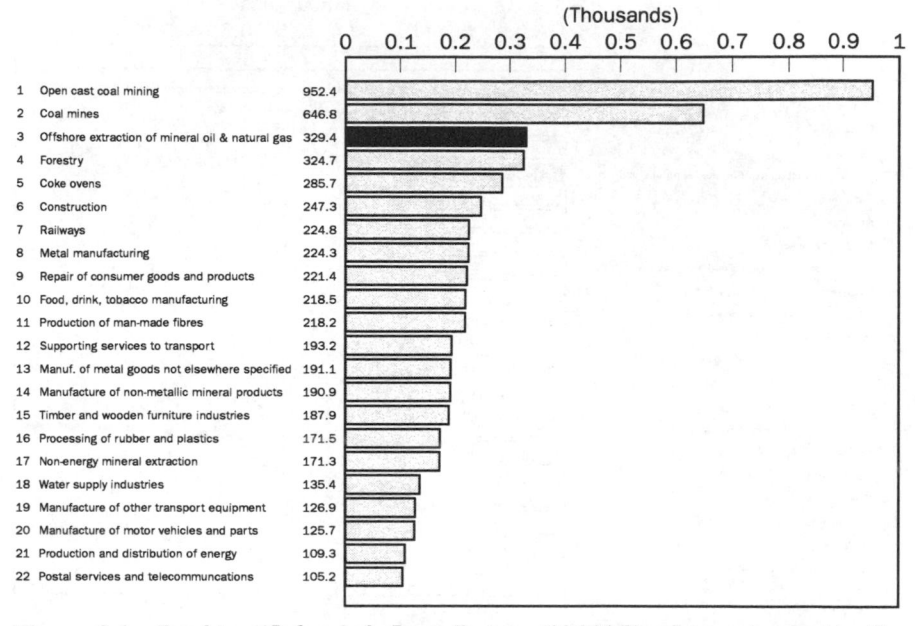

Figure 8.4 *Ranking of Industries by Injury Rate per 100,000 Employees, using Combined Incident Rates (fatalities and serious injuries) 1992/93: offshore rate only, using Grampian employment figures*
Source: OSD and Grampian Regional Council

(2) *Coal Mines*, and (3) *Forestry*, i.e. an overall ranking of fourth. Since, however, not all of the managerial employees actually perform directly offshore-related work, the previous assessment of offshore injury rates as third most dangerous is probably more realistic. This rank order of 'third most dangerous industry' not merely is a contingent feature of the most recent available statistics, but can be shown to be a continuing trend since 1990 (see Table 8.7).

By itself this ranking still does not represent a ranking of generic industry groups. If *Open Cast Coal Workings* and underground *Coal Mines* are combined into one category of coal extraction industries, then *Offshore Oil and Gas Extraction* ranks as the UK's second most dangerous industry. This represents a position startlingly at variance with that claimed by the operators. However, given that privatized coal companies have no legal obligation placed upon them to report their accident rates, the possibility of future comparisons with offshore oil and gas is now remote. In addition, the extensive use of contractors in the privatized coal industry has produced similar pressures to those offshore towards under-reporting of lost time incidents.[29]

This picture is confirmed when the 'hardest' figure of all, fatalities alone,

Table 8.7 *Ranking of Industries by Injury Rates per 100,000 Employees using Combined Incident Rates (fatalities and serious injuries) 1990/91,1991/92,1992/93 and Three-Year Average: Offshore Rates Disaggregated*

		1990/1	1991/2	1992/3	Average 1990/3
1.	Open cast coal mining	–	729.2	952.4	840.8
2.	Coal mines	651.7	709.3	646.8	669.3
3.	**Offshore extraction of mineral oil and natural gas**	370.0	318.5	329.4	**339.3**
4.	Forestry	291.7	307.7	324.7	308.0
5.	Coke ovens	200.0	428.6	285.7	304.8
6.	Construction	289.3	247.3	247.3	261.3
7.	Railways	245.9	224.6	224.8	231.8
8.	Metal manufacturing	231.2	222.5	224.3	226.0
9.	Repair of consumer goods and products	206.7	193.2	221.4	207.1
10.	Food, drink, tobacco manufacturing	227.5	204.6	218.5	216.9
11.	Production of man-made fibres	269.8	112.9	218.2	200.3
12.	Supporting services to transport	160.0	172.6	193.2	175.3
13.	Manufacture of metal goods not elsewhere specified	208.1	221.1	191.1	206.8
14.	Manufacture of non-metallic mineral products	209.5	214.5	190.9	205.0
15.	Timber and wooden furniture industries	200.5	190.1	187.9	192.8
16.	Processing of rubber and plastics	182.4	178.0	171.5	177.3
17.	Non-energy mineral extraction	199.2	179.7	171.3	183.4
18.	Water supply industries	145.6	126.4	135.4	135.8
19.	Manufacture of other transport equipment	130.8	138.0	126.9	131.9
20.	Manufacture of motor vehicles and parts	142.4	114.7	125.7	127.6
21.	Production and distribution of energy	135.6	113.2	109.3	119.4
22.	Postal services and telecommunications	118.7	89.3	105.2	104.4

Source: HSC Annual Report, various years; HSE/OSD Offshore accident and incident statistics report, various years.

is examined. The fatality rate for the whole oil and gas extraction industry, averaged over the eight-year period 1986/87 to 1993/94, is reported in the HSE's published data (HSC, 1995c: 8). This confirms a ranking of third equal most dangerous industry. In this case, workforce numbers include both the onshore and offshore segment of the oil and gas extraction industry. Again this makes the oil industry's view of its relative safety somewhat difficult to sustain, even when relying wholly on the HSE's data, and reflects how powerful corporate interests seek to misuse statistical information to influence policy agendas (see Table 8.8).

Table 8.8   *Average Fatality Rate 1986/87 to 1993/94*

	Average rate per 100,000 employees
Extraction of minerals/ores other than coal, oil and gas	25
Forestry	21
Extraction of mineral oil and natural gas	15*
Coal extraction	15
Railways	10

*This excludes the 167 fatalities in the Piper Alpha disaster. The average with these deaths would have been 64 per 100,000 employees.
Source: HSC Health and Safety Statistics 1994/95: 8.

Offshore Safety: An Improving Picture?

As important to the debate on offshore safety as the comparative position relative to other industries is the record of the industry over time. This section examines the industry's long-term safety record, and more specifically the changes in offshore safety following the post-Piper Alpha regulatory reconstruction. This analysis again concentrates on serious injuries and fatalities, which tend to be less subject to the vagaries of reporting.

UKOOA's view of the long-term accident trend is shown to be progressively downward (Figure 8.5). Despite industry claims to the contrary, accident data for the offshore oil industry using fatalities and serious injuries alone show a rising trend from the inception of the industry until the present day. This rising trend applies to both raw fatalities and serious injuries; although it is more marked in the case of serious injuries (see Figures 8.6a and 8.6b).

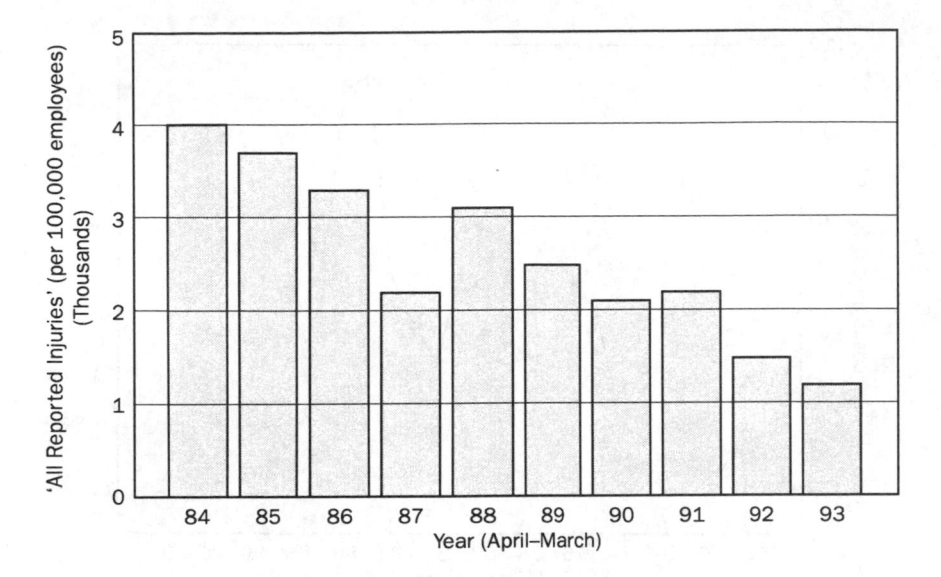

Figure 8.5 *Rate of Offshore Accidents, 'All Reported Injuries' (including over three-day injuries) per 100,000 Employees, 1984–93, as presented by UKOOA*
Source: Hughes, 1994b

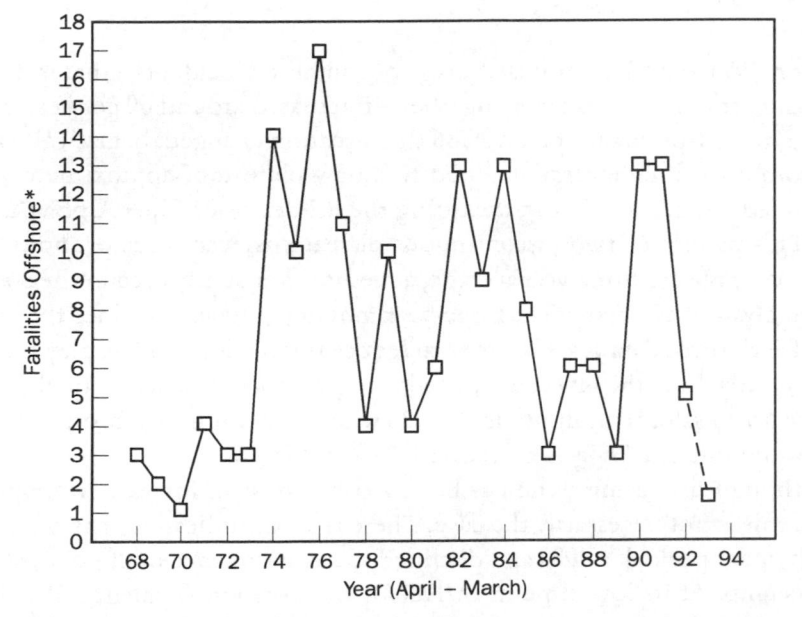

Figure 8.6a *Fatalities – UK Offshore Sector 1968–93*
*excluding Piper Alpha
Source: DEn Brown Books and HSE/OSD

393

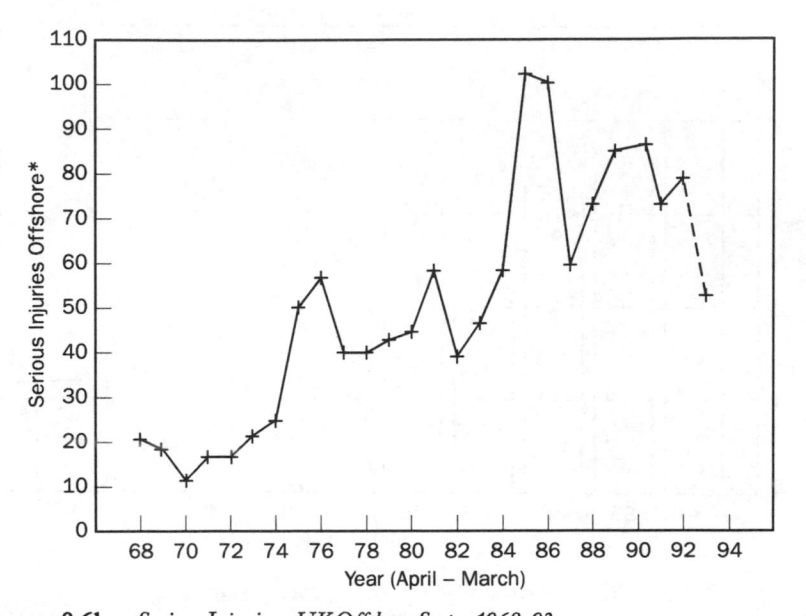

Figure 8.6b *Serious Injuries – UK Offshore Sector 1968–93*
* excluding Piper Alpha
Source: DEn Brown Books *and HSE/OSD.*

From 1975 to 1985 the annual average of combined incidents – that is, fatalities and serious injuries taken together – fluctuated around 60 per year. Following the oil-price slump in 1985/86 this situation changed dramatically and the combined incident rate jumped to a new plateau of approximately 90 combined incidents per year, excluding the 167 deaths of Piper Alpha (Table 8.9). This pattern of two discontinuous plateaux is even more pronounced when we apply the three-year average, a method frequently used in the statistical analysis of accidents. The three-year moving average combines the average of each three data years in order to reduce fluctuations and display trends more clearly. Like the raw data figure it suggests there has been a qualitative *deterioration* of safety conditions in 1985/86 which has continued through Piper Alpha and into the 1990s (see Figures 8.7a and 8.7b).

Although this rising trend has been attributed to an increase in employment, this is not necessarily the case. There is some indication that offshore employment peaked in 1984 and declined as a consequence of the 1985/86 oil price slump. At its lowest point in 1986/87 offshore employment fell below 18,000. Since 1988 this declining trend has reversed and offshore employment figures appear to reach peak 1984 levels again, to be followed by a further recent decrease from 1991/92 onwards. This pattern is documented in both

Table 8.9   *Combined Incidents (fatalities and serious injuries) 1975–92*

Year	No
1975	63
1976	77
1977	56
1978	44
1979	53
1980	49
1981	65
1982	52
1983	56
1984	72
Annual Average: Pre-Slump Phase **58.7**	
1985	111
1986	104
1987	65
1988	80
1989	89
1990	100
1991	86
1992	84
Annual Average Post-Slump Phase **89.9**	

Sources: DEn Brown Books, various years; OIAC (1993) Report on 1991 Accident Statistics; HSE (1994) Accident and Incident Statistics Report, 1993.

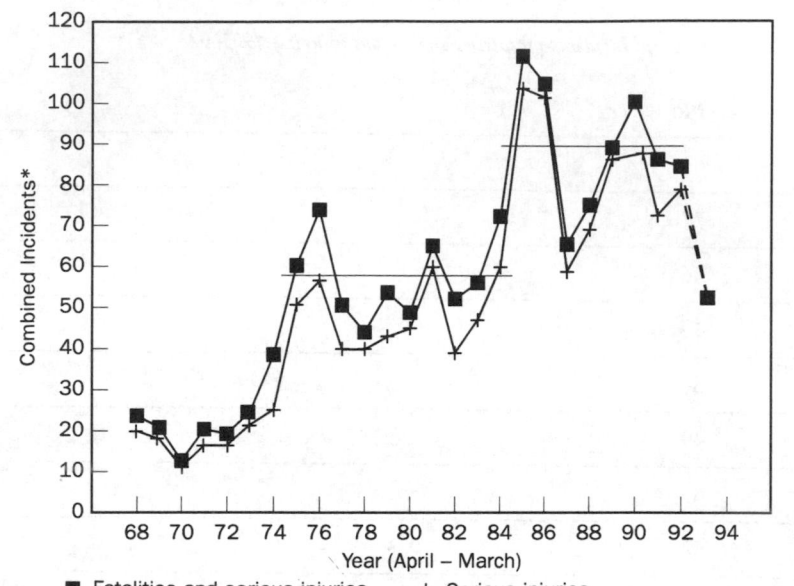

■ Fatalities and serious injuries   + Serious injuries

Figure 8.7a   *Combined Incidents (fatalities and serious injuries) UK Offshore Sector 1968–93*
*excluding Piper Alpha
Source: DEn Brown Books, and HSE/OSD

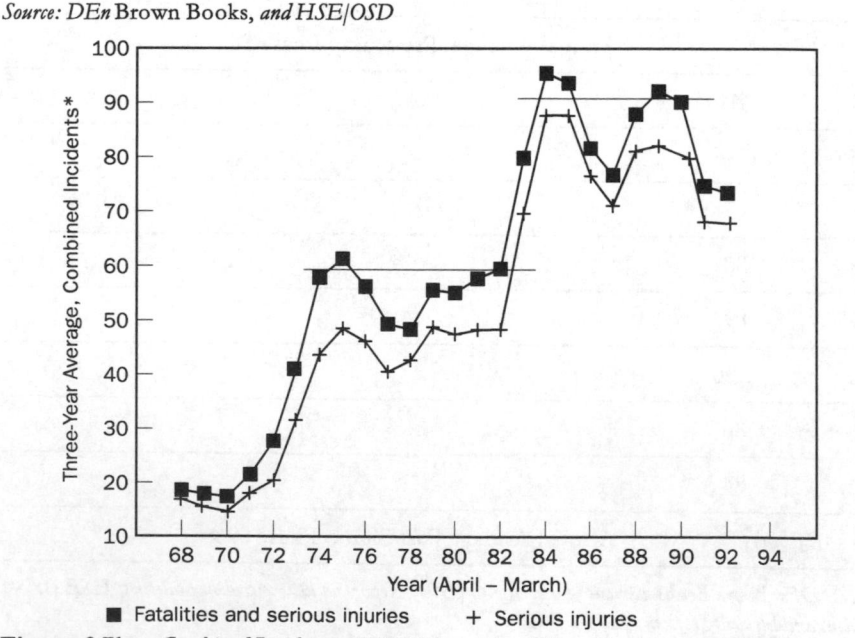

■ Fatalities and serious injuries   + Serious injuries

Figure 8.7b   *Combined Incidents – UK Offshore Sector, Three-Year Average 1968–92*
*excluding Piper Alpha
Source: DEn Brown Books, and HSE/OSD

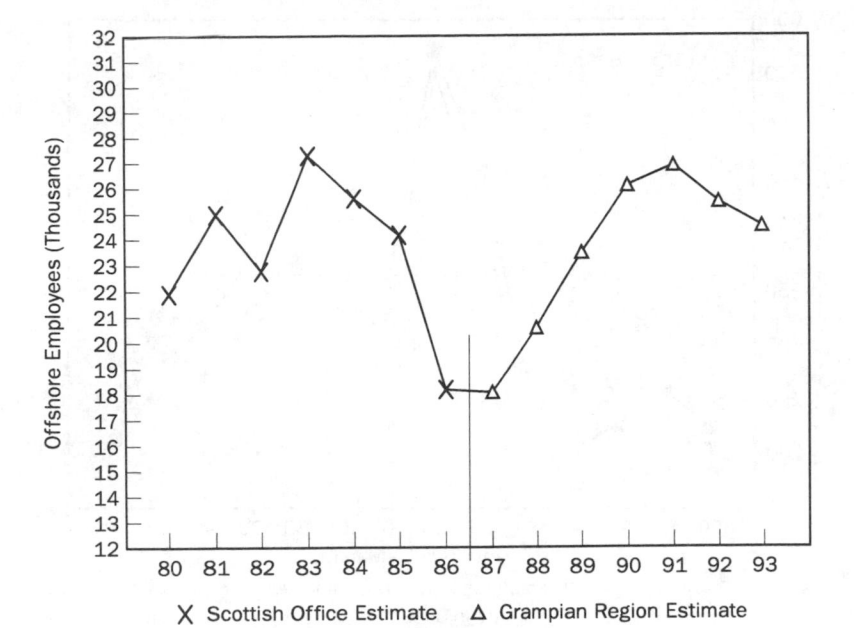

Figure 8.8   *Composite Offshore Workforce Count 1980–93*

Grampian Region employment figures (Grampian Regional Council, 1994) and figures collected by the Scottish Office (Scottish Office, Industry Department, 1993). There is some indication that the Grampian figures, which represent the most reliable offshore employment estimates for more recent years, underestimate offshore employment in the early 1980s up until 1986. According to Scottish Office production and output figures, the output index for the year 1985 exceeded that for 1990 (Scottish Office, 1995, Table 3). Yet Grampian Region's estimates report an offshore workforce of only 21,200, that is 5000 workers less than the 1990 figure of 26,200. In order to compensate for this underestimation we have combined Scottish Office employment figures up until 1986 with Grampian figures from 1987 onwards (see Figure 8.8). The combined workforce estimate of Figure 8.8 represents our best estimate of the workforce, which we utilize for our calculation of combined incident rates.

Figure 8.9a shows the combined incident rates for the years from 1980 to 1993, calculated from the raw data on fatalities and serious injuries divided by our time series of workforce employees (see also Table 8.10). The previous caveats apply with regard to the 1993 figure. Using these figures the plateau pattern of a low pre-1984 accident regime and a high post-1984 accident regime

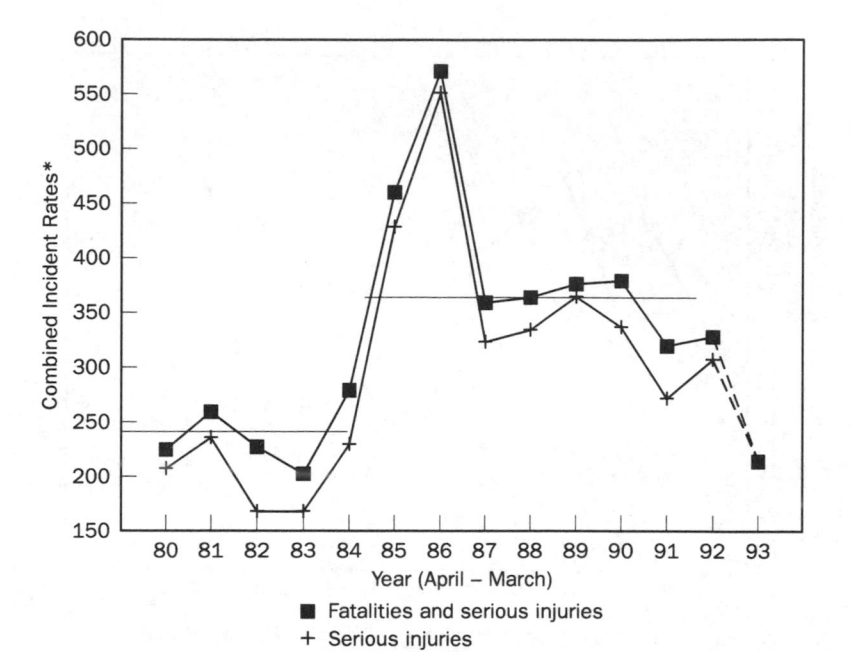

Figure 8.9a   *Combined Incident Rates – UK Offshore Sector per 100,000 Employees 1980–93*
*excluding Piper Alpha
Source: DEn Brown Books *and HSE/OSD*

is even more pronounced, with a massive spike in the combined incident rate
in excess of 550 incidents per 100,000 employees occurring in 1986. The years
following 1986 up until 1992 display a lower rate of incidents, yet the rates
remain significantly above pre-1984 levels. This pattern is confirmed when
rates based on the three-year average of combined incidents are plotted (see
Figure 8.9b). Here we see a more pronounced downward trend following the
year 1988. This decline is in part an artefact resulting from the inclusion of the
less reliable 1993 figure and should not be taken as evidence for a substantive
downward trend which converges with 1983 levels.

While this broad analysis locates the post-Piper Alpha reconstruction in
the high plateau of a degraded safety environment, it does not allow for an
explicit comparison of pre- with post-Piper Alpha conditions. In testing the
impact of the early period of regulatory reconstruction, we have used five
years of post-Piper Alpha safety statistics (1989–93) which can be compared
to the pre-Piper Alpha period (1984–88). This time frame should allow us to
give some indication of the comparative safety record of the two periods.

Table 8.11 lists the raw data for combined incidents, that is, fatalities and
serious injuries, for the years from 1984 to 1993 inclusive. Fatalities and serious

Table 8.10 *Combined Incident Rates (fatalities and serious injuries) per 100,000 Employees 1980–93*

Year	Workforce	Source	Comb. Incidents	Raw Rate	Average	Rate with 3 Year Average Combined Incidents
1980	21,875	[Scot. Office]	49	224		254.48
1981	25,125	"	65	259		220.23
1982	22,925	"	52	227		251.54
1983	27,500	"	56	204	pre 1985:	218.18
1984	25,825	"	72	279	238	308.49
1985	24,125	"	111	460		396.55
1986	18,200	"	104	571		512.82
1987	23,650	[Grampian Region]	65	275		350.95
1988	23,175	"	80	345		336.57
1989	23,600	"	89	377		379.94
1990	26,200	"	100	382		349.87
1991	27,000	"	86	319		333.33
1992	25,500	"	84	329	post 1985:	295.42
1993	24,500	"	53	216	363	

Notes:
With regard to incidents 1980 stands for April 1980 to March 1981.
Scot. Office workforce estimates represent the midpoint of a high/low estimate.
Data on Combined Incidents are from DEn *Brown Book*, and HSE/OSD reports (various eds).
Piper Alpha fatalities have been excluded.

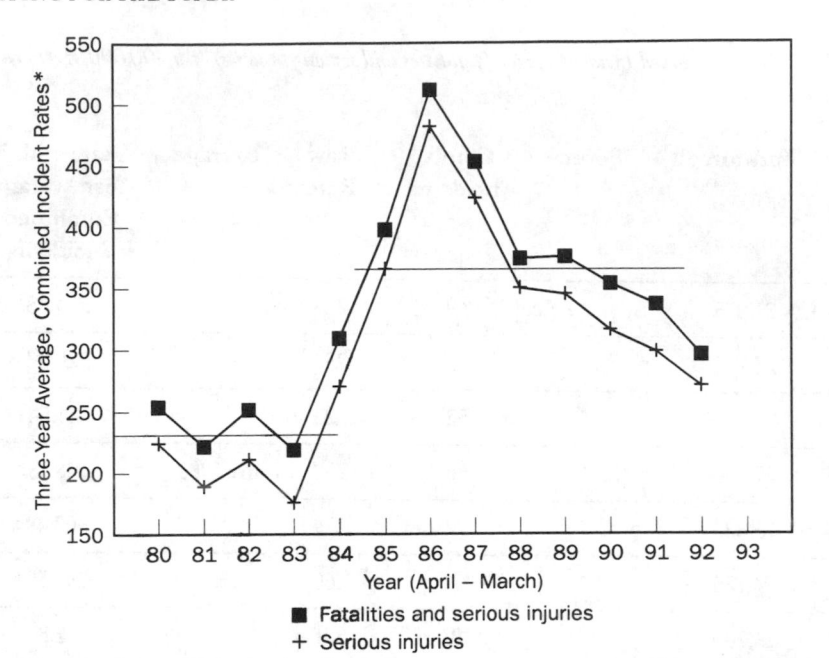

Figure 8.9b *Combined Incident Rates – UK Offshore Sector per 100,000 Employees, Three-Year Average 1980–92*
*excluding Piper Alpha
Source: DEn Brown Books *and HSE/OSD*

injuries resulting from the Piper Alpha disaster have again been excluded. Yearly counts represent incidents which occurred from 1 April to 31 March. The time series has been divided into a pre- and post-Piper Alpha section. In order to present a more detailed analysis of where precisely these accidents have occurred, the workforce has been disaggregated into three broad occupational groupings: (a) construction, maintenance and production workers, (b) drilling workers, and (c) workers employed in sea and air transport. We also present the aggregate data for all three groupings, which may be considered as particularly high risk.

Construction, maintenance and production workers face roughly comparable risks of slips, trips, falls and falling objects. Platform and exploration drilling workers commonly encounter a substantial risk of injury from the operation of machinery. Workers employed in sea and air transport have been grouped together as their activities are generically similar. Reported accident data include only incidents which occur on the installation itself or within a surrounding 500-metre zone.

For construction, maintenance and production workers, the annual average of combined incidents reported in Table 8.11 shows a small decrease from

Table 8.11 *Combined Incidents (fatalities and serious injuries) by Major Occupation Group 1984–93*

Year	Construction Maintenance Production	Drilling	Sea & Air Transport	All Three Groups
Pre Piper Alpha				
1984	18	7	7	32
1985	49	26	5	80
1986	38	15	10	63
1987	21	14	6	41
1988	31	27	4	62
Average	**31.4**	**17.8**	**6.4**	**55.6**
Post Piper Alpha				
1989	23	33	9	65
1990	18	32	11	61
1991	33	22	13	68
1992	39	25	3	67
1993	31	10	7	48
Average	**28.8**	**24.4**	**8.6**	**61.8**
Diff. Means Test				
T Value	0.38	1.17	1.11	0.67
P Value	Pre > Post	Pre < Post	Pre < Post	Pre < Post
one tailed	0.36	0.14	0.16	0.27

Source: HSE/OSD Offshore accident and incident statistics reports; Grampian Region survey data for employment (unpublished).

the pre- to the post-Piper Alpha period. A statistical test indicates that this decrease from the pre- to the post-Piper Alpha period is not significant. For drilling, however, there has been a substantial increase in the annual combined incidents of 6.6 per cent from the pre- to the post-Piper Alpha period, an increase which is possibly statistically significant. A similar increase in average annual incidents can be observed for workers employed in sea and air transport. The combined annual average incidents for all three groupings also shows an increase from the pre- to the post-Piper Alpha period; however, the statistical significance of this increase cannot be fully confirmed. However, overall there exists no indication yet for the *expected decrease* of incidents accompanying the new regulatory regime or the creation of a new 'safety culture'.

Again, we have recalculated the raw data on combined incidents of Table 8.11 into combined incident *rates* in Table 8.12. Currently, estimates of employment by broad occupation are utilized from Grampian Regional Council. While these data permit us to construct similar occupational categories as reported in OSD accident statistics, there are some problems resulting from the underestimation of the offshore workforce by Grampian statistics for the early to mid 1980s. This underestimation of the workforce, when used as a denominator, is likely to yield unrealistically high incident rates for the pre-Piper Alpha period, which will bias a comparison of incident rates in favour of the post-Piper years. The data in Table 8.12 nevertheless roughly follow the pattern established in Table 8.11, with some decline in the incident rates for construction, maintenance and production workers and an increase for drilling workers and workers engaged in sea and air transport. Again the average combined annual incident rate for all three groups shows an increase which in this case is not statistically significant. This is possibly due to the underestimation of the denominator in the pre-Piper phase. The data from Tables 8.11 and 8.12 are presented in Figures 8.10a and 8.10b respectively. Despite bias in the pre-Piper rate, our analysis of combined rates broadly confirms the patterns identified on the basis of raw data: there is no indication of a significant improvement in offshore safety in so far as fatalities and serious injuries in risky occupations are concerned. These long-term rates, although considerably more realistic than those of UKOOA, may well merit further refinement. The fact that they mirror the raw data may be taken as an indication of their general reliability.

Table 8.12 *Combined Incident Rates (fatalities and serious injuries) by Major Occupation Group1984–93*

Year	Construction Maintenance Production		Drilling		Sea & Air Transport		All Three Groups	
	Workers	Rate	Workers	Rate	Workers	Rate	Workers	Rate
Pre Piper Alpha								
1984	11,630	0.155	7400	0.095	2800	0.250	21,830	0.147
1985	10,280	0.477	7730	0.336	2800	0.179	20,810	0.384
1986	10,700	0.355	5750	0.261	2050	0.488	18,500	0.341
1987	11,200	0.188	4500	0.311	1950	0.308	17,650	0.232
1988	11,200	0.277	6200	0.435	2200	0.182	19,600	0.316
Average		**0.291**		**0.288**		**0.281**		**0.284**
Post Piper Alpha								
1989	10,500	0.219	6400	0.516	2200	0.409	19,100	0.340
1990	11,600	0.155	6900	0.464	2500	0.440	21,000	0.290
1991	15,600	0.212	7800	0.282	2400	0.542	21,900	0.311
1992	15,600	0.250	6800	0.368	2400	0.125	20,900	0.321
1993	15,500	0.200	5600	0.179	2300	0.304	23,400	0.205
Average		**0.207**		**0.362**		**0.364**		**0.293**
Diff. Means Test								
T Value	1.37		0.89		0.91		0.20	
P Value	Pre > Post		Pre < Post		Pre < Post		Pre < Post	
one tailed	0.12		0.20		0.20		0.43	

Sources: HSE/OSD Offshore accident and incident statistics reports; Grampian Region survey data for employment (unpublished).

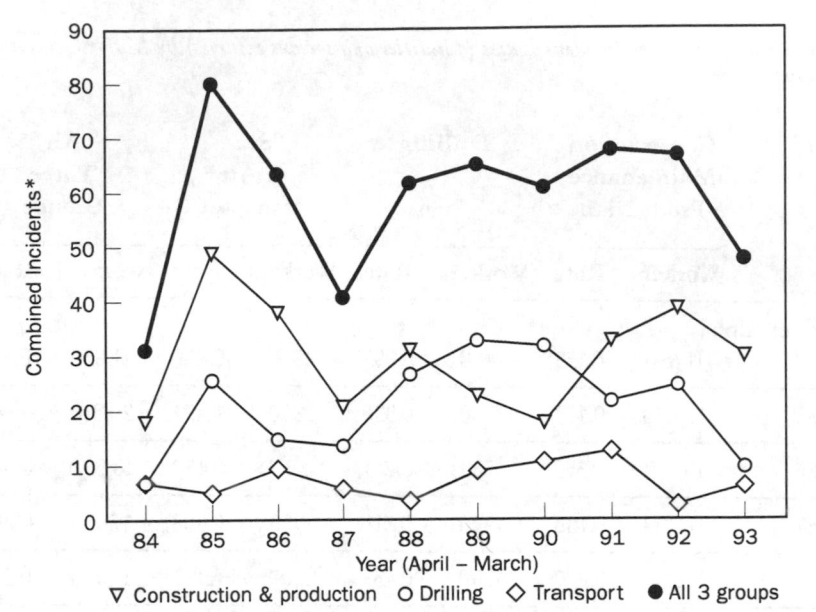

Figure 8.10a   *Combined Incidents – UK Offshore Sector by Major Occupation Group 1984–93*
*excluding Piper Alpha
Source: DEn Brown Books and HSE/OSD

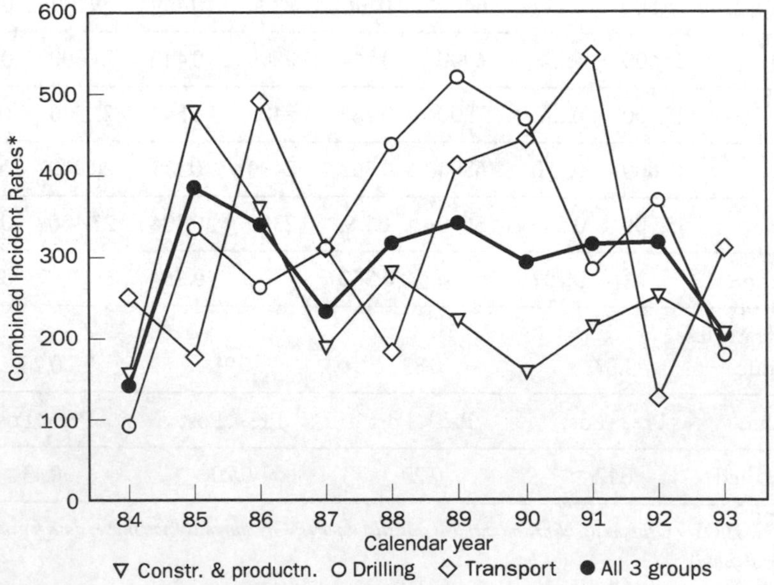

Figure 8.10b   *Combined Incident Rates – UK Offshore Sector per 100,000 Employees by Major Occupation Group 1984–93*
*excluding Piper Alpha
Source: DEn Brown Books, HSE/OSD, and Grampian Region

Recently the offshore operators have suggested that the downturn in reported incidents in the most recent period (1994/95) indicates a substantial improvement in offshore safety (UKOOA, 1996). In the view of the operators this can be taken as proof of the overall viability of the Safety Case approach and the policies they claim to have implemented. To this our previous cautionary remarks on the validity of recently reported data apply. Today, it has to be conceded that, due to the recent implementation of the Safety Case, there are insufficent data points for its full evaluation. Any proper systematic quantitative analysis of the Safety Case regime must await further incident data over a much longer period, possibly even as much as a decade. The operators' portrayal of the current regime as the best of all worlds must therefore be regarded with caution. It is exemplified in the following quotation from Hughes: 'It is easy to overlook the improvements in safety performance which were already being achieved in the greater part of the UK sector, almost entirely as a result of the industry's own efforts' (Hughes, 1994b). This is clearly an argument for the virtues of industry-driven self-regulation, for which 'insufficient credit' has been given, as against new external regulatory impositions. The operators now appear to claim that the Safety Case approach which had been advocated by the industry at the Cullen inquiry in 1989/90 was already best-practice currency. If this had been the case, and the Safety Case was indeed as effective as the government and industry seem to believe, we should have expected to see substantial safety improvements even before the formal Safety Case regulations had been fully bedded in across the industry.

At the time of writing (1996) we have to conclude that if safety in relevant high-risk offshore occupations has worsened since Piper Alpha, it has not done so substantially. Most importantly, it has as yet not improved significantly. There are real grounds for concern that there will be an actual worsening of offshore safety in the near future, as the anticipated 'start-up effects' of new post-Cullen regulations are likely to wear off and the process of mutual accommodation between regulators and regulated is consolidated. The wider contextual dimension which we also need to take into account points to the possibility of a worsening of safety conditions due to cost-cutting. The CRINE programme, as well as the wider overall political tendency towards deregulation of health and safety in the UK, may impact negatively on the safety regime offshore.

In some sense, the drive to cost-cutting and its effects on safety represent a recurrent cyclical phenomenon in the offshore oil industry. Pike (1993) has addressed the dramatic effects of the 1985/86 downturn on the level of activity and the structure of the oil industry. This downturn had equally if not more dramatic effects on offshore safety. After several years of postponement of essential maintenance activities, a renewed investment cycle, resulting in an upturn in activity offshore, provided the context of the Piper Alpha disaster. In the wake of the disaster, a new imperative was established in terms of more rapid completion of previously postponed maintenance and costly new investment in safety technology. This investment took place against the background of a stagnant sales take, and contributed to the profits squeeze the industry experienced. Between 1989 and 1991 the cost of producing a barrel of crude in the UK sector rose from $2.50 to $4.00, significantly higher than in any other oil province. Figure 8.11 shows the price of Brent Crude, the price marker for North Sea oil, and the revenue of companies operating in the UK sector, for the years from 1976 to 1992. The massive drop in the crude oil price in the years from 1985 to 1986 was accompanied by a roughly proportional drop in oil revenues. From roughly 1988 onward, however, the decline in oil revenues in the UK sector continued, while the oil price recovered. Figure 8.12 shows that the massive increase in expenditures which the industry was facing from 1987 onwards, and which accelerated from 1988/89 onwards after Piper Alpha, could not be matched by rising sales. Given the mature character of its reservoir, as well as safety concerns, the UK oil province was, at least

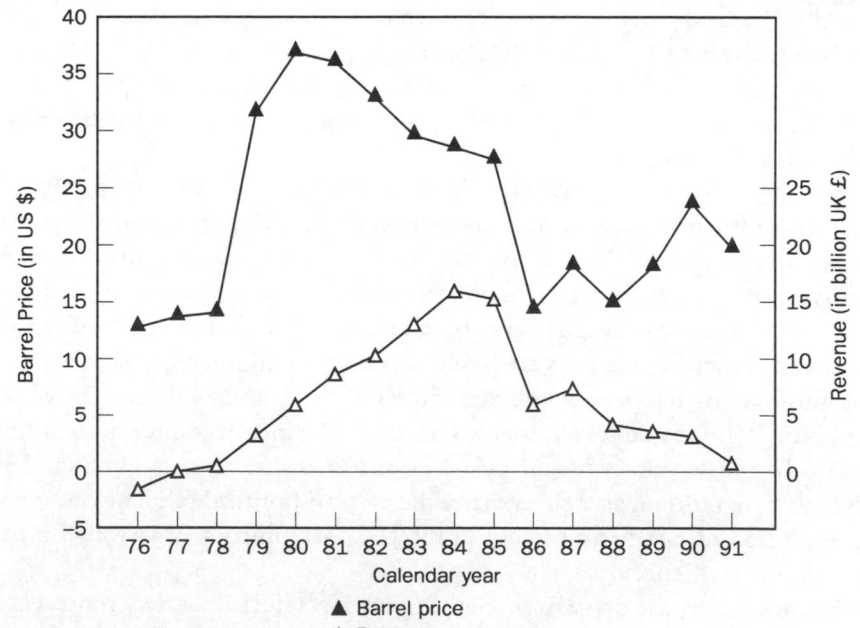

Figure 8.11 *Oil Price and Revenue – UK Offshore Sector 1976–91*
Source: DTI, Digest of UK Energy Statistics

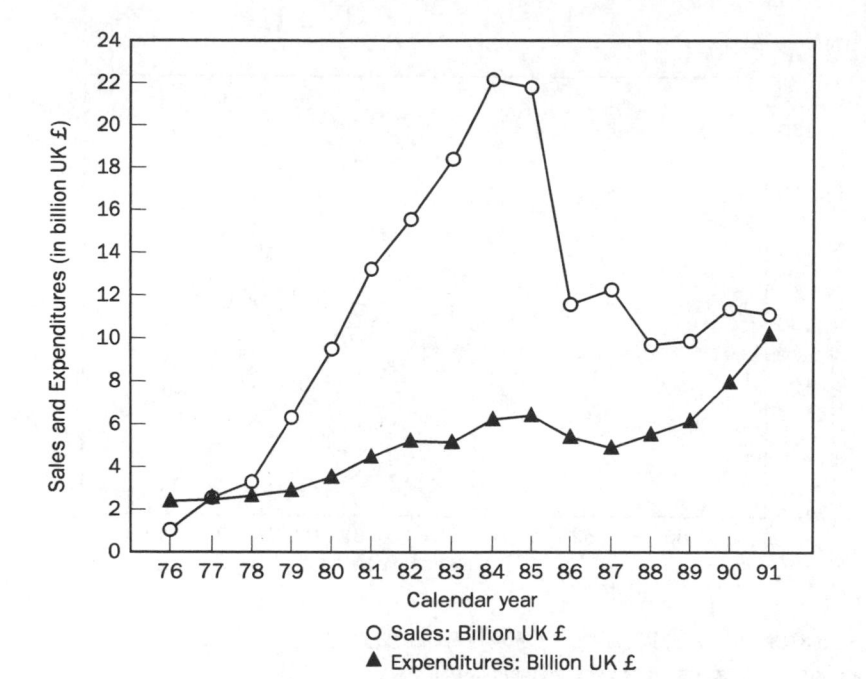

Figure 8.12 *Sales and Expenditures – UK Offshore Sector 1976–91*
Source: DTI, Digest of UK Energy Statistics

until the very recent period, unable to capitalize on the renewed increase of the oil price.

The effects of the employer-dominated offshore industrial relations system became apparent when the massive slump in the oil price cut profits by two thirds in 1985/86. Facing this sudden profits squeeze, the employers embarked on an unprecedented campaign of wage and benefits cuts which resulted in the complete erosion of the offshore 'wage premium'. Even where the workers had a collective agreement, as in the case of the Hook-up construction agreement, the unions were powerless to prevent a steady drop in wages (Figure 8.13). It is likely that this period of wage cuts was accompanied by increased pressure on the labour force, resulting in extended hours and reductions in time off.

Indeed, we would suggest that the dramatic increase in incidents post-1985/86 can be directly attributed to the intensification of the labour process; and even more, that there is an explicit correlation between the level of labour utilization and the levels of incidents. This relationship is visible when we use the relative wage of hook-up construction workers – the largest group for which we have wage data available – as an index of exploitation, or employer

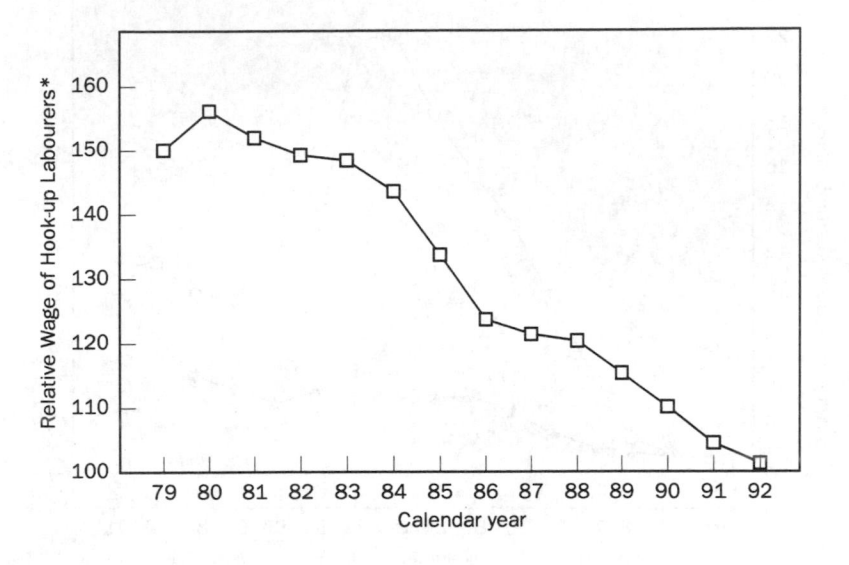

Figure 8.13 *Relative Wages – UK Offshore Sector 1979–92*
*calculated as percentage of average male earnings
Source: IDS Reports

power. Statistically, this index correlates very closely with the level of combined incidents previously plotted (see Figures 8.7a and 8.7b); or in other words, intensified labour utilization, measured by relative wage, explains most of the variation in accidents over the years at hand. This pattern is illustrated in the 'cluster effect' produced in Figure 8.14. Overall, the plot shows that as the relative wage rate declines, or workforce exploitation increases, accidents went up. When splitting our time series between the years 1984 and 1985, we can identify a move from a low-accident, relatively high-wage regime to one of high accidents and low wages. This dramatic bifurcation of clusters corresponds to the discontinuity in combined incident data earlier observed in the form of a new higher incident plateau following the 1985/86 downturn. It signifies a close link between industrial relations and occupational safety, in which a shift in the balance of power to the side of capital led to a decline in offshore safety. It could well be that the current CRINE programme will introduce similar future discontinuities, with concomitant deteriorated safety levels. What can be said with certainty on the basis of this analysis, is that whenever the industry's profits have been under pressure in the past, safety levels have been sacrificed to the concerns of the bottom line.

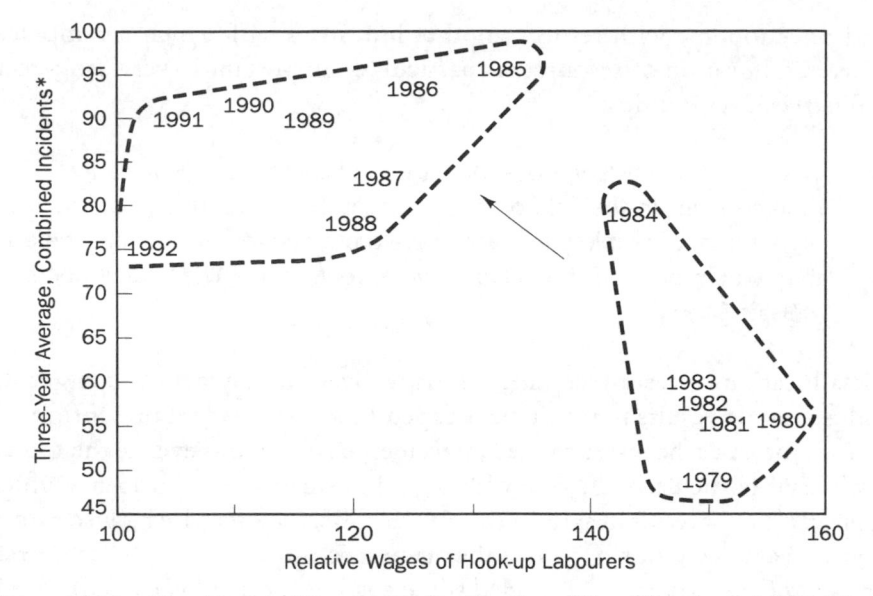

Figure 8.14 *Plot of Relative Wages by Combined Incidents (Three-Year Average) 1979–92*
*excluding Piper Alpha
Source: IDS Reports and HSE Annual Reports

The Costs of Accidents

Both the offshore industry and the regulator appear to have been preoccupied with output. Phillips (1976), an early critic of the Robens report, has
already stressed the neglect of 'economic deterrence' in the regulatory system
envisaged by the Robens Committee. Robens emphasized the need to create
voluntary compliance and self-regulation rather than reliance on 'negative'
punitive sanctions. This philosophy was intrinsic to the onshore regulatory
regime administered by the HSE. Economic deterrence, as a regulatory
device, would seek to reinstate consideration of 'the potential effectiveness
of economic sanctions in the promotion of safety' (Phillips, 1976: 148). Those
in favour of such deterrence argue that in the absence of realistic economic
sanctions, companies do not bear the true costs of accidents arising out of
employment. If they are not made liable for damages and, at the same time,
medical services are subsidized or free, distortions in the national distribution of resources will arise. As Phillips argues, 'Misallocation of accident
costs prevents the achievement of efficient allocation of productive
resources. Not only is the allocation between industries affected: so, within
a particular industry, is the allocation between safety and other inputs' (1976:
148). The absence of economic deterrence can result in output being too high

409

and price too low with respect to other industries with which it competes. This misallocation of resources is particularly important in very dangerous industries. Says Phillips:

> The distortion in dangerous industries is likely to have substantial repercussions in the field of safety, for the high level of output implies a higher level of employment and therefore a greater number of accidents than would occur if the industry were bearing its full accident costs. (1976: 149)

Misallocation of resources, then, leads to over-employment in dangerous industries and results in insufficient expenditure on accident prevention.

In some cases the losses created by accidents are obvious even to the industry. This is particularly the case with regard to smaller-scale incidents which typically do not result in serious injuries. Small incidents which cause minor injuries have been shown to cause the deepest commercial loss. An HSE draft of Safety Case regulations included some costings of small versus large accidents (HSE, 1992a). These showed that, whereas large accidents might cost the industry on average between £120 and £260 million per year (around £1 million per platform), small incidents which caused no major injuries cost around £940 million per year (around £3.75 million per platform). As Mac-Farlane (1993a) comments, 'The figure may not be precise, but the orders of magnitude probably are'.

From this analysis it may be concluded that the incidence of high-cost small accidents resulting in minor injuries can be reduced by tying the level of deterrence to the cost of accidents. The economic theory of law in such instances advocates the so-called 'cheapest cost avoidance rule' as determinant of the optimal level of deterrence. The cheapest cost avoidance rule was established by Calabresi (1970) with the purpose of allocating the liability for accident losses most efficiently. The result of accident in this view is that of a loss to victims and third parties, whereas preventing accidents requires consuming resources. Calabresi's rule asserts that the goal of accident law and deterrence must be to minimize the sum of these two costs. In other words, if the losses of accidents are high, and penalties on employers' negligence effect a substantial reduction in the accident rate, the fines imposed on firms should be high. If by contrast the losses due to accidents are comparatively small, and/or fines are unlikely to act as incentive to accident reduction, economic deterrence is pointless.

A recent HSE study (HSE, 1993c) provides estimates of the cost of health and safety management failures at a national level (see also Davies and Teasdale,

1994). Among the five organizations participating in this study were a construction firm, a food manufacturer, a transport company, an NHS hospital and a North Sea oil production platform, Chevron's Ninian Northern. The platform was staffed by between 100 and 120 people, including subcontractors. The study included only those accidents which participating organizations agreed could have been prevented by the application of existing procedures or other cost-effective measures. All accidents were costed irrespective of whether they caused injuries or ill health, and both direct costs and opportunity costs were taken account of, as well as whether the costs could be recovered from insurance. The results are summarized in Table 8.13. The data show that losses of a significant scale are incurred in all cases. Had the losses not been incurred, most of the money saved would have contributed to profits. Yet most of the costs could not be recovered from insurance cover, contrary to the employers' popular belief that they could (Le Guen, 1994: 32).

Table 8.13   *The Costs of Accidents in Selected Industries**

	Total loss (£000's)	Annualized loss (£000's)	Representing
1. Construction Site		245	700† 8.5% of tender price
2. Creamery	244	975	1.4% of operating costs
3. Transport Company	49	196	1.8% of operating costs 37% of profits
4. Oil Platform	941	3764	14.2% of potential output
5. Hospital	99	397	5% of annual running costs

*Figures quoted are actual at time of study; no adjustment has been made for inflation.
  Study 1 lasted 18 weeks; studies 2–5 for 13 weeks each.
†Represents total length of contract (54 weeks).
Source: HSE, 1993c, The Costs of Accidents at Work: 16

So far as the offshore oil platform was concerned, there were 262 preventable events in 13 weeks costing over £940,000. This was said to be equivalent to shutting the platform down for one day a week at a cost of around £3.75 million per year. Of these losses only one part in twelve was insured, thus around 48 days a year of production was being totally lost (MacFarlane,

1993a: 5). Le Guen (1994), the head of HSE's Risk Assessment Policy Unit, observed that the number of incidents is considerable; in most cases the average cost of individual incidents is small; but the ratio of events resulting in injury or ill health to those where only damage to property occurred was high (particularly so in oil production). In other words, looking at the sum total of accidents occurring in the firms, the case studies revealed that damage to persons vastly exceeded damage to property. This bears important consequences with regard to enforcement strategies, since employers will be primarily concerned with damage to their property. Compliance in these instances cannot be enforced on the basis of a cost-avoidance or cost-benefit rationale. In order to protect human life, avoiding potential property loss due to accidents has to be secondary to preventing suffering and harm to individuals and their families. Hence deterrence has to be based on sanctions sufficiently high not only to compensate the victims for losses but also to prevent the perpetrators from repeating the action which caused the accident.

This introduces a notion of culpability which is captured neither in current cost-benefit literature nor in the penalties imposed by the regulators or courts.

Further Cases for Corporate Killing

Today, culpability is often thought of in connection with issues of corporate crime (Wells, 1993; Pearce and Tombs, 1992). The unsatisfactory outcome of the trial arising from the *Herald of Free Enterprise* sinking has led to an intense public debate in which disaster action groups and the trade unions have pressed for urgent changes in the law (Bergman, 1993; TUC, 1995a). In this regard, the most recent report of the Law Commission on involuntary manslaughter signals a long-overdue recognition that the law in this area has been defective in terms of ensuring an appropriate penalty structure and attribution of blame (Law Commission, 1996). Both the Ocean Odyssey and the Cormorant Alpha disasters would seem to be appropriate examples of where a new charge of corporate killing could be considered.

Ocean Odyssey

Ocean Odyssey, or 'Ocean Oddity' as it was known to the men on board, was originally named Ocean Ranger II, but had changed its name after its sister rig Ocean Ranger I capsized off Newfoundland in 1982 with the loss of 84 lives. On 22 September 1988, a matter of three months after Piper Alpha, Ocean Odyssey blew up while drilling for oil 130 miles off Aberdeen. Timothy Williams the radio operator, on his first trip offshore, died at the age of 25 when the blowout engulfed the rig. He had no survival certificate and had not been given a safety induction into the rig's layout. During the emergency evacuation of the 67-man crew, shortly before it was engulfed in flames, he was ordered by the installation manager to return from his lifeboat to his station in the radio room. There he was trapped and eventually overcome after twenty desperate minutes. His last message was a plea for instructions to find a safe exit.

Just after Lord Cullen concluded the public inquiry into Piper Alpha in Aberdeen, Sheriff-Principal Ireland had embarked upon what turned out to be the longest and, at £5 million, most expensive Fatal Accident Inquiry (FAI) in Scottish legal history. The Ocean Odyssey FAI in 125 days of evidence opened to scrutiny the exploration and drilling side of the industry, paralleling aspects of Lord Cullen's investigation into the management practices on the production side. Both catalogued a flagrant disregard for the safety and welfare of the offshore workforce. What was revealed was an industry where the huge financial outlays in the exploration for oil had generated a routinely reckless culture of risk-taking in which the shutting-down of operations was almost unthinkable. There was much talk at the Ocean Odyssey inquiry by Arco, the drilling company to whom Odeco, the rig owners, had leased the rig, about 'deep water drilling at the frontier of technology', 'testing technology to the limit' and other such macho phrases designed to blur the line between exploration and excess.[30] The fact was Arco personnel were drilling a high-pressure well, which all their experience told them was inherently extremely dangerous. When signs of real trouble in controlling the well did appear, they appear to have been ignored long beyond the point of any regard for safety. Eight days before the blowout, the rig had been visited by a DEn inspector who had found nineteen faults.

The two companies, Arco and Odeco, were less than helpful during the FAI proceedings. Sheriff-Principal Ireland was unable to compel either four senior Arco personnel, or Odeco's installation manager, to appear before the inquiry. As persons not resident in Scotland they could not be forced to attend an FAI. Arco appeared consistently unwilling to instruct its employees to testify. At one stage the court attempted the unique step of travelling to Eire to hear evidence on commission from Arco's drilling supervisor, Jack Browne. Lacking the testimony of the key individuals added substantially to the difficulties facing the inquiry. At least two of the Arco personnel were reportedly still employed by the company in Norway and Indonesia, while

Odeco's installation manager, a US citizen, was believed to be still working for that company in the Far East.

Much of Arco's case sought to reject allegations of negligent behaviour and shift the focus of blame onto an alleged equipment failure of the rig's crucial blowout preventer component. Evidence was given of lack of management co-ordination and communication, and of the disregard of basic safety procedures on the rig. It emerged that a welder had been so terrified at the amount of gas escaping that he had been unwilling to light his torch. Eventually, after nights without sleep, he succeeded in being 'medivac'd' off the rig. On the morning of the explosion senior drilling staff, previously under severe pressure from shore-based management to get results, had heated arguments amongst themselves as to whether to shut the well down.

When Sheriff-Principal Ireland's carefully considered 67-page findings were eventually delivered, they detailed 'flagrant error of judgement' and 'reckless disregard for the safety of the men on board' (Ireland, 1991: 8 and 55). Arco dismissed these criticisms as 'lamentable'. The Sheriff observed that Arco had only fortuitously been compelled to lay the evidence gleaned from its own technical inquiry before the court. This was as a result of the presence in Scotland of the one senior Arco representative, the operations manager, responsible for compiling it. Such a general unwillingness to assist the FAI was described by the Sheriff as 'deplorable'. Had such a statement come from a private individual, said Arco's managing director, the company 'would be seeking legal recourse at this time'.[31] This was probably sufficient provocation for the Crown Office to seek a *criminal* prosecution in the Scottish High Court, again a first in Scottish legal history involving an offshore oil company, for breaches under the Mineral Workings Act and the Health and Safety at Work Act. It was remarkable also because, unlike the English Coroner's Court, a Fatal Accident Inquiry does not determine whether there is a criminal case to answer, but rather seeks to establish the precise cause of death with a view to making recommendations to prevent a recurrence of a similar fatality. Fatal Accident Inquiries are typically held *after* any prosecution has been disposed of, or when criminal proceedings are not contemplated, as attendant publicity could prejudice subsequent proceedings. However, in this case the public clamour for a prosecution in relation to Ocean Odyssey might have made action of some sort hard to avoid.[32] On conclusion of the prosecution, Arco, the drilling operator, was eventually fined the record sum of £250,000 in August 1993, while Odeco, the rig owner, was fined £25,000. The fine for Arco represented 0.03 per cent of the annual profits for the previous year of the parent company Atlantic Richfield, hardly a deterrent which could effectively prevent similar future transgressions. Moreover, in several contemporary cases including one against Atlantic Drilling resulting in a fine of £100,000 following a fatality, this amount was halved on appeal. The legal power to compel the attendance of witnesses at a Fatal Accident Inquiry has still not been secured. This situation leaves the Scottish judiciary at a continuous disadvantage when faced with a footloose multinational industry and its elusive managers.

It took twenty months from the date of the disaster for the Ocean Odyssey inquiry to be set up, and it took a full five years before the courts imposed penalties on the companies responsible. Such protracted proceedings are by no means unusual. In the 1970s Carson had noted similar delays in holding Fatal Accident Inquiries, compounded it would appear by considerable administrative and jurisdictional problems. The latter arose from the uneven and protracted development of offshore safety law, the different procedural requirements of the Scottish legal system and the lack of familiarity with these in the London-based DEn (Carson, 1982: 258–67). Not all of these problems had been resolved despite the passing of the Fatal Accidents and Sudden Deaths Inquiry (Scotland) Act 1976. A norm of two years or more before holding an FAI has remained fairly constant throughout the history of the North Sea.

In November 1993, an Aberdeen sheriff publicly criticized a delay of three years in bringing a prosecution following an offshore fatal accident when he imposed a fine of £75,000 on a drilling company for breach of Section 3 of HSWA. The company concerned was once again Odeco Drilling (UK). It transpired that since the fine of £25,000 imposed as a result of the Ocean Odyssey fatality in August 1993, Odeco Drilling (UK) had been wound down as a company. It was now lying dormant with no or few assets and the realistic prospect of recovering the fine was thought to be remote. The assets of the company had been transferred to the Diamond M Corporation, to whom Odeco's holding company Murphy Oil had disposed of its drilling operations in January 1992. A perusal of Odeco Drilling (UK) Ltd.'s 1991 company accounts, prepared by auditors Peat Marwick, covering the last complete year of the company's operations, is less than revealing. These are the statutory lodged accounts of a UK-domiciled subsidiary of a foreign-owned and controlled company.

In 1993, Odeco received a (self-nominated) British Safety Council award for its lost time accident record over the previous decade. Meanwhile, the outstanding £75,000 fine was paid in December 1993. Presumably it amounted to a small amount in terms of Murphy Oil's annual profits of $110 million and overall capitalization of $1.9 billion. It did not warrant the further negative publicity or possible legal impediments on future activities which non-payment might have entailed. Nevertheless, there was no strict legal obligation to make payment of the fine, as a result of the intervening corporate restructuring. Some of the delay in bringing the Ocean Odyssey case to court may well be attributed to the fact that the original incident investigation occurred while the DEn was still the responsible agency. In the aftermath of the Odeco prosecution, the HSE was keen to point out that if it investigated an incident in the Scottish sector of the North Sea which it felt warranted prosecution, it would forward a report to the Procurator Fiscal. The Fiscal's office would then decide on whether to proceed to court, the matter then being out of the hands of the HSE. The appointment of a full-time Fiscal (prosecuting officer) in Aberdeen, with the oil industry as a specific remit, could be seen as a step towards more prompt action by the legal authorities, although it is by no means clear that a more pro-active prosecution strategy has been formally sanctioned. Nevertheless, the following remarks by the Senior Procurator Fiscal Depute appointed for this task are an indication that issues of corporate responsibility are now given some importance. With the discomfort caused by cases like Ocean Odyssey very much in mind, he has observed, 'It is a pity that we cannot more directly link Company Directors to actions for which they are responsible and which are carried out at their behest within the corporate concern, when it is applicable.'[33]

Cormorant Alpha

A different illustration of possible corporate culpability and the difficulties in prosecuting companies which operate in the offshore sector is given by the Cormorant Alpha disaster.

On 14 March 1992, Bristow's Super Puma G–TIGH with seventeen men on board crashed into the sea near the Cormorant Alpha whilst shuttling to the nearby Safe Supporter accommodation barge. The Safe Supporter barge, normally connected to the platform, had pulled away from the platform some 72 hours previously, due to storm damage to its moorings. As soon as G–TIGH hit the sea it turned turtle and rapidly sank. There was no time to pull out the life rafts stowed inside the cabin, although incredibly one did break free and, partially inflated, allowed some men to cling to it and survive. Eleven men lost their lives in what should have been a routine two-minute flight. The appalling weather included one of the longest periods of freezing recorded in over six years. Wave heights in the North Sea exceeded eleven metres and winds were gusting to 65 knots. Two reports, one from the Fatal Accident

Inquiry held by Sheriff Jessop of Aberdeen and another from the Department of Transport's Air Accident Investigation Branch (AAIB), put most of the blame on the dismissed commander, Captain Jonathan Shelbourne. In turning the aircraft away from the strong gusting wind he had inadvertently allowed the airspeed, and the height of the helicopter, to decrease. Remedial action taken in the last seconds of the flight was insufficient to prevent the ditching. A survivor said, 'it was like a car going down hill out of gear'.[34] Both reports agree that the freezing blizzard conditions were not the cause of the accident; but they are at variance on the significance of the weather in the chain of events that led up to the disaster. Sheriff Jessop completely discounted it, saying: 'There is no reason why the flight should not have been safely carried out with reference to the weather conditions.' The Air Accident Investigation Branch report of May 1993 suggested that the flight should not have taken place at all.

It is an essential feature of the certification of the Super Puma that flight in cloud, fog, snow or rain must not take place in sub-zero temperatures unless there is a 500 ft layer of warm air above the surface of the sea into which the aircraft can descend and shed accumulated ice. It is also a requirement that the commander, prior to take-off, plan the flight. He is required to have regard to the performance capability of the aircraft and the weather expected en route. The AAIB report suggests that there was little possibility of the flight being carried out in accordance with the flight manual in this regard. Meteorological reports obtained by the crew prior to departure showed snow showers and sub-zero temperatures from sea level up. What the reports did not show was the presence of an unusual turbulent Arctic weather formation approaching the Cormorant Alpha. This is known as the Polar Low, a weather system only encountered once in several years. An urgent telex warning of the imminent approach of such a Polar Low, logged into the Cormorant Alpha radio room, was not passed to the pilot. Even without this, it was the coldest day recorded by the offshore weather service since record-keeping began. Helideck fire monitors were frozen solid on at least three other platforms in the area.[35] Hence there seems little doubt that the flight should never have taken place, given these weather conditions.

The explanation of why it did may be found in documents obtained by *Blowout* — documents which were never presented in evidence to the Fatal Acident Inquiry or to the AAIB. Read in conjunction with the AAIB report these point to conclusions which are disturbing. Says the AAIB report: 'A major factor in the accident was a hasty and ill-considered flight manoeuvre', but other factors include the commander's 'position of responsibility in the company'. Captain Shelbourne, in addition to being the commander of

G–TIGH, was Chief Pilot at Sumburgh Airport, responsible to Bristow's General Manager (Scotland) for the commercial and administrative management of the operation there. His other responsibilities included liaison with the client Shell Expro. Extreme weather had curtailed routine flying, with the two in-field aircraft based in the Brent Field in their hangars. Freight was required on the Brent Alpha and personnel required to be shuttled around the field including Cormorant Alpha. G–TIGH was on contract, and Shell requested it be used to the maximum. The limiting factors to this included the weather reports which showed an absence of the required 500 ft band of positive-temperature air over the sea. The assessment had to be made by whoever was to agree to the client's requested flying programme. It was the helicopter commander who did so, without reference to any superior authority. He was, as the AAIB report points out, effectively his own superior. As base manager, the relationship between Bristow and Shell fell very much within his ambit of responsibilities. He was required to maximize the company assets. The flight appears to have taken place in contravention of the relevant airworthiness directives despite the fact that, as the AAIB observes, it 'was not required under an emergency situation, and the maintenance of a public transport standard was paramount, even at the expense of perceived commercial emphasis'. A 'commercial emphasis' was implicated in the decision to undertake the flight to the Shell field. Had vital freight not been delivered, the Brent Alpha might have had to shut down the following day. In Captain Shelbourne's mind, there may have been little doubt as to what the company required of him in these circumstances.

In the unusually cold period from 11 to 14 January 1987, the meteorological reports show the North Sea to have been dominated by an intense anticyclone over Norway. The situation was unstable and unusually cold, with a Polar Low again developing to the north. Throughout that week heavy snow and hail showers were prevalent with warnings of airframe icing of moderate to severe extent in shower cloud. The question can be raised as to whether Bristow continued to fly its helicopters in contravention of the airworthiness directive relating to flying in icing conditions during this period. Moreover, the company appears to have picked up extra business due to the fact that competitors' helicopters did not fly. Senior Bristow managers expected its pilots to fly. The Area Manager, Mr A. MacGregor, had issued a memorandum to pilots on 16 January 1987. In this he congratulated those pilots who continued operations during the spate of bad weather. It was, he said, 'most laudable'. The memorandum went on to say, 'we flew over one hundred hours "ad-hoc" during the week and stole a march on other operators by our endeavours' (internal memo, A. MacGregor to D. Smith, 16 January 87). In 1992,

MacGregor was promoted to Deputy Managing Director of Bristow. The question being asked in the aftermath of the Cormorant Alpha crash was whether a company enthusiasm to 'steal a march' on competitors, exhibited in 1987, did not also colour the decision to fly G–TIGH on the night of 14 March 1992?

Since the tragedy, Shell on its own initiative has introduced an Adverse Weather Working Policy, uniquely so amongst North Sea operators. Despite employers' persistent denials that disciplinary action had been taken against workers who refused to fly because they feared for their safety, contrary evidence has emerged. One contractor employee, Tommy Roe, who died during the disaster, had previously received a written warning from Press Offshore (now AMEC) for reluctance to board a helicopter in bad weather. Tommy Roe's offence was described as, 'Failure to accept instructions from HLO (helicopter landing officer) prior to boarding helicopter'. This unfortunate individual was 'reminded' that 'any future misconduct or poor performance will be dealt with in accordance with the disciplinary procedure'.[36] An AMEC company memo from senior management on the beach instructed that written warnings 'issued to potential NRBs' had to be adequately filed. Tommy Roe and his fellow workers knew the inevitable consequences for their jobs of further protests.[37] As the Fatal Accident Inquiry got underway it transpired that several men had expressed apprehension about the flight. The Cormorant Alpha Helicopter Landing Officer (HLO) maintained no official complaint had been made to him. Tommy Roe, who had received the written disciplinary warning, had himself complained repeatedly at being made to sit in a seat he regarded as particularly unsafe. This was colloquially known as the 'dead man's seat'. It was an additional and cramped middle seat at the rear of the helicopter from which easy access to escape routes was restricted. Its use has subsequently been discontinued from Super Puma North Sea flights for Shell.

Five of the deceased were recovered along with the wreckage. Six more died on the surface while awaiting rescue. The six survivors claimed that but for the survival suits all would have perished in the freezing waters. One survivor had lasted more than 90 minutes in the sea. This in turn provoked the question as to why rescue had taken so long to carry out. First on the scene, some twenty minutes after the alarm was raised, was the standby vessel, closely followed by a Norwegian supply vessel. The sea was so rough that the standby vessel could not launch its fast rescue craft. The Norwegian supply vessel played a crucial role. One of its crew, with only a rope tied round him, dived into mountainous 50-foot waves in a repeated attempt to rescue a survivor. Counsel, press and onlookers at the Fatal Accident Inquiry were ordered to stand by Sheriff Jessop as the whole court applauded the bravery of Norwegian seaman Knut Rogne.

During the inquiry there was some concern at the time taken to mount the rescue operation. The Norwegian helicopter pilot based on the Gullfaks accommodation vessel had offered immediate assistance in response to the Mayday call put out from the Cormorant Alpha. He claimed he could have been at the scene fifteen minutes earlier but had remained on standby for those vital minutes after the initial offer of help was refused. Shell's own two in-field helicopters in the Brent Field were on the Safe Gothia in their hangar. One was out of commission awaiting a parts delivery from the fateful Super Puma, while the other helicopter took 40 minutes to deploy in the emergency. This was the only offshore-based dedicated rescue helicopter in the UK's northern sector of the North Sea. There was no regulatory requirement for such a Search and Rescue helicopter to be in place. This was not the case, however, for the installation standby vessel. The Offshore Installations (Operational Safety Health and Welfare) Regulations (SI 1976, No. 1019) require the installation Helicopter Landing Officer 'to have ensured that before any helicopter lands or takes off, the vessel standing by to render assistance to the installation has been informed that helicopter operations are to take place'. The Fatal Accident Inquiry heard that, in contravention of these regulations, it was not the current practice on any Shell installation to inform the standby vessel of helicopter movements (Jessop, 1993: para 26.4). The Cormorant Alpha installation manager, whose ultimate responsibility it was, admitted that he did not ensure that these regulations were complied with. Nor did the senior Shell Helicopter Landing Officers who carried out periodic audits of the on-board Helicopter Landing Officers. The standby vessel, *Seaboard Support*, was in fact two miles away attempting to avoid the weather. Had it not been so, 'the death of some of the survivors of the accident might have been prevented' said the Fatal Accident Inquiry report (1993: para 36.5). Nevertheless, no charges were laid against the operator for regulatory breach, it being deemed 'not in the public interest'.

The Cormorant Alpha Fatal Accident Inquiry was an in-depth inquiry into this important area of North Sea safety. The Chinook crash inquiry had been very much more restricted in its scope, dealing primarily with the contributory influence of technical modifications to the aircraft. Sheriff Jessop was to pay tribute to the role of counsel for the bereaved at the Cormorant Alpha inquiry, in opening up a range of issues upon which he was able to make observations in his final determination. Six of the victims were members of the electricians' union. On the eve of the inquiry, Paul Gallagher, general secretary elect of the EETPU, and one of the TUC appointees on the Health and Safety Commission, wrote to the relatives intimating that the union now intended to withdraw legal representation since, 'based on previous experience of fatal accident inquiries, the cost of representation would not materially affect the outcome of your claim for compensation.'[38] The union had estimated that it would cost £150,000 to provide representation. For the widows of the victims the point was not simply the amount of compensation, but rather the desire to see justice done and to ensure that the truth be exposed. OILC, which had four members on the flight, two of whom died, stepped in with legal representation for all of the deceased and survivors with the exception of the captain and co-pilot, who were each independently represented by counsel appointed by the pilots' union, BALPA. The EETPU view of OILC's intervention as revealed by Pat O'Hanlon, its Scottish Executive Councillor, is quoted:

> Nobody can alter the technical fact-finding work of the Fatal Accident Inquiry. All OILC is doing is displaying a fine turn of amateur dramatics to try to boost their recruitment efforts offshore. This cynical manipulation of people's emotions should be rejected.[39]

An interest-free loan of £30,000 to OILC from the Statoil Club of OFS, the Norwegian offshore union, enabled solicitor for OILC, Sandy Kemp, to be fielded at the inquiry. Sheriff Jessop noted that without the presence of such counsel 'much of the evidence would not have been properly tested' (1993, para 41.2). The questioning of witnesses 'brought out many points which might prevent a similar accident occurring in the future' (1993: para 41.3). It would have been 'unfortunate had they not participated in the inquiry on the ground of cost' (1993: para 41.2). Sheriff Jessop recommended a change in the law to allow the granting of legal aid or the award of expenses to those with 'limited means but with a real interest' in such inquiries. The crippling legal costs of representation at such enquiries has already been highlighted by Sheriff Risk in his Determination on the Brent Spar disaster. The government subsequently chose, however, not to amend the legal aid provisions in line with Sheriff Jessop's recommendation. The decision of the Procurator Fiscal's office not to prosecute, despite Shell's apparent admission of breach of regulations with respect to standby vessel precautions, was surprising.

The relatives of the victims and the survivors embarked on litigation against Bristow in the UK, and then in the courts of Texas and Louisiana against Shell and Exxon, Esso's US parent company. They were seeking compensation beyond that which, under the outmoded Warsaw convention on aviation accident compensation, restricts payment to those involved in a civil aircraft disaster to a sum in the region of £90,000. With the prospect of US litigation, Shell sought and obtained interim interdicts in Scotland and injunctions in England against bereaved families and survivors, some 63 individuals in all. They were to be prevented from pursuing an award in the American courts. Violation of this court order, Shell warned, could result in the families and survivors concerned being 'subject to bodily imprisonment'. Faced with such legal harassment, even case-hardened lawyers involved in the proceedings reeled in disbelief. Shell confirmed: 'the action reflects the company's belief that the appropriate forum for a resolution of this matter is Scotland'.[40] Any reference to imprisonment, said Shell, was 'legal jargon'.

Shell's attempt to block compensation cases in the US courts proved not entirely successful and the initial interdicts sought in the Scottish High Court and south of the border were recalled.[41] Then, in late December 1994, a Texas district court judge in Brazoria County ruled that Exxon ultimately controlled the Shell–Esso joint venture operating installations like Cormorant Alpha and was responsible for its aviation policy. Judge Neil Caldwell ruled that Exxon could be held to conduct its business from the State of Texas, despite the company's attempt to avoid jurisdiction being granted by 'moving' its registered headquarters in the US and other legal manoeuvres (Caldwell, 1994).[42] In Judge Caldwell's view there appeared to be:

> reasonable grounds to allege that the co-venturers SUKL/EEPUKL (Shell UK Ltd/Esso Exploration and Production UK Ltd.) appear to have been responsible for the crash of the G-TIGH because of their unrelenting push to reduce NPT (non-productive time) by way of reducing WOW (waiting on weather). By using the Super Puma G-TIGH (upgraded equipment) in storm conditions when WOW had previously caused NPT (non-productive time), the co-venturers (Shell/Esso) achieved their goal of reducing NPT and, not coincidentally, caused the death of eleven (11) men and permanent disability of a remaining six (6). (1994: para. 53)

The ruling potentially opened the way for US-level settlements to be awarded to the victims of the disaster, although further legal challenges from Shell/Esso continued. In April 1995 Shell/Esso and the relatives and survivors returned to the Court of Session in Edinburgh. The companies had obtained an interdict order prohibiting the survivors and relatives from taking any steps to secure transfer of the US proceedings from a Texas State court to a federal court. Now the survivors and relatives asked for the interdict against them to be withdrawn, as they had been threatened that if the transfer went ahead, they would be summoned for breach of interdict. There was also the threat of a £1 million expenses claim for costs incurred in defending the US proceedings. US attorneys acting for the deceased were described by Shell's QC as 'dogs straining at the leash'. The legal moves were justified as getting 'the handlers to order the dogs to sit down'.[43] Shell did attempt, unsuccessfully as it turned out, to have the interdict enforced. An article in Shell's house magazine for employees by Richard Wiseman, Head of Shell UK, Legal Division, put forward the company's position: 'We are not fighting Texas jurisdiction to avoid paying huge damages as has been alleged by the media on several occasions. Shell UK is a British company with no operations outside the UK.'[44] The ability of such oil companies to persevere financially, through long and tedious court battles, is unfortunately greater than that of the pursuers or plaintiffs. Judge Caldwell's initial determination of jurisdiction in favour of the latter could not detract from this crucial asymmetry. In the end, when faced with the imminent prospect of US court proceedings going ahead, Shell proposed an out-of-court settlement which was reached in early 1996, nearly four years after the disaster. As yet, the size of this settlement remains undisclosed. While the families received substantially greater compensation than they would have obtained in the British courts, the imposition of 'gagging clauses' left unanswered vital questions about corporate culpability.

Sheriff Jessop, at the Fatal Accident Inquiry, recommended that 'a review of helicopter safety in the North Sea 'be undertaken as a matter of urgency' (1993: para 38.9). The regulatory body was the Civil Aviation Authority (CAA). During the inquiry the CAA had admitted that it altered its minimum safety standards *only in response* to an accident or near-miss. It was given seven major areas of priority investigation. These were: restrictions on operations in adverse weather, the adequacy of in-field 'search and rescue' facilities, the positioning of standby vessels during shuttling, the mandatory use of survival suits, the effectiveness of life jackets in combination with survival suits, the automatic deployment of flotation bags on helicopters and the possibility of fitting externally mounted life-rafts to helicopters.

Up to half a million helicopter flights take place offshore each year. The announcement in November 1993 that the CAA had set up a review of offshore helicopter passenger safety and survivability was certainly welcomed by the workforce. As yet, the CAA was said to have failed as an effective regulator and appeared to lack familiarity with the rigours of helicopter travel in the offshore environment. One senior Bristow's pilot, with 27 years' experience of North Sea helicopter operations, has written:

The regulators: If I have one criticism of the CAA it is that it is getting more remote from the industry's need to grow and develop. All the bad weather work has been wasted. All the early low visibility approach minima and the offshore rig detection ranges were withdrawn in 1986 and have never been replaced.

I do not consider that many of the CAA airworthiness test pilots are competent in the operational use of helicopters. They should not be involved in the simulation of bad weather operations, which are entirely to do with the use of the aircraft, until they are competent and experienced in that area themselves. It is a fact that in the mid-1980s a CAA test pilot flying as co-pilot in the Super Puma said, 'I didn't realise that helicopters could operate in weather like this'. (Gordon, 1992: 11)

The review had come after three major disasters in the North Sea in six years, resulting in 62 helicopter fatalities. Overall, since 1969 a total of 113 men had died as a result of helicopter incidents in the UK sector of the North Sea, of which about three-quarters were not listed as oil-related fatalities. The clamour for such a review from unions and political figures was now irresistible. Evidence from an HSE investigation begun after the Brent Spar crash found aviation deficiencies in half of the 82 oil and gas installations surveyed. On two rigs, problems were so serious that the inspectors banned operations.

Shell had voluntarily taken the Brent Spar out of operation some time after the July 1990 tragedy. The installation was to achieve renewed notoriety in 1995 during its final decommissioning. Shell, with the support of the British government, but in the face of opposition from governments of other European countries, proposed to dump the installation and its toxic contents in the deep waters of the Atlantic. Harried by Greenpeace activists and a growing Europe-wide consumer boycott, Shell eventually capitulated and in the process exposed a damaging split with its co-venturer Esso which we examine in Chapter 11. The weight of expert scientific evidence was eventually to confirm Shell's estimate of sea-disposal for Brent Spar as less damaging environmentally than onshore disposal.[45] The episode focused public concern on Shell in such a way as to seriously undermine its carefully constructed environmentally-sensitive image. In their jubilation over Shell's climbdown, Greenpeace campaigners declared, 'Three months ago, no-one had heard of the Brent Spar . . . and look at it now'.[46] In the world of environmental activism this was probably true. In the world of the offshore workforce, however, Brent Spar, on which a total of nine men lost their lives, would remain yet another enduring memory of the human price of North Sea oil.

As the CAA review continued, issues of helicopter travel remained deeply contentious for the North Sea workforce, proving again the impossibility of a strict compartmentalization of safety and industrial relations. As the final submissions were being made at the Cormorant Alpha inquiry in January 1993, 30 workers who refused to board a helicopter shuttle to Piper Bravo in severe weather had their wages docked, in an act of retaliation by their employer.[47] Once again, elected safety representatives resigned in protest after the incident. Finally, on the Tiffany, in an incident previously referred to, nine men were suspended on the spot for similar reasons and were sent ashore without pay for three and a half weeks. Their crime had been to ask if Agip had an 'adverse weather policy' and whether, in the stormy seas prevailing, the standby vessel would be able to launch its fast rescue craft. The question was not unreasonable given what had occurred during the Cormorant Alpha disaster. The construction supervision had an answer to the men's concerns. In the time-honoured parlance of the North Sea, the responsible supervisor reportedly replied – 'How the *fuck* would I know?'

Sheriff Jessop recommended that all North Sea companies should 'consider the availability of rescue resources' in 'any safe system of work involving helicopter shuttling' in adverse weather (1993: para 37.7). The CAA review reported in March 1995 almost exactly three years after the disaster. It contained a number of recommendations, including suggestions to improve life-saving jacket design in response to criticism which emerged from those involved in the crash, and modification of cabin layouts of aircraft, as well as further research into helicopter crashworthiness and flotation capabilities. However, in relation to Sheriff Jessop's call for consideration of flying restrictions in bad weather, the report was contradictory. It argued both for managers to consider restrictions in adverse weather with an 'emphasis on the importance of comparing likely survival and rescue times at the most remote points of flight', but suggested that it would be 'impracticable' to specify 'the prohibition of offshore flights in weather unsuitable for ditching' (CAA, 1995).

In 1996 the role of helicopters in the North Sea became a renewed source of controversy. This followed the announcement by Shell, subsequently temporarily rescinded, that the Search and Rescue facility provided by the Bell 212 on the Safe Gothia for the Brent field was to be withdrawn, following completion of the refurbishment programme. This facility had played a major role in medical evacuation and rescue over the years, including the Cormorant Alpha disaster. It was to be replaced by reliance on the Coastguard S–61, located in Sumburgh, nearly one hour's flying time away. Shell's primary reason for withdrawal was cost considerations amounting to £4 million per year, a burden not shared by other operators using the facility.[48]

The Price of Regulatory Failure

The issue of corporate crime and negligence, its prevention and prosecution, is a matter of contention. This is perhaps nowhere more obvious than in the offshore environment, where corporate interests are particularly powerful, while the human toll of corporate negligence can be particularly high.

Today, views on how corporations who violate safety regulations should be dealt with differ widely. Yet within social and legal theory there are some common themes (Ginsberg, 1965). One such theme is that the type and scale of punishment should fit the type of crime committed (Silving, 1961). Serious offences resulting in considerable harm to society should be met with weighty sanctions, whereas minor offences whose resultant harm to society is small should be met with lesser sanctions.

According to this rule, offshore incidents such as the Chinook crash, the Piper Alpha explosion, the Brent Spar helicopter crash, or the Cormorant Alpha disaster, resulting in multiple deaths, or as in the case of Ocean Odyssey, where fortuitously there was one fatality and not more, should be met with stringent sanctions. Yet the sanctions which can be imposed on a wrong-doer are not unlimited. The natural desire for vengeance ultimately cannot provide a basis for legal and political action against a corporate wrongdoer. The concern of an enlightened morality is not to suppress the natural desire for vengeance, but to control or minimize it (Cohen, 1940). Equally however, corporate crimes cannot go unsanctioned. If corporations escape prosecution – as we observe offshore – for even the most blatant forms of misconduct, it will be difficult to uphold a sense of justice in the community by the formal repudiation of acts which violate accepted standards of conduct. Ultimately the punishment of corporate misconduct is necessary, not because it is a deterrent, but because it is the emphatic denunciation of a crime. Sanctioning the corporation is necessary, not because – as Calabresi (1976) suggests – there are measurable benefits from such sanctions, but because it is critical for a society to state that the negligent treatment of employees, the endangering of the workforce, is unacceptable.

From this perspective, the current offshore regulatory regime, with its focus on cost and benefits, is fundamentally flawed. The flaws of cost-benefit-based decision making, in the context of fatality risks, has been examined by Kelman (1981) and more recently by Dorman (1996). Kelman has suggested that the act of 'pricing' a condition or a risk, changes it fundamentally. By pricing an accident we lose our capacity to experience feelings such as horror or revenge, or similar attitudinal responses which can change our behaviour. Moreover, pricing alters the way individuals view themselves and society.

Unpriced values provoke solidarity since they are deeply rooted in the feelings and values we share as social beings. By introducing prices we reduce these values to the level of commodities towards which people are socialized to respond individualistically or competitively. The pricing of benefits and costs of accidents systematically excludes moral and social claims. It ultimately represents an antihumanist denial of the social nature of human beings and their rights.

The sanctioning of corporate misconduct crucially involves the preservation of workers' rights. From a moral point of view, a corporate crime is not a crime because it is denounced or penalized, but rather because there is a reason why it is condemned. Punishment is justified because there are rights which are worth defending. Concretely, the overriding aim of the denunciation of safety offences is not that sanction will improve the operator's conduct, but rather that certain rights must be protected – such as the right to a safe working environment and reasonable hours, as well as the right to refuse dangerous or unreasonable orders from management without recrimination or detriment (Durkheim, 1933).

The deeply disturbing implication of our analysis is that in the context of negligence and crime offshore, standards of justice have often been suspended and, as a consequence, the rights of workers have been undermined. In the very context where the defence of rights with regard to safety would have been essential, corporations have on the whole been able to escape serious penalty or prosecution. There are several reasons for this. Apart from factors such as the bias of an essentially conservative judiciary, and the government's aversion to sanctioning business, the operators' own conduct has played a principal role. From the inception of the industry, the oil majors have been unwilling to admit to any form of wrongdoing, even where substantial evidence was mounted against them. That such a policy of asserting non-guilt was adopted by individual operators and, later on, in the context of the Piper Alpha inquiry, by UKOOA, was not accidental. Asserting the infallibility of the operators was part and parcel not only of the justification of the enormous power oil majors had accumulated, but also of the close ties to the government which they entertained.

This position was helped by the legislator's own stance on health and safety in the workplace. Carson (1985) identified a historical trajectory in which the 'conventional' routes of strict-liability enforcement were substituted by Factory Acts which in their implementation shielded negligent employers from broader political recriminations and 'de-classed' health and safety issues. Although in Britain these Acts were replaced by broader legislation in the form of the Health and Safety at Work Act 1974, this pattern of decriminalization was effectively preserved. The Robens Report on Health and Safety at Work, the precursor of the Health and Safety at Work Act, suggested that '... any idea that standards generally should be rigorously enforced through the extensive use of legal sanctions is one that runs counter to our general philosophy' (1972: para. 255). Perhaps more revealing was Robens' view of corporate criminality. The report concluded that:

> the traditional concepts of criminal law are not readily applicable to the majority of infringements which arise under this type of legislation ... [Few offences] arise from reckless indifference to the possibility of causing injury ... The typical infringement arises rather through carelessness, oversight or lack of knowledge or means, inadequate supervision or sheer inefficiency. (1972: para. 261)

With its basic rejection of the view that employers offend through 'reckless indifference', Robens subscribed to a view of corporate negligence that amounted essentially to the wholesale decriminalization of corporate action (Woolf, 1973).

It was this view which at root informed the assumptions of the post-Cullen reconstruction. Lord Cullen's enthusiasm for Lord Robens' approach to health and safety legislation is a matter of record. In his keynote lecture to the Royal Society of Edinburgh, Lord Cullen (1996) concluded with a section entitled 'The Path to Self-Regulation'. This describes the evolution of UK safety legislation as a smooth trajectory moving from the Robens report, the Health and Safety at Work Act of 1974, to the offshore Safety Case regulations. For Cullen, self-regulation was desirable for several reasons, including above all the avoidance of over-regulation of the operators. This concern with the needs of the operators is perhaps most apparent when Cullen states that '... the more specific the language the greater the risk of it being over-rigid, obsolescent, unduly complex, let alone unable to cover every contingency' (Cullen 1996: 9). In the same section, Cullen specifically stresses that:

> It was considerations such as these [meaning the avoidance of over-regulation] which led me to recommend in the field of offshore safety [that] while there would be a continuing need for some regulation which prescribed detailed measures, the principal regulations should take the form of requiring that stated objectives are met. (Cullen, 1996: 9)

Underlying Cullen's view was a set of assumptions about employers which

Baldwin (1987) had earlier, in the context of Robens, described as the 'consensual paradox'. Said Baldwin:

> Consensual regulation, as well as assuming that optimal safety conditions coincide with optimal profit-maximizing conditions, is aimed at the well-informed, well-intentioned and well-organized employer, who would present few problems if left wholly to self-regulate. But many hazards relate to the ill-informed, ill-intentioned, and ill-organized employer who is left untouched by consensual regulation. (Baldwin, 1995: 153).

What is puzzling is that Lord Cullen applied the consensual regulation view to the offshore industry, where the preconditions for its successful implementation, even from evidence to his own inquiry, appear to be so tenuous. Offshore, as was particularly obvious in the 1986 oil price slump, safety and profits always stood in open conflict. At a 1994 conference on CRINE including Norwegian and UK regulators, oil industry executives and workforce representatives, Eric Brandie, Loss Prevention Manager for Chevron UK, stated openly that fashionable claims that 'good safety' was 'good business' were fundamentally flawed. Said Brandie:

> Some influential parties associated with the industry continue to argue that stringent safety and environmental standards make industry more competitive because, to the extent [that] they encourage companies to re-engineer their technology, they may result in processes that bring about higher standards of safety, whilst also lowering costs and/or improving quality. These arguments contribute to a belief that there need not be any trade-offs between expenditure on health, safety and environmental management issues, and company productivity and profitability.
>
> The 'win-win' rhetoric, although having tremendous appeal, may be somewhat unrealistic. The reality is that health, safety, and environmental costs in general, are rising substantially through the international scene, with little real economic payback guaranteed in a number of cases. (OFS/OILC, 1995: 44)

Apart from unrealistic assumptions about employers' attitudes towards safety matters, both Robens', and later on, Cullen's favourable view of self-regulation were based on a misconstruction of the 'prescriptive' approach to health and safety regulation. Baldwin argues that Robens overstated the extent to which the 'mandatory' model of enforcement applied before 1972. Without going into details, the false opposition of goal-setting to 'inefficient' prescriptive regulation is best illustrated by the US example. In the United States today, health and safety legislation is based on two components. One component is a system of primarily prescriptive regulations, and the other is collective bargaining on health and safety matters: that is, the inclusion of provisions requiring safety investment or workforce involvement in safety matters within plant-level agreements. As yet, no convincing evidence has been found which would suggest that this approach has harmed US competitiveness (Kelman, 1980; Dorman, 1996).

A 1993 International Labour Organisation (ILO) report on safety on offshore petroleum installations concluded that, although some goal-setting regulations have been introduced, the US system was 'in most respects the prototype of . . . a compliance regime': i.e., a system of prescriptive rule which specifies in some technical detail the characteristics of equipment and procedures that are thought to be required for safe operations (ILO, 1993: 54). This prescriptive regime is accompanied by an extensive inspection programme, which checks on the compliance of installation operators with all aspects of the regulations. Between 1990 and 1993 an average of 10,000 inspections per year have been conducted. Each drilling and production installation must be inspected at least once a year. For these mandatory inspections, advance notice is given. In addition, a minimum of 10 per cent of production installations and 50 per cent of drilling installations are inspected each year without notice, using the regulator's own fleet of helicopters. Operators are also required to record certain data and report these to the regulators. Of the approximately half a million individual items checked by the inspectors (including for instance 160 key components of a drilling rig), over 99 per cent of all items are typically found to be satisfactory. For the others, operators receive a citation requiring that the problems be corrected within seven days. If important enough, the inspectors will shut off a component part of an installation or close the entire complex down, a measure which has been imposed several times in the past. Serious violations that are 'knowing and wilful' can be subject to immediate criminal prosecution (ILO, 1993: 55).

Despite the complexity of the system, the ILO report concludes that the US offshore regulatory regime appears to meet with a reasonable degree of satisfaction on the part of the public and even the operators. Above all, the 'prescriptive' US regime serves the purpose for which it was designed, namely the avoidance of major accidents, as was noted in an independent comparative study carried out under the auspices of the US National Research Council in 1989 (ILO, 1993: 56). In 1991, for instance, the lost time injury frequency offshore for the US stood at 5.4 lost time and fatal incidents per million man hours, whereas its European counterpart was almost three times as high with 20.4. Although there are, as we have previously suggested, some problems with lost time injury measures, the sheer magnitude of this difference suggests that there are some advantages to the 'prescriptive' US regime.

Indeed, today there is – in the context of the corporate manslaughter debate – some evidence that many members of the legal community would prefer a US-style regime for the prosecution of industrial accidents. In its report on involuntary manslaughter, the Law Commission, for instance, takes a position which implicitly opposes the consensual views and practices of Robens and Cullen. The Law Commission recommends the introduction of the crime of corporate killing, where a death has been caused 'by a failure, in the way in which the corporation's activities are managed or organized, to ensure the health and safety of persons employed in or affected by those activities' (Law Commission, 1996: 110). To avoid the evasion of liability by the corporation – which has marked many previous prosecutions – the report further recommends that 'it should be possible for a management failure on the part of a corporation to be a cause of a person's death even if the immediate cause is the act or omission of an individual' (Law Commission, 1996: 112). In this context, the Law Commission recommends that the new offence of corporate killing should be applied to instances where 'the defendant's conduct in causing the death falls far below what could reasonably be expected' (Law Commission, 1996: 110).

The key rationale for adopting the broader notion of liability is that previous prosecutions, arising from disasters such as the *Herald of Free Enterprise*, or the *Marchioness* sinking, failed on the grounds that intent could not be ascribed to the corporate body since it lacked a 'controlling mind'. Yet the scale of recent disasters in the UK cannot be overstated. In the years from 1986 to 1989 alone, over 500 persons were killed in multi-death incidents, nearly half of whom were killed offshore.

It is perhaps symptomatic of the deficiencies of the consensual approach, that the Law Commission's recommendation construed a notion of corporate liabilty which was in its broad lines established in a turn-of-the-century American case. In the oft-cited case of New York Railroads (NY Railroad *v.* US, 1909), the US Supreme Court upheld a statute which required that:

> ... omission or failure of any officer, agent, or other person acting for or
> employed by any common carrier, acting within the scope of his
> employment, shall in every case be also deemed to be the act, omission,

or failure of such carrier, as well as that person. (Cited in Wells, 1993:116)

In other words, the US Supreme Court condoned the prosecution of a corporation in cases where the court was unable to prove intent of the corporation to commit the respective offence. After thirty years of a systematic decriminalization of the corporation, of which the post-Cullen offshore reconstruction has become an integral part, there finally appears some recognition of the need to move away from the 'consensual' misconception of corporate misconduct and negligence, and address the need for prosecution and criminalization.

Notes

1. DEn *Onstream*, No. 60, 5 August 1977.
2. Letter from I. P. Smith, Principal Inspector NII, to author, 10 March 1994.
3. ibid.
4. Piper Alpha Public Inquiry, 18 January 1990, Day 173: 61E and 62E.
5. *Hansard*, Vol. 181, 1990–91, Written Answer, 21 November 1990, col. 152.
6. *Hansard*, Vol. 181, 1990–91, Written Answer, 28 November 1990, col. 416.
7. *Hansard*, Vol. 181, 1990–91, 21 November 1990, col. 192.
8. *Hansard*, Vol. 240, Written Reply, 30 March 1994.
9. DEn *Onstream*, No.76, 26 May 1978, p. 17.
10. Piper Alpha Public Inquiry, 12 December 1989, Day 158: 28D.
11. *Hansard*, Vol. 181, 1990–91, Written Answer, 18 November 1990, col. 415.
12. *Hansard*, Vol. 181, 1990–91, Written Answer, 21 November 1990, cols. 149–50.
13. Provisional figures informally supplied by HSE.
14. Letter from J. Pearson, Section Head, to R. Allison, Chief Executive OSD, May 1996.
15. Piper Alpha Public Inquiry, 16 January 1990, Day 172: 60C.
16. See note 13, *above*.
17. *Safety Management*, March 1996, Vol. No. 3, pp. 2–3; *IRS Employment Review*, March 1996, No. 603 (Health and Safety Bulletin, p. 3).
18. Piper Alpha Public Inquiry, 12 December 1989, Day 157: 18A.
19. *Hansard*, Vol. 240, Written Reply, 30 March 1994.
20. R. G. Craig, Senior Procurator Fiscal Depute, Aberdeen, 2 February 1995, personal communication.

21. Harold Hughes, letter to Mr Padraig Flynn, Commissioner for Social Affairs, 27 July 1994.

22. ibid.

23. E&P Forum Position Paper on the Working Time Directive, Revision of Directive 93/104/EC, Exclusion of 'Other Work at Sea', Brussels, 1996. This suggests the trends in safety performance are also improving at European level within the industry using combined UK, Netherlands and Denmark rates as indicators. Norwegian figures are excluded, however. See Annex 1.

24. See note (a)2, Serious Injury, notice of casualty or other accident involving loss of life or danger to life on or near to an offshore installation, HSE form OIR/9A.

25. Interview with J. Molloy, Brent Delta safety representative, recorded 1 February 1996.

26. BBC TV *Frontline Scotland*, 'Paying for the Piper', 16 May 1996.

27. Excerpts from interview with HSE inspector kindly supplied by David Whyte from 'Safety management in the offshore oil industry', (unpublished PhD thesis, forthcoming), John Moores University, Liverpool.

28. Alan Campbell, personal communication.

29. *Labour Research*, Vol. 84, No. 12, December 1995, pp. 17–18.

30. *Scotsman*, 22 August 1990.

31. *Scotsman*, 9 November 1991.

32. *Press and Journal, Scotsman, Herald*, 9 November 1991.

33. ibid, see note 20 *above*

34. *Oilman*, 5 December 1992.

35. *Blowout*, Issue No. 46, December 1995/January 1996, p.8.

36. *Blowout*, Issue No. 25, June 1992.

37. *Blowout*, Issue No. 46, December 1995/January 1996.

38. *Scotsman*, 25 October 1992.

39. AEEU *Offshore Bulletin*, November 1992.

40. *Scotsman*, 11 April 1994.

41. *Scotsman*, 7 June 1994.

42. *Press and Journal*, 29 December 1994.

43. *Scotsman*, 7 April 1995.

44. *Expro Update*, May 1995, p.7.

45. *Scotsman*, 19 October 1995.

46. *Scotsman*, 21 June 1995.

47. *Scotsman*, 22 January 1993.

48. *Scotsman*, 24 January 1996; *Blowout*, Issue 48, June 1996, pp. 6–7.

PART 4 THE FUTURE

The final section of our book takes us back to the other dimension of the post-Cullen offshore world: the attempt to restabilize industrial relations activity. The reconstruction of offshore safety was predicated upon an explicitly consensualist and sectionalist trade union movement. It was incorporated, where necessary, at a general level so as not to impinge on contested day-to-day issues of safety and industrial relations at the workplace.

OILC, however, had developed perspectives which radically challenged the predetermined role of the established offshore unions. Chapter 9 describes how the unofficial OILC committee was now inexorably propelled towards a new identity as an independent offshore industrial union, in the face of the unwillingness of the established unions to sustain a comprehensive approach to the problems of the North Sea. The key turning-points in this trajectory are documented and reconstructed through particpant observation of these events, again using extensive tape recordings.

Chapter 10 charts the early years of development of OILC as an industrial union. The problems it faced, both internally, in terms of increasingly fierce disagreements over its future direction, and externally, in terms of the hostility of the established unions acting increasingly in concert with the employers, are described and analysed. The making of the new OILC union, the pressures and uncertainties which shaped it, are seen as symptomatic of a wider crisis in British trade unionism which achieved particularly sharp expression in the offshore context.

Finally, the scale of transformation of the internal structure of the industry itself over this period is analysed in Chapter 11. It is suggested that a critical turning point for the oil and gas industry was marked out during the early 1990s. The timing, if not the scale of these changes had to do with the challenge posed by the offshore workforce, a challenge that we conclude in Chapter 12 has only been partially contained in the longer term by the implementation of a new labour regime and safety set-up: a regime which remains fundamentally unsafe.

9 STRIKING OUT: SETTING A NEW AGENDA

In resuming the tangled history of trade unionism offshore, it is useful to remind ourselves that what had already transpired – the trauma of Piper Alpha, the dramatic labour insurrection of 1989 and again of 1990 – meant that the offshore workforce had come to see itself in a new way. It would no longer tolerate the role of passive victim, far less silent witness to perceived injustice. The workforce had found its 'collective voice' and it could not now be silenced (Greenfield and Pleasure, 1993). That voice was the OILC. Once mobilized by the OILC, the offshore workforce saw that body as 'the legitimate and powerful expression of the collective voice of the workers ... directed to ... the establishment of a particular system of industrial justice' (Greenfield and Pleasure, 1993: 172).

OILC had crystallized the new-found identity and collective unity of the offshore workforce in a series of interrelated demands for recognition and participation in safety. Up until this moment, the voice of OILC had been exercised on behalf of the existing trade union movement. Paradoxically, at the moment of its greatest strength, when it could easily have persuaded the workforce to pursue a path of independent action, OILC had focused its energies in a different direction, namely on rebuilding the legitimacy of and loyalty towards the established unions rather than to itself as an unofficial committee. Yet that support for the official trade union movement was necessarily provisional. It was predicated upon two things: the genuine desire and capacity of these trade unions to resolve their existing differences and with that, a real intervention in the new arena of offshore safety following Lord Cullen's report. What follows in this chapter charts the unravelling of that provisional support for and loyalty to the existing trade union structures.

The Cullen report had at least offered the trade unions an opportunity for future direct involvement in safety offshore. The OILC-led industrial action of the summer of 1990 had not produced a decisive outcome. It did not persuade the employers to co-operate with the unions in organizing ballots on recognition which would have enabled trade union involvement in safety matters. At best, there was a stalemate, with the established union leaderships searching for a new accommodation with the employers in the post-Cullen atmosphere of *rapprochement*. Such moves were viewed with increasing suspicion by the OILC. OILC now carried the legacy of over 500 workers still blacklisted as a result of their participation in the industrial unrest. The employers, and UKOOA in particular, were not slow to read signs of hesitation on the part of the unions over conducting an independently organized ballot on recognition. Statements of the national union officer, Tom MacLean, welcoming the Cullen report and suggesting less urgency for a ballot, were interpreted by the operators as evidence of a trade union 'backtrack'.[1]

But the employers were not waiting passively for their labour problems to resolve themselves. Operators such as Mobil began introducing the new concept of a 'core team' of secure employment among the contracting workforce. This had potentially divisive results, especially among those deemed excluded from the core. The 'core contracts' offered a 'guarantee' of three years' work to contractor employees, together with various fringe benefits. This was the carrot. The stick was the weapon that the employers had always used, fear, in particular of blacklisting and the threat of unemployment. On Mobil's Beryl Alpha, overtime working was again compulsory, while the company had threatened a downmanning if the workforce failed to co-operate in meeting overtime requirements.[2] This kind of pressure was crucial in repressing the remaining militancy as 1990 drew to a close. Those workers who now worked offshore knew full well that hundreds of their colleagues remained stranded 'on the beach' with no immediate prospect of reinstatement. It was a salutary reminder of where the ultimate balance of power in the industry lay. Shell's OPRIS bar remained in place for those who had taken action in the East Shetland Basin, although some had managed to trickle back offshore, working for other contractors elsewhere in the North Sea. But not only construction workers had to pay the price for activism. One hundred and seven catering workers were blacklisted by Shell and effectively prevented from re-employment in any other part of the North Sea. Shell had commented that it 'did not see why other operators should be obliged to import problems onto their platforms'.[3]

The joint arbitration panels, which the contractors and unions had agreed upon in the wake of the previous year's action, at last began their work. From early November there were to be a number of 'test cases' for dismissed workers with key contractors such as Vauldale, Press Offshore and Wood Group. Contractors such as Asco-Smidt, who were not with the OCC, refused to hold such panels. In addition, some 300 applications had been lodged for Industrial Tribunal hearings for unfair dismissal, although the dates for these would be many months away. In any event, only one-fifth of those workers dismissed had applied for a hearing before the closing date for application had passed. The only remaining challenge to the employers in the form of industrial action was in the Morecambe Bay area, where workers had embarked on a strike, ultimately successful, to achieve full parity with the Northern sector. The key contractors, George Craig Services and Cape Scaffolding, now agreed to meet the officials. These employers were impressed by their failure to persuade scaffolders who had been flown offshore, to break a continuing strike of 350 men. Although the Morecambe Bay strike was essentially a 'domestic' dispute, behind the scenes OILC provided the finance and logistics to maintain heliport picket-lines. This enabled these workers in the western gas field to secure an important advance, bringing parity of rates with the northern sector.

Almost unnoticed by the media, the 1990 Employment Act received Royal Assent on 1 November. Expectations that the Act would have been in place even before the 1990 summer industrial action commenced had proved incorrect. The 1990 Act had in view precisely the kind of unofficial action that OILC had initiated, but its origins were in the train and London Underground drivers' unofficial strikes the previous year. To a lesser extent strikes by the London steel erectors and dockworkers in 1989 also lay behind the Act, as did the 1989 action of offshore workers. Unofficial strikes now had to be formally 'repudiated' by their trade unions which would otherwise face penalties, up to and including sequestration of their funds. For the first time, unofficial strike leaders could be individually singled out and selectively dismissed within 24 hours. So too could any groups of workers who took industrial action seeking to secure the reinstatement of strike leaders. In December 1990, Eric Hammond, general secretary of the EETPU, warned all shop stewards and branch secretaries of the implications for the union of taking unofficial action, including even a simple go-slow.[4] Gavin Laird of the AEU wrote a similar communication.[5] The overtime ban, which OILC still sought to retain, albeit with limited success after the cessation of the strikes and sit-ins, was now identified as the kind of unofficial action which the unions would repudiate. When exhausted workers refused to 'turn to' after being fog-bound on an installation for three days, having endured three consecutive nights of 'hard-lie' on the installation cinema floor, management distributed the *union* warning memos to the contractor workforce in order to secure a resumption of work. Unions were now co-opted into a policing role.

OILC's future as an unofficial activist committee had become increasingly problematic by the autumn of 1990. This new legislation raised questions as to its entire future strategy. The advantages of being a purely *ad hoc* body were now reduced, and OILC had to consider whether having a rule book, office bearers and a constitution was more advantageous. As the incentive of union officials to discipline unofficial action was strengthened by the new legislation, the tensions between the different levels within trade unions, especially where official leaders were seen to be 'compromising', were also heightened. Inherent divisions between the various unions also now reasserted themselves offshore, heightened by a legislative context which reinforced the growing polarization of official and unofficial movements.

The Slide to Sectionalism

The major source of tension between OILC and the official trade unions was exemplified in the growing disintegration of the one-table approach. Catering workers had now received an offer from COTA, the catering employers' association, which amounted to 14.5 per cent over nine months. This offer was calculated to buy off future unrest in this sector, although it still only produced an average wage of £16,000 per year for catering workers. Fred Higgs, as national secretary for the oil industry section of the TGWU, recommended acceptance, as the employers had also agreed to talks on union recognition for catering workers in the southern sector. The TGWU had suspended industrial action over COTA's attempt in the early summer to impose a two-tier wage system between production and drilling platforms. Once again, and much to the embarrassment of COTA employers on fixed installations, the drilling companies refused to honour the deal. A settlement which Higgs had characterized as a 'step towards a single agreement covering all offshore workers', lay in shambles by the end of the year with threats of industrial action renewed.

But this was nothing compared to the divisions created by the engineering and construction unions. As promised, John Wakeham, Secretary of State for Energy, had met national engineering union officials including Jimmy Airlie, responsible for the Scottish area, and Tom MacLean of the constructional section, to discuss the Cullen report. It was an event duly photographed and recorded in the AEU journal.[6] Airlie and MacLean chose this moment to announce that the unions had also made a 'breakthrough' in their campaign for recognition. The OCC had suggested private exploratory talks with the unions after months of deadlock. According to a letter from Les Balcombe, OCC secretary, talks covering both maintenance and construction, would 'investigate the possibilities of negotiating an agreement'.[7] This, said MacLean, was a 'major breakthrough' for the unions.[8] There was talk of preventing further industrial unrest and of a no-strike deal. The employers' offer of talks was conditioned by the context of four or five major new hook-ups, including the Miller field, the biggest offshore construction project since the Brae Bravo. When the OCC discovered that what they thought had been a confidential letter was publicly quoted by the unions, they were appalled. An angry spokesperson accused the unions of 'trying to hype the meeting ... and railroad the OCC into arriving with an offer'.[9] There was even talk of possible OCC withdrawal.

What started as a union triumph ended in chaos when it transpired that three construction unions, AEU, EETPU and GMB had been invited to talks. The fourth signatory to the Offshore Construction Agreement, MSF, was to be excluded. The OCC argued that MSF did not have significant membership among the employees of the contracting companies. MSF did, however, represent a small number of sheet metal workers, acquired by the amalgamation of the National Union of Sheet Metal Workers. Now excluded, MSF immediately called for a boycott of the talks, only to be informed by the other three unions that they intended to proceed regardless. This was a particularly ironic twist, since it had been the MSF officials who had been most reluctant of all to abandon the Hook-up agreement in January 1990 as a prelude to the summer of industrial action. Then, MSF had been the only union to re-initial the agreement. MSF was not the only union to view these prospective talks with doubts. NUS (now RMT) had always had a cautious, even ambivalent, attitude to the one-table approach. A letter from Keith Jobling, RMT national official, to a disgruntled shop steward reveals the full extent of the reassertion of sectional interest. Once it had become clear that RMT were to be excluded from any talks with employers, said Jobling:

> there is no way I am going to jeopardise our vast number of offshore agreements with companies which we have obtained over a number of years because we have been told by the OCC, ... and from Tom MacLean ... that we are not to be invited to any talks ... It is a sad day when I have to write letters like this. However, I am employed as a senior official of RMT, ex-NUS, and my remit is to look after the members of that union.[10]

This view of the need to preserve existing agreements had in fact been supported by the local RMT officials who in their autumn branch report stated that:

this OILC/National Offshore Committee is tying up too much of our time for negligible return [and] gives rise to the conclusion that A) at national level we should participate and B) at a local level we should distance ourselves from the OILC and give a higher profile to RMT.[11]

Norrie McVicar, who as local official for NUS in Aberdeen had been an active participant in the offshore saga, wrote to a key union offshore activist, Jerry Chambers, also a leading member of OILC Standing Committee. McVicar viewed the campaign for the single-table Continental Shelf Agreement with hindsight:

The Continental Shelf Agreement – from its conception – has in my view been impractical and unworkable, in particular, the way it was set down in the draft UKCS Agreement and portrayed by the offshore workers, i.e. a single agreement covering the terms and conditions of all offshore workers with negotiations involving every man and his dog, if you pardon the expression![12]

From the point of view of OILC these various manoeuvres by the unions were little more than an attempt to reinstate the previous sectional agreements. Talk of no-strike deals also did not sit well with the OILC committee, composed of activists for whom the right to withdraw labour was seen as integral to effective trade unionism. When the National Offshore Committee met in early December it endorsed the TGWU and RMT seeking separate agreement with COTA, although the issue of the dismissed catering workers remained unresolved.[13] The construction unions intended to engage in purely sectional talks with their employers. The EETPU, for its part, had long indicated its intention to meet the electrical contractors to discuss renewing the SJIB agreement, ostensibly, as national official Hector Barlow claimed, due to pressure on the officers from the union's membership.[14] By 1991 all vestiges of the one-table approach had been dissolved. Official union co-ordinated industrial action for a comprehensive offshore agreement was no longer on the agenda.

The only glimmer of optimism for the offshore workforce was the announcement by Shell of a 'goodwill gesture'. The 'temporary OPRIS bar', the offshore blacklist, would be lifted by the company from 1 January 1991. For those languishing onshore, it meant that a four-month punishment period of unemployment now had an end in sight. Shell's action was part of the employers' attempt to build on the post-Cullen optimism that a 'new era' was about to begin in the North Sea. More immediately, a number of Opposition

MPs had taken every opportunity to remind the government that the plight of the dismissed workforce remained an obstacle to any new beginning off-shore. At a private meeting with Colin Moynihan MP, who had now replaced Morrison as the Minister responsible for oil, Ronnie McDonald had reiterated the need for Shell's blacklist to be rescinded before any progress could be made towards restoring industrial peace offshore.

Moynihan had promised to make contact with Shell management. Shell's 'goodwill gesture' came the following week. As a further measure to restore its benevolent face, Shell announced a new anti-victimization initiative. In future, all decisions which resulted in the dismissal of a safety representative would be reviewed by a senior onshore Shell executive along with the respective contractor's management. As a Shell spokesperson put it, the company wished to start the New Year with 'a clean slate . . . mindful of criticisms of politicians and others to which we are not impervious'.[15]

Welcome though these developments were to offshore workers, they were offset by OCC's signals that the joint employer/union arbitration panels would not now be going ahead. The employers felt these panels were not capable of dealing with the situation where there had been mass dismissals. If there was to be a single decisive illustration of the impotence of the trade unions in the face of unilateral employer diktat, this was surely it. Meanwhile, despite Shell's 'no victimization' announcement, two vocal safety representa-tives on the Brent Bravo, one of them, Jake Boyle, a prominent OILC activist, were soon to be inexplicably 'down-manned'. Brian Ward, Shell's Production Director, had been quoted in the company press release on the new 'anti-victimization' policy: 'The revised procedures should go a long way towards reassuring those who have been concerned about rumours of victimisation in the past, particularly on safety. Safeguards for Safety Representatives are par-ticularly important.'[16] In the North Sea, however, it was business as usual.

The lack of power of the local union officials in advancing the cases of the dismissed workers was mirrored at the highest levels of the trade union hierar-chy. The TUC had called a meeting of the Offshore Safety Group in December 1990 to review the way forward after Cullen. All the key national officers, along with Allan Tuffin, a TUC-nominated commissioner on the HSC, were present. It was clear that some had barely read the report. The Cullen report was to be treated, at best, as a potential lever to ensure more government resources for the HSE in the future. There was no discussion of a coherent future strategy for offshore unionization, nor of direct workforce involvement in health and safety through their trade unions. In the ranks of OILC there was now a growing disillusionment with the official union movement, coupled with a deep sense of frustration at the lack of any broader longer-term perspective.

By the end of the year the committee was convinced that it had entered 'a whole new phase of inevitable confrontation'.[17] The issue for 1991 would be whether these accumulated tensions could be resolved within, or in opposition to, the established structures of the trade union movement.

The *Blowout* Controversy

Over the early part of the New Year of 1991, differences over how to resolve the problems of offshore unionism became crystallized in a bitter internal division on OILC's Standing Committee. This conflict centred around a referendum, suggested by the *Blowout* editor, on the creation of a single new offshore union. The need to analyse the issues facing the offshore trade union movement had been recognized as paramount, in the wake of the industrial action. The lessons of previous struggle needed to be drawn and a new agenda had to be developed. Contributions to the debate were invited from members of the Standing Committee and about ten written submissions were produced. These, together with the analysis of a mass of documentary material detailing the whole evolution of offshore trade unionism from its inception up to and including the Cullen report, formed the basis of a discussion document which was the product of this collective authorship.

This document was titled *Striking Out: New Directions for Offshore Workers and their Unions* (OILC, 1991a). *Striking Out* was to be the first attempt at a detailed and comprehensive historical overview of how the trade unions had reached the current impasse. It ran to 60,000 words and was to become required reading throughout the industry. Its writing was the result of intensive research over the period between December 1990 and early February 1991. On the Standing Committee of OILC there was impatience over the seemingly endless delay, in fact only a matter of weeks, in producing the first draft of the discussion document. It was heightened by the feeling among certain leading members of the committee that the discussion document would arrive at politically unpalatable proposals. Within OILC, there had always been a barely concealed tension between those who had now lost, or had never had, any faith in the established trade unions, and those who still sought to resolve the issues in the framework of the official labour movement. This divergence now resurfaced in internal OILC debates.

By early February the Standing Committee had become a battleground of oppositional factional intrigue. It was led by the editor of the *Blowout* newspaper, Neil Rothnie. Rothnie's forceful and fluent rhetorical style had swayed the opinions of many workers at OILC meetings who otherwise had little in common with his far-Left politics. In early 1989 he approached the OILC Standing Committee with the offer to produce a newspaper for the offshore workforce.[18] This had become the *Blowout*. Over the space of fourteen issues, the *Blowout* had developed from little more than a cyclostyled news-sheet into a lively tabloid-style monthly publication. Rothnie himself had come onshore in order to devote himself full-time to editing the newspaper. He received a wage and expenses from OILC funds to cover his salary and the publication costs of the *Blowout*, amounting to £2000 per month.

As the discussion document's first draft was being prepared, the debate on the Standing Committee intensified. In early January 1991 a number of possible scenarios had been discussed, including whether by inter-union agreements, confederation or dual membership, a new inter-union structure with effective executive powers could be created from within the established IUOOC trade unions. Any of the above might enable a solution to the problem of effective organization offshore within the framework of the official labour movement. In late January, however, an inconclusive 'summit' meeting between OILC and IUOOC, at which only four of the seven unions attended, made such options appear impractical. The IUOOC unions now appeared to attempt to marginalize the OILC as a body which had 'outlived its usefulness' in the new climate of co-operation offshore. Ronnie McDonald, as chairperson of OILC, nevertheless argued, 'the drastic solution of a breakaway union, I personally feel to be politically unattainable'.[19] These issues were debated when the Standing Committee met again in early February to hear the first formal presentation of the draft discussion document.

As McDonald painstakingly took the Standing Committee through the draft of the *Striking Out* discussion document, the IUOOC as presently constituted was regarded as wholly 'discredited'. For committee members, the detailed analysis of how the IUOOC was first constituted simply as a local Aberdeen committee, the narrow terms of its relations with UKOOA, excluding industrial relations issues, and the long history of inter-union strife which had held back the development of effective offshore unionism, came as a visible shock. While *Striking Out* sought to keep open the possibility of a renovated inter-union body with effective executive powers, those grouped around the *Blowout* polarized the debate in terms of an immediate demand for a single offshore union. At a meeting with his supporters a few days previously in the *Blowout* office in Glasgow, Rothnie had proposed that the next issue of the newspaper endorse an article calling for a referendum on the question of a single offshore union among the *Blowout* readership. With the newspaper, including a ballot form, about to go to the printers, a quick decision was critical. For Rothnie, the *Blowout* article was 'an attempt, long overdue, to see what the offshore oil worker wants as his future'. *Striking Out* was sharply criticized. Far from putting the offshore oil-worker 'at the centre of his own destiny', it was held that it 'looks to forces which have failed us time and again'.[20] The *Blowout* referendum, by contrast, was said to make an attempt to generate 'the widest possible debate' among the offshore workforce.

There had been an agreed Standing Committee timetable for discussion of the draft document before it was to be presented more widely. This was now being overturned by *Blowout* as its 'referendum' undercut the agenda which the discussion document was seeking to create. The *Blowout* referendum in that sense pre-empted the debate just when it started. This was likely to alienate allies in the Labour Party shadow cabinet and in the trade union movement. Not least among these was Campbell Christie, General Secretary of the STUC, who had devoted much energy to assisting the offshore workforce. For McDonald, the option of OILC forming itself into a single union would consign it to becoming 'a UDM [Union of Democratic Mineworkers] of the Left'. It would be a 'renegade organisation' which would immediately exclude not just the OILC's official labour movement supporters, but those 'trade union stalwarts offshore' who had provided the backbone of the OILC organization.

The purpose of the discussion document was 'to engineer an intervention at the highest levels of the labour movement from outwith the circle of existing vested interests' among the established trade unions. The analysis presented in the document argued that the unions had become trapped in a 'sectional cul-de-sac', in part of their own making, which only such a high-level intervention could resolve. For Rothnie and some of his supporters this smacked of élitist reliance on discredited union officialdom, but for others such views were persuasive. As the argument intensified, erstwhile key supporters of the 'referendum' began to shift their ground. One of them, Jamie Jamieson, articulated his doubts: 'We wouldn't be here without Ronnie and I personally should have showed more faith in him. We should give the document a chance.'[21] Rothnie asserted the 'editorial independence' of *Blowout* and its freedom from editorial control by OILC's Standing Committee:

> Look, you have not convinced me that your opinion is correct. It is just an opinion that this page in the paper is going to jeopardise everything. My own belief as editor of *Blowout* is, edition 15 will be exactly as successful as the previous ones. There has not been a sudden change between 14 and 15. The whole question of censorship of *Blowout* is a major question. You cannot expect me on the one hand to pretend that *Blowout* is an independent paper and on the other hand to give in to the pressure of the committee.

But heavy pressure there certainly now was. McDonald's view of the damaging repercussions of the proposed *Blowout* single-union referendum was shared by the majority. With policy yet to be decided, to publish *Blowout* in the proposed form would jeopardize the interests of the committee, of which Rothnie himself was a member. Said McDonald, 'I don't know if you regard yourself as part of this collective or if you do so only up to that point where your role as editor of *Blowout* takes place.' As the debate moved towards a formal vote, Rothnie asked for 'leave' to consider the request to hold back the referendum from this issue of the paper.

> I need to reflect at some length on what has gone on here and I cannot guarantee to do what you ask. One possible compromise would be to issue a statement in the paper that it is not the official paper of the OILC, and I need to go and think about this.

With that, Rothnie left the meeting.

Over the next few days events were to move rapidly. Despite considerable efforts on the part of McDonald, exchanges with Rothnie indicated he would not reconsider his position. Faced with this, McDonald took the decision to 'freeze' the monthly £2000 cheque covering Rothnie's wages and the printing costs of the *Blowout*, and delayed the paper's publication. An emergency Standing Committee subsequently endorsed this decision.[22] Rothnie's wages were reinstated after two days, while the emergency Standing Committee drafted a policy decision indicating its unanimous position of support for McDonald. This was conveyed by a 'peace mission' to seek reconciliation with Rothnie. On the crucial issue of the 'independent' role of *Blowout*, the Standing Committee was now united. Either the paper served as a weapon in the armoury of the OILC's struggle or it must go its own way. The contentious single-union referendum must be withdrawn.

The *Blowout* controversy pointed to problems of democratic accountability in OILC. Since its inception, OILC had tended to emphasize its informal, open and democratic structure at the expense of formal collective responsibility. It was a legacy which, whatever its original benefits in terms of generating genuine debate, was to be carried at considerable cost to the organization both immediately and in the longer term. Although defeated on the Standing Committee, Rothnie fought a rearguard action to preserve as much of the contentious material as possible whilst agreeing to conform to the Standing Committee's policy. *Blowout*'s publication went ahead with the offending referendum and supporting editorial removed. In its place was left a 'blank page' in the middle of which was reproduced a highlighted facsimile of the policy decision of OILC Standing Committee bordered by a surrounding black box. Beneath the policy decision was a disclaimer referring readers to another 'discussion contribution' calling for a single offshore union, printed on the facing page. Although the referendum had been withdrawn and the authority of the committee prevailed, much damage had been done by the opening-up of a basic split in the OILC leadership which would not easily heal. Not long after, Rothnie relinquished the editorship of *Blowout* and returned offshore. Rothnie had failed to use the *Blowout* referendum to derail the discussion which *Striking Out* was intended to initiate. But he had only just failed.

The Document Launch

As OILC prepared to launch *Striking Out* at the STUC Congress in April, informal behind-the-scenes talks between the OCC and the three larger construction unions, the AEU, GMB and EETPU, but excluding MSF, were proceeding. The contractors had already conducted discussions in their own ranks on what kind of package to offer, in order to defuse further industrial unrest or 'threat of disruption'. The OCC offer, hailed yet again by Tom MacLean, wearing his hat as secretary of the inter-union National Engineering Construction Committee, as a 'significant breakthrough', came in the form of an imposed pay rise under the OCC's Model Terms and Conditions. This was worth approximately an average increase of 10 per cent. This covered the 8000 maintenance 'post-construction' workforce. It was the third wage rise the employers had confirmed in seventeen months, which on average amounted to an overall wage increase for the contractors' workforce of 41 per cent. Such imposed pay awards were accepted with tacit union approval.

The unions now agreed to begin formal talks to reinstate the Hook-up agreement to cover the expected work on major new platforms involving some 2000 of the workforce. In return, the OCC agreed that it would have 'talks' with the local officials with a view to reinstating all the men who were dismissed in the dispute. OILC pointed out that the imposed wage rise would merely keep wages in line with inflation, while 'the main issues which have concerned the offshore workforce for over a decade remain unacknowledged', in particular the marginalization of the trade unions in the safety process.[23]

A rather shamefaced group of local union officials presented themselves at the OILC's Glasgow mass meeting to explain these events. The group had not been present or consulted during the talks with the OCC, but was merely summoned to London to hear the national officials' report. Airlie and MacLean had told them in no uncertain terms either to come up with a 'realistic alternative' to negotiations with the contractor employers, or 'toe the line'. As Bob Eadie of the EETPU, not the most militant of local union officials, put it, 'The way that meeting was conducted it was almost like going down there to be mugged by the national officials.'[24] Tommy Lafferty of the AEU was more forthright in his opposition to the agreement: 'The facts of the matter are at the present time, as far as I'm concerned, the trade union movement can gain nothing by signing a Hook-up agreement.'

According to this view, the Model Terms and Conditions did at least offer a new uniformity in wages and conditions throughout the northern and southern sectors, but it was an imposed agreement without trade union input. The national officials had sought to argue that by acceding to the Model Terms for post-construction and renegotiating the Hook-up agreement, they would eventually secure a comprehensive collective agreement. As it was, said Lafferty, the Hook-up 'only covered 5 per cent of members for 10 per cent of their working lives'. If a comprehensive collective bargaining agreement could not be attained, then the unions should retain the status quo, said Lafferty. He had written to national officials on behalf of local officials:

> I am completely convinced that signing a Hook-up agreement would be a disaster for all unions, but in particular the construction section ... Prior to 1989 the offshore was covered by Hook-up, SJIB and a dozen or more contracts of employment. Today because of the actions of 1989 and 1990 the offshore is covered by three or four contracts of employment with no union input to any of them. To agree that this position would continue and our only involvement would be a reintroduction of the Hook-up, the only period of work UKOOA wants covered, would be devastating to our members. By our support over the last two years in particular, we had had hundreds of lapsed members and new entrants joining our ranks. I believe that a return to Hook-up would result in all this good being wasted and a probable loss of members who have stuck with us from day one. I believe we must either refuse any new offer on Hook-up only, or at least let the offshore members decide by any means possible.[25]

Lafferty was soon to feel the full force of national officers' disapproval for airing such views publicly. A typical reaction from the floor of the mass meeting, was, 'If the unions sign the Hook-up agreement it's treachery. It's a betrayal of the men who went on the sit-ins in support of union recognition.

If they do sign it I'll go so far as to say I'm tearing my union card up . . .'[26] Lafferty and the other local officials were caught in the crossfire between the increasingly disillusioned workforce and the rapidly retrenching national officials. The catering workers had now also accepted the imposition of the two-tier settlement under COTA arrangements, as between the production platforms and the drilling rigs in the northern sector. At least they had been given 'the luxury of being consulted' by their leadership, observed one OILC activist. The frustration caused by the ongoing delays in the Industrial Tribunals for the dismissed workers, now amounting to some five months, was added to by the contractors' offer to give some men their jobs back, but only if they agreed to forgo their right to an Industrial Tribunal hearing. It was into this somewhat volatile atmosphere that *Striking Out* was launched in the spring of 1991.

The Launch and the Sinking

The launch of *Striking Out* (OILC, 1991a) took place in a packed and expectant press conference at the STUC annual conference in Dundee. The deficiencies of the existing inter-union committee and the collapse of the one-table approach were analysed in detail. *Striking Out* stated:

> The one-table approach, developed over the winter of 1989/90 and within which the offshore workforce was induced to take on the oil companies, was created on legs which were already sinking in the quicksand of sectionalism. The inescapable conclusion is that the IUOOC, no matter what attempts are made to 'restructure' it, is not currently a vehicle capable of organising the UK Continental Shelf. (OILC, 1991a: 82)

The questions that the document posed were crucial ones. For OILC, the logic of Lord Cullen's admittedly brief remarks about trade union input into offshore safety suggested at least one way forward. Lord Cullen referred to 'putting the trade unions' contentions to the test' in the review of the offshore safety regulations SI 971. The trade unions, said Cullen, might have a case to argue for appointing safety representatives where they had 'achieved recognition in relation to a substantial aspect of labour relations and had a substantial membership on the installation' in question.

The entity with which Lord Cullen was concerned was the individual offshore installation. The onshore 1977 Safety Representatives and Safety Committee's Regulations promulgated under Section 2 of the HSWA placed the onus of responsibility with the individual employer. Cullen felt that in the offshore context this should be the operator of the installation responsible for devising a Safety Case. Offshore, however, there existed a multi-employer and multi-union environment. *Striking Out* argued, 'As matters stand at the moment, our analysis has shown that no individual union can cross the numerical threshold of viability which entitles it to claim recognition' (OILC, 1991a: 96).

The way forward, said the document, was some form of confederal structure, specifically, an Offshore Federation. This could effectively pool union memberships on each installation. The final pages of the document argued the case for an Offshore Federation if the alternative demand for a single off-shore union was not acceptable to the established unions.

> How then is the log-jam to be broken? From platform representatives and ordinary workers across the UK Continental shelf, there is a growing clamour for change. It comes from both within the memberships of existing unions, and from those who have felt unable to join the existing unions. It is taking the form of a simple and straightforward demand – a single union. If the offshore workforce are to be denied this demand, it must be for compelling reasons. It has to be demonstrated that it is not simply because of the need to preserve existing sectional fiefdoms, or because of bureaucratic or organisational rigidity in the labour movement. The only acceptable reason for not moving forward to a single union *now*, must be that there is a better, more constructive direction to follow. It is up to the labour movement to convince the offshore workforce, as the offshore workforce has tried to convince the labour movement in this document, that a new direction within the framework of the movement can be found. What is required, and what the OILC is seeking to engineer is an intervention, from without the circle of vested interests, but from *within* the labour movement. This process by its very nature involves the direct participation of a third party, be it the STUC and/or the TUC....
>
> It is perfectly feasible, for instance, for every union to form its own offshore section, and for those sections to be organised in a confederal structure, which could in itself seek a Certificate of Independence. Dual membership of the Offshore Federation and of the individual's own union would breach no law or convention and virtually, at a stroke, would cross that threshold of viability stipulated by Lord Cullen for the purposes of recognition (1991a: 99).

From the floor of the launch press conference came the inevitable question – what if the unions say 'no' to the idea of an Offshore Federation? McDonald put his answer unequivocally:

> If they say 'no', they have declared unilaterally that the North Sea is a no-go area for them. They will have admitted that the only thing that's on offer is the crumbs that fall off the table. The inescapable conclusion therefore will be that the offshore workforce themselves will be entitled to seek the solution that they see is appropriate and if that means the foundation of an offshore workers' union there would be little to invalidate the case for it.[27]

While OILC was launching the *Striking Out* document, Airlie and MacLean were holding a secret meeting with the OCC in nearby Arbroath. It had been the intention to finalize at this meeting a new 'deal' based on the Hook-up which would distract from the publicity surrounding the discussion document. An agreement did not materialize but Airlie was able to announce at a press conference that the employers had now agreed to a 'joint panel' to consider the cases of the dismissed workers and that there had been 'significant progress'. The reinstatement of dismissed workers would remove a major obstacle to re-signing the Hook-up. For 'post-Hook-up' there was now a 'de facto agreement' in the form of the Model Terms and Conditions. The Cullen report, said Airlie, was a 'watershed' in creating rights and opportunities for workers in the industry. Lord Cullen, he claimed, had given employees certain 'key' opportunities, specifically 'the right to elect their safety representatives'. With a nod and a wink, Airlie confided to the press. 'You know fascism was undermined in Spain and in Portugal by democrats standing in elections for syndicalist and fascist unions. In other words, what I'm saying to you is this, it's like flinging the fox in the chicken coop'.[28] Whether the trade unions would succeed in taking over the existing non-union offshore safety committees remained to be seen. With no more than 30 per cent of the offshore workforce unionized, it seemed unlikely that much advance could be made within such structures. Something new was required.

The response of the official unions to the questions posed by *Striking Out* was far from sympathetic. The AEU's national press officer, Charlie Whelan, had been particularly assiduous in priming journalists. On the eve of the STUC conference, a press comment spoke of the unions believing 'OILC is becoming too politically motivated by a handful of extremists'.[29] The *Daily Telegraph* quoted Gavin Laird as speaking of 'unfortunate tendencies developing'. Jimmy Airlie, meanwhile, declared of the continuing search for an agreement with the employers, 'We have nothing to be ashamed of'.[30] According to Laird, any criticism of existing union strategy was 'singularly unfortunate'.[31] Questioned on his response to the discussion document, Airlie was dismissive: 'I don't want to be unkind to the lads, but it's whining and offers no solution to the problem. It is not realistic.'[32]

Talk of a 'breakaway' union was 'suicide' in Airlie's opinion, and he issued a warning to OILC.

> I hope they don't take that step. I hope they recognise that there is always a role for rank and file activists in particular ... But history is littered with the corpses of those who thought they could take a different route from the official movement.

It was a warning that was reiterated by Airlie during the following day's debate on the floor of the STUC conference. The irony of Jimmy Airlie, a former leader of the Clydeside shop stewards' 'work-in', now attacking rank and file activists, was not lost on observers of these proceedings. But then, the shop stewards from the Caterpillar occupation had experienced similar treatment during the STUC annual conference only a few years previously (Woolfson and Foster, 1988). Press comment spoke of 'the uneasy peace' between the unions and OILC now at 'new breaking point'.[33] While publicly Airlie claimed to be 'conciliatory', privately, both he and the other officials, with the notable exception of MSF, were reported to be incandescent with fury over the *Striking Out* document. Whether they had actually read it or not was a debatable question.

The Open Breach

The knee-jerk reaction to *Striking Out* on the part of the official union movement was probably inevitable. No individual union was willing to contemplate surrendering its offshore members to the new Offshore Federation proposed by OILC. The open breach between OILC and the unions, particularly the AEU executive, was confirmed the following week at the union's lay delegate National Committee meeting at Eastbourne. Here MacLean warned of 'pressure groups' which 'overextend' themselves, especially when they involve 'academics with a job for life', who have the luxury of recommending workers to go on strike and perhaps lose their jobs. At the Eastbourne AEU National Committee, a motion was put that there should be a delegate conference called to consult the membership before the re-signing of any Hook-up agreement. Airlie intervened, and the executive called for 'rejection' of the motion.

For OILC the summary rejection of *Striking Out* heightened what was already a deep crisis facing the organization. With the re-signing of the Hook-up imminent, it became increasingly difficult to argue that a solution existed within the official labour movement. But inside OILC's Standing Committee the dominant view was still to attempt a solution which would keep the organization within the mainstream of the movement.

> We're not going to do anything to short-circuit the political process, frustrated as we may feel. There is still a result there for us. The document has presented an irrefutable argument based on a raft of sound analysis. There is a simple choice either for a confederal structure or a single union.[34]

The next few months over the summer, leading up towards the autumn 1991 Labour Party and TUC annual conferences, provided the time-scale which would resolve the issue once and for all.

At both the STUC and the union's own National Committee, the AEU executive had been successful in foreclosing discussion of *Striking Out* in order to prepare the way for re-signing the Hook-up. But it failed to take into consideration the grass-roots sympathy for OILC's arguments in the trade union movement, gathering strength all the time as the discussion document circulated. It also failed to anticipate the rearguard resistance of the Hook-up unions' own local officials. Thus, when the recently announced 'joint panel' of three local union officials and three OCC company representatives first met in Aberdeen at the end of April 1991 to consider the reinstatement of the dismissed workers, they found themselves unable to agree on common terms of reference. The cases of 450 workers were to be considered but the OCC sought to exclude those who still had an outstanding Industrial Tribunal Form No. 1 (IT1) lodged for unfair dismissal. Those who had since found other work, whether onshore or offshore, even if only for one trip, were also to be excluded, as were those who had been dismissed in a 'normal redundancy'. The two sides could not agree on the composition of the joint panel, nor indeed whether its results would be binding. Eventually they broke up in disarray, much to the fury of Airlie. The full force of his anger was vented on Tommy Lafferty, as the local official chiefly to blame for what was seen as an act of 'sabotage'. Airlie knew that without the reinstatement of the dismissed workers the re-signing of the Hook-up agreement would be extremely difficult.

When the national officers met the OCC in early May, for the third time, no Hook-up agreement transpired. Yet, with several major hook-ups in view over the next few years, both sides had compelling reasons for seeking an early accommodation. At a reconvened meeting of the joint panel, the contractors had further narrowed the criteria for considering dismissed workers to such an extent that by July 1991 they were only prepared to consider a handful of cases limited to OCC member companies.[35] This took no account of 30 dismissed catering workers who had 'stood shoulder to shoulder with the bears'. As well as advising their members to withdraw their Industrial Tribunal claims, the unions settled a few scores of their own. The EETPU argued that dismissed members of the rival electricians' union, the EPIU should not be considered by the panel. Workers who had lost their jobs in pursuit of recognition rights for the trade unions during the 'summer of discontent' now turned away from those unions, which it seemed were prepared to go to any lengths in order to secure an agreement with the contractor employers.

From one such union stalwart on the Standing Committee came the question, 'What else can we do, bar going down to London with baseball bats to get the national officers to change their minds?' From an exasperated Tommy Lafferty there came no words of comfort:

> I just don't know, I honestly don't, and I believe if you attempt to send a delegation down to London you won't find them. They have certainly switched . . . from giving OILC every assistance that they could, they have now turned anti-OILC. The time will come when you will no longer be allowed to use any of these premises (of the AEU) for your meetings. That is already beginning to happen. I've been told to distance myself from OILC.[36]

But there was a far greater imperative which made the kind of obstacles put in the way of re-signing the Hook-up agreement by the local officials, and OILC, particularly unacceptable to the AEU executive. This had to do with discussions now taking place with the EETPU, seeking to secure a merger between these two unions. Such a merger would not only bring the EETPU back into the fold of the TUC, but would create a right-wing trade union bloc that would powerfully dominate the entire civil engineering construction industry both offshore and onshore. It would create a new-generation 'super-union', able both to absorb smaller rivals and to project a 'business-friendly' appeal to employers. Re-signing the Hook-up agreement in this context was a necessary demonstration for the AEU in terms of its ability to bring troublesome rank-and-file elements into line.

The Test Cases

The quest by AEU for a 'business-friendly' relationship with the offshore employers had until 1991 proved somewhat problematic. The joint employer–union panel had been a farcical expedient so far as reinstating dismissed workers was concerned. The proceedings of the long-delayed Industrial Tribunals which finally commenced in late May, almost nine months after the initial dismissals in August 1990, proved to be not much better. The first test case led by Tommy Lafferty was on behalf of workers with less than two years' continuous service.[37] The only grounds for claiming unfair dismissal were that such dismissals had been 'by reason of trade union activities'. John Dick, employed by Aberdeen Scaffolding, had been an OILC activist and spokesperson on the Brent Bravo during the sit-in. In a decision described as 'devastating' by Lafferty, the tribunal found that John Dick had failed to show he had been engaged in the 'activities of an independent trade union' under the terms of Section 58 of the Employment Protection Act, a decision subsequently confirmed on appeal.[38] The fact that employees were taking part in OILC-led industrial action when dismissed was deemed to be a separate and irrelevant point. At least half of the applications lodged for hearings were negatively affected by this decision.

The test case for those with more than two years' service fared little better. Another employee of Aberdeen Scaffolding, Harry Bell, had taken part in the Safe Gothia sit-in and had been duly dismissed. With Ian Truscott, advocate, appearing for Aberdeen Scaffolding and two other QCs present, one for the OCC and the other for Press Offshore, the AEU lawyer had a difficult job on his hands. David Bremner, the Industrial Relations Officer for Aberdeen Scaffolding, painted a lurid picture of 'anarchy' and intimidation during the sit-in on the Safe Gothia, claiming he required the services of a 'minder' to protect himself from unruly behaviour by the men. The 'minder' in question was 'Cowboy' John McCormack, ex-British and European middleweight champion, now working as a contract worker in the North Sea. He promptly took the next train to Aberdeen in order to tell the tribunal that he had never in his life been 'minder' for anyone. Far from anarchy prevailing offshore, said McCormack, the atmosphere was more 'like a boy Scouts outing'. However, Bell proved to be a poor witness under sharp cross-examination, again by Truscott. After a further delay of over a month, the tribunal ruled that Harry Bell's dismissal was not unfair, quoting a judgement by Lord Denning that 'a concerted refusal to leave' constituted industrial action. Therefore the tribunal held that it had no proper jurisdiction to hear the case and Mr Bell's dismissal for breach of contract was deemed to be fair.[39] Eighteen other cases claiming unfair dismissal were time-barred as none of the applications had been made within the statutory three-month period after dismissal.[40]

The débâcle over both the joint panel and the Industrial Tribunal test cases served to strengthen the resolve of OILC to develop 'into a more strenuous and effective organisation in its own right'.[41] If the unions would not pursue the outstanding Industrial Tribunal cases effectively, then OILC would take up the cudgels. For the first time, OILC began taking initiatives that ran directly counter to the established unions. In the first instance, this involved bringing in heavyweight legal representation at the tribunals to match the employers on equal terms. The test cases were to be taken to appeal. The issue of the dismissed and victimized workers was also raised at parliamentary level in detailed submissions by OILC to hearings of the Energy Select Committee (Energy Select Committee, 1991: 64). Just as OILC was achieving a measure of input in the national political arena, its marginalization in the trade union movement was intensifying.

The Re-signing of the Hook-up

The third anniversary of the Piper Alpha disaster in early July 1991 had been marked by the unveiling of Sue Jane Taylor's magnificent bronze sculpture of three oil workers, situated in Aberdeen's Hazelhead Park. Offshore, the oil companies and contractor employers did not quite succeed in maintaining a 'business as usual' approach. Workers on the Brent Bravo held an hour's stoppage in remembrance. A reading took place on the Safe Gothia of survivors' testimony to the Cullen inquiry, from the opening pages of *Striking Out*. Several poems of remembrance composed by the workers were recited. Occidental posted a memo for personnel on the Claymore and *Tharos*, allowing a one-minute silence. Press Offshore allowed fifteen minutes but docked the pay of those who took a full hour.

By August, with the TUC annual conference now only a matter of a couple of weeks away, it looked increasingly unlikely that the hoped-for political intervention which *Striking Out* had called for was going to materialize. Discussions on the OILC Standing Committee were increasingly preoccupied with the possibility of the formation of a new oil-workers' union. OILC's crisis was seen as symptomatic of a deeper crisis in British trade unionism in which its increasingly remote bureaucratic structures of 'super-unions' remained unresponsive to the needs of particular groups of rank and file workers (Fairbrother and Waddington, 1990). The approach of the official movement was criticized as being circumscribed by a weak-kneed 'legalism', which had prevented them from confronting the employers directly. Instead, unions were placing their faith in a future Labour government to rectify the legislative impediments facing trade unions. At OILC meetings the view was put: 'We're going to have to break the mould' with the 'formation of a union specific to offshore safety'.[42] The unions' drive to renegotiate a Hook-up agreement with the employers underscored how the established trade unions were continuing to co-operate in their own marginalization. In allegedly wasting the limited opportunities for an effective say in offshore safety presented by Lord Cullen, the established unions were seen to have set the scene for a final confrontation.

This confrontation came in late August on the steps of the STUC's elegant terraced headquarters in Glasgow's West End. Dozens of OILC supporters, including dismissed workers, gathered to lobby union officials and employers' representatives who were there to re-sign the Hook-up agreement. Also lobbying outside the STUC were officials from MSF, excluded from discussions with the employers. MSF had called for the re-signing to be cancelled while the TUC disputes' committee considered their complaint against the AEU, EETPU and GMB. At the top of the steps, OILC supporters unfurled a banner declaring 'UNIONS BIN CULLEN'. As they entered the STUC building, Airlie, MacLean and the OCC representatives were forced to duck beneath this banner. A somewhat bemused Campbell Christie, arriving on the scene, was quick to reassure the assembled throng. 'We're just providing a facility here. We're not involved. It's not our agreement.' In a grand gesture of defiance, the AEU had hired the wood-panelled boardroom of the STUC for the re-signing of the Hook-up to be witnessed by the assembled press corps. This was to be no shamefaced hole-and-corner affair.

But the press conference was to prove an awkward affair. The Hook-up agreement, outlined by David Odling, chairman of the OCC, would provide wage increases of between 13 and 16 per cent, giving a top craftsman an annual wage of £30,000. Airlie, endorsing the agreement, spoke enthusiastically of 'an amnesty with the past', of the need for 'dialogue' with the employers 'to provide the best wages and conditions and security of employment' for the unions' members.[43] In classic pugilistic style, Airlie defended the agreement:

> We're not going to say that the agreement is the most perfect agreement we've ever signed. I've signed agreements man and boy ... I've never signed a perfect agreement yet ... But I'll argue this. What's the alternative to an agreement? It's no agreement ... And we believe it's a good agreement. Time will tell who is right ... We are entering into this agreement in a spirit of co-operation and heralding a new dawn.

Illustration 8 *Jimmy Airlie at STUC Headquarters*

As the assembled press shuffled under the weight of rhetoric, the serious questioning began. How was it that an agreement had been signed which effectively excluded most of his membership? Airlie drew attention to the joint employer–trade union 'Statement of Intent' which had been issued. It spoke of getting 'away from an attitude of "us" and "them"'. Signing the Hook-up was effectively 'a foot in the door', said Airlie, towards an eventual post-Hook-up agreement. David Odling was keen to bolster Airlie. It was, Odling said, 'an important move in that direction'. What was needed was to rebuild 'confidence and trust between employers and employees and their representatives', a process that would take time, especially after the 'mistrust' of the last two years. 'In the fullness of time', intoned Odling, 'it may well lead to a different relationship between us.' But what about the Continental Shelf Agreement? Surely re-signing the Hook-up is a defeat, asked another.

Airlie responded:

> We were never under any illusions that we were going to win a
> Continental Shelf Agreement, a collective agreement that covered all
> workers. I think we've made advances. This agreement compared with
> the old agreement is superior. That's all workers have done historically.
> We've never stormed the Winter Palace in a month!

At this, the correspondent from the *Morning Star* looked somewhat
bemused. When it came to a question about the fate of the dismissed workers,
Tom MacLean had a ready answer. There were now no more than 50 people
dismissed whose names would be submitted on a list to the employers. Their
future employment had been 'guaranteed' at the earliest opportunity. There
was a subtle but important difference between MacLean's language, however,
and that used by the OCC, which freelance researcher Paul Laverty was to
pick up. The OCC representative, David Odling, had spoken merely of an
undertaking to give the matter of the dismissed workers 'positive attention',
somewhat less than MacLean's 'guarantee' for these 50 workers. Laverty's
question to MacLean hit the mark but Airlie quickly spotted the
'interloper'. *Blowout* reproduced the ensuing recorded dialogue:

Airlie:	Let's see your [press] pass.
Questioner:	I didn't ask the question of you, Mr Airlie. I just heard that use of the word 'guarantee' and I just want to clarify that.
Odling:	Well, first things first. There are three thousand [30 per cent] less people employed by our members than there were a year ago. (Interjection: With respect, what about the fifty on the list?)
Odling:	But how are we to decide that some of the fifty are not part of the three thousand? It's impossible – is the overlap one, none, twenty-five, forty-nine, whatever? You cannot be quite so specific.
Questioner:	What he [MacLean] had to say is meaningless then.
Odling:	What we have said is there is no blacklist and we will treat those chaps on an equal basis with everybody else when it comes to recruitment. Individual employers and individual employees who've had a disagreement might not be able to repair that damage any more than if you fell out with your employer. We will treat those guys without discrimination.
Questioner:	This has really opened a can of worms, because to do that does not smack of a 'guarantee'. And Mr MacLean, if you

	would just listen to what Mr Odling has said, that seems to indicate that that list is simply meaningless. If he is saying we will treat them as part of that 30 per cent, he could quite easily be saying that fifty ...
Airlie:	Which newspaper do you represent?
Questioner:	I'm a freelance, sir. My name is Paul Laverty.
Airlie:	What paper do you represent?
Questioner:	I'm a freelance, sir. I'm going to write ...
Airlie:	For who? Where's your NUJ card?
Questioner:	I'm asking ...
Airlie:	You're a wee Trot! Now, get out! Come on, where's your NUJ credentials? Get out!
Questioner:	Why does that question upset you, Mr Airlie? Will you answer the question?
MacLean:	Let's try and deal with the question ... What is factual is that there is 30 per cent less [employed] this year than there was at the same time last year. Now how do we recruit or reinstate people in companies who are no longer involved? The only way we can do this is for the OCC to take the matter on board and they have agreed to do that. So they will be recruiting people who were involved with other companies in order to alleviate matters. Let me say again, we are absolutely sure that by the time the Miller field is manned, the list we are left with will no longer be there, and that's the point. That's a guarantee as far as I'm concerned.
Questioner:	That's a guarantee?
Airlie:	It's our Press conference but we don't tell the NUJ who to send. He is NOT a member of the Press. You'll admit that. Now please ...
Questioner:	I'm a freelance, sir ...
Airlie:	You are NOT a freelance, sir! Where's your NUJ card?
Questioner:	Listen, I'm not going to be intimidated.
Airlie:	Then, get out! Tom [Lafferty], see him out!
Lafferty:	That'll be _____ right! He might _____ wallop me![44]

As the proceedings descended into farce, they were quickly brought to a halt. Outside the STUC building, the officials had to endure further taunts of 'sell-out' from the waiting OILC protesters. With his colleagues, Odling also made a swift exit, but found he was being pursued along the pavement by a persistent little bald-headed man tugging at his sleeve. 'Mr Odling, stop a minute, please. You've got to listen to me. My son was killed on Piper Alpha.' It was Gavin Cleland. Odling had to stop and listen as 'wee Gavin' castigated the Hook-up agreement. It was precisely the kind of offshore agreement which had left the unions powerless on safety issues with tragic results.

OILC's view was that the agreement represented 'a squalid little sectional deal signed on the backs of the sacked workers'. The trade unions had 'endorsed their own marginalization'. The *Scottish Daily Express* next day welcomed the agreement in glowing terms, commenting: 'The dissenting voice of Ronnie McDonald, who led last year's dispute, is an echo from the past. His out-of-date eloquence has no place in modern industry where prosperity comes through partnership of common goals and not conflict.'[45]

It was an editorial which seemed to echo the thinking of the AEU leadership.

The TUC Annual Conference

By another of the peculiar twists which characterize the North Sea saga, the September 1991 annual conference of the TUC was held, not in the traditional haunts of Brighton, Bournemouth or Blackpool, but in Glasgow, the city which was home to many of the offshore workforce. OILC members who had been lionized as the heroes of the hour at the two previous TUC conferences now found themselves refused admission. The conference was being held in the vast iron and glass hangar which claimed for itself the grand title of the Scottish Exhibition and Conference Centre. While outside an OILC lobby basked in the heat of a rare Indian summer, inside the delegates sweltered beneath a blanket of stultifyingly boring debates. The exclusion of OILC, refused permission to display their publicity material on conference stalls, provoked much sympathetic fraternizing between the visiting delegates and OILC supporters, now characterizing themselves as 'outcasts in their own city'. Inside the conference centre everyone from British Nuclear Fuels to Butlin's had laid out their wares for the TUC delegates. When other rank-and-file groups such as the 'Pergamon 23', sacked employees of Robert Maxwell, tried to display OILC leaflets at their stall, a zealous TUC official tore them up in rage.

If there was one word to describe this TUC conference which all the media from the *Sun* to the *Morning Star* were agreed upon, it was 'tedious'. The issue which was expected to provoke real debate, but which TUC officials were determined to smother, was whether the union movement should call upon a future Labour government to repeal the entirety of the Conservative anti-trade union laws. With a general election in prospect, possibly as soon as November, but certainly before the next TUC conference in the autumn of 1992, it was important for the trade unions not to be seen to be 'rocking the boat'. It was argued that a wholesale repeal of this legislation, or worse, a split on the issue, would provide damaging political ammunition for the Conservatives to attack the Labour Party.

The straw man of the conference was Arthur Scargill of the mineworkers' union, the NUM. Scargill received the ritual rubbishing from the right wing of the trade union movement, led by TUC General Secretary Norman Willis himself. The NUM motion demanded the comprehensive repeal of the employment legislation passed since 1979. This was 'clinging to outmoded images of class war', in Willis's words. Bill Jordan of the AEU, sporting the union delegation tartan tie, also solemnly admonished, 'Look East, Arthur, the world is changing. Real people power is sweeping away yesterday's people, yesterday's ideas.' But Arthur Scargill could certainly not be defeated by mere debating rhetoric. There had been 'no holding of postal ballots' before the political changes in Eastern Europe, he wryly observed. The TUC leadership was easily able to prevail over 'dinosaurs of class struggle', like Scargill and his supporters. Willis wrote to the *Morning Star* berating the newspaper for joining the rest of the media in its characterization of the annual conference as 'tedious'.

> They [the media] would have been delighted had we gone against our members' opinions and passed the [NUM] motion.
> Instead we have a specific forward-looking policy which has the support of trade unionists, the support of public opinion as a whole.[46]

As for the 'future Prime Minister', Neil Kinnock was careful to keep his distance from the conference itself. Kinnock arrived in time for the TUC General Council's private dinner but departed almost immediately after, without addressing the delegates at the conference hall. Kinnock was already on his way to Aberdeen, which was hosting a major oil multinational jamboree, the 'Offshore Europe' conference. As a guest of BP, Kinnock was flown offshore for a visit to the Forties Delta installation. Had he lingered slightly longer at the TUC conference, he might have had the opportunity of speaking to some of the dismissed workforce from the Forties Delta. They would have given him a rather different picture of offshore life to that presented by the oil company.

But Kinnock was not the only Labour leader whose favourable regard was assiduously cultivated by the industry. His successors, John Smith and Tony Blair, had both been guests, with their wives, of Conoco at weekend seminars in the exclusive Gleneagles Hotel in Scotland. So, too, had deputy Labour leader John Prescott and his wife. Both Blair and Prescott were to endure Conservative 'counter-sleaze' allegations for failing, although technically not required to do so at that time, to declare these visits in the Register of Members' Interests. A scrutiny of the Conoco guest list at Gleneagles over a two-year period shows the presence of senior figures from all major political parties.[47] But if the Labour leadership was keen to make friends with big business both at home and abroad in its search for a return from fifteen years in the political wilderness, the same could not be said of its treatment of its traditional allies in the trade union movement.

The Labour Party in its dealings with the TUC in the early 1990s was confronted by a very different kind of animal to that of the 1970s. From a peak of over 12 million affiliated members in 1979, the tide of political, economic, occupational and legislative change had served to erode much of the TUC's former strength. By 1991, membership had dropped to about 9.6 million. In 1979 trade union density was nearly 57 per cent. Nevertheless the trade union movement still covered almost 44 per cent of employees in 1991 (Kessler and Bayliss, 1995: 154). Moreover, in terms of the actual internal conduct of Labour Party affairs from branch level to leadership elections, the trade union movement continued to have considerable influence. Neil Kinnock's dream of 'modernizing' the party with the introduction of 'one member one vote' and ending the trade union 'block vote' in leadership elections was still some way off. The Labour Party conference of September 1993 was to see these changes forced through by a mere whisker under Kinnock's successor, John Smith, with the enthusiastic support of then Shadow employment spokesperson Tony Blair.

While a comprehensive commitment to reverse the anti-union laws was neither sought nor desired by the TUC leadership, many at the sharp end of shop-floor struggle expected proposals to repeal the more draconian aspects of Conservative legislation on secondary picketing and sympathy action. Instead, the TUC had been persuaded to accept proposals which left in place much of the Conservative legislation of the 1980s in exchange for a Labour Party commitment to statutory rights to union recognition from employers. The TUC's own modest proposals on union recognition were put forward as the focus of debate at the 1991 Glasgow conference, while more controversial demands were ignored. For OILC, the issue of recognition had more than a passing interest and the TUC's proposals were subjected to the closest scrutiny.

Union Recognition

The 1977 Grunwick dispute had shown that even where a statutory measure for union recognition by employers was in place, it was ineffective without appropriate legal penalties. The TUC's own consultative document to the 1991 congress recognized this. It provided a detailed analysis of the failures of this period created by the absence of 'clear statutory recognition criteria' (TUC, 1991a: para 3.4ff). The repeal of these very recognition procedures was among the first measures of the Thatcher government, in the 1980 Trade Union Act. In the initial formulation of the TUC's new recognition proposals, there had even been the suggestion that companies who failed to award full negotiating rights where a union had recruited the majority of the workforce, should face fines, including the sequestration of assets. 'Trigger-figures' were suggested for a 'step-by-step' approach towards full recognition, beginning with a minimum threshold for all employees to have legal rights to basic representation by their union, regardless of the level of membership; facilities, such as time off for union duties and training where 10 per cent support existed; to be consulted annually on pay and conditions where there was 30 per cent union support; up to full negotiating rights after 50 per cent support had been demonstrated to an appropriate agency. Specification of precise thresholds was latterly not considered helpful, as it might assist employers in legally *de*recognizing unions. The need for innovative structures to take account of particular industrial situations where individual union memberships might not reach the majority threshold was recognized.

> In sectors where there are traditionally a number of different unions for a particular group of employees, it may be difficult for any one union to reach the necessary threshold for recognition. Consideration might be given to allowing joint union application [for recognition], under the legislation. (TUC, 1991a: para 6.10).

This was precisely the argument for the formation of an Offshore Confederation put forward by OILC. The TUC also had a stated policy of the need for individual trade unions and the TUC itself to actively pool resources on health and safety. Nevertheless, for the TUC, statutory recognition procedures 'would very much be the last resort for a union'. Conciliation was 'the TUC's preferred route to new recognition arrangements' (1991a: para 6.8). The law would be there to deal with intractable employers such as at Grunwick, but the TUC of the 1990s was more anxious to demonstrate the persuasive power of good industrial relations as an incentive to employer co-operation.

> Employers ... would see the benefits through improved relationships at the workplace which would result from consultation and might be prepared to grant full recognition rights once membership had increased without the union needing to use the law. (1991a: para 6.7)

The moderation of the TUC was overlain with a whole new collaborationist language of consultation and co-operation between 'social partners' derived from European legislation. Pre-Maastricht, before the British government had decisively rejected the Social Chapter, there had been much excitement in trade union circles over the 'European option' (TUC, 1991b). The TUC anticipated continuing consultation at European level as a national 'social partner'. Indeed, in an attempt to import the 'social dialogue' of Europe into the unfriendly climate of British industrial relations, the 1991 TUC conference had been hosted under the proud banner, 'Social Partnership at Work'. The slogan summed up the real aspirations of the right wing of the trade union movement. Its implications became joltingly clear to Gordon Douglas, one of the excluded OILC supporters lobbying outside the TUC conference hall. Gordon was a member of the AEU, blacklisted as a result of participation in the offshore dispute. It is easy to imagine his consternation when, unable himself to acquire an AEU entry pass, he spotted Bill Murray of Press Offshore management, the very man who had dismissed him during the dispute, now entering the conference hall. On his lapel was a visitor's pass issued by the AEU. This surely was a perfect example of 'Social Partnership at Work'.

In fact, the AEU, like OILC, had arrived at the conference with fresh documentary ammunition meant to silence critics. OILC had produced a new document, 'Crisis in Offshore Trade Unionism' (OILC, 1991b). This was a distillation of previous arguments in *Striking Out* set out for the TUC delegates in a shortened pamphlet form. It pointedly denounced the Hook-up agreement as part of the attempt by the AEU and EETPU to form a 'craft super-union'. The AEU for its part had recently announced the formation of a special 'offshore section' and now published the first edition of its own *Offshore News*, in which the re-signing of the Hook-up was lauded as marking 'a return to peace and harmony offshore'. Previous 'disruption' was blamed on 'unofficial bodies based mainly in Aberdeen'. The AEU's own previous tacit support and encouragement to OILC was pointedly omitted from mention. OILC was condemned for 'a lack of responsibility and a tendency to anarchy'. Tom MacLean now queried, 'It is for those involved to decide what was really achieved.' Referring to those who remained dismissed, *Offshore News* observed, 'The truth is there was an aftermath of suffering, problems with dismissals and discrimination which was duly handed over to the unions to rectify.'[48] Readers were invited to understand that rectification had in fact occurred, since the Hook-up had been signed 'to the satisfaction of all parties'. All, that is, except MSF, who used the occasion of the TUC conference to pursue the other three union signatories, threatening a formal complaint under the TUC's Bridlington rules, and, of course, the dismissed workers.

OILC: An Independent Union

The war of words between OILC and AEU could not get any fiercer. It was now exacerbated by deep personal antipathy between McDonald and Airlie. A last-minute attempt by MSF at the TUC conference, to salvage the proposal of an Offshore Federation to include *all* the unions, was again resisted by the three Hook-up agreement union signatories. Five unions which publicly supported the Offshore Federation were MSF, TGWU, RMT, NUMAST and EPIU. However, the 'big three', AEU, EETPU and GMB remained implacably opposed at national level, even though their local officials at IUOOC level had supported the concept and had been present at the TUC conference meeting.

The upshot of these events was to accelerate the demand among the offshore workforce for the formation of a single union under the auspices of OILC. As Gordon Douglas put it at the Standing Committee, 'The unions have finally unshackled us'.[49] But from Jake McLeod, an EPIU official and regular attender at OILC meetings, came a warning. It was based on the bitter experience of his own union's long sojourn in the cold after leaving the EETPU to form a pro-TUC breakaway electricians' union:

> You will be outside the labour and trade union movement. You'll be sitting on the outside looking in. Friends to the OILC, when it comes to the crunch, they will not remain your friends, and I'll tell you that now. They'll remain entrenched in the TUC disciplines. They will close ranks. They'll shut the door.

Three positions emerged on the Standing Committee, each with vocal proponents. The first, hostile to any breakaway, argued that OILC should throw its weight behind the 'Offshore Federation' formed at the TUC conference out of the five unions. The second argued that OILC should become 'a membership organisation' but that it should not yet seek certification as an independent trade union. This position was seen as not necessarily mutually exclusive to the first. A third position, attracting overwhelming support, advocated that OILC immediately set in motion the necessary procedures to become an independent certificated union. A series of internal discussions took place over a period of three weekends to thrash out a consensus opinion among OILC's offshore supporters. The key meetings were conducted in the incongruous setting of Glasgow's Holiday Inn hotel, as the AEU had now officially barred OILC from its premises. With the last of these meetings due to take place on Sunday 29 September, the fledgling 'Offshore Federation' met again to discuss forming a confederated body. This proposal was dismissed by the AEU, with MacLean saying that it was 'not a properly constituted meeting' and 'totally meaningless'. Airlie, for his part, described the five union confederation as simply 'a lot of hot air'.[50]

With the Labour Party annual conference taking place the following week, the question was whether the breach could be healed at what was now the moment of rupture. Much frantic manoeuvring over the following days, involving Labour's oil spokesperson Frank Doran MP as would-be mediator, was to no avail. Even a late 'conversion' by the three Hook-up agreement unions failed to prevent the split. From the platforms offshore, particularly the OILC strongholds of the Forties, Claymore and the Brents, the message had come through to the Standing Committee – 'Go for it.' But there was little in the way of euphoria when, during the Labour Party conference in Brighton, OILC announced it would now seek to become an independent trade union to represent the interests of offshore workers.[51]

At the Labour Party conference, the eight established unions had finally got round the table together under the chairmanship of Alec Ferry of the Confederation of Shipbuilding and Engineering Unions (CSEU). An Offshore Federation would be formed, as a sub-committee of the CSEU, although with none of the executive control and pooling of membership envisaged in *Striking Out*. The AEU, EETPU and GMB had reluctantly agreed to join this Offshore Federation but the 'price' of their co-operation was that OILC be excluded from any future role. This was unacceptable to OILC which saw itself as having an essential contribution to make to the future debate over the emerging offshore safety regime, a contribution which it felt it had already made with considerably greater effect than the established unions.

Among informed sections in the wider trade union movement, there was a view that the AEU had been happy to goad OILC into breaking with the established unions. Either way, win or lose, it would be to the AEU's advantage. If OILC failed, it would serve to confirm Airlie's prophecy that it had become just another 'corpse' outside of the mainstream. If, on the other hand,

OILC had any degree of impact as an independent union, it would simply accelerate the pressure on the employers to seek an accommodation with established unions such as the EETPU and AEU or their future merged incarnation. Flanked by MacLean, Airlie was quick to denounce the OILC as 'pariahs'. Also by his side, and vociferous in his condemnation, was Rab Wilson, the Nigg Bay convener. Others, such as Campbell Christie of the STUC, expressed their regret at the 'mistaken judgement' of OILC. He made it clear that there would be no recognition for the new offshore union, either from the TUC or the STUC. 'All this will do', said Christie, 'is create another player offshore, and make getting a solution further away, whereas I think we were on the point of making substantial progress'.[52] From the independent Norwegian offshore workers' union OFS, however, came an unqualified enthusiastic welcome and the promise of formal co-operation across the British/Norwegian sector line. From the 'bears' offshore would come the most important response of all. Within a week of its formation announcement, over 260 had joined the new OILC union. It was a beginning, but if OILC did not succeed in turning discontent with the established unions into mass membership, then the new union would be stillborn. After all of the tempestuous struggles of the last two years, a bitter contest for the support of the offshore worker was about to begin.

OILC: What Kind of Union?

In her pioneering study of breakaway unions conducted in the 1950s, Shirley Lerner (1961) points out that unofficial strikes often act as a precursor to union membership secession. Unofficial action is not simply activity which lacks the stamp of formal official approval; it often involves the creation of a new authority, control and democratic structure among the rank and file. Whilst unofficial action does not inevitably lead to a breakaway, it typically makes some tension between members' objectives and those of union leaderships inevitable. Where the rank-and-file membership have led independent industrial action, as in the case of OILC, the degree of cohesion, and of tension with the leadership, is likely to be all the greater. Lerner points out, however, that one crucial ingredient is needed before a breakaway occurs:

> While an unofficial strike may terminate in a breakaway, the strike does not cause the breakaway ... members do not secede without first becoming thoroughly disillusioned with their union and first believing their union is incapable of much improvement. (Lerner, 1961: 194)

In the case of OILC, the unofficial strike of 1990 had been an event which generated both cohesion and rank and file momentum. The common experience of OILC's industrial action, in overcoming previous offshore sectional identities, was not matched by the underlying institutional structure of the established unions. This structure was characterized by a fragmented, competitive, and at times divisive unionism. The OILC's own organizational resources, meanwhile, were severely depleted after the industrial action. In that sense *Striking Out* alone did not offer an immediately attractive alternative to many offshore workers.

The mismatch between the experience of industrial action, its demands and consequences, and the responses of existing unions, however, became dramatically pronounced from the late autumn of 1990 onwards. New legal impediments made OILC's continued existence as an unofficial committee difficult. The established unions' euphoric reception of Cullen's recommendations masked their retreat from previous plans for a ballot on industrial action. This was followed by their failure to avail themselves of the opportunities created in the post-Cullen reconstruction. Had the established unions combined their separate memberships the way could well have been opened for the eventual appointment by trade unions of safety representatives at installation level. By 1991, official union leaderships had effectively redefined their objectives, in what had to be seen as a retreat from the one-table approach and the central goal of a Continental Shelf Agreement. Events along the way, the hostile response to *Striking Out*, the re-signing of limited sectional agreements, the attempted marginalization of OILC, the last-minute and half-hearted endorsement of an inter-union confederation, cumulatively led to an inevitable and final break.

The OILC's disillusion with the established unions was powerfully re-asserted in opposition to the re-endorsement of sectional agreements, particularly the re-signing of the Hook-up agreement. The disillusion was on a scale that matched and even surpassed that which followed the 1979 offshore strike defeat. Official union leadership, especially that of the AEU and EETPU, was seen to pursue objectives unacceptable to the rank-and-file body. Secession was the culmination of a process of mutual disenchantment which took over a year to complete, from the ending of the industrial action in the early autumn of 1990 until the following winter of 1991.

Lerner has commented on such separations, 'Solidarity (between official and unofficial levels) breaks down gradually, but some of its more obvious manifestations are outgrowths of crisis situations' (Lerner, 1961: 187).

OILC had analysed and documented what it perceived as the 'crisis' offshore of trade unionism in *Striking Out*. But in breaking away from the established unions it provoked a crisis within its own organization. OILC now argued that the existing unions had failed, and were incapable of promoting necessary change in the future. The question remained, what kind of union would OILC become, in order for it to succeed where others had failed. Becoming a union on its own involved changing from a purely *ad hoc* rank-and-file group to a properly constituted body with a constitution and rule book, elected officials, branches, membership subscription dues and benefits. All these were to be worked out, not least to satisfy the rigorous demands of the Certification Officer of the Board of Trade who could refuse or endorse the legal status of OILC as a bona fide independent trade union.

One of the key issues which OILC had to clarify was how to differentiate itself from the existing unions in the industry. In order for OILC not to become 'just another offshore union', it had to acquire a different kind of 'personality', one that spanned the divisions in the workforce which the existing union structures had perpetuated. As a rank-and-file body, OILC had been able to achieve such a profile during the action of 1990, bringing together catering and construction workers and evoking tacit support from other groups of the workforce, even including direct employees of the operators. The question now was whether OILC would be able to consolidate that unity within an independent trade union organization, especially given the heterogeneity of the workforce.

One way forward for OILC lay in the concept of industrial unionism. The model of craft unionism had its roots in Britain's history as the oldest capitalist country. It was often seen as an obstacle to working-class unity. The formation of general unions in the late 19th century, organizing the semi-skilled and unskilled workers, was a development away from craft unionism but it cut across the development of industrial unionism. The Webbs (1926) in their *History of Trade Unionism* describe the concept of industrial unionism as:

> an organisation based on the whole of an industry such as engineering, housebuilding, mining or the railway service, in which all the operating crafts and grades of workers would be associated in a single industrial union, in contrast with the earlier conception of the separate organisation of each craft. (Webbs, 1926: 548)

In certain variants of the model of industrial unionism, it was seen as a different kind of union structure as well as the basis of creating a new social order in which unions would be agents of revolutionary change. Both the early Guild Socialists and the Syndicalist movement were proponents of industrial unionism. As an aspiration, it has remained a continuing theme in the debates on the Left of the labour and trade union movement. Will Paynter, former secretary of the NUM, for instance, highlights the influence of industrial unionism among the South Wales Miners (Paynter, 1970: 94). In his analysis of the debates at the TUC Congresses of 1925–27 and 1962–64 on the issue of union structures, Paynter provided a reasoned and 'moderate' defence of the advantages of industrial unionism. It was based on his experiences within the NUM, which he described as 'the nearest approach to an industrial union in this country' (1970: 96-123). The miners, together with the fire-fighters, provide two contemporary historical examples which were to feature in the key debates within OILC as it began moving towards independent union status. The Fire Brigades Union (FBU), which was a frequently cited example of a successful industrial union, had started its life as a breakaway union. Indeed its recently published history showed some striking parallels with the development of OILC (Bailey, 1992).

The example of the FBU illustrates the different types and outcomes of sectionalism. Citing similar examples, Kelly (1988) has argued that the term sectionalism has been used in a pejorative and ill-defined manner, which has failed to distinguish fundamentally different phenomena. A similar argument in defence of the positive dimensions of sectionalism was advanced in the context of Upper Clyde Shipbuilders' labour force (Foster and Woolfson, 1986), in opposition to earlier views by Hyman (1980) who attributed a narrow, purely economistic character to sectionalism. According to Kelly, sectionalism can take different forms. Competitive sectionalism involves actions by one group of workers that are taken at the expense of another. Beneficial sectionalism, by contrast, refers to actions by a group of workers that promote the interests of wider sections of the working class (Kelly, 1988: 145–6).

What is important here is that it is the cohesion of the sectional grouping which provides the initial springboard for the generalization of narrower sectional demands into wider, more all-embracing objectives. Thus, the sectional combativeness of the engineering construction workforce lay at the core of the new OILC union. The wider cross-sectional unity, at first encapsulated at unofficial level in the demand for a single-table approach and a UK Continental Shelf Agreement, was now given organizational embodiment by the formation of a breakaway industrial union. OILC, in these terms, represented an instance of beneficial sectionalism. OILC's programme was at root an industry-wide agenda, aimed at uniting the workforce across occupational boundaries. Its concerns, also, were those most central to the workforce as a whole, namely matters of health and safety as well as issues of representation. Its consciousness was based on a common understanding of the nature of power relations in the offshore environment, which was further advanced through the experience of industrial struggle. Only an industrial union offered the vehicle for consolidation of these transformed occupational identities. For the offshore worker, OILC was a 'class bargainer' in Kerr's sense (1959), with a broad set of demands and an equally broad perspective seeking to establish a counterweight to a dominant employer. In that sense, OILC did not present an 'obstacle to the coherent radicalization of the objectives of industrial struggle' (Hyman, 1980) but rather its realization.

OILC's claim to industrial unionism rested in the first instance on its status as the only union specifically dedicated to offshore workers. Yet, as a union, OILC was still embryonic, with its core activists and membership mainly drawn from the engineering construction sector. To become an industrial union in any meaningful sense it would need to make substantial inroads into the catering and the drilling sectors, and even perhaps among the direct employees of the operators themselves. The growth of OILC as an independent union, however, would be in the teeth of opposition from the existing unions. Lerner's study has shown how fiercely established unions attempted to combat their 'breakaway' rivals. Acting as a union, OILC would have even less prospect of securing comprehensive negotiating and bargaining rights than its competitors. Most 'breakaway' unions in Lerner's account remained small organizations which never developed the industrial muscle of the dominant established unions. Employers, if they could, generally preferred to deal with the latter, usually more moderate unions. As Lerner (1961: 71) pointed out, the TUC consistently opposed 'breakaway' unions 'not only because their formation represented a breach of solidarity but also because they increased the number of competing unions.'

What was unique about OILC was its profile as a 'safety union'. If OILC could continue to serve as a channel for workforce discontents in this area, it would find a justification for its existence. OILC was poised to make major interventions in the post-Cullen reconstruction of North Sea safety. Whether these interventions would help to recruit the kind of membership numbers needed for OILC to survive as an independent entity, never mind to challenge the existing unions, remained to be seen. If OILC was to prosper, it would need to prove its relevance to the interests of the offshore workforce at platform level. The next twelve months would be make or break for OILC, the union.

Notes

1. Chris Ryan, UKOOA, 'Speaking Out', BBC Scotland 6 November 1990.
2. OILC Mass Meeting, 22 November 1990.
3. OILC Standing Committee, 8 November 1990.
4. Letter from E. Hammond, EETPU General Secretary, to all shop stewards, concerning industrial action, 14 December 1990.
5. Letter from G. Laird, AEU General Secretary, to all branch officials and shop stewards, 25 January 1991.
6. AEU *Journal*, February 1991.
7. *Financial Times*, 19 December 1990.
8. AEU News Release, 18 December 1990.
9. Note 7 *above*.
10. Letter from Keith Jobling, NUS, to Mick Avery, n.d.
11. RMT Aberdeen Branch Report, July–September 1990.
12. Letter from R. McVicar to J. Chambers, 21 August 1991.
13. National Offshore Committee Minutes, 7 December 1990.
14. National Offshore Committee Minutes, 29 October 1990.
15. BBC Radio Scotland, 19 December 1990.
16. Shell UK Exploration and Production, Press Release, 19 December 1990.
17. OILC Mass Meeting, 13 December 1990.
18. Letter from Jim Murphy to R. McDonald, 10 May 1989.
19. OILC Standing Committee, 7 January 1991.
20. OILC Standing Committee, 4 February 1991.
21. Ibid.
22. OILC Standing Committee, 7 February 1991.
23. OILC Press Statement, 18 March 1991.
24. OILC Mass Meeting, 21 March 1991.
25. Letter from T. Lafferty to T. MacLean, 25 March 1991.
26. Note 24 *above*.
27. OILC Press Conference, 16 April 1991.
28. AEU Press Conference, 6 April 1991.
29. *Herald*, 15 April 1991.
30. *Daily Telegraph*, 15 April 1991.
31. *Financial Times*, 15 April 1991.
32. Note 28, *above*.
33. *Herald*, 18 April 1991.
34. OILC Standing Committee, 29 April 1991.
35. Letter from T. Lafferty to T. MacLean, 16 July 1991.

36. OILC Mass Meeting, 20 June 1991.

37. The Industrial Tribunals (Scotland) Case No: S/3171/90, Aberdeen, 21 May 1991.

38. Dick *v* Aberdeen Scaffolding Company Ltd EAT/400/91.

39. Bell *v* Aberdeen Scaffolding Company Limited, Case No. S/2721/90, Aberdeen 1 July 1991.

40. *Scotsman*, 2 July 1991.

41. OILC Mass Meeting, 4 July 1991.

42. OILC Mass Meeting, 21 August 1991.

43. AEU Press Conference, 28 August 1991.

44. *Blowout*, Issue No. 20, September/October 1991.

45. *Scottish Daily Express*, 29 August 1991.

46. Letter from Norman Willis, TUC General Secretary, to the *Morning Star*, 23 September 1991.

47. A list of participants in Conoco seminars includes some of the key figures in Scottish and national political life, as well as in the trade union movement, including at least three former secretaries of the IUOOC. The purpose of the seminars is described in an invitation to Campbell Reid as providing 'a useful brief for people prominent in public life and helpful generally in disseminating knowledge about issues of vital importance to us' (Letter from George S. Edwards, Public Affairs, Conoco, to Campbell Reid, Secretary IUOOC, 14 November 1980). The following is a list of some of those who participated in Conoco seminars between April 1978 and April 1980.

Politics
Rt Hon. John Biffen, MP, former Conservative Energy Spokesman
Rt Hon. Lord Campbell of Croy, former Secretary of State for Scotland
Rt Hon. Lord Chalfont, former Labour Minister of State
Douglas Crawford, former SNP Economics Spokesman
Dick Douglas, MP for Dunfermline
Michael English, MP, Commons Expenditure Committee
Douglas Henderson, MP, SNP Spokesman on Employment
Lord Hughes, former Minister of State for Scotland
Russell Johnston, MP, Leader of Scottish Liberal Party
Lord Kennet, Member, European Parliament
Ian Lloyd, MP, Chairman, Select Committee on Energy
Rt Hon. Dr J. Dickson Mabon, MP, former Minister of State for Energy
Sir Tom McCaffrey, Chief Assistant to the Leader of the Opposition
John Osborn, MP, Vice-Chairman, Conservative Energy Committee

Arthur Palmer, MP, Vice-Chairman, Select Committee on Energy
Alex Pollock, MP for Moray & Nairn
Michael Portillo, Special Adviser to the Secretary of State for Energy
George Robertson, MP for Hamilton
Trevor Skeet, MP, Vice-Chairman of the Conservative Energy Committee
Rt Hon. John Smith, MP, former Energy Minister and Trade Secretary
Iain Sproat, MP for South Aberdeen
Allan Stewart, MP for East Renfrewshire
Lord Strabolgi, Opposition Energy Spokesman, House of Lords
Edward Taylor, MP, Shadow Secretary of State for Scotland
William C. Wolfe, Chairman of the Scottish National Party
Mark Wolfson, MP for Sevenoaks

Unions
Tom Dougan, Regional Officer, AUEW
William Dougan, Chairman, Scottish TUC
Robert Garland, General Secretary, Foundry Section, AUEW
Thomas Lafferty, Executive Council Member, AUEW
Gavin Laird, Member, General Council of the TUC
James Milne, General Secretary, Scottish TUC
John D. Pollock, General Secretary, Educational Institute of Scotland
William P. S. Reid, District Secretary, TGWU
Adam Souza, Area Secretary, EETPU

Local Government
Provost Thomas Clarke, President, Convention of Scottish Local Authorities
(COSLA)
Cllr William Fitzgerald, President, COSLA
Lord Provost William J. Fraser, City of Aberdeen
Douglas Macnaughton, Chief Executive, Grampian Regional Council
I. A. Duncan Miller, Convener, Tayside Regional Council
Cllr Sandy Mutch, Convener, Grampian Regional Council
Cllr Charles O'Halloran, Convener, Strathclyde Regional Council
Sir George Sharp, Convener, Fife Regional Council

48. AEU, *Offshore News*, Issue No. 1, September 1991.
49. OILC Standing Committee, 19 September 1991.
50. *Observer*, 29 September 1991.
51. OILC Press Conference, 3 October 1991.
52. BBC Radio Scotland, 'Head On', 8 October 1991.

10 THE FUTURE OF OFFSHORE TRADE UNIONISM

Forming OILC the Union

The formal rupture of OILC with the established unions had occurred at the tail end of 1991. This chapter analyses the conflicts and tensions that arose both within OILC and between OILC and the established unions from 1991 to 1995. The first months of 1992 were occupied by the construction of a framework for OILC that would satisfy the demands of the Certification Officer for documentation of the organization's activities as a bona fide union. More importantly, a new membership structure which provided for internal democracy had to be created. By early February 1992 OILC had obtained an official listing as a trade union, thus initiating a two-year 'probationary' period prior to achieving its full Certificate of Independence. The immediate requirements facing OILC were to put together a rule book and constitution, and to hold a national conference at which these could be adopted and office bearers selected. In the period following the OILC's foundation as a union, the most urgent task was to recruit the volume of membership that would make the union a sustainable financial entity. After the first flush of over 200 new members, recruitment had been slow, although steady. Over the first months at the turn of the year, there was a period during which OILC teetered precariously on the brink of financial collapse. OILC activists, in the main those still 'blacked' as a result of the action, had daily canvassed offshore workers travelling to and from the rigs at the main railway station in Glasgow with membership recruitment leaflets and *Blowouts*. By March, membership had reached the 1000 mark and the union had secured basic financial viability. For the first time 'drill hands' on exploration rigs had joined up with the union, giving some credence to OILC's claims to industrial unionism, although the numbers involved were still very small. On three drilling rigs, the Borgny Dolphin, the Sedco 710 and the Ocean Alliance, recruitment had taken place. On a few installations such as the Claymore, which had retained its organizational infrastructure relatively intact during the 1990 action, OILC members constituted the majority of active trade unionists on the platform. On the Claymore, total membership reached 114 and covered all departments including over 30 electricians, about 48 engineers and scaffolders, some 14 painters, a dozen pipefitters and several welders, riggers, platers, roustabouts, mechanical workers and the helideck crew. OILC was to claim, accurately if somewhat grandiosely, 'In the twenty-five year history of the offshore oil and gas industry, no single union has made such a comprehensive penetration of a single installation.'[1]

On other installations such as the Brent Bravo and Cormorant Alpha, where there had been organizational strength before the action, followed by the subsequent 'wipe out' of activists, support for OILC began to be built up again, although somewhat more slowly. Perhaps most encouraging of all, on new hook-ups such as the Miller field, recruitment to OILC was successfully taking place, in particular among disaffected members of the established unions, which yet again renegotiated a Hook-up agreement in early 1992. This new agreement involved a substantial increase in working time of 91 hours per year and the loss of 'radius money'.[2] These and other sources of discontent provided fertile recruiting ground for OILC. OILC's stated target of 3000 members to be recruited by 1993 nevertheless proved overly optimistic.[3]

OILC members were amongst the offshore fatalities during this period, two of them in the Cormorant Alpha helicopter tragedy. Angry workers from the platform appeared at OILC meetings, bitter that their colleagues had perished in what they felt was a helicopter flight which should never have taken place. Once again OILC was in the forefront of the campaign for safety offshore and provided an immediate channel for safety representatives from Cormorant Alpha to express their concerns directly, in a face-to-face meeting between Chris Fay of Shell and the union. OILC's existence was a reality which could not be ignored by the operators. The contractor employers meanwhile found that they faced over a dozen Industrial Tribunal cases in which OILC was providing active legal support for its members. By the end of January 1992 OILC won its first case at an Industrial Tribunal, resulting from the unfair dismissal of a safety representative by Smedvig for a minor breach of safety procedures. Although the tribunal did not recommend reinstatement, and held that the sacked worker had contributed 25 per cent towards his dismissal, an award of £9389 was made, duly adjusted in accordance with the apportioned blame.[4] It was a signal victory which in itself provided important arguments for the eventual extension of legal protection to offshore safety representatives. But more dramatic successes were to follow.

The previous initial test cases led by the AEU, for workers dismissed and victimized as a result of employer retaliation during the 1990 dispute, had been unsuccessful. In 1990, OILC had secured the assistance of John Hendy QC in the case for Jim Byrne, a maintenance worker on the Brent Charlie, against Wood Group Engineering.[5] Opposite Hendy, who was widely recognized as a champion of trade union rights, advocate Ian Truscott appeared for Wood Group, supported by well-known Aberdeen solicitor David Burnside, no stranger to offshore affairs. The weighty employers' team being fielded signalled the recognition that the stakes had been upped by the presence of Hendy. OILC had made it clear that it would pursue the cases of victimized workers much more aggressively than the established unions.

The case involved a worker, Jim Byrne, who had taken part in the initial 24-hour stoppage on 2 August on the Brent Charlie and was locked out when he and the other strikers attempted to return to work on 3 August. He was recalled ashore by his employer but when he refused to leave the platform, was dismissed along with those who had embarked on the sit-in. Byrne had remained offshore until 25 August when Shell finally obtained its High Court interdict enabling the platforms and flotels to be cleared of striking contractors' employees. Spokesman for the men on the Brent Charlie had been one John Goddard, also a Wood Group employee. He had supported the initial stoppage and the subsequent decision to sit in on the Safe Gothia. Goddard had actually addressed the mass meeting calling for the occupation, but later that same day had telephoned Wood Group management indicating that 'he might be able to persuade two or three people to leave the platform'.[6] Further telephone exchanges ensued in which Goddard indicated his desire to leave the platform the next day but was prevailed upon by Wood Group management 'to remain on board' to monitor the activities of the occupiers, on the understanding that he would not be dismissed if he did so.[7] He remained in the sit-in for a further six days and as a reward for his services was the only 'striker' to be re-employed by the company in the immediate aftermath of the dispute.

Goddard's role was described by Wood Group legal representatives as that of 'a mediator between the workforce and themselves'.[8] Jim Byrne had been 'appalled' when he learned of Goddard's duplicitous activities. These were described by Hendy as those of an *agent provocateur*, an undercover agent or a double agent'[9] and 'in itself sufficient to make the dismissal unfair'.[10] The tribunal agreed that the dismissal of Jim Byrne was unfair on the grounds that it was 'unreasonable to attempt to instruct the workers to come ashore by threat of dismissal'.[11] The employers had refused to discuss union recognition during the 1989 action and had rejected workers' attempts to raise the issue of recognition through grievance procedure in May 1990. Wood Group's formal position was cited in evidence, namely that the company acknowledged the 'apparent feeling' among the workforce for trade union recognition but did not feel it was 'in the best interests of the workforce'.[12] Wood Group's opinion had not changed since then. Therefore it was not reasonable to require Byrne and his colleagues to 'come ashore for discussions which they all knew would be pointless'.[13] In December 1992 Wood Group took the case to an Employment Appeal where it was again unsuccessful.[14] The outcome of the Byrne case did much to redress the negative result of the previous test cases. A marker had been put down by OILC. Henceforth, where known activists had been targeted, full legal redress would be sought. Over the spring of 1992, more than a dozen other cases were pending which the new union would represent and eventually go on to win or in which it was to achieve an out-of-court settlement.

Perhaps most significant was the successful Industrial Tribunal and appeal fought on behalf of Frank McEachen, a worker with the catering contractor *SAS* on the semi-submersible, Sedco 704. As an employee in the drilling sector, the union activist McEachen was likely to be a target of hostility. McEachen had been an active shop steward with the TGWU on a fixed installation where shop stewards were recognized by the employers under the COTA agreement, before transferring to 'semis'. Although no longer a shop steward, and with less than two years' service, he remained active as a trade unionist in this more hostile environment by continuing to organize meetings on grievances, including a one-minute stoppage to commemorate Piper Alpha, ostensibly with company 'approval'. He was subsequently dismissed after a single verbal warning alleging a failure to carry out an order, despite a previously excellent work record. In 1992 McEachen had taken his case to an Industrial Tribunal which had ruled that his dismissal was unfair under section 58(1)(b) of the Employment Protection (Consolidation) Act 1978. In other words, he was deemed to have been victimized by reason of his trade union membership.[15] At last, a victimized offshore trade unionist had achieved legal compensation of a kind and had secured reinstatement. It was a historic first, in terms of redressing employer victimization of trade unionists in the offshore industry, and another signal victory for OILC.

OILC: An Organization in Transition

In the early summer of 1992, OILC convened its first national conference at the University of Stirling. The presence of observers from the Norwegian OFS union and messages of support from socialist organizations, trades councils and political groups added to the sense of occasion. Among many groups of rank-and-file trade unionists there was a continuing sympathy for OILC, if anything heightened by its formal exclusion from the mainstream trade union movement. It was reported to the conference that OILC membership had reached 1500. That figure, in itself healthy enough for the first nine months of the existence of the union, concealed less encouraging trends. During May and June recruitment had virtually stopped and was now down to a mere trickle of three or four per day. While the first thousand members had been recruited relatively quickly, the next thousand would not be quite so easy to recruit, said Ronnie McDonald, now 'interim' union General Secretary. The target membership of 3000 still remained, but with the down-manning of contract labour on the Miller and Piper Bravo hook-ups, OILC memberships were beginning to lapse. OILC's strategy had not focused exclusively on hook-up recruitment, but this was clearly a core constituency.

The conference also showed that as a union, OILC was still very much a transitional organization. Its membership remained small and it was without a firm financial base, properly developed delegate structure, elected committees or even formal motions to consider. Perhaps, given its prior history as a rank-and-file organization, this was not so surprising. The adoption by conference of the Constitution and Rules of OILC marked a start of the process of formalizing the affairs of the organization.[16] Again, a gut resistance to what was seen as the possibility of creating yet another impotent union bureaucracy remained a strong undercurrent in the debates which ensued over the Constitution. The model proposed was one in which there would be 'the minimum of bureaucracy at national level'. The intention was to retain OILC's 'open and democratic' structure whilst 'remaining as close to the membership as possible'.[17]

The formal requirements of the Certification Officer were met by the election of a General Secretary and Chairperson, the latter responsible for chairing annual conference, which would be the supreme governing body of the union. In between conferences there was to be an Organising Committee which would perform the executive functions of the union (Rule 10). The Organising Committee would be the democratically elected executive council and its composition comprised six office bearers: the General Secretary, a

First and Second Deputy General Secretary, a Chairperson and a First and Second Deputy Chairperson (Rule 11). This, said McDonald, was to be the committee of 'doers' rather than 'talkers'. The legacy of OILC's open structure of debate was retained with the preservation of the Standing Committee as a wider forum for discussion. Nomination to the Organising Committee was to be made from the membership of the Standing Committee and election to the Organising Committee would be by general ballot of the entire membership (Rule 11). The Standing Committee had an advisory function but was subordinated to the authority of the Organising Committee. It was to comprise area representatives and installation representatives. Glasgow, Liverpool, Hull and Aberdeen were to have area committees, now given a formal footing, which in turn could send one representative per ten members to the Standing Committee (Rule 13). Each installation on which there were three or more members was entitled to elect representatives who would both attend annual conference and be members of the area committees and the Standing Committee (Rule 14). With this constitution, an attempt was made to preserve the workplace character of the organization while accommodating the geographical dispersion of the union's membership.

Union Democracy

OILC had a sound democratic structure, in theory. In practice, the full development of union democracy was to prove somewhat more difficult. Placing area committees on a formal footing was necessary if OILC was to be a properly national union rather than a mainly Scottish, or even more narrowly, a West of Scotland-based organization. Yet the fact was that there had been problems in ensuring the full accountability of the various areas to the organizational centre during OILC's unofficial life. Now that it was an official trade union body, these problems were exacerbated. While the area committees in the South remained relatively weak and undeveloped, the West of Scotland area committee, centred on Glasgow, contained the bulk of the membership. In some of the other areas, the Standing Committee had been seen in the past as dominated by a 'Glasgow agenda', where the majority of the activists were based. As the union began to develop, a competing agenda began to emerge between the Glasgow area and the union's administrative headquarters in Aberdeen. Glasgow members of the Standing Committee began to criticize the 'style of leadership' of the General Secretary, and what was seen as 'a failure to consult' committee members in making decisions. The previous *ad hoc* organization of OILC had given room for the General Secretary's personal discretion and control over the affairs of OILC. Now, as full-time General Secretary of OILC, Ronnie McDonald was charged with carrying out its day-to-day functions, which created frictions in the new broader decision-making process. Added to that was the geographical separation involved between Glasgow and Aberdeen, which in itself was a recipe for potential difficulties.

But there was another, much more fundamental dynamic to the eventual schisms which were to beset OILC as a union and which were to do so much to hold back its progress as an effective force. The roots of this dynamic lay in the 'problems of transition' from rank-and-file body to official trade union, much more than in the individual personalities of the actors involved. These schismatic tendencies, a feature noted in Lerner's study (1961: 138ff), were already apparent at OILC's first national conference at Stirling in 1992. In part, they were a hangover from the previous factionalism of the *Blowout* controversy, in which Neil Rothnie had been the leading dissident voice. During the first Stirling conference disagreements crystallized around the future shape of the Organising Committee. In the absence of a properly developed delegate structure, the OILC conference had elected an interim Organising Committee from those members present. In future years OILC would need to ballot the entire membership in any contested election for a position on this committee. While the Constitution and Rule Book had specified a committee of six, the actual number elected by conference was thirteen. Rothnie had moved rejection of the entire Constitution and Rule Book unsuccessfully. But the argument for a broader executive body had prevailed, based on a feeling that a larger committee would be somehow more 'democratic'. Of those nominated, members of the Glasgow area committee dominated by a factor of two to one. Just as importantly, most of those nominated to the Organising Committee were prominent activists dismissed in 1990 who had since remained blacklisted and now no longer worked offshore. Several had secured one or two trips offshore since the 1990 dispute, but their position as offshore workers remained insecure. Others were permanently blacklisted. A few were dismissed, with tribunals pending. Of the remaining members of the Organising Committee, only a handful of the 'old guard' had continuous employment offshore and still remained activists. A new cohort of activists had yet to evolve from those who had joined the industry since 1990 (although a couple of 'newcomers' were nominated for the committee). This imbalance between those working offshore and those not created weaknesses for OILC's organization on the installations at this time. A new generation of representatives actually working on the rigs was inadequately represented on the new Organising Committee.

One key task facing OILC was to address itself to those changes accompanying the reconstruction of safety offshore as the new post-Cullen regime was being put in place. This required a forward-looking, if critical, perspective. Yet the main executive body of OILC, the Organising Committee, which emerged from its founding conference was dominated by individuals who had paid a high personal price for their participation in the 1990 industrial action. Their perspective was largely framed by the industry as they had known it. Here were the roots of damaging divisions which had already been partially articulated in conference debates. Whether or not any real changes in health and safety had in fact occurred in the North Sea since Piper Alpha, was a matter of sharp disagreement. This was best summed up in a heated conference exchange between two participants:

'You cannot deny that there have been changes. The HSE is something which wasn't there before.'

'I don't think there *has* been any change. It's the same puppet with a different mask on.'[18]

Such disagreements revealed deeper divergences in OILC about what were the key issues facing the workforce. The fact that many of the offshore workforce still 'did not know what OILC stood for' was perhaps a reflection of an identity crisis for the new union, which had still to be resolved.

OILC: Schism

The second national conference of OILC took place, once again at Stirling, in August 1993. The union had had a full year to establish itself and it was now time for serious stocktaking. While membership recruitment and growth were still taking place, the total of 2774 members was still below the 3000 target. It suggested that OILC was likely to remain a small union for some time to come (see Fig. 10.1). The total of 2774 comprised those who had at one time or another been union members, but in fact only 1723 were fully paid up members, while a further 313 were suspended for non-payment of dues, taking the membership to just over 2000. By 1996, over a quarter of the membership had already lapsed entirely, perhaps not quite so surprising given the downturn in employment in the industry. Many workers had found alternative work onshore, in particular those who were formerly employed on hook-up work (see Fig. 10.2). The strong underlying support for OILC had not directly translated itself into membership. OILC stickers, worn defiantly

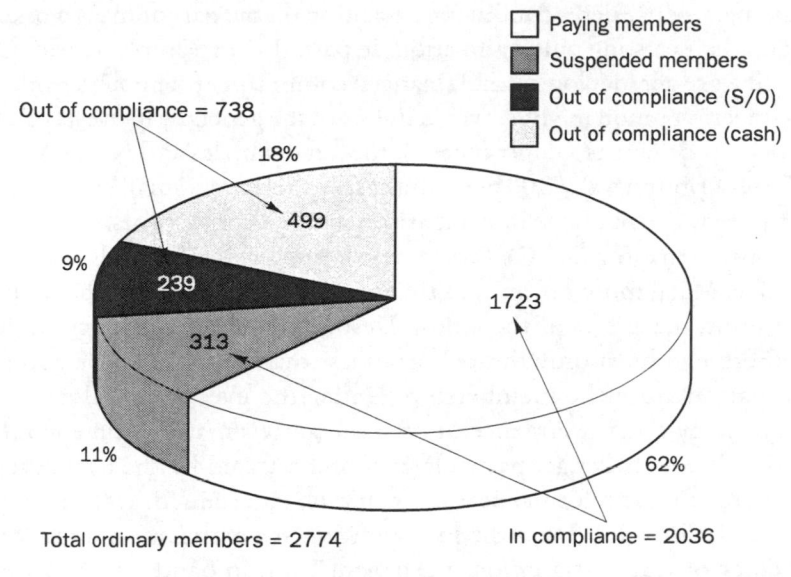

Figure 10.1 *OILC Membership Breakdown (Cumulative) 1993*
Source: OILC

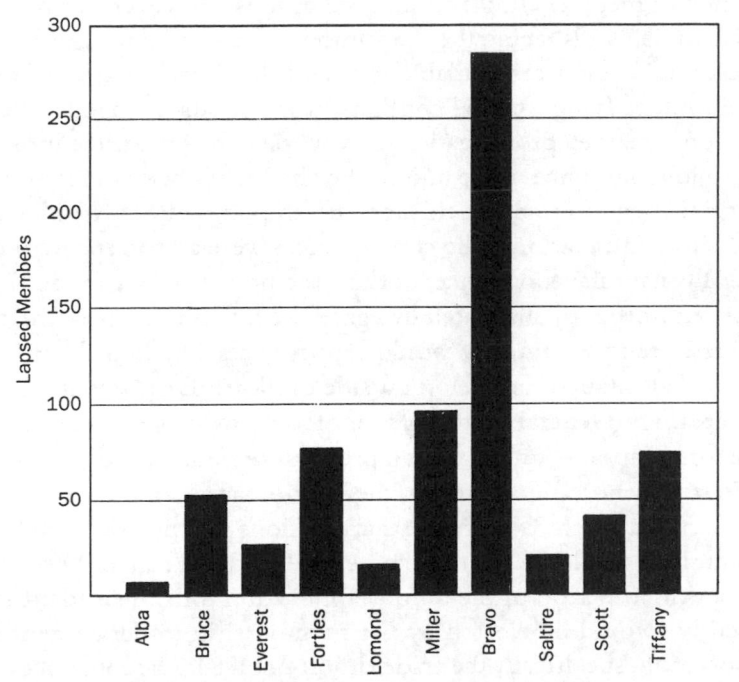

Figure 10.2 *OILC Lapsed Members on Hook-up (Cumulative) 1996*
Source: OILC

on hard hats, concealed a continuing hesitation on the part of many workers to abandon their existing union affiliation. In part, this was simply because OILC required a greater ideological and financial commitment. The subscription for an engineering union member was in line with the generally low level of union dues paid in Britain as against other European countries and North America. OILC subscription was £8.00 per month, still a relatively small amount out of an offshore wage, but large by comparison with its 'competitors'.

The problems for OILC's future development did not only include its small size. Much more central was the issue of the level of membership participation in the affairs of the union. Despite the union's democratic structure, there had been only limited progress towards more active collective participation from the membership. Under the ever-watchful eye of the employers any open resurgence of offshore activism at this time would be seen as a direct challenge, particularly if orchestrated by the new renegade union with which no formal dealings could be entertained. Yet activism offshore at platform level was the precondition for activism in terms of the democracy of OILC as a union. Each went hand in hand, especially given its formative rationale as a union which rejected the passive and ineffectual participation of members in the established unions. However, given also the sheer scale of demands facing the new union at a day-to-day organizational level, the limited resources available to it and the draining away of crucial energies in intensifying internal conflicts, it is not surprising membership participation remained problematic. Many workers had made the individual decision to join but, once in the union, they had remained as individuals. It had proved difficult to translate this membership into effective collectivism on the offshore installations. The consequences were all too apparent at the second OILC national conference, both in the poor turnout and in the virtual absence of properly mandated delegates with a direct link to the membership offshore to whom they would report back. The hoped-for branch structure had also failed to develop outside of North East Scotland and the Glasgow area. The General Secretary's report acknowledged these problems in a terse formulation – 'unless we can progress organizationally we are finished'.[19] In strictly bureaucratic terms, the interim nature of the union's status with the Certification Officer meant that elections for the executive Organising Committee would be required to be held in the spring of 1994, that is, within a specified period of the union's application for independent status. The executive would be elected by the membership under current trade union legislation, specifically the Trade Union Act 1984. The conduct of these elections was to prove critical in the subsequent internal dispute which was to threaten the very survival of the union.

By early 1993, the branch structure of OILC still remained embryonic. Partly in consequence, OILC's general forum for discussion, the Standing Committee, was never properly turned into the open assembly of oil workers which it had been during 1989/90. Its role as sounding board and advisory body to the executive Organising Committee, providing a continuing link with the views of workers on the platforms, proved impossible to recreate. The Organising Committee, mainly Glasgow-based and largely no longer offshore, became increasingly detached from the membership of the union and inward-looking. Divorced from the day-to-day decisions being taken in Aberdeen, some within the Organising Committee became more and more hostile towards the union's General Secretary, who, it was felt, 'was not properly consulting' with the Organising Committee. In early February 1993, the base of the Organising Committee narrowed still further with the temporary resignation of one of the most prominent OILC activists from the North East of England, Peter Douglass, followed by several other threatened and actual resignations over the following two or three months. By then, an openly critical discussion document was presented to the Organising Committee by one of its leading members, Gerry Chambers. This called for an urgent review of the way decisions were being arrived at, for delegation of the General Secretary's various responsibilities and for 'the means for fuller participation by the organisers (to be) provided'.[20]

The trigger for the breach between this group within the Organising Committee and the General Secretary was the eventual opening of a much-delayed OILC Social Club, a venture which, it was hoped, would enhance the financial and organizational resources of the union. The Social Club had opened in the summer of 1993 but by the early autumn it was clear that all was not going well. It had been agreed that the manager of the venture should be a member of the Organising Committee, and in the event Willie Stevenson, the chairman of OILC, was elected to the post. By mid-August, figures of the first eight weeks' turnover indicated that the wage bill was too high, raising the prospect of cutting staff. It was a suggestion to which the Organising Committee, and Willie Stevenson in particular, were strongly opposed, even after discussion with OILC's accountant and lawyer and the attempt to agree upon a business plan.

On the Organising Committee there was now open hostility between Ronnie McDonald and Gerry Chambers with the latter calling for the General Secretary to relinquish the posts of editor of *Blowout* and a number of other duties, on the grounds that the General Secretary 'held too many positions to himself and that this was having a detrimental effect on the development of the union'.[21] Chambers had hoped to be appointed as a full-time development officer for the union. OFS, the Norwegian union, had already agreed to part-fund such a post but it was becoming clear that McDonald was reluctant to see this job filled by Chambers. Neither OILC's finances nor the even more problematic finances of the Social Club now permitted this. However, broader issues of delegation and financial accountability had also become personalized between McDonald and Chambers. Willie Stevenson dramatically announced his resignation as Social Club steward, citing 'interference from the General Secretary' in the management.[22] An unsuccessful attempt by the Organising Committee to have Stevenson reinstated further added to the frictions.

As this dispute intensified, the Glasgow area of OILC had reconstructed itself as a West of Scotland OILC branch. It now provided an organized and increasingly embittered focus of dissent in which Stevenson and Chambers were able to mobilize vocal support from other Organising Committee members who had long resented the OILC General Secretary's style of leadership. By October 1993 a list of 23 points of complaint was drafted by Chambers. Meanwhile, the Organising Committee made some attempts to strengthen its links to the offshore workforce by co-opting five new members from offshore installations.[23] This meant that as an enlarged body it was now even less of an effective executive committee while still not the democratic forum of the previous Standing Committee. The new co-optees were catapulted into an environment already soured by animosity and discontent. Those who continued to stomach this atmosphere of intrigue, charge and counter-charge were eventually enmired in the factional infighting. Others, particularly those Organising Committee members still active offshore, resigned. In fact, the co-options, if anything, only delayed tackling the unresolved issue of developing OILC installation branches and area branches. These could have provided the proper basis for a democratic union executive elected by and accountable to the membership. As it was, the development of the union as an effective force was becoming increasingly subordinated to its internal difficulties.

By the end of 1993 Gerry Chambers, now the leading spokesperson for the dissident group, authored a further document, detailing seven pages of criticism. Attempts to find some *rapprochement* between the General Secretary and the dissident group within the Organising Committee disintegrated in rancorous argument, as 1993 drew to a close. As the union entered 1994 it was locked in a downward spiral of internal fratricide. A series of three Special Conferences of the union were called in the spring of 1994 to find a way forward and, equally importantly, to put in place the procedures for an open election of a new Organising Committee by the membership. The existing

Organising Committee, including the General Secretary, had been elected to office at the 1992 OILC conference by acclamation, and confirmed in office at the following year's conference in a similar manner. Formal election of officers was now a necessity for full certification of the union under law to be achieved. However, far from breaking out of the deadlock which now paralysed the union's internal structures, the three Special Conferences in February and March 1994 only underscored the irrretrievable breakdown in the relationship between the General Secretary and the dissident group. Occasionally, in the midst of these protracted debates over internal affairs, over who did, or did not do or say what, to whom, when, where and why, a shaft of reality would pierce through. 'The main enemy is UKOOA, not in here', said a voice from the floor. 'The reason we've not raised our membership is we're too busy fighting each other.' But these were hopeless pleas, disconnected fragments quickly submerged in the torrents of abuse.

In fact, the first Special Conference in Aberdeen in February 1994 had less than a dozen ordinary members present. The second Special Conference in Glasgow in March had more members present, approximately 40 from the West of Scotland and sixteen from Aberdeen, but proceedings quickly degenerated into near farce as chairman Willie Stevenson led a walkout after the failure of a motion censuring an OILC member. It was an indirect attack on one of the General Secretary's supporters, designed to whittle away McDonald's support. Chambers and a few others also walked out, and while fierce arguments could be heard outside the hall, a new chair was appointed and business resumed, with Chambers and then Stevenson returning to sit in the body of the meeting. Once again Chambers had a lengthy document entitled 'OILC Development Strategy', together with resolutions to limit the power of the General Secretary, to present to the conference. Among these was a proposal to remove from the Rule Book all reference to the Standing Committee, which would now be known as the Organising Committee, while the Organising Committee in turn would henceforth be called the Executive Committee and would comprise the six national officers of the union as before. Behind these seemingly Byzantine manoeuvres, which only scholars of union procedures might care to examine closely, lay a much less complex intention. Under these proposed rule changes, only the existing Organising Committee (that is, the opponents of the General Secretary) would provide the personnel from which the new Executive Committee would be nominated and elected. Procedural chaos had been the hallmark of the second Special Conference in Glasgow, with the motion on the 'Method of Appointment' of the executive and national officers remitted to the third and final Special Conference in Newcastle, fourteen days later.

This third meeting comprised the dissident rump of the previous Special Conference with only a handful of local members present, including Peter Douglass, now having resumed his position on the Organising Committee, and one or two other members from the North East of England. No North East branch existed as such. Yet again, the atmosphere degenerated into slander and threats of violence, as an attempt was made to re-instate Willie Stevenson in the chair. Following this débâcle two local members resigned. It was the end of the line so far as reconstituting the internal democracy of OILC was concerned. Even as these events were unfolding, the dissident group had taken legal advice with a view to re-establishing their control over the affairs of OILC Social Club. Now they formally addressed their complaints to the Certification Officer, accusing the General Secretary of failure to abide by the Rule Book. In particular, the allegedly unauthorized use on the union's behalf of American Express cards by both the General Secretary and his administrative assistant was queried. Under the Trade Union Reform and Employment Rights Act 1993, the Certification Officer was empowered to direct a trade union 'to produce such relevant documents relating to its financial affairs as may be specified'.[24] Under Section 37E(1) of that Act, the approach the Certification Officer had received from the dissident group was being formally treated as a complaint. He directed that he be provided with 'copies of all monthly statements relating to both charge cards with appropriate explanations' within two weeks.

A full-scale assault on the General Secretary's leadership of the union was now being mounted. This included the holding of a press conference at the STUC annual conference. Stevenson and Chambers, flanked by Deputy General Secretary of the STUC Bill Speirs, seeking to make public OILC's internal divisions, issued a lengthy statement denouncing McDonald's 'self-aggrandisement'.[25] The statement concluded, 'We are aware that there is a danger that the Union will be critically damaged. However, Mr McDonald, by his conduct . . . has already brought it to the brink.' It was a sorry episode in which the deep internal divisions of OILC became the gleeful public property of the media and the established unions, courtesy of OILC members themselves.

The Special Conferences had not resolved the terms of reference for the elections to the union's executive. On that basis the General Secretary proceeded to begin the electoral process in terms of the existing union rules. Otherwise, the Organising Committee would become a self-perpetuating oppositional clique. There was a risk, however, of further legal entanglement. As McDonald put it:

If this election is met by a court challenge on the basis that I have acted unconstitutionally, I will have to show the court that the mitigating factor in this was the total gridlock we were in. I either had to walk away, leaving them in charge, or take my responsibilities as General Secretary in hand and implement to the absolute letter the existing Constitution and Rule Book.[26]

The first step was to revive regular meetings of the Standing Committee, which was reconstituted following a mass mailing to the membership seeking new nominations. As per the Rule Book, nominations for the Organising Committee, were in turn drawn from the Standing Committee, which elected six national officers unopposed in May 1994. None of the dissident group stood for election. Indeed, under current rules, the two chief protagonists, Chambers and Stevenson, would in any event have been disbarred as 'out-of-trade' members.

It appeared that OILC was, at last, back on track as a union. The Certification Officer indicated, after examining the financial affairs of the union, that he had not found anything which substantiated the original complaint and, therefore, required formal investigation.[27] However, the weekly meetings in Glasgow provided a continuing focus of opposition. Eventually OILC's new Organising Committee was forced to suspend the branch. Legal entanglement of the union took a new turn with a further complaint by the dissident group to the Certification Officer concerning the conduct of the election of the new Organising Committee. In addition, there was confirmation that application was being made to the Commissioner for the Rights of Trade Union Members (CROTUM) for funding to pursue the union through the courts. The Commissioner had been specifically appointed by Conservative government legislation to provide financial support to just such dissident members within trade unions who wished to launch legal actions against their union executive, and had achieved prominence a few years before as part of the legal wolf-pack tearing at the heels of the NUM leadership in the aftermath of the miners' strike (see Milne, 1994: 70). Now the CROTUM was to become an increasingly intrusive element in the affairs of OILC.

Meanwhile, over a number of months prior to this, the dissident group were already receiving advice from legal counsel and access to a firm of solicitors. Since none of the chief protagonists had steady employment, it was a matter of speculation where they received access to funds to deploy legal resources in the period before the CROTUM arrived on the scene. It may have been purely coincidental that the firm of solicitors which corresponded on behalf of the dissidents was the same firm as that employed by one of the largest North Sea contractors.

The further complaint to the Certification Officer was a carefully judged challenge to the legitimacy of the new Organising Committee, which the dissident group refused to accept. It is of interest because of the wider ramifications for the trade union movement. The election process, it was alleged, had failed to comply with the provisions of Chapter IV of the Trade Union and Labour Relations (Consolidation) Act 1992. Specifically, one of the requirements of elections for executive positions was that the trade union shall appoint an independent person, 'the scrutineer', to supervise the conduct of the elections. A hearing before the Certification Officer, at which Chambers appeared for eight other complainants, took place in October 1994. The issue facing the Certification Officer was, whether the law required a trade union to appoint a scrutineer under section 49 of the 1992 Act where an election was uncontested and a ballot, therefore, was not required. This had never been properly considered before in any previous union election.

OILC's lawyer argued that a scrutineer need only be appointed where an election was contested and that the use of the term 'election' could not be extended to include 'uncontested election'. Section 49 could only apply where an election was contested, otherwise the Act was drafting nonsense. It had originally been the Trade Union Act 1984 which required the election of members of a trade union executive committee, and the Employment Act 1988 which introduced the requirement to appoint a scrutineer, both now consolidated in the 1992 Act. A scrutineer appointed to supervise an uncontested election might be thought to be a plain absurdity. Indeed, the Certification Officer as much as conceded this in an Observation appended to his decision:

> My decision, which I am convinced is the only one compatible with the statutory provisions, may seem to lack some common sense. Certainly it would seem to require the scrutineer in the case of an uncontested election to produce a largely vacuous report.[28]

He argued, however, that even when there was no actual ballot, the scrutineer was still required to ensure that no candidate had been unreasonably excluded from standing. If Parliament had wished to limit scrutiny to elections resolved by ballots, it could have expressly done so, but it had not. Parliament could also have said no scrutineer need be appointed in an uncontested election but did not. The Certification Officer argued such omissions were intentional rather than simply the result of sloppy drafting during the consolidation process. The union was therefore found to be in breach of the 1992 Act.

On legal grounds, this decision was heavily criticized, or in the more gentlemanly language of the legal profession 'with the greatest respect, very much doubted', by the authoritative legal compendium *Harvey on Industrial Relations and Employment Law* (*Harvey*, 1995, Issue 113: M/402ff). While the case stands 'as authority unless and until overturned', it was the view of *Harvey* that the Certification Officer's own admission that his decision might be deficient in common sense, 'may not in itself provide a ground for appeal, but it comes close to it' (*Harvey*, 1995, M/403D, M/402). By failing to specify whether the failure to appoint a scrutineer was 'material', although 'it might well be', the Certification Officer also provided new ammunition for the dissident group, even though he had specifically left it to 'the union to decide how to proceed'. In other words, no instruction was given to re-run the elections even though OILC had indicated its prior willingness to do so.

It would appear that the matter had been laid to rest. However, within a matter of days a letter to OILC arrived in Aberdeen claiming that 'the only legitimate Committee to exist . . . is the original Organising Committee' and summoning McDonald to a meeting in Glasgow on 29 December.[29] A further letter on 30 December announced the intention of the 'original Organising Committee' to call a new election on 2 January 1995 and the initiation of disciplinary action against the General Secretary.[30] Another unsuccessful attempt to involve the Certification Officer in new actions against the OILC failed in January 1995.[31] The communication from the dissident group to the Certification Officer indicated further recourse to the CROTUM was planned 'with a view to applying for a legal Enforcement Order' in order to force a re-run of the election. Such an order could only be obtained as a result of court action, contesting which would be a further drain on OILC's already meagre financial resources. The activity of the dissident group now began to take on bizarre proportions, posing a serious threat to the survival of the union.

Once again, the internal divisions within OILC were spilled across the pages of the press as 'the original Organising Committee' now 'suspended' McDonald from office 'in absentia' after his non-attendance at a three-man 'disciplinary hearing'.[32] At the same time, the union's bank was contacted and instructed by the dissidents to freeze all accounts until further notice. All advertisers in *Blowout* were also contacted. A counter-attempt to discipline those responsible for this damaging manoeuvre, in turn, backfired on the union. It appeared to provide the necessary pretext for the CROTUM to authorize funding long-threatened court action. The current leading figure among the dissidents, Peter Douglass, was given financial assistance to obtain a High Court interdict forbidding a disciplinary hearing by the executive, while CROTUM was also able to finance the pursuit of an order specifically to enforce a re-run of the election within 21 days. This OILC now again offered to do, and duly invited new nominations to the Standing Committee as a preliminary step. An interdict was also granted by Lord Cameron in March 1995 to prevent OILC proceeding with disciplinary action against the dissidents, an interdict which OILC again had not the funds to contest. In the event, Peter Douglass was invited by the General Secretary to stand for office so that, once and for all, the campaign of disruption could be brought to an end.

Here matters stood in the spring of 1995, with any further challenge to OILC leadership doomed to failure, as the dissident group itself began to splinter under its own internal pressures. The challenge from Douglass for the position of OILC chairperson failed decisively in a balloted contest in June 1995 by 390 votes to 135. It had, however, done much to undermine the credibility of OILC, as rumour and allegation circulated both on and offshore. Moreover, the union had been virtually paralysed, just at the moment of the employers' offensive in terms of the CRINE programme, when attendant job cuts and changes in working conditions were being introduced across the industry.

How far there was involvement of the security services against OILC is more difficult to tell. The recourse to the Certification Officer, the intervention of CROTUM, and the allegations about union finances, bore similarities in some respects to the campaign by the media and intelligence services against the NUM (Milne, 1994). As a review of Milne's book in *Blowout* observed:

> It's a fair bet that every trade union has its MI5 or Special Branch placemen. Given the events of late, even the tiny OILC would appear not to be exempt. In fact, it would be most remiss of the authorities if they had failed to infiltrate an organization that had the power to shut down the North Sea oilfield.[33]

OILC Confronts the Employers

Despite its internal problems, OILC continued to slowly build its organization on offshore platforms over this period. The £1.3 billion redevelopment of the Brent field, with massive reconstruction of the topsides of all four platforms, once again brought large numbers of construction 'bears' offshore.

This redevelopment was a crucial aspect of the shift in emphasis from oil recovery to exploitation of natural gas reserves. A key consideration for the operators was the containment of costs, bringing, in turn, pressure on the major contractors. The Brent Bravo was to be shut down for over a year from July 1994, while sequential shutdown work was to begin on the Brent Charlie in 1995 and on the Delta in 1997. Delays in the Brent Bravo work, with potential effects on the other platforms, had already led to client anxiety concerning the need to limit expenditures to the original budget. The Brent redevelopment typified the new 'partnering' relationship between clients Shell/Esso and offshore contractors, developed under the CRINE programme. Any prospect of the revival of a combative workforce would therefore be an extremely unwelcome development for the employers in the North Sea.

Just at the moment when the accommodation with the established trade unions was expected to yield the benefits of a quiescent workforce, OILC proved to be the wild card. Activists on the Brent Charlie and Brent Delta were instrumental in organizing a ballot of Wood Group personnel in March and April 1995. The question on the ballot sheet was simple:

Do you want trade union representation on your terms and conditions? Tick one box 'Yes' ☐ 'No' ☐ If 'Yes', which trade union?

The results were unequivocal, as Table 10.1 shows.

In fact, the outcome of the ballot should not have been at all surprising,

Table 10.1 *Wood Group Employees' Ballot on Union Representation and Union Choice*

	Papers issued	Papers returned	Yes	No
Brent Charlie	219	213	212	1
Brent Delta	145	136	134	2
TOTAL	364	349	346	3

	OILC	MSF	AEEU	Amalgamated AEEU/OILC	GMB	No preference
Choice of union	292	3	25	1	10	15

Source: OILC

given the erosion of terms and conditions which had taken place for the contractor workforce since the gains of 1989/90. In consequence, 57 Wood Group employees registered a grievance under the terms of their contract. OILC activists were to take Sir Ian Wood, currently ranked 108th among the 500 richest people in Britain, at his word. Sir Ian was reminded of his statement during the 1990 dispute when he had proclaimed in a BBC Radio Scotland discussion programme, 'We do recognise trade unions. All our agreements cover the right of any of our employees who are in trade unions to be represented by that trade union in any dispute that takes place.[34]

In one respect, however, the position of Wood Group had changed since then. Prior to OILC becoming a trade union, the Terms and Conditions of Employment did indeed stipulate the right of employees to be represented by a trade union in the company grievance procedure. More recently, there had been a new stipulation in the Terms and Conditions of Employment. Such representation had to be exclusively from a TUC registered trade union recognized by the Offshore Contractors Association. A letter to Sir Ian Wood from OILC seeking clarification of the new Terms and Conditions, produced the following response from Wood Group:

> We have for many years had regular dialogue with Trade Unions registered with the TUC. This association has worked well and has given a high degree of comfort in our dealings on industrial relations matters. We would not wish to see this disturbed and our Terms and Conditions of Employment reflect this.[35]

OILC had achieved overwhelming density among the majority of Wood Group's offshore employees on the Brent platforms. Its claim to recognition in its own right might at first glance have appeared irresistible. But the breakthrough on the Brents had still to reckon with the power of the established unions. Lerner had observed in her earlier study of breakaway unions:

> New unions (whether or not formed as a result of a secession) are generally smaller and weaker than the established unions. Of course, ... they may grow stronger than the recognized unions in individual firms and compel individual employers to grant them negotiating rights in spite of the opposition of the established unions. But they rarely match the combined strength of the established unions. (1961: 194)

'Combined strength' of the established TUC unions was being exercised collectively with the contractor employers to resist encroachment by OILC.

This employers' 'dialogue' with the TUC unions has been documented previously in our analysis. While current employment law did not compel an employer to recognize trade unions, the Trade Union and Labour Relations (Consolidation) Act 1992 did specifically recognize the right of employees to join a union of their choice. This 'freedom of choice' was precisely in order to undercut the TUC unions' hegemony in industrial relations matters.[36] Having created the space for competitive unionism, the employers, courtesy of Conservative government legislation, had now to live with the consequences for the management of offshore industrial relations. But again Lerner's observation holds true here:

> The argument that employers use breakaway or new unions as catspaws against the established unions has little validity in Great Britain today. Employers' associations oppose breakaway unions and new unions almost as strongly as do established unions. (1961: 195)

Wood Group was to continue to rebuff OILC for the next ten months, eventually provoking the Brent Charlie and Delta workforce to work to rule. But nothing in law compelled Wood Group to negotiate with the workforce's chosen union. In the aftermath of the 1990 dispute the company had established a 'Workers Forum' to enable elected spokespersons to represent its workers. When this non-union consultative arrangement looked as if it would pursue contentious issues it had been allowed to wither and die. Faced with the results of the ballot of its employees seeking collective representation through OILC, the idea of the Workers Forum was hastily revived by Wood Group management.

Other successful ballots were to be held, most notably on the drilling rig, Divy Stena, in the autumn of 1995. Again the workforce voted for trade union representation (73 to 1) and overwhelmingly for representation by OILC (64 votes). The personnel manager, working for Stena's employment agency front, Northern Marine Management, was none other than George Simpson, an ex-RMT official. He was able to offer an immediate 6 per cent pay rise in order to quench the desire for unionism in the form of OILC. In a subsequent ballot, employees unanimously rejected management attempts to impose new terms and conditions without consultation. Faced with this, Stena then attempted to exploit an anomaly in current employment law, whereby an employer may choose to confer recognition on a particular union for the purpose of that union endorsing terms and conditions. Such terms and conditions may then cover all employees whether or not members of the favoured union. In this case, unions from the largely defunct British Seafarers Joint Council, RMT,

NUMAST and the AEEU, were revived to perform this role. Such was the price to ensure that OILC remained out in the cold.

Today OILC, on its own, finds it difficult to break out of this isolation. If OILC were to enter into an eventual amalgamation with a sympathetic TUC union, the barrier against its influence could be breached. It was with some consternation that the TUC learned in Spring 1995 of ongoing discussions taking place between OILC and the NUM with a view to possible future merger between the two unions. In a letter to Scargill from John Monks, the TUC General Secretary, it was pointed out that the TUC unions operating in the North Sea regarded OILC as a 'breakaway organization'. Monks observed:

> In the light of my past point and in regard to the TUC's and NUM's position on the breakaway UDM, you will readily understand that it is my expectation that NUM would not enter into any form of relationship with OILC.[37]

The label of 'breakaway' was rejected by OILC on the grounds that as a union it did not seek to adopt a pro-employer stance or undermine existing bargaining structures, since 'Such structures do not exist on any meaningful level in the offshore oil and gas industry. It is, to all intents and purposes, an unorganised province.'[38] The established unions had 'sold the pass' by re-signing the Hook-up agreements and thus accepting their continuing derecognition in post-construction. OILC, therefore, 'as a new union, is entitled to strive to organise'.

Whether OILC is more properly characterized as a 'breakaway' or simply a 'new' union, remains a matter for debate. There was a powerful logic in the amalgamation of two industrial unions in the energy sector, covering coal and oil and gas. The ferocity of the established unions' reaction to the merger proposal was such that even a veteran combatant like Scargill ruefully observed, in private, that he had achieved the one thing that he had never before succeeded in doing – 'uniting the Left and the Right in the TUC General Council!' If the NUM persisted in its strategy then there was the threat of expulsion from the TUC.[39] Yet OILC, despite its difficulties and the forces ranged against it, seemed set to persist, with or without employer or TUC recognition. Intimations of OILC's early demise were not borne out. Lerner's study noted:

> Although most splinter unions die after a short period, others continue to exist year after year without any prospect of securing recognition. The

ability to live in spite of all odds, the sheer stubbornness of splinter unions, is truly amazing. (1961: 197)

Perhaps, given the circumstances of OILC's formation and its subsequent history, it was not so amazing after all.

The AEEU Super-union

The established unions with offshore interests mobilized their full resources both to prevent the growth of OILC and to undermine its credibility. As far back as the autumn of 1991 a whispering campaign had been set in motion by Tom MacLean, chairman of the National Offshore Committee, within days of the announcement that OILC was to seek independent status as a union. MacLean had asked AEU solicitors to inquire into payments from the offshore hardship fund, which had been set up in 1990 to help victimized workers and their families during the dispute. The press statement read: 'The AEU is most concerned about who is receiving payment from the fund and whether those receiving payment are in fact dismissed oil workers in hardship.'[40]

The hardship fund had been set up under the auspices of the STUC as a charitable trust, with a prominent board of trustees, including the head of the Church of Scotland Industrial Mission, the Rev. Dr Hugh Ormiston, the president of the FBU, Ronnie Scott, plus Mike Morris, assistant principal at Lauder College and Jurgen Thomaneck, president of Aberdeen Trades Council. The trustees angrily issued a rebuttal statement, and the STUC deputy General Secretary, Bill Speirs, further expressed 'complete faith in the integrity of the fund's trustees'. It was only the start of a continuing campaign of smear and innuendo directed at OILC and its General Secretary's 'gold card lifestyle' and 'expensive motorcar'. In fact, the hardship fund had produced two fully audited sets of accounts itemizing the disbursements totalling some £60,590 of voluntary donations before it was finally wound down in the autumn of 1992.[41]

The offshore oil industry was probably marginal to AEU's concerns. The AEU's need to combat OILC influence was driven by a wider concern to develop a 'business-friendly' strategy towards employers, both offshore and on. If OILC was allowed to survive as the 'living rejection' of such employer-dominated bargaining arrangements as the offshore Hook-up agreement, then its example could have a profoundly destabilizing effect in key onshore bargaining arrangements. These included the onshore engineering and construction industry agreement, the National Agreement for the Engineering Construction Industry (NAECI). The NAECI was characterized by its critics as 'a no-strike agreement in all but name'.[42] While work on large onshore construction sites had declined during the 1980s, major current projects governed by NAECI included the Shellhaven refinery and the Sellafield and Sizewell B power stations. In a bid to consolidate its mutual sectional courtship with the EETPU, the AEU had tried unsuccessfully to vote EETPU executive member Paul Bevis into the chair of the union side of the NAECI joint council. This manoeuvre, in anticipation of future merger, was in breach of the tradition that the chair of the joint union side always went to the third co-venturer in NAECI, the GMB.

Shop stewards in the onshore engineering construction industry, like their offshore counterparts, were becoming increasingly dissatisfied with these manoeuvres and at the way the employers were seeking to use the unions to police collective agreements. In the 'feast and famine' of a highly casualized industry, site level activism and militancy had been integral to the identity of the former Constructional Engineering Union (CEU) which had organized the scaffolders, riggers and steel erectors. Since its amalgamation with the mechanical engineers, the CEU membership had formed the core of the AEU's membership in this industry. The virtue of NAECI in the eyes of Tom MacLean, as leader of the NAECI unions, was precisely that it had ended the 'anarchy' which had prevailed in the industry in the 1960s and 1970s.[43] The NAECI, in centralizing control over wages and conditions in national-level negotiations, had to some extent eroded local-level militancy and organization. With the downturn in the construction industry, after a short boom in the late 1980s, clients and contractors increasingly now abandoned centralized bargaining. The space for a renewed employers' offensive on wages and conditions had been created. The workforce were beginning to demand to be consulted by a ballot before any new agreement was signed, and for a number of proposed objectionable clauses to be withdrawn. Among these were the loss of a Friday tea-break, reduction in overtime payment and the imposition of a lengthy dispute procedure culminating in binding arbitration during which no officially backed industrial action could be taken. In exchange, the employers in 1992 had offered a cut in the working week from 39 to 38 hours and a 4.1 per cent pay increase.

It was the NAECI agreement which the steel erectors on London building sites had come up against during their successful unofficial strike in 1989. In the immediate aftermath of that strike, pay increases of 9.4 to 15.2 per cent on basic rates, plus a London accommodation allowance supplement of £4.03 per day had been conceded to prevent a further repetition of such action.[44]

Several of those blacklisted shop stewards had ended up working under false names in the North Sea to escape employer victimization. With the downturn in the industry, such temporary concessions needed to be withdrawn. Here too, in the onshore sector, were worrying rumblings of rank-and-file discontent. These eventually erupted into a rank-and-file boycott of the agreed increase, unofficial stoppages and the temporary formation of a national *ad hoc* NAECI shop stewards' committee, the Combined Sites Liaison Committee, bearing striking similarities to the early formation of OILC.[45] If this could not be contained by the AEU executive, or if it were to receive impetus from discontent offshore, it would have made it very difficult for the AEU to present itself as a credible suitor to the EETPU or to retain credibility in its policing role in the eyes of the employers.

Outside the construction industry, the 'business-friendly' strategy also prevailed. The AEU had its eye upon a single-union agreement with the Toyota car company for its new plant in Derbyshire opening in 1992, the most important since Nissan arrived on Tyneside in 1986. As the 'beauty contest' at Toyota unfolded, MSF denounced the 'Dutch auction' of five competing union bids for company recognition in a motion at that year's autumn TUC conference. The 'alien approach' of some foreign investors had resulted, said MSF, in 'civil rights being abandoned at every turn'. What MSF sought was a TUC code of conduct that would prevent unions offering 'no-strike deals' in exchange for membership advantage. In fact, experience at Nissan suggested that where such single-union agreements existed, less than half the potential membership took up the opportunity of joining the union. Gavin Laird, speaking against the MSF motion at the TUC, described it as a 'racist and negative piece of contraband'.[46] The terms of the Toyota deal, eventually secured by the AEU, were to include a two-year pay freeze after an initial pay settlement and a binding arbitration 'no disruption' clause.[47] While both sides were keen to emphasize that this was not a 'no-strike' agreement, critical observers maintained that the effect of such agreements was to produce a workplace unionism that was almost totally incorporated into management structures, with little independent initiative or identity. The credibility of MSF's stance, however, was somewhat dented the following year, after another 'beauty contest', when it too signed a single union deal with the Japanese company Toray Textiles Europe Ltd., on a greenfield site in Nottinghamshire, which involved binding pendulum arbitration by ACAS.

The belligerent stance of the AEU towards other unions, not just OILC, mirrored its willingness to accommodate employers. If anything it intensified with the final consummation of the merger process between the AEU and the EETPU. The new 835,000-strong super-union, the AEEU (Amalgamated

Engineering and Electrical Union) was proclaimed on the symbolic 1 May 1992. It formed a new powerful bloc in the trade union movement leaning heavily towards the right wing. A ballot of AEU members had previously endorsed the merger by 86.5 per cent in a 35 per cent turnout while a similar EETPU ballot produced a vote of 84.5 per cent in favour in a 41.4 per cent turnout.[48] The way was now open for the EETPU to gain readmittance to the TUC by the back door, which it finally succeeded in doing at the following year's, 1993 TUC annual conference, after the usual horse-trading, including a promise from the electricians henceforth to abide by TUC rules.[49]

The AEEU was now poised to take control of the mechanical engineering and construction industry both onshore and offshore. Indeed, when the successful merger was eventually completed in 1992, other NAECI signatory unions, the TGWU and MSF, as well as the GMB, were predictably squeezed out. The AEEU concluded single-union deals to replace the NAECI at the new Mobil refinery in Stanford Le Hope, Essex, and at Esso's refinery at Mossmorran in Fife.[50] Rank-and-file discontent, which had initially surfaced in parallel with OILC's own disaffection with the official union leadership, was to rumble on and resurface in 1993, and again in 1994, when MacLean abandoned plans for selective strikes financed by a weekly £5 levy on the membership. Further concessions of hard-won rights in a trade-off for a minimal pay rise, including more flexibility and redundancies, were negotiated against the wishes of site representatives.[51] Site-level demands for democratic consultation, ignored by the leadership before the endorsement of the national agreeement, continued to provoke unrest among the onshore construction workforce. In order to head this off, a regional consultative structure of officials and shop stewards was finally set up, so that by early 1995 an employers' offer of 3.3 per cent on basic rates was endorsed by shop stewards by 2 to 1, and thereafter by site meetings.[52]

The setting up of a new AEEU Civil and Building Trades Section, likewise indicated the comprehensive ambitions of the new 'super-union'. The AEEU construction section would carry forward the EETPU's previous membership raids on the building workers' union UCATT, into further incursions in the building industry and civil engineering industry.[53] The AEEU's broader offensive had succeeded in poaching several hundred members from both UCATT and the TGWU, as well as undermining two national agreements, the National Joint Building Industry Working Rules Agreement and the Civil Engineering Conciliation Board. This offensive resulted in a list of complaints to the TUC. A disputes committee eventually awarded £100,000 to UCATT and £7000 to the TGWU as compensation for the subscriptions lost by the two unions to the AEEU through membership poaching over the previous two years. The 'fine' levied on the AEEU, unprecedented in its severity in the TUC's history, was evidence of the TUC determination to prevent the outbreak of membership recruitment warfare between competing unions at a time when union memberships overall were experiencing sharp decline and recent employment law eroded its former policing procedures under the Bridlington rules.

The TUC disputes committee rejected an AEEU application to be granted recognition in the two national agreements in the construction industry which it had tried to undermine. Any further attempts to seek membership in the industry would be permitted only 'within very strict limits' and the AEEU was enjoined to give reports on its activities in this area to the TUC disputes committee every four months.[54] The AEEU, for its part, was expected to examine the legal standing of the ruling. Paul Gallagher, General Secretary of the electricians' section, was rumoured to have warned that the AEEU could well contemplate a future outside the realms of the TUC, thus resurrecting the threat to create a rival right-wing trade union centre. Indeed, just two weeks after these fines were imposed, the AEEU announced a further recruitment drive to sign up building workers.[55]

Tommy Lafferty

The new Amalgamated Engineering and Electrical Union (AEEU) was characterized by aggressive membership recruitment in the onshore construction industry, the smothering of rank-and-file discontent and a compliant approach to employers. This approach was transposed into offshore activities. Following its merger with the EETPU, the AEU's previously precarious 'offshore section' was put on an entirely new war footing. The enemy was OILC and any other competitor unions offshore, and the AEEU's ally was the contractor employers. The new strategy required new officials who were 'uncontaminated' with the virus of OILC activism and who would unquestioningly pursue the employer-friendly approach which the union was seeking to develop.

The final break with the past in offshore affairs was marked by significant personnel changes at local level in Aberdeen. As the amalgamation reached its consummation, it was important that the key official with offshore responsibilities would at all times follow the union's diktat. This the present incumbent, Tommy Lafferty, had notably failed to do. Lafferty was the AEU organizer for the Construction Section in the North of Scotland, whose own long union career had embraced all the ups and the many downs of the offshore industry's trade union saga. In a bitter re-election contest he had been defeated by Rab Wilson, the Nigg Bay convener, in late 1991. That Wilson should have made the challenge was a surprise to many in the union. Wilson had taken over from Lafferty as yard convener at Nigg in the mid-seventies, when Lafferty moved north to become the convener at the Flotta terminal. As there was no full-time organizer for the North East and for the oil industry, a new post was created, and Lafferty was initially appointed. Thereafter he was re-elected unopposed throughout the 1980s. As a divisional delegate in the grass-roots democracy inherited from the Constructional Engineering Union (CEU), Wilson had every opportunity to call to account the activities of Lafferty, as his Divisional Organiser. This he had not done. Now he announced his candidature.

Lafferty claimed that Wilson's use of the AEU logo on his election posters had made it appear as if Wilson were the 'official' union-backed candidate. Such unauthorized use, while not a breach of rule, was subsequently expressly forbidden by the AEU.[56] Wilson had now muted his earlier criticisms of the Hook-up agreement voiced during the AEU National Conference in the spring. In the autumn 1991 election period he had proved his loyalty to the AEU leadership by echoing official condemnation of OILC's announced move to independent union status. The election vote was 785 to 663, in a 36.9 per cent return, close enough for Lafferty to seek legal counsel with a view to challenging the ballot result and Wilson's conduct of the campaign. Many of Lafferty's own members in the north who could have voted failed to do so. But 166 ballot papers had allegedly been incorrectly sent to former members of the Construction Section not entitled to vote, including 65 distributed to lapsed union members from Invergordon alone. After lengthy correspondence between Lafferty and the AEU General Secretary, Gavin Laird, the union's view was that 'the mistakes which have been made do not invalidate the result of the election'.[57] In the end, Wilson's election remained unchallenged, although unsurprisingly, relations between the two men sharply deteriorated thereafter.

Lafferty had previously been sent a dossier in August 1991 from Tom MacLean. This was compiled by an unnamed third party, some believe the Offshore Contractors Council. The dossier's purpose was, in MacLean's words, 'to demonstrate to me that you, as a Full Time Official are not pursuing the policies of the Union with regard to the Offshore Industry.'[58] Included in the dossier was a précis of Lafferty's questions to Ronnie McDonald at the Industrial Tribunal for John Dick, the test case conducted by Lafferty for those with under two years' service who were dismissed as a result of the dispute in 1990. The dossier implied that Lafferty had been overly sympathetic to

OILC. Lafferty was accused of attempting to show 'that OILC, while an unofficial body, did enjoy a high level of recognition by companies and legislators'.[59] Also included was a transcript of an August 1991 radio interview, broadcast on the first anniversary of the 1990 industrial action, in which Lafferty attacked the continuing blacklisting of activists by the employers and the delay in progressing tribunals for the dismissed workers.[60] In MacLean's formulation, 'The statements, as enclosed, would appear to demonstrate your hostility towards the OCC and Clients and your support for OILC'.[61] This was clearly out of line with the AEU's overall accommodation with the OCC which, by August 1991, was rapidly moving towards the re-signing of the Hook-up agreement. MacLean's warning was explicit: 'Please make sure in future that statements made by you are consistent with the agreed policies of the Union as laid down by the Executive Council'.[62]

Local officials had already been drummed into line at a stormy meeeting with the national officials referred to in the previous chapter. Lafferty, however, committed the unforgivable mistake of continuing to oppose the Hook-up agreement and of supporting the OILC. The AEU's payback came with the election of Wilson and the deposing of Lafferty after seventeen years in the post as a full-time official.

To add to this blow, Lafferty suffered a grievous personal loss in the suicide of his son. Lafferty took his own life six weeks later in October 1993. It was at this point that allegations were made public of possible fraud in the conduct of a Piper Alpha Hardship Fund of which Lafferty was the sole trustee. This led the AEEU to order the account to be frozen. The sum involved, some £17,000, had been donated by workers in the construction industry at the time of the disaster, but was never combined into the Lord Provost of Aberdeen's Fund, the main source paying out compensation from public donations. When it looked as if relatives of victims would be means-tested, the AEU had held the money back. Since then, everyone had forgotten about it. Lafferty's error had been his failure to pass on control of the fund to Wilson following his election defeat. It was typical of Lafferty's cavalier attitude to the bureaucratic niceties to have allowed the fund to become mixed up with his personal finances. Indeed, probably the only paperwork Lafferty ever organized with anything like meticulous detail was the file detailing his correspondence with union head office in his attempt to have the election contest with Rab Wilson re-run.[63]

Lafferty was a combative official who had come up the hard way and whom the construction bosses feared for his straight talking. He had been on the 'wrong' side on the 1979 strike and the 'bears' never allowed him to forget it. But Piper Alpha had been a turning point in his life and he had stood shoulder to shoulder with rank-and-file struggles since then. Bob Ballantyne, a Piper Alpha survivor, summed up this tragic suicide: 'Tommy Lafferty was affected deeply by Piper Alpha and he looked after us when other people didn't.'[64] Lafferty had driven to Glasgow and parked on the top floor of a multi-storey car park, from which he had fallen to his death. Piper survivors and dependants had already unexpectedly received cheques from Lafferty earlier that week. Inside Lafferty's car were found more neatly addressed brown envelopes containing further sums of money to be distributed.

Lafferty's long-time compatriot in the offshore union scene, Bob Eadie, the EETPU official, was also to depart. Initially a reluctant supporter of OILC during the 1990 action, he had ensured that the EETPU participated in the demand for a Continental Shelf Agreement and ensured that the electricians' own sectional SJIB agreement had been suspended temporarily in favour of the 'one-table approach'. His replacement, who arrived in the renamed and refurbished AEEU office in Aberdeen, was Bobby Buirds. Buirds, a former electricians' shop steward on the Tern hook-up in 1988–89, had previously been based in the EETPU office in Edinburgh. As a shop steward he had been one of the most vocal critics of the Hook-up agreement during the initial hostilities launched by OILC in the summer of 1989. Now he had become an implacable foe of the OILC and a defender of the very agreement, the Hook-up, which he and other founding members of OILC had fought to reject.

The Established Unions: New and Existing Inter-union Bodies

The AEU had been a reluctant party to the hastily cobbled 'unity' achieved at the end of 1991, which resulted in the established unions agreeing to participate in an Offshore Federation of sorts. It was to prove an equally reluctant participant in all further attempts to forge inter-union unity offshore, especially following its amalgamation with the EETPU. A year later, due to AEEU stalling, the Offshore Federation was still a matter of contentious discussion. An attempt to establish the Offshore Federation, as a sub-committee of the long-existing onshore-based inter-union body, the Confederation of Shipbuilding and Engineering Unions, foundered dramatically in late November 1992. After fifteen minutes, the AEEU walked out. The bone of contention was the refusal of the other unions present to agree to the exclusion of the pro-TUC 'breakaway' electricians' union, the EPIU. The electricians' section of the merged AEEU had no wish to see its breakaway rival achieve any part in offshore affairs. Five months earlier, in June 1992, a bid by the EPIU to affiliate directly to the Confederation of Shipbuilding and Engineering Unions had also been narrowly defeated on a card vote by the AEEU. The hostility of the old EETPU leadership to the presence of the EPIU in any forum of the trade union movement remained undiminished in the new AEEU. The EPIU duly lodged a complaint with the TUC.

The other established unions with offshore interests meanwhile attempted to keep the idea of the Offshore Federation alive. A new body was given the confusingly similar title of the Offshore Industry Unions Co-ordinating Committee (OIUCC), separate from the long-established Inter Union Offshore Oil Committee discussed in Chapter 2. The IUOOC had continued to meet as before with the oil company employers on the previous purely consultative basis over this period, but, unlike the new inter-union body, *with* the participation of the AEEU. Even dedicated union activists were beginning to find it difficult to steer their way through this maze of inter-union committees.

The new-formed Offshore Industry Unions Co-ordinating Committee (OIUCC), as an inter-union body, began the laborious task of attempting to improve co-operation between the established unions. Proposals to sort out clearly defined 'spheres of interest', co-ordinated training and research facilities, the establishment of a newsletter and the formation of committees of safety representatives from all the installations of a particular company, were voiced at its first meeting. In addition, demands for appointment of company-based Senior Safety Representatives plus Senior Safety Representatives at platform level along Norwegian lines, and the creation of local area-based inter-union committees, were also aired at the first conference of the OIUCC.[65] When nearly a year and a half later the second conference was convened in March 1995, progress on most of these items was still negligible.

Some more substantial progress was made by the established unions in the training of safety representatives offshore. In 1995 an infusion of European Union funds to the TUC provided £95,000 for a handbook and distance-learning package for offshore safety representatives. A further £124,000 of EU money enabled a series of meetings between officials to strengthen international co-operation among oil unions from the UK, Netherlands, Ireland, Denmark and Norway. The focus of these meetings was the proposed review of the Working Time Directive and the potential opportunities for oil unions created by the European Works Council Directive. The European Works Council Directive eventually came into effect in 1996. Although the UK government had opted out of such social provisions at Maastricht, the possibility existed of UK representatives being invited by another Member country to participate in Works Councils in certain circumstances. A list of half a dozen 'largest companies', oil operators who spanned more than one European country, was being prepared in the hope of exploiting this somewhat tenuous opening. There was also the beginning of a formal arrangement between UK and Norwegian unions, with a link-up of offshore membership services between TGWU, RMT and NOPEF (the Norwegian Oil and Petrochemical Workers Union). This complemented a more long-standing agreement between MSF and NOPEF for joint membership services.[66]

Domestic issues, however, were hardly moving forward at all under the Offshore Industry Unions Co-ordinating Committee. Local area inter-union committees had still to be set up, an offshore newsletter produced, and co-ordinated research facilities put in place. Training for safety representatives, now mainly under TUC auspices, was slowly getting off the ground, but even with distance-learning facilities, in the absence of statutory rights for time off for training and the right of the safety representatives to embark on the course of their choice, take-up of such courses would inevitably be limited. By the second conference of the new offshore inter-union committee in the spring of 1995 there were at least some concrete proposals being considered on the critical issue of defining 'spheres of interest' offshore, the cause historically of so much debilitating inter-union friction.[67] However, as one close observer of these events noted in a confidential report to the oil industry, 'What was not discussed at the Conference were the difficulties that there will be in reaching agreement with certain of the unions who have recruited widely and are reluctant to give up members.'[68] Even if the affiliated unions could agree on spheres of influence amongst themselves, there would still be the question of the AEEU's non-participation; without AEEU, creation of an Offshore Federation would be impossible. One decision of the first conference was to simplify the name of the new inter-union body. By the second conference it was known as the Offshore Unions Co-ordinating Committee (OUCC). So far as most of the offshore workforce was concerned, this body, whatever its name, remained largely unknown and irrelevant. The oil companies, meanwhile, simply declined to meet the new body, preferring instead the existing consultative arrangements with the longer-established tried and trusted IUOOC.

The IUOOC, although shaken by the events of the previous few years, continued to function as a limited inter-union forum. Here too the ambitions of the AEEU proved a disruptive force. Claiming that the merger between the electricians and engineers was not yet organizationally complete, the AEEU demanded two votes on the IUOOC for each union. MSF had opposed this. An attempt by the AEEU to seize the chair of the IUOOC had also been defeated.[69] Long discussions as to how the IUOOC should promote itself and on the need to counteract 'a definite swing to OILC by the local press' by becoming more 'pro-active', indicated a continuing lack of direction.[70] Then, in September 1994, the AEEU hosted its own 'European Offshore Oil and Gas Industry Conference', cocking a snook at affiliates on both old and new inter-union committees.

Even where the IUOOC could have had a degree of effectiveness in shaping offshore affairs, for example through its nominated directors on the Offshore Petroleum Industry Training Organisation (OPITO), it failed to intervene in key safety discussions covering the new Offshore Safety Induction and Emergency Training Course. This course was reduced in 1994 from 4.5 to 2.5 days training as part of cost-saving rationalization. Bobby Buirds of the AEEU, as nominee of the IUOOC on the OPITO Working Group charged with drafting the new training modules, had been unable to attend the relevant meetings of OPITO's Working Group.[71] The reductions in survival training, with their potential safety implications, had apparently been achieved largely without opposition from the established unions, who increasingly acceded to the operators' cost-cutting agenda. Thus, while the established unions, with TUC support, now had greater access to considerable financial and organizational inputs, the longer-term impact of these initiatives, both at domestic and international level, remained uncertain. Linkages remained uneven at union leadership level, and equally so between these leaderships and the offshore workforce at platform level. In that sense neither the existing nor the newly created inter-union body appeared capable of resolving the long-standing problems of offshore trade unionism, far less of meeting the new challenge of CRINE.

The Trade Union Consultative Committee: 'Super-union' Sectionalism

The difficulties the AEEU created for inter-union co-operation, and the continuing stagnation of the original inter-union body, the IUOOC, were augmented by another development in the offshore scene. In 1992, a new 'Trade Union Consultative Committee' was established which involved the employers, grouped in the Offshore Contractors Council, and the two key signatory Hook-up unions, the AEEU and its junior partner, the GMB. This signalled a further twist in the spiral of offshore 'super-union' sectionalism. The AEEU heralded the new consultative committee with the contractors as 'a significant movement by negotiation towards union recognition for offshore post-construction work'.[72] Whether 'negotiation' played any part in the setting up of the committee was doubtful. Even more doubtful was any prospect of comprehensive 'post-construction' recognition emerging from its deliberations. What was much more likely was that the contractors were willing to agree to a partial accommodation with the two dominant signatory Hook-up unions. This would act in the mutual interest both of contractor employers and unions as a hedge against any growth in support for OILC and to bolster the credibility of the Hook-up unions as a force capable of delivering 'real results' to their memberships. More importantly, this consultative committee provided the contractor employers with a useful vehicle for 'educating' the trade unions into the necessary 'realities' resulting from the CRINE programme. In 1992/93 the operators' cost-cutting project was in full force. As a consequence the numbers of employees offshore declined sharply. There was also pressure on the contractors to cut back on the charges which they had pushed up by between 20 and 30 per cent during the surge of offshore activity in the early 1990s. The expectations of the contract labour force were to be dampened down.

The real objectives behind the establishment of the Trade Union Consultative Committee with the offshore contractors can be discerned from the constitution and remit of the new joint body. The contractors fielded six employer members, while the union side fielded six representatives, two each from the engineering and electrician sectors of the AEEU and two from the GMB, thus underscoring the hegemony of the AEEU in offshore affairs. On a strict pro rata membership basis, the two places reserved for the GMB may even have been generous. The Trade Union Consultative Committee was to meet once a quarter to consider issues of safety and training. A further objective was 'working together to ensure that the offshore contracting industry is cost-effective', the central objective of the CRINE programme. Finally, the committee would establish a database of contractor employees, perhaps to replicate the employment agency function of the electricians' union joint industrial board, the SJIB, with the electrical contractor employers. Nowhere was the establishment of comprehensive collective bargaining arrangements mentioned. Nevertheless, the AEEU claimed, 'there is the possibility it [the Trade Union Consultative Committee] can take on a more formal role'.[73]

The storm of criticism from other unions with offshore interests led the AEEU to counter that these unions had 'achieved nothing with other groups of employers'. Accordingly, said the AEEU, 'This move forward by our Union does not prevent co-operation between Unions, but gives that necessary lead forward as an example for other Unions to follow.'[74] Such a rationale was identical to that of the EETPU in its previous vigorous defence of the SJIB agreement, the only limited area of post-construction recognition hitherto. In practice, the Trade Union Consultative Committee, as an employer-dominated forum, was hardly capable of doing more than magnifying the sectional divisiveness which had all along dogged the development of off-shore unionism. The MSF union, formerly also a Hook-up agreement co-signatory, was yet again excluded from this new body. Roger Spiller, its aggrieved official, commented, 'Another cosy deal is being set up and that won't be to the advantage of the workforce. It knocks on the head the idea that the AEEU, in particular, is prepared to co-operate with colleagues in other unions.'[75]

By the summer of 1994 the Trade Union Consultative Committee had pro-gressed to a 'more formal arrangement'. There would be an agreed agenda with joint secretaries and agreed minutes of the discussions collated by the joint chairpersons, Bobby Buirds from the union side and George Beattie of AOC International, and chair of the OCC, from the employers.[76] However, a union request that such committee minutes be distributed offshore was regarded as 'ill-advised', after discussion at national level between Ian Bell, secretary of OCC and Tom MacLean. Any briefing put out to the platforms 'Could be misconstrued by other people and, therefore, it would only be put out if there was an issue where a joint agreement had been reached for a par-ticular item'.[77]

'Other people' in this context was a thinly veiled reference to OILC. Even in terms of its own restricted remit, the Trade Union Consultative Committee seemed little more than a talking shop. A reading of minutes reveals union concerns about three-week work rotas being introduced by operators such as Chevron. Also raised were issues of excessive overtime, helicopter shuttling in bad weather and unfair selection procedures for redundancy due to client pressure to remove individuals whose 'face didn't fit'. All these, key issues for offshore union members, were met with evasion or, in the case of helicopter flights, the threat that 'if the man continually refuses to shuttle ... then they (the employers) will have to look at the individual's ability to work in an off-shore environment'.[78] The dangers of the minutes being 'misconstrued by other people' were amply confirmed by an additional item of business on which there did seem to be agreement between unions and employers. This recorded George Beattie's 'dismay' that the OILC General Secretary, Ronnie McDonald, had yet again been invited to speak on health and safety at a major oil industry conference. Beattie asked the unions 'whether they could use their influence to prevent McDonald appearing at these seminars'. For the union side, Bobby Buirds replied that 'it was up to the OCC to stop sending people to these seminars'. Companies running these seminars were doing so for profit and thus if no-one turned up there would be no profit. 'Economic pressure' should 'stop the companies using McDonald'. However, the trade union side 'agreed to do their part in trying to prevent companies giving Ronnie McDonald a platform'.[79] With joint agreement on concerns such as these, it was not surprising that progress in other areas remained slow. Just how slow can be seen by examining those sectional 'gains' the AEEU did succeed in achieving over this period.

The Hook-up Agreement 1992–95

The re-signing of the Hook-up agreement in late August 1991 was a significant moment in the evolution of the North Sea saga. It was the turning point in OILC's relations with the established unions. On the positive side, for the first time, one Hook-up agreement covered both northern and southern North Sea waters and wage rates between the two sectors had been equalized. Yet, following a year in abeyance as an accompaniment of the 1990 industrial action, the agreement epitomized the reinstatement and the limitations of sectional bargaining. This was never more so than in the early 1990s, with the last burst of fourteen new North Sea fields coming on stream between 1990 and 1992. Thereafter the focus of offshore activity and oil investment began to shift elsewhere. Hook-ups as such were rapidly becoming an area of declining activity. They would hardly figure at all in the development of the new Atlantic oil province west of Shetland where floating production units rather than fixed platforms were to be the norm. Nevertheless, some half-a-dozen major projects were undertaken during the early 1990s which could have provided the seed-bed for more sustained trade union recruitment and growth. AEEU claims to have as many as 6000 members offshore were generally regarded as being completely unrealistic by other unions.[80] On the Miller and Piper Bravo hook-ups, fewer than 70 of a total of 700 possible members were paying union members, and similar numbers were lapsed.[81] Such figures were in no way atypical. They had previously led to calls from shop stewards on the Miller project for an amnesty from the £45 rejoin fee for out-of-compliance members, in an effort to boost recruitment. A report of a visit offshore by officials of the Hook-up signatory unions, following unrest over the re-signing of the 1993 Hook-up agreement, describes a platform meeting of nearly 300 at which only 40 were members in compliance and able to vote, of whom 39 were against the deal and only one in favour.[82]

The 1992 Hook-up agreement had been re-signed, bringing wage rises roughly in line with inflation at 6 per cent for the majority of the skilled craftsmen workforce.[83] The engineering union leadership felt sufficiently combative over this contentious agreement to attempt to append a general motion on offshore safety at the 1992 STUC annual conference, with the congratulatory words, 'Congress welcomes agreements such as the Hook-up Agreement'.[84] As much as anything, this was to signal to the rest of the trade union movement the rejection of the charge by OILC that it was a 'bankrupt' agreement.

With the CRINE programme of cost-cutting now coming fully into play, the context within which wage bargaining took place altered radically. By 1993, Hook-up agreement offers were of a different order to earlier years. Shop stewards from the East Brae, Alba and Scott hook-ups were participants in the formulation of the 1993 claim. At a meeting in Aberdeen with Bobby Buirds and Rab Wilson it was agreed that a demand for a 10 per cent increase on all rates be pressed, a guarantee that there would be no change in the current two-on-two-off work cycle, and that a union agreement be sought for all post-construction work.[85] A subsequent report by Bobby Buirds in the AEEU *Offshore Bulletin* made clear that the contractor employers were in no position to make such substantial concessions. The *Offshore Bulletin* noted, 'The offer made by the OCC would rank as the poorest offer ever made for the Hook-up Agreement, and was one of the toughest negotiations in the agreement history.'[86]

In formulating the claim, AEEU officials had sought to involve the workforce representatives, who now returned offshore to consult the membership. In these meetings, described as 'very lively' and 'frank', a complete rejection of the OCC's latest offer was voiced. A further meeting between national officials and the OCC, however, produced little significant movement, leading the AEEU to ballot its offshore membership on the employers' final offer. This historic first in 'democracy at work', as the AEEU heralded it, produced a disturbing insight into the real scale of union weakness offshore. Yet this was an area which should have been one of its few offshore strongholds. Out of a total Hook-up workforce of 3550, nearly half (45 per cent) were not union members. They were therefore ineligible to vote. Of the 1950 who could vote, only 49 per cent, again almost exactly half, actually did so, that is, just under 1000 workers. Of these, the ballot result was 56 per cent in favour of acceptance and 44 per cent against, yet again a roughly even split. Effectively, the 1993 Hook-up deal was endorsed by significantly less than a fifth (17 per cent) of the total Hook-up workforce.[87] The manifest inadequacy of this state of affairs produced a plea to the membership: 'The AEEU needs more Shop Stewards offshore as there are too many people prepared to load the gun but not fire the bullets.'[88]

By 1993 the mood of the contract workforce had reverted to old fears of employer blacklisting and general apathy. With further client pressure on the contractors to cut costs set to intensify into the mid-1990s, the outlook for offshore unionism was bleak. An indication of this shift in the balance of power was crystallized by the Hook-up negotiations when there was direct interference by the clients with normal redundancy selection procedures, to ensure that only those whose faces 'fitted' would be re-employed. Some contract workers were now being offered their own jobs back at inferior rates and conditions. Others were dispensed with entirely. While UKOOA claimed that the companies were merely ensuring 'the correct skills mix', union leaders voiced their worry that 'Fear is once again prevalent amongst the offshore workforce and, unless matters improve, it could have a long-term damaging effect on industrial relations.'[89]

Although the Trade Union Consultative Committee set up in 1993 was not a negotiating body, it now conveniently served to ensure that the signatory unions to the Hook-up agreement entered into negotiations with the employers with a 'realistic' set of expectations. The OCC *Annual Report* for 1994 notes that 'relations with this committee were strengthened during the Hook-up agreement negotiations'.[90] The OCC chairman observed:

> It was gratifying to note that the Offshore Hook-up Agreement was renegotiated with the trade unions at a very competitive rate for 1994. The OCC and the trade unions are aware of the projected decline in Hook-up agreements in the near future, and as such see the need to remain competitive in a declining market.[91]

The actual level of pay increase agreed from 1 January 1994 was 1.6 per cent, identical to that imposed by the contractors under the Model Terms and Conditions from 1 April 1994, a derisory amount compared to previous years.

By 1994, the CRINE programme had been identified by the AEEU as the culprit behind contractor parsimony. But by this time the downturn in the industry was extensive. A Hook-up agreement of 2.1 per cent for 1995 was accepted, even though no members were currently employed under the agreement. The logic on the part of the AEEU was that this nominal raise 'may stem the hawks on the employers' side from reducing any rates imposed under the OCC Model Terms'.[92] From 1 April 1995, the imposed Model Terms rise of 2.1 per cent did indeed match the Hook-up rate. This figure disguised other changes in the Model Terms and Conditions which made the rise considerably less, nearer 1.8 per cent, at a time when the headline inflation rate was 3.4 per cent.[93] Among these changes was a reduction of the 'core status' guaranteeing employment from one year to four months, together with the loss of four days paid leave per annum. In addition, those reporting sick off-shore would now only be paid for a maximum of twelve hours. Previous custom and practice had allowed two days' paid sick time offshore. Employees were now under financial pressure to return to work early, with obvious implications for the health and safety of their co-workers as well as for the reporting of accidents. Employees would also be required to co-operate in the assessment of their 'competence' on a quarterly basis. The scrutiny of their 'individual performance' could, in the eyes of the workforce, leave the door open to subtle and not-so-subtle employer abuse. Absent completely from the AEEU's bargaining agenda was any serious consideration of comprehensive union recognition, although it remained the supposed rationale for union participation in the Trade Union Consultative Committee. The AEEU's game plan was failing to realize the hoped-for benefits of 'super-unionism'. Indeed, if anything, the 'super-union' strategy simply magnified the relative impotence resulting from the sectional cul-de-sac of the Hook-up agreement and the AEEU's broader employer-friendly strategy.

The AEEU: A Merger of Convenience

The difficulties encountered by the AEEU offshore were compounded by more general difficulties which the process of merger of the engineering and electricians' unions was experiencing as a whole. Gavin Laird, as General Secretary, detailed the difficulties which had been faced in consolidating the structure of the newly merged union. In a speech to the 1994 National Committee of the engineering section of the union, prior to its dissolution as part of the merger process, Laird addressed 'the progress on the amalgamation or lack of it'.[94] He refuted the suggestion that the engineering union was 'less financially sound than the EETPU' and that the EETPU would be taking over a 'financial failure'. Laird, threatening to resign, said, 'I have to say I think we are giving more than we are getting. I have to say I think the spirit of compromise is one-sided'.[95]

Despite the merger, the EETPU, complained Laird, 'speak and vote on virtually every major issue as a single entity'.[96] While limited progress had been made on rationalizing some aspects of administration, duplication and administrative over-staffing remained, allegedly 'costing the members millions of pounds'.[97] More crucially, there had been an almost complete failure to harmonize the two unions' rule books within a single rule book. Just before Christmas 1993, said Laird, 'the lack of a positive approach almost wrecked the whole process and no meetings took place for five weeks.'[98] Problems and disagreements over the powers of the new union's Policy Conference, attendance at this by full-time officials, and the participation of the new executive in the crucial Standing Orders Committee had been resolved. However, the basic political structure of the merged union and the contentious element of lay participation still remained to be tackled. The Rules subcommittee had met on twenty-one occasions, said Laird, but had 'managed to agree only two rule changes of any significance and upset everyone in the process.'[99] In particular there had been no agreement on placing a new rule book before the members to be voted upon. Nor was agreement reached on the structure of the new AEEU Conference and on ending the continuing duplication of officials at all levels of the two unions. After two years, said Laird, 'nowhere near 50 per cent' of the new rule book had been written.[100] Speaking of the need to find a way 'of breaking through this impasse' and of compromise as 'a two-way process', Laird provided a depressing catalogue of facts and figures detailing the reluctance of the EETPU to preserve the more democratically accountable structures of union government which the engineering union had brought to the merger.[101] The deadline for putting a new rule book before the members was 1 May 1996, that is, within four years of the original 'amalgamation'. But with the shape of the 1995 national delegate conference still in contention, and each side of the joint executive only meeting in the presence of their legal advisers, the prospects for a unified AEEU were looking increasingly poor.

Laird was subsequently to retire as General Secretary three years early on full salary. This retirement 'hamper', worth up to £500,000 for officials prepared to retire at 55, was the AEEU's solution to thinning out the new union's top-heavy executive. Laird himself duly received a knighthood in 1995. It had been a long journey from Communist shop steward in the giant Singer sewing-machine factory at Clydebank to the top of his union. But along the way he had also collected a string of lucrative directorships, including serving on the board of Scottish Television, GEC, Britannia Life, acting as a non-executive director of the Bank of England and Scottish Enterprise, and membership of the Arts Council, the Forestry Commission and the Highlands and Islands Development Board. Laird had also been a director of BNOC between 1976 and 1986. But it was as non-executive director of Greater Manchester Buses North, sold on after six months to FirstBus, Britain's largest privatized operator, following a management–employee buyout, that Sir Gavin attracted most unfavourable publicity. He had received an 'exit bonus' of £27,000 from Greater Manchester Buses North plus a salary of £18,000 for chairing the management buyout team, as well as £40,000 profit on share dealings in the company. Local shop stewards in Manchester had raised questions about the appropriateness of his initial appointment, which had found the workforce agreeing to a 6 per cent pay cut and lower holiday entitlements on Laird's recommendation, to achieve savings of more than £2 million a year and ensure the success of the privatized concern. When the scale of their former leader's rewards became known, shop stewards called for an official union inquiry.[102]

Additional questions about Sir Gavin's involvement in the Greater Manchester bus deal were raised in June 1996. Sir Gavin confirmed that he had been a paid member for about three years of Murray Johnstone's private acquisitions partnership. He was one of seven directors who shared a total of £1.3 million paid by Murray Johnstone, the advisers of the management buyout team, as a 'success fee'.[103]

The Sectional Tail

For the other established unions on the offshore scene, the picture was also mixed. 'Partnership' agreements were locking in the engineering construction contractors with the operators' cost-cutting programme with predictable results, both in the Hook-up agreement and the employer-imposed Model Terms and Conditions. The dependent layer of catering contractors, under similar pressures, meanwhile embarked on a ferocious new round of inter-firm cut-throat competition. The employers' association COTA (the Catering Offshore Trades Association) came under severe strain in much the same way as during the downturn of the mid-1980s. The limited arrangements with the unions, sanctioned by the operators, again now looked likely to disintegrate. Cost-reduction pressure from the operators tempted one or two major catering companies to attempt to steal a march on their competitors by cutting wages in an attempt to lower overall tender costs. The threatened withdrawal from COTA by one of the largest contractors, Compass, indicated both the fragility of COTA and its dependency on a generally supportive environment sanctioned by the operators. The sudden removal of Compass exposed the catering sector to a revival of a competitive contract war. It also revealed just how tenuous was the signatory unions' foothold in the COTA arrangement, and how limited was the ability of the TGWU and RMT to preserve previous terms and conditions. An increase of 5.9 to 6.4 per cent on hourly rates awarded in September 1991, though restricted to northern waters installations, was the last major concession of any substance made to catering staff. By 1994 the COTA employers were offering 2.5 per cent on basic pay, while manning levels were being cut back by about one-fifth. For the third year running, in 1994, no increase at all was on offer to catering crews on drilling units or in the southern sector.

The real severity of the impact of CRINE and the weakness of the established offshore unions was best judged by the experiences of the direct employees of the oil operators themselves. MSF had made steady if limited progress in extending recognition with respect to representational rights for employees, particularly in the Shell field. By mid-1993 this had resulted in successful ballots on nine Shell installations, including most of the Brent complex.[104] In both northern and southern sectors, the operators had begun to extend work tours to three weeks, as part of the cost-cutting exercise. In the one company with which MSF did have full collective bargaining rights, Phillips Petroleum, it did prove possible to resist unilaterally imposed shift changes, but not elsewhere.[105] The years following 1993/94, however, saw intensifying job cuts both onshore and offshore among all major operators as 'flatter' management structures were introduced across the North Sea.[106] By 1996 major operators such as Chevron had attempted to dismiss nearly half their employees. Indeed, Chevron, one of the longest-term players in the North Sea was to dispose of its Ninian field assets to Oryx. BP forced its staff to accept unilateral changes in terms and conditions under threat of redundancy.

The shock of these cuts had begun to rival the downturn of the mid-1980s. Formerly loyal operators' staff began to withdraw their co-operation with the companies. Typical here was the resignation of all but a couple of employee representatives on the Shell Staff Consultative Committee in the Brent field.[107] Where MSF had previously secured a foothold, it was to some extent able to ensure that redundancies were 'sensitively' handled in a 'fair' manner that limited improper selection. On the other hand, with redundancy settlements rumoured to be as high as £50,000, and with at least some prospect of re-employment by a major contractor, former oil company employees had every incentive to go quietly.

Where there was no union presence, employers such as Conoco were able to redouble their resistance to any involvement of a 'third party' between themselves and their employees.[108] Any possibility of the imposed shift changes and job cuts having a deleterious effect on safety was vigorously denied by the companies. While the situation for union recognition offshore was unpromising, the threat of redundancy and lump sum offers was used to force through actual union derecognition in the onshore oil industry. At the BP Grangemouth facility, following the example of Shell UK at its onshore refineries of Stanlow and Shellhaven, union derecognition was achieved in 1995.[109]

This exclusion of unions as an unwelcome 'third party', more than anything underscored the general weakness of the established UK trade unions throughout the oil industry and the need for a new alternative approach of a more concerted nature to be developed. The most likely scenario for offshore unionism was intensified inter-union sectionalism, an increasingly restricted scope of existing fragmentary collective bargaining arrangements, and continuing undiminished hostility towards OILC. All of this was likely to occur within the context of an increasingly cost-driven employers' offensive and a radical programme of employment restructuring in the offshore industry, which in the future was likely to be not only increasingly 'union-free' but also 'employee-free'.

The Contemporary Politics of Offshore Unionism

The story of OILC's formation as a union presents a unique opportunity to observe the making of a new kind of industrial union in the 1990s. Organization theory proposes that new organizational solutions – such as the setting up of a new union – typically encounter a host of gestation problems (Greiner, 1972). A decision to delegate functions to a committee, for instance, creates problems of supervision and control by the grass roots. Multiple committee structures invite rivalry over jurisdiction and resources, as we observed in the context of OILC's Standing Committee and its Organising Committee. Additional problems arise from tensions between leadership and members.

Once the decision to create a formal union structure was made by OILC, incentives for competition for posts, new rivalries and discontents were created which had been largely unknown to the previous informal organization. The evolving conflicts were heightened by the personal sacrifices many OILC activists had made. Out of these sacrifices grew strong and often uncompromising convictions about what was the way forward for OILC, and perhaps more importantly, what rights and positions certain individuals should have.

The outbreak of a debilitating conflict within OILC, however, was not inevitable. One ingredient which brought it to the fore was outside factors: namely, the hostile industrial relations climate created through Conservative employment legislation, and the adversarial attitude of the existing unions towards the challenge of a 'breakaway'. Equally important was the historical weakness of trade unionism offshore. As an informal organization, OILC could avoid many of the rigidities and problems of a formal union structure.

Nor was it bound within existing sectional agreements. With the legal requirements of certification, much of the potential for a flexible, responsive organizational set-up was precluded. For OILC, the longer-term objective of displacing the established unions with a developed industrial union whilst matching the aspirations of many of the offshore workforce seemed unlikely to be easily achievable. Given the array of hostile forces which surrounded it, even after overcoming many of its internal difficulties, the most likely scenario was that it would remain locked within a 'small union ghetto' (Lerner, 1961). An analysis of OILC cumulative membership in mid-1996 revealed that its recruitment was overwhelmingly in the engineering and construction constituency. Catering, drilling, administration, helideck crews, seamen and divers together comprised under 20 per cent of the total OILC membership, suggesting that the new union still had a long way to go before it could claim that it had comprehensively recruited from across the industry's workforce (see Figure 10.3). On the positive side, with approximately 1500 offshore members, OILC's membership exceeded that of any other offshore union. Despite the clear preference of specific sectors of the workforce to be represented by OILC on particular rigs and installations, it was improbable that

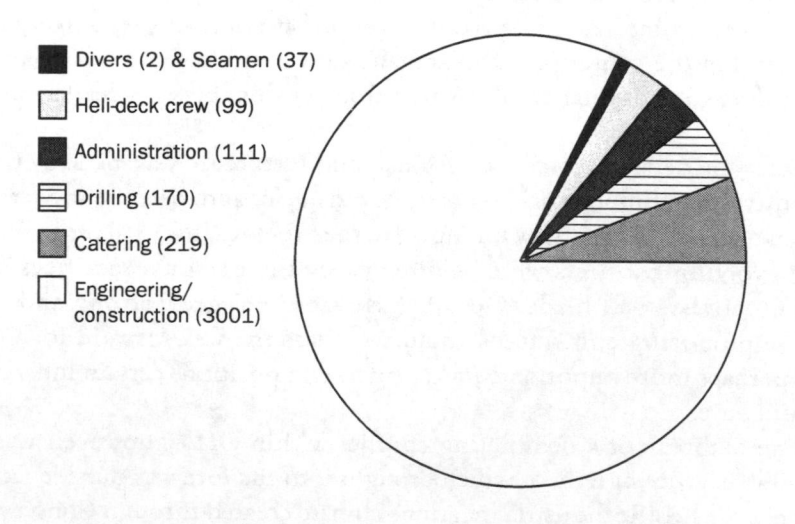

Figure 10.3 *OILC Membership (Cumulative) 1996*
Source: OILC

any formal collective bargaining rights would be conceded by the employers. Their interest lay in consolidating relationships with the established unions, who shared with these employers a mutual desire to exclude the OILC. Finally, Conservative employment legislation had created the instruments which could be used by 'policy entrepreneurs', such as a cohesive dissident group, to damage the growth and evolution of the new OILC union. Restrictive certification procedures and CROTUM interventions provided discontented members with the opportunity to disrupt what might otherwise have been a more focused development (Hendy, 1993).

In the first instance, membership recruitment among those working off-shore became an imperative for the new union to survive. It was an imperative only met with some difficulty. Further, membership recruitment brought with it a new source of tension. This tension was rooted in differences between the day-to-day concerns and perspectives of members currently working offshore and those of the pre-existing leading OILC activists, many of whom were now excluded from offshore employment and wedded to broader but unrealized demands shaped by the struggles of 1989 and 1990.

The hostile industrial relations climate of the 1980s and 1990s also impacted on the conduct of established unions towards each other. For some unions it meant adopting an openly aggressive and competitive stance towards former partners: a process which could only be detrimental to the union movement as a whole. This pattern became particularly apparent in the case of the AEEU. As the new AEEU 'super-union' sought to demarcate its territory offshore and onshore, a transposition of competitive sectionalism at a higher, more intensified level took place. AEEU's merger out of the AEU and the EETPU had produced an uneasy alliance between an engineering union with a more democratic and open structure, in which historically the Left was able to play some role, an electricians' union which had stifled internal democracy in the name of anti-Communism. For the AEU it was important to show to employers and its new partner that it was able to control unofficial challenges. In the petrochemical industry, the merged AEEU was willing to break previous sectional alliances to pursue overtly single-union deals. In the construction industry its strategy involved raiding parties on vulnerable rivals such as the Left-oriented building workers' union, UCATT. The other side of AEEU's hostility towards fellow unions was an increasingly collaborationist stance towards employers. Under CRINE, however, this revival of 'business unionism' could hardly pay off (Jacoby and Werma, 1989). In this sense, the AEEU's model of modern competitive unionism was essentially negative in its outcome, and failed to deliver the goods.

By contrast to this type of business union, OILC's commitment to industrial unionism and its critical attitude towards offshore employers and their role in the post-Cullen reconstruction presented a serious problem. Most paradoxically, just at the moment when union power was gathered by the newly merged AEEU leadership, it was forced to counter OILC's push for the creation of effective workplace union representatives offshore, with its own programme of 'consultation' with the membership. OILC's mere existence was a continuing reminder, not just of the democratic deficiencies of the existing unions, but also of the inadequacy of the agreements they had defended. By the mid-1990s, Hook-up agreement wage increases deteriorated to nominal levels, while post-hook-up recognition was as far away as ever. This was obvious despite the formation of a new exclusive consultative committee with the employers. Creative inter-union initiatives which attempted to counter sectionalist tendencies had been replaced by agendas which actively impeded the unity of offshore workers. The hopes and initiatives of the early 1970s, the anger and unrest following Piper Alpha, had now been dissipated into a dualism of existing competitively poised unions, and the alternative of a broad but still underdeveloped industrial union.

In the final analysis, the truly troubling aspect of the lack of creative initiative by existing unions is that it is almost certain to have strengthened the already overpowering position of the offshore employers. Despite its internal problems, OILC by merely surviving has been able to represent the unpalatable 'Left alternative' to this established collaborationist offshore unionism. Yet OILC has done much more than survive. In the ongoing debate about the nature of workforce representation and safety offshore, it has continued to exercise an influence out of all proportion to its size. As such, its significance for the offshore worker, as well as for UK trade unionism as a whole, cannot be overestimated.

Notes

1. *Morning Star*, 12 February 1992.
2. OILC Mass Meeting, 30 January 1992.
3. OILC Mass Meeting, 26 March 1992.
4. *Press and Journal*, 28 January 1992.
5. See Case No. S/2816/90, The Industrial Tribunals (Scotland), Aberdeen, 6–8 April 1992.
6. ibid. para 4G.
7. ibid. paras 4H, 5A.
8. ibid. para 6A.

9. ibid para 10A.

10. ibid.

11. ibid. para 11B.

12. See note 5 *above*, p. 3.

13. ibid. para 11B.

14. Employment Appeals Tribunal/447/92, 2 December 1992.

15. See Case No. S/3398/91, The Industrial Tribunals (Scotland), Aberdeen, 16 April 1992 and Employment Appeals Tribunal/414/92, 18 November 1992.

16. OILC Constitution and Rules, 1992.

17. OILC First Conference, Stirling, 28 June 1992.

18. ibid.

19. OILC Second Conference, Stirling, 28 August 1993.

20. Minutes of OILC Organising Committee, 19 February 1993.

21. Minutes of OILC Organising Committee, 6 September 1993.

22. Minutes of OILC Organising Committee, 7 October 1993.

23. ibid.

24. Letter from Certification Office to R. McDonald, 19 April 1994.

25. Press statement of members of the OILC Organising Committee, 20 April 1994.

26. Press Conference transcript, April 1994.

27. Letter from Certification Office to R. McDonald, 13 May 1994.

28. *Re Offshore Industry Liaison Committee* (D/7/94), 25 November 1994, Certification Officer.

29. Letter from P. Douglass to R. McDonald, 11 December 1994.

30. Letter from P. Douglass, 30 December 1994.

31. Letter from J. G. Chambers to Certification Officer, 3 January 1995; Letter from Certification Officer to J. G. Chambers, 4 January 1995.

32. *Scotsman*, 14 January 1995; *Press and Journal*, 31 January 1995.

33. *Blowout*, Issue No. 43, March 1995, p. 10.

34. BBC Radio Scotland, 'Headlines', with Ruth Wishart, September 1990.

35. Letter from J. A. Lee, Director, Contract Support Services, Wood Group Engineering, to R. McDonald, 16 May 1995.

36. See the Trade Union and Labour Relations (Consolidation) Act 1992, Section 146.

37. Letter from J. Monks to A. Scargill, 12 April 1995.

38. *Blowout*, Issue No. 45, July 1995.

39. BBC Radio Scotland News, 17 July 1995.

40. AEU Press Statement, 13 October 1991.

41. *Blowout*, Issue No. 27, September 1992.

42. *Morning Star*, 21 January 1992.

43. *Morning Star*, 1 June 1992.

44. IDS Report 562, February 1990, p. 7.

45. *Morning Star*, 10 January 1992.

46. *Morning Star*, 11 September 1991.

47. *Financial Times*, 6 September 1991.

48. *Morning Star*, 5 March 1992.

49. *Morning Star*, 23 September 1993.

50. *Morning Star*, 2 March 1993.

51. *Morning Star*, 10 June 1994.

52. AEEU *Offshore Bulletin*, December 1994 (consultative structure).

53. *Morning Star*, 3 September 1993.

54. *Morning Star*, 15 March 1995.

55. *Morning Star*, 1 April 1995.

56. AEU *Journal*, December 1991.

57. Letter from G. Laird to T. Lafferty, 14 April 1992.

58. Letter from Tom MacLean to T. Lafferty, 19 August 1991.

59. OCC Industrial Tribunals: Note of Comments made by Ronnie McDonald, n.d.

60. BBC Radio Scotland, Aberdeen, 2 August 1991.

61. Note 58 *above*.

62. ibid.

63. T. Lafferty, Personal File, in authors' possession.

64. *Scotsman*, 30 October 1993.

65. Offshore Industry Unions Co-ordinating Committee, Documents and Conference Report, 30–31 October 1993, Glasgow.

66. MSF *Offshore News*, October 1992.

67. Offshore Unions Co-ordinating Committee, Documents and Conference Report, Appendix 1, 25 March 1995, Glasgow.

68. Full citation permission refused.

69. Minutes of IUOOC, 29 January 1992.

70. Minutes of IUOOC, 31 March 1993.

71. Minutes of IUOOC, 7 September 1994.

72. AEEU *Offshore Bulletin*, November 1992, p. 5.

73. ibid.

74. ibid.

75. *Scotsman*, 30 September 1992.

76. AEEU *Offshore Bulletin*, July 1994, p. 6.

77. Offshore Consultative Committee, Trade Union Minutes, 25 January 1995.

78. ibid. p. 3.

79. ibid.

80. MSF *Offshore News*, January 1993.

81. ibid.

82. MSF *Offshore News*, April 1993.

83. IDS, No. 619, January 1992, p. 5.

84. *Blowout*, Issue No. 24, March – April 1992.

85. Minutes of Review of Offshore Hook-up Agreement, AEEU Aberdeen Office, 7 October 1993.

86. AEEU *Offshore Bulletin*, July 1993, p. 2.

87. ibid. for the figures cited in text.

88. ibid.

89. Notes of a meeting between IUOOC and UKOOA, Aberdeen, 7 September 1994.

90. Offshore Contractors Council, *Annual Report*, 1994, p. 6.

91. ibid.

92. AEEU *Offshore Bulletin*, January 1995, p. 8.

93. *Guardian*, 13 April 1995.

94. G. Laird, text of speech to AEU National Committee, 1994.

95. ibid.

96. ibid.

97. ibid.

98. ibid.

99. ibid.

100. ibid.

101. ibid.

102. *Scotland on Sunday*, 26 May 1996.

103. *Scotland on Sunday*, 2 June 1996.

104. MSF *Offshore News*, August 1993.

105. MSF *Offshore News*, October 1992.

106. *Financial Times*, 28 April 1995.

107. MSF *Offshore News*, August 1993.

108. MSF *Offshore News*, December 1993.

109. *Herald*, 6 April 1995.

11

The Restructuring of Britain's Offshore Oil and Gas Industry

By January 1996 the architects of the Cost Reduction Initiative could claim virtually complete success in their original objectives. Within three years costs had been brought down by at least a third in most areas of capital expenditure. The refurbishment of the two great pipeline infrastructures was largely complete. Very considerable progress had been made in linking into this infrastructure outlying wells using non-staffed, subsea collection systems and improving the production from the old Brent and Forties fields. It was this additional production which had contributed to the record output levels of 1995 – with the proportionate amount of oil going through the pipelines now back to its early 1980s levels. The amount of gas flowing was far greater. At the January 1996 CRINE Conference John D'Ancona, one of the scheme's principal architects during his period in the Department of Trade and Industry, claimed 'no major change of culture and practice has ever overtaken the oil and gas industry as quickly as CRINE. In a few short years the whole approach to development in the UKCS has been revolutionised and the influence of CRINE and CRINE thinking is now taking hold all over the world'.[1]

To understand the wider significance of these changes for the balance between capital and labour, two key questions must be answered. One concerns the impact on the industry's structure and the other on its technology. In terms of the industry's structure the crisis of 1992 was handled in a very different way to that of 1986. In the earlier crisis the process was largely left to market forces. Part of the burden fell on labour; part on the supply industry itself. In 1992 a direct attack on labour was out of the question. Politically, in terms of industrial relations, there could be no outright cuts in wages and conditions. Instead the supply industry had, at least in the short run, to absorb the great bulk of the cost reduction through cuts in capacity and profits. The key question concerns the way in which this was done. It is clear that, in contrast to 1986, the Cost Reduction Initiative represented an industry-wide process of rationalization that was co-ordinated and planned. The question relates to the depth and effectiveness of this planning. Was it simply a short-term expedient whereby costs were absorbed for two or three years until the labour situation stabilized? Or did it represent a more fundamental restructuring – by which the character of the supply industry was changed, paths were opened up for the entrance of new, smaller firms and the beginnings of an indigenously-owned and locally based industry took root?

A similar question concerns the character of the technology. Historically, in other industries, pressure from organized labour has, on occasion, served to push forward the process of technological change. Did this also happen in the UKCS? The post-1992 period saw a shift to low-cost solutions and the use of basic standardized equipment. How far was the objective of these new systems primarily to reduce the amount of labour that would be required offshore, and how far was it simply to cut immediate capital costs or even to abandon those areas that would require large-scale research and development? Answers to these questions have much to tell us about the depth of the crisis and the degree to which managements saw labour militancy as a long-term danger.

Restructuring the Supply Industry

The dilemma regarding the structure of the supply industry was put bluntly by the managing director of Shell, Heinz Rothermund, to the December 1994 CRINE Conference. In 1986/87, the reduction in the size of the supply industry had ultimately enabled the suppliers to hold the oil companies to ransom. Could the same happen again? If, asked Rothermund, the oil companies continued out-sourcing their own functions and at the same supporting the growth of super-contractors, would they not eventually be back 'at the same situation as twenty five years ago – with everything getting done by the same set of people' (CRINE Secretariat, 1994: 3). In our earlier analysis of the origins of CRINE in 1992–93 we noted this danger. The cost reduction initiative was essentially at the expense of supply industry. The gold-plating on orders had to be removed. Suppliers had to work co-operatively to use the cheapest technology. We noted that the ability to impose these new terms depended not so much on CRINE itself as on the restored market power of the traditional oil majors, especially BP and Shell. With five leading oil companies controlling over 70 per cent of the orders, they could very easily use this power to ensure

Table 11.1 *Types of Expenditure (oil only) 1989–94 (billion£)*

Type of expenditure	1989	1990	1991	1992	1993	1994
Development	1.7	2.5	3.3	3.7	3.2	2.5
Operating	1.8	2.3	2.6	2.6	2.8	3.0
Exploration	1.2	1.6	2.0	1.5	1.2	0.9

Source: DTI, 1995

that the objectives of CRINE were met. The trend in expenditure away from exploration shown in the 1995 *Energy Report* illustrates the overall reorientation of activity within the UKCS.

Yet the basic contradiction remained. The overall costs generated by the supply industry had to be cut by a third. Whatever the power of the operators to control this process, the supply industry would still end up smaller. And this could in the future shift the balance back in favour of the suppliers. The Scottish Office employment survey conducted in summer 1994 revealed a 15 per cent fall in oil-related employment over the previous twelve months. Proportionately, the fall was slightly less marked in Grampian than in other Scottish regions, reflecting the effects of the geographical regrouping. But the fall was sharp none the less, and particularly marked in construction and metal manufacturing (both with a 49 per cent reduction in their workforces). Over the preceding twelve months, between 7 and 10 per cent of all firms appear to have ceased trading, and another 5 per cent to have moved way from the oil industry as their main market (Scottish Office Industry Department, 1995: 5, 7, 9). Over the same period the gross trading profits of contracting companies fell from £260 million to £130 million, and reduced the overall share of the supply companies in the gross profits of the industry from 3.5 to 1.6 per cent (DTI, 1996: 175). This itself reveals the degree to which, at least in the short run, the costs of the crisis were borne by the supply industry.

The surveys of 1992 and 1993 revealed the problems faced by smaller companies and the degree to which the bulk of orders were going to a small group of big contractors (Foster *et al.*, 1993; Foster *et al.*, 1994). Further survey work has confirmed this trend. The MAI Consultants' report for Scottish Enterprise in August 1995 concluded that smaller subcontractors were being squeezed out of the market. In subsequent comment the industrial development manager for Scottish Enterprise expressed concern at the threat this posed to continued small-firm creation within the supply industry. Earlier in 1994 a survey by the the *Scotsman* drew similar comment. The managing director of one specialist engineering firm described the new structure as facing small firms with a 'broken ladder'. Five or six big contractors were cornering the market, and although they could offer a range of services, they did not invest in their development and would ultimately impose higher costs on the industry. John Wils of Hamilton Oil, one of the UKCS independents, argued that the creation of large multi-specialism service companies increased the overhead costs for any particular specialist function.[2]

The industry leaders have, as our earlier quotation from Rothermund demonstrated, been only too well aware of these dangers. D'Ancona at the 1996 CRINE conference spoke of 'an introspective gang of four or five major contractors who wish to see the whole UKCS development philosophy geared to their interests'. He went on to make it clear that the oil companies would not concede this position easily. 'One could see a situation in which the main effect of partnering could undermine all that CRINE is trying to achieve. It hasn't and won't but that is only because the guardians of both will not presently permit it.'[3]

So there can be no doubt about the intent of the oil companies. They wanted to effect a long-term and fundamental change. The question is how much they were willing to invest in this objective. There seem have been three main ways in which interventions took place. The first was for the oil companies to use their own market power to promote competition within the supply industry. John Cross of BP has summed up some of the lessons drawn by his company from the process of establishing partnerships. Writing in the *Harvard Business Review* in 1995 he examined how BP's exploration division contracted out its entire information technology needs between 1993 and 1994. BP selected three different contractors, one French, one American and one British (a subsidiary of BT), and required them to work co-operatively but competitively. BP imposed relatively short contracts (just two years in one case) with the possibility of renewal, and insisted on continued market testing (Cross, 1995: 100–2). This resulted, Cross claimed, in an improved service at much cheaper costs. Information technology, because of the relatively deep and global character of the market available, probably represented a relatively easy option. The geographically less mobile area of engineering services might be more difficult. None the less, the same principles of relatively short original contracts and continued market testing seem to have been applied more generally.

The second path of intervention has been through government agencies. In the period since 1991 the Department of Trade and Industry has, as we saw in Chapter 6, sought to regroup the industry in one region and to promote indigenous ownership and small-firm formation. Tim Eggar, speaking in December 1994, noted that the Department of Trade and Industry's financial support for the CRINE Secretariat has been specifically 'on behalf of the small and medium enterprises whose support is needed but who find it difficult to commit financially to the initiative'. Vic Tuft, director of the CRINE Secretariat, stressed the need to ensure that 'our strategies do not drive out these smaller specialist suppliers in favour of the larger "one stop" contractors. If the benefits of CRINE were to exclude the suppliers, especially the smaller ones, that would not only be unjust but plain stupid' (CRINE Secretariat, 1994: 2).

The third arm of industrial intervention appears to have been through the banking system. Financial support has been repeatedly extended to maintain the independence of locally owned specialist firms in key areas. It is difficult to be precise about how this has operated, or even to categorize it as strategic intervention at all. It does, however, appear to be relatively systematic. We noted that in the first stages of CRINE in 1992 a couple of big UK-owned contractors were refinanced through the City of London and emerged with BP and ex-BP personnel on their boards. Between 1994 and 1996 the finance company 3i intervened on four occasions, usually with assistance from other banks, to rescue local specialist suppliers and facilitate management buy-outs. In November 1995, BW Mud, controlling 20 per cent of the UK well-stimulation market, was refinanced and an ex-BP employee installed as company chairman. Director of 3i, Keith Mair, explained the intervention in these terms: 'BW's primary competitors are all subsidiaries of multi-national service companies. Our intervention maintains BW's independence, which ensures a healthy competitive environment in this segment of the North Sea service industry'. 3i had intervened in June 1994 to enable the UK-owned Bond Group to consolidate its position as the biggest helicopter supply firm for both the UK and Norwegian sectors, and in February 1994 to finance the expansion of the UK-owned Pressure Products Group. In February 1996, 3i stepped in again to finance the management buyout of the sixth biggest UK-owned North Sea service company, Rigblast.[4]

So, as an interim conclusion, it does seem possible to argue that the oil companies did want to achieve a long-term structural change in the supply industry and were involved in a range of tactics that were, in sum, relatively unprecedented. The question is, how much they were willing to put into this? Did it extend to a willingness to invest in structural change – to temporarily pay more in order to create a technologically better equipped and more competitive local industry?

The degree to which the banks were having to rescue local firms from takeover might indicate that margins were being squeezed in the longer term. By 1995–96 even the biggest UK contractors were in difficulties. In the summer of 1995, the Dutch firm Heerema, leader in the new deep water technology of Floating Storage and Loading Systems, started buying up UK dock facilities from the ailing giant of the UK offshore supply industry, Trafalgar House. In December 1995, the Norwegian firm Kvaerner launched a hostile bid for the second biggest UK supply firm AMEC. It acquired 26 per cent of the shares but met firm resistance from the Board and institutional investors from the City of London. In March 1996, Kvaerner made a successful bid for Trafalgar House.[5]

These events, therefore, lead us on to our second question: the degree to which the pressures of the Cost Reduction Initiative might have weakened rather than enhanced the technological competitiveness of the UK supply industry. Whatever the desire of the UK oil majors for a competitive supply base, the vulnerability of UK firms to external takeover might indicate that their competitiveness had been damaged.

The evidence on this question would seem to be relatively evenly balanced. The ability of Dutch, Norwegian and French supply firms to buy into the UK supply industry may not necessarily indicate that the UK companies were technologically weak. On the contrary, it may simply mean that they were financially vulnerable. Margins had been cut across the UKCS. Firms involved in construction work and rig building had been particularly badly hit by the UK industry's switch from development to maintenance. By 1993 the rig yards were operating at only 20 per cent capacity.[6] Consequently firms whose work was based primarily outside the UKCS, such as Kvaerner and Heerema, would have the cash balances for expansion at a time when UK-based firms, such as AMEC and Trafalgar House, were showing only minimal profits.

Nor is it automatically the case that low-cost solutions are going to be technologically inferior to more expensive ones. It was precisely the move to simple, standard procedures and relatively low-technology processes which characterized the first stage in the development of Japanese flexible production systems. The developments in the UKCS could potentially be just as innovative, and this has been repeatedly argued by the architects of CRINE. Persuasive evidence of the resulting competitive advantages would be the increasing ability of the UK supply industry to penetrate overseas markets. In 1994 the Offshore Supplies Office estimated that a third of the UK supply industry's turnover was now generated outside the UKCS (DTI, 1994: 65). The Wood Group, the third biggest UK supply firm, confirmed this estimate in its annual report for 1994–95.[7] It reported that a third of its own sales were now outside the UKCS – and that this represented a tenfold increase since 1990. This impression of significant advance in improving cost-effectiveness is further supported by the decision of the Norwegian government to launch its own counterpart to CRINE in autumn 1994. This came two years later than the UK programme and drew its main proposals from the experience of CRINE. The founding document is in places reproduced almost word for word from the 1993 DTI report (Norwegian Ministry of Industry and Energy, 1994). Its overall stress is also the same: the need to reduce costs by developing standard procedures and technologies.

Yet there are also arguments on the other side. If UK supply firms have been increasing their external sales, they have been losing market share in the UKCS. Separate reports by the Offshore Supplies Office and MacKay Consultants in summer 1995 both record a slippage over the previous year. MacKay Consultants attributed this to the impact of EU Competition Directives on contract allocation and to the enhanced presence of foreign companies within the UKCS. This was particularly marked in two areas that were crucial for the future: subsea systems and installation barges. A couple of months before, the managing director of the Wood Group used his annual report to call for the protection of the UKCS against Norwegian contractors 'who come and go as they please' and who were producing a 'totally lop-sided playing field'.[8] So, as well as the evidence of strength, there also appears to be a definite perception of competitive weakness on some fronts.

Critics of CRINE within the industry have portrayed it as weakening supply firms' wider competitiveness in three ways. The first is in terms of resources. Research and development budgets had been severely cut as the big service companies fought to contain contract costs, and in doing so, it is argued, their long-term development capacity has been damaged. The second problem has been structural. Smaller specialist firms are either squeezed out altogether or, if employed, only have the status of subcontractors. This loss of direct contact with the operator has, it is suggested, deprived the specialist firms of the opportunity for full involvement in design and sometimes meant that less than the best engineering solutions are adopted. The third impediment is cultural. The imposition of standard technologies across the whole sector could quickly lead to an environment of technological conservatism. The large service companies have good economic reasons for perpetuating 'their own' sector standards once they are established. When Vic Tuft, the director of the CRINE Secretariat, observed that the enforcement of common technology standards across the UKCS was not intended to create a 'Fortress Britain', he was pointing to a consequence that was as potentially real as it was unwanted.[9]

What, then, is the overall picture? In terms of structure there is no doubt that the UK supply industry is today smaller and more concentrated than it was in 1990. There would also seem to be considerable evidence that the UK oil majors, and UK government agencies, have exercised themselves to nurture 'national champions' among the large service companies and to sustain key UK specialist firms. It is probably because of this that there has been a fairly comprehensive movement by externally owned supply firms to secure alliances with UK-owned supply firms. In contrast to the 1980s, therefore, it seems correct to conclude that there has been a detailed attempt to consolidate a locally rooted and sustainable supply base, and to concentrate geographically it in the Aberdeen area, and this has met with some success.

The key question, however, is what kind of supply base, and it is here that the issue of technology is important. On this front there would seem to be two quite different stories to tell. The first is positive. Cheap but robust standardized technologies have indeed served to cut the costs of pipeline and platform maintenance, minimize the amount of labour required to sustain production offshore, and, in particular, maximize the potential for the development of subsea collection. Quite a number of these technologies have been transferable to other oil provinces and explain the increase in overseas orders for the UK supply industry – assisted, no doubt, by the increased levels of overseas investment by the UK oil majors themselves. To this extent it can be claimed that the level of worker resistance in 1989 and the early nineties did profoundly affect the character of the restructuring. By temporarily blocking off the opportunity for directly cutting wages and conditions, the breakdown in industrial relations does seem to have pushed the industry towards the only alternative: new technological systems. This stimulus for innovation has a long pedigree. In the later nineteenth century the United States' lead over Britain in developing mass production techniques had much to do with the relative scarcity, and strong bargaining position, of skilled labour in America (Habakkuk, 1962).

But there is also another side to this story. Innovation has occurred in areas associated with the maintenance of mature fields and their infrastructure. It has not occurred, in terms of locally owned supply firms, in specialisms associated with exploration and development and in particular at the frontiers of such activity in deep ocean extraction. Exploration work, of course, is where the biggest reductions in UKCS expenditure have occurred. In the 1970s and 1980s the UKCS was in the front-line of offshore development, and the high costs paid at this stage to the mainly US-owned multinational supply companies reflected this. By the mid-1990s it is the Gulf of Mexico that has been setting the records for the largest and deepest offshore structures.[10] As we

will see later, the one significant area where the new ground was being broken
on the UKCS in the 1990s was in the deep waters west of the Shetlands, and it
is notable that it is here that reliance on externally owned companies has been
heaviest. When work started in 1994, no UK-based contractor had the capacity
to build the floating production and storage vessels required. The design and
production had to be supplied from Switzerland, Italy, Finland and the
Netherlands, and much of the supporting technology has come from US
and Norway.[11] This very fact produced a major conflict between the DTI
and the oil operators in April 1994. Tim Eggar saw the importation of floating
production systems as a direct threat to the new 'UK first' orientation of his
Ministry. For a period he appeared to be threatening to withhold development permissions unless the operators committed themselves to the use of
UK supply. The oil operators, on their side, protested that such development
was not within the technical capacity of the UK, and sought to draw support
on this point from the Offshore Supplies Office.[12] The oil companies were
not willing to invest either time or capital in the indigenous development of
technologies for deep sea exploration. Weakness in this area is of no little
significance. In terms of future trends in global production it is deep-water
extraction that is likely to become increasingly important.

So the role of the restructured supply base is very specific: to sustain
production in an existing mature and otherwise uncompetitive oil and
gas province and in doing so to maintain the revenue flow for the biggest
of the established producers. Here change has been fundamental. To answer
our earlier questions, there has been a willingness to invest, both directly
and through government agencies, in a long-term change in the industry's
structure, and also in technologies that are, in terms of CRINE priorities,
labour-saving. But this willingness does not extend to the advanced technologies needed for deep-water extraction and the requirements of the new
frontiers of oil exploration.

Here the contrast with the Norwegian sector is particularly instructive
and matches the differences in the political economy of the two provinces.
In Norway the bulk of private national capital has always been invested in
the supply side of the industry rather than in production. Correspondingly,
Norwegian supply firms have enjoyed a significantly privileged position in
their relations with the Norwegian state and its companies. The Norwegian
supply industry entered high-technology areas earlier and had begun to
penetrate foreign markets by the late 1980s. In the period since then, pressures for cost reduction have been manifestly less urgent than in the UKCS.
Norwegian supply firms in consequence have been able to sustain higher
profit levels through the 1990s and had the cash balances to permit them

to develop their position in the forefront of world technology.

This leaves the UK oil and gas companies with significant concerns. They have tamed their own supply industry and gone some way to develop low-cost production and maintenance technologies that are transferable internationally. But it has been at the expense of the industry's technological depth and its structural robustness. And within a smaller workforce, labour militancy remains a recurring possibility in an inherently volatile industry. How far these local difficulties will actually matter for the UK oil companies mainly depends on what happens on the larger world canvas – which is what we must look at next.

The Restructuring of British Oil and Gas: The UK Oil Companies

In his 1996 annual report, the BP Chief Executive John Browne adopted a distinctly bullish tone: 'We are a company that has reduced costs everywhere and dramatically cut its debt'. It was, he claimed, self-help, not higher oil prices, that had produced this result. The group had cut costs by US $2 billion since 1992 and this was contributing up to 80 per cent of the improved profit performance. The dividend had now been restored, the company had reduced its debt from US $15 billion to US $8 billion and capital expenditure would rise from US $4.5 billion in 1995 to US $5 billion in 1996. Shell Transport, reporting at the same time, indicated similar improvements in profit levels.[13]

Part of this improvement can be put down to restructuring at global level. In BP's case its total workforce has been cut by half since 1992 – from 120,000 to 60,000. But changes within the UKCS had assisted as well. The reduction in PRT was generating an additional income of over $0.5 billion a year for BP by 1994. The company's profits on capital employed in the North Sea had risen from 2.4 per cent in 1990 to 14 per cent in 1994. Shell benefited proportionately on a somewhat larger UKCS capital base (Rutledge and Wright, 1996).

When we examined the change of tax policy in 1993, we noted that it formed part of a cluster of decisions which fundamentally affected the domestic and international orientation of British energy policy in the three years after 1993. These policy decisions were the liberalization of the UK gas market, the parallel involvement in the European Union to liberalize the energy market, the final stage in the shutdown of the UK coal industry and the associated removal of limits on the proportion of UK electricity production that could be generated from fuels other than coal. In less directive form the British government gave strong diplomatic support for the opening of new overseas areas to investment by UK oil majors. Taking all these developments together, we propose that they represented a re-orientation of policy away from the United States and towards the European Union – and involved the adoption of a more independent stance by the UK oil majors. What, then, has happened since?

In terms of the American alliance it is important to to be clear what is proposed. It is not that there has been any decisive breach. On the contrary, American firms remain very important partners in the UKCS and their continuing investment is critical for its future. What is being argued is that the special and strategic character of the previous relationship has ended. In the 1970s and early 1980s these strategic objectives determined the pace of extraction and thereby the source of investment and the character of the supply industry. Only the United States had sufficient capital. Only US firms possessed the necessary technology: fast development precluded the lead-in time required by UK firms to acquire high-technology specialisms. This effectively accorded US firms a privileged position they did not enjoy for very long in the Norwegian sector.

In some respects this alliance was already losing its special character in the mid-1980s. Once OPEC had been broken, there was little reason for either government to treat investments in the UKCS any differently from other commercial arrangements. At the same time, the importance of the oil revenues for the UK government and for the country's balance of payments did make it vital that investment was maintained. As a result. there was no challenge to existing arrangements, and, as we saw, the introduction of PRT development relief in 1986 actually served to enhance the pace of external investment. What happened in the early 1990s was that these inherited arrangements fell apart. The tax regime, the structure of the supply industry and even the pattern of labour relations came to be seen as actively incompatible with the interests of the biggest of the UK's multinational firms.

The new arrangements which replaced them gave no special place to US interests and cleared away many of the industrial practices that had been part and parcel of the previous production regime. The transformation of the supply industry meant that the UKCS no longer constituted a high-profit venue for US multinational supply firms. More centrally for the development of UKCS, United States firms have started to lose their dominant position as oil operators. In the mid-1990s the sea-bed west of the Shetlands was licensed for exploration. The amount of oil and gas was estimated to be potentially comparable to some of the biggest fields east of the Shetlands – although in much deeper waters and far more difficult to extract. Two unusual occurrences were associated with the distribution of licences. First, BP and Shell were allocated licences in 1993 two years ahead of other companies, in order, according to the Energy Minister, to expedite exploration. Then, when the other licences were allocated in May 1995, 62 per cent of the territory went to non-US companies – which was almost exactly opposite to the proportion allocated in the 1970s and 80s.[14] The lower US proportion probably reflected pessimistic assessments by the US oil majors of the commercial risks involved rather than any change of practice by the DTI. But this reduction of US commitment west of the Shetlands was associated with another change of considerable symbolic magnitude: the end of the Shell–Esso partnership. This partnership had been the driving force for development in the UKCS east of the Shetlands, and the two firms had controlled around 35 per cent of all investment since the 1970s. But for the waters west of the Shetlands, Shell's partner now became the other UK oil major, BP.

East of the Shetlands the partnership continues, and Esso shares in the benefits derived by Shell from lower production costs and the reorientation of activity back towards the old pipeline infrastructures. Even here, however, there is evidence of tension. When Shell sought to dump the derelict Brent Spar rig in the Atlantic in 1995, it found itself the object of an international campaign of protest. In Germany in particular, it was subject to a consumer boycott that temporarily reduced its market share to the benefit of rival oil companies. The directors of Shell made it known that they felt that Esso had effectively stabbed them in the back. Although Esso was no less responsible for Brent Spar, the company refused to enter the controversy or make any public statement in support of its trading partner. The *Financial Times* ran a centre-page feature on the difficulties this was creating for Shell.[15]

In step with this erosion of the pre-existing relationship with the United States, British involvement with the European Union has become correspondingly more active. A key focus has been the development of energy policy. The years since 1990 have witnessed strenuous attempts to prise open the heavily protected European energy market. The major European states are energy importers. Most have created state-controlled monopolies for energy generation and distribution, and have sought to sustain internal power supplies, coal in Germany and nuclear power in France, in order to guarantee a degree of self-sufficiency. Apart from Britain no country possesses major energy companies which control large external reserves. By contrast, Britain and its multinational oil companies control exportable surpluses of oil. In terms of gas, Britain's potential is even bigger. One of the major objectives of the refurbishment plans for the UKCS pipeline infrastructures was to permit more effective gas collection for export to the European market.

By January 1992 Britain had succeeded in securing EU Directives by which the creation of a single European market in energy would begin in January 1993 for industrial consumers. Full energy liberalization was projected for 1996. Since 1992, however, a number of obstacles have impeded progress, and rendered the ultimate benefits for Britain much more problematical. There have been two problems. One has been the defiance of the energy Directives by France and Italy, and the absence of political will within the European Union to ensure compliance. Both France and Italy wish to protect their own energy producers and to avoid external dependence (DTI, 1995: 1, 63; DTI, 1996: 1, 22–3). Britain, on the other hand, has increasingly lacked the necessary allies within the EU to enforce its interests, and this political weakness has been compounded by a further difficulty. British gas faces competition from pre-existing supplies of Norwegian gas.

Britain began to deregulate its own internal energy market in the early 1990s. British Gas was deprived of its internal monopoly on distribution, and coal lost its safeguarded position as the fuel stock for electricity. The main objective seems to have been to expand the internal market for gas and to give UKCS oil companies an incentive to invest in increased production levels – and, in consequence, to bring down domestic prices. This has indeed happened. But, at the same time, gas prices have also fallen internationally, and at the same time Norway has been able to exploit its more developed gas infrastructure and its pre-existing pipeline links into the European Union to consolidate its position. Statoil was forecasting in November 1995 that its new pipeline and gas production facilities would be commissioned well ahead of the UK's 'Interconnector-Link' with Belgium and that it would be able to increase existing market shares in Germany from 14 per cent to 30 per cent and in France from 21 per cent to 37 per cent. The same month in 1995, Norway inaugurated the world's biggest gas processing plant employing 3000 people (Mollet, 1994).[16]

Britain still possesses the potential to undercut Norway. Germany in particular has good reason to want to take gas from the cheapest sources possible and to reduce its currently high energy costs. But Britain has yet to get its gas into the European network. The lead operator for the Interconnector is the privatized utility, British Gas, and this company is in fierce conflict with the UKCS oil and gas operators over the terms of their gas supply contracts, and in acute financial crisis as a result of the fall in gas prices. These problems, together with continued footdragging over European energy liberalization, make the original prospects for the European market still elusive.

The same chequered history also applies to the attempts by the British oil majors to replenish their external oil supplies. In the medium to long run this remains essential if these companies are to retain their global character. Some significant advances have been made. BP, in addition to its now mature fields in Alaska, is developing a new and very large oil province in Colombia. It has also had some success in Algeria. But the opportunities perceived in the early 1990s have not yet been secured. John Browne of BP then spoke of political changes since 1989 as opening up 'huge areas of the world ... closed to the industry by the barriers of ideology' (Browne, 1991: 1). He instanced the joint ventures then being established with Statoil to operate in Vietnam and other countries previously within the Soviet sphere. In subsequent years joint work with Statoil has gone ahead in Angola, Vietnam and Azerbaijan. But the outcome has been mixed. Exploration results in Vietnam have proved disappointing – although BP has secured a gas field in the Mekong delta. The Angolan civil war still threatens stability in the potentially very lucrative fields in the north of that country. In Azerbaijan major oil concessions have been successfully negotiated with the government, and together with other concessions negotiated by US oil firms in Kazakhstan on the eastern shore of the Caspian, the potential output comes near to half that of the whole UKCS. But the oil companies have so far failed to secure the pipelines that can get the oil out of the region. The cheapest exit route is along existing pipelines into Chechnya and then on to Russia – pipelines blocked by the struggle for secession in Chechnya. Alternative pipeline routes through Georgia to the Black Sea or through Turkey to the Mediterranean would be very expensive to construct. The US State Department has indicated that strategic reasons preclude a pipeline through Iran.[17]

In general BP's exploration activity has been shaped by its previous over-concentration of investment in Alaska and the UKCS. It has made a late entry into the new areas of cheap-cost oil. An *Economist* feature on BP's corporate policy in 1995 drew attention to the degree to which all its new investments were in politically high-risk areas.[18] This criticism applies somewhat less to the UK's other oil major, Shell, but much of Shell's new investment in overseas fields has also tended to be in frontier areas. Shell's pre-existing base of external supply has always been bigger than BP's. It has had major centres of production in the United States, in Africa largely in Nigeria, in the Near East mainly in Oman and Abu Dhabi, and in the Far East mainly in Malaysia. Shell has, however, been actively expanding its assets in Colombia, Brunei and Oman and undertaking exploration in Rumania, in Vietnam and offshore in China. The company has also acquired joint ventures in Siberia and the Russian Far East on Sakhalin. John Jennings spoke in his 1996 annual report of 'massive planned investment' in these Russian oil and gas fields.[19]

Neither company publishes detailed statistics on the capital invested in specific ventures overseas. It is, however, clear that these investments have increased sharply since 1991, and that a significant amount of the necessary cash has come from the UKCS. An analysis by Wood Mackenzie in May 1996 showed that the UKCS was moving towards record levels of income generation, and that, in net terms after tax and replacement costs, this would reach £7 billion per annum in real terms towards the end of the decade. However, the survey also found that for the top ten operators only 40 per cent of their aggregate net cash flow would be reinvested in the UKCS. 'While opportunities may exist for some in the deep waters west of Britain, others will view this as too high a risk and look elsewhere to invest'. The period to the end of the century 'is likely to see the attention of some cash-rich players directed overseas towards less mature provinces and assets where there may be greater potential for reserve-replacement'.[20]

A Temporary Stabilization

So, what is the final balance? Economically, the years since 1992 have seen a relatively successful attempt to stabilize costs in the UKCS. In some respects this has been achieved through the genuine development of standardized, labour-saving technologies. In other respects it has, despite efforts to the contrary, been at the expense of the size and vigour of the supply industry. The key drive has been the release of funds for investment elsewhere. The transformation of technology has been restricted to the existing infrastructure and investment in new labour-saving technologies was not comprehensive. It did not extend to the more demanding areas required for the new exploration frontier west of the Shetlands. The traditional colonial imperatives of Britain's oil industry reasserted themselves. The stabilization must therefore be seen as temporary. The concentration of control within the supply industry could easily result in circumstances where the suppliers could again take the offensive on the cost front. For the oil companies themselves the short-run turnaround in the UKCS has been critical for their fortunes. This was especially so for the two UK oil majors who were the most heavily exposed. These companies have now secured the cash they needed for transforming the character of their holdings in the UKCS, notably towards greater gas extraction, and for re-expanding their investments abroad. These developments have not involved any decisive break with the previous international alignments. But they have shifted the balance. US firms are no longer the leading force in new UKCS investment, and the production regime with which they were previously identified has been profoundly modified. In the UKCS, the alliance between Shell and Exxon is, for new exploration, replaced by that between Shell and BP. Externally, BP's chosen partner, at least in areas of previous Soviet influence, is the Norwegian state firm, Statoil. In terms of markets, the focus has shifted to Europe. A deregulated energy industry within the European Union appears to hold great potential for UK-based firms, and especially for those controlling gas supplies.

Yet all these prospects remain unsecured. The biggest single setback has been the failure to achieve a fully deregulated energy market in Europe. The slippage in the timetable has left UK producers with a serious oversupply of gas and brought acute financial crisis for the lead operator for the European market, British Gas. The incapacity of the post-Thatcher Conservatives to develop a coherent policy on Europe has so far dissipated the political alliances which would otherwise have been essential.

This leaves a very uncertain legacy for industrial relations and health and safety. Cutting costs remains essential for company balance sheets in the UKCS. Yet cost reductions inevitably also impact on labour and on health and safety. It is already apparent that an increasing proportion of cost-savings are being drawn directly from labour. By 1995 and 1996, wage settlements were near or below the industrial average onshore. As the memories of 1990 fade, so it is once more seen as safe to seek revenue from this source rather than at the expense of the supply industry or by enhancing labour-saving technology. The same switch of priorities may also be true for health and safety.

In sum, therefore, relations between capital and labour face a potentially fraught and difficult future. Obvious sources of volatility remain. On the one hand, the windows of opportunity for overseas investment, so promising in 1991, may close – precipitating much more investment back into the UKCS. This could recreate the same problems of overheating as occurred in 1989. Moreover, there is also a pressing obligation on the labour front. By the end of the decade the exemption from the EU Working Time Directive will expire, and, unless reinstated, the new requirements will very significantly tighten labour market constraints. Conversely, investments in other areas of the globe may expand still further and the current OPEC quota system disintegrate. In this case the price of oil will come down sharply. In either set of circumstances, significant challenges will be created for the management of the UKCS (UKOOA, 1995b: 2).[21]

Notes

1. *Aberdeen Petroleum Review*, 7 February 1996.

2. *Financial Times*, 9 August 1995 and *Aberdeen Petroleum Review*, 3 August 1995 for the report of MAI consultants to Scottish Enterprise; *Scotsman*, 19 September 1994 for the feature by Steven Tinsley.

3. *Aberdeen Petroleum Review*, 7 February 1996.

4. *Aberdeen Petroleum Review*, 29 June 1994 (Bond), 29 November 1995 (BW Mud) and 20 March 1996 (Rigblast).

5. *Aberdeen Petroleum Review*, 14 June 1995 (Heerema), 14 December 1995 (AMEC) and 6 March 1996 (Trafalgar House).

6. *Aberdeen Petroleum Review*, 9 February 1994, citing report by MacKay consultants.

7. *Aberdeen Petroleum Review*, 17 May 1995 for annual report of the Wood Group.

8. *Aberdeen Petroleum Review*, 16 August 1995 (OSO and McKay reports), 17 May 1995 (Wood Group AGM).

9. *Aberdeen Petroleum Review*, 31 May 1995.

10. *Petroleum Economist*, Vol. 62, 12 December 1995: feature on Deep Water Technology.

11. *Aberdeen Petroleum Review*, 2 February 1994.

12. Record Note of luncheon meeting between Executive Officers and Mr Tim Eggar at the Royal Horseguard Hotel, 25 April 1994 (UKOOA mimeo typescript marked Highly Confidential) and accompanying letter from Tim Eggar of 26 April 1996 and memo from Harold Hughes (9 May 1994): UKOOA Archive, Offshore Information Centre, Aberdeen. The correspondence reflects bitter exchanges in which UKOOA functionaries accused the Minister of saying that the oil 'should stay in the ground' if UK technology was not used. The UKOOA transcript reads:

> It became clear that he [the Minister] was switching the discussion to the issue of floating production systems, in which he again clearly expected the industry to take some general position across companies to ensure that the UK market for such systems was fully delineated, and that UK suppliers were thereby encouraged to enter the market ... The President [of UKOOA] and I decided not to say that at a recent ... meeting we had attended the OSO officials had confirmed ... that they did not see hull construction for floating production systems as now being within UK capability.

13. *Financial Times*, 12 May 1996 (Royal Dutch Shell); *Aberdeen Petroleum Review*, 23 May 1996.

14. *Aberdeen Petroleum Review*, 9 March 1993 (Licences to BP and Shell) and 24 May 1995 (allocation of blocks).

15. *Financial Times*, 1 July 1995. It may only be of historic interest that the Pearson Group, which owns the *Financial Times*, grew out of the Cowdray oil assets now incorporated in Shell.

16. *Aberdeen Petroleum Review*, 27 July 1994 (Eggar's statement on importance of gas in 15th Licensing Round), 22 November 1995 (Statoil market projections), 6 December 1995 (Troll gas project).

17. *Shell Review* 1993; BP Annual report and accounts 1993 and 1995; *Financial Times*, 10 May 1996 for statement by Cor Herkstoeter on Royal Dutch investment priorities; *Financial Times*, 18 and 29 April 1996 (Caspian pipeline arrangements); *Aberdeen Petroleum Review*, 17 April 1996 for assessment of BP's external partnership with Statoil, by Barry Halton, BP's Senior Public Affairs Adviser.

18. *Economist*, 20 January 1996, p. 81.

19. *Aberdeen Petroleum Review*, 18 April 1966.

20. *Aberdeen Petroleum Review*, 7 May 1996.

21. The 1995 UKOOA document *Towards 2020* lists six potentially destabilizing factors. They are: lower oil and gas prices, adverse fiscal changes, CRINE lessons not fully implemented, application of the Working Time Directive to the offshore industry, restricted gas demand, and exclusion of the expected acreage from future UKCS licensing rounds.

12 CONCLUSION: AN UNSAFE FUTURE

In April 1996 the Energy Minister Tim Eggar was able to celebrate the continuing achievements of the British oil and gas industry. Introducing the 1996 Energy Report, he noted that the industry 'was still setting records decades after the first offshore oil fields were discovered'. Output levels for both oil and gas were the highest ever and new investment amounted to 18 per cent of the UK industrial total. Corporate income from the sector had been restored to £18 billion and included a record contribution from gas at £4 billion. Eggar ended by stressing the importance of new European markets for the industry:

> The prospective UK–Belgian interconnector will allow new gas developments to find profitable continental sales opportunities. The Government is determined that our European partners should be aware of the benefits of liberalisation of markets and we will continue to press this issue wherever we can. (DTI, 1996)

A decade earlier, in 1985, a similar congratulatory tone was adopted – just before the industry was plunged into crisis by the oil price collapse of that year.

Over the intervening years much had indeed changed. The internal structure of the industry had been transformed. Quite new relationships existed between operators and contractors. Government had become directly involved in technological development. Managements had taken a comprehensive responsibility for safety. Labour had temporarily become organized, and managements were now seeking to implement quite new perspectives for labour relations.

This Conclusion will attempt to assess the character of this transformation. It has been our argument that these changes amounted to a critical turning-point for the industry and for its wider position within the British economy.

More specifically, three basic propositions have been advanced. The first is that these years witnessed the crisis and disintegration of a production regime originally imported from the United States in the 1970s. The second is that its replacement coincided with a reorientation of the industry away from a previously close strategic alliance with the United States and towards more specifically UK-determined objectives – both in terms of the opening of the European energy market and the resumption of the traditional over-seas investment priorities of the UK oil majors. The third proposition concerns the role of labour. We have argued that it was the collective action of the workforce in the years after Piper Alpha that both precipitated the crisis and played a key role in determining the character of its resolution. This did not happen in a unilateral way. There were other forces at work. But neither the crisis of the early 1990s nor its resolution can be understood unless labour's capacity for collective action is taken into account.

Safety and the Re-establishment of Managerial Control

The main body of our narrative has already identified the potential impor-tance of safety within offshore industrial relations. Piper Alpha was a critical turning-point. Trade union activists had long argued that the industry was grievously unsafe. Yet even among those directly at risk this perspective had been effectively marginalized. The scale of the Piper Alpha disaster, its obvious link to oppressive management styles and inadequate government supervision, and the focus of attention on these issues by the Cullen inquiry suddenly combined to give this perspective a widespread public legitimacy. Popular discussion of the offshore industry became framed by the perception that safety had been systematically sacrificed to corporate profit. Within the breakdown of managerial authority, culminating in the rig occupations of 1989 and more especially of 1990, the issue of safety was manifestly central.

In the battle to re-establish managerial control, safety was no less important. Managements quickly realized the collective penalties of failure – and also the opportunities to be gained by seizing the initiative. Safety was not a matter which could be left to individual employers. As Piper Alpha demonstrated, lapses by one operator could easily throw the whole industry into turmoil and penalize every operator. Within a few months of the disaster, UKOOA was preparing the agenda for strategic change that it was to take into the Cullen inquiry and which was to profoundly modify its outcome. Safety had to become basic to the industry's culture. And it had to be management, and no one else, that took prime responsibility for changing the safety environment.

This was the key theme of UKOOA's expert witnesses at the inquiry and it was hammered home at UKOOA's own conference in December 1990. The dangers of any alternative outcome were clear. Were prime responsibility to be vested externally within an inspectorate, or even worse, given to trade-union appointed committees, then management would lose a major part of its credibility and authority. Conversely, by claiming central responsibility, management would be able to drive the changes and be the originator of 'thought, innovation and the introduction of improved safety techniques' (Hughes, 1990: 42). This was why the proposal for the introduction of Formal Safety Assessments (or the Safety Case) was so important to UKOOA. It enabled each individual operator to set the agenda among its own workers. If there was to be a goal-oriented safety culture on these terms, then management would be able to determine its content and themselves organize the participation of the workforce. Managers had to become the safety crusaders. As another participant at the UKOOA conference put it:

> Reorganise your priorities and put safety right at the top. And believe me, this may just turn out to be the best management decision you'll ever take. It'll turn out to be good for morale, good for people, good for productivity, good for profits and basically good for everyone with a stake in your company. (McKee, 1990: 55)

Two years later the Cost Reduction Initiative presented safety management as an integral part of reorganization. Goal-setting and the creation of a safety culture made it possible to dispense with prescriptive procedures – at the same time that changes in systems of communication would create a far more open and responsive atmosphere. The creation of non-adversarial relations had to extend through the workforce: 'such sweeping changes emphasise the importance of involving the workforce in the formulation and development of new approaches' (DTI, 1993a: 4.5.3).

Preceding chapters have detailed the success of UKOOA's interventions in determining the outcome of the Cullen inquiry and in modifying the implementation of its recommendations on safety. They have also revealed that the actual consequences, as represented by offshore death and injury statistics, are by no means as good as the new system's propagandists have sometimes claimed. We will now seek to consider why this should have been the case and why the new arrangements are intrinsically unlikely to secure any fundamental improvement in the future.

The core organizing concept for the new safety regime is that of safety culture. Cullen had endorsed it quite unproblematically – no doubt influenced by the powerful advocacy of McKee of Conoco and Rimington of HSE in the course of the inquiry. He formulated his position thus:

> It is essential to create a corporate atmosphere or culture in which safety is understood to be, and is accepted as, the number one priority. Management have to communicate the safety philosophy at all times and at all levels within the organisation but most particularly by their everyday decisions and actions in tackling the many issues that arise in operating in the North Sea. (1990: Ch. 18.47)

Cullen was aware that an integrated safety culture was not a simple matter of exhortation or management 'mission statements'. It concerned the actual realities of daily work practice. He stressed that not only had management to 'communicate' but, he said, 'it is essential that the whole workforce is committed to and involved in safe operations' (1990: Ch. 18.48).

The problem with the type of safety culture espoused by the oil companies is that its limits were very carefully defined in both theory and practice. It assumed and demanded consensus. It excluded the real-life inconsistencies and contradictions that arose between management and the shopfloor. John Morgan, senior UK executive of BP exploration, made this very clear in 1992:

> Any organisation that has a legitimate interest in safety is welcome to work with my organisation so long as they are working with the grain of what I have been describing and in a way that will add to it. But it should also be made clear that any organisation using safety to work a different agenda will be a potential hindrance to the alignment inherent in what I have been describing. (Morgan, 1992)

At the UKOOA safety conference in 1990 Harold Hughes dealt directly with the issue of trade union involvement:

> The present arrangement offshore provides every employee with the right to elect (and be elected as) safety representatives. This is different from the situation onshore where safety representatives are appointed by recognised trade unions. We are pleased that Lord Cullen recognises the merit and democratic basis of the present offshore regulation. (Hughes, 1990: 44)

For the oil employers contending with the fraught industrial relations of 1990, safety culture represented an ideal vehicle for re-establishing more general control and legitimacy. It reproduced quite exactly the 'common values' assumptions of Human Resource Management and provided a platform on which the new type of consensual relations could be built. On this basis trade union representation was unnecessary. Safety was above conflicts of interest: an effective safety culture had to involve all employees at every level. As the CBI's 1990 document on safety put it: 'the safety culture of an organisation could be described as the ideas and beliefs that all members of an organisation share about risks, accidents and ill-health' (CBI, 1990: 5–6; see also Bibbings, 1992).

In this sense safety culture was indeed a new and innovative concept in an offshore context. Its proponents focused particularly on communication. Authoritarian and command styles of management had to go. The new stress was on involvement, explanation and understanding. In 1992 the Oil Industry Advisory Committee established a working group concentrating on 'how to create safety through good quality communications . . . Particular attention is being paid to the key role of supervisors'.[1] Within the industry this concern for systems of communication quickly extended beyond safety to styles of work and productivity. The research undertaken for BP by Steward and Dawson underlined the productivity gains to be secured by changing communication patterns and achieving a routine sharing of knowledge. Even in the macho world of drilling, shouting had to give way to talking (Steward and Dawson, 1993). By 1994 OIAC was recommending the procedures familiar from land-based flexible manufacturing: team meetings, tool box discussions, safety circles (OIAC, 1994). Key offshore contractors such as Smedvig were now propounding a coherent programme of organizational culture change to secure workforce involvement, accompanied by intensive management re-education and detailed psychometric employee selection procedures (Ramsay, 1994).[2]

There can be no doubt about the formal success of this initiative. It profoundly modified management practice. And at the same time as marginalizing trade union interventions on safety, it has placed management securely in command of the safety agenda – as much as anything as a result of the highly technical process by which safety cases are drawn up. But in terms of any long-term effectiveness in reducing accidents, very considerable doubts remain. This is precisely because its definition of culture is manifestly artificial – and real-life communication is considerably more complex than what is presumed.

Chris Wright has produced a particularly insightful analysis of the survival patterns of different groups of workers on Piper Alpha. Some groups, he found, had perished almost entirely. Others, like the divers, largely survived.

Wright finds that these different survival rates were closely correlated with two characteristics. One was the degree to which the group itself was, as a working collective, closely integrated. The other was the degree to which it was not incorporated into a wider system of control. The divers survived because they had previously worked out their own informal routines as to how to respond to a crisis and disregarded official procedures. Others perished because they followed the official emergency instructions, made their way to the galley accommodation and then obediently waited for instructions which never came. For Wright this emphasizes the importance of informal and internally generated understandings of safety (Wright, 1993). It also corresponds with the findings of Wright's associated research on offshore fatal accident inquiries. Wright discovered that fatalities only rarely resulted from sudden and exceptional violations of safe practice. The usual cause was a lack of fit between prescribed procedures and actual working routines. What people did as a normal part of working life was itself potentially dangerous. There may have been prescribed safe procedures. But, for one reason or another, they were felt to be inappropriate and not observed. Hence again the importance of internally generated work-group understandings of safety (Wright, 1986; 1994).

All this might appear to support the arguments for a corporate safety culture which covers all employees and penetrates from the top of the hierarchy to its base. But this ignores one crucial factor: the social context of communication. People's position within a social hierarchy affects the way they listen to others – and what they say. Stephen Tombs looked at one aspect of this phenomenon in his research on the Piper Alpha disaster. He sought to explain why management had systematically disregarded certain types of information on safety hazards prior to the explosion. His conclusion is that this occurred when the information came from individual workers outside the recognized management chain. Such information was written off as generalized grumbling. This, claims Tombs, was an example of 'distorted communication'. Effective, undistorted communication demands mutuality and trust, and will fade and disappear in so far as relations are hierarchical, authoritarian and conflictual (Tombs, 1991).

The converse of this is that people will not say what they mean in socially oppressive situations. This phenomenon has been most fully explored by James Scott. He argues that quite different types of language will be used by the same people in different social circumstances. In public communications with those in dominant positions they will only use what they perceive to be 'accepted' formulations. In private, with others in the same circumstances, they will use quite different terms that match what they perceive to be their real situation. Scott calls this the 'hidden transcript'. An example would be the informal group perceptions of hazard that enabled the divers to escape from Piper Alpha. The divers as a group had a strong enough integration to articulate among themselves a critical awareness of their work situation – and to disregard official procedures. This is similar to the evolution of other normal (but dangerous) working routines. A critical awareness of them will crystallize within and between work-group members only when safety has arisen as an issue in this social context – as it did after Piper Alpha. Scott argues that such hidden transcripts will remain hidden until the socially oppressive circumstances have been removed – or until they are effectively challenged (Scott, 1990).

It is this perception that underlies the argument for direct trade union involvement in health and safety, and specifically for the trade union appointment of health and safety committees. Trade union-based representation, because it is distinctly separate from the management, has a unique ability to access this hidden transcript and enhance it. As a safety procedure, the use of trade union representatives recognizes that power relations in the workplace are inherently unequal, and acts on this assumption. 'Safety culture', by contrast, presumes a level of equality and consensus that does not exist (Fairbrother, 1996). In 1991, BP issued its Charter of Rights. Thousands of copies were distributed to its staff promising 'fair reward', 'respect for the individual' and 'a safe working place'.[3] Yet these promises were made at the very time when hundreds of offshore employees remained victimized for taking collective action to demand trade union recognition. Employees who wished to prosper no doubt felt constrained to give public acknowledgement to the rights which BP had conferred. Their private feelings may have been very different.

Hence, the problem with the type of safety culture being promulgated in the North Sea is that, in these circumstances, it is likely to be counterproductive. It will tend to diminish rather than enhance any active growth of critical safety awareness among shopfloor workers, and it will do so for two reasons. In so far as corporately supervised social structures are created, and separate work-group solidarity is weakened, so the social robustness of the 'hidden transcript' will be eroded. Isolated individuals will not articulate heretical thoughts, and normally unsafe work routines will not be subject to collective scrutiny. And in so far as management seizes the issue of safety and makes it part of its own rhetoric of control, safety will be less likely to figure as part of the internal critique of the work group.

What has happened since 1991 tends to substantiate this. Attitudes to safety appear to be becoming progressively more passive and routine. In 1992 an

Aberdeen University research team was commissioned to carry out a review of the safety committee system introduced in the UKCS in 1989. Set up as a very belated response to the disaster, this safety committee system was based on the election of representatives as against their appointment by trade union which occurred onshore. The survey of 2500 employees and 160 safety representatives revealed a relatively high knowledge of safety procedures and of the identity of safety representatives, compared to the situation onshore. It also revealed an evenly divided position among the sample of employees about the merits of the onshore system for the trade union appointment of safety representatives. The fact that almost half the sample did not seen any benefit in trade union appointments was seized upon by UKOOA to justify the retention of the existing system (Spaven *et al.*, 1993).

However, the survey also revealed a significant change in the character of safety representatives over the period. Those taking up post in 1989 and 1990 were mostly trade union members. Those taking up post in 1991 and 1992 included only a small minority of trade union members. Those in the earlier cohort included many more elected in contested elections; those in the second had more who were effectively management appointees. The occupational profile of safety representatives also shows that over a fifth of the total surveyed were in supervisory or management grades and only a third drawn from manual workers or construction trades. While this profile is not broken down by date of appointment, the presumption must be that those coming into post from 1991 would tend to be more frequently drawn from non-manual grades. Already, therefore, the management espousal of safety culture might be seen to have been distancing those most at risk from direct involvement in safety monitoring (Vulliamy, 1993). The authors of the Aberdeen report noted, in associated articles, an increasing isolation of safety representatives from their constituents and a measure of confusion about their role, giving rise to 'the possibility of conflicts of interest' (Spaven and Wright, 1993a).

> In some cases confusion over the role of safety representative has led managers attempting to impose safety duties on them such as carrying out a specified number of audits of work permits. In other cases, safety representatives with a particularly pro-active approach had encountered tensions with their constituents who saw them policing their work practices rather than representing their interests and concerns. (Spaven and Wright, 1993b: 31)

The report, not surprisingly, recorded that 'there was considerable disillusionment among present and previous safety representatives'. What has happened since tends to bear out our presupposition that workforce involvement has become more routine and passive. As we noted in Chapter 7, the 1995 HSE Interim Report on 1992 Safety Case regulations indicated significant communication problems in terms of the general workforce. The specifications of Safety Cases are highly technical, and many safety representatives have found it difficult to make any effective response – either at the level of formulating Safety Cases or assimilating them after approval. For the workforce as a whole this narrowing of direct involvement appears to have been even more marked.

So our prognosis for offshore safety tends to match that of Colin MacFarlane (MacFarlane, 1993a). Repetitions of major disasters like that at Piper Alpha are, hopefully, much more unlikely. The scale of capital expenditure since 1990 should have made structures less dangerous. In addition, the Safety Case procedure has involved managements in a systematic consideration of safety which was previously lacking. Hence, the multiple failure of systems ought to be avoidable. Yet most offshore accidents have never been of this catastrophic variety. They have involved the death and injury of individual workers, and it is here that the weakness of the new system is most apparent. Avoidance of individual accidents demands a critical consciousness of safety that penetrates actual working routines. Technical Safety Cases and the new-style safety culture tend, for the reasons we have given, to inhibit rather than develop this awareness.

Let us give a couple of illustrations of the type of circumstances we are talking about. Every winter there is the danger of at least one 'bridge incident' resulting in either the total loss of, or structural damage to, the connecting bridge between the flotel and the installation as a consequence of bad weather. Of the fifteen major occurrences and innumerable minor incidents recorded over a period of twelve years, five had involved the total loss of the bridge. The workforce and the unions campaigned year in year out for threshold limits on wave height and wind speed to be established for the mandatory closure of the bridge. Such criteria are applied by regulation in regard to crane use offshore.

On Brent Charlie in January 1992, workers refused to cross the bridge during bad weather and were threatened with disciplinary action. An acrimonious debate ensued in which three sets of interests emerged. First, there were the men who were acting in a spontaneous collective manner in refusing to cross the bridge. Second, there was the employer, and contract management, insisting that the men should cross. Third, there was the installation management, Shell, seeking to avoid becoming involved in a dispute between contractor and workforce, but claiming that the bridge was within its safe operating envelope. So, while ostensibly not taking sides, Shell tacitly supported the contract management. In the stand-off which developed, and as the weather worsened, the flotel lurched into a deep trough, activating the bridge auto-lift system. In the process of disengaging itself, structural and secondary damage was inflicted on the installation, vindicating the workforce's refusal to cross.[4]

The operators have continued to maintain that the 'safe operating envelope' of the bridge extends right to the point where the automatic lift mechanism intervenes. This lift mechanism is activated only when the extreme limit has been reached. Experience clearly shows that, before that point is reached, there is no margin for error. In the autumn of 1994 there was an almost exact re-run of the earlier incident on the Brent Charlie in which an offshore worker crossing from the Safe Gothia had a narrow escape. His account, in his own words, minuted by Shell Safety Department, was reprinted in *Blowout*.

> When I reached the far end of the bridge I heard warning bells. I started to descend down the stairs to the platform. Halfway down the stairs, the bridge lifted about 3 to 4 feet, shuddering violently. I grabbed the hand rail to hang on. Suddenly the bridge lifted again to a height of about 10 feet. I heard someone on the platform shout 'JUMP! FOR FUCK'S SAKE, JUMP!' On hearing this, I jumped from the stairs onto the landing platform in time to see it [the bridge] lift right up, and ran down the rest of the stairs to the Brent Charlie.[5]

It was the previous contention of the workforce that real danger occurs well in advance of the situation deteriorating to the point where automatic mechanisms operate. The Shell representative on the Safe Gothia had advised of the intention to close the bridge due to deteriorating weather expected in an hour's time. The incident occurred, however, within 45 minutes of this warning. Refusal to cross the bridge, essentially a safety judgement by the workers, became identified as a direct challenge to management preroga-tives. In the previous Brent Charlie incident the workforce spokesperson had been subsequently NRB'd.

Crossing the bridge in adverse weather conditions is exactly one of those routines of offshore life that are taken as normal. They are risky but accepted. In the first incident the workforce retained enough of its own collective cri-tique of what constituted dangerous practice to resist. In the second, two years later, an individual followed what was normal practice and almost lost his life. It is precisely at this day-to-day level that the greatest danger exists, and developments on this front since 1990 are not encouraging. The dissemination of a management-controlled safety culture has gone hand in hand with an erosion of collective shopfloor organization, and this would seem to have weakened both the ability to generate a rank-and-file safety consciousness and the capacity to assert it. What is more, this has happened at a time when the new safety procedures have served to strengthen managerial prerogative.

The Aberdeen University report makes an important point here. It identifies a largely unnoticed consequence of the shift from a detailed prescriptive regime to a more generalized goal-setting one. This is that goal-setting places even greater discretion in the hands of management in exercising their prerogative to interpret company policy and procedures. What is seen by management as flexibility and legitimate discretion can be seen by the workforce as potentially dangerous 'grey areas' (Spaven et al., 1993: 79–80). The authority of the safety representatives, caught between pressures from above and below, is that much more easily undermined. On at least two major installations, Shell's Brent Charlie in early 1994 and AGIP's Tiffany in late 1993, there have been mass resignations from the safety committee. On Brent Charlie, contractors' safety representatives for Wood Group resigned under pressure from a mass meeting when a dispute over 'call-outs' during the prescribed eight-hour rest period could not be resolved through the mechanisms of the safety committee. The issue was only finally settled through grievance procedures covering industrial relations. The Brent Charlie workforce, with a core crew on a five-year contract, felt sufficiently frustrated with the perceived weakness of the safety representatives to resort to using them as a direct industrial relations bargaining counter with management. On the Tiffany platform men were run off for refusal to shuttle on helicopters during weather severe enough for the accommodation barge to have lifted its bridge and pulled away.[6] The Tiffany safety committee, in disarray, could not intervene on behalf of the workforce. Yet where such interventions over safety are made and do become issues of contention, managerial prerogatives are easily asserted.

This takes us back to the original promulgation of the new safety culture in 1990. Then, and in the years that followed, the employers have had a very clear vision of how it should operate. They were willing to draw a line under what had gone before. They implicitly, and sometimes explicitly, criticized old-style management styles, and stressed the importance of discussion and communication. They publicly supported measures to prevent any victimization of safety representatives carrying out their functions, and backed both the 1992 Offshore Safety (Protection Against Victimisation) Act and the related sections of the 1993 Trade Union Reform and Employment Rights Act which extended the same protection to all employees and did so in line with the EU Directive of the previous year.[7] What they were not willing to tolerate was the involvement of trade unions. The UKOOA Director General, Harold Hughes, made this very clear in 1990. His organization defended the right of every employee to be freely elected as a safety representative. He contrasted the merits of this democratic principle, already operating offshore under SI 971, with the trade union-based system in force everywhere else in the UK. Hughes ended his speech to the 1990 UKOOA safety conference on a prophetic note. In identifying UKOOA with the principles outlined in the Cullen report, he expressed his confidence that their influence would soon extend more widely (Hughes, 1990: 46).

Since 1990 this has come to seem increasingly more likely. The 1989 offshore regulations (SI 971) look set to become the pattern for all UK workplaces (Kidger, 1992). European Union legislation now directs that consultation on safety matters should take place with all employees and not just trade unionists (HSC, 1995d; Walters *et al.*, 1993). In line with this legislation, the Health and Safety Executive finally decided in October 1995 not to recommend any change in the existing SI 971 regulations. Over the previous five years the offshore trade unions had failed to establish even the limited foothold, recommended in the Aberdeen report, by which trade union-nominated representatives would be able to compete for election alongside non-union representatives. The unions had also failed to secure the opening which Lord Cullen had offered. No union succeeded in establishing a sufficiently 'substantial' membership on any particular installation to claim the more formal rights for union-appointed safety representatives which Cullen had proposed. This singular defeat for the unions offshore came at precisely the moment when the whole onshore safety representative system was undergoing extensive reappraisal (Storey and Barker, 1993a; 1993b). European Union legislation now appears to have made the development of a new onshore system unavoidable. A system of trade union-based representation, which confines rights in law solely to collectively organized workplaces, will now increasingly become a thing of the past, despite evidence of an enhanced safety record (Reilly *et al.*, 1995; Walters and Gourlay, 1990; TUC, 1995b). The new systems introduced offshore after 1990 are likely to become the norm unless decisively challenged – either by an exposure of their unsafe character or by organized labour itself.

Organized Labour

Perhaps the most remarkable feature of the oil workers' occupations of 1989 and 1990 is that they occurred at all. They took place in an industry where union members were in a relatively small minority, where most employers had long refused union recognition and where there was no tradition of collective bargaining. They occurred at a time when the level of strike activity within the UK as a whole was at a historic low and in the face of some of the most oppressive anti-trade union legislation in the western world. Yet the occupations took place, and did so with sufficient force to necessitate a permanent restructuring of the industry.

We have argued that much of the effectiveness of this industrial action derived from the circumstances in which it arose. It needed to take a form which evaded the legal ban on solidarity action or the requirement for ballots. It relied on workplace organization that had to be created very quickly and demanded the active mobilization of the workforce for a specific end. And its effectiveness stemmed from the way it challenged the authority of management. It was not a strike in the classical sense: the workers remained on the platforms. It involved workers in progressively withdrawing from the jurisdiction of their employers, first through the overtime ban and then through sit-ins. In doing so the workforce developed their own alternative command structure. Intransigent managers were left humiliated. Those who sought to negotiate were drawn into tacit complicity.

As a form of industrial action, the tactic of sit-in had inherent weaknesses. It was limited in time; it could not have been prolonged much beyond a month. It relied on the commitment of a relatively small core of activists who were very vulnerable to exclusion and victimization. It involved isolated groups of workers separated by hundreds of miles of sea and with no sure method of communication – and depended on securing sufficient unity across the UKCS to be able to hit the operators at just that moment when they required to undertake their maintenance operations. Yet because of the physical interconnection of the pipeline infrastructure, it could potentially inflict very heavy losses running into tens of millions of pounds. Stopping the oil, as Funkhouser noted in the mid-1970s, gave organized labour an immensely powerful lever (cited in Harvie, 1994). To this extent, the occupations were a form of action that was quite appropriate to the offshore oil industry. Few other groups of workers possess the potential to exercise such a strategic grip over a crucial sector of the economy. The very capital intensity of the oil industry could put its relatively small workforce, once organized, in a commanding position.

However, at the same time as these specific features, there are some more general lessons that it is important to note. The first concerns the long-term viability of union-free styles of management. The occupations of 1989 and 1990 occurred in an industry where there were no comprehensive structures of collective bargaining. At this level, the offshore oil industry was rather similar to many other areas of the economy that dispensed with trade unions in the 1980s, and which have been presented as harbingers of a union-free future (McLoughlin and Gourlay, 1994). Offshore managerial authority crumbled very quickly once challenged. Because of the lack of established negotiating structures, managers had restricted options for limiting conflict. Moreover, the demand itself, the right to collective bargaining, proved a powerful one and was not easily denied without the further undermining of managerial authority.

The second lesson concerns the way in which this challenge was launched. It did not emerge wholly spontaneously from the rank and file. Nor was it the result of a top-down initiative by the leadership of one union. It stemmed from the emergence of a common perspective among union activists at local level which drew upon a reservoir of previous experience. It was this perspective that initially served to unite both officers and lay members across a number of different unions. Without this it would not have been possible to access the organizational resources of the existing trade union structures or to unite the loyalties of a diversity of union members within the industry. In so far as the trade union movement in Britain retains a formal structural unity – through the TUC and its regional structures and trades councils – this potential for united intervention remains critical, if largely unrealized. The ambitions of 'super-unions', however, increasingly appear to undermine even this potentiality, allowing sectionalist tendencies to be systematically exploited by the employer. Against this, the industrial union OILC poses a perhaps unpalatable but necessary counterpoint, which itself has forced business-friendly unions to adopt an even more belligerent stance.

The third lesson concerns the future. New forms of management have now been instituted. They seek to co-opt workers through longer-term contracts, personal development programmes and a 'culture' of institutional responsiveness. In some cases this programme of incorporation has extended to the adoption of Works Councils. The outcomes for management have in general been good. Formal trade union organization has been marginalized. The OILC has not disappeared but neither has it grown to the point where it can displace the established unions, and nowhere has it secured bargaining rights. The two main TUC-affiliated unions, the AEEU and GMB, have been forced back to their previous role as enforcers of highly limited sectional agreements for hook-up contracts. The steady decline in the level of negotiated wage increases in this sector mirrors their diminishing influence. But this does not necessarily mean that in the longer run the new forms of management will be any more successful than the old. Marginalizing organized labour is not the same as restoring the status quo. The experience of collective action remains. So does the organization which led it: the OILC. Moreover, there is also an additional factor: the international one. Strong organizational links are developing with organized labour in the Norwegian sector. Workers in this sector have a strong interest in ensuring that their own wages and conditions do not move too far out of line with those of their British counterparts. This support will probably be enough to ensure that a core of militant trade unionism continues in the UKCS, however harsh the local environment. The logic of this internationalism also extends elsewhere in the UK.

Hence, to sum up, the outlook for management – within the inherent unpredictability of the oil industry – remains unsecured. An industry with fewer workers does not necessarily deprive those workers of power. Small numbers can often exert disproportionate power. In the same measure, labour's prospects for collective organization depend very largely on recreating, though inevitably in a new way, that alliance of cross-union commitment that proved so effective in 1989 and again in 1990.

An Unsafe Future

This study has focused on a particular and quite limited episode in the recent history of British industrial relations. It has sought to document the upsurge in rank-and-file activism which occurred within the UK offshore oil industry in the years after Piper Alpha and which ultimately resulted in the formation of a new union. It has attempted to demonstrate that the origins of this struggle lay in a production regime which showed scant regard for health and safety and which was associated with the worst industrial disaster in recent British history. But in telling this story a more basic point has become very clear. This is the continuing capacity of organized labour to determine the wider direction of economic and political change. The ultimate outcome for labour organization in the UKCS has been relatively small. But the restoration of management control has been accompanied by profound changes in the organization of the offshore oil industry and in its wider orientation within the British economy. These changes cannot be solely attributed to labour militancy. Most were likely to occur in some form anyway. But their timing and character was very significantly affected by the action of the oil workers, and it is this that we will now attempt to sum up.

First, there is the timing of the industry's internal restructuring and the character of the Cost Reduction Initiative. The cost explosion of 1990–91 was in no small part the result of management attempts to buy off the demand for trade union recognition. Correspondingly, the residual strength of rank-and-file organization meant that the subsequent restructuring could not be at the expense of the workforce. To have taken the 1986 route and slashed wages and conditions would have relighted fires that had by then scarcely been extinguished. So the restructuring of 1992–93 had to be at the expense of the supply industry. The result was a fundamental change in technological assumptions and procedures. In terms of the technologies required for cheapening the labour costs of maintenance and production in developed fields, it can be claimed that major advances have been made. The innovation of basic standardized systems, themselves largely derivatives of pre-existing technology, has now provided UK supply companies with internationally saleable products which it previously lacked. But it has also taken them out of the market for more advanced technologies, and here the UK is even more heavily dependent on external companies than before.[8]

The second consequence has been for the dynamics of the oil industry's development in the UKCS. It was again on the cards that the UK oil majors in particular would have pushed for changes in the tax system so as to permit the redirection of investment to the refurbishment of the traditional core of the UKCS. The effect of the militancy of the late 1980s and early 1990s was to convince the government that it could no longer ride two horses. It could not safely combine its subsidy of investment in the exploration and development of new areas with the maintenance of effective production conditions in the old fields on which the UKCS depended. A choice had to be made. This choice was no doubt also powerfully conditioned by perceptions of the European market for gas – a commodity whose expanded production was closely related to refurbishing the UKCS infrastructure. But the basic lesson of 1989–91 was that the investment tap had at least partly to be turned off if a grip on the labour market was to be re-established. The 15 per cent drop in the employed workforce between 1992 and 1993 was one clear outcome.

The third consequence was for the character of the production regime. We have just examined the centrality of 'safety culture' to the redevelopment of management authority. This was not just a matter of responding to the tragic indictment of Piper Alpha. It was symbolic of a new beginning. Again there has been genuine innovation. Control over labour could not simply be sustained in the old way by upping the number of unemployed – an instrument that could anyway be removed overnight by the implementation of the EU Working Time Directive. A more fundamental relationship had to be built up between management and a smaller, more concentrated and more stable core workforce. There had to be investment in labour itself. Education and training had to be given a new place. And patterns of communication had to change. Managements had to move with some deliberation away from the now obsolete practices of the 1970s to decisively new relationships – most cogently outlined in the 1993 DTI report. These did not include trade union recognition. But they did seek to incorporate workers within a new value system that recognized joint interests and a measure of consultation. The new perspective sought consensus and was essentially compatible with the social philosophy of the European Union. BP is one of those UK companies that have now committed themselves to the establishment of Works Councils – though, in BP's case, it has done so without any attempt to consult or involve the trade union movement.[9]

This takes us to the changed international alignment away from the United States. Again, as we have noted, this shift was already underway in the 1980s and was fairly inevitable. Commercial relations were bound to replace strategic considerations as the world oil market changed. There was also the transformation in global politics that occurred in 1990. These factors all had their independent effects on the assumptions of the UK oil majors. But the breakdown in industrial relations did add a further and critical dimension. Both Shell and, especially, BP were locked into the UKCS to a much greater extent than their American partners. For them the UKCS had previously represented a source of oil that was politically trouble-free and reliable. This was its great attraction in the 1970s. By 1990-91 this was no longer true, and the two UK companies had to contemplate drastic surgery to rescue themselves: deflating the entire sector, salvaging and nailing down a local supply base, negotiating a costly social partnership deal with its workforce and, crucial in order to guarantee a reliable cash flow into the future, securing a new opening to the EU energy market for gas. These objectives had to be achieved quickly and without too much regard for the sometimes conflicting interests of American partners. And in the same way that in the 1960s political turmoil in ex-colonial areas precipitated UK investment into the North Sea, the uncertain industrial relations and declining profitability of the UKCS now pushed investment in the other direction. In the 1970s the main interests of UK and US oil majors coincided in the fast development of the UKCS. In the 1990s they were increasingly competitors in the global search for oil and oil markets.

In our discussion of the place of BP and Shell within the British state system in the 1930s and again in the 1950s, we noted the scale of interlock which existed with the banking institutions of the City of London. In 1951, when 14 per cent of the country's profit income came from these two companies, the closest of relations existed between the companies' directors, the leading merchant banks and the state apparatus. Today these links persist. Sitting on the board of BP are Sir James Glover, previously commander-in-chief of UK land forces, and Lord Wright, previously head of the diplomatic service. Shell has Lord Robert Armstrong, previously head of the civil service. The banks are still present – Bank of England, Barclays, ING Baring, John Swire Holdings, Barclays – together with the major UK industrial groupings (Inchcape, Pilkington, BAT, BOC, RTZ, Booker Tate). But there is also a new dimension. While Shell retains its close links with ex-Empire interests in Africa and the Far East, BP has developed a significant level of interlinkage with the EU. Peter Sutherland, previously an Irish EU commissioner, is a director. The company chair, David Simon, is on the advisory board of the Deutsche Bank. The director with responsibilities for former Soviet territories is Rolf Stronberg, an advisory board member for the Dresdner Bank and Gerling Konzern, while C. Hahn brings with him directorships of the Commerzbank, Thyssen, Volkswagen and Gerling.[10]

Some of these directors may be purely ornamental. But the very nature of the oil industry demands governmental and diplomatic support. BP's biggest overseas oil find since 1990 is in Colombia. The potential output of this field is equivalent to one-fifth of the entire UKCS output. The British government, from the level of prime minister down, have been involved in ensuring supportive relations with the Colombian government. Since 1992 the DTI and Scottish Enterprise have been mobilized to ensure the maximum use of UK supplies. The Colombian government has been persuaded to establish a special army brigade of 5000 men to protect BP installations against civilian unrest and trade union organization. The British government has in turn used its influence to mitigate the effects of UN sanctions imposed on Colombia as a result of human rights abuses.[11] Shell has had equal need of external governmental and diplomatic support. Its biggest single source of oil outside the UK and the USA is Nigeria. Throughout 1995 and 1996, Shell's operations in that country have been threatened by pro-democracy campaigners who claim to have won the elections. The military government, which provides protection for Shell's business, has in turn required the full sympathy and understanding of the UK government to avoid an international boycott. In terms of the European Union, links at governmental level are even more crucial. In the future BP will no doubt seek to draw advantage from its growing links with banking and business circles in Germany.

The battle of workers in the UKCS for trade union rights and safe working conditions was, therefore, not one that took place in isolation. It did not cause these developments. The new move overseas was intrinsically likely to happen in some form or other as the UK oil majors sought to compensate for declining UKCS yields. Yet the converse is also true. The timing and content of these changes, of critical importance for the wider international alignments of British capital, cannot be understood without looking at the dynamics of industrial relations in the North Sea. Such is the nature of the oil industry that the actions of a very few thousand workers on desolate oil rigs in the North Sea remain intimately tied to those of their counterparts in Ogoniland, Cusiana, Abu Dhabi, Siberia, Baku and, not least, the Norwegian waters of the North Sea, only separated from the UK sector by an invisible line on the map.

Notes

1. OIAC *Bulletin* No 7, 11/92.
2. Ramsay was to assume a key role in 1995 as director of OPITO.
3. BP, Charter of Rights, 1991.
4. BBC TV Scotland, *Focal Point*, 23 January 1992.
5. *Blowout*, Issue No. 41, October/November 1994.
6. *Blowout*, Issue No. 35, December 1993.
7. This legislation still remains weaker than that in Norway and does not include the right to halt dangerous work (see Miller, 1993). Nor does UKOOA's public support for legislation against victimization mean that victimization has become a thing of the past. Over a quarter of the current safety representatives questioned in the 1992 Aberdeen University survey knew of specific instances of victimization, and almost one in five had themselves failed to raise safety issues for fear of victimization. One well-known instance of victimization being used to silence critics occurred during the construction of Elf's Piper Bravo platform, which was eventually commissioned in 1991. A design engineer, Colin Jewell, and an electrical supervisor, Bob Nortcliff, separately voiced public fears about the safety of the technology being used. Both suffered victimization. In 1994–95, the platform suffered an associated series of gas leaks and fires for which the operators were first served with a safety notice and then fined £5000 by the HSE (*Blowout*, October/November 1990; *Scotsman*, 9 December 1991; *Herald*, 2 November 1994; *Blowout*, May/June 1994; *Blowout*, October/November 1994).
8. Will Hutton, *Observer*, 2 June 1996, quoting staff from the Marine

Technology Directorate.

9. Lionel Fulton, Labour Research Department, personal communication.

10. BP *Annual Report* 1995, Shell Trading and Transport plc entries in *Directory of Directors* 1995.

11. Michael Gillard in *Scotland on Sunday*, 9 June 1996, pp. 2 and 16.

POSTSCRIPT

This book has been about the development and crisis of a production regime that excluded organized labour and substituted supervisory diktat for negotiation – and the consequences of this for health and safety. This regime originated in the early 1970s. It was temporarily challenged but never shifted by the subsequent Labour governments. It found its apogee under the Conservative governments of Mrs Thatcher. Its crisis was short and spectacular, but, like the Thatcher administration itself, was equally swiftly replaced.

The new regime of the 1990s sought to carry forward the same essence, the exclusion of organized labour, but to do so in a new way: by enveloping the individual worker in a culture of manifold discussion and powerless consultative committees which leave management assumptions supreme. As one of its academic analysts has recently put it very succinctly, 'A new labour process is being developed where direct communication between managers and workers eliminates the need for unions.'[1]

A key argument of this book has been that this non-union production regime did not develop spontaneously as a result of factors internal to the offshore work process. On the contrary, it has depended at all critical points on power exercised at state level. Its introduction in the early 1970s depended on a sudden and new-found convergence of interest between British and American capital. Its ability to side-step attempts to introduce onshore health and safety systems in the later 1970s was directly related to pressures brought on the Labour government by the oil companies and associated banks. The marginalization of BNOC has a similar origin.

In the crisis of the early 1990s the state-level interventions were no less critical – even if their character and content had changed. The Department of Trade and Industry acted as the midwife for the restructuring of the industry from 1992, and did so on terms set by the two big UK companies. The 'profound change of culture' based on the sharing of knowledge and co-operative work practices shifted the balance of power between operators and contractors, and maintained, in new ways, the power of management over labour.

The year 1996 and the approach of a new general election supply a final test for the perceived power of the oil companies and their potential for intervention at state level. The Labour Party has for two decades indicated concern for the working conditions of offshore oil workers and the lack of collective bargaining rights. On occasion, the Labour Party has indicated intentions to bring back into public ownership those companies and utilities privatized by the previous government, to ensure greater social accountability of transnational companies and to remove at least some of the legal restrictions on free collective bargaining. Given wider developments in the Labour Party since 1994, it is perhaps not surprising that it should have abandoned every one of these commitments. What is instructive is the degree to which Labour and the leading oil companies have publicly sought to match their political agendas. Those leading the party have made it clear to all that they recognize the extra-parliamentary power of the oil companies, and that they intend to respect it.

In May 1996 Aberdeen City Council organized a conference at which representatives of the oil industry and the Labour Party were able to discuss the 'Future of the UK oil and gas industry'. The conference was co-sponsored by Amerada Hess and heard submissions from spokespersons from the leading companies including Shell and BP. George Robertson, the Shadow Scottish Secretary, stressed the degree to which his party understood the importance of oil and gas and sought a 'new partnership' which 'sees government and business working together'. Robertson noted the need to 'build on' the new safety regime introduced by Cullen, but also the requirement to 'reduce costs' in the new circumstances and 'to ensure that regulation is transparent, efficient and effective by eliminating unnecessary bureaucracy'. In terms reminiscent of Tory ministers at the DTI, Robertson warned against commercial complacency:

> 'Competition will remain fierce and the task of the next government will be to enable our industries to become world beaters in global markets. But if we are to do that, we must have a strong home base from which to build and that home base in turn needs stability.'[2]

Robertson made no mention of collective bargaining rights or of any intent to increase levels of accountability or control. The Shadow Energy Minister, John Battle, assured the industry: 'Labour understands that stability is essential to long-term strategic investments in the difficult terrain in which you operate. We have no intention of introducing special taxes. We have no proposals to change the fiscal regime.' Perhaps the most bizarre and revealing speech was that made by Martin O'Neill, the Labour MP chairing the House of Commons Select Committee on Trade and Industry. He spoke of the party's understanding of the problems faced by the industry as a result of unwelcome aspects of EU regulation, and, in particular, the dangers posed by the end of the UK's exemption from the Working Time Directive. Previously, it had been expected that the Labour Party's general endorsement of the Social Chapter might lead to the end of a situation in which UK oil workers were compelled to work much longer shifts than their Norwegian counterparts and longer than that which was legally permissible elsewhere in the EU. On this occasion, however, O'Neill noted the benefits for safety purposes of long shifts offshore:

> The longer workers are away from an installation in the North Sea the more difficult it is to sustain a safety culture. One of the greatest sources of risk of accident in the North Sea comes from helicopter accidents, and that is an increased risk if more helicopter flights are required.

He promised that a Labour government would be able to put these arguments more convincingly to its European partners than the current Conservative government was able to do.[3]

Four months later, during the 1996 TUC Conference, the Labour leader, Tony Blair, boarded a helicopter and was flown out to inaugurate the new Andrew field, by its operators, BP. This is an honour usually reserved for government ministers or minor royalty. At the TUC, Blair had stated that a Labour government would have no special relationship with the trade union movement; that it would be equally committed to its relationship with business; and reiterated an intention to uphold the Conservative 'reform' of industrial relations. After inaugurating the new BP field, in which trade unions were not recognized, Blair was asked to comment on trade union rights offshore. He answered: 'This is a matter for the employers and individual employees. I don't envisage any change there.'[4]

It might perhaps be argued that Labour's shift to the right on industrial relations offshore might be seen simply as part of much wider political changes. But there is also another political party that is, in its own way, even more revealing. This is the Scottish National Party, which has, by contrast, moved towards the left over the past decade. Its policy of 'Independence in Europe' encompasses a commitment to abandon Trident and any involvement with nuclear weapons, to consider certain limited increases in direct and indirect taxation to pay for public sector housing and education programmes, to launch major job creation initiatives and to restore levels of benefit, pensions and student grants. It even contemplates action by an independent Scottish parliament to restore public ownership of some utilities, and possibly the creation of a state-sponsored Scottish steel industry. But it makes no mention at all of any action to increase levels of social accountability in oil and gas — an omission that can hardly be accidental. The entire financial basis of the SNP programme rests on assumptions about oil and gas revenues. Three-quarters of the additional expenditure will be met from this source, not by increasing taxation but simply by taking 90 per cent of the existing tax revenues away from the English. Like Labour, there is an explicit commitment not to change the character of the fiscal regime, and certainly no suggestion that the SNP would in any way interfere with the prerogatives of those who own the industry.[5] So, here again, we see political leaders bowing to the power of the UK oil majors in order to prevent any attack on their party's fitness to govern.

The British oil majors have recently made it brutally clear to the Conservative government that they have specific political objectives and wish to see them met. In September 1996, Shell and BP took a leading part in launching a deeply embarrassing challenge to the government on its lack of clear policy on European monetary union. They joined a dozen other major UK companies, with a total turnover of £150 billion a year, in signing the 5 September letter to the press demanding an explicit commitment that the UK enter the EMU in the first wave of states in 1999. If the government failed to make this commitment, the letter argued, the UK would lose its ability to 'influence decision-making in one of the largest markets in the world'.[6]

A new political era is clearly approaching. The oil companies know this. So do those who aspire to exercise governmental power. This new era will be more international in scope, more aligned to the European Union and more dependent on the language of social partnership. But the content of the UK's offshore production regime will remain the same. Those who control the UK oil and gas industry remain convinced that their interests are incompatible with the presence of organized labour and the right to collective bargaining. This conviction is the story of our book. The oil companies have seen the power of organized labour and realized their weakness in face of it. How far organized labour will be able to draw once more upon the sources of their collective strength will depend as much on their own actions as on the political conditions created by a new government.

Notes

1. *Herald*, 12 September 1996.

2. Press statement issued by the Labour Party, 30 May 1996.

3. *Aberdeen Petroleum Review*, 5 June 1996.

4. *Herald*, 11 September 1996.

5. SNP, *Power for Change: Towards a Better Scotland*, SNP, Edinburgh, November 1995.

6. *Financial Times*, 5 September 1996.

Afterword

I am very pleased to be able to write the Afterword for this book. In doing so I can pay my personal tribute to those who died on Piper Alpha. My argument in *The Other Price of Britain's Oil* was always vulnerable to the empirical charge that, for all my criticisms of the British regulatory regime, no major disaster had yet occurred. Anticipating this criticism, I suggested that the complacency of the UK authorities would only retain a semblance of credibility as long as such an eventuality did not take place in the British sector. That credibility has been utterly destroyed, as this book more than amply demonstrates. I derive no satisfaction from having been right all along.

I embarked on my own research intent only upon an analysis of the offshore occupational health and safety record and regulatory regime. Very quickly however, I came to realize that such an analysis would only make sense within the context of a much broader political economy of North Sea oil. Where I scratched the surface on these matters, this book has dug deep. It has accomplished what I was only beginning to recognize as necessary when I finished.

Yet I confess to that same sense of *déjà vu* with which I was left at the end of my own earlier work. To be sure, and Piper Alpha apart, a lot has happened in the intervening decade and a half. These events and the changing configuration of forces are charted in this work. I am still left wondering, however, just how much has fundamentally changed with regard to the basic dynamics of occupational health and safety.

While it would be petty to underestimate the progress made under the Offshore Safety Division of the Health and Safety Executive since the new post-Cullen regime has been in place, it is important to realize that the regulators are operating within a political economy the fundamental parameters of which remain unchanged in several respects. Where I indicted acquiescence and the priority allocated to speed as a consequence of external factors and internal exigencies, the new regulators have now to take account of cost-reduction policies and practices resulting from a similar combination of forces. Thus while the previous Department of Energy inspectors may have pleaded the need to balance the requirements of rapid production against those of safety, their successors might now cite cost reduction as the analogous trade-off.

While the fundamental inseparability of occupational health and safety from industrial relations has in the past been recognized onshore, it has never been recognized in the offshore working environment. Onshore, organized workers could exercise some countervailing force to the power of capital in a way that, as this book shows, has been far more difficult to achieve offshore. There, he who pays the piper really does still call the tune.

W G Carson
Auckland, New Zealand
November 1996

BIBLIOGRAPHY

Aaronovitch, S. (1961) *The Ruling Class: A Study of British Finance Capital*, London: Lawrence and Wishart.

Abelson, R. P. (1959) 'Modes of resolution of belief dilemmas', *Journal of Conflict Resolution*, Vol. 3, pp. 343–52.

Aberdeen People's Press (1976) *Oil Over Troubled Waters: A Report and Critique of Oil Developments in North East Scotland*, Aberdeen.

Andersen, S. S. (1993) *The Struggle over North Sea Oil and Gas: Government Strategies in Denmark, Britain and Norway*, Scandinavian University Press.

ASTMS (1976) Industrial relations in the oil companies: an ASTMS view (unpublished document).

Atkinson, F. and Hall, S. (1983) *Oil and the British Economy*, London: Croom Helm.

Bailey, V. (1992) *Forged in Fire: The History of the Fire Brigades Union*, London: Lawrence and Wishart.

Baldwin, R. (1987) 'Health and safety at work: consensus and self-regulation' in R. Baldwin and C. McCrudden (eds) *Regulation and Public Law*, London: Weidenfeld and Nicolson.

Baldwin, R. (1995) *Rules and Government*, Oxford: Clarendon Press.

Ball, M. (1979) 'Cost-benefit analysis: a critique' in I. Grove and M. More (eds) *Issues in Political Economy: a Critical Approach*, London: Macmillan, pp. 63–88.

Balogh, Lord (1974) 'The North Sea oil blunder', *The Banker*, Vol. 124, pp. 281–8.

Bamberg, J. H. (1994) *The History of the British Petroleum Company: The Anglo-Iranian Years 1928–1950*, Cambridge: Cambridge University Press.

Bank of England Quarterly Bulletin (1986) 'North Sea oil and gas', December.

Barratt Brown, M. (1970) *After Imperialism*, London: Heinemann.

Barrell, A. C. (1991) Evidence to Energy Select Committee, Seventh Report, HC343, London: HMSO.

Barrell, A. C. (1993) Speech to Offshore Europe '93, Aberdeen, reprinted in *Safety Management*, October 1993.

Barrell, A. C. (1994a) 'North Sea safety after Piper Alpha', 1994 Royal Academy of Engineering and Royal Society of Edinburgh Lecture. London: The Royal Academy of Engineering.

Barrell, A. C. (1994b) 'The HSE position and the safety case regime', paper presented to the Offshore Safety Case Management Conference, reprinted in *Safety Management*, June 1994.

Beck, M. and Woolfson, C. (1995) The hidden deregulation of Britain's offshore oil industry, Department of Economics Discussion Paper No. 9511, University of St Andrews.

Bem, D. J. (1970) *Beliefs, Attitudes and Human Affairs*, Belmont, CA: Wadsworth.

Benn, T. (1989) *Diaries 1973–76: Against the Tide*, London: Hutchinson.

Benn, T. (1990) *Diaries 1977–80: Conflicts of Interest*, London: Hutchinson.

Bercusson, B. (1994) *Working Time in Britain: Towards a European Model, Part 1: The European Directive*, London: Institute of Employment Rights.

Bergman, D. (1993) *Disasters: Where the Law Fails – a New Agenda for Dealing with Corporate Violence*, London: Herald Families Association.

Bibbings, R. (1992) 'Towards a stronger safety culture: a union view' in HSE (1992b) (Proceedings of Conference), Aberdeen.

Blumay, C. and Edwards, H. (1993) *The Dark Side of Power: The Real Armand Hammer*, London: Simon and Schuster.

Bonefeld, W., Brown, A. and Burnham, P. (1995) *A Major Crisis? The Politics of Economic Policy in Britain in the 1990s*, Aldershot: Dartmouth Publishing Co.

Bowers, J., Brown, D. and Gibbons, S. (1993) *Trade Union Reform and Employment Rights Act 1993: A Practical Guide*, London: Longman.

Braithwaite, J. (1985) *To Punish or Persuade?* Albany: New York University Press.

Brandie, E. (1994) 'Achieving the balance between safety and cost reduction' in OFS/OILC (1995), pp. 43–7.

Bresnen, M. (1990) *Organising Construction*, London: Routledge.

British Petroleum Company (1994) *BP Statistical Review of World Energy*, June.

Brody, D. (1980) *Workers in Industrial America*, New York: Oxford University Press.

Bromley, S. (1987) The State, capital and the oil industry: with special reference to Britain and Norway (unpublished PhD thesis), University of Cambridge.

Bromley, S. (1991) *American Hegemony and World Oil: The Industry, the State System and the World Economy*, Cambridge: Polity Press.

Browne, E. J. P. (1991) Speech at Fifth International Offshore Northern Seas Petroleum Conference, Stavanger, Norway, 19 November (mimeo, BP).

Buchan, J. McD. (1984) Approaches and attitudes of managers to collective bargaining in North East Scotland (unpublished PhD thesis), Robert Gordon Institute of Technology Business School, Aberdeen.

Burgoyne Report (1980) *Offshore Safety*, Cmnd 7866, London: HMSO.

CAA (Civil Aviation Authority) (1995) *Review of Helicopter Offshore Safety and Survival*, 1 March, London.

Cairns, J. A. and Harris, A. H. (1988) 'Firm location and differential barriers to entry in the offshore oil supply industry', *Regional Studies*, Vol. 22, No. 6, pp. 499–506.

Calabresi, G. (1970) *The Costs of Accidents: A Legal and Economic Analysis*, New Haven: Yale University Press.

Calabresi, G. (1976) 'Some thoughts on risk distribution and the law of tort', *Yale Law Journal*, Vol. 70, pp. 499–553.

Caldwell, Judge N. (1994) Determination of 23rd Judicial District Court, Brazoria County, Texas, in the case of Mr and Mrs Andrew Innes and children Scott Alexander Innes and Andrew David Innes *et al.* vs Shell UK Exploration and Production Ltd. *et al.*, 23 December.

Cameron, Lord (1991) 'Shell UK Ltd. v McGillivray, Opinion', *Scots Law Times*, Reports: pp. 667–73.

Cameron, P. (1983) *Property Rights and Sovereign Rights: The Case of North Sea Oil*, London: Academic Press.

Carrigan, D. (1985) 'Deteriorating terms and conditions offshore in the post-construction sector – a trade union response', Discussion Paper, November.

Carson, W. G. (1982) *The Other Price of Britain's Oil*, Oxford: Martin Robertson.

Carson, W. G. (1985) 'Hostages to history: some aspects of the occupational health and safety debate in historical perspective' in W. B. Creighton and N. Cunningham (eds) *The Industrial Relations of Health and Safety*, Sydney: Croom Helm.

Cave-Brown, A. (1978) *Operation World War III?*, London: Arms and Armour Press.

Cazenove & Co. (1972) *The North Sea: The Search for Oil and Gas and the Implications for Investment*, September.

CBI (1990) *Developing Health and Safety Culture*, London: CBI.

Chevron (1994) *Chevron Alba Fact File*, London: Chevron UK Ltd.

Cohen, R. M. (1940) Note, *Yale Law Review*, Vol. 49.

Committee of Public Accounts (1973) *North Sea Oil and Gas*, First Report, Session 1972–73, 14 February, London: HMSO.

Corti, G. and Frazer, F. (1983) *The Nation's Oil: A Story of Control*, London: Graham and Trotman.

CRINE Secretariat (1993) Cost Reduction Initiative for the New Era Report, St Paul's Press, November.

CRINE Secretariat (1994) *Crine Watch 1994 Conference Special Edition*, December.

Cross, J. (1995) 'IT outsourcing: British Petroleum', *Harvard Business Review*, May–June, pp. 94–102.

Cullen, The Hon. Lord (1990) *The Public Inquiry into the Piper Alpha Disaster*, Vols 1 and 2, London: HMSO.

Cullen, The Hon. Lord (1996) 'The development of safety legislation', Royal Academy of Engineering and Royal Society of Edinburgh lecture, University of Strathclyde.

Davies, N. and Teasdale, P. (1994) *The Costs to the British Economy of Work Accidents and Work-Related Ill Health*, London: HSE Books.

Davis, K. (1970) *Administrative Law Treatise*, St Paul: West Publishing Company.

Dawson, S., Willman, P., Banford, M. and Clinton, A. (1988) *Safety at Work: The Limits of Self-regulation*, Cambridge: Cambridge University Press.

Department of Employment (1977) Report of a Court of Inquiry into a trade dispute at Dyce Airport, Aberdeen, between Bristow Helicopters Limited and members of the British Airline Pilots Association, conducted by the Hon. Lord McDonald MC, Cmnd 6951, London: HMSO.

DEn (Department of Energy) (1968–91) *Brown Books: Development of Oil and Gas Resources in the United Kingdom*, London: HMSO.

DEn (1976a) *The Offshore Energy Technology Board: Strategy for Research and Development*, Energy Paper No. 8, London: HMSO.

DEn (1976b) *North Sea Costs Escalation Study*, London: HMSO.

DEn (1989) *Safety Representatives and Safety Committees on Offshore Installations: Guidance Notes*, London: HMSO.

Det Norske Veritas (1993) Submission to HSE on draft Prevention of Fire etc. Regulations, 13 November.

Donovan, Lord (1968) Royal Commisssion on Trade Unions and Employers' Associations, *Report*, London: HMSO.

Dorman, P. (1996) *Markets and Morality: Economics, Dangerous Work and the Value of Human Life*, Cambridge: Cambridge University Press.

Downs, A. (1957) *An Economic Theory of Democracy*, New York: Harper and Row.

Drake, C. D. and Wright, F. B. (1983) *Law of Health and Safety At Work: The New Approach*, London: Sweet and Maxwell.

DTI (Department of Trade and Industry) (1993a) *Report of Working Group on Competitiveness in the UKCS*, February, London.

DTI (1993b) *Review of the Implementation and Enforcement of EC Law in the UK*, London: Crown Copyright.

DTI (1994) *The Energy Report 1994: Vol. I Markets in Transition, Vol. II Oil and Gas Resources of the UK*, London: HMSO.

DTI (1980–95) *Digest of UK Energy Statistics*, London: HMSO.

DTI (1995) *The Energy Report 1995: Vol. I Markets in Transition, Vol. II Oil and Gas Resources of the UK*, London: HMSO.

DTI (1996) *The Energy Report 1996: Vol. I Change and Opportunity, Vol. II Oil and Gas Resources of the UK*, London: HMSO.

Durkheim, E. (1933) *The Division of Labor in Society*, New York: Macmillan.

Edwards, P. K. (1992) 'Industrial conflict: themes and issues in recent research', *British Journal of Industrial Relations*, Vol. 30, September, pp. 361–404.

Elbaum, B. (1984) 'The making and shaping of job and pay structures in the iron and steel industry' in P. Osterman (ed.) *Internal Labor Markets*, Cambridge, MA: MIT Press, pp. 71–107.

Emmott, R. (1993) 'How inspections of offshore installations are organised' in J. Foster and C. Woolfson (eds) (1993), pp. 39–46.

Energy Select Committee (1991) *Offshore Safety Management*, Seventh Report, HC 343, London: HMSO.

Fairbrother, P. (1996) 'Organize and survive: unions and health and safety – a case study of an engineering unionized workforce', *Employee Relations*, Vol. 8, No. 2, pp. 2–88.

Fairbrother, P. and Waddington, J. (1990) 'The politics of trade unionism: evidence, policy and theory', *Capital and Class*, Vol. 41, Summer, pp. 15–56.

Feagin, J. R. (1990) 'Extractive regions in developed countries: a comparative analysis of oil capital', *Urban Affairs Quarterly*, Vol. 24, No. 4, pp. 591–619.

Feinstein, C. H. (1972) *National Income, Expenditure and Output of the UK*, Cambridge: Cambridge University Press.

Foster, J. (1993) 'Labour, Keynesianism and the welfare state' in Fyrth, J. (ed.) *Labour's High Noon: The Government and the Economy 1945–1951*, London: Lawrence and Wishart, pp. 20–36.

Foster, J., Lipka, J., Maguiness, H. and Munro, A. (1994) 'Competition and co-operation in the UK offshore oil industry', Working Paper available from Department of Applied Social Studies, University of Paisley.

Foster, J., Maguiness, H. and Munro, A. (1993) 'Scotland's oil and gas con-tracting industry and the Petroleum Revenue Tax', Fraser of Allander Institute, *Quarterly Economic Commentary*, Vol. 14, No. 4, pp. 76–83.

Foster, J. and Woolfson, C. (1986) *The Politics of the UCS Work-in: Class Alliances and the Right to Work*, London: Lawrence and Wishart.

Foster, J. and Woolfson, C. (eds) (1993) *Workforce Involvement and Health and Safety Offshore: Power, Language and Information Technology*, Proceedings of International Conference, November, Glasgow: STUC.

Friedman, M. (1975) *Unemployment and Inflation*, London: Institute of Economic Affairs.

Friedman, M. (1977) *From Galbraith to Economic Freedom*, London: Institute of Economic Affairs.

Funkhouser, R. (1951) 'Remarks by Ambassador Richard Funkhouser before the National War College, December 4, 1951 – the problem of Near Eastern oil' in United States Senate (1974).

Gardner, R. (1956) *Sterling-Dollar Diplomacy*, Oxford: Oxford University Press.

Garfit, T. (1989) The making of the UK engineering construction industry: a case study of multi-employer and multi-union bargaining, Warwick Papers in Industrial Relations, No. 26, University of Warwick.

Ginsberg, M. (1965) *On Justice in Society*, London: Heinemann.

Gordon, A. (1992) 'Helicopter innovation', *Aerospace*, May.

Goss, R. M. (1977) 'Finance' in *Our Petroleum Industry*, British Petroleum.

Grampian Regional Council Economic Development Unit (1994) Offshore workforce estimates, Aberdeen.

Greenfield, F. A. and Pleasure, R. J. (1993) 'Representatives of their own choosing: finding workers' voice in the legitimacy and power of their unions' in B. E. Kaufman and M. Kleiner (eds) *Employee Representation: Alternatives and Future Directions*, Madison, WI: Industrial Relations Research Organisation, pp. 169–96.

Greiner, L. E. (1972) 'Evolution and revolution as organizations grow', *Harvard Business Review*, July/August.

Habakkuk, H. J. (1962) *American and British Technology in the Nineteenth Century*, Cambridge: Cambridge University Press.

Hall, J. N. (1991) 'An oil company's approach to reviewing offshore safety' in Institute of Marine Engineers (1991).

Hall, R. (1995) Regulating health and safety offshore in Britain and Norway (unpublished MA thesis), Keele University.

Hallwood, P. (1990) *Transaction Costs and Trade between Multinational Corporations: A Study of Offshore Oil Production*, Boston: Hyman Unwin.

Hardie, F. W. (1991) 'Offshore accommodation design – past, present and future' in Institute of Marine Engineeers (1991).

Harrington, J. M. (1994) 'Working long hours and health: no unequivocal scientific evidence to support or refute a 48 hour week', *British Medical Journal*, Vol. 308, June, pp. 1581–2.

Harris, A., Lloyd, M. and Newlands, D. (1988) *The Impact of Oil on the Aberdeen Economy*, Aldershot: Avebury.

Harvey (1995) *on Industrial Relations and Employment Law*, Issue 113, London: Butterworths.

Harvie, C. (1994) *Fool's Gold: The Story of North Sea Oil*, London: Hamish Hamilton.

Hawkins, K. and Hutter, B. M. (1993) 'The response of business to social regulation in England and Wales: an enforcement perspective', *Law and Policy*, Vol. 15, No. 3, July.

Hendy, J. (1993) *A Law Unto Themselves – Conservative Employment Laws*, London: Institute of Employment Rights, 3rd edition.

Hiller, E. T. (1928) *The Strike: A Study in Collective Action*, Chicago University Press.

Howie, D. and Lipka, J. (1993) *Contracts in the Offshore Oil Industry: A Comparison of the UK and Norwegian Sectors*, Glasgow: STUC.

HSC (Health and Safety Commission) (1992) *Consultative Document on Proposals for Offshore Installations (Safety Case) Regulations*, HSC CD 41, London: Department of Employment.

HSC (1993) *Annual Report 1992/93*, London: HMSO.

HSC (1994a) *Consultative Document on Draft Offshore Installations and Pipe-line Works (Management and Administration) Regulations*, HSC CD 70, London: HMSO.

HSC (1994b) *Supplementary Consultation on the Draft Offshore Installations and Pipeline Works (Management and Administration) Regulations*, London: OSD/HSE.

HSC (1994c) *Draft Proposals for the Reporting of Injuries, Diseases and Dangerous Occurrences Regulations 199–*, HSC CD 74, London: HMSO.

HSC (1994d) *Annual Report 1993/94*, London: HMSO.

HSC (1994e) *Plan of Work 1994/95*, London: HMSO.

HSC (1995a) The role and status of Approved Codes of Practice, HSC CD 85, London: HMSO.

HSC (1995b) *Annual Report 1994/95*, London: HMSO.

HSC (1995c) *Health and Safety Statistics 1994/95*, London: HMSO.

HSC (1995d) Draft Proposals for Health and Safety Consultation with Employees: Regulations and Guidelines, HSC CD 96, London: HMSO.

HSC (1996a) Commission completes role and status review of Approved Codes of Practice, C11: 96, News Release, 22 February.

HSC (1996b) *Annual Report 1995/96*, London: HMSO.

HSE (Health and Safety Executive) (1991a) *Annual Report 1990/91*, London: HMSO..

HSE (1991b) 'Notice of casualty or other accident involving loss of life or danger to life on or near to an offshore installation', OIR/9A.

HSE (1992a) *Draft Offshore Installation (Safety Case) Regulations 199–* London: HMSO.

HSE (1992b) *Health and Safety in the Offshore Oil and Gas Industries*, Proceedings of Conference, 6–7 April, Aberdeen.

HSE (1992c) *A Guide to the Offshore Installations (Safety Case) Regulations 1992: Guidance on Regulations L30*, London: HMSO.

HSE (1993a) *Draft Offshore Installations (Prevention of Fire and Explosion, and Emergency Response) Regulations 199- and Approved Code of Practice*, Consultative Document, London: HSE.

HSE (1993b) *Offshore Safety Case Assessment*, OSD/SC C5O 11/93.

HSE (1993c) *The Costs of Accidents at Work*, London: HMSO.

HSE (1994) Offshore accident and incident statistics report 1993, OTO 94 010.

HSE (1995a) *An Interim Evaluation of the Offshore Installation (Safety Case) Regulations 1992*, London: HMSO.

HSE (1995b) Prevention of fire and explosion, and emergency response on offshore installations, *Offshore Installations (Prevention of Fire and Explosion, and Emergency Response) Regulations 1995 and Approved Code of Practice*, London: HMSO.

HSE (1995c) Offshore accident and incident statistics report 1994, OTO 95 953.

HSE (1996) Offshore accident and incident statistics report 1995, OTO 96 950.

Hughes, H. (1990) 'The offshore industry's response to Lord Cullen's recommendations', *Offshore Safety: The Way Ahead*, paper presented to Conference organized by the Exploration and Production Discussion Group of the Institute of Petroleum, 22 November.

Hughes, H. (1991) 'The offshore industry's response to Lord Cullen's recommendations', *Petroleum Review*, Vol. 45, p. 528.

Hughes, H. (1992) 'Towards a goal-setting regime – plans and issues – the operators' view' in HSE (1992b) (Proceedings of Conference).

Hughes, H. (1994a) 'The operators' response', paper presented to Conference on Offshore Safety Case Management, reprinted in *Safety Management*, Vol. 10, No. 6, pp. 48–50.

Hughes, H. (1994b) 'Developments of safety, health and environmental standards and regulation systems in North-West Europe', paper presented to Eighth Offshore Northern Seas Conference, Stavanger, Norway.

Hughes, H. (1995) Letter to Mr Padraig Flynn, Commissioner for Social Affairs of the European Union, 27 July.

Hughes, H. and Taylor, B. (1995) 'Offshore safety: an update of progress', paper presented to Leith International Conference, Aberdeen, 24 October.

Hyman, R. (1980) 'Trade unions, control and resistance' in G. Esland and G. Salaman (eds) *The Politics of Work and Occupation*, Milton Keynes: Open University Press, pp. 303–34.

IDS (Income Data Services) (1975) Report No. 200, January

IDS (1977a) No. 248 'Setting the Pace in North Sea Agreements', pp. 3–6, January.

IDS (1977b) No. 259 'New Agreement for North Sea Oil Ships', pp. 4–5, June.

IDS (1979) No. 314 'ARA Offshore Services', p. 7, October.

IDS (1980) No. 322 'Mechanical Construction Engineering-Site Agreement', p. 2, February.

IDS (1981) No. 346 'Offshore Construction Agreement', pp. 5–6, February.

IDS (1988) No. 530 'North Sea Supply Vessels: Derecognition', p. 7, October.

ILO (International Labour Organisation) (1993) *Safety and related issues pertaining to work on offshore petroleum installations*, International Labour Organisation Sectoral Activities Programme, Geneva: ILO.

Institute of Marine Engineers (1991) *Offshore Operations Post Piper Alpha*, Proceedings of Conference, 6–8 February, London.

Ireland, R. D. QC, Sheriff-Principal (1991) Determination in Fatal Accident Inquiry into the death of Timothy John Williams on board Ocean Odyssey, Aberdeen, 8 November.

IRRR (*Industrial Relations Reviews and Reports*) (1975) 'Industrial relations in the North Sea', No. 116, November, pp. 2–4.

IRRR (1977) 'The growth of trade union organisation in the North Sea oil and gas industries', No. 146, February, pp. 8–13; 19–27.

IRRR (1978) 'Recognition: review of ACAS reports', *Legal Information Bulletin* No. 106, 8 February.

IRRR (1989) 'Unions explore "single-table" bargaining', No. 441, June, pp. 3–4.

Jack, M. (1968) 'The purchase of the British Government's shares in the British Petroleum Company 1912–1914', *Past and Present*, Vol. 39, April, pp. 139–68.

Jacoby, S. M. and Werma, A. (1989) 'Enterprise unions in the United States', Working Paper, Los Angeles: UCLA Institute of Industrial Relations.

James, P. (1993a) 'The European Community: a way forward for worker health and safety?' in J. Foster and C. Woolfson (eds) (1993) pp. 63–73.

James, P. (1993b) *The European Community: A Positive Force for UK Health and Safety Law?* London: Institute of Employment Rights.

Jessop, A. S., Sheriff (1993) Determination of the Cormorant Alpha Fatal Accident Inquiry, Aberdeen, March.

Jessop, B. (1983) 'The capitalist state and the rule of capital: problems in the analysis of business associations', *West European Politics*, Vol. 6, No. 2, April, pp. 139–62.

Jessop, B., Bennett, K., Bromley, S. and Ling, T. (1988) *Thatcherism*, Cambridge: Polity Press.

Jones, G. (1981) *The State and the Emergence of the British Oil Industry*, London: Macmillan.

Kalt, J. and Zupan, M. (1984) 'Capital and ideology in the economic theory of politics', *American Economic Review*, Vol. 74, pp. 279–300.

Kalt, J. and Zupan, M. (1990) 'The apparent ideological behavior of legislators: testing for principal–agent slack in political institutions', *Journal of Law and Economics*, Vol. 33, pp. 103–31.

Karsh, B. (1958) *Diary of a Strike*, Urbana: University of Illinois Press.

Kelly, J. (1988) *Trade Unions and Socialist Politics*, London: Verso.

Kelman, S. (1980) 'Occupational safety and health administration' in J. Wilson (ed.) *The Politics of Regulation*, New York: Basic Books, pp. 36–60.

Kelman, S. (1981) *What Price Incentives? Economists and the Environment*, Boston: Auburn House Publications.

Kerr, C. (1959) 'The impacts of unions on the level of wages' in C. A. Myers (ed.) *Wages, Prices, Profits and Productivity*, New York: The American Assembly, Columbia University.

Kessler, S. and Bayliss, F. (1995) *Contemporary British Industrial Relations*, London: Macmillan (2nd edition).

Kidger, P. (1992) 'Should union appointed or elected safety representatives be the model for the UK?', *Human Resource Management Journal*, Vol. 2, No. 4, pp. 21–35.

Klein, B. (1984) 'Contract costs and administered prices: an economic theory of rigid wages', *American Economic Review*, Vol. 74, p. 332.

Kochan, T. (1980) *Collective Bargaining and Industrial Relations*, Homewood, IL: Irwin.

Kochan, T., Katz, H. and McKersie, R. (1986) *The Transformation of American Industrial Relations*, New York: Basic Books.

Labour Party Scottish Council (1973) *North Sea Oil and the Scottish Economy*, Glasgow.

Law Commission (1996) *Legislating the Criminal Code: Involuntary Manslaughter*, HC Paper No. 171, London: HMSO.

Lazonick, W. (1991) *Business Organization and the Myth of the Market*, Cambridge: Cambridge University Press.

Lazonick, W. (1993) 'Industry clusters versus global webs: organizational capabilities in the American economy', *Industrial and Corporate Change*, Vol. 2, No. 1, pp. 1–14.

Le Guen, J. (1994) 'Reaping the rewards of risk assessment', *Safety Management*, Vol. 10, No. 3, pp. 32–3.

Lenin, V. I. (1971) *Imperialism*, Selected Works in One Volume, London: Lawrence & Wishart, pp. 169–263 (2nd edition).

Lerner, S. W. (1961) *Breakaway Unions and the Small Trade Union*, London: Allen & Unwin.

Lewis, R. and Simpson, B. (1981) *Striking a Balance? Employment Law after the 1980 Act*, Oxford: Martin Robertson.

McDonald, R. (1989) 'One union offshore?', OILC Discussion Paper, 5 September.

McDonald, R. (1991) Minutes of Evidence to Energy Select Committee, 19 June 1991, in Energy Select Committee (1991).

MacFarlane, C. (1993a) 'Maximising safety through better project management: understanding the problems that projects leave behind' paper presented to IIR Conference, Aberdeen, July.

MacFarlane, C. (1993b) 'Participation: the lost strand in offshore safety' in J. Foster and C. Woolfson (eds) (1993), pp. 11–18.

McKee, R. E. (1990) 'Good management is the key to offshore safety', *Offshore Safety: The Way Ahead*, Paper presented to Conference organized by the Exploration and Production Discussion Group of the Institute of Petroleum, 22 November.

McLoughlin, I. and Gourlay, S. (1994) *Enterprise Without Unions: Industrial Relations in the Non-Union Firm*, Buckingham: Open University Press.

Mazmanian, D. A. and Sabatier, P. A. (1983) *Implementation and Public Policy*, Glenview, IL: Scott, Foresman and Co.

Meredeen, S. (1988) *Managing Industrial Conflict: Seven Major Disputes*, London: Hutchinson.

Middleton, R. J. (1977) 'The North Sea Oil Action Committee: a sucessful pressure group' paper presented at Department of Business Studies, Robert Gordon Institute of Technology, Aberdeen, September.

Miller, K. (1982) 'Factory occupations in Scotland', *Industrial Law Journal*, Vol. 11, pp. 115–17.

Miller, K. (1993) 'Worker participation in health and safety matters offshore' in J. Foster and C. Woolfson (eds) (1993), pp. 30–6.

Miller, K. and Woolfson, C. (1994) 'Timex: industrial relations and the use of the law in the 1990s', *Industrial Law Journal*, Vol. 23, No. 3, pp. 209–25.

Mills, D. M. (1972) *Industrial Relations and Manpower in Construction*, Cambridge MA: MIT Press.

Milne, S. (1994) *The Enemy Within: MI5, Maxwell and the Scargill Affair*, London: Verso.

Ministry of Power (1967) Inquiry into the causes of the accident to the drilling rig Sea Gem, Report, London: HMSO.

Mitchell, B. R. (1962) *British Historical Statistics*, Cambridge: Cambridge University Press.

Mollet, P. (1994) 'Unified energy policy climbs to the top of agenda', *Petroleum Economist*, August 1994, p. 43.

Molloy, J. (1993) 'Workforce involvement in safety case development' paper presented at a conference on *Offshore Safety Cases: The Living Documents – Where Next?*, 1–2 December 1993, London: IBC Technical Services Ltd.

Moore, R. (1991) *The Price of Safety: The Market, Workers' Rights and the Law*, London: Institute of Employment Rights.

Morgan, J. (1992) 'Towards a stronger safety culture' in HSE (1992b) (Proceedings of Conference), Aberdeen.

Nationwide Building Society (1975) *Annual Report*.

NEDO (National Economic Development Office) (1970) *Large Sites Report*, London: HMSO.

Nichols, T. (1986) 'Industrial injuries in British manufacturing in the 1980s', *Sociological Review*, Vol. 34, No. 2, pp. 290–306.

Nichols, T. (1994) Research Note: 'Problems in monitoring the safety of British manufacturing at the end of the twentieth century', *Sociological Review*, Vol. 42, No. 1, February, pp. 104–10.

Nichols, T. and Armstrong, P. (1973) *Safety or Profit: Industrial Accidents and the Conventional Wisdom*, Bristol: Falling Wall Press.

Noreng, O. (1980) *The Oil Industry and Government Strategy in the North Sea*, London: Croom Helm.

North Sea Oil Action Committee (1973) *North Sea Oil Exploitation: A Campaign Plan for Action*, Aberdeen, 31 March.

Norwegian Ministry of Industry and Energy (1994) Norwegian Offshore Sector's Competitive Standing. Report presented by Steering Group of the Development and Operations Forum for the Norwegian Petroleum Sector, September.

Odeco (1991) Odeco Drilling (UK) Ltd., Directors' Report and Financial Statement, 31 December, Peat Marwick.

Odell, P. (1981) *Oil and World Power*, London: Penguin, (6th edition).

OFS/OILC (1995) *Offshore Safety in a Cost Conscious Environment: From British and Norwegian Perspectives*, Proceedings of Conference, 15–16 November 1994, Stavanger.

OIAC (1992) *Guidance on Multi-skilling in the Petroleum Industry*, London: HMSO.

OIAC (1993) Report on 1991 accident statistics, OIAC/93/03.

OIAC (1994) *Playing Your Part: How Offshore Workers Can Help Improve Health and Safety*, London: HMSO.

OILC (1991a) *Striking Out: New Directions for Offshore Workers and their Unions*, Aberdeen: OILC.

OILC (1991b) *Crisis in Offshore Trade Unionism* Aberdeen: OILC.

OILC (1992) Constitution and Rules.

OILC (1993) Comments on the *Draft Offshore Installation (Prevention of Fire and Explosion and Emergency Response) Regulations and Approved Code of Practice*, submitted to HSE/OSD, 3 December.

OILC (1994) Comments on the *Draft Offshore Installations and Pipeline Works (Management and Administration) Regulations*, submitted to HSE/OSD, June.

OILC (1995) Comments on the *Draft Offshore Installations and Wells (Design and Construction) Regulations (DRC)* submitted to HSE/OSD, 29 September.

Olson, M. (1965) *The Logic of Collective Action: Public Goods and Theory of Groups*, Cambridge, MA: Harvard University Press.

Overbeek, H. (1990) *Global Capitalism and Global Decline: the Thatcher Decade in Perspective*, London, Unwin and Hyman.

Pape, R. P. (1992) 'Risk assessment in UK offshore installation safety cases', paper presented to Risk Assessment: International Conference, 1992.

Parry, C. and MacFarlane, C. (1994) 'Cost cutting and improved safety in drilling' in OFS/OILC (1995), pp. 34–8.

Patterson, R. (1995) 'Offshore safety – the new regime: Part 2 implementation', paper presented to Leith International Conference, Aberdeen, 24 October.

Paynter, W. (1970) *British Trade Unions and the Problem of Change*, London: Allen & Unwin.

Pearce, F. and Tombs, S. (1992) 'Realism and corporate crime' in R. Matthews and J. Young (eds) *Issues in Realist Criminology*, London: Sage, pp. 70–101.

Penrose, E. (1968) *The Large International Firm in Developing Countries*, London: George Allen and Unwin.

Perrow, C. (1984) *Normal Accidents*, New York: Basic Books.

Phillips, J. (1976) 'Economic deterrence and the prevention of industrial accidents', *Industrial Law Journal*, Vol. 5, pp. 148–53.

Pike, W. J. (1993) 'The oil price crisis and its impact on Scotland's North Sea development', *Scottish Economic and Social History*, Vol. 13, pp. 56–71.

Pondy, L. R. (1967) 'Organisational conflict: concepts and models', *Administrative Science Quarterly*, Vol. 12, No. 2, pp. 296–320.

Porter, M. (1990) *The Competitive Advantage of Nations*, London: Macmillan.

Pressman, J. L. (1978) *Federal Programmes and City Politics: The Dynamics of the Aid Process in Oakland*, Berkeley: University of California Press.

Pressman, J. L. and Wildavsky, A. (1974) *Implementation*, Berkeley: University of California Press.

Punchard, E. (1989) *Piper Alpha: A Survivor's Story*, London: W. H. Allen.

Ramsay, J. (1994) 'Creating the right culture for workforce involvement' in OFS/OILC (1995) (Proceedings of Conference), pp. 15–17.

Reilly, B., Paci, P. and Hall, P. (1995) 'Unions, safety committees and workplace injuries', *British Journal of Industrial Relations*, Vol. 33, No. 2, pp. 275–88.

Riches, P. A. (1991) 'After Piper Alpha – the insurance aspects' in Institute of Marine Engineers (1991), Proceedings of Conference.

Rimington, J. (1991) Minutes of Evidence to Energy Select Committee, 3rd July 1991 in Energy Select Committee (1991).

Robens, The Hon. Lord (1972) *Safety and Health at Work*, Report of the Committee 1970–72, Cmnd 5034, London: HMSO.

Robinson, C. and Morgan, J. (1978) *North Sea Oil in the Future: Economic Analysis and Government Policy*, London: Trade Policy Research Centre, Macmillan.

Roncaglia, A. (1985) *The International Oil Market*, London: Macmillan.

Ross, J. (1983) *Thatcher and Friends: The Anatomy of the Tory Party,* London: Pluto.

Roth, A. (1984) *Parliamentary Profiles,* London: Parliamentary Profiles.

Rother, E. (1992) 'European safety legislation from 1993', paper presented to Fourth North Sea Safety Conference, 29 October 1992, London.

Rutledge, I. and Wright, P. (1996) 'Taxing the second North Sea oil boom: a fair deal or a raw deal?' Division of Adult and Continuing Education, University of Sheffield, January.

Salmond, A. and Walker, J. (1986) 'The oil price collapse: some effects', Fraser of Allander Institute, *Quarterly Economic Commentary,* Vol. 12, No. 2, pp. 63–9.

Sampson, A. (1976) *The Seven Sisters: The Great Oil Companies and the World They Made,* London: Hodder and Stoughton.

Saville, R. (1993) 'The commanding heights' in J. Fyrth (ed.) *Labour's High Noon: The Government and the Economy 1945–1951,* London: Lawrence and Wishart, pp. 37–60.

Scott, J. C. (1990) *Domination and the Arts of Resistance: Hidden Transcripts,* New Haven and London: Yale University Press.

Scottish National Party (SNP) (1996) *Power for Change: Towards a Better Scotland,* Edinburgh: SNP.

Scottish Office (1995) Statistical Bulletin – Industry Series, Edinburgh.

Scottish Office Industry Department (1993) The 1990, 1992 and 1993 oil related surveys: Employment results final report, ESU Research Paper No. 33, October, HMSO.

Scottish Office Industry Department (1995) The 1994 oil related survey: employment results final report, ESU Research Paper No. 37, May, HMSO.

Sefton, A. (1994) 'Workforce involvement – the Regulator's view' in OFS/OILC (1995), pp. 9–12.

Sewel, J. and Penn, R. (1996) 'Trade unionism in a hostile environment: an account of attempts to organize the North Sea off-shore oil industry between 1970 and 1990' in R. Penn, M. Rose and D. Gallie (eds) *Trade Unionism in Recession,* Oxford: Oxford University Press, pp. 286–318.

Shell Expro (1993) 'ALARP in practice: an industry view: Shell Expro', paper presented to Offshore Safety Case Conference, 1–2 April 1993.

Silving, H. (1961) in G. O. W. Mailler (ed.) *Essays in Criminal Science,* Ch. 5.

Spaven, M., Ras, H., Morrison, A. and Wright, C. (1993) *The Effectiveness of Offshore Safety Representatives and Safety Committees: A Report to the Health and Safety Executive, Vol. 1: Survey, Analysis, Conclusions and Recommendations,* Aberdeen: Offshore Study Group.

Spaven, M. and Wright, C. (1993a) 'The effectiveness of offshore safety representatives and safety committees: a response to Vulliamy' in J. Foster and C. Woolfson (eds) (1993), pp. 92–5.

Spaven, M. and Wright, C. (1993b) 'Safety representation in the offshore industry', *The Safety and Health Practitioner*, November 1993, pp. 29–31.

Spiller, P. T. (1990) 'Politicians, interest groups and regulators: a multiple-principals agency theory, or "Let them be bribed" ', *Law and Economics*, Vol. 33, pp. 65–101.

Stadnachenko, A. (1975) *The Monetary Crisis of Capitalism: Origin, Development*, Moscow: Progress Publishers.

Steward, K. and Dawson, S. (1993) 'Breaking the silence: can the talking begin and will it continue: a study of communication and team work on offshore oil installations' in J. Foster and C. Woolfson (eds) (1993), pp. 37–8.

Stock Exchange Year-Book (1939) London.

Stock Exchange Official Year Book (1973–4) London.

Storey, C. and Barker, R. (1994a) 'The safety representative is an endangered species? Part 1: Rise and fall of the workplace watchdog', *Health and Safety at Work*, July, pp. 33–6.

Storey, C. and Barker, R. (1994b) 'The safety representative is an endangered species? Part 2: Future survival of the workplace watchdog', *Health and Safety at Work*, August, pp. 12–15.

STUC (1973) 76th *Annual Report*, Aberdeen.

STUC (1974) 77th *Annual Report*, Rothesay.

Sutherland, V. J. and Cooper, C. L. (1991) *Stress and Accidents Offshore*, Houston: Gulf Publishing.

Taylor, B. G. S. (1991) 'The UK offshore operators response to Piper Alpha and Lord Cullen's report', paper presented to Society of Petroleum Engineers First International Conference on Health, Safety and Environment, The Hague, 10–14 November, pp. 349–56.

Thom, A. (1989) Managing labour under extreme risk: collective bargaining in the North Sea oil industry (unpublished PhD thesis), Aberdeen: Robert Gordon Institute of Technology.

Todd, I. (1995) 'Offshore safety: the new regime: Part 1 development', paper presented to Leith International Conference, Aberdeen, 24 October.

Tombs, S. (1991) 'Piper Alpha and the Cullen Inquiry: beyond "distorted communication"?' in R. F. Cox and M. H. Walter (eds) *Offshore Safety and Reliability*, London and New York: Elsevier, pp. 28–41.

TUC (1989) *Prospects for a Single Bargaining Table*, Special Review Body, London: Congress House.

TUC (1991a) *Trade Union Recognition: A Consultative Document*, London: Congress House.

TUC (1991b) *Towards 2000: A Consultative Document*, May, London: Congress House.

TUC (1995a) *Paying the Price for Deaths at Work: The TUC Response to the Law Commission's Consultation on 'Involuntary Manslaughter'*, Law Commission Consultation Paper No. 135, London: Congress House.

TUC (1995b) *The Future of Union Workplace Safety Representatives: A TUC Health and Safety Report*, October, London: Congress House.

Turnbull, P., Woolfson, C. and Kelly, J. (1992) *Dock Strike: Conflict and Restructuring in Britain's Ports*, Aldershot: Avebury.

Turner, H. A. (1963) *The Trend of Strikes*, Leeds: Leeds University Press.

Turner, H. A., Clack, G. and Roberts, G. (1967) *Labour Relations in the Motor Industry*, London: Allen and Unwin.

UKOOA (1987) *The United Kingdom Offshore Operators Association*, London: UKOOA.

UKOOA (1988) Employment Practices Committee Information Booklet, London: UKOOA.

UKOOA (1995a) *Offshore Safety – Setting the Record Straight*, London: UKOOA.

UKOOA (1995b) *Towards 2020: Future Oil and Gas Production in UK Waters*, London: UKOOA.

UKOOA (1996) Official statistics confirm offshore industry's improving safety performance, Press Release, 18 March, London: UKOOA.

United States Senate (1974) Hearings before the Subcommittee on Multinational Corporations of the Committee on Foreign Relations, Ninety-Third Congress, Second Session on Multinational Petroleum Companies and Foreign Policy, February 20 and 21, March 27 and 28, Part 7, Washington: US Government Printing Office.

Vulliamy, D. (1993) 'Review of the S1 971 report on the effectiveness of offshore safety representatives' in J. Foster and C. Woolfson (eds) (1993), pp. 87–91.

Walters, D., Dalton, A. and Gee, D. (1993) *Worker Representation on Health and Safety in Europe*, Brussels: European Trade Union Technical Bureau for Health and Safety.

Walters, D. and Gourlay, S. (1990) *Statutory Employee Involvement in Health and Safety at the Workplace*, HSE Contract Report 20/1990, London: HMSO.

Webb, S. and B. (1920) *The History of Trade Unionism*, London: Longman, Green & Co.

Wells, C. (1993) *Corporations and Criminal Responsibility*, Oxford: Clarendon Press.

Whyte, D., Tombs, S. and Smith, D. (1996) 'Offshore safety management in the "New Era": Perceptions and experiences of workers' in *Major Hazards Onshore and Offshore*, Vol. II, *Symposium Series*, No. 139, Rugby: Institute of Chemical Engineers, pp. 35–51.

Wildavsky, A. (1979) *Speaking Truth to Power: The Art and Craft of Policy Analysis*, Boston: Little, Brown and Co.

Wilson, Sir H. (1978) *The Financing of North Sea Oil*, Committee to Review the Functioning of Financial Institutions: Research Report No. 2, London: HMSO.

Woolf, A. D. (1973) 'Robens Report: the wrong approach?', *Industrial Law Journal*, Vol. 2, pp. 88–95.

Woolfson, C. and Beck, M. (1995) 'Seven years after Piper Alpha: safety claims and the new Safety Case regime', University of Glasgow Working Paper.

Woolfson, C. and Beck, M. (1996) 'Deregulation: the contemporary politics of "health and safety" ' in A. McColgan (ed.) *The Future of Labour Law*, London: Mansell, pp. 171–205.

Woolfson, C. and Foster, J. (1988) *Track Record: The Story of the Caterpillar Occupation*, London: Verso.

Wraith, R. E. and Lamb, G. B. (1971) *Public Inquiries as an Instrument of Government*, London: Allen & Unwin.

Wright, C. (1986) 'Routine deaths: fatal accidents in the oil industry', *Sociological Review*, Vol. 34, No. 2, pp. 265–89.

Wright, C. (1993) 'The effect of work group organisation on responses to a total emergency in the offshore industry' in J. Foster and C. Woolfson (eds) (1993), pp. 59–62.

Wright, C. (1994) 'A fallible safety system: institutionalised irrationality in the offshore oil and gas industry', *Sociological Review*, Vol. 42, No. 1, pp. 79–103.

Wybrow, P. (1982) 'The Scottish labour movement and the offshore oil industry' in T. Dickson (ed.) *Capital and Class in Scotland*, Edinburgh: Donald, pp. 251–77.

Yergin, D. (1991) *The Prize: The Epic Quest for Oil, Money and Power*, New York: Simon and Schuster.

Name Index

Subject Index